DB2 9 for Linux, UNIX, and Windows
Database Administration
Certification Study Guide

DB2 9

for Linux, UNIX, and Windows Database Administration Certification Study Guide

Roger E. Sanders

MC Press Online, LP
Lewisville, TX 75077

DB2 9 for Linux, UNIX, and Windows Database Administration Certification Study Guide
Roger E. Sanders

First Edition

First Printing—October 2007
Second Printing—May 2009

© 2007-2009 Roger Sanders. All rights reserved.

MC Press offers excellent discounts on this book when ordered in quantity for bulk purchases or special sales, which may include custom covers and content particular to your business, training goals, marketing focus, and branding interest.

For information regarding permissions or special orders, please contact:
MC Press
Corporate Offices
125 N. Woodland Trail
Lewisville, TX 75077 USA

For information regarding sales and/or customer service, please contact:
MC Press
P.O. Box 4300
Big Sandy, TX 75755-4300 USA

ISBN 10: 158347-077-8
ISBN 13: 978-158347-077-0

Dedication

To Mark Hayakawa,
my good friend and "plucky sidekick"
on numerous "Pros from Dover" tours

Acknowledgments

A project of this magnitude requires both a great deal of time and the support of many different individuals. I would like to express my gratitude to the following people for their contributions:

Susan Dykman – Information Management Certification Program Manager, IBM Information Management
Susan invited me to participate in the DB2 9 exam development process, and provided me with screen shots of the IBM Certification Exam Testing software. Susan also reviewed the first chapter of the book and provided valuable feedback.

Susan Visser – IBM Press, Data Management Program Manager IBM Toronto Lab
Once again, Susan's help was invaluable; without her help, this book would not have been written. Susan paved the way for me to acquire the rights to the Version 8.1 manuscript and move to MC Press when Pearson Education decided not to publish an updated version of my Version 8.1 book. Susan also reviewed many of the chapters as they were written, and she made sure the appropriate subject-matter experts at the IBM Toronto Lab reviewed portions of the manuscript as well.

Dr. Arvind Krishna – Vice President, IBM Data Servers and Worldwide Information Management Development
Dr. Krishna provided me with the Foreword for this book.

Reed M. Meseck – Senior Competitive Specialist, IBM Information Management Software
Reed helped Dr. Arvind Krishna develop the Foreword for this book.

Brant Davison – Program Director, IBM Information Management Software
Brant worked with me to ensure that Dr. Arvind Krishna received the materials he needed to develop the Foreword for this book.

Jason Gartner – Executive Assistant to Arvind Krishna
Jason worked with Reed Meseck and Dr. Arvind Krishna to make sure I received the Foreword for this book in a timely manner.

Rick Swagerman – Sr. Technical Manager, DB2 SQL and Catalog Development IBM Toronto Lab

Rick provided me with detailed examples illustrating how the UPDATE/DELETE NO ACTION and UPDATE/DELETE RESTRICT rules of referential constraints work. His examples were converted into some of the illustrations you see in Chapter 4, and Rick reviewed the final draft of many of these drawings for accuracy and completeness.

Dale McInnis – Sr. Technical Staff Member, DB2 High Availability IBM Toronto Lab

Dale reviewed the material in Chapter 7 – High Availability for accuracy and completeness; the valuable feedback he provided was incorporated into the chapter.

I would also like to thank my wife Beth for her help and encouragement, and for once again overlooking all of the things that did not get done while I worked on yet another (my 15th) book.

About the Author

Roger E. Sanders is the President of Roger Sanders Enterprises, Inc. He has been designing and developing database applications for more than 20 years and has been working with DB2 and its predecessors since it was first introduced on the IBM PC (as part of OS/2 Extended Edition). He has written articles for publications such as *Certification Magaz*ine and *IDUG Solutions Jour*nal, authored tutorials for IBM's developerWorks Web site, presented at numerous International DB2 User's Group (IDUG) and Regional DB2 User's Group (RUG) conferences, taught classes on DB2 fundamentals and database administration (DB2 for Linux, UNIX, and Windows), writes a regular column called "Distributed DBA" in *DB2 Magazine*, and is the author of the following books:

- *Using the IBM System Storage N Series with Databases* (IBM RedBook; co-author)

- *DB2 9 Fundamentals Certification Study Guide*

- *Integrating IBM DB2 with the IBM System Storage N Series* (IBM RedBook; co-author)

- *Using IBM DB2UDB with IBM System Storage N Series* (IBM RedBook; co-author)

- *DB2 Universal Database V8.1 Certification Exam 703 Study Guide*

- *DB2 Universal Database V8.1 Certification Exam 701 and 706 Study Guide*

- *DB2 Universal Database V8.1 Certification Exam 700 Study Guide*

- *DB2 UDB Exploitation of NAS Technology* (IBM RedBook; co-author)

- *All-In-One DB2 Administration Exam Guide*

- *DB2 Universal Database SQL Developer's Guide*

- *DB2 Universal Database API Developer's Guide*

- *DB2 Universal Database Call Level Interface Developer's Guide*

- *ODBC 3.5 Developer's Guide*

- *The Developer's Handbook to DB2 for Common Servers*

In addition, Roger holds the following professional certifications:

- IBM Certified Advanced Database Administrator—DB2 9 for Linux, UNIX, and Windows

- IBM Certified Application Developer—DB2 9

- IBM Certified Database Administrator—DB2 9 DBA for Linux, UNIX, and Windows

- IBM Certified Database Associate—DB2 9 Fundamentals

- IBM Certified Advanced Database Administrator—DB2 Universal Database V8.1 for Linux, UNIX, and Windows

- IBM Certified Database Administrator—DB2 Universal Database V8.1 for Linux, UNIX, and Windows

- IBM Certified Developer—DB2 Universal Database V8.1 Family

- IBM Certified Database Associate—DB2 Universal Database V8.1 Family

- IBM Certified Advanced Technical Expert—DB2 for Clusters

- IBM Certified Solutions Expert—DB2 UDB V7.1 Database Administration for UNIX, Windows, and OS/2

- IBM Certified Solutions Expert—DB2 UDB V6.1 Application Development for UNIX, Windows, and OS/2

- IBM Certified Specialist—DB2 UDB V6/V7 User

About This Book

This book is divided into two parts:

- Part 1 – DB2 UDB Certification (Chapter 1)

  This section consists of one chapter (Chapter 1), which is designed to introduce you to the DB2 Professional Certification Program that is available from IBM. In this chapter, you will learn about the different certification roles available, along with the basic prerequisites and requirements for each role. This chapter also explains what's involved in the certification process, and it includes a tutorial on the IBM Certification Exam testing software, which you will encounter when you go to take any IBM certification exam.

- Part 2 – DB2 9 Database Administration Concepts (Chapters 2–8)

  This section consists of seven chapters (Chapters 2 through 8), which are designed to provide you with the concepts you will need to master before you can pass the DB2 9 for Linux, UNIX, and Windows Database Administration exam (Exam 731).

  Chapter 2 is designed to introduce you to the various aspects of server management. In this chapter, you will learn how to configure servers, instances, and databases, as well as how to configure client communications. You will also learn how to configure a database for Automatic Maintenance, how to schedule tasks, how to use the Self-Tuning Memory Manager, how to throttle utilities, and how to obtain detailed information from the Notification log that can be used to resolve problems when they occur.

  Chapter 3 is designed to teach you everything you need to know about how data in a DB2 9 database is physically stored. In this chapter, you will learn how to create a DB2 9 database and you will discover what a DB2 9 database's underlying structure looks like, as well as how that structure is mapped to files and directories. You will also learn how table spaces are used, how to obtain information about a table space, how to cluster data using range-clustered tables, how to partition data with table (range) partitioning, how to manipulate XML data and create XML indexes, and how to configure a table to use data row compression.

Chapter 4 is designed to provide you with information about creating tables, indexes, and views. In this chapter, you will learn how to create base tables, indexes, and views and you will learn when and how the following constraints should be applied: NOT NULL, default, check, unique, referential integrity, and informational. You will also learn how to obtain information from the system catalog, and how to administer a server, instance, or database using the GUI tools that are available with DB2 9.

Chapter 5 is designed to introduce you to the various tools that are available for monitoring a database's performance. In this chapter, you will learn how to configure and use the snapshot monitor, one or more event monitors, the Health Monitor (via the Health Center), and the Explain facility. You will also learn how to analyze the information produced by these tools to locate weaknesses in database and/or application design.

Chapter 6 is designed to provide you with everything you need to know about DB2 9's data movement and data management utilities. In this chapter, you will learn how to use the Export utility to extract data from a database and store it in an external file and how to use the Import and Load utilities to move data stored in external files into database tables. You will also learn how to reorganize data in a table, how to update statistics that are used by the DB2 Optimizer when selecting a data access path to use to respond to a query, and how to rebind existing packages once statistics have been updated. Finally, you will learn how to use the db2look, db2move, db2batch, and db2advis utilities.

Chapter 7 is designed to introduce you to the concept of database backup and recovery and to the various tools available with DB2 9 that can be used to return a damaged or corrupted database to a useable and consistent state. In this chapter, you will learn what transaction logging is, how transaction logging is performed, and how log files are used to restore a damaged database. You will also learn how to make backup images of a database or a table space using the Backup utility, how to perform version recovery using the Restore utility, how to reapply transaction records stored in logs to perform a roll-forward recovery operation using the Rollforward utility, and how to restore a database using information stored in the recovery history log file using the Recover utility. You will also learn how to set up a High Availability Disaster Recovery (HADR) environment and how to configure a database for dual logging.

Chapter 8 is designed to introduce you to the concept of database security and to the various authorization levels and privileges that are recognized by DB2. In this chapter, you will learn how and where users are authenticated, how authorities and privileges determine what a user can and cannot do while working with a database, and how authorities and privileges are given to and taken away from individual users and/or groups of individual users. You will also learn how to restrict access to specific columns and/or rows in a table using Label-Based Access Control (LBAC).

The book is written primarily for IT professionals who have a great deal of experience working with DB2 9, have already taken and passed the DB2 9 Fundamentals exam (Exam 730), and would like to take (and pass) the DB2 9 for Linux, UNIX, and Windows Database Administration exam (Exam 731). However, any individual who would like to learn the skills needed to administer one or more DB2 9 databases will benefit from the information found in this book.

Conventions Used

Many examples of DB2 9 administrative commands and SQL statements can be found throughout this book. The following conventions are used whenever a DB2 command or SQL statement is presented:

[ ]   Parameters or items shown inside of brackets are required and must be provided.

< >   Parameters or items shown inside of angle brackets are optional and do not have to be provided.

| Vertical bars are used to indicate that one (and only one) item in the list of items presented can be specified

,...   A comma followed by three periods (ellipsis) indicate that multiple instances of the preceding parameter or item can be included in the DB2 command or SQL statement

The following examples illustrate each of these conventions:

Example 1

```
REFRESH TABLE [TableName ,...]
<INCREMENTAL | NON INCREMENTAL>
```

In this example, at least one *TableName* value must be provided, as indicated by the brackets ([ ]), and more than one *TableName* value can be provided, as indicated by the comma-ellipsis (, . . .) characters that follow the *TableName* parameter. INCREMENTAL and NON INCREMENTAL are optional, as indicated by the angle brackets (< >), and either one or the other can be specified, but not both, as indicated by the vertical bar (|).

Example 2

```
CREATE SEQUENCE [SequenceName]
<AS [SMALLINT | INTEGER | BIGINT | DECIMAL]>
<START WITH [StartingNumber]>
<INCREMENT BY [1 | Increment]>
<NO MINVALUE | MINVALUE [MinValue]>
<NO MAXVALUE | MAXVALUE [MaxValue]>
<NO CYCLE | CYCLE>
<NO CACHE | CACHE 20 | CACHE [CacheValue]>
<NO ORDER | ORDER>
```

In this example, a *SequenceName* value must be provided, as indicated by the brackets ([ ]). However, everything else is optional, as indicated by the angle brackets (< >), and in many cases, a list of available option values is provided (for example, NO CYCLE and CYCLE); however, only one can be specified, as indicated by the vertical bar (|). In addition, when some options are provided (for example, START WITH, INCREMENT BY, MINVALUE, MAXVALUE, and CACHE), a corresponding value must be provided, as indicated by the brackets ([ ]) that follow the option.

SQL is not a case-sensitive language, but for clarity, the examples provided are shown in mixed case—command syntax is presented in uppercase while user-supplied elements such as table names and column names are presented in lower case. However, the examples shown can be entered in any case.

Although basic syntax is presented for most of the DB2 commands and SQL statements covered in this book, the actual syntax supported may be much more complex. To view the complete syntax for a specific command or to obtain more information about a particular command, refer to the *IBM DB2, Version 9 Command Reference* product documentation. To view the complete syntax for a specific SQL statement or to obtain more information about a particular statement, refer to the *IBM DB2, Version 9 SQL Reference, Volume 2* product documentation.

Contents

Foreword

We live in a world of information. But how did we get here? We started with the goal of reaching the moon, and conquering the task of moving data between a tiny spacecraft and the earth, and then storing that data in a reliable and quickly accessible way.

We developed new technologies, new systems, and new software to transmit, process, and store that data. Today, we live in an era where processing power continues to soar, and where the sky is the limit for storage capacity. The result has been an unprecedented flood of data.

Today, the goal is not just storing data, but providing ubiquitous access to information. We live in a world of information, and increasingly we expect our world to be an On Demand world: always on, always available, where information is increasingly rich and dynamic, immediate and instantaneous.

We access information with our laptops, our cell phones, our Blackberrys—at our desks and on the road. Increasingly your success is dependent upon your ability to easily access and connect that information across the organization and across the globe.

IBM's goal is to help our customers and partners transform from data and information management to Information On Demand. Information On Demand is about getting the right information to the right people, at the right time, in the right context.

Today, the greatest competitive advantages are often gained from uncovering data you already have and connecting it easily, seamlessly and ubiquitously: Information as a Service. Only IBM has the vision and the breadth of products and services to make this vision a reality and DB2 is the Data Server for your On Demand world.

Data servers are a critical element of your IT foundation, and DB2 is the Data Server of choice for customers running a broad spectrum of applications, from On-Line Transaction Processing to Data Warehousing, from Web Services to Analytics, from small to extreme data volume. From the no-charge DB2

Express-C to advanced capabilities for transactional and dynamic warehousing applications, IBM offers the right data server for the job.

Today, DB2 runs in the top 25 banks worldwide, 23 of the top 25 U.S. retailers, and 9 of the top 10 global life and health insurance providers. DB2 is the choice of a growing number of ISVs and customers running ISV applications such as SAP. Last year alone, over 4,500 new customers chose DB2 to run their businesses. And with the delivery of DB2 9, we are seeing that growth accelerate. We now have over 450,000 customers using IBM Data Servers to run their businesses across industries and across the globe.

DB2 is the only data server that consistently delivers leading performance in TPC-C, TPC-H and SAP application benchmarks. But more importantly, DB2 continues to deliver reliability and security for your business and applications.

DB2 9 provides another proof point of what makes IBM different - from the invention of database technology in 1966 to support the Apollo space program; to the invention of the relational data model in the 70s; to the 68 patented innovations in DB2 9, to the more than 3,000 data management patents—IBM continues to lead in innovations that help our clients deliver business results.

Information is the fabric of global businesses, and data server professionals will continue to be critical to the delivery, management, and governance of this corporate asset. Roger Sanders has provided a tremendous opportunity to learn more about DB2, and I encourage you to take advantage this opportunity and learn skills you can leverage to deliver more value to your business. Your time spent will be valuable to you and your colleagues.

Arvind Krishna
IBM Corporation
Vice President
Data Servers and Information Management Development

Preface

One of the biggest challenges computer professionals face today is keeping their skill sets current with the latest changes in technology. When the computing industry was in its infancy, it was possible to become an expert in several different areas, because the scope of the field was relatively small. Today, our industry is both widespread and fast paced, and the skills needed to master a single software package can be quite complex. Because of this complexity, many application and hardware vendors have initiated certification programs to evaluate and validate an individual's knowledge of their technology. Businesses benefit from these programs, because professional certification gives them confidence that an individual has the expertise needed to perform a specific job. Computer professionals benefit, because professional certification allows them to deliver high levels of service and technical expertise, and, more importantly, because professional certification can lead to advancement or new job opportunities within the computer industry.

If you've bought this book (or if you are thinking about buying this book), chances are you have already decided you want to acquire one or more of the IBM DB2 Professional Certifications available. As an individual who holds ten IBM DB2 professional certifications, let me assure you that the exams you must pass in order to become a certified DB2 professional are not easy. IBM prides itself on designing comprehensive certification exams that are relevant to the work environment an individual holding a particular certification will have had some exposure to. As a result, all of IBM's certification exams are designed with the following questions in mind:

- What are the critical tasks that must be performed by an individual who holds a particular professional certification?

- What skills must an individual possess in order to perform each critical task identified?

- How frequently will an individual perform each critical task identified?

You will find that to pass a DB2 certification exam, you must possess a solid understanding of DB2—and for some of the more advanced certifications, you must understand many of DB2's nuances as well.

Now for the good news. You are holding in your hands what I consider to be the best tool you can use to prepare for the DB2 9 Fundamentals exam (Exam 730). When IBM began work on the DB2 9 certification exams, I was invited once again to participate in the exam development process. In addition to helping define the exam objectives, I authored several exam questions, and I provided feedback on many more before the final exams went into production. Consequently, I have seen every exam question you are likely to encounter, and I know every concept you will be tested on when you take the DB2 9 Fundamentals exam (Exam 730). Using this knowledge, along with copies of the actual exam questions, I developed this study guide, which not only covers every concept you must know in order to pass the DB2 9 Fundamentals exam (Exam 730) but also covers the exam process itself and the requirements for each DB2 9 certification role available. In addition, you will find, at the end of each chapter, sample questions that are worded just like the actual exam questions. In short, if you see it in this book, count on seeing it on the exam; if you don't see it in this book, it won't be on the exam. If you become familiar with the material presented in this book, you should do well on the exam.

CHAPTER 1

IBM DB2 9 Certification

Recognized throughout the world, the Professional Certification Program from IBM offers a range of certification options for IT professionals. This chapter is designed to introduce you to the various paths you can take to obtain DB2 9 Certification from IBM and to describe the testing software you will use when you sit down to take your first DB2 9 certification exam.

DB2 9 Certification Roles

One of the biggest trends in the IT industry today is certification. Many application and software vendors now have certification programs in place that are designed to evaluate and validate an individual's proficiency with the vendor's latest product release. In fact, one of the reasons the Professional Certification Program from IBM was developed was to provide a way for skilled technical professionals to demonstrate their knowledge and expertise with a particular version of an IBM product.

The Professional Certification Program from IBM is made up of several distinct certification roles that are designed to guide you in your professional development. You begin the certification process by selecting the role that's right for you, and familiarizing yourself with the certification requirements for that role. The following subsections are designed to help get you started by providing you with the prerequisites and requirements associated with each DB2 9 certification available.

IBM Certified Database Associate – DB2 9 Fundamentals

The *IBM Certified Database Associate – DB2 9 Fundamentals* certification is intended for entry-level DB2 9 users who are knowledgeable about the fundamental concepts of DB2 9 for Linux, UNIX, and Windows; DB2 9 for zSeries (OS/390); or DB2 9 for iSeries (AS/400). In addition to having some hands-on experience with DB2 9, some formal training, or both, individuals seeking this certification should:

- Know what DB2 9 products are available and be familiar with the various ways DB2 9 is packaged

- Know what DB2 9 products must be installed in order to create a desired environment

- Know what features and functions are provided by the various tools that are shipped with DB2 9

- Possess a strong knowledge about the mechanisms DB2 9 uses to protect data and database objects against unauthorized access and/or modification

- Know how to create, access, and manipulate basic DB2 objects, such as tables, views, and indexes

- Be familiar with the different types of constraints that are available and know how each is used

- Be familiar with how XML data can be stored and manipulated

- Possess an in-depth knowledge of Structured Query Language (SQL), Data Definition Language (DDL), Data Manipulation Language (DML), and Data Control Language (DCL) statements that are available with DB2 9

- Have a basic understanding of the methods used to isolate transactions from each other in a multi-user environment

- Be familiar with the methods used to control how locking is performed

In order to acquire the IBM Certified Database Associate – DB2 9 Fundamentals certification, candidates must take and pass one exam: the **DB2 9 Family Fundamentals** exam (Exam 730). The roadmap for acquiring the IBM Certified Database Associate – DB2 9 Fundamentals certification is illustrated in Figure 1–1.

*Figure 1–1: IBM Certified Database Associate – DB2 9 Fundamentals
certification roadmap.*

IBM Certified Database Administrator – DB2 9 for Linux, UNIX, and Windows

The *IBM Certified Database Administrator – DB2 9 for Linux, UNIX, and Windows* certification is intended for experienced DB2 9 users who possess the knowledge and skills necessary to perform the day-to-day administration of DB2 9 instances and databases residing on Linux, UNIX, or Windows platforms. In addition to being knowledgeable about the fundamental concepts of DB2 9 and having significant hands-on experience as a DB2 9 Database Administrator (DBA), individuals seeking this certification should:

- Know how to configure and manage DB2 9 instances

- Know how to configure client–server connectivity

- Be able to obtain and modify the values of environment/registry variables

- Be able to obtain and modify DB2 Database Manager (instance) and database configuration file parameter values

- Know how to use Automatic Maintenance and the self-tuning memory manager

- Know how to create DB2 9 databases

- Possess a strong knowledge about SMS, DMS, and automatic storage table spaces, as well as be familiar with the management requirements of each

- Know how to create, access, modify, and manage the different DB2 9 objects available

- Know how to manage XML data

- Be able to create constraints on and between table objects

- Know how to capture and interpret snapshot monitor data

- Know how to create and activate event monitors, as well as capture and interpret event monitor data

- Know how to capture and analyze Explain information

- Know how to use the DB2 Control Center and other GUI tools available to manage instances and databases, create and access objects, create tasks, schedule jobs, and view Explain information.

- Possess an in-depth knowledge of the Export, Import, and Load utilities.

- Know how to use the REORGCHK, REORG, REBIND, RUNSTATS, db2look, db2move, and db2pd commands

- Know how to perform database-level and table space-level backup, restore, and roll-forward recovery operations

- Have a basic understanding of transaction logging

- Be able to interpret information stored in the administration notification log

- Possess a strong knowledge about the mechanisms DB2 9 uses to protect data and database objects against unauthorized access and/or modification

Candidates who have either taken and passed the **DB2 V8.1 Family Fundamentals** exam (Exam 700) or acquired the IBM Certified Database Administrator – DB2 V8.1 for Linux, UNIX, and Windows certification (by taking and passing Exams 700 and 701) must take and pass the **DB2 9 for Linux, UNIX, and Windows Database Administration** exam (Exam 731) to acquire the IBM Certified Database Administrator—DB2 9 for Linux, UNIX, and Windows certification. All other candidates must take and pass both the **DB2 9 Family Fundamentals** exam (Exam 730) and the **DB2 9 for Linux, UNIX, and Windows Database Administration** exam (Exam 731). The roadmap for acquiring the IBM Certified Database Administrator – DB2 9 for Linux, UNIX, and Windows certification can be seen in Figure 1–2.

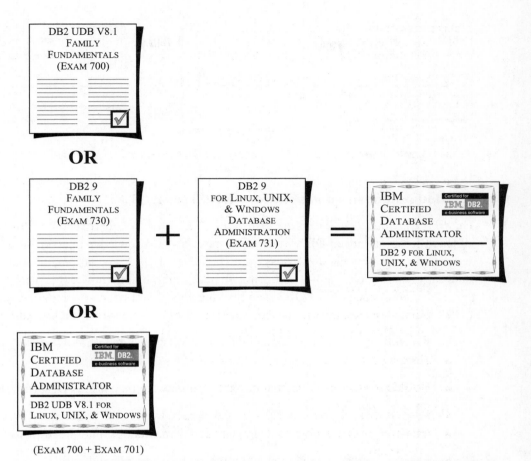

Figure 1–2: IBM Certified Database Administrator – DB2 9 for Linux, UNIX, and Windows certification roadmap.

Candidates who already hold the IBM Certified Database Administrator – DB2 V8.1 for Linux, UNIX, and Windows certification may opt to take the **DB2 9 for Linux, UNIX, and Windows Database Administration Upgrade** exam (Exam 736) to acquire the IBM Certified Database Administrator – DB2 9 for Linux, UNIX, and Windows certification. This exam, which is half the length and half the cost of the **DB2 9 for Linux, UNIX, and Windows Database Administration** exam (Exam 731), is designed to test a candidate's knowledge of the new features and functions that are provided in DB2 9. Essentially, the upgrade exam provides certified DB2 Version 8.1 DBAs an accelerated approach for acquiring an equivalent Version 9 certification. This accelerated approach is outlined in Figure 1–3.

(EXAM 700 + EXAM 701)

Figure 1–3: The accelerated approach for acquiring IBM Certified Database Administrator – DB2 9 for Linux, UNIX, and Windows certification.

IBM Certified Database Administrator – DB2 9 for z/OS

The *IBM Certified Database Administrator – DB2 9 for z/OS* certification is intended for experienced DB2 9 users who possess the knowledge and skills necessary to perform the day-to-day administration of DB2 9 instances and databases residing on OS/390 platforms. In addition to being knowledgeable about the fundamental concepts of DB2 9 and having significant hands-on experience as a DB2 9 Database Administrator, individuals seeking this certification should:

- Know how to convert a logical database design to a physical database design

- Know how to create, access, modify, and manage the various DB2 9 objects available

- Know how to interpret the contents of system catalogs and directories

- Possess a strong knowledge about the activities associated with enabling stored procedures

- Be familiar with the different types of constraints available and know how each is used

- Possess an in-depth knowledge of the Structured Query Language (SQL), Data Definition Language (DDL), Data Manipulation Language (DML), and Data Control Language (DCL) statements that are available with DB2 9

- Know the difference between static and dynamic SQL

- Know how to manage storage allocation with tools such as VSAM DELETE, VSAM DEFINE, and STOGROUP

- Be familiar with DB2 Disaster Recovery

- Possess a basic understanding of the different object statuses available (for example: RECP, GRECP, LPL, and RESTP)

- Be able to describe the effects of COMMIT frequency

- Know how to capture and analyze Explain information

- Know how to capture and analyze DB2 Trace data

- Be able to determine the best characteristics for an index

- Be able to describe the benefits of data sharing

- Be able to describe the features that enable around-the-clock availability

- Know how to use the REORG, BIND, REPAIR, UNLOAD, RUNSTATS, LOAD, and MODIFY utilities, including being able to restart a failed utility

- Know how to use the DISPLAY, START, STOP, ALTER, RECOVER, and TERM UTILITY commands

- Possess a basic understanding of the CHECK DATA/INDEX/LOB utility

- Be able to demonstrate how DB2I is used

- Be able to identify the functions of the Control Center

- Possess a strong knowledge about the mechanisms DB2 9 uses to protect data and database objects against unauthorized access and/or modification

Candidates who have either taken and passed the **DB2 V8.1 Family Fundamentals** exam (Exam 700) or acquired the IBM Certified Database Administrator – DB2 V8.1 for z/OS and OS/390 certification (by taking and passing Exams 700 and 702) must take and pass the **DB2 9 for z/OS Database Administration** exam (Exam 732) to acquire the IBM Certified Database Administrator – DB2 9 for z/OS certification. All other candidates must take and pass both the **DB2 9 Family Fundamentals** exam (Exam 730) and the **DB2 9 for z/OS Database Administration** exam (Exam 732). The roadmap for acquiring the IBM Certified Database Administrator – DB2 9 for z/OS certification can be seen in Figure 1–4.

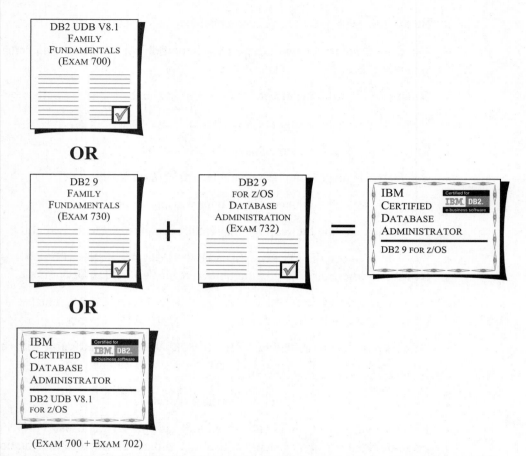

Figure 1–4: IBM Certified Database Administrator – DB2 9 for z/OS and OS/390 certification roadmap.

IBM Certified Application Developer – DB2 9 Family

The *IBM Certified Application Developer – DB2 9 Family* certification is intended for intermediate- to advanced-level application developers who possess the knowledge and skills necessary to create applications that interact with DB2 9 databases residing on supported platforms, including Linux, AIX, HP-UX, Sun Solaris, Windows, zSeries (z/OS, OS/390), and iSeries (AS/400). In addition to being knowledgeable about the fundamental concepts of DB2 9 and having strong skills in embedded SQL programming, ODBC/CLI programming, JDBC programming, or SQLJ programming, individuals seeking this certification should:

- Be familiar with the naming conventions used to identify DB2 9 objects

- Know what authorities and privileges are needed in order to access data within an application

- Possess an in-depth knowledge of the complex database objects available with DB2 9

- Possess an in-depth knowledge of the Structured Query Language (SQL), Data Definition Language (DDL), Data Manipulation Language (DML), and Data Control Language (DCL) statements that are available with DB2 9

- Know the difference between static and dynamic SQL

- Possess an in-depth knowledge of the SQL functions available

- Know when to use Embedded SQL, CLI/ODBC, JDBC, SQLJ, PHP, PERL, PYTHON, .NET, and XML

- Be able to execute queries across multiple tables and/or views

- Be able to identify the types of cursors available, as well as know when to use cursors in an application and what their scope will be

- Be able to work with materialized query tables (MQTs)

- Be able to identify the results of XML parsing and XML serialization

- Possess an in-depth knowledge of XML document encoding management

- Know how XML schemas are validated

- Be able to execute and identify the results of an XQuery expression

- Be familiar with the SQL/XML functions that are available with DB2 9

- Be able to establish a connection to a database within an Embedded SQL, CLI/ODBC, JDBC, SQLJ, or .NET application

- Possess the ability to analyze the contents of an SQL Communications Area (SQLCA) data structure

- Possess the ability to obtain and analyze CLI/ODBC diagnostic information

- Possess the ability to obtain and analyze JDBC trace, SQL exception, and JDBC error log information

- Possess the ability to obtain and analyze .NET diagnostic information

- Be able to query tables across multiple databases, including federated databases

- Possess the ability to create triggers and identify their results

- Know how to cast data types

- Know when to use compound SQL, parameter markers, and distributed units of work

- Know when to use user-defined functions (UDFs) and stored procedures

- Know how to create user-defined functions (UDFs) and stored procedures

- Be familiar with the DB2 Developer Workbench

Candidates who have either taken and passed the **DB2 V8.1 Family Fundamentals** exam (Exam 700) or acquired the IBM Certified Application Developer – DB2 V8.1 Family certification (by taking and passing Exams 700 and 703) must take and pass the **DB2 9 Family Application Development** exam (Exam 733) to acquire the IBM Certified Application Developer – DB2 9 Family certification. All other candidates must take and pass both the **DB2 9 Family Fundamentals** exam (Exam 730) and the **DB2 9 Family Application Development** exam (Exam 733). The roadmap for acquiring the IBM Certified Application Developer – DB2 9 Family certification can be seen in Figure 1–5.

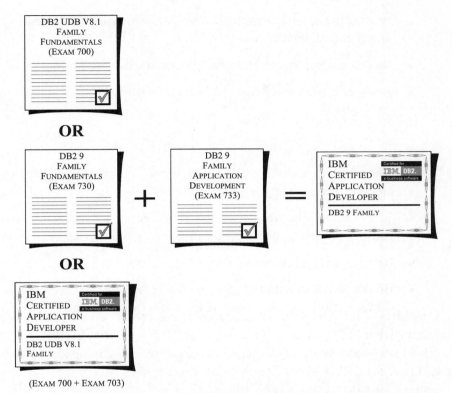

Figure 1–5: IBM Certified Application Developer – DB2 9 Family certification roadmap.

IBM Certified Advanced Database Administrator – DB2 9 for Linux, UNIX, and Windows

The *IBM Certified Advanced Database Administrator – DB2 9 for Linux, UNIX, and Windows* certification is intended for lead database administrators who possess extensive knowledge about DB2 9 and who have extensive experience using DB2 9 on one or more of the following supported platforms: Linux, AIX, HP-UX, Sun Solaris, and Windows. In addition to being knowledgeable about the more complex concepts of DB2 9 and having significant experience as a DB2 9 Database Administrator, individuals seeking this certification should:

- Know how to design, create, and manage SMS, DMS, and automatic storage table spaces

- Know how to design, create, and manage buffer pools

- Be able to take full advantage of intrapartition parallelism and interpartition parallelism

- Be able to design and configure federated database access

- Know how to manage distributed units of work

- Be able to develop a logging strategy

- Be able to create constraints on and between table objects

- Know how to perform database-level and table space-level backup, restore, and roll-forward recovery operations

- Be able to use the advanced backup and recovery features available

- Know how to implement a standby database using log shipping, replication, failover, and fault monitoring

- Be able to identify and modify the DB2 Database Manager and database configuration file parameter values that have the most impact on performance

- Possess a strong knowledge of query optimizer concepts

- Be able to correctly analyze, isolate, and correct database performance problems

- Know how to manage a large number of users and connections, including connections to host systems

- Know how to create, configure, and manage a partitioned database spanning multiple servers

- Be able to create and manage multidimensional clustered tables

- Know when the creation of an index will improve database performance

- Be able to identify and resolve database connection problems

- Possess a strong knowledge about the external authentication mechanisms that DB2 9 uses to protect data and database objects against unauthorized access and/or modification

- Know how to implement data encryption using Label-Based Access Control (LBAC)

To acquire the IBM Certified Advanced Database Administrator – DB2 9 for Linux, UNIX, and Windows certification, candidates must hold the IBM Certified Database Administrator – DB2 9 for Linux, UNIX, and Windows certification, and they must take and pass the **DB2 9 for Linux, UNIX, and Windows Advanced Database Administration** exam (Exam 734). The roadmap for acquiring the IBM Certified Advanced Database Administrator – DB2 9 for Linux, UNIX, and Windows certification can be seen in Figure 1–6.

Figure 1–6: IBM Certified Advanced Database Administrator – DB2 9 for Linux, UNIX, and Windows certification roadmap.

IBM Certified Solution Designer – DB2 Data Warehouse Edition V9.1

The *IBM Certified Solution Designer – DB2 Data Warehouse Edition V9.1* certification is intended for individuals who are knowledgeable about the fundamental concepts of IBM's DB2 Data Warehouse Edition (DWE), Version 9.1. In addition to having the knowledge and skills necessary to design, develop, and support DB2 data warehouse environments using DB2 DWE, anyone seeking this certification should:

- Be able to explain how data warehouse and front-end analytics impact Business Intelligence Analytics architecture

- Know the difference between a multidimensional database and a relational database warehouse

- Know how metadata affects analytical queries

- Be able to select appropriate front-end features based on criteria such as presentation needed, level of interactivity required, Web versus FAT client, static versus dynamic, and end user skill level

- Know how to translate data warehouse-based analytics into schemas, aggregations, and SQL

- Know when to use the DB2 Design Advisor versus the CV Advisor

- Be able to explain how the DB2 Query Patroller fits into warehouse-based analytics

- Be able to distinguish between logical and physical data models

- Be able to describe the architecture of DB2 DWE in terms of its components

- Be able to describe the architecture of DB2 DWE in terms of the three physical nodes used and where they are installed

- Be able to identify the hardware needed to install DB2 Data Warehouse Edition

- Know how to create a Data Design Project in the Project Engineer as a container for physical data modeling

- Know how to reverse-engineer an existing DB2 schema (or a schema subset)

- Know how to design or modify a physical data model that describes a data warehouse (including constraints), as well as perform an impact analysis to identify all model–database dependencies

- Be able to view the contents of database objects

- Be able to identify candidate fact and dimension tables in a data warehouse

- Be able to create cube models and cubes

- Know how to define levels and hierarchies

- Know how to define and create a dimension object

- Know how to create materialized query tables (MQTs), as well as troubleshoot ineffective MQTs

- Know how to perform Import and Export operations

- Be able to create a data-mining project in the Project Explorer

- Know how to formulate a data-mining task from a business problem, define a preprocessing function to prepare data for data mining, edit properties of mining operators, apply a visualizer operator to a data-mining flow, run a data-mining flow against a data warehouse, and view the results of any data-mining flow run

- Be able to describe use cases for the SQL Warehousing Tool

- Know how to create, setup, and navigate a Data Warehouse Project using the DB2 DWE Design Studio

- Be able to describe the concepts of dataflows, subflows, and control flows, as well as build dataflows and subflows by adding, connecting, and defining properties of SQL Warehousing Dataflow Operators

- Know why, when, and how to use a data station in a dataflow

- Be able to prepare and deploy a Data Warehouse Project application to a test or production environment, using the DB2 DWE Administration Console

- Be able to set up and perform Query Workload Management

- Know how to set up and perform Historical Analysis

- Know how to administer, maintain, and tune the Query Patroller

In order to acquire the IBM Certified Solution Designer – DB2 Data Warehouse Edition V9.1 certification, candidates must take and pass one exam: the **DB2 Data Warehouse Edition V9.1** exam (Exam 716). The roadmap for acquiring the IBM Certified Solution Designer – DB2 Data Warehouse Edition V9.1 certification is illustrated in Figure 1–7.

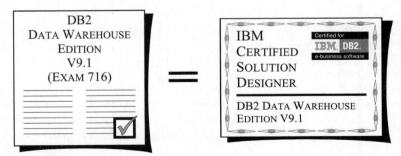

Figure 1–7: IBM Certified Solution Designer – DB2 Data Warehouse Edition V9.1 certification roadmap.

The Certification Process

A close examination of the IBM certification roles available quickly reveals that, in order to obtain a particular DB2 9 certification, you must take and pass one or more exams that have been designed specifically for that certification role. (Each exam is a software-based exam that is neither platform- nor product-specific.) Thus, once you have chosen the certification role you wish to pursue and have familiarized yourself with the requirements for that particular role, the next step is to prepare for and take the appropriate certification exam or exams.

Preparing for the Certification Exams

If you have experience using DB2 9 in the context of the certification role you have chosen, you may already possess the skills and knowledge needed to pass the exam(s) required for that role. However, if your experience with DB2 9 is limited (and even if it is not), you can prepare for any of the certification exams available by taking advantage of the following resources:

- Formal Education

  IBM Learning Services offers courses that are designed to help you prepare for DB2 9 certification. A listing of the courses recommended for each certification exam can be found using the Certification Navigator tool provided on IBM's "Professional Certification Program from IBM" Web site (*www.ibm.com/certify*). Recommended courses can also be found at IBM's "DB2 Data Management" Web site (*www.ibm.com/software/data/education/learningcontent.html*). For more information on course schedules, locations, and pricing, contact IBM Learning Services or visit their Web site.

- Online Tutorials

  IBM offers a series of seven interactive online tutorials designed to prepare you for the DB2 9 Fundamentals exam (Exam 730). These tutorials can be found at *www-128.ibm.com/developerworks/offers/lp/db2cert/db2-cert730.html*.

  IBM also offers a series of interactive online tutorials designed to prepare you for the DB2 9 for Linux, UNIX, and Windows Database

Administration exam (Exam 731) and the DB2 9 Family Application Development exam (Exam 733). These tutorials can be found at *www-128.ibm.com/developerworks/offers/lp/db2cert/db2-cert731.html* and *www-128.ibm.com/developerworks/offers/lp/db2cert/db2-cert733.html*.

- Publications

  All the information you need to pass any of the available certification exams can be found in the documentation that is provided with DB2 9. A complete set of manuals comes with the product, and the manuals are accessible through the Information Center once you have installed the DB2 9 software. DB2 9 documentation can also be downloaded from IBM's Web site in both HTML and PDF formats. (The IBM Web site containing the DB2 9 documentation can be found at *www.ibm.com/software/data/db2/library*.)

  Self-study books (such as this one) that focus on one or more DB2 9 certification exams or roles are also available. Most of these books can be found at your local bookstore or ordered from many online book retailers. A listing of possible reference materials for each certification exam can be found using the Certification Navigator tool provided on IBM's "Professional Certification Program from IBM" Web site (*http://www.ibm.com/certify*).

  In addition to the DB2 9 product documentation, IBM often produces manuals, known as "RedBooks," that cover advanced DB2 9 topics (as well as other topics). These manuals are available as downloadable PDF files on IBM's RedBook Web site (*www.redbooks.ibm.com*). Or, if you prefer to have a bound hard copy, you can obtain one for a modest fee by following the appropriate links on the RedBook Web site. (There is no charge for the downloadable PDF files.)

  A list of possible reference materials for each certification exam can be found using the Certification Navigator tool provided on IBM's "Professional Certification Program from IBM" Web site (*www.ibm.com/certify*). Ordering information is often included with the listing.

- Exam Objectives

  Objectives that provide an overview of the basic topics covered on a particular certification exam can be found using the Certification Navigator tool provided on IBM's "Professional Certification Program from IBM" Web site (*www.ibm.com/certify*). Exam objectives for the DB2 9 for Linux, UNIX, and Windows Database Administration exam (Exam 731) can also be found in Appendix A of this book.

- Sample Questions and Exams

  Sample questions and practice tests allow you to become familiar with the format and wording used on the actual certification exams. They can also help you decide whether you possess the knowledge needed to pass a particular exam. Sample questions, along with descriptive answers, are provided at the end of every chapter and in Appendix B of this book. Sample exams for each DB2 9 certification role available can be found using the Certification Exam tool provided on IBM's "Professional Certification Program from IBM" Web site (*www.ibm.com/software/data/education/cert/assessment.html*). There is a $10 charge for each exam taken.

It is important to note that the certification exams are designed to be rigorous. Very specific answers are expected for most exam questions. Because of this, and because the range of material covered on a certification exam is usually broader than the knowledge base of many DB2 9 professionals, you should take advantage of exam preparation resources if you want to guarantee your success in obtaining the certification(s) you desire.

Arranging to Take a Certification Exam

When you are confident that you are ready to take a specific DB2 9 certification exam, your next step is to contact an IBM-authorized testing vendor. The DB2 9 certification exams are administered by Pearson VUE, by Thompson Prometric, and, in rare, cases by IBM (for example, IBM administers the DB2 9 certifications free of charge at some of the larger database conferences, such as the International DB2 User's Group North American conference). However, before you contact either testing vendor, you should visit their Web site (*www.vue.com/ibm* and *www.2test.com*, respectively) and use the navigation tools provided there to locate a testing center that is convenient for you. Once you have located a testing center, you can then contact the vendor and make arrangements to take the certification exam. (Contact information for the testing vendors can also be found on their respective Web sites; in some cases, you can schedule an exam online.)

You must make arrangements to take a certification exam at least 24 hours in advance, and when you contact the testing vendor, you should be ready to provide the following information:

- Your name (as you want it to appear on your certification certificate)

- An identification number (if you have taken an IBM certification exam before, this is the number assigned to you at that time; if not, the testing vendor will supply one)

- A telephone number where you can be reached

- A fax number

- The mailing address to which you want all certification correspondence, including your certification welcome package, to be sent

- Your billing address, if it is different from your mailing address

- Your email address

- The number that identifies the exam you wish to take (for example, Exam 731)

- The method of payment (credit card or check) you wish to use, along with any relevant payment information (such as credit card number and expiration date)

- Your company's name (if applicable)

- The testing center where you would like to take the certification exam

- The date when you would like to take the certification exam

Before you make arrangements to take a certification exam, you should have paper and pencil or pen handy so that you can write down the test applicant identification number the testing center will assign you. You will need this information when you arrive at the testing center to take the certification exam. (If time permits, you will be sent a letter of confirmation containing the number of the certification exam you have been scheduled to take, along with corresponding date, time, and location information; if you register within 48 hours of the scheduled testing date, you will not receive a letter.)

> If you have already taken one or more of the certification exams offered, you should make the testing vendor aware of this and ask them to assign you the same applicant identification number that was used before. This will allow the certification team at IBM to quickly recognize when you have met all the exam requirements for a particular certification role. (If you were assigned a unique applicant identification number each time you took an exam, you should go to the IBM Professional Certification Member Web site (*www.ibm.com/certify/members*) and select Member Services to combine all of your exam results under one ID.)

With the exception of the DB2 9 for Linux, UNIX, and Windows Database Administration Upgrade exam (Exam 736), each certification exam costs $150 (in the United States). Scheduling procedures vary according to how you choose to pay for the exam. If you decide to pay by credit card, you can make arrangements to take the exam immediately after providing the testing vendor with the appropriate information. However, if you elect to pay by check, you will be required to wait until the check has been received and payment has been confirmed before you will be allowed to make arrangements to take the exam. (Thompson Prometric recommends that if you pay by check, you write your registration ID on the front and contact them seven business days after the check is mailed. At that time, they should have received and confirmed your payment, and you should be able to make arrangements to take the exam for which you have paid.)

If, for some reason, you need to reschedule or cancel your testing appointment after it is made, you must do so at least 24 hours before your scheduled test time. Otherwise, you will still be charged the price of the exam.

Taking an IBM Certification Exam

On the day you are scheduled to take a certification exam, you should arrive at the testing center at least 15 minutes before the scheduled start time, to sign in. As part of the sign-in process, you will be asked to provide the applicant identification number you were assigned when you made arrangements to take the exam and two forms of identification. One form of identification must feature a recent photograph, and the other must show your signature. Examples of valid forms of identification include a driver's license (photograph) and a credit card (signature).

Once you are signed in, the exam administrator will instruct you to enter the testing area and select an available workstation. The exam administrator will then enter your name and identification number into the workstation you have chosen, provide you with a pencil and some paper, and instruct you to begin the exam when you are ready. At that point, the title screen of the IBM Certification Exam testing software should be displayed on the computer monitor in front of you. Figure 1–8 illustrates what this screen looks like.

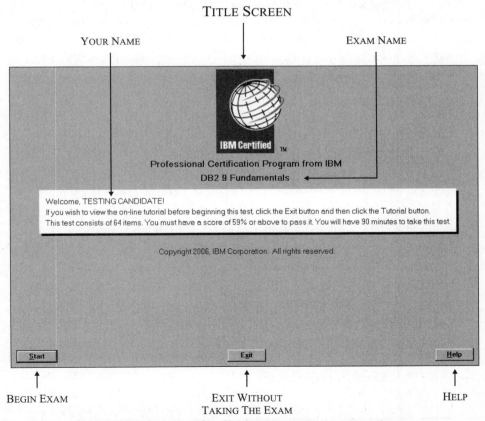

Figure 1–8: Title screen of the IBM Certification Exam testing software.

As you can see in Figure 1–8, the title screen of the IBM Certification Exam testing software consists of the IBM Certification Logo along with the title "Professional Certification Program from IBM," the name of the exam that is about to be administered (for example, the title screen shown in Figure 1–8 indicates that the DB2 9 Family Fundamentals exam is about to be administered), and a welcome message containing your name and some basic information on how to get started. Before proceeding, you should do the following:

- Verify that the exam you are about to take is indeed the exam you expected to take. If the name of the exam shown on the title screen is different from the name of the exam you had planned to take, bring this to the attention of the exam administrator immediately.

- Verify that your name is spelled correctly. The way your name appears in the welcome message shown on the title screen reflects how it has been stored in the IBM Certification database. This is how all correspondence to you will be addressed, and more importantly, this is how your name will appear on the certification credentials you will receive if you pass the exam.

In addition to telling you which exam is about to be administered, the title screen of the IBM Certification Exam testing software lets you know how many questions you can expect to see on the exam you are about to take, what kind of score you must receive in order to pass, and the time frame in which the exam must be completed. With one exception, each exam contains between 50 and 70 questions and is allotted 90 minutes for completion. The DB2 9 for Linux, UNIX, and Windows Database Administration Upgrade exam (Exam 736) contains 38 questions and is allotted 60 minutes for completion. Although each certification exam must be completed within a predefined time limit, you should never rush through an exam just because the "clock is running"; the time limits imposed are more than adequate for you to work through the exam at a relaxed, but steady pace.

When you are ready, begin by selecting the "Start" push button located in the lower left corner of the screen (refer to Figure 1–8). If instead you would like a quick refresher course on how to use the IBM Certification Exam testing software, select the "Help" push button located in the lower right corner of the screen. (If you panic and decide you're not ready to take the exam, you can select the "Exit" push button located between the "Start" and "Help" push buttons at the bottom of the screen to get out of the testing software altogether, but I recommend you talk with the exam administrator about your concerns before selecting this push button.)

If you plan to take a quick refresher course on how to use the IBM Certification Exam testing software, make sure you do so before you select the "Start" push button to begin the exam. Although help is available at any time, the clock does not start running until the "Start" push button is selected. By viewing help information before the clock is started, you avoid using what could prove to be valuable testing time reading documentation instead of answering test questions.

Once the "Start" button on the title screen of the IBM Certification Exam testing software is selected, the clock will start running, and the first exam question will be presented in a question panel that looks something like the panel shown in Figure 1–9.

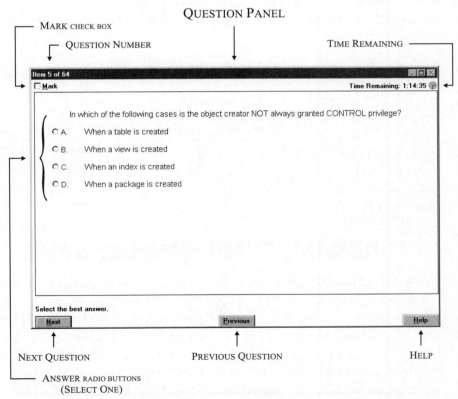

Figure 1–9: Typical question panel of the IBM Certification Exam testing software.

Aside from the question itself, one of the first things you may notice when you examine the question panel of the IBM Certification Exam testing software is the question number displayed in the top left corner of the screen. If you answer the questions in the order they are presented, this portion of the screen can act as a progress indicator because the current question number is displayed along with the total number of questions contained in the exam.

Immediately below the question number, you will find a special check box that is referred to as the "Mark" check box. If you would like to skip the current question for now and come back to it later, or if you're uncertain about the answer(s) you have chosen and would like to look at this question again after you have completed the rest of the exam, you should mark this check box (by placing the mouse pointer over it and pressing the left mouse button). When every question has been viewed once, you will be given the opportunity to review just the marked questions again. At that time, you can answer any unanswered questions remaining as well as reevaluate any answers about which you have some concerns.

Another important feature found on the question panel is the "Time Remaining" information that is displayed in the top right corner of the screen. As the title implies, this area of the question panel provides continuous feedback on the amount of time you have available to finish and review the exam. If you would like to see more detailed information, such as the actual wall-clock time at which you began the exam and the time frame within which you are expected to complete the exam, you can view that information by selecting the clock icon located just to the right of the "Time Remaining" information. When you select this icon (by placing the mouse pointer over it and pressing the left mouse button), a dialog similar to the one shown in Figure 1–10 is displayed.

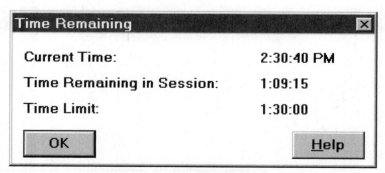

Figure 1–10: Time Remaining dialog.

Obviously, the most important part of the question panel is the exam question itself, along with the corresponding list of possible answers provided. Take the time to read each question carefully. When you have located the correct answer in the list provided, you should mark it by selecting the answer radio-button positioned just to the left of the answer text (by placing the mouse pointer over the desired answer radio-button and pressing the left mouse button). Once you have selected an answer for the question being displayed (or marked it with the "Mark" check box), you can move to the next question by selecting the "Next" push button, which is located in the lower left corner of the screen (refer to Figure 1–9).

If at any time you would like to return to the previous question, you can do so by pressing the "Previous" push button, located at the bottom of the screen, just to the right of the "Next" push button. If you would like to access help on how to use the IBM Certification Exam testing software, you can do so by selecting the "Help" push button located in the lower right corner of the screen. It is important to note that although the "Next" and "Previous" push buttons can be used to navigate through the questions, the navigation process itself is not cyclic in nature—that is, when you are on the first question, you cannot go to the last question by selecting the "Previous" push button (in fact, the "Previous" push button will not be displayed if you are on the first question). Likewise, when you are on the last question, you cannot go to the first question simply by selecting the "Next" push button. However, there is a way to navigate quickly to a specific question from the item review panel, which we will look at shortly.

Although in most cases only one answer in the list provided is the correct answer to the question shown, there are times when multiple answers are valid. On those occasions, the answer radio-buttons will be replaced with answer check boxes, and the question will be worded in such a way that you will know how many answers are expected. An example of such a question can be seen in Figure 1–11.

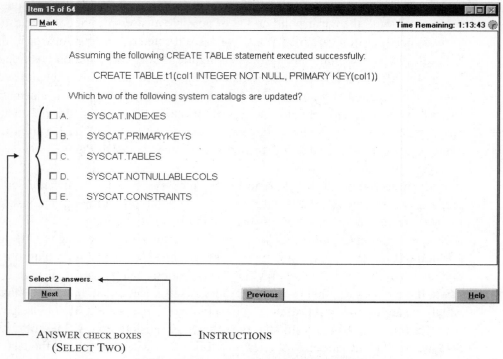

☐ Mark   Time Remaining: 1:13:43

Assuming the following CREATE TABLE statement executed successfully:

   CREATE TABLE t1(col1 INTEGER NOT NULL, PRIMARY KEY(col1))

Which two of the following system catalogs are updated?

☐ A.   SYSCAT.INDEXES

☐ B.   SYSCAT.PRIMARYKEYS

☐ C.   SYSCAT.TABLES

☐ D.   SYSCAT.NOTNULLABLECOLS

☐ E.   SYSCAT.CONSTRAINTS

Select 2 answers.

   Next   Previous   Help

ANSWER CHECK BOXES   INSTRUCTIONS
  (SELECT TWO)

Figure 1–11: Question panel for questions expecting multiple answers.

These types of questions are answered by selecting the answer check box positioned just to the left of the text *for every correct answer found*. (Again, you do this by placing the mouse pointer over each desired answer check box and pressing the left mouse button.)

Once in a while, an illustration or the output from some diagnostic tool will accompany a question. You will be required to view that illustration or output (referred to as an exhibit) before you can successfully answer the question presented. On those occasions, a message instructing you to display the exhibit for the question will precede the actual test question, and a special push button called the "Exhibit" push button will be positioned at the bottom of the screen, between the "Previous" push button and the "Help" push button. An example of such a question can be seen in Figure 1–12.

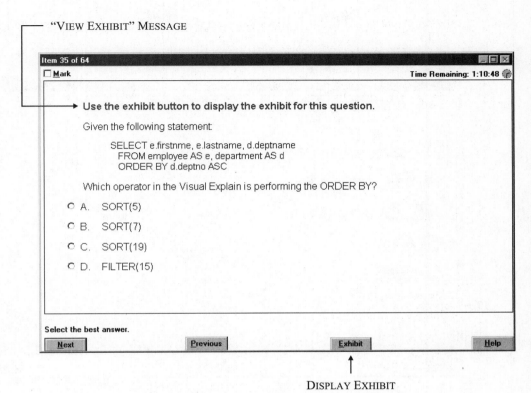

Figure 1–12: Question panel for questions that contain an exhibit.

To view the exhibit associated with such a question, you simply select the "Exhibit" push button located at the bottom of the screen. This action will cause the corresponding exhibit panel to be displayed. (A sample exhibit panel can be seen in Figure 1–13.)

EXHIBIT PANEL

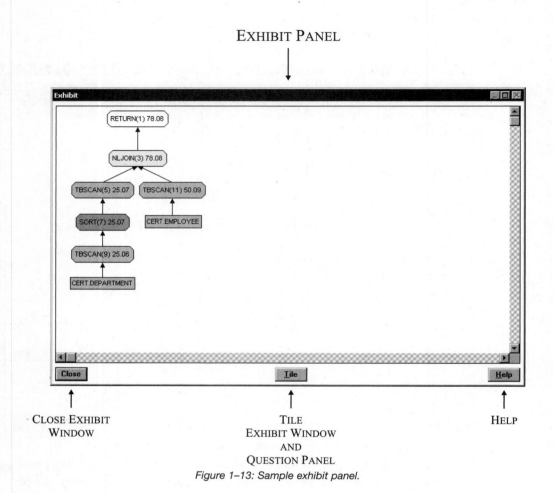

CLOSE EXHIBIT
WINDOW

TILE
EXHIBIT WINDOW
AND
QUESTION PANEL

HELP

Figure 1–13: Sample exhibit panel.

Exhibit panels are relatively simple. In fact, once an exhibit panel is displayed, there are only two things you can do with it: You can close it by selecting the "Close" push button located at the bottom of the screen, or you can tile it (i.e., make it share screen real estate) with its corresponding question panel by selecting the "Tile" push button, which is located beside the "Close" push button. Aside from having to view the exhibit provided, the process used to answer questions that have exhibits is no different from the process used to answer questions that do not.

When you have viewed every exam question available (by selecting the "Next" push button on every question panel shown), an item review panel that looks something like the panel shown in Figure 1–14 will be displayed.

ITEM (QUESTION) REVIEW PANEL

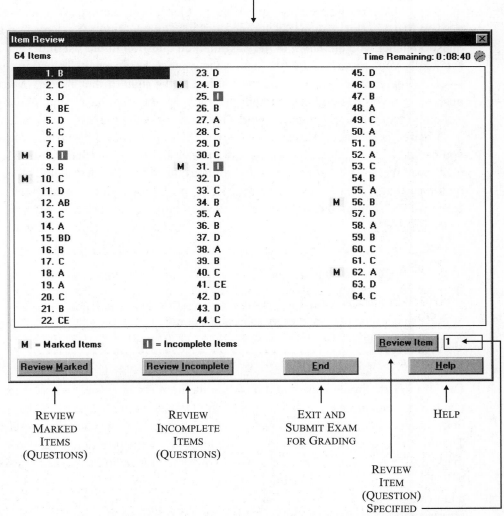

Figure 1–14: Item (question) review panel of the IBM Certification Exam testing software.

As you can see in Figure 1–14, the item review panel contains a numerical listing of the questions that make up the certification exam you are taking, along with the answers you have provided for each. Questions that you marked (by selecting the "Mark" check box) are preceded by the letter "M," and questions that you skipped or did not provide the correct number of answers for are assigned the answer "I" to indicate they are incomplete. By selecting the "Review Marked" push button located in the lower left corner of the screen (refer to Figure 1–14), you can quickly go back through just the questions that have been marked. When reviewing marked items in this manner, each time the "Next" push button is selected on a question panel, you are taken to the next marked question in the list until eventually you are returned to the item review panel. Likewise, by selecting the "Review Incomplete" push button located just to the right of the "Review Marked" push button, you can go back through just the questions that have been identified as being incomplete. (Navigation works the same as when the "Review Marked" push button is selected.) If, instead, you would like to review a specific question, you can do so by highlighting that question's number or typing that question's number in the entry field provided just to the right of the "Review Item" push button (which is located just above the "Help" push button in the lower right corner of the screen) and selecting the "Review Item" push button.

> If you elect to use the "Review Item" push button to review a particular question, the only way you can return to the item review screen is by selecting the "Next" push button found on that question panel and every subsequent question panel presented until no more question panels exist.

One of the first things you should do when the item review panel is displayed is resolve any incomplete items found. (When the exam is graded, each incomplete item found is marked incorrect, and points are deducted from your final score.) Then, if time permits, you should go back and review the questions that you marked. It is important to note that when you finish reviewing a marked question, you should unmark it (by placing the mouse pointer over the "Mark" check box and pressing the left mouse button) before going on to the next marked question or returning to the item review panel. This will make it easier for you to keep track of which questions have been reviewed and which have not.

As soon as every incomplete item found has been resolved, the "Review Incomplete" push button is automatically removed from the item review panel. Likewise, when there are no more marked questions, the "Review Marked" push button is removed from the item review panel. Thus, when every incomplete and marked item found has been resolved, the item review panel will look similar to the one shown in Figure 1–15.

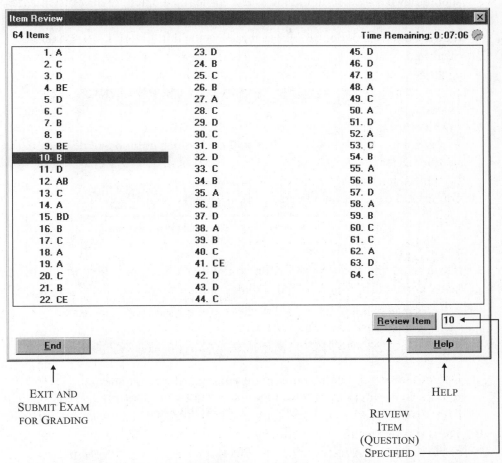

Figure 1–15: Item (question) review panel with all incomplete and marked items (questions) resolved.

Keep in mind that even when the "Review Incomplete" and "Review Marked" push buttons are no longer available, you can still go back and review a specific question by highlighting that question's number or typing that question's number in the entry field provided and selecting the "Review Item" push button (refer to Figure 1–15).

As soon as you feel comfortable with the answers you have provided, you can end the exam and submit it for grading by selecting the "End" push button, which should now be located in the lower left corner of the item review panel. After you select this push button (by placing the mouse pointer over it and pressing the left mouse button), a dialog similar to the one shown in Figure 1–16 should be displayed.

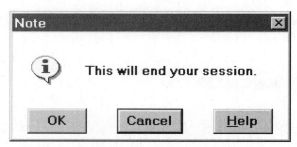

Figure 1–16: End exam session confirmation dialog.

If you select the "End" push button on the item review panel before all incomplete items found have been resolved, a dialog similar to the one shown in Figure 1–17 will be displayed instead.

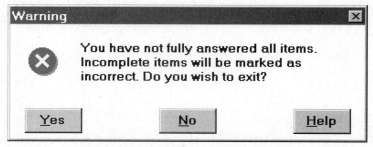

Figure 1–17: Ending exam with incomplete items warning dialog.

Both of these dialogs give you the opportunity to confirm your decision to end the exam and submit it for grading or to reconsider and continue resolving and/or reviewing exam questions. If you wish to do the former, you should select the "OK" or the "Yes" push button when one of these dialogs is presented; if you wish to do the latter, you should select the "Cancel" or "No" push button, in which case you will be returned to the item review panel. Keep in mind that if you select the

"Yes" push button when the dialog shown in Figure 1–17 is displayed, all incomplete items found will be marked as being wrong, and this will have a negative impact on your final score.

As soon as you confirm that you do indeed wish to end the exam, the IBM Certification Exam testing software will evaluate your answers and produce a score report that indicates whether you passed the exam. This report will then be displayed on an exam results panel that looks something like the panel shown in Figure 1–18, and a corresponding hard copy (printout) will be generated.

EXAM RESULTS PANEL

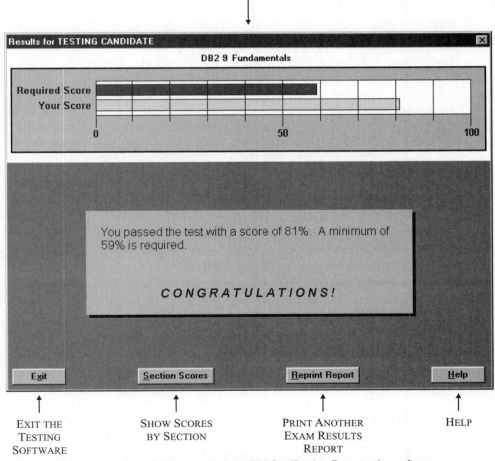

Figure 1–18: Exam results panel of the IBM Certification Exam testing software.

As you can see in Figure 1–18, the exam results panel shows the required score along with your actual score in a horizontal percentage bar graph. Directly below this graph is a message that contains the percentage score you received, along with the percentage score needed to pass the exam. If you received a passing score, this message will end with the word "Congratulations!" However, if you received a score that is below the score needed to pass, the message you see will begin with the words "You did not pass the test," and your score will follow.

Each certification exam is broken into sections, and regardless of whether you pass or fail, you should take a few moments to review the score you received for each section. This information can help you evaluate your strengths and weaknesses; if you failed to pass the exam, it can help you identify the areas you should spend some time reviewing before you take the exam again. To view the section scores for the exam you have just completed, you simply select the "Section Scores" push button located at the bottom of the screen. This action will cause a section scores panel similar to the one shown in Figure 1–19 to be displayed.

Section Scores Panel

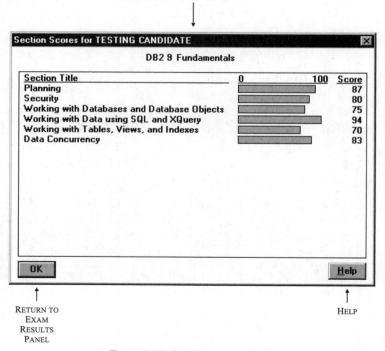

Figure 1–19: Section scores panel.

When you have finished reviewing your section scores, you may return to the exam results panel by selecting the "OK" push button located at the bottom left corner of the screen. From there, you can exit the IBM Certification Exam testing software by selecting the "Exit" push button, which is also located at the bottom left corner of the screen.

Shortly after you take a certification exam (usually within five working days), the testing vendor sends your results, along with your demographic data (e.g., name, address, phone number) to the IBM Certification Group for processing. If you passed the exam, you will receive credit toward the certification role the exam was designed for, and if the exam you took completes the requirements that have been outlined for a particular certification role, you will receive an email (at the email address you provided during registration) containing a copy of the IBM Certification Agreement and a welcome package that includes a certificate suitable for framing (in the form of a PDF file), camera-ready artwork of the IBM certification logo, and guidelines for using the "IBM Certified" mark. (If this email cannot be delivered, the welcome package will be sent to you via regular mail.) You can also receive a printed certificate, along with a wallet-sized certificate, via regular mail by going to the Web site referenced in the email you receive and requesting it—you will be asked to provide your Fulfillment ID and Validation Number (also provided in the email) as verification that you have met the requirements for certification.

Upon receipt of the welcome package, you are officially certified, and can begin using the IBM Professional Certification title and trademark. (You should receive the IBM Certification Agreement and welcome package within four to six weeks after IBM processes the exam results.) However, if you failed to pass the exam and you still wish to become certified, you must make arrangements to take it again (including paying the testing fee again). There are no restrictions on the number of times you can take a particular certification exam; however, you cannot take the same certification exam more than two times within a 30-day period.

CHAPTER 2

Server Management

Twenty and one-half percent (20.5%) of the DB2 9 for Linux, UNIX, and Windows Database Administration exam (Exam 731) is designed to test your knowledge about basic DB2 server management. The questions that make up this portion of the exam are intended to evaluate the following:

- Your ability to create and manage DB2 instances

- Your ability to view and modify DB2 system registry variables

- Your ability to view and modify DB2 Database Manager configuration information

- Your ability to view and modify database configuration information

- Your ability to configure client/server connectivity

- Your ability to configure clients and servers using DB2 Discovery

- Your ability to gain exclusive control of a database

- Your ability to schedule jobs

- Your ability to use Automatic Maintenance

- Your ability to throttle utilities

- Your ability to use DB2's Self-Tuning Memory Manager (STMM)

- Your ability to interpret information found in the Administration Notification Log

This chapter is designed to introduce you to the various concepts you need to be familiar with in order to manage a DB2 server. This chapter will also provide you with information about some of the tools that are available for server management.

Working with Instances

DB2 sees the world as a hierarchy of objects. Workstations (or servers) on which DB2 has been installed occupy the highest level of this hierarchy. When any edition of DB2 is installed on a workstation, program files for a background process known as the DB2 *Database Manager* are physically copied to a specific location on that workstation, and in most cases, an *instance* of the DB2 Database Manager is created. Instances occupy the second level in the hierarchy and are responsible for managing system resources and databases that fall under their control. Although only one instance is created initially, several instances can exist on a single server. Each instance behaves like a separate installation of DB2, even though all instances within a system share the same DB2 Database Manager program files (unless each instance is running a different version of DB2). And although multiple instances share the same binary code, each runs independently of the others and has its own environment, which can be modified by altering the contents of its associated configuration file.

Databases make up the third level in the hierarchy and are responsible for managing the storage, modification, and retrieval of data. Like instances, databases work independently of each other. Each database has its own environment (also controlled by a set of configuration parameters), as well as its own set of grantable authorities and privileges to govern how users interact with the data and database objects it controls. Figure 2–1 shows the hierarchical relationship between systems, instances, and databases.

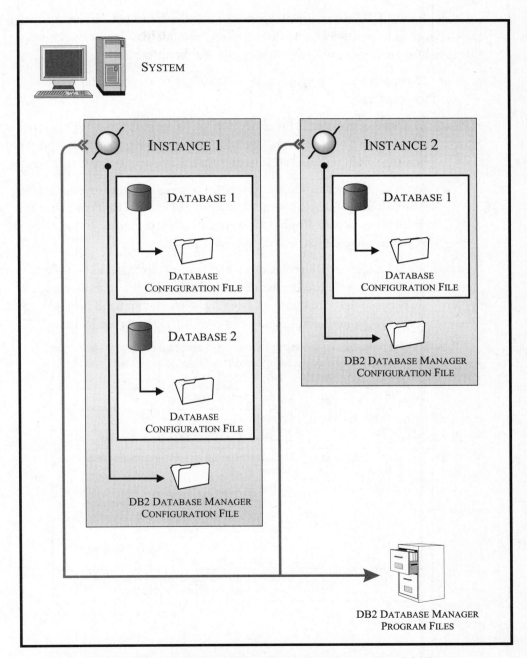

Figure 2-1: Hierarchical relationship between systems, instances, and databases.

Although most DB2 environments consist of one instance per server, at times it is advantageous to create multiple instances on the same physical workstation. Reasons for creating multiple instances include the following:

- To separate your development environment from your production environment.

- To obtain optimum performance for special applications. (For example, you may choose to create an instance for one or more applications and then fine-tune each instance specifically for the application(s) it will service.)

- To prevent database administrators from accessing sensitive data. (For example, a company's payroll database could reside in its own instance, in which case owners of other databases in other instances on the same server would be unable to access payroll data.)

As you might imagine, DB2 provides several commands that can be used to create and manage instances. These commands, which are referred to as system commands because they are executed from the system command prompt rather than from the DB2 Command Line Processor (CLP), are shown in Table 2.1.

Table 2.1 DB2 Instance Management Commands	
Command	**Purpose**
db2icrt [*InstanceName*]	Create a new instance.
db2idrop [*InstanceName*]	Delete (drop) an existing instance.
db2ilist	List all instances that have been defined.
db2imigr [*InstanceName*]	Upgrade (migrate) an existing instance to a newer version of DB2.
db2iupdt [*InstanceName*]	Update an existing instance to take advantage of new functionality that is provided when product fix packs are installed. (Also used to convert a 32-bit instance to a 64-bit instance.)
db2start	Start the DB2 Database Manager background processes for the current instance.
db2stop	Stop the DB2 Database Manager background processes for the current instance.

Although basic syntax is presented for the instance management commands shown in Table 2.1, the actual syntax supported may be more complex. To view the complete syntax for a specific DB2 command or to obtain more information about a particular command, refer to the *IBM DB2, Version 9 Command Reference* product documentation.

Attaching to an Instance

The default instance for a system is defined by the DB2INSTANCE environment variable, and in many cases, this is the instance that all instance-level operations are performed against. If you need to perform an operation against a different instance, you must first change the value assigned to the DB2INSTANCE variable by executing the command set DB2INSTANCE=[*InstanceName*] (export DB2INSTANCE=[*InstanceName*] on Linux and UNIX), where *InstanceName* is the name assigned to the instance that you want to make the default instance, or you must *attach* to that instance. Applications and users can attach to any instance by executing the ATTACH command. The basic syntax for this command is:

```
ATTACH <TO [InstanceName]>
<USER [UserID] <USING [Password]
    <NEW [NewPassword] CONFIRM [NewPassword]>>>
```

where:

InstanceName   Identifies the name assigned to the instance to which an attachment is to be made. (This instance must have a matching entry in the local node directory.)

UserID   Identifies the user (by authorization ID) under whom the instance attachment is to be made.

Password   Identifies the password that corresponds to the authorization ID specified.

NewPassword   Identifies the password that is to replace the current password associated with the authorization ID specified.

Thus, if you wanted to attach to an instance named DB2_PROD using the authentication ID DB2ADMIN and the password IBMDB2, you could do so by executing an ATTACH command that looks something like this:

```
ATTACH TO db2_prod USER db2admin USING ibmdb2
```

Instance-level attachments can also be made using the Attach dialog, which can be activated by selecting the appropriate action from the Systems menu found in the Control Center. Figure 2–2 shows the Control Center menu items that must be selected to activate the Attach dialog; Figure 2–3 shows how the Attach dialog looks when it is first activated.

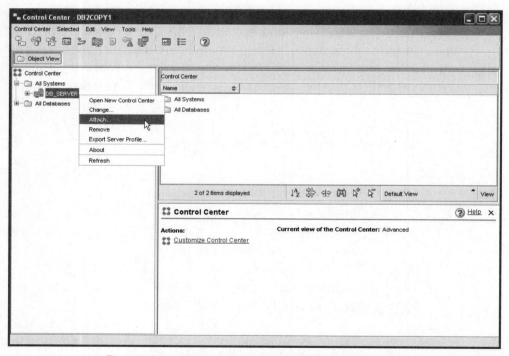

Figure 2–2: Invoking the Attach dialog from the Control Center.

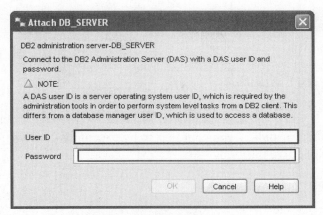

Figure 2–3: The Attach dialog.

Detaching from an Instance

Once an attachment to an instance has been made and all necessary tasks have been performed against that instance, the instance attachment should be terminated if it is no longer needed; by terminating an instance attachment, you eliminate the potential to accidentally perform new operations against the wrong instance. The easiest way to terminate an attachment to an instance is by establishing an attachment to another one. That's because an application or user can be attached to only one instance at a time—if an attachment is made to another instance, the current instance attachment is automatically terminated.

Applications and users can also detach from an instance by executing the DETACH command. The basic syntax for this command is:

DETACH

As you can see, the DETACH command requires no additional parameters.

Starting and Stopping an Instance

The DB2 Database Manager background processes that are associated with a particular instance must be active and ready to process requests before any operation can be performed against the instance or a database under the instance's control. If they are not already running, these background processes can be started by executing the START DATABASE MANAGER command. The basic syntax for this command is:

```
START [DATABASE MANAGER | DB MANAGER | DBM]
```

or

```
db2start </D>
```

Thus, if you wanted to start the DB2 Database Manager background processes for the default instance, you could do so by executing a command that looks something like this:

```
START DATABASE MANAGER
```

If at any time you want to stop the DB2 Database Manager background processes, you can do so by executing the STOP DATABASE MANAGER command. The basic syntax for this command is:

```
STOP [DATABASE MANAGER | DB MANAGER | DBM]
<FORCE>
```

or

```
db2stop
```

Therefore, if you wanted to stop the DB2 Database Manager background processes for the default instance, you could do so by executing a command that looks something like this:

```
STOP DATABASE MANAGER
```

Quiescing an Instance

Because any number of users can be granted access to an instance or one or more databases under an instance's control, it can be difficult, if not impossible, to coordinate the work efforts of everyone who is using a specific instance at any given point in time. This can present a problem if a Database Administrator needs exclusive access to a particular instance for a short period of time, for example to perform a maintenance operation. Because of this, individuals holding the proper authority can place an instance in a "restricted access" or "quiesced" state; when an instance is quiesced, all users are forced off the instance, all active transactions are immediately rolled back, and all databases under the instance's control are put into quiesced mode. Instances (and databases) can be placed in quiesced mode by executing the QUIESCE command. The basic syntax for this command is:

```
QUIESCE
[INSTANCE [InstanceName] | DATABASE | DB]
<USER [UserName] | GROUP [GroupName]>
[IMMEDIATE | DEFER <WITH TIMEOUT [Minutes]>]
<FORCE CONNECTIONS>
```

where:

InstanceName   Identifies the name assigned to the instance that is to be placed in quiesced mode.

UserName   Identifies the name of a specific user who is to be allowed access to the instance or database specified while it is in quiesced mode.

GroupName   Identifies the name of a specific group of users who are to be allowed access to the instance or database specified while it is in quiesced mode.

Minutes   Specifies a time, in minutes, to wait for applications to commit their current transaction before quiescing the instance/database. If no value is specified, the default value is 10 minutes.

Thus, if you wanted to place an instance named DEV_INST into quiesced mode immediately, but allow a user named DB2ADMIN to continue to have access to it, you could do so by executing a QUIESCE command that looks something like this:

```
QUIESCE INSTANCE dev_inst
FOR USER db2admin
IMMEDIATE
```

Eventually, an instance or database that has been put into quiesced mode will need to be returned to a normal state. Instances and databases can be removed from quiesced mode by executing the UNQUIESCE command. The basic syntax for this command is:

```
UNQUIESCE [INSTANCE [InstanceName] | DB]
```

where:

InstanceName   Identifies the name assigned to the instance that is to be taken
                     out of quiesced mode.

Therefore, if you wanted to take an instance named DEV_INST out of quiesced
mode, you could do so by executing an UNQUIESCE command that looks like this:

```
UNQUIESCE INSTANCE dev_inst
```

You can also quiesce and unquiesce instances and databases by selecting the
Quiesce or Unquiesce action from either the Instances menu or the Databases
menu found in the Control Center. Figure 2–4 shows the Control Center menu
items that must be selected in order to activate the Quiesce instance dialog.
Figure 2–5 shows how this dialog might look when it is first activated.

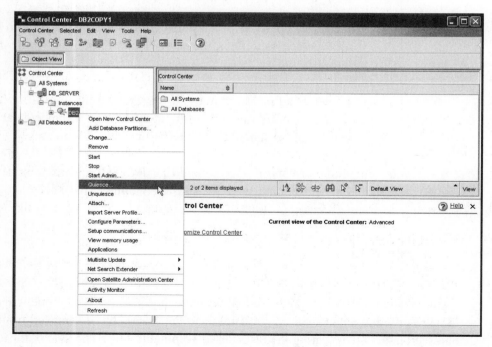

Figure 2–4: Invoking the Quiesce dialog from the Control Center.

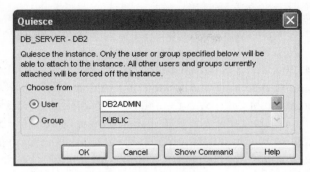

Figure 2–5: The Quiesce dialog.

It is important to note that only users with System Administrator (SYSADM) or System Control (SYSCTRL) authority are allowed to quiesce an instance; once an instance is in a quiesced state, only users with System Administrator (SYSADM), System Control (SYSCTRL), or System Maintenance (SYSMAINT) authority, users who are members of a group specified (if a group name was specified when the instance was placed in quiesced mode), and users with the user name specified (if a user name was specified when the instance was placed in quiesced mode) are allowed to connect to the instance.

Similarly, only users with System Administrator (SYSADM) or Database Administrator (DBADM) authority are allowed to quiesce a database; once a database is in a quiesced state, only users with System Administrator (SYSADM), System Control (SYSCTRL), System Maintenance (SYSMAINT), or Database Administrator (DBADM) authority, users who are members of a group specified (if a group name was specified when the database was placed in quiesced mode), and users with the user name specified (if a user name was specified when the database was placed in quiesced mode) are allowed to connect to the database.

A Word About the DB2 Administration Server (DAS) Instance

All of the tools that come with DB2 (such as the Control Center) require a separate instance that operates independently of, yet concurrently with, all other instances that have been defined for a particular workstation. For this reason, a special instance, known as the DB2 Administration Server (DAS) instance, is also created as part of the DB2 installation process. In contrast to other instances, only one DAS instance can exist on a single workstation. (The DB2 global-level profile registry variable DB2ADMINSERVER contains the name of the DAS instance that has been defined for a particular workstation.)

Once created, the DAS instance runs continuously as a background process whenever the system it was created on is online; the DAS instance is usually activated automatically each time the workstation it resides on is started (or rebooted). Furthermore, the DAS instance must be running on every DB2 server that you wish to administer remotely. That's because, among other things, the DAS instance provides remote clients with the information needed to establish communications with other instances. (It is important to note that in order to administer a server from a remote client, a user must have System Administration (SYSADM) authority for the DAS instance used. Furthermore, once a remote instance and database have been registered on a client workstation, the user must hold the authorities and privileges needed to perform administrative tasks.)

In addition to enabling remote administration of DB2 servers, the DAS instance assists the Control Center and the Configuration Assistant in the following:

- Providing job (task) management, including the ability to schedule and run user-defined shell scripts/batch files that contain both DB2 and operating system commands.

- Scheduling jobs, viewing the results of completed jobs, and performing administrative tasks against jobs executed either remotely or locally (by using the Task Center).

- Providing a means for discovering information about the configuration of other DAS instances, DB2 instances, and databases using DB2 Discovery. (The Configuration Assistant and the Control Center use such information to simplify and automate the configuration of client connections to DB2 servers; neither tool will be able to "discover" a server if the DAS instance for that server is not running.)

Configuring the DB2 System Environment

During normal operation, the behavior of the DB2 Database Manager is controlled, in part, by a collection of values that define the DB2 operating environment. Some of these values are operating system environment variables, and others are special

DB2-specific system-level values known as environment or registry variables. Registry variables provide a way to centrally control the database environment. Three different registry profiles are available, and each controls the database environment at a different level. The registry profiles available are as follows:

The DB2 Global-Level Profile Registry. All machine-wide environment variable settings are kept in this registry; one global-level profile registry exists on each DB2 workstation. If an environment variable is to be set for all instances, this profile registry is used.

The DB2 Instance-Level Profile Registry. The environment variable settings for a particular instance are kept in this registry; this is where the majority of the DB2 environment variables are set. (Values defined in this profile registry override any corresponding settings in the global-level profile registry.)

The DB2 Instance Node-Level Profile Registry. This profile registry level contains variable settings that are specific to a partition (node) in a multi-partitioned database environment. (Values defined in this profile registry override any corresponding settings in the global-level and instance-level profile registries.)

> DB2 looks for environment variable values in the DB2 global-level profile registry first, then in the DB2 instance-level profile registry, and finally, in the DB2 instance node-level profile registry. (Additional values may be set in individual sessions, in which case DB2 will see these values last.)

A wide variety of registry variables are available, and they vary depending on the operating system being used. A complete listing can be found in Appendix B of the *IBM DB2, Version 9 Performance Guide* product documentation.

So how do you determine which registry variables have been set, and what they have been set to? Or more importantly, how do you assign values to one or more registry variables? One way is by executing the db2set system command. The basic syntax for this command is:

```
db2set
<[Variable] = [Value]>
<-g | -gl | -i [InstanceName]>
<-all>
<-null>
<-r [InstanceName]>
<-n [DASNode] <-u [UserID] <-p [Password]>>>
<-l | -lr>
<-v>
<-ul | -ur>
<-h | -?>
```

where:

Variable   Identifies the registry variable whose value is to be displayed, set, or removed.

Value   Identifies the value that is to be assigned to the registry variable specified. If no value is provided, but a registry variable is specified, the registry variable specified is deleted.

InstanceName   Identifies the instance profile with which the specified registry variable is associated.

DASNode   Identifies the name of the node where the DB2 Administration Server instance resides.

UserID   Identifies the authentication ID that will be used to attach to the DB2 Administration Server instance.

Password   Identifies the password (for the authentication ID) that will be used to attach to the DB2 Administration Server instance.

All other options shown with this command are described in Table 2.2.

Table 2.2 db2set Command Options	
Option	**Meaning**
-g	Indicates that a global profile variable is to be displayed, set, or removed.
-gl	Indicates that a global profile variable stored in LDAP is to be displayed, set, or removed. This option is only effective if the registry variable DB2_ENABLE_LDAP has been set to YES.
-i	Indicates that an instance profile variable is to be displayed, set, or removed.
-all	Indicates that all occurrences of the registry variable, as defined in the following, are to be displayed: • The environment (denoted by [-e]) • The node-level registry (denoted by [-n]) • The instance-level registry (denoted by [-i]) • The global-level registry (denoted by [-g])
-null	Indicates that the value of the variable at the specified registry level is to be set to NULL.
-r	Indicates that the profile registry for the given instance is to be reset.
-n	Indicates that a remote DB2 Administration Server instance node name is specified.
-u	Indicates that an authentication ID that will be used to attach to the DB2 Administration Server instance is specified.
-p	Indicates that a password for the authentication ID specified is provided.
-l	Indicates that all instance profiles will be listed.
-lr	Indicates that all registry variables supported will be listed.
-v	Indicates that the db2set command is to be executed in verbose mode.
-ul	Accesses the user profile variables. (This parameter is supported only on Windows operating systems.)
-ur	Refreshes the user profile variables. (This parameter is supported only on Windows operating systems.)
-h	-?	Displays help information. When this option is specified, all other options are ignored, and only the help information is displayed.

It is important to note that if the db2set command is executed without options, a list containing every registry variable that has been set for the current (default) instance, along with its value, will be returned.

Thus, if you wanted to find out which registry variables have been set for each profile available, you could do so by executing a db2set command that looks like this:

```
db2set -all
```

And when this command is executed, the output produced might look something like this:

```
[e] DB2PATH=C:\DB2_ESE\SQLLIB
[i] DB2_ENABLE_AUTOCONFIG_DEFAULT=NO
[i] DB2_XML_RUNSTATS_PATHVALUE_K=300
[i] DB2_XML_RUNSTATS_PATHID_K=300
[i] DB2ACCOUNTNAME=db_server\db2admin
[i] DB2INSTOWNER=db_server
[i] DB2PORTRANGE=60000:60003
[i] DB2INSTPROF=C:\DB2_ESE\SQLLIB
[i] DB2COMM=TCPIP, NPIPE
[g] DB2_EXTSECURITY=YES
[g] DB2SYSTEM=DB_SERVER
[g] DB2PATH=C:\DB2_ESE\SQLLIB
[g] DB2INSTDEF=DB2
[g] DB2ADMINSERVER=DB2DAS00
```

On the other hand, if you wanted to see the current value of the DB2COMM registry variable for all DB2 instances, you could do so by executing a db2set command that looks something like this:

```
db2set -l DB2COMM
```

And finally, if you wanted to assign a value to the DB2COMM registry variable for all DB2 instances on a server, you could do so by executing a db2set command that looks something like this:

```
db2set -g DB2COMM=[Protocol, ...]
```

where:

Protocol Identifies one or more communications protocols that are to be started when the DB2 Database Manager for the instance is started. Any combination of the following values is valid: NPIPE, TCPIP, and SSL.

Thus, if you wanted to set the DB2COMM instance level registry variable such that the DB2 Database Manager would start the TCP/IP communication manager each time any instance is started, you could do so by executing a db2set command that looks like this:

```
db2set -g DB2COMM=TCPIP
```

You can remove the value assigned to any registry variable by providing just the variable name and the equal sign as input to the db2set command. Thus, if you wanted to disable the DB2COMM instance level registry variable for an instance named PAYROLL, you could do so by executing a db2set command that looks like this:

```
db2set -i PAYROLL DB2COMM=
```

Another way to view and/or change registry variable settings is by using a tool known as the DB2 Registry management tool. The DB2 Registry management tool is activated by selecting the DB2 Registry action from the Configure menu found in the Configuration Assistant. Figure 2–6 shows the Configuration Assistant menu items that must be selected in order to activate the DB2 Registry management tool; Figure 2–7 shows how the main dialog of the DB2 Registry management tool might look after it has been activated.

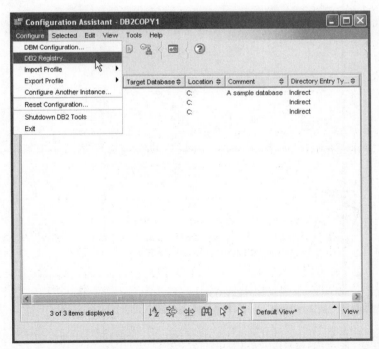

Figure 2–6: Invoking the DB2 Registry management tool from the Configuration Assistant.

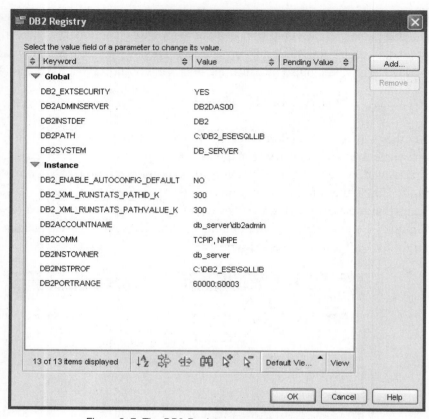

Figure 2–7: The DB2 Registry management tool dialog.

Although registry variables can be set at any time, the DB2 Database Manager must be stopped and restarted before any changes made will take effect.

Configuring Instances and Databases

Along with the comprehensive set of registry variables available, DB2 uses an extensive array of configuration parameters to control how system resources are allocated and utilized on behalf of an instance and a database. Unfortunately, the default values provided for many of these configuration parameters were produced with very simple systems in mind. (The goal was for DB2 to run out of the box, on virtually any platform, not for DB2 to run optimally on the platform on which it is installed.) Thus, even though the default values provided for these configuration parameters are sufficient to meet most database needs, you can usually greatly improve overall system and application performance simply by changing the values of one or more configuration parameters. In fact, the values assigned to DB2 configuration parameters should always be modified if your database environment contains one or more of the following:

- Large databases

- Databases that normally service large numbers of concurrent connections

- One or more special applications that have high performance requirements

- A special hardware configuration

- Unique query or transaction loads

- Unique query or transaction types

In Chapter 5 – "Analyzing DB2 Activity," we'll look at ways to measure transaction loads and performance to determine how configuration parameter values should be altered. For now let's take a closer look at the configuration parameters available.

The DB2 Database Manager Instance Configuration

Whenever an instance is created, a corresponding DB2 Database Manager configuration file is also created and initialized as part of the instance creation process. Each DB2 Database Manager configuration file is made up of approximately 85 different parameter values, and most control the amount of system resources that are allocated to a single DB2 Database Manager instance. The parameters that make up a DB2 9 DB2 Database Manager configuration file are shown in Table 2.3.

Table 2.3 DB2 Database Manager Instance Configuration Parameters		
Parameter	Value Range/Default	Description
agent_stack_sz	8–1,000 4K Pages Default: 16	Specifies the amount of memory (in pages) that is to be allocated by the operating system for each DB2 agent used.
agentpri	-1, 41–128 4K Pages or 0–6 4K Pages, depending on the operating system being used. Default: -1	Specifies the execution priority that is to be given, by the operating system scheduler, both to all agents and to other DB2 Database Manager instance processes and threads.
aslheapsz	1–524,288 4K Pages Default: 15	Specifies the amount of memory (in pages) that is to be shared between a local client application and a DB2 Database Manager agent. The application support layer heap represents a communication buffer between the local application and its associated agent. This buffer is allocated as shared memory by each DB2 Database Manager agent that is started.
audit_buf_sz	0–65,000 4K Pages Default: 0	Specifies the amount of memory (in pages) that is to be used to store audit records that are generated by the audit facility. If this parameter is set to 0, no audit buffer is used.
authentication	CLIENT, SERVER, SERVER_ENCRYPT, KERBEROS, KRB_SERVER_ENCRYPT, DATA_ENCRYPT, DATA_ENCRYPT_CMP, GSSPLUGIN, GSS_SERVER_ENCRYPT Default: SERVER	Specifies how and where user authentication takes place. If this parameter is set to CLIENT, authentication takes place at the client workstation. If this parameter is set to SERVER, the user ID and password are sent from the client workstation to the server workstation so that authentication can take place at the server. The value SERVER_ENCRYPT provides the same behavior as SERVER, except that any passwords sent over the network are encrypted. A value of DATA_ENCRYPT means the server accepts encrypted SERVER authentication schemes and user data is encrypted.
catalog_noauth	YES, NO Default: YES	Specifies whether users without System Administrator (SYSADM) authority are allowed to catalog and uncatalog nodes, databases, or DCS and ODBC directories.
clnt_krb_plugin	Any valid character string Default: NULL or "IBMkrb5"	Specifies the name of the default Kerberos plug-in library to be used for client-side authentication and local authorization. This plug-in library is used when the client is authenticated using KERBEROS authentication.

Parameter	Value Range/Default	Description
clnt_pw_plugin	Any valid character string Default: NULL	Specifies the name of the User ID–Password plug-in library to be used for client-side authentication and local authorization. This plug-in library is used when the client is authenticated using CLIENT, SERVER, or SERVER_ENCRYPT authentication.
comm_bandwidth	0.1–100,000 Megabytes per second Default: -1	Specifies the calculated value for the communications bandwidth (in megabytes per second) that is to be used by the DB2 Optimizer to estimate the cost of performing certain SQL operations between the database partition servers of a partitioned database system.
conn_elapse	0–100 Seconds Default: 10	Specifies the number of seconds within which a TCP/IP connection between two nodes is to be established. (If a connection is not established within the time specified by this parameter, other attempts are made up to the number of times specified by the *max_connretries* parameter. If all attempts made fail, an error is returned.)
cpuspeed	-1, 10^{-10} -1 Default: -1	Specifies the speed of the CPU, in milliseconds per instruction, being used by the workstation on which DB2 has been installed.
dft_account_str	Any valid character string Default: NULL	Specifies the default charge-back accounting string that is to be used when connecting to DRDA servers.
dft_mon_bufpool	ON, OFF Default: OFF	Specifies the default value of the snapshot monitor's buffer pool switch.
dft_mon_lock	ON, OFF Default: OFF	Specifies the default value of the snapshot monitor's lock switch.
dft_mon_sort	ON, OFF Default: OFF	Specifies the default value of the snapshot monitor's sort switch.
dft_mon_stmt	ON, OFF Default: OFF	Specifies the default value of the snapshot monitor's statement switch.
dft_mon_table	ON, OFF Default: OFF	Specifies the default value of the snapshot monitor's table switch.
dft_mon_timestamp	ON, OFF Default: ON	Specifies the default value of the snapshot monitor's timestamp switch.
dft_mon_uow	ON, OFF Default: OFF	Specifies the default value of the snapshot monitor's unit of work (UOW) switch.
dftdbpath	Any valid character string Default: Drive C: (Windows) or instance user's home directory (UNIX).	Specifies the default drive (Windows) or directory path (UNIX) that is to be used to store new databases. (If no path is specified when a database is created, the database is created in the location identified by this parameter.)

Table 2.3 DB2 Database Manager Instance Configuration Parameters (continued)

Table 2.3 DB2 Database Manager Instance Configuration Parameters (continued)		
Parameter	**Value Range/Default**	**Description**
diaglevel	0–4 Default: 3	Specifies the type of diagnostic errors that will be recorded in the database administration notification log file and the DB2 diagnostics log file (db2diag.log).
diagpath	Any valid character string Default: NULL	Specifies the fully qualified path where DB2 diagnostic information is to be stored.
dir_cache	YES, NO Default: YES	Specifies whether directory cache support is enabled. (If this parameter is set to YES, then node, database, and DCS directory files are cached in memory. This reduces connect overhead by eliminating directory file I/O and minimizing the directory searches required to retrieve directory information.)
discover	DISABLE, KNOWN, SEARCH Default: SEARCH	Specifies the type of DB2 Discovery requests that are supported. (If this parameter is set to SEARCH, then search discovery, in which the DB2 client searches the network for DB2 databases, is supported. If this parameter is set to KNOWN, then known discovery, in which the discovery request is issued against the administration server specified by the user, is supported. If this parameter is set to DISABLE, the workstation will not respond to any type of discovery request.)
discover_inst	ENABLE, DISABLE Default: ENABLE	Specifies whether this instance can be detected by DB2 Discovery requests.
fcm_num_buffers	AUTOMATIC, 128–65,300 (32-bit), 128–524,288 (64-bit) Buffers Default: AUTOMATIC	Specifies the number of 4KB buffers that are to be used for internal communications (messages) both among and within database servers When set to AUTOMATIC, FCM monitors resource usage and incrementally releases resources if they are not used within 30 minutes. If the database manager cannot allocate the number of resources specified when an instance is started, it scales back the configuration values incrementally until it can start the instance.
fcm_num_channels	AUTOMATIC, 128–120,000 (32-bit), 128–524,288 (64-bit) Channels Default: AUTOMATIC	Specifies the number of channels that are to be used for internal communications (messages) both among and within database servers. (An FCM channel represents a logical communication end point between EDUs running in the DB2 engine.) When set to AUTOMATIC, FCM monitors channel usage, incrementally allocating and releasing resources as requirements change.

Parameter	Value Range/Default	Description
Table 2.3 DB2 Database Manager Instance Configuration Parameters (continued)		
fed_noauth	YES, NO Default: NO	Specifies whether authentication at the instance is to be bypassed (because authentication will happen at the data source). (When *fed_noauth* is set to YES, *authentication* is set to SERVER or SERVER_ENCRYPT, and *federated* is set to YES, then authentication at the instance is bypassed.)
federated	YES, NO Default: NO	Specifies whether federated database object support is enabled (i.e., whether applications can submit distributed requests for data being managed by DB2 Family and Oracle database management systems).
fenced_pool	-1, 0–*max_coordagents* Default: *max_coordagents*	Specifies the maximum number of fenced processes that may reside at the database server. (Once this limit is reached, no new fenced requests may be invoked.)
group_plugin	Any valid character string Default: NULL	Specifies the name of the group plug-in library that will be used for all group lookups.
health_mon	ON, OFF Default: ON	Specifies whether the health of the instance and database objects that have been configured in the Health Center is to be monitored. (When turned on, the DB2 Health Monitor collects information from these objects and takes actions when an object is considered unhealthy. The monitor can be started and stopped dynamically by modifying the switch setting.)
indexrec	RESTART, RESTART_NO_REDO ACCESS, ACCESS_NO_REDO, Default: RESTART	Specifies when the DB2 Database Manager will attempt to rebuild invalid indexes and whether any index build will be redone during roll-forward or HADR log replay on the standby database. This parameter is used only if the database configuration parameter *indexrec* is set to SYSTEM.
instance_memory	AUTOMATIC, 8–4,294,967,295 4K Pages Default: AUTOMATIC	Specifies the amount of memory that should be reserved for instance management, including memory areas that describe the database under the instance's control. The memory allocated by this parameter establishes the maximum number of databases that can be active at the same time and the maximum number of agents that can be active at any given time. (If this parameter is set to AUTOMATIC, DB2 will calculate the amount of instance memory needed for the current configuration.)

Table 2.3 DB2 Database Manager Instance Configuration Parameters (continued)		
Parameter	**Value Range/Default**	**Description**
intra_parallel	SYSTEM, YES, NO Default: NO	Specifies whether the DB2 Database Manager instance can use intrapartition parallelism.
java_heap_sz	0–524,288 4K Pages Default: 2,048	Specifies the maximum amount of memory (in pages) that is to be used by the Java interpreter to service Java DB2 stored procedures and user-defined functions.
jdk_path	Any valid character string Default: NULL	Specifies the directory under which the Software Developer's Kit (SDK) for Java™, to be used for running Java stored procedures and user-defined functions, is installed. CLASSPATH and other environment variables used by the Java interpreter are computed using the value of this parameter.
keepfenced	YES, NO Default: YES	Specifies whether a fenced process is to be kept after a fenced call is completed. (If this parameter is set to NO, a new fenced process is created and destroyed for each fenced invocation; if set to YES, a fenced process is reused for subsequent fenced calls.)
local_gssplugin	Any valid character string Default: NULL	Specifies the name of the default GSS API plug-in library to be used for instance-level local authorization when the value of the authentication database manager configuration parameter is set to GSSPLUGIN or GSS_SERVER_ENCRYPT.
max_connections	-1, 1–64,000 Default: -1 (*max_coordagents*)	Specifies the maximum number of applications that can be connected to the instance.
max_connretries	0–100 Default: 5	Specifies the number of connection retries that can be made to a database partition server. If the value specified for this parameter is exceeded, an error is returned.
max_coordagents	-1, 0–*maxagents* Default: -1 (*maxagents–num_initagents*)	Specifies the maximum number of coordinating agents that can exist on a node at one time. This parameter is used to limit the number of coordinating agents or to control the workload in a database.
max_querydegree	ANY, 1–32,767 Default: ANY	Specifies the maximum degree of intrapartition parallelism that is to be used for any SQL statement executing on this instance of the DB2 Database Manager.

Table 2.3 DB2 Database Manager Instance Configuration Parameters (continued)		
Parameter	**Value Range/Default**	**Description**
max_time_diff	1–1,440 Minutes Default: 60	Specifies the maximum time difference, in minutes, that is permitted among the system clocks of the database partition servers listed in the db2nodes.cfg file.
maxagents	1–64,000 Default: 200 (400 on a partitioned database server)	Specifies the maximum number of DB2 Database Manager agents that can exist simultaneously, regardless of which database is being used. (An agent facilitates the operations between the application and the database.)
maxcagents	-1, 1–*max_coordagents* Default: -1 (*max_coordagents*)	Specifies the maximum number of DB2 Database Manager agents that can be concurrently executing a DB2 Database Manager transaction. This parameter can be set to the same value as the *maxagents* parameter.
maxfilop	2–1,950 (UNIX), 2–32,768 (Windows) Default: 64	Specifies the maximum number of files that can be open per application. The value specified in this parameter defines the total database and application file handles that can be used by a specific process connected to a database.
mon_heap_sz	0–60,000 4K Pages Default: 40, 66, or 90, depending on the operating system used.	Specifies the amount of memory (in 4KB pages) to allocate for database system monitor data.
nname	Any valid character string Default: NULL	Specifies the name of the node or workstation. Database clients use this value to access database server workstations using NetBIOS. If the database server workstation changes the name specified in *nname,* all clients that access the database server workstation must catalog it again and specify the new name.
nodetype	N/A	Read-only. Provides information about the DB2 products that you have installed on your machine.
notifylevel	0–4 Default: 3	Specifies the type of administration notification messages that are to be written to the administration notification log. (For Windows NT, notifications are written to the Windows NT event log. For all other operating systems and node types, notifications are written to the notification file called *instance.nfy.* Notifications can be written by DB2, the Health Monitor, and the Capture and Apply programs, as well as by user applications.)

Table 2.3 DB2 Database Manager Instance Configuration Parameters (continued)		
Parameter	**Value Range/Default**	**Description**
num_initagents	0–*num_poolagents* Default: 0	Specifies the initial number of idle agents that are to be created in the agent pool when the DB2 Database Manager is started.
num_initfenced	0–*max_connections* + (*maxagents* - *max_coordagents*) Default: 0	Specifies the initial number of idle, nonthreaded, fenced processes that are to be created in the fenced pool when the DB2 Database Manager is started. (This parameter can be used to reduce the initial startup time required for running non-threadsafe C and COBOL routines.)
num_poolagents	-1, 0–*maxagents* Default: -1 (*maxagents* / 2)	Specifies the size to which the idle agent pool is allowed to grow.
numdb	1–256 Default: 3 (Windows) or 8 (UNIX)	Specifies the maximum number of local databases that can be active (that is, that can have applications connected to them) at one time.
query_heap_sz	2–524,288 4K Pages Default: 1,000	Specifies the maximum amount of memory (in 4 KB pages) that can be allocated for the query heap. The query heap is used to store each query in the agent's private memory.
release	N/A	Read-only. Specifies the release level of the DB2 Database Manager configuration file.
resync_interval	1–60,000 Seconds Default: 180	Specifies the time interval (in seconds) after which a Transaction Manager (TM), Resource Manager (RM), or Sync Point Manager (SPM) should retry to recover any outstanding in-doubt transactions found in the TM, RM, or SPM. This parameter value is used only when transactions are running in a distributed unit of work (DUOW) environment.
rqrioblk	4,096–65,535 Bytes Default: 32,767	Specifies the size (in bytes) of the buffer that is used for communication between remote applications and their corresponding database agents on the database server.
sheapthres	0–2,097,152 4K Pages Default: 0	Specifies the instance-wide soft limit on the total amount of memory (in pages) that is to be made available for sorting operations.
spm_log_file_sz	4–1,000 4K Pages Default: 256	Specifies the size (in 4KB pages) of the Sync Point Manager (SPM) log file.
spm_log_path	Any valid character string Default: sqllib/spmlog	Specifies the directory where Sync Point Manager (SPM) log files are to be written.
spm_max_resync	10–256 Default: 20	Specifies the number of agents that can simultaneously perform resynchronization operations.

Table 2.3 DB2 Database Manager Instance Configuration Parameters (continued)		
Parameter	**Value Range/Default**	**Description**
spm_name	Any valid character string Default: Derived from TCP/IP hostname.	Specifies the name of the Sync Point Manager (SPM) instance that is to be used by the DB2 Database Manager.
srvcon_auth	CLIENT, SERVER, SERVER_ENCRYPT, KERBEROS, KRB_SERVER_ENCRYPT, GSSPLUGIN, GSS_SERVER_ENCRYPT Default: NULL	Specifies how and where user authentication is to take place when handling incoming connections at the server; used to override the current authentication type.
srvcon_gssplugin_ list	Any valid character string Default: NULL	Specifies the GSS API plug-in libraries that are supported by the database server. If the authentication type is GSSPLUGIN and this parameter is NULL, an error is returned; if the authentication type is KERBEROS and this parameter is NULL, the DB2-supplied Kerberos module or library is used.
srv_plugin_mode	UNFENCED Default: UNFENCED	Specifies whether plug-ins are to run in fenced mode or unfenced mode. At this time, unfenced mode is the only supported mode.
srvcon_pw_plugin	Any valid character string Default: NULL	Specifies the name of the default User ID–Password plug-in library to be used for server-side authentication. By default, the DB2-supplied User ID–Password plug-in library will be used if no other library is specified.
start_stop_time	1–1,440 Minutes Default: 10	Specifies the time, in minutes, in which all nodes of a partitioned database must respond to DB2START, DB2STOP, and ADD DBPARTITIONNUM commands.
svcename	Any valid character string Default: NULL	Specifies the name of the TCP/IP port that a database server will use to await communications from remote client nodes. This parameter should be set to the service name associated with the main connection port so that when the database server is started, it can determine on which port to listen for incoming connection requests.
sysadm_group	Any valid character string Default: NULL	Specifies the group name that has System Administrator (SYSADM) authority for the DB2 Database Manager instance.
sysctrl_group	Any valid character string Default: NULL	Specifies the group name that has System Control (SYSCTRL) authority for the DB2 Database Manager instance.

Table 2.3 DB2 Database Manager Instance Configuration Parameters (continued)		
Parameter	Value Range/Default	Description
sysmaint_group	Any valid character string Default: NULL	Specifies the group name that has System Maintenance (SYSMAINT) authority for the DB2 Database Manager instance.
sysmon_group	Any valid character string Default: NULL	Specifies the group name that has System Monitor (SYSMON) authority for the DB2 Database Manager instance.
tm_database	1ST_CONN, Any valid database name Default: 1ST_CONN	Specifies the name of the Transaction Manager (TM) database for each DB2 Database Manager instance. The TM database is a special database that is used as a logger and coordinator and to perform recovery for in-doubt transactions.
tp_mon_name	CICS, MQ, ENCINA, CB, SF, TUXEDO, TOPEND, blank, or Any valid character string Default: blank	Specifies the name of the transaction processing (TP) monitor product being used.
trust_allclnts	YES, NO, DRDAONLY Default: YES	Specifies whether all clients are treated as trusted clients. If set to YES, the server assumes that a level of security is available at the client and the possibility that users can be validated at the client. If set to DRDAONLY, the server assumes that a level of security is available at the client only if the client is DB2 for OS/390 and z/OS, DB2 for VM and VSE, or DB2 for OS/400.
trust_clntauth	CLIENT, SERVER Default: CLIENT	Specifies whether a trusted client is authenticated at the server or the client when the client provides a user ID and Password combination for a connection.
util_impact_lim	1–100 Percent Default: 10	Specifies the percentage that the execution of a throttled utility will impact a database workload. For example, a value of 10 indicates that a throttled backup operation will not impact the current database workload by more than 10 percent.
Adapted from Table 62 and Table 63 on pages 265–268 of the DB2 9 Performance Guide manual		

The contents of the DB2 Database Manager configuration file for a particular instance can be displayed by attaching to the instance and executing the GET DATABASE MANAGER CONFIGURATION command. The syntax for this command is:

```
GET [DATABASE MANAGER | DB MANAGER | DBM]
[CONFIGURATION | CONFIG | CFG]
<SHOW DETAIL>
```

Thus, if you wanted to view the contents of the DB2 Database Manager configuration file for the current instance, you could do so by executing a GET DATABASE MANAGER CONFIGURATION command that looks like this:

```
GET DBM CFG
```

You can change the value assigned to a particular DB2 Database Manager configuration file parameter by attaching to the instance and executing the UPDATE DATABASE MANAGER CONFIGURATION command. The syntax for this command is:

```
UPDATE [DATABASE MANAGER | DB MANAGER | DBM]
[CONFIGURATION | CONFIG | CFG]
USING [[Parameter] [Value] |
       [Parameter] [Value] AUTOMATIC |
       [Parameter] AUTOMATIC |
       [Parameter] MANUAL ,...]
<IMMEDIATE | DEFERRED>
```

where:

Parameter   Identifies one or more DB2 Database Manager configuration parameters (by keyword) whose values are to be modified. (In many cases, the keyword for a parameter is the same as the parameter name itself.)

Value   Identifies the new value or values that are to be assigned to the DB2 Database Manager configuration parameter(s) specified.

If the AUTOMATIC keyword is specified as the value for a particular parameter, DB2 will automatically adjust the parameter value to reflect the current resource requirements. (Refer to Table 2.3 to identify the configuration parameters that can be set using the AUTOMATIC keyword.) If a value is specified along with the AUTOMATIC keyword, the value specified may influence the automatic calculations performed.

If the DEFERRED clause is specified with the UPDATE DATABASE MANAGER CONFIGURATION command, changes made to the DB2 Database Manager configuration file will not take effect until the instance is stopped and restarted. If the IMMEDIATE clause is specified instead, or if neither clause is specified, all changes made to the DB2 Database Manager configuration file will take effect immediately—provided that the necessary resources required are available.

So if you wanted to configure the current instance such that the maximum number of applications that can be executing concurrently at any given point in time is 100, you could do so by executing an UPDATE DATABASE MANAGER CONFIGURATION command that looks like this:

```
UPDATE DBM CFG USING MAXCAGENTS 100
```

Or, if you wanted to specify the name of the TCP/IP port that the current instance is to use to receive communications from remote clients, you could do so by executing an UPDATE DATABASE MANAGER CONFIGURATION command that looks like this:

```
UPDATE DBM CFG USING SVCENAME db2c_db2inst1
```

The values assigned to all DB2 Database Manager configuration file parameters can be returned to their factory settings by attaching to the appropriate instance and executing the RESET DATABASE MANAGER CONFIGURATION command. The syntax for this command is:

```
RESET [DATABASE MANAGER | DB MANAGER | DBM]
[CONFIGURATION | CONFIG | CFG]
```

Thus, if you wanted to return the DB2 Database Manager configuration file parameters for the current instance to their system default settings, you could do so by executing a RESET DATABASE MANAGER CONFIGURATION command that looks like this:

```
RESET DBM CFG
```

The contents of a DB2 Database Manager configuration file can also be viewed or altered using the DBM Configuration dialog, which can be activated by selecting the Configure Parameters action from the Instances menu found in the Control Center. Figure 2–8 shows the Control Center menu items that must be selected to activate the DBM Configuration dialog; Figure 2–9 shows how this dialog might look after it has been activated.

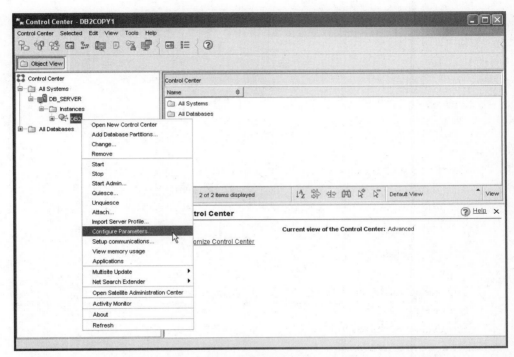

Figure 2–8: Invoking the DBM Configuration dialog from the Control Center.

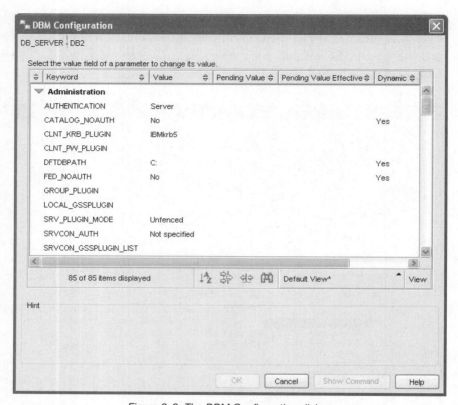

Figure 2–9: The DBM Configuration dialog.

Database Configurations

Just as a DB2 Database Manager configuration file is created and initialized whenever a new instance is created, a database configuration file is created and initialized each time a new database is created. Each database configuration file is made up of approximately 105 different parameters, and just as most DB2 Database Manager instance configuration parameters control the amount of system resources that will be allocated to a single DB2 Database Manager instance, many of the database configuration file parameters control the amount of system resources that will be allocated to a database during normal operation. The parameters that make up a database configuration file are shown in Table 2.4.

Parameter	Value Range / Default	Description
alt_collate	IDENTITY_16BIT Default: NULL	Specifies the collating sequence that is to be used for Unicode tables in a non-Unicode database.
app_ctl_heap_sz	1–64,000 4K Pages Default: 128 or 512	Specifies the maximum size (in 4KB pages) of memory that is to be allocated for the application control heap. The application control heap is used to share information among agents working on behalf of the same application at a node in an MPP or an SMP system.
appgroup_mem_sz	1–1,000,000 4K Pages Default: 10,000, 20,000, 30,000 or 40,000	Specifies the maximum size of the application group shared memory segment.
applheapsz	16–60,000 4K Pages Default: 64, 128, or 256	Specifies the number of private memory pages that are to be available for use by the DB2 Database Manager on behalf of a specific agent or subagent.
archretrydelay	0–65,535 4K Seconds Default: 20	Specifies the number of seconds to wait after a failed archive attempt before trying to archive the log file again. Subsequent retries will take effect only if the value of the *numarchretry* database configuration parameter is at least 1.
auto_maint	ON, OFF Default: ON	Enables or disables automatic maintenance for the database. This is the parent of all the other automatic maintenance database configuration parameters (*auto_db_backup*, *auto_tbl_maint*, *auto_runstats*, *auto_stats_prof*, *auto_prof_upd*, and *auto_reorg*). When this parameter is disabled, all of its children parameters are also disabled, but their settings, as recorded in the database configuration file, do not change. When this parent parameter is enabled, recorded values for its children parameters take effect.
auto_db_backup	ON, OFF Default: ON	Enables or disables automatic backup operations for the database.
auto_tbl_maint	ON, OFF Default: ON	Enables or disables automatic table maintenance operations for the database. This parameter is the parent of all table maintenance parameters (*auto_runstats*, *auto_stats_prof*, *auto_prof_upd*, and *auto_reorg*). When this parameter is disabled, all of its children parameters are also disabled, but their settings, as recorded in the database configuration file, do not change. When this parent parameter is enabled, recorded values for its children parameters take effect.

Table 2.4 DB2 Database Configuration Parameters

Table 2.4 DB2 Database Configuration Parameters (continued)

Parameter	Value Range / Default	Description
auto_runstats	ON, OFF Default: ON	Enables or disables automatic table RUNSTATS operations for the database.
auto_stats_prof	ON, OFF Default: ON	Enables or disables automatic statistical profile generation for the database.
auto_prof_upd	ON, OFF Default: ON	Enables or disables automatic RUNSTATS profile updating for the database.
auto_reorg	ON, OFF Default: ON	Enables or disables automatic table and index reorganization for the database.
autorestart	ON, OFF Default: ON	Specifies whether the DB2 Database Manager is to automatically issue a RESTART DATABASE command when it detects that the database is in an inconsistent state (which is the case if the last database connection was disrupted or if the database was not terminated normally during the previous session). If this parameter is set to ON, a database is restarted automatically if necessary. If this parameter is set to OFF, the database must be restarted manually.
avg_appls	AUTOMATIC, 1–*maxappls* Default: AUTOMATIC	Specifies the average number of active applications that normally access the database. The SQL optimizer uses this parameter to help estimate how much buffer pool memory will be available for the chosen access plan at application run time.
backup_pending	N/A	Read-only. Indicates whether a full backup of the database must be made before it can be accessed. If this parameter is set to NO, the database is in a usable state. If this parameter is set to YES, an OFFLINE backup must be performed before the database can be used.
blk_log_dsk_ful	YES, NO Default: NO	Specifies whether applications should hang whenever the DB2 Database Manager encounters a log-full error. This configuration parameter can be set to prevent disk-full errors from being generated when DB2 cannot create a new log file in the active log location.
catalogcache_sz	-1, 8–524,288 4K Pages Default: -1	Specifies the amount of memory (in pages) that is to be used to cache system catalog information.
chngpgs_thresh	5–99% Default: 60	Specifies the level (percentage) of changed pages at which the asynchronous page cleaners will be started, if they are not currently active.

Table 2.4 DB2 Database Configuration Parameters (continued)		
Parameter	Value Range / Default	Description
codepage	N/A	Read-only. Identifies the code page that was used to create the database.
codeset	N/A	Read-only. Identifies the code set that was used to create the database.
collate_info	N/A	Read-only. Identifies the collating sequence used by the database.
country (region)	N/A	Read-only. Identifies the country/territory code used to create the database.
database_consistent	N/A	Read-only. Indicates whether the database is in a consistent state. If this parameter is set to YES, all transactions have been committed or rolled back so that the data is consistent. If this parameter is set to NO, a transaction is pending, or some other task is pending on the database.
database_level	N/A	Read-only. Identifies the release level of the DB2 Database Manager that can use the database.
database_memory	AUTOMATIC, 0–4,294,967,295 4K Pages Default: AUTOMATIC	Specifies the minimum amount of shared memory that is to be reserved for the database's shared memory region. (If this parameter is set to AUTOMATIC, DB2 will calculate the amount of memory needed for the database and allocate it at database activation time.)
dbheap	32–524,288 4K Pages Default: 300, 600, or 1,200	Specifies the size, in pages, of the database heap, which is used to hold control information on all open cursors accessing the database. Both log buffers and catalog cache buffers are allocated from the database heap.
db_mem_thresh	0-100 Percent Default: 10	Specifies the maximum percentage of committed, but currently unused, database shared memory that the DB2 Database Manager will allow before starting to release committed pages of memory back to the operating system
dft_degree	-1, 1–32,767 Default: 1	Specifies the default value for the CURRENT DEGREE special register and the DEGREE bind option.
dft_extent_sz	2–256 4K Pages Default: 32	Specifies the default extent size (in pages) that will be used when new table spaces are created if no extent size is specified.

Table 2.4 DB2 Database Configuration Parameters (continued)

Parameter	Value Range / Default	Description
dft_loadrec_ses	1–30,000 Default: 1	Specifies the default number of sessions that will be used during the recovery of a table load operation. This parameter is only applicable if roll-forward recovery is enabled.
dft_mttb_types	ALL, NONE, FEDERATED_TOOL, SYSTEM, and/or USER Default: SYSTEM	Specifies the default value for the CURRENT MAINTAINED TABLE TYPES FOR OPTIMIZATION special register.
dft_prefetch_sz	AUTOMATIC, 0–32,767 4K Pages Default: AUTOMATIC	Specifies the default prefetch size (in pages) that will be used when new table spaces are created if no prefetch size is specified.
dft_queryopt	0–9 Default: 5	Specifies the default query optimization class to use when neither the SET CURRENT QUERY OPTIMIZATION statement nor the QUERYOPT option on the bind command is used. The query optimization class is used to direct the DB2 Optimizer to use different degrees of optimization when compiling SQL queries and XQuery expressions.
dft_refresh_age	ANY, 0–99,999,999,999,999 Default: 0	Specifies the default value to use for the refresh age of summary tables if the CURRENT REFRESH AGE special register has not been set. (This parameter is used to determine whether summary tables are to be considered when optimizing the processing of dynamic SQL queries.)
dft_sqlmathwarn	YES, NO Default: NO	Specifies whether arithmetic errors and retrieval conversion errors are handled as errors or as warnings during SQL statement compilation.
discover_db	ENABLE, DISABLE Default: ENABLE	Specifies whether information about the database is to be returned when a DB2 Discovery request is received at the server.
dlchktime	1,000–600,000 Milliseconds Default: 10,000	Specifies the frequency with which the DB2 Database Manager checks for deadlocks among all applications connected to the database.
dyn_query_mgmt	ENABLE, DISABLE Default: DISABLE	Specifies whether queries that exceed thresholds are trapped by the DB2 Query Patroller. If this parameter is set to ENABLE and the cost of the dynamic query exceeds the trap threshold for the user or group (as specified in the Query Patroller user profile table), the query will be trapped. If this parameter is set to DISABLE, no queries are trapped.

Table 2.4 DB2 Database Configuration Parameters (continued)		
Parameter	**Value Range / Default**	**Description**
failarchpath	Any valid character string Default: NULL	Specifies a path to which DB2 will try to archive log files if they cannot be archived to either the primary or the secondary (if set) archive destinations because of a media problem.
groupheap_ratio	1–99 Percent Default: 70	Specifies the percentage of memory (in the application group shared memory set) devoted to the application group shared heap.
hadr_db_role	N/A	Read-only. Indicates the current role of the database, if it is part of a high availability disaster recovery (HADR) environment. Valid values are STANDARD, PRIMARY, or STANDBY.
hadr_local_host	Any valid character string Default: NULL	Specifies the local host for high availability disaster recovery (HADR) TCP communication. Either a host name or an IP address can be used.
hadr_local_svc	Any valid character string Default: NULL	Specifies the TCP service name or port number for which the local high availability disaster recovery (HADR) process accepts connections.
hadr_remote_host	Any valid character string Default: NULL	Specifies the TCP/IP host name or IP address of the remote high availability disaster recovery (HADR) node.
hadr_remote_inst	Any valid character string Default: NULL	Specifies the instance name of the remote server. Administration tools, such as the Control Center, use this parameter to contact the remote server. High availability disaster recovery (HADR) also checks whether a remote database requesting a connection belongs to the declared remote instance.
hadr_remote_svc	Any valid character string Default: NULL	Specifies the TCP service name or port number that will be used by the remote high availability disaster recovery (HADR) node.
hadr_syncmode	SYNC, NEARSYNC, ASYNC Default: NEARSYNC	Specifies the high availability disaster recovery (HADR) synchronization mode, which determines how primary log writes are synchronized with the standby when the systems are in peer state.
hadr_timeout	1–4,294,967,295 Default: 120	Specifies the time (in seconds) that the high availability disaster recovery (HADR) process waits before considering a communication attempt to have failed.

Parameter	Value Range / Default	Description
Table 2.4 DB2 Database Configuration Parameters (continued)		
indexrec	SYSTEM, RESTART, RESTART_NO_REDO ACCESS, ACCESS_NO_REDO, Default: SYSTEM	Specifies when the DB2 Database Manager will attempt to rebuild invalid indexes and whether any index build will be redone during roll-forward or HADR log replay on the standby database. (The value SYSTEM indicates that the value of the DB2 Database Manager configuration parameter *indexrec* is to be used.)
locklist	AUTOMATIC, 4–524,288 4K Pages Default: AUTOMATIC	Specifies the maximum amount of memory (in pages) that is to be allocated and used to hold the lock list.
locktimeout	-1, 0–32,767 Seconds Default: -1	Specifies the number of seconds that an application will wait to obtain a lock.
logarchmeth1	OFF, LOGRETAIN, USEREXIT, DISK, TSM, VENDOR Default: OFF	Specifies the media type of the primary destination for archived log files and whether archival logging is to be used.
logarchmeth2	OFF, LOGRETAIN, USEREXIT, DISK, TSM, VENDOR Default: OFF	Specifies the media type of the secondary destination for archived logs. If this path is specified, log files will be archived to both this destination and the destination specified by the *logarchmeth1* database configuration parameter.
logarchopt1	Any valid character string Default: NULL	Specifies the options for the primary destination for archived logs (if required).
logarchopt2	Any valid character string Default: NULL	Specifies the options for the secondary destination for archived logs (if required).
log_retain_status	N/A	Read-only. Indicates whether log files are being retained for use with roll-forward recovery operations
logbufsz	4-4,096 (32-bit), 4-65,535 (64-bit) 4KPages Default: 8	Specifies the amount of memory (in pages) that is to be used to buffer log records before they are written to disk.
logfilsiz	4-524,286 4K Pages Default: 1,000	Specifies the amount of disk storage space (in pages) that is to be allocated to log files that are used for data recovery. This parameter defines the size of each primary and secondary log file used.
loghead	N/A	Read-only. Identifies, by name, the log file that is currently active.
logpath	N/A	Read-only. Specifies the current path being used to store log files
logindexbuild	ON, OFF Default: OFF	Specifies whether index creation, recreation, or reorganization operations are to be logged so that indexes can be reconstructed during DB2 roll-forward recovery operations or high availability disaster recovery (HADR) log replay procedures.

Table 2.4 DB2 Database Configuration Parameters (continued)		
Parameter	**Value Range / Default**	**Description**
logprimary	2-256 Default: 3	Specifies the number of primary log files that will be used for database recovery
logretain	RECOVERY, NO Default: NO	Specifies whether active log files are to be retained as archived log files for use in roll-forward recovery (also known as archival logging).
logsecond	-1, 0–254 Default: 2	Specifies the number of secondary log files that can be used for database recovery.
max_log	0–100 Percent Default: 0	Indicates whether there is a limit to the percentage of log space that a transaction can consume and, if so, specifies what that limit is.
maxappls	AUTOMATIC, 1–60,000 Default: AUTOMATIC	Specifies the maximum number of concurrent applications (both local and remote) that can connect to the database at one time. (If this parameter is set to AUTOMATIC, DB2 will dynamically allocate the resources it needs to support new applications.)
maxfilop	2–32,768 (Windows) 2–1,950 (UNIX) Default: 64	Specifies the maximum number of file handles that a database agent can have open at one time.
maxlocks	AUTOMATIC, 1–100 Default: AUTOMATIC	Specifies a percentage of the lock list held by an application that must be filled before the DB2 Database Manager performs lock escalation.
min_dec_div_3	YES, NO Default: NO	Specifies whether the results of decimal division arithmetic operations are to always have a scale of at least 3.
mincommit	1–25 Default: 1	Specifies the number of COMMIT SQL statements that are to be processed before log records are written to disk.
mirrorlogpath	Any valid character string Default: NULL	Specifies the location where a second copy of active log files is to be stored.
multipage_alloc	N/A	Read-only. Specifies whether new storage for SMS table spaces is allocated one page at a time or one extent at a time.
newlogpath	Any valid character string Default: NULL	Specifies an alternate path to use for storing recovery log files.
num_db_backups	1–32,768 Default: 12	Specifies the number of database backup images to retain for a database. (After the specified number of backups is reached, old backups are marked as expired in the recovery history file.)
num_freqvalues	0–32,767 Default: 10	Specifies the number of "most frequent values" that are to be collected when the WITH DISTRIBUTION option is specified with the RUNSTATS command.

Parameter	Value Range / Default	Description
num_iocleaners	AUTOMATIC, 0–255 Default: AUTOMATIC	Specifies the number of asynchronous page cleaners that are to be used by the database.
num_ioservers	AUTOMATIC, 1–255 Default: AUTOMATIC	Specifies the number of I/O servers that are to be used on behalf of database agents to perform prefetch I/O and asynchronous I/O needed by utilities such as backup and restore.
num_log_span	0–65,535 Default: 0	Number of active log files that a single active transaction is allowed to span.
num_quantiles	0–32,767 Default: 20	Specifies the number of quantiles (values in a column that satisfy a RANGE predicate) that are to be collected when the WITH DISTRIBUTION option is specified with the RUNSTATS command.
numarchretry	0–65,535 Default: 5	Specifies the number of times that the DB2 Database Manager is to try archiving a log file to the primary or the secondary archive directory before attempting to archive log files to the failover directory.
numsegs	N/A	Read-only. Specifies the number of containers that will be created within the default SMS table spaces of the database.
overflowlogpath	Any valid character string Default: NULL	Specifies the location where archived log files needed for roll-forward and rollback operations are stored.
pagesize	N/A	Read-only. Identifies the value that was used as the default page size when the database was created.
pckcachesz	AUTOMATIC, 32–128,000(32-bit), 32–524,288 (64-bit) 4K Pages Default: AUTOMATIC	Specifies the amount of application memory (in pages) that will be used to cache packages for static and dynamic SQL statements and XQuery expressions.
rec_his_retentn	-1, 0–30,000 Days Default: 366	Specifies the number of days that historical information on backups is to be retained in the recovery history file.
release	N/A	Read-only. Identifies the release level of the database configuration file.
restore_pending	N/A	Read-only. Indicates whether the database is in "Restore Pending" state.
restrict_access	N/A	Read-only. Indicates whether the database was created using the restrictive set of default actions (i.e., whether it was created with the RESTRICTIVE clause specified in the CREATE DATABASE command).

Table 2.4 DB2 Database Configuration Parameters (continued)

Table 2.4 DB2 Database Configuration Parameters (continued)		
Parameter	**Value Range / Default**	**Description**
rollfwd_pending	N/A	Read-only. Identifies whether a roll-forward recovery operation needs to be performed on the database. (If this parameter is set to NO, neither the database nor any of its table space is in "Roll-forward Pending" state. If this parameter is set to DATABASE, the database needs to be rolled forward before it can be used. If this parameter is set to TABLESPACES, one or more table spaces in the database need to be rolled forward.)
self_tuning_mem	ON, OFF Default: ON	Enables or disables the self-tuning memory manager for the database. When this parameter is set to ON, the memory tuner dynamically distributes available memory resources as required between all memory consumers that are enabled for self-tuning.
seqdetect	YES, NO Default: YES	Specifies whether the DB2 Database Manager can monitor I/O and, if sequential page reading is occurring, can activate I/O prefetching on behalf of the database.
sheapthres_shr	AUTOMATIC, 250–2,097,152 (32-bit), 250–2,147,483,647 (64-bit) 4K Pages Default: 5,000	Specifies the maximum amount of memory (in pages) that is to be used at any one time to perform sort operations.
softmax	1–100 * *logprimary* Percent Default: 100	Specifies the maximum percentage of log file space to be consumed before a soft checkpoint is recorded.
sortheap	AUTOMATIC, 16–524,288 (32-bit), 16–4,194,303 4K Pages Default: AUTOMATIC	Specifies the maximum number of private memory pages to be used for private sorts or the maximum number of shared memory pages to be used for shared sorts.
stat_heap_sz	1,096–524,288 4K Pages Default: 4,384	Specifies the maximum size of the heap space (in pages) that is to be used when creating and collecting table statistics (using the RUNSTATS command).
stmtheap	128–524,288 4K pages Default: 2,048 (32-bit), 4,096 (64-bit)	Specifies the heap size (in pages) that is to be used for precompiling and binding SQL statements.
territory	N/A	Read-only. Identifies the territory code used to create the database.
trackmod	YES, NO Default: NO	Specifies whether database modifications are to be tracked so that the BACKUP utility can detect which subsets of the database pages must be examined by an incremental backup and potentially included in the backup image.

Table 2.4 DB2 Database Configuration Parameters (continued)

Parameter	Value Range / Default	Description
tsm_mgmtclass	Any valid character string Default: NULL	Specifies how the server should manage backup versions or archive copies of the objects being backed up. The TSM management class is assigned from the TSM administrator.
tsm_nodename	Any valid character string Default: NULL	Specifies the node name that is to be used to override the default setting for the node name associated with the Tivoli Storage Manager (TSM) product. The node name is needed to allow you to restore a database that was backed up to TSM from another node.
tsm_owner	Any valid character string Default: NULL	Specifies the owner name that is to be used to override the default setting for the owner associated with the Tivoli Storage Manager (TSM) product. The owner name is needed to allow you to restore a database that was backed up to TSM from another node.
tsm_password	Any valid character string Default: NULL	Specifies the password that is to be used to override the default setting for the password associated with the Tivoli Storage Manager (TSM) product. The password is needed to allow you to restore a database that was backed up to TSM from another node.
userexit	ON, OFF Default: OFF	Specifies whether a user exit program used for archiving or retrieving log files can be called the next time the database is opened. (If this parameter is set to OFF, a user exit function cannot be called. If this parameter is set to ON, a user exit function can be called.)
user_exit_status	N/A	Read-only. Indicates whether the database has been configured to use a user exit program to store archive log files.
util_heap_sz	16–524,288 4K Pages Default: 5,000	Specifies the maximum amount of shared memory that can be used simultaneously by the Backup, Restore, and Load utilities.
vendoropt	Any valid character string Default: NULL	Specifies additional parameters that DB2 might need to use to communicate with storage systems during backup, restore, or load copy operations.

Adapted from Table 64 and Table 65 on pages 269–273 of the DB2 9 Performance Guide manual

The contents of the database configuration file for a particular database can be displayed by executing the GET DATABASE CONFIGURATION command. The syntax for this command is:

```
GET [DATABASE | DB] [CONFIGURATION | CONFIG | CFG]
FOR [DatabaseAlias]
<SHOW DETAIL>
```

where:

DatabaseAlias   Identifies the alias assigned to the database that configuration information is to be displayed for.

Thus, if you wanted to view the contents of the database configuration file for a database named SAMPLE, you could do so by executing a GET DATABASE CONFIGURATION command that looks like this:

```
GET DB CFG FOR sample
```

The value assigned to a particular database configuration file parameter can be changed by executing the UPDATE DATABASE CONFIGURATION command. The syntax for this command is:

```
UPDATE [DATABASE | DB]
[CONFIGURATION | CONFIG | CFG]
FOR [DatabaseAlias]
USING [[Parameter] [Value] |
       [Parameter] [Value] AUTOMATIC |
       [Parameter] AUTOMATIC |
       [Parameter] MANUAL ,...]
<IMMEDIATE | DEFERRED>
```

where:

DatabaseAlias   Identifies the alias assigned to the database for which configuration information is to be modified.

Parameter   Identifies one or more database configuration parameters (by keyword) whose values are to be modified. (In many cases, the keyword for a parameter is the same as the parameter name itself.)

Value   Identifies the new value(s) that are to be assigned to the
                            database configuration parameter(s) specified.

If the AUTOMATIC keyword is specified as the value for a particular parameter, DB2
will automatically adjust the parameter value to reflect the current resource
requirements. (Refer to Table 2.4 to identify the configuration parameters that can be
set using the AUTOMATIC keyword.) If a value is specified along with the AUTOMATIC
keyword, the value specified may influence the automatic calculations performed.

If the DEFERRED clause is specified with the UPDATE DATABASE CONFIGURATION
command, changes made to the database configuration file will not take effect
until all connections to the corresponding database have been terminated and a
new connection is established. If the IMMEDIATE clause is specified instead, or if
neither clause is specified, all changes made to the database configuration file
will take effect immediately—provided the necessary resources are available.
(Applications running against a database at the time database configuration
changes are made will see the change the next time an SQL statement is
executed.)

So if you wanted to configure a database named SAMPLE such that any application
connected to the database will wait up to 10,000 seconds to acquire a lock before
rolling back the current transaction, you could do so by executing an UPDATE
DATABASE CONFIGURATION command that looks like this:

```
UPDATE DB CFG FOR sample USING LOCKTIMEOUT 10000
```

Or if you wanted to configure a database named SAMPLE to use archival logging
and instruct it to store a second copy of the active log files in a directory named
MIRRORLOGS that resides on drive E:, you could do so by executing an UPDATE
DATABASE CONFIGURATION command that looks like this:

```
UPDATE DB CFG FOR sample USING LOGARCHMETH1 LOGRETAIN MIRRORLOGPATH
E:/mirrorlogs
```

The values assigned to all database configuration file parameters can be returned
to their system defaults by executing the RESET DATABASE CONFIGURATION
command. The syntax for this command is:

```
RESET [DATABASE | DB]
[CONFIGURATION | CONFIG | CFG]
FOR [DatabaseAlias]
```

where:

DatabaseAlias   Identifies the alias assigned to the database whose configuration
information is to be modified.

Therefore, if you wanted to return the database configuration file parameters for a
database named SAMPLE to their system default settings (thereby losing any
configuration changes made), you could do so by executing a RESET DATABASE
CONFIGURATION command that looks like this:

```
RESET DB CFG FOR sample
```

You can also view or alter the contents of a database configuration file by using
the Database Configuration dialog, which can be activated by selecting the
Configure Parameters action from the Databases menu found in the Control
Center. Figure 2–10 shows the Control Center menu items that must be selected to
activate the Database Configuration dialog; Figure 2–11 shows how this dialog
might look after it has been activated.

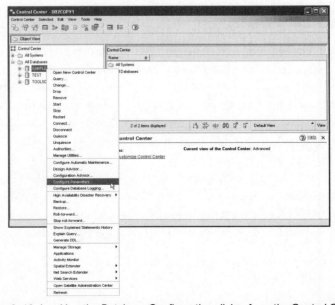

Figure 2–10: Invoking the Database Configuration dialog from the Control Center.

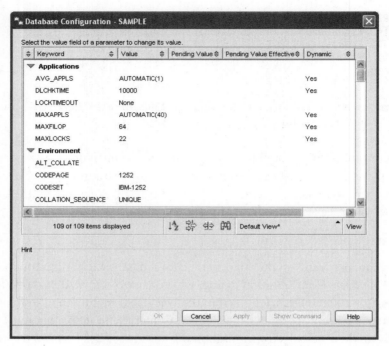

Figure 2–11: The Database Configuration dialog.

The Configuration Advisor

With such a broad range of configuration parameters to choose from, deciding where to start and what changes to make can be difficult. Fortunately, DB2 comes packaged with a tool to help you get started; that tool is the Configuration Advisor. The Configuration Advisor is designed to capture specific information about your database environment and recommend or make changes to configuration parameters based on the information provided.

You can activate the Configuration Advisor by selecting the Configuration Advisor action from the Databases menu found in the Control Center. Figure 2–12 shows the Control Center menu items that must be selected to activate the Configuration Advisor; Figure 2–13 shows how the Configuration Advisor looks when it is first activated.

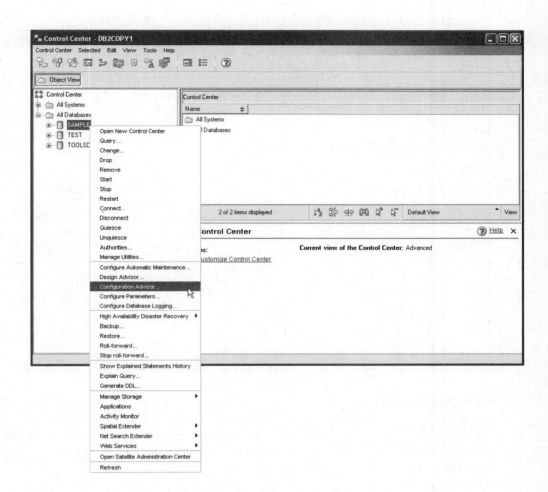

Figure 2–12: Invoking the Configuration Advisor from the Control Center.

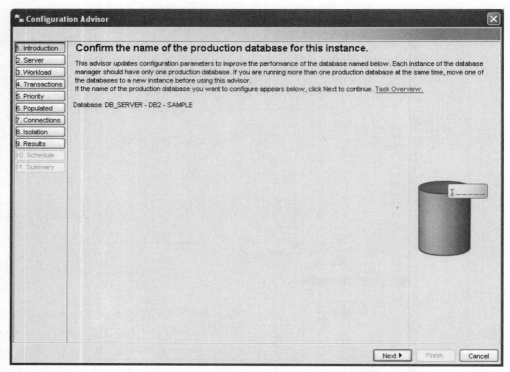

Figure 2–13: The Configuration Advisor dialog.

Once the Configuration Advisor wizard is activated, you simply follow the directions shown on each panel presented to describe your server environment and to explain what a typical transaction workload for your database looks like. When you have provided the information requested, the Configuration Advisor will recommend changes that should improve overall performance if made to instance and/or database configuration parameters. At that time, the "Finish" push button displayed in the lower right corner of the wizard (see Figure 2–13) will be enabled, and when this button is selected, the recommended configuration parameter changes may be applied.

In DB2 9, the Configuration Advisor is automatically invoked whenever you create a database using the Create Database Wizard. (This behavior can be changed by assigning the value NO to the DB2_ENABLE_AUTOCONFIG_DEFAULT registry variable.)

The AUTOCONFIGURE Command

If you prefer to work with commands instead of GUI tools, the functionality provided by the Configuration Advisor can also be obtained by executing the AUTOCONFIGURE command (which calls the Design Advisor under the covers). The basic syntax for this command is:

```
AUTOCONFIGURE
USING [[Keyword] [Value] ,...]
APPLY [DB ONLY | DB AND DBM | NONE]
```

where:

Keyword   Identifies one or more special keywords that are recognized by the AUTOCONFIGURE command. The following values are valid for this parameter: mem_percent, workload_type, num_stmts, tpm, admin_priority, is_populated, num_local_apps, num_remote_apps, isolation, and bp_resizable.

Value   Identifies the value associated with the keyword provided. Table 2.5 lists the values that are valid for each keyword recognized by the AUTOCONFIGURE command.

Table 2.5 AUTOCONFIGURE Command Keywords and Values		
Keyword	**Valid Values / Default**	**Description**
mem_percent	1–100 Default: 25	Percentage of available server memory (RAM) the DB2 Database Manager is to use when performing database operations.
workload_type	simple, complex, mixed Default: mixed	The type of workload that usually is run against the database. Valid values are as follows: simple–database is used primarily for transaction processing (for example, order entry and OLTP); complex–database is used primarily to resolve queries (for example, data warehousing); and mixed–database is used to resolve queries and to process transactions. Simple workloads tend to be I/O-intensive and mostly transactions, whereas complex workloads tend to be CPU-intensive and mostly queries.
num_stmts	1–1,000,000 Default: 10	Average number of SQL statements executed within a single transaction (i.e., between commits). NOTE: If unknown, choose a number greater than 10.

Table 2.5 AUTOCONFIGURE Command Keywords and Values (continued)		
Keyword	**Valid Values / Default**	**Description**
tpm	1–200,000 Default: 60	Average number of transactions executed per minute (estimated). NOTE: The DB2 Performance Monitor can help you get a more accurate TPM measurement.
admin_priority	performance, recovery, both Default: both	Type of activity for which the database should be optimized. Valid values include the following: performance—database should be optimized for transaction performance (slower backup/recovery); recovery—database should be optimized for backup and recovery (slower transaction performance); or both—database should be optimized for both transaction performance and backup/recovery (both are equally important).
is_populated	yes, no Default: yes	Indicates whether the database currently contains data. Valid values are as follows: yes—the database contains data; and no—the database does not contain data.
num_local_apps	0–5,000 Default: 0	Number of local applications that will be connected to the database at one time.
num_remote_apps	0–5,000 Default: 10	Number of remote applications that will be connected to the database at one time. Allocating memory to handle all connections needed (both local and remote) ensures that users never have to wait for an existing connection to be terminated before they can get connected. However, over-allocating memory for connections can result in wasted resources. The DB2 Performance Monitor can help you determine how many connections are actually acquired within a specified time frame.
isolation	RR, RS, CS, UR Default: RR	Isolation level used by most applications that access the database. Valid values include the following: RR—Repeatable Read (large number of locks acquired for long periods of time); RS—Read Stability (small number of locks acquired for long periods of time); CS—Cursor Stability (large number of locks acquired for short periods of time); and UR—Uncommitted Read (no locks acquired).
bp_resizeable	yes, no Default: yes	Indicates whether buffer pools are resizable. Valid values are: yes—buffer pools are resizable; and no—buffer pools are not resizable.

If the APPLY DB ONLY clause is specified with the AUTOCONFIGURE command, database configuration and buffer pool changes recommended by the Design Advisor will be applied to the appropriate database configuration file; if the APPLY DB AND DBM clause is specified, database configuration and buffer pool changes recommended will be applied to the database configuration file, and instance configuration changes recommended will be applied to the appropriate DB2 Database Manager configuration file. If the APPLY NONE clause is specified instead, change recommendations will be displayed, but not applied.

Thus, if you wanted to determine the best configuration to use for an OLTP database named SAMPLE that uses resizable buffer pools and is populated, and you wanted to review any configuration changes recommended before applying them to the appropriate database configuration file, you could do so by executing an AUTOCONFIGURE command that looks like this:

```
AUTOCONFIGURE USING workload_type complex,
  is_populated yes,
  bp_resizable yes
APPLY NONE
```

Or if you wanted to determine the best configuration to use if 60 percent of a system's memory will be available for the DB2 Database Manager to use when performing database operations, and if the instance controlled only one database (named SAMPLE) and you wanted to automatically update the appropriate configuration files to reflect any configuration changes recommended, you could do so by executing an AUTOCONFIGURE command that looks like this:

```
AUTOCONFIGURE USING mem_percent 60 APPLY DB AND DBM
```

On the other hand, if you wanted to determine the optimum configuration to use if 60 percent of a system's memory will be available for a DB2 Database Manager instance, and the instance controls two active databases that need to use memory equally, you could obtain this configuration by executing an AUTOCONFIGURE command that looks like this *for each database*:

```
AUTOCONFIGURE USING mem_percent 30 APPLY DB AND DBM
APPLY NONE
```

The AUTOCONFIGURE command (and the Configuration Advisor) will always recommend that a database be configured to take advantage of the Self-Tuning Memory Manager. However, if you run the AUTOCONFIGURE command against a database that resides in an instance where the SHEAPTHRES configuration parameter has been assigned a value other than zero, the sort memory heap database configuration parameter (SORTHEAP) will not be configured for automatic tuning. Therefore, you must execute the command UPDATE DATABASE MANAGER CONFIGURATION USING SHEAPTHRES 0 before you execute the AUTOCONFIGURE command if you want to enable sort memory tuning.

Configuring Communications

In a typical client/server environment, databases stored on a server are accessed by applications stored on remote client workstations using what is known as a distributed connection. In addition to providing client applications with a way to access a centralized database located on a remote server, a distributed connection also provides a way for administrators to manage databases and servers remotely.

In order to communicate with a server workstation, each client must use some type of communications protocol that is recognized by the server. Likewise, each server must use some type of communications protocol to detect inbound requests from client workstations. In most cases, the operating system being used on both workstations provides the communications protocol support needed; however, in some cases, this support may be provided by a separate add-on product. In either case, both clients and servers must be configured to use a communications protocol that is recognized by DB2. DB2 9 recognizes the following communications protocols:

- NetBios

- Transmission Control Protocol/Internet Protocol (TCP/IP) (which is used today in an overwhelming majority of cases)

- Named pipe

When DB2 is installed on a workstation, it is automatically configured to take advantage of any communications protocols that have been set up for that particular workstation (provided the protocols found are recognized by DB2). At that time, information about each supported communications protocol available is collected and stored in the configuration files for both the DAS instance and the default instance as they are created. However, this information is not updated automatically when a new protocol is activated or when an existing protocol is reconfigured. Instead, you must manually configure communications for each instance before such changes will be reflected.

Manually Configuring Communications

The easiest way to manually configure communications or make communications configuration changes is by using the Setup communications dialog, which can be activated by selecting the appropriate action from the Instances menu found in the Control Center. Figure 2–14 shows the Control Center menu items that must be selected in order to activate the Setup communications dialog; Figure 2–15 shows how the Setup communications dialog might be used to configure the TCP/IP protocol for a particular instance.

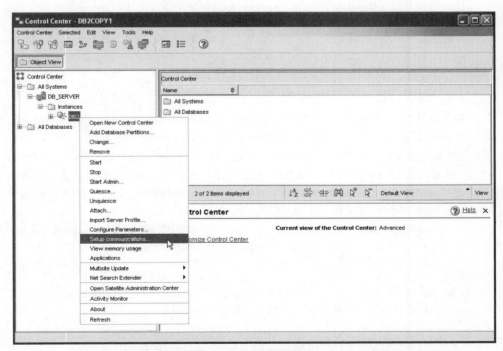

Figure 2–14: Invoking the Setup communications dialog from the Control Center.

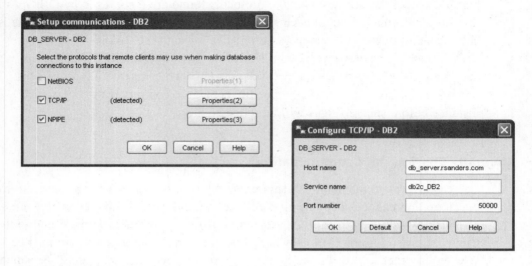

Figure 2–15: The Setup communications dialog and the Configure TCP/IP dialog.

If you choose to manually configure communications without using the Setup communications dialog, the steps you must follow can vary according to the communications protocol being used. For example, if you wanted to configure a server to use TCP/IP, you would have to perform the following steps (in any order):

1.   Assign the value TCPIP to the DB2COMM registry variable.

   Whenever you manually configure communications for a server, you must update the value of the DB2COMM registry variable before an instance can begin using the desired communications protocol. The value assigned to the DB2COMM registry variable is used to determine which communications managers will be activated when the DB2 Database Manager for a particular instance is started. (If the DB2COMM registry variable is not set correctly, one or more errors may be generated when the DB2 Database Manager attempts to start protocol support during instance initialization.)

The DB2COMM registry variable is assigned the value TCPIP by executing a db2set command that looks something like this:

```
db2set DB2COMM=TCPIP
```

Before a DB2 client can communicate with a DB2 server, the DB2 server must be configured to accept inbound requests for the communications protocol the client has been configured to use. Therefore, in order for a specific communications protocol to be used between a client and a server, the value assigned to the DB2COMM registry variable on both the client and the server workstation must include the keyword for that particular protocol. With DB2 9, valid keywords are TCPIP and NPIPE.

2. Assign the name of the TCP/IP port that the database server will use to receive communications from remote clients to the *svcename* parameter of the DB2 Database Manager configuration file.

   The *svcename* parameter should be set to the service name associated with the main connection port so that when the database server is started, it can determine which port to listen on for incoming connection requests. This parameter is set by executing an UPDATE DATABASE MANAGER CONFIGURATION command that looks something like this:

   ```
   UPDATE DBM CFG USING SVCENAME db2c_db2inst1
   ```

3. Update the services file on the database server, if appropriate.

   The TCP/IP services file identifies the ports that server applications will listen on for client requests. If you specified a service name in the *svcename* parameter of the DB2 Database Manager configuration file, the appropriate service name-to-port number/protocol mapping must be added to the services file on the server. (If you specified a port number in the *svcename* parameter, the services file does not need to be updated.)

The default location of the services file depends on the operating system being used: on UNIX-based systems, the services file is located in: /etc/services; on Windows servers, the services file is located in %SystemRoot%\system32\drivers\etc. An entry in the services file for a DB2 database server might look something like this:

```
db2c_db2inst1          50001/tcp
```

A Word About DB2's Directory Files

Because databases can physically reside anywhere on a network, each DB2 Database Manager instance must know where databases that fall under its control physically reside, as well as how to establish connections to those databases on behalf of users and applications. To keep track of this information, DB2 9 uses a special set of files known as directory files (or directories). Four types of directories exist:

- System database directory

  The system database directory resides in a file named *sqldbdir* that is created automatically when the first database for an instance is created. Information about the new database is then recorded in the system database directory, and as additional databases are cataloged, information about those databases is recorded as well.

- Local database directory

  Any time a DB2 database is created in a new location (i.e., a drive or a directory), a local database directory file is also created at that location. Information about that database is then recorded in the local database directory, and as other databases are created in that location, information about those databases is recorded in the local database directory as well. Thus, although only one system database directory exists for a particular instance, several local database directories can exist, depending on how databases have been distributed across the storage available.

- Node directory

  Unlike the system database directory and the local database directory, which are used to keep track of what databases exist and where they are stored, the node directory contains information that identifies how and where remote systems or instances can be found. A node directory file is created on each client workstation the first time a remote server or instance is cataloged. As other remote instances or servers are cataloged, information about those instances or servers is recorded in the node directory as well. Entries in the node directory are then used in conjunction with entries in the system database directory to make connections and instance attachments to DB2 databases stored on remote servers.

- Database Connection Services (DCS) directory

  Using an add-on product called DB2 Connect, it is possible for DB2 for Linux, UNIX, and Windows clients to establish a connection to databases on a DRDA Application Server, such as DB2 for OS/390 or z/OS databases on System/370 and System/390 architecture host computers; DB2 for VM and VSE databases on System/370 and System/390 architecture host computers; and iSeries databases on Application System/400 (AS/400) and iSeries computers. Because the information needed to connect to DRDA host databases is different from the information used to connect to LAN-based databases, information about remote hosts or iSeries databases is kept in a special directory known as the Database Connection Services (DCS) directory.

Once a server has been configured for communications, any client that wishes to access a database on the server must be configured to communicate with the server, *and* entries for both the server and the remote database must be added to the system database and node directories on the client workstation.

Cataloging and Uncataloging a Node

Nodes (servers) are usually cataloged implicitly whenever a remote database is cataloged via the Configuration Assistant. However, if you want to explicitly catalog a node (i.e., add an entry to the node directory for a particular server), you can do so by executing a CATALOG...NODE command that corresponds to the communications protocol that will be used to access the server being cataloged. Several forms of the CATALOG...NODE command are available, including the following:

- CATALOG LOCAL NODE

- CATALOG LDAP NODE

- CATALOG NAMED PIPE NODE

- CATALOG TCPIP NODE

The syntax for all of these commands is very similar, the major difference being that many of the options available with each are specific to the communications protocol for which the command has been tailored. Because TCP/IP is probably the most common communications protocol in use today, let's take a look at the syntax for that form of the CATALOG...NODE command.

The syntax for the CATALOG TCPIP NODE command is:

```
CATALOG <ADMIN> [TCPIP | TCPIP4 | TCPIP6] NODE [NodeName]
REMOTE [IPAddress | HostName]
SERVER [ServiceName | PortNumber]
<SECURITY SOCKS>
<REMOTE INSTANCE [InstanceName]>
<SYSTEM [SystemName]>
<OSTYPE [SystemType]>
<WITH "[Description]">
```

where:

NodeName	Identifies the alias to be assigned to the node to be cataloged. This is an arbitrary name created on the user's workstation and is used to identify the node.
IPAddress	Identifies the IP address of the server where the remote database you are trying to communicate with resides.
HostName	Identifies the host name, as it is known to the TCP/IP network. (This is the name of the server where the remote database you are trying to communicate with resides.)
ServiceName	Identifies the name of the service with which the DB2 Database Manager instance on the server uses to communicate.
PortNumber	Identifies the port number with which the DB2 Database Manager instance on the server uses to communicate.
InstanceName	Identifies the name of the server instance to which an attachment is to be made.
SystemName	Identifies the DB2 system name that is used to identify the server workstation.
SystemType	Identifies the type of operating system being used on the server workstation. The following values are valid for this parameter: AIX, WIN, HPUX, SUN, OS390, OS400, VM, VSE, and LINUX.

Description   A comment used to describe the node entry that will be made in the node directory for the node being cataloged. The description must be enclosed by double quotation marks.

Thus, if you wanted to catalog a node for a Linux server named DB2HOST that has a DB2 instance named DB2INST1 that listens on port 60000 and assign it the alias RMT_SERVER, you could do so by executing a CATALOG TCPIP NODE command that looks something like this:

```
CATALOG TCPIP NODE rmt_server
REMOTE db2host
SERVER 60000
OSTYPE LINUX
WITH "A remote Linux TCP/IP node"
```

Regardless of how a node was cataloged, it can be uncataloged at any time by executing the UNCATALOG NODE command. The syntax for this command is:

```
UNCATALOG NODE [NodeName]
```

where:

NodeName   Identifies the alias assigned to the node to be uncataloged.

So if you wanted to uncatalog the node that was cataloged in the previous example, you could do so by executing an UNCATALOG NODE command that looks like this:

```
UNCATALOG NODE rmt_server
```

Cataloging and Uncataloging a DB2 Database

Before you can access a database stored on a remote server, you must catalog the database on the client workstation. Fortunately, cataloging a database is a relatively straightforward process and can be done using the Control Center or the Configuration Assistant or by executing the CATALOG DATABASE command. The basic syntax for the CATALOG DATABASE command is:

```
CATALOG [DATABASE | DB] [DatabaseName]
<AS [Alias]>
<ON [Path] | AT NODE [NodeName]>
```

```
<AUTHENTICATION [AuthenticationType]>
<WITH "[Description]">
```

where:

DatabaseName   Identifies the name that has been assigned to the database
                  to be cataloged.

Alias   Identifies the alias that is to be assigned to the database
                  when it is cataloged.

Path   Identifies the location (drive or directory) where the
                  directory hierarchy and files associated with the database to
                  be cataloged are physically stored.

NodeName   Identifies the node where the database to be cataloged
                  resides. The node name specified should match an entry in
                  the node directory file (i.e., should correspond to a node
                  that has already been cataloged).

AuthenticationType Identifies where and how authentication is to take place when
                  a user attempts to access the database. The following values
                  are valid for this parameter: SERVER, CLIENT, SERVER_ENCRYPT,
                  KERBEROS TARGET PRINCIPAL [*PrincipalName*] (where
                  PrincipalName is the fully qualified Kerberos principal name
                  for the target server), DATA_ENCRYPT, and GSSPLUGIN.

Description   A comment used to describe the database entry that will be
                  made in the database directory for the database to be
                  cataloged. The description must be enclosed by double
                  quotation marks.

Thus, if you wanted to catalog a database that physically resides in the directory
/home/db2data and has been assigned the name TEST_DB, you could do so by
executing a CATALOG DATABASE command that looks something like this:

```
CATALOG DATABASE test_db AS test
ON /home/db2data
AUTHENTICATION SERVER
```

Just as there are multiple ways to catalog a DB2 database, there are multiple ways
to uncatalog one: by using the Control Center, by using the Configuration
Assistant, or by executing the UNCATALOG DATABASE command. The syntax for the
UNCATALOG DATABASE command is:

```
UNCATALOG [DATABASE | DB] [DatabaseAlias]
```

where:

DatabaseAlias   Identifies the alias assigned to the database to be uncataloged.

So if you wanted to uncatalog a database that has both the name and the alias
TEST_DB, you could do so by executing an UNCATALOG DATABASE command that
looks like this:

```
UNCATALOG DATABASE test_db
```

DB2 Discovery

It's easy to see how manually configuring communications between client and
server workstations can become an involved process, especially in complex
network environments. And as we have just seen, establishing communications
between clients and servers is only the beginning; before a client can send requests
to a DB2 server for processing, both the server and the database stored on the
server must be cataloged on the client workstation as well.

DB2 Discovery allows you to easily catalog a remote server and a database (and set
up a distributed connection between a client and a server) without having to know
any detailed communication-specific information. Here's how DB2 Discovery
works. When invoked from a client workstation, DB2 Discovery broadcasts a
discovery request over the network, and each DB2 server on the network that has
been configured to support the discovery process responds by returning a list of
instances found on the server, information about the communication protocol each
instance supports, and a list of databases found within each instance. The Control
Center and the Configuration Assistant can then use this information to catalog any
instance or database returned by the discovery process.

To process a discovery request, DB2 Discovery can use one of two methods: (1) search and (2) known. When the search discovery method is used, the entire network is searched for valid DB2 servers and databases, and a list of all servers, instances, and databases found is returned to the client, along with the communications information needed to catalog and connect to each. In contrast, when the known discovery method is used, the network is searched for a specific server using a specific communications protocol. (Because the client knows the name of the server and the communications protocol used by that server, the server is said to be "known" by the client.) Again, when the specified server is located, a list of all instances and databases found on the server is returned to the client, along with the information needed to catalog and connect to each one.

> A search discovery can take a very long time (many hours) to complete if the network that the client and server are on contains hundreds of machines. Furthermore, some network devices, such as routers, may actually block a search discovery request.

Whether a client can launch a DB2 Discovery request, and if so, how, and whether a particular server will respond, and if so, how, are determined by the values of parameters found in the configuration file for the DAS instance, the DB2 Database Manager configuration file for each instance (both on the client and on the server), and the database configuration file for each database within an instance. Specifically, these parameters control

- whether a client can launch a DB2 Discovery request;

- whether a server can be located by DB2 Discovery, and if so, whether the server can be located only when the search discovery method is used or when either the search or known discovery method is used;

- whether an instance can be located with a discovery request; and

- whether a database can be located with a discovery request.

The DAS instance, DB2 Database Manager (instance), and database configuration parameters that are used to control the behavior of DB2 Discovery are described in Table 2.6.

Table 2.6 Configuration Parameters That Control the Behavior of DB2 Discovery		
Parameter	Values/Default	Description
Client Instance (DB2 Database Manager Configuration File)		
discover	DISABLE, KNOWN, SEARCH Default: SEARCH	Identifies the DB2 Discovery action that is to be used by the client instance. If this parameter is set to SEARCH, the client instance can issue either search or known discovery requests; if this parameter is set to KNOWN, the client instance can issue only known discovery requests; and if this parameter is set to DISABLE, the client instance cannot issue discovery requests.
discover_inst	ENABLE, DISABLE Default: ENABLE	Specifies whether this instance can be detected by other DB2 Discovery requests.
Server DAS Instance (DAS Configuration File)		
discover	DISABLE, KNOWN, or SEARCH Default: SEARCH	Identifies the DB2 Discovery action that is to be used when the server is started. If this parameter is set to SEARCH, the server will respond to both search and known discovery requests; if this parameter is set to KNOWN, the server will respond only to known discovery requests; and if this parameter is set to DISABLE, the server will not respond to discovery requests.
Server Instance (DB2 Database Manager Configuration File)		
discover	DISABLE, KNOWN, SEARCH Default: SEARCH	Identifies the DB2 Discovery action that is to be used by the server instance. If this parameter is set to SEARCH, the server instance can issue either search or known discovery requests; if this parameter is set to KNOWN, the server instance can issue only known discovery requests; and if this parameter is set to DISABLE, the server instance cannot issue discovery requests.

Table 2.6 Configuration Parameters That Control the Behavior of DB2 Discovery (continued)		
Parameter	**Values/Default**	**Description**
discover_inst	ENABLE or DISABLE Default: ENABLE	Identifies whether information about a particular instance found on a server will be included in the server's response to a discovery request. If this parameter is set to ENABLE, the server will include information about the instance in its response to both search and known discovery requests. If this parameter is set to DISABLE, the server will not include information about the instance (nor will it include information about any databases that come under the instance's control) in its response to discovery requests. This parameter provides a way to hide an instance and all of its databases from DB2 Discovery.
Server Database (Database Configuration File)		
discover_db	ENABLE or DISABLE Default: ENABLE	Identifies whether information about a particular database found on a server will be included in the server's response to a discovery request. If this parameter is set to ENABLE, the server will include information about the database in its response to both search and known discovery requests. On the other hand, if this parameter is set to DISABLE, the server will not include information about the database in its response to discovery requests. This parameter provides a way to hide an individual database from DB2 Discovery.

As you can see, it is possible to enable or disable DB2 Discovery at the server level, instance level, and database level, as well as control how clients (and servers) initiate discovery requests. It is also possible to configure a server so that DB2 Discovery will not see one or more of its instances or databases when discovery requests are made. Figure 2–16 shows how the configuration parameters that control the behavior of DB2 Discovery can be used to prevent DB2 Discovery from seeing certain instances and databases stored on a server.

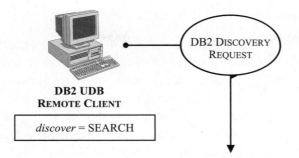

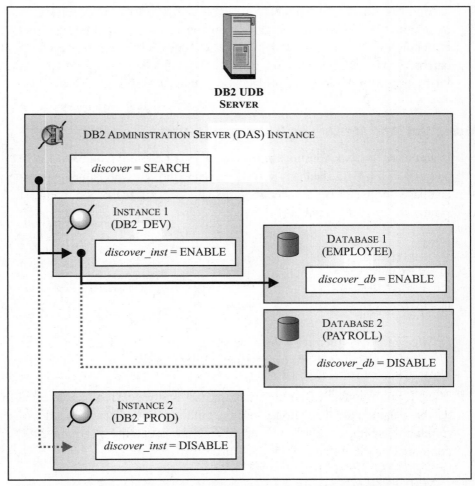

Figure 2–16: Controlling what instances and databases can be seen by DB2 Discovery. In this example, the server, Instance 1, and Database 1 will be returned by a discovery request; Instance 2 and Database 2 will not.

Taking Control of a Server

Because any number of clients can access a server, and in turn, any number of users can be granted the privileges needed to work with a particular database, it can be difficult, if not impossible, to coordinate the work efforts of everyone using a specific database at any given point in time. This can create a problem because there are times when a Database Administrator will need all users to stop using a particular instance or database so that routine maintenance operations can be performed. If your organization is small, it may be possible to contact each database user and ask them to disconnect long enough to perform any necessary maintenance operations. But what if your organization consists of several hundred users? Or what if an employee went home early and inadvertently left an instance attachment or database connection open? How can you find out which users and applications are interacting with the instance or database you need exclusive access to?

Finding Out Who Is Using an Instance or a Database

If you have System Administrator (SYSADMN) or System Control (SYSCTRL) authority for a DB2 database server, you can find out who is using an instance or a database on that server by executing the LIST APPLICATIONS command. The basic syntax for this command is:

```
LIST APPLICATIONS
<FOR [DATABASE | DB] [DatabaseAlias]>
<SHOW DETAIL>
```

where:

DatabaseAlias   Identifies the alias assigned to the database for which application information is to be obtained.

Thus, if you wanted to find out what applications are currently connected to a database named SAMPLE (along with the authorization IDs associated with the users running those applications), you could do so by executing a LIST APPLICATIONS command that looks something like this:

```
LIST APPLICATIONS FOR DATABASE sample
```

And when this command is executed, you might see output that looks something like this:

```
Auth Id   Application  Appl.   Application Id          DB      # of
          Name         Handle                          Name    Agents
--------  -----------  ------  ----------------------  ------  -------
RSANDERS  db2taskd     148     *LOCAL.DB2.070601164915  SAMPLE  1
RSANDERS  db2stmm      147     *LOCAL.DB2.070601164914  SAMPLE  1
RSANDERS  db2bp.exe    146     *LOCAL.DB2.070601164913  SAMPLE  1
```

You can also find out what applications are attached to an instance (or connected to a database within that instance) by selecting the Applications action from the Databases menu found in the Control Center. Figure 2–17 shows the Control Center menu items that must be selected in order to activate the Applications dialog. Figure 2–18 shows how this dialog might look if an application is connected to a database within the instance specified.

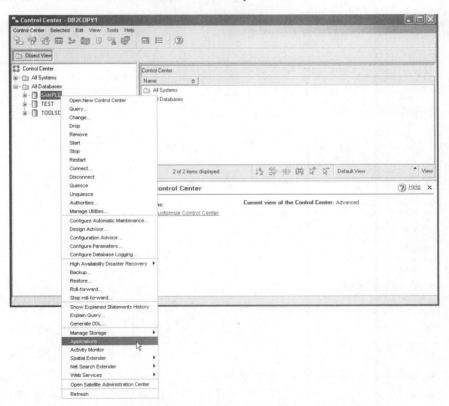

Figure 2–17: Invoking the Applications dialog from the Control Center.

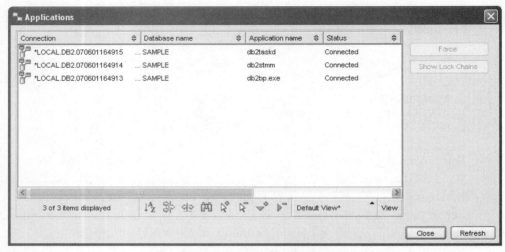

Figure 2–18: The Applications dialog.

The FORCE APPLICATION Command

Once you know what applications are using a particular instance or database, you can terminate one or more of those applications prematurely by executing the FORCE APPLICATION command (assuming you have SYSADMN or SYSCTRL authority). The basic syntax for this command is:

```
FORCE APPLICATION ALL
```

or

```
FORCE APPLICATION ([ApplicationHandle] ,...)
```

where:

ApplicationHandle   Identifies the handle associated with one or more applications whose instance attachments or database connections are to be terminated.

Thus, if you wanted to force all users and applications connected to databases stored on a server named DB_SERVER to terminate their database connections, you could do so by executing a FORCE APPLICATION command that looks something like this:

```
FORCE APPLICATION ALL
```

On the other hand, if you wanted to force a specific application whose handle is 148 (refer to the sample output shown for the LIST APPLICATIONS command to see where this value came from) to terminate its connection to a database named SAMPLE, you could do so by executing a FORCE APPLICATION command that looks something like this:

```
FORCE APPLICATION (148)
```

It is important to note that when an application's instance attachment or database connection is terminated by the FORCE APPLICATION command, any SQL operations that have been performed by the application but have not yet been committed are rolled back.

In order to preserve database integrity, only applications that are idle or that are performing interruptible database operations can be terminated when the FORCE APPLICATION command is processed. (For example, applications in the process of creating or backing up a database would not be terminated; applications in the process of restoring a database would be terminated, and the restore operation would have to be rerun before the database would be usable.) In addition, the DB2 Database Manager for the instance cannot be stopped during a force operation; the DB2 Database Manager must remain active so that subsequent instance-level operations can be handled without having to restart the instance. Finally, because the FORCE APPLICATION command is run asynchronously, other applications or users can attach to the instance or connect to a database within the instance after this command has been executed. Multiple FORCE APPLICATION commands may be required to completely terminate all instance attachments and database connections.

If you are using the Applications dialog to see which users or applications are currently attached to an instance or connected to a database, you can terminate instance attachments and database connections by highlighting one or more entries in the list shown on the Applications dialog and selecting the "Force" push button located in the upper right corner of the screen (refer to Figure 2–18).

Using the Task Center

As you might imagine, terminating instance attachments and database connections
with the FORCE APPLICATION or QUIESCE commands can have a significant impact
on all users and applications affected. A better alternative is to schedule
maintenance operations so that they are performed at a time when there is little or
no database activity. That's where the Task Center comes in. The Task Center is an
interactive GUI application that allows users to organize task flow, schedule
frequently occurring tasks, run tasks, and send notifications about completed tasks
to other users. Figure 2–19 shows how the Task Center might look on a Windows
XP server after a Database Backup task has been created.

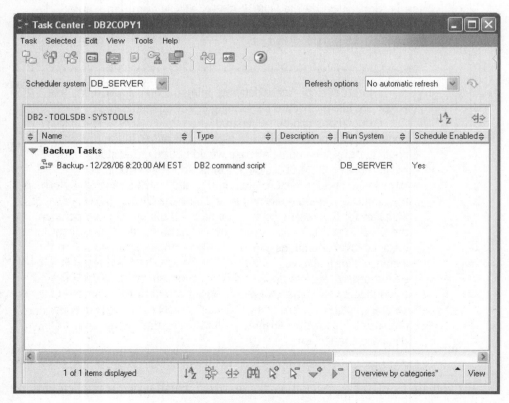

Figure 2–19: The Task Center.

So just what is a *task*? A task is a script together with any associated success
conditions, schedules, and notifications. Users can create a task within the Task

Center, generate a task by saving the results from a DB2 dialog or wizard (for example, the Backup Wizard can be used to create a database backup operation that can be scheduled to run at regular intervals), create a script within another tool and save it to the Task Center, or import an existing script. Such scripts can contain DB2 commands, SQL statements, operating system commands, or any combination of the three. Although a task is not just a script, a script is often an integral part of a task; once a script has been created, the process of converting it into a task involves

- scheduling when the script will run,

- specifying success and failure conditions,

- specifying actions that should be performed when the script executes successfully and when it fails, and

- specifying email addresses (including pager addresses) that should be notified when the script has completed or if the script failed. (The task center can either notify contacts or place information in the Journal.)

With the Task Center, it is also possible to create a grouping task, which is a special task that combines several scripts into a single logical unit of work. When the grouping task meets the success or failure conditions that you define, any follow-on tasks are run. For example, you could combine three backup scripts into a grouping task and then specify a table reorganization operation as a follow-on task that is to be executed if all of the backup scripts execute successfully.

The Task Center uses success code sets (the return codes or range of return codes that, if received, indicate the task was executed successfully) to evaluate the success or failure of any task it executes; codes that fall outside the range specified indicate failure. In addition, the Task Center evaluates the SQLCA return code of every SQL statement executed in a DB2 script, and if any statement fails, the entire task fails. Regardless of whether a task completes successfully or fails, any number of actions can be performed, including the following:

- Running another task

- Scheduling another task

- Disabling another scheduled task

- Deleting itself

So just who can create and schedule tasks? Anyone who has the authorities and privileges needed to execute the task. In fact the Task Center provides a way for a user who creates a task to grant read, write, and execute (run) privileges to other users for the task being created. This can be useful when a number of different users are creating and maintaining tasks.

●●●

To use the Task Center, you must first create a tools catalog. If you did not create a tools catalog when you installed DB2, you can create one by executing the CREATE TOOLS CATALOG command.

●●●

The DAS Configuration and the Task Center

To a certain extent, the behavior of the task center is controlled through parameters found in the DAS instance configuration file. Just as a DB2 Database Manager configuration file is created and initialized whenever a new instance is created, a DAS instance configuration file is created and initialized when the DAS is created. The parameters that make up a DAS instance configuration file are shown in Table 2.7.

Table 2.7 DAS Instance Configuration Parameters		
Parameter	Value Range/Default	Description
authentication	SERVER_ENCRYPT, KERBEROS_ENCRYPT Default: SERVER_ENCRYPT	Specifies how and where DAS user authentication takes place.
contact_host	Any valid TCP/IP host name Default: NULL	Specifies the location (which is a DB2 administration server's TCP/IP hostname) where the contact information used for notification by the Scheduler and the Health Monitor is stored. If a location is not specified, the DAS assumes the contact information is local.
das_codepage	Any valid character string Default: NULL	Identifies the code page used by the DB2 administration server. If this parameter is null, the default code page of the system is used.
das_territory	Any valid character string Default: NULL	Identifies the territory used by the DB2 administration server. If this parameter is null, the default territory of the system is used
dasadm_group	Any valid character string Default: NULL	Specifies the group name that has DAS Administrator (DASADM) authority for the DAS instance.

Table 2.7 DAS Instance Configuration Parameters (continued)		
Parameter	Value Range/Default	Description
db2system	Any valid character string Default: TCP/IP host name	Specifies the name that is used by users and database administrators to identify the DB2 server system. (DB2 Discovery returns this name as a DB2 system that contains instances and databases.)
discover	DISABLE, KNOWN, SEARCH Default: SEARCH	Specifies the type of DB2 Discovery requests that are supported by the server. (If this parameter is set to SEARCH, then search discovery, in which the DB2 client searches the network for DB2 databases, is supported. If this parameter is set to KNOWN, then known discovery, in which the discovery request is issued against the administration server specified by the user, is supported. If this parameter is set to DISABLE, the workstation will not respond to any type of discovery request.)
exec_exp_task	YES, NO Default: NO	Specifies whether expired tasks are to be executed when the Scheduler is turned on. (The Scheduler only detects expired tasks when it starts up.) For example, if you have a job scheduled to run every Saturday, and the Scheduler is turned off on Friday and then restarted on Monday, the job scheduled for Saturday is now an expired task. If *exec_exp_task* is set to YES, the Saturday job will run immediately when the Scheduler is restarted.
jdk_64_path	Any valid character string Default: NULL	Specifies the directory under which the 64-bit Software Developer's Kit (SDK) for Java™, to be used for running DB2 administration server functions, is installed.
jdk_path	Any valid character string Default: NULL	Specifies the directory under which the Software Developer's Kit (SDK) for Java™, to be used for running DB2 administration server functions, is installed.
sched_enable	ON, OFF Default: OFF	Specifies whether the Scheduler is running. The Scheduler allows tools such as the Task Center to schedule and execute tasks at the administration server.
sched_userid	Any valid character string Default: NULL	Specifies the user ID that is to be used by the Scheduler to connect to the tools catalog database—if the tools catalog database is remote to the DB2 administration server.

Table 2.7 DAS Instance Configuration Parameters (continued)		
Parameter	**Value Range/Default**	**Description**
smtp_server	Any valid SMTP server TCP/IP hostname Default: NULL	Identifies the SMTP server that the Scheduler will use to send email and pager notifications (when it is on).
toolscat_db	Any valid character string Default: NULL	Identifies the tools catalog database that is used by the Scheduler. (The tools catalog database contains task information created by the Task Center and the Control Center and must exist before the Task Center can be used.)
toolscat_inst	Any valid character string Default: NULL	Identifies the instance name that is used by the Scheduler, along with *toolscat_db*, to identify the tools catalog database.
toolscat_schema	Any valid character string Default: NULL	Identifies the schema of the tools catalog database that is used by the Scheduler. (The schema is used to uniquely identify the set of tools catalog tables and views within the database.)
Adapted from Table 66 on pages 273–274 of the DB2 9 Performance Guide manual		

You can display the contents of the DAS instance configuration file by executing the GET ADMIN CONFIGURATION command. The syntax for this command is:

```
GET ADMIN [CONFIGURATION | CONFIG | CFG]
```

The value assigned to a particular DAS instance configuration file parameter can be changed by executing the UPDATE ADMIN CONFIGURATION command. The syntax for this command is:

```
UPDATE ADMIN [CONFIGURATION | CONFIG | CFG]
USING [[Parameter] [Value] ,...]
```

where:

Parameter Identifies one or more DAS instance configuration parameters (by keywords) whose values are to be modified.

Value Identifies the new value(s) that are to be assigned to the DAS instance configuration parameter(s) specified.

So if you wanted to turn the Scheduler on so that tasks in the Task Center will be executed, you could do so by executing an UPDATE ADMIN CONFIGURATION command that looks like this:

```
UPDATE ADMIN CFG USING SCHED_ENABLE ON
```

The values assigned to all DAS instance configuration file parameters can be returned to their system defaults by executing the RESET ADMIN CONFIGURATION command. The syntax for this command is:

```
RESET ADMIN [CONFIGURATION | CONFIG | CFG]
```

Automatic Maintenance

Although the Task Center can be used to schedule maintenance operations, for some administrators, it can be time-consuming to determine whether and when to run some of the more resource-intensive maintenance utilities. With automatic maintenance (a new feature introduced in DB2 9), you specify your maintenance objectives, and the DB2 Database Manager will use the objectives you have identified to determine whether one or more maintenance activities need to be performed. If it is determined that a maintenance operation is required, that operation will be performed during the next available maintenance window (a maintenance window is a time period, specified by you, in which all automatic maintenance activities are to be executed).

Automatic maintenance can be used to perform the following maintenance operations:

- **Create a backup image of the database.** Automatic database backup provides users with a solution to help ensure their database is being backed up both properly and regularly, without their having to worry about when to back up or having any knowledge of the syntax for the BACKUP command.

- **Data defragmentation (table or index reorganization).** This maintenance activity can increase the efficiency with which the DB2 Database Manager accesses tables. Automatic reorganization manages offline table and index reorganization without users having to worry about when and how to reorganize their data.

- **Data access optimization (running RUNSTATS).** The DB2 Database Manager updates the system catalog statistics on the data in a table, the data in a table's indexes, or the data in both a table and its indexes. The DB2 Optimizer uses these statistics to determine which path to use to access data in response to a query. Automatic statistics collection attempts to improve the performance of the database by maintaining up-to-date table statistics. The goal is to allow the DB2 Optimizer to always choose an access plan based on accurate statistics.

- **Statistics profiling.** Automatic statistics profiling advises when and how to collect table statistics by detecting outdated, missing, and incorrectly specified statistics and by generating statistical profiles based on query feedback.

When a DB2 9 database is created, automatic maintenance is enabled by default; enablement of the available automatic maintenance features is controlled using the automatic maintenance-specific database configuration parameters available (*auto_maint*, *auto_db_backup*, *auto_tbl_maint*, *auto_runstats*, *auto_stats_prof*, *auto_prof_upd*, and *auto_reorg*). These parameters represent a hierarchical set of switches that can be set to ON or OFF.

The easiest way to configure automatic maintenance and define maintenance windows is by using a special tool known as the Configure Automatic Maintenance wizard. You can activate this tool by selecting the Configure Automatic Maintenance action from the Databases menu found in the Control Center. Figure 2–20 shows the Control Center menu items that must be selected in order to activate the Configure Automatic Maintenance wizard. Figure 2–21 shows how the first page of this wizard looks on a Windows XP server.

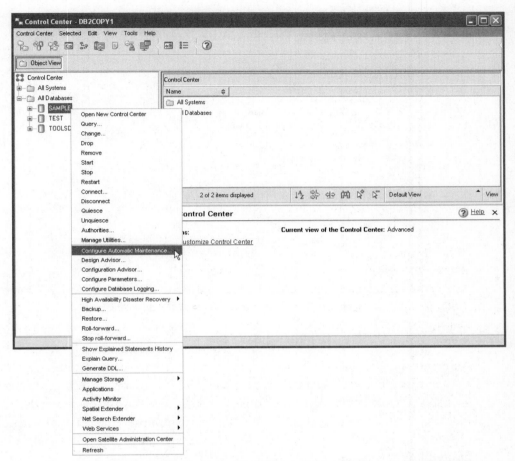

Figure 2–20: Invoking the Configure Automatic Maintenance wizard from the Control Center.

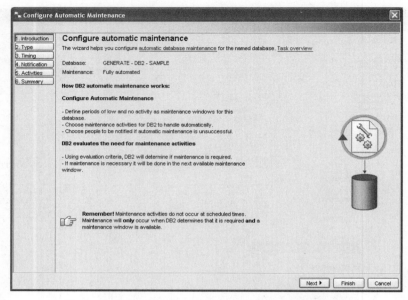

Figure 2–21: The Configure Automatic Maintenance wizard.

DB2's Adaptive Utility Throttling System

Automatic maintenance activities consume system resources when they are run, so their execution can affect database performance. Additionally, offline database backup and table/index reorganization operations can restrict access to tables, indexes, or the entire database. To minimize system impact, the resource usage of some automatic maintenance activities can be regulated using DB2's adaptive utility throttling system.

The adaptive utility throttling system allows maintenance utilities to be run concurrently with workloads during critical periods, while keeping their impact on the system within acceptable limits. This also allows utilities to be automatically assigned more computing resources during off-peak times, and to be scaled back during periods of high activity. The following maintenance operations can take advantage of utility throttling:

- Statistics collection
- Backup operations
- Rebalancing operations
- Asynchronous index cleanups

Setting an Impact Policy

To control utility throttling, you must establish an impact policy. The impact policy refers to the instance-wide limit that all throttled utilities can cumulatively have on the production workload; once such a policy is established, it's the system's responsibility to ensure that the policy is obeyed. To define the impact policy for all throttled utilities, you simply assign a value between 1 and 100 to the *util_impact_lim* DB2 Database Manager configuration parameter.

For example, to set the instance-wide limit that all throttled utilities can cumulatively have on production workloads to 10 percent (or in other words, to ensure performance degradation from all throttled utilities will not impact the system workload by more than 10 percent), you would assign the util_impact_lim configuration parameter the value 10 by executing an UPDATE DATABASE MANAGER CONFIGURATION command that looks like this:

```
UPDATE DATABASE MANAGER CONFIGURATION USING UTIL_IMPACT_LIM 10
```

As you would expect, a throttled utility will usually take longer to complete than an unthrottled utility. If you find that a utility is running for an excessively long time, you can increase the value assigned to the *util_impact_lim* configuration parameter, or you can disable throttling altogether by setting the *util_impact_lim* configuration parameter to 100. (If *util_impact_lim* is set to 100, no utility invocations will be throttled. In this case, the utilities can complete faster, but they most likely will have an undesirable impact on workload performance.)

Executing a Utility in Throttled Mode

Defining an impact policy doesn't mean that all utility invocations will run throttled. In fact, by default, utilities run unthrottled even when an impact policy has been defined. To execute a utility in throttled mode, you must either enable throttling at the time the utility is invoked, or you must enable throttling after the utility has been started.

To enable throttling when a utility is invoked, you must specify the UTIL_IMPACT_PRIORITY option with the command that is used to execute the utility. (Currently, the only commands that recognize the UTIL_IMPACT_PRIORITY clause are BACKUP DATABASE and RUNSTATS.) Keep in mind that an impact policy must be defined (via the *util_impact_lim* configuration parameter) before the UTIL_IMPACT_PRIORITY clause will have any affect on these commands.

The UTIL_IMPACT_PRIORITY clause takes an optional relative priority argument (a value between 0 and 100 where 0 is OFF), which is used to differentiate amongst the importance of throttled utilities. A throttled utility with a high priority will run more aggressively than one with a low priority.

Changing a Running Utility's Impact Priority

If you want to change the impact priority (level of throttling) of a utility that is already running, you can do so by executing the SET UTIL_IMPACT_PRIORITY command. With this command, you can

- Throttle a running utility that was started in unthrottled mode,
- Unthrottle a running throttled utility (disable throttling), and
- Reprioritize a running throttled utility. (This capability is useful if multiple simultaneous throttled utilities are running and one is more important than the others.)

The syntax for the SET UTIL_IMPACT_PRIORITY command is:

```
SET UTIL_IMPACT_PRIORITY  [UtilityID] TO [Priority]
```

where:

UtilityID   Identifies the running utility, by ID, whose priority is to be changed.

Priority   Specifies an instance-level limit on the impact associated with running the utility specified. A value of 100 represents the highest priority; a value of 1 represents the lowest. Setting *Priority* to 0 will force a throttled utility to continue running unthrottled; setting *Priority* to a non-zero value will force an unthrottled utility to continue running in throttled mode.

Thus, if you wanted to force an active unthrottled backup operation whose utility ID is 1 to continue running in throttled mode, you could do so by executing the following command:

```
SET UTIL_IMPACT_PRIORITY 1 TO 20
```

Once this statement is executed, the cumulative impact of the Backup operation and other concurrently executing throttled utilities will be less than the percent impact value assigned to the *util_impact_lim* configuration parameter; the value 20 defines the throttling importance of the Backup operation with respect to other throttled utilities.

Obtaining Information about Running Utilities

If you want to find out which, if any, utilities are running against an instance and what their current impact priority is, you can do so by executing the LIST UTILITUES command. The syntax for this command is:

```
LIST UTILITIES
<SHOW DETAIL>
```

So, if someone started Backup operation for a database named SAMPLE and you wanted to obtain detailed information about the operation, you could execute a LIST UTILITIES command that looks like this:

```
LIST UTILITIES SHOW DETAIL
```

Assuming the backup operation was started unthrottled, the information returned would look something like this:

```
ID                                = 1
Type                              = BACKUP
Database Name                     = SAMPLE
Partition Number                  = 0
Description                       = offline db
Start Time                        = 06/02/2007 10:35:31.442019
State                             = Executing
Invocation Type                   = User
Throttling:
    Priority                      = Unthrottled
Progress Monitoring:
    Estimated Percentage Complete = 46
        Total Work                = 49310404 bytes
        Completed Work            = 22696620 bytes
        Start Time                = 06/02/2007 10:35:31.466054
```

If you wanted to change the impact priority of this backup operation, you would do so by executing a SET UTIL_IMPACT_PRIORITY command with the utility ID 1 specified.

Self-Tuning Memory Manager

Although utility throttling can help reduce the impact the execution of a utility has on production workloads, how well (or poorly) workloads perform often depends on how resources such as memory are utilized by the server. And as we saw earlier, the DB2 Database Manager configuration and database configuration parameters control how system resources are allocated for instances and databases. In DB2 9, a new memory tuning feature, known as the Self-Tuning Memory Manager, simplifies the task of configuring memory-related database parameters by automatically setting values for these parameters after measuring and analyzing how well each DB2 memory consumer is using the allocated memory available. The following memory consumers can be enabled for self-tuning:

- Buffer pools (controlled by the ALTER BUFFERPOOL and CREATE BUFFERPOOL statements)
- Package cache (controlled by the *pckcachesz* configuration parameter)
- Locking memory (controlled by the *locklist* and *maxlocks* configuration parameters)
- Sort memory (controlled by the *sheapthres_shr* and the *sortheap* configuration parameters)
- Database shared memory (controlled by the *database_memory* configuration parameter)

When a database is not enabled for self-tuning, the entire database will use a specified amount of memory, distributing it across the database memory consumers as required. However, when a database has been enabled for self-tuning, the memory tuner responds to significant changes in database workload characteristics, adjusting the values of memory configuration parameters and buffer pool sizes to optimize performance. If the current workload requirements are high, and there is sufficient free memory on the system, more memory will be consumed by the database. Once the workload's memory requirements drop, or if the amount of free memory available on the system becomes too low, some database shared memory is released. It is important to note that because self-tuning memory management bases its tuning decisions on database workload, workloads with changing memory characteristics limit its ability to tune effectively. If a workload's memory characteristics are constantly changing, self-tuning memory will tune memory less frequently and will repeatedly tune toward shifting target conditions.

Self-tuning is enabled for a database by assigning the value ON to the *self_tuning_mem* database configuration parameter. Specific memory areas that are controlled by a memory configuration parameter can be enabled for self-tuning by assigning the value AUTOMATIC to the configuration parameter; you can enable buffer pools for self-tuning by setting their size to AUTOMATIC, using either the CREATE BUFFERPOOL or the ALTER BUFFERPOOL SQL statement. However, because the memory tuner trades memory resources between different memory consumers, there must be at least two memory consumers enabled for self-tuning in order for self-tuning to be active. (Not to mention the fact that the database itself must have the *self_tuning_mem* database configuration parameter set to ON.)

Once a database and two or more memory consumers have been configured for self-tuning, the current memory configuration for the database can be obtained by executing the GET DATABASE CONFIGURATION command. Changes made by self-tuning are recorded in memory tuning log files, which reside in the *stmmlog* subdirectory of the instance. (The first file created will be assigned the name *stmm.0.log*, the second will be assigned the name *stmm.1.log*, and so on.) Each memory tuning log file contains summaries of the resource demands for each memory consumer at the time a tuning operation was performed. Tuning intervals can be determined by examining the timestamps for the entries made in the memory tuning log files.

Problem Determination

Because the potential for errors to occur can never be completely eliminated from a database environment, DB2 comes equipped with a variety of tools that can be used to help pinpoint the cause in the event an error does occur. And in many cases, these tools can provide recommendations that, when followed, may resolve the situation that caused the error to be generated in the first place.

When an error occurs within a database system, the DB2 Database Manager notifies the user by generating a specific error code and presenting this code in a variety of ways. If the Command Line Processor (CLP) is being used when an error occurs, the error code generated, along with a corresponding message, will be displayed at the CLP prompt. On the other hand, if any of the administration tools that come with DB2 are being used when an error occurs, the error code generated, along with a corresponding message, will be displayed in a pop-up dialog and recorded in the Journal, along with the date and time the error occurred.

Obtaining Information About An Error Code

When an error code is returned by the DB2 Database Manager, there are a variety of ways in which you can find out what that error code means:

- By looking up the error code generated in the *IBM DB2 9 Message Reference Volume 1 or Volume 2* product documentation.

- By executing the GET ERROR MESSAGE API (this API must be executed from within an application program).

- By instructing the DB2 Database Manager to provide information associated with the error code generated. You can tell the DB2 Database Manager to provide information associated with an error code by executing a command that consists of a question mark followed by the error code from the DB2 Command Line Processor (CLP). For example, if you wanted to view information associated with the error code CCA3002N, you could do so by executing the command ? CCA3002N from the CLP. The results returned would look something like this:

```
CCA3002N An I/O error occurred.

Explanation:

An error was encountered while attempting to open, read, change the file
position or close a file.

User Response:

If a file name was specified, verify that the file name is valid and
that the user has permission to access the file. Also check for any disk
and operating system errors.
```

Reason codes

In some cases, an error message will contain a reference to what is known as a reason code. Reason codes are used when a single error code can be generated by several different events, and they are designed to provide additional information associated with the error code returned. For example, the error message associated with the error code SQL0866N looks something like this:

```
Connection redirection failed. Reason code: "[ReasonCode]"
```

where:

ReasonCode   Identifies the reason code associated with the error message. Usually, this is a numerical value. (For error code SQL0866N, *ReasonCode* can be the number 1 or 2.)

In most cases, you can find out what a particular reason code means by looking up the error code generated in the *IBM DB2 9 Message Reference, Volume 1* or the *IBM DB2 9 Message Reference, Volume 2* product documentation, or by instructing the DB2 Database Manager to provide information about the error code with which the reason code is associated.

First Failure Data Capture (FFDC)

One of the most important diagnostic tools available with DB2 is a facility known as First Failure Data Capture (FFDC). FFDC runs quietly in the background until a significant event occurs, and at that time, diagnostic information about the event is automatically captured by the DB2 Database Manager and recorded in special ASCII-format files. This information contains crucial details that may help in the diagnosis and resolution of problems. And because this information is collected at the actual time an event takes place, the need to reproduce errors in order to obtain diagnostic information is greatly reduced or in some cases eliminated. The information captured by FFDC is externalized in several different ways, including the following:

DB2 diagnostic log file entries. Whenever any significant event occurs, an entry containing diagnostic information about that event is automatically recorded in a file named "db2diag.log," which acts as the primary diagnostic log file for DB2.

Administration notification log entries. When significant events occur, supplemental information for any SQL return code generated is written to the Windows Event Log (on Windows NT, Windows 2000, and Windows XP systems) or to a file named *"InstanceName*.nfy"—where *InstanceName* is the name of the instance that generated the information (on all other supported operating systems). This information is noncryptic and can be viewed with the Windows Event Viewer (on Windows systems) or with any text editor (on all other systems).

Dump files. In some cases, when a DB2-specific process or thread fails, extra information is logged in external binary dump files (that are assigned a name based on the ID of the failing process/thread). These files are more-or-less unreadable and are intended to be forwarded to DB2 Customer Support for interpretation.

Trap files. If the DB2 Database Manager cannot continue processing because a trap, segmentation violation, or exception has occurred, it generates a trap file that contains the sequence of function calls made for the last steps executed before the trap, segmentation violation, or exception event occurred.

Core files (UNIX only). If DB2 terminates abnormally on a UNIX platform, the operating system will generate a core file, which is a binary file that contains information similar to the information recorded in a DB2 trap file. (Core files may also contain the entire memory image of the terminated DB2 process.)

Where FFDC information is stored

By default, all FFDC information collected on a UNIX platform is stored in the directory *$HOME/sqllib/db2dump,* where *$HOME* is the home directory of the instance owner. On Windows platforms, if the location of the instance directory has not been stored in the DB2INSTPROF environment variable, FFDC information collected is stored in the directory *DB2Path\DB2Instanc*e, where *DB2Path* is the path stored in the DB2PATH environment variable and *DB2Instance* is the value stored in the DB2INSTDEF environment variable (which is "DB2" by default). On the other hand, if the location of the instance directory has been stored in the DB2INSTPROF environment variable, FFDC information is stored in the directory *Drive:\DB2InstProfile\DB2Instance,* where *Drive* is the drive referenced in the DB2PATH environment variable, *DB2InstProfile* is the name of the instance profile directory, and *DB2Instance* is the value stored in the DB2INSTDEF environment variable.

However, where FFDC information is actually recorded is controlled by the value of the *diagpath* parameter of a DB2 Database Manager instance's configuration file. Thus, if you wish to change the location where all FFDC information is stored, you do so by changing the value of this parameter (which contains a null string when an instance is first created).

Regardless of where FFDC information is stored, it is up to the System Administrator to ensure that the location used is cleaned periodically; DB2 does not automatically remove dump files, trap files, and core files that are generated by the FFDC tool.

Controlling how much FFDC information is collected

The type (which controls the amount) of administrative and diagnostic information recorded is also controlled by parameters (*notifylevel* and *diaglevel*) in a DB2 Database Manager instance's configuration file. Based on their current value, these parameters tell FFDC what type of administrative and diagnostic information to collect:

0. Do not collect administrative information and diagnostic data (not recommended).

1. Collect administrative information and diagnostic data for severe (fatal or unrecoverable) errors only.

2. Collect administrative information and diagnostic data for all types of errors (both severe and non-severe) but not for warnings.

3. Collect administrative information and diagnostic data for all errors and warnings.

4. Collect administrative information and diagnostic data for all errors and warnings, including informational messages and other internal diagnostic information.

When an instance is first created, the *notifylevel* and *diaglevel* parameters in a DB2 Database Manager instance's configuration file are set to 3 by default, and administrative information/diagnostic data for errors and warnings is collected by FFDC whenever such events occur. However, these parameters should be set to 4 (except in parallel database environments where this setting can cause too much data to be produced) whenever possible. This is particularly true when DB2 is set up initially, each time configuration parameter values are changed, or whenever a large number of errors seem to be occurring. However, it is important to keep in mind that if the *diaglevel* configuration parameter is set to 4, DB2 will run more slowly when the DB2 Database Manager for the instance is first started, when an initial connection to a database within the instance is established, and each time an error condition occurs.

The DB2 diagnostic log file

Earlier, we saw that whenever any significant event occurs, an entry containing diagnostic information about that event is automatically recorded in a file named "db2diag.log," which acts as the primary diagnostic log file for DB2. The db2diag.log file is an ASCII format file made up of diagnostic records that have been generated by the FFDC tool. Each record (or entry) in this file contains either information about a particular administrative event that has occurred or specific error information. Entries for administrative events are valuable because they indicate whether events such as backup and restore operations were started and if so, whether they finished successfully. Entries for error information, on the other hand, are useful only when trying to diagnose an external symptom, or if the source of a particular error has been isolated and you are looking for more information (for example, if an application receives an unexpected SQL code or if a database crashes). If a database is behaving normally, error information entries are not important and can usually be ignored.

Once created, the db2diag.log file grows continuously. As a result, the most recent entries are always found near the end of the file. If storage space for this file becomes an issue, the existing file can be deleted—a new db2diag.log file will be created automatically the next time one is needed.

The administration notification log

In earlier versions of DB2, the DB2 diagnostics log (db2diag.log file) acted as a single diagnostic facility that could be used by both system/database administrators and DB2 Customer Service. Unfortunately, because diagnostic information needed by system/database administrators is very different from that needed by DB2 Customer Service personnel, and because the information needed by DB2 Customer Service personnel is often cryptic (i.e., memory structure dumps, internal return codes, and benign diagnostic entries) and is useful only to people with a working knowledge of the DB2 source code, forcing this one file to serve two purposes often caused system and database administrators to become unnecessarily concerned about file entries they did not understand. To remedy this situation, IBM introduced the user-friendly administration notification log in Version 8.1. This log is designed to drastically change the diagnostic landscape of DB2; now the administration notification log serves as the primary diagnostic facility for system and database administrators, and the DB2 diagnostics log exists for the sole purpose of providing special, customized information to DB2 Customer Service personnel.

One of the noticeable differences about administration notification log entries as opposed to DB2 diagnostic log entries is the lack of confusing hex dumps. Meaningful, helpful messages that were reviewed and written with the help of real, professional DB2 database administrators (DB2 customers) are provided in their place. Most of these messages provide supplemental information for each associated SQL return code value returned to an application or the CLP. Other messages provide notification of unexpected errors or asynchronous events such as a crash, a signal from the operating system, or a sub-optimal configuration. The format of administration notification log entries and DB2 diagnostic log entries are essentially identical. However, all messages written to the administration notification log are written using the end-user language specified during the installation process (messages written to the DB2 diagnostics log are always written English, regardless of the end-user language used).

Another significant difference is that on Windows platforms, administration notification log entries are written to the Windows Event Log, rather than a predefined file. However, when a predefined file is used (which is the case on all non-Windows platforms), this file behaves like the DB2 diagnostics log: Once created, it grows continuously; the most recent entries are always found near the end of the file; and if the file is deleted, a new one will be created automatically the next time it is needed.

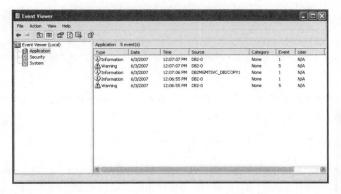

Figure 2–22: The Windows Event Viewer.

It is important to note that entries written to the Windows Event Log can be viewed using the Windows Event Viewer. Figure 2–22 shows how a DB2 administration notification log entry might appear in the Windows Event Viewer on a Windows XP server.

Interpreting DB2 diagnostic log and administration notification log entry headers

Every entry in the administration notification log file and the DB2 diagnostic log file begins with a specific set of values that are intended to help identify the particular event the entry corresponds to. Because this block of information is recorded for all entries and because it is always recorded in a specific format, it is referred to as the entry header. Figure 2–23 illustrates how a typical administration notification log entry header looks.

Figure 2–23: Individual components of an administration notification log/DB2 diagnostic log entry header

All entry headers consist of the following components (refer to the numbered bullets in Figure 2–23):

1. A timestamp that identifies when the entry was made.

2. The db2diag.log file's record ID. This ID specifies the file offset at which the current message is being logged (for example, "907855") and the message length (for example, "435") for the platform where the DB2 diagnostic log was created.

3. The diagnostic level associated with the error message. Valid values are Info, Warning, Error, Severe, and Event.

4. The unique identifier that has been assigned (by the operating system) to the process that generated the entry. This value is more applicable in a UNIX environment where DB2 operates using multiple processes. In a Windows environment, DB2 operates with multiple threads rather than multiple processes; therefore, the process ID provided is usually that of the main DB2 executable. (If the application is operating in a Distributed Unit Of Work [DUOW] environment, the Process ID shown will be the DUOW correlation token.)

5. The unique identifier that has been assigned (by the operating system) to the thread that generated the entry.

6. The name of the process that generated the entry.

7. The name of the instance that generated the entry.

8. The number that corresponds to the node that generated the entry. If a nonpartitioned database is being used, the node number will always be 000.

9. The name of the database for which the entry was generated.

10. The application handle that has been assigned to the application for which the process that generated the event is working. This value consists of the coordinator partition number followed by the coordinator index number, separated by a dash.

11. The unique identifier that has been assigned to the application for which the process that generated the event is working. To find out more about a particular application ID, perform the following tasks:

    - Use the LIST APPLICATIONS command on a DB2 server or the LIST DCS APPLICATIONS command on a DB2 Connect gateway to obtain a list of application IDs. Search this list for the application ID; once you have found it, you can obtain information about the client experiencing the error, such as its node name and its TCP/IP address.

    - Use the GET SNAPSHOT FOR APPLICATION command to view a list of application IDs.

    - Execute the command db2pd -applications -db [*DatabaseName*].

12. The authorization ID of the user who was working with the instance or database when the entry was generated.

13. The product name ("DB2 UDB"), component name ("buffer pool services"), and function name ("sqlbAlterBufferPoolAct") that generated the message (as well as the probe point [90] within the function). If the entry was generated by a user application that executed the db2AdminMsgWrite() API, this component of the entry header will read "User Application." (Applications can write messages to the administration notification log file and the DB2 diagnostic log file by invoking the db2 AdminMsgWrite() API.)

To find out more about the type of activity performed by the function that produced the entry, look at the fourth letter of its name. The following shows some of the letters used in the fourth position of DB2 function names, along with the type of activity each function performs:

b: Buffer pool management and manipulation

c: Communications between clients and servers

d: Data management

e: Database engine processes

o: Operating system calls (such as opening and closing files)

p: Data protection (such as locking and logging)

r: Relational database services

s: Sorting operations

x: Indexing operations

In the entry shown in Figure 2–23, the fourth letter of the function named sqlbAlterBufferPoolAct—*b*—indicates that the message was generated by a function that was attempting to perform some type of buffer pool management and manipulation operation.

14. A message that describes the event that was logged.

The db2diag utility

For the most part, the information found in the administration notification log file and the DB2 diagnostic log file is easy to read once you understand the format used. However, searching through a large DB2 diagnostic log file can be time-consuming, particularly if the log file spans several months. To aid in problem determination, DB2 9 provides a utility that can be used to filter and format the information available in the db2diag.log file. This utility is known as the db2diag utility, and it is activated by executing the db2diag command. There are several options available with this command; to find out more, execute any of the following commands from the DB2 Command Line Processor:

- db2diag -help (Provides a short description of the options available)

- db2diag -h brief (Provides descriptions for all options without examples)

- db2diag -h notes (Provides usage notes and restrictions)

- db2diag -h examples (Provides a small set of examples to help you get started)
- db2diag -h tutorial (Provides examples for all options available)

- db2diag -h all (Provides a comprehensive list of options available)

Practice Questions

Question 1

Which of the following authorities should a user have in order to quiesce an instance named DB2INST1?

○ A. SYSADM

○ B. SECADM

○ C. SYSMAINT

○ D. SYSMON

Question 2

Which of the following commands will start a default instance named DB2INST1?

○ A. START db2inst1

○ B. START DB MANAGER

○ C. db2start i db2inst1

○ D. START DBMGR

Question 3

A DB2 server contains two instances named TEST and PROD. The instance named TEST is the default instance. Which of the following commands must be executed before an attempt is made to start the instance named PROD?

○ A. db2set DB2_INSTANCE=prod

○ B. UPDATE DBM CFG USING DB2INSTANCE prod

○ C. set DB2INSTANCE=prod

○ D. UPDATE DBM CFG USING DB2_INSTANCE prod

Question 4

Which of the following commands will assign the value TCPIP to the variable DB2COMM for all instances on a DB2 server?

○ A. db2set DB2COMM=TCPIP

○ B. db2set –g DB2COMM=TCPIP

○ C. db2set –all DB2COMM=TCPIP

○ D. set DB2COMM=TCPIP

Question 5

If the following command is executed:

```
db2set DB2COMM=
```

What will happen?

○ A.   The value assigned to the DB2COMM registry variable will be displayed.

○ B.   A list of communications protocols that are recognized by the server will be assigned to the DB2COMM registry variable.

○ C.   The value assigned to the global DB2COMM variable will be copied to the DB2COMM registry variable for the default instance.

○ D.   The DB2COMM registry level variable for the default instance will be deleted.

Question 6

Which of the following commands can be used to obtain information about how memory has been allocated for a database named SAMPLE?

○ A.   GET DB CFG FOR sample SHOW DETAIL

○ B.   GET MEMORY USAGE FOR sample

○ C.   GET DBM CFG

○ D.   GET CFG DETAILS FOR sample

Question 7

Which of the following DB2 Database Manager configuration parameters is used to control the maximum number of applications that can be executing concurrently in an instance?

○ A.   NUM_INITAGENTS

○ B.   MAXCAGENTS

○ C.   MAX_COORDAGENTS

○ D.   MAXAGENTS

Question 8

Which of the following commands disables roll-forward recovery for a database named SAMPLE and causes the database to create a duplicate copy of the transaction log files in a separate location?

○ A.   UPDATE DB CFG FOR sample USING LOGARCHMETH1 LOGRETAIN;
       UPDATE DB CFG FOR sample USING NEWLOGPATH D:\dup_logs;

○ B.   UPDATE DB CFG FOR sample USING LOGARCHMETH1 OFF;
       UPDATE DB CFG FOR sample USING MIRRORLOGPATH D:\dup_logs;

○ C.   UPDATE DB CFG FOR sample USING LOGARCHMETH1 LOGRETAIN;
       UPDATE DB CFG FOR sample USING LOGSECOND D:\dup_logs;

○ D.   UPDATE DB CFG FOR sample USING LOGARCHMETH1 OFF;
       UPDATE DB CFG FOR sample USING LOGARCHMETH2 DISK:
       D:\dup_logs;

Question 9

A database administrator successfully executed the following commands:

```
UPDATE DBM CFG USING SHEAPTHRES 37500
UPDATE DB CFG FOR sample USING SORTHEAP 2500
```

Assuming each sort operation performed against the SAMPLE database consumes 10 MB of memory, what is the maximum number sort operations that can be run concurrently?

○ A.   5
○ B.   10
○ C.   15
○ D.   20

Question 10

Which of the following database configuration parameters is used to force an application to wait indefinitely to obtain a lock on a table?

○ A.   LOCKLIST
○ B.   LOCKTIMEOUT
○ C.   DLCHKTIME
○ D.   MAXLOCKS

Question 11

A database administrator executes the following commands:

```
CONNECT TO sample;
UPDATE DB CFG FOR sample USING SORTHEAP 25;
UPDATE DB CFG FOR sample USING UTIL_HEAP_SZ 32;
COMMIT;
```

Assuming sufficient memory is available, when will the changes take place?

- ○ A. The next time the instance is stopped and restarted.
- ○ B. The next time the SAMPLE database is stopped and restarted.
- ○ C. Immediately after the commands are executed.
- ○ D. The changes will not take place because the database was not placed in quiesce mode first.

Question 12

A database administrator successfully changes the value of the SORTHEAP database configuration parameter while a running application is accessing the database. When will the application see the effects?

- ○ A. When a new SQL statement is executed.
- ○ B. When a new transaction is started.
- ○ C. When a new database connection is established.
- ○ D. When the application terminates and is restarted.

Question 13

Which of the following commands will recommend and make configuration changes for an instance named DB2INST1?

- ○ A. AUTOCONFIGURE USING db2inst1 APPLY
- ○ B. AUTOCONFIGURE USING mem_percent 60 APPLY db2inst1
- ○ C. AUTOCONFIGURE USING mem_percent 60 APPLY DBM ONLY
- ○ D. AUTOCONFIGURE USING mem_percent 60 APPLY DB AND DBM

Question 14

After running the AUTOCONFIGURE command, a database administrator noticed that the SORTHEAP database configuration parameter for a database named SAMPLE had not been set to AUTOMATIC, even though the SELF_TUNING_MEM configuration parameter had been set to ON.

In order to get the desired results, which of the following commands must be executed before the AUTOCONFIGURE command is run again?

○ A. UPDATE DBM CFG USING SHEAPTHRES 0

○ B. UPDATE DB CFG FOR sample USING SHEAPTHRES_SHR AUTOMATIC

○ C. UPDATE DBM CFG USING SHEAPTHRES AUTOMATIC

○ D   UPDATE DB CFG FOR sample USING SHEAPTHRES_SHR 0

Question 15

Given the following information about a DB2 server:

Instance name: db2inst1
Port number: 60000
Service name: db2c_db2inst1
Host name: db2host
Host TCP/IP address: 10.205.15.100
Protocol: TCP/IP
Database name: PROD_DB

Assuming the following entry has been made to the services file:

```
db2c_db2inst1              60000/tcp
```

Which two of the following commands must be executed to correctly configure communications for the server?

❏ A. UPDATE DBM CFG USING SVCENAME db2c_db2inst1

❏ B. UPDATE DBM CFG USING SVCEPORT 60000

❏ C. db2set DB2COMM=TCPIP

❏ D. UPDATE DBM CFG USING NNAME db2host

❏ E. db2set DB2COMM=TCP/IP

Question 16

A database administrator wants a database on a server to be seen by DB2 Discovery. Which of the following is true?

○ A. The database must be activated before it can be seen by DB2 Discovery.

○ B. The database must be cataloged on the server before it can be seen by DB2 Discovery.

○ C. The DAS on the server must be running and the DISCOVER configuration parameter for the DAS must be set to KNOWN or SEARCH.

○ D. The DISCOVER configuration parameter for the database must be set to KNOWN or SEARCH.

Question 17

A database server has one instance named DB2INST1 and two databases named SALES and PAYROLL. Which of the following commands will allow the DB2INST1 instance and the SALES database, but prevent the PAYROLL database from being seen by DB2 Discovery?

○ A. UPDATE DBM CFG USING DISCOVER_INST SEARCH;
UPDATE DB CFG FOR sales DISCOVER_DB SEARCH;
UPDATE DB CFG FOR payroll USING DISCOVER_DB DISABLE;

⊘ B. UPDATE DBM CFG USING DISCOVER_INST ENABLE;
UPDATE DB CFG FOR sales DISCOVER_DB ENABLE;
UPDATE DB CFG FOR payroll USING DISCOVER_DB DISABLE;

○ C. UPDATE DBM CFG USING DISCOVERY SEARCH;
UPDATE DB CFG FOR sales DISCOVER_DB ENABLE;
UPDATE DB CFG FOR payroll USING DISCOVER_DB DISABLE;

○ D. UPDATE DBM CFG USING DISCOVERY ENABLE;
UPDATE DB CFG FOR sales DISCOVER_DB ENABLE;
UPDATE DB CFG FOR payroll USING DISCOVER_DB DISABLE;

Question 18

A LIST APPLICATIONS command returned the following output:

```
Auth Id   Application Appl.    Application Id               DB      # of
          Name        Handle                                Name    Agents
_____  _____ _____  _____  _____  _____
RSANDERS  db2taskd    148      *LOCAL.DB2.070601164915      SAMPLE  1
RSANDERS  db2stmm     147      *LOCAL.DB2.070601164914      SAMPLE  1
RSANDERS  db2bp.exe   146      *LOCAL.DB2.070601164913      SAMPLE  1
```

Which two of the following commands will terminate all of the applications that are currently running?

- ☑ A. FORCE APPLICATION (146, 147, 148)
- ☐ B. FORCE APPLICATION (LOCAL.DB2.070601164915, LOCAL.DB2.070601164914, LOCAL.DB2.070601164913)
- ☐ C. FORCE APPLICATION (db2taskd, db2stmm, db2bp.exe)
- ☑ D. FORCE APPLICATION ALL
- ☐ E. FORCE ALL APPLICATIONS

Question 19

Which of the following must exist before the Task Center can be used to schedule a daily database backup operation for a database named SAMPLE?

- ○ A. A special database named TOOLSDB
- ⊘ B. A special set of tables known as the tools catalog
- ○ C. A table space named SYSTOOLSPACE in the SAMPLE database
- ○ D. A schema named TOOLSCAT in the SAMPLE database

Question 20

A database administrator wants to temporarily disable the Task Center. Which of the following can be used to achieve this objective?

- ○ A. Assign the value OFF to the SCHED_ENABLE registry variable.
- ○ B. Assign the value OFF to the SCHED_ENABLE parameter in the DB2 Database Manager configuration.
- ○ C. Assign the value OFF to the SCHED_ENABLE parameter in the database configuration for the TOOLSDB database.
- ⊘ D. Assign the value OFF to the SCHED_ENABLE parameter in the DAS (ADMIN) configuration.

Question 21

Which of the following configuration parameters can be used to control how the Task Center behaves when the Scheduler is stopped and restarted?

- ○ A. JOURNAL_TASKS
- ○ B. SCHED_RESTART
- ⊘ C. EXEC_EXP_TASK
- ○ D. SCHED_ENABLE

Question 22

Which of the following activities can NOT be performed with Automatic Maintenance?

○ A. Database-level backups

⊘ B. Snapshot monitoring

○ C. Statistics collection and statistics profiling

○ D. Table and index reorganization

Question 23

A database administrator needs to create a new DB2 9 database and wants offline table and index reorganization operations to be performed automatically whenever the database's data becomes fragmented. Which of the following is the minimum set of steps required to meet this objective?

⊘ A. Create the new database using the CREATE DATABASE command

Define an appropriate maintenance window

○ B. Create the new database using the CREATE DATABASE command

Assign the value ON to the AUTO_MAINT database configuration parameter

Define an appropriate maintenance window

○ C. Create the new database using the CREATE DATABASE command

Assign the value ON to the AUTO_REORG database configuration parameter

Define an appropriate maintenance window

○ D. Create the new database using the CREATE DATABASE command

Assign the value ON to the AUTO_MAINT database configuration parameter

Assign the value ON to the AUTO_REORG database configuration parameter

Define an appropriate maintenance window

Question 24

A database administrator wants to ensure that backup operations performed against a database named SAMPLE will not impact a production workload by more than 20 percent. Which of the following commands can be used to achieve this objective?

○ A. UPDATE DBM CFG USING UTIL_IMPACT_LIM 80

○ B. UPDATE DBM CFG USING UTIL_IMPACT_PRIORITY 80

⊘ C. UPDATE DBM CFG USING UTIL_IMPACT_LIM 20

○ D. UPDATE DBM CFG USING UTIL_IMPACT_PRIORITY 20

Question 25

A LIST UTILITIES SHOW DETAIL command returned the following output:

```
ID                              = 1
Type                            = BACKUP
Database Name                   = SAMPLE
Partition Number                = 0
Description                     = offline db
Start Time                      = 06/02/2007 10:35:31.442019
State                           = Executing
Invocation Type                 = User
Throttling:
    Priority                    = 20
Progress Monitoring:
    Estimated Percentage Complete = 46
        Total Work              = 49310404 bytes
        Completed Work          = 22696620 bytes
        Start Time              = 06/02/2007 10:35:31.466054
```

Which of the following commands will allow the backup operation to continue running unthrottled?

◉ A. SET UTIL_IMPACT_PRIORITY 1 TO 0

○ B. SET UTIL_IMPACT_LIM 1 TO 0

○ C. SET UTIL_IMPACT_PRIORITY 1 TO 100

○ D. SET UTIL_IMPACT_LIM 1 TO 100

Question 26

Which of the following memory consumers can NOT be tuned automatically by the Self-Tuning Memory Manager as the database workload changes?

○ A. Buffer pools

○ B. Locking memory

◉ C. Utility memory

○ D. Database shared memory

Question 27

Where are changes made by the Self-Tuning Memory Manager recorded?

◉ A. In memory tuning log files.

○ B. In the DB2 Diagnostics Log File

○ C. In the Administration Notification Log

○ D. In the Journal

Question 28

A notification log entry indicates that an error was generated by a function named sqlpsize. What does the fourth letter in the function name indicate?

- ○ A. The error occurred during a buffer pool management/manipulation operation.
- ○ B. The error occurred during a data management operation.
- ⦿ C. The error occurred during a data protection operation.
- ○ D. The error occurred during a sort operation.

Question 29

Which of the following statements about the DB2 Diagnostics Log File is NOT true?

- ○ A. Once created, the DB2 Diagnostics Log File grows continuously.
- ○ B. If the DB2 Diagnostics Log File is deleted, a new one will be created.
- ○ C. The db2diag utility can be used to filter and format the information stored in the DB2 Diagnostics Log File.
- ⦿ D. If the DB2DIAG_RESTART DB2 Database Manager configuration parameter is set to YES, the DB2 Diagnostics Log File will be deleted and recreated whenever an instance is restarted.

Question 30

Which of the following components of an administration notification log/DB2 diagnostic log entry header record can be used in conjunction with the LIST APPLICATIONS command to obtain the name of the application that caused the entry to be generated?

- ○ A. PID
- ○ B. TID
- ⦿ C. APPID
- ○ D. APPHDL

Answers

Question 1

The correct answer is **A**. Only users with System Administrator (SYSADM) authority or System Control (SYSCTRL) authority are allowed to quiesce an instance. Once an instance has been placed in a quiesced state, only users with System Administrator (SYSADM), System Control (SYSCTRL), or System Maintenance (SYSMAINT) authority, users who are members of group specified (if a group name was specified when the instance was placed in quiesced mode), and users with the user name specified (if a user name was specified when the instance was placed in quiesced mode) are allowed to connect to the instance.

Question 2

The correct answer is **B**. If they are not already running, the DB2 Database Manager background processes that are associated with a particular instance can be started by executing the START DATABASE MANAGER command. The basic syntax for this command is:

```
START [DATABASE MANAGER | DB MANAGER | DBM]
```

or

```
db2start </D>
```

Thus, if you wanted to start the DB2 Database Manager background processes for the default instance, (regardless of its name) you could do so by executing a command that looks like this:

```
START DB MANAGER
```

Question 3

The correct answer is **C**. The default instance for a system is defined by the DB2INSTANCE environment variable and in many cases this is the instance that all instance-level operations are performed against. If you need to perform an operation against a different instance, you must first change the value assigned to the DB2INSTANCE variable (by executing the command set DB2INSTANCE=[*InstanceName*] (export DB2INSTANCE=[*InstanceName*] on Linux and UNIX) where *InstanceName* is the name assigned to the instance that you want to make the default instance) or you must *attach* to that instance. Applications and users can attach to any instance by executing the ATTACH command.

Question 4

The correct answer is **B**. The db2set system command is used to determine which registry variables have been set and what they have been set to, or to assign values to one or more registry variables. The –g option indicates that a global profile variable is to be displayed, set, or removed so Answer B is correct. The –all option indicates that all occurrences of the registry variable (environment, node, instance, and global) are to be displayed, so answer C is not valid and answer A will only set the DB2COMM variable for the default instance.

Question 5

The correct answer is **D**. You can remove the value assigned to any registry variable by providing just the variable name and the equal sign as input to the db2set command. Thus, if you wanted to disable the DB2COMM instance level registry variable for an instance named TEST, you could do so by executing a db2set command that looks like this:

```
db2set –i TEST DB2COMM=
```

Question 6

The correct answer is **A**. The contents of the database configuration file for a particular database can be displayed by executing the GET DATABASE CONFIGURATION command. The syntax for this command is:

```
GET [DATABASE | DB] [CONFIGURATION | CONFIG | CFG]
FOR [DatabaseAlias]
<SHOW DETAIL>
```

where:

DatabaseAlias   Identifies the alias assigned to the database that configuration information is to be displayed for.

Thus, if you wanted to view the contents of the database configuration file for a database named SAMPLE, you could do so by executing a GET DATABASE CONFIGURATION command that looks like this:

```
GET DB CFG FOR sample SHOW DETAIL
```

Question 7

The correct answer is **B**. The MAXCAGENTS DB2 Database Manager configuration parameter is used to specify the maximum number of DB2 Database Manager agents that can be concurrently executing a DB2 Database Manager transaction. (An agent facilitates the operations between the application and the database.) NUM_INITAGENTS specifies the initial number of idle agents that are to be created in the agent pool when the DB2 Database Manager is started; MAX_COORDAGENTS specifies the maximum number of coordinating agents that can exist on a node at one time; and MAXAGENTS specifies the maximum number of DB2 Database Manager agents that can exist simultaneously, regardless of which database is being used.

Question 8

The correct answer is **B**. The LOGARCHMETH1 database configuration parameter is used to specify the media type of the primary destination for archived log files and whether or not archival logging is to be used. If this parameter is set to OFF, circular logging is used and roll-forward recovery is not possible; if this parameter is set to LOGRETAIN, archival logging is used and roll-forward recovery is possible. The MIRRORLOGPATH database configuration parameter specifies the location where a second copy of active log files is to be stored.

NEWLOGPATH specifies an alternate path to use for storing recovery log files; LOGSECOND specifies the number of secondary log files that can be used for database recovery; and LOGARCHMETH2 specifies the media type of the secondary destination for archived logs.

Question 9

The correct answer is **C**. The SHEAPTHRESH DB2 Database Manager configuration parameter is used to specify the instance-wide soft limit on the total amount of memory (in pages) that is to be made available for sorting operations; the SORTHEAP database configuration is used to specify the maximum number of private memory pages to be used for private sorts, or the maximum number of shared memory pages to be used for shared sorts. Each sort operation consumes 10 MB or 2,500 pages (10,000 K / 4K page size = 2,500 4K pages). The total amount of memory available for sorts is 37,500 pages and each sort operation can consume up to 2,500 pages of memory, so 37,500 / 2,500 = 15.

Question 10

The correct answer is **B**. The LOCKTIMEOUT database configuration parameter is used to specify the number of seconds that an application will wait to obtain a lock—if this parameter is assigned the value -1, applications will wait indefinitely to obtain a needed lock. The LOCKLIST database configuration parameter is used to specify the maximum amount of memory (in pages) that is to be allocated and used to hold the lock list; the DLCHKTIME configuration parameter is used to specify the frequency at which the DB2 Database Manager checks for deadlocks among all applications connected to the database; and the MAXLOCKS configuration parameter is used to specify a percentage of the lock list held by an application that must be filled before the DB2 Database Manager performs lock escalation.

Question 11

The correct answer is **C**. The value assigned to a particular database configuration file parameter can be changed by executing the UPDATE DATABASE CONFIGURATION command. The syntax for this command is:

```
UPDATE [DATABASE | DB]
[CONFIGURATION | CONFIG | CFG]
FOR [DatabaseAlias]
USING [[Parameter] [Value] |
       [Parameter] [Value] AUTOMATIC |
       [Parameter] AUTOMATIC |
       [Parameter] MANUAL ,...]
   <IMMEDIATE | DEFERRED>
```

where:

DatabaseAlias Identifies the alias assigned to the database that configuration information is to be modified for.

Parameter Identifies one or more database configuration parameters (by keyword) whose values are to be modified. (In many cases, the keyword for a parameter is the same as the parameter name itself.)

Value Identifies the new value(s) that are to be assigned to the database configuration parameter(s) specified.

If the DEFERRED clause is specified with the UPDATE DATABASE CONFIGURATION command, changes made to the database configuration file will not take until all connections to the corresponding database have been terminated and a new connection is established. If the IMMEDIATE clause is specified instead, or if neither clause is specified, all changes made to the database configuration file will take effect immediately—provided the necessary resources are available.

Question 12

The correct answer is **A**. If the IMMEDIATE clause is specified with the UPDATE DATABASE CONFIGURATION command, or if neither clause is specified, all changes made to the database configuration file will take effect immediately—provided the necessary resources are available. Applications running against a database at the time configuration changes are made will see the change the next time an SQL statement is executed.

Question 13

The correct answer is **D**. The AUTOCONFIGURE command is designed to capture specific information about your database environment and recommend and/or make changes to configuration parameters based upon the information provided. The basic syntax for this command is:

```
AUTOCONFIGURE
USING [ [Keyword] [Value] ,...]
APPLY [DB ONLY | DB AND DBM | NONE]
```

where:

Keyword   One or more special keywords are recognized by the AUTOCONFIGURE command. Valid values include: mem_percent, workload_type, num_stmts, tpm, admin_priority, is_populated, num_local_apps, num_remote_apps, isolation, and bp_resizable.

Value   Identifies the value that associated with the keyword provided.

If the APPLY DB ONLY clause is specified with the AUTOCONFIGURE command, database configuration and buffer pool changes recommended by the Design Advisor will be applied to the appropriate database configuration file; if the APPLY DB AND DBM clause is specified, database configuration and buffer pool changes recommended will be applied to the database configuration file and instance configuration changes recommended will be applied to the appropriate DB2 Database Manager configuration file. If the APPLY NONE clause is specified instead, change recommendations will be displayed, but not applied.

Question 14

The correct answer is **A**. The AUTOCONFIGURE command (and the Design Advisor) will always recommend that a database be configured to take advantage of the Self Tuning Memory Manager. However, if you run the AUTOCONFIGURE command against a database in an instance where the SHEAPTHRES configuration parameter has been assigned a value other than zero, the sort memory heap database configuration parameter (SORTHEAP) will not be configured for automatic tuning. Therefore, you must execute the command UPDATE DATABASE MANAGER CONFIGURATION USING SHEAPTHRES 0 before you execute the AUTOCONFIGURE command if you want to enable sort memory tuning.

Question 15

The correct answers are **A** and **C**. If you choose to manually configure communications, the steps you must follow can vary according to the communications protocol being used. For example, if you wanted to configure a server to use TCP/IP, you would have to perform the following steps:

1. Assign the value TCPIP to the DB2COMM registry variable.

   The value assigned to the DB2COMM registry variable is used to determine which communications managers will be activated when the DB2 Database Manager for a particular instance is started. The DB2COMM registry variable is assigned the value TCPIP by executing a db2set command that looks something like this:

   ```
   db2set DB2COMM=tcpip
   ```

2. Assign the name of the TCP/IP port that the database server will use to receive communications from remote clients to the *svcename* parameter of the DB2 Database Manager configuration file.

   The *svcename* parameter should be set to the service name associated with the main connection port so that when the database server is started, it can determine which port to listen on for incoming connection requests. This parameter is set by executing an UPDATE DATABASE MANAGER CONGIGURATION command that looks something like this:

   ```
   UPDATE DBM CFG USING SVCENAME db2c_db2inst1
   ```

3. Update the services file on the database server.

   The TCP/IP services file identifies the ports that server applications will listen on for client requests. If you specified a service name in the *svcename* parameter of the DB2 Database Manager configuration file, the appropriate service name-to-port number/protocol mapping must be added to the services file on the server. (If you specified a port number in the *svcename* parameter, the services file does not need to be updated.)

An entry in the services file for a DB2 database server might look something like this:

```
db2c_db2inst1        50001/tcp
```

Question 16

The correct answer is **C**. In addition to enabling remote administration of DB2 servers, the DAS instance assists the Control Center and the Configuration Assistant in providing a means for discovering information about the configuration of other DAS instances, DB2 instances, and databases using DB2 Discovery. (The Configuration Assistant and the Control Center use such information to simplify and automate the configuration of client connections to DB2 servers; neither tool will be able to "discover" a server if the DAS instance for that server is not running.) If the *discover* DAS configuration parameter is set to SEARCH, the server will respond to both search and known discovery requests; if this parameter is set to KNOWN, the server will only respond to known discovery requests; and if this parameter is set to DISABLE, the server will not respond to discovery requests.

A database can be "hidden" from a discovery request by setting its *discover_db* configuration parameter to DISABLE. (By default, this configuration parameter is set to ENABLE.)

Question 17

The correct answer is **B**. The *discover_inst* DB2 Database Manager configuration parameter is used to specify whether or not information about a particular instance found on a server will be included in the server's response to a discovery request. If this parameter is set to ENABLE, the server will include information about the instance in its response to both search and known discovery requests. If this parameter is set to DISABLE, the server will not include information about the instance (nor will it include information about any databases that come under the instance's control) in its response to discovery requests.

The *discover_db* database configuration parameter is used to specify whether or not information about a particular database found on a server will be included in the server's response to a discovery request. If this parameter is set to ENABLE, the server will include information about the database in its response to both search and known discovery requests. On the other hand, if this parameter is set to DISABLE, the server will not include information about the database in its response to discovery requests.

Question 18

The correct answers are **A** and **D**. You can terminate one or more running applications prematurely by executing the FORCE APPLICATION command (assuming you have SYSADMN or SYSCTRL authority). The basic syntax for this command is:

```
FORCE APPLICATION ALL
```

or

```
FORCE APPLICATION ( [ApplicationHandle] ,... )
```

where:

ApplicationHandle   Identifies the handle associated with one or more applications whose instance attachments and/or database connections are to be terminated.

Thus, if you wanted to force all users and applications connected to databases stored on a server named DB_SERVER to terminate their database connections, you could do so by executing a FORCE APPLICATION command that looks something like this:

```
FORCE APPLICATION ALL
```

On the other hand, if you wanted to force a specific application whose handle is 148 to terminate its processing, you could do so by executing a FORCE APPLICATION command that looks like this:

```
FORCE APPLICATION (148)
```

Question 19

The correct answer is **B**. In order to use the Task Center, you must first create a set of tables known as the tools catalog. If you did not create a tools catalog when you installed DB2, you can create one by executing the CREATE TOOLS CATALOG command. The tools catalog can reside in its own database, or in a database that contains other data.

Question 20

The correct answer is **D**. To a certain extent, the behavior of the task center is controlled through parameters found in the DAS instance configuration file. The SCHED_ENABLE DAS configuration parameter is used to identify whether or not the Scheduler is running. The Scheduler allows tools such as the Task Center to schedule and execute tasks at the administration server. Therefore, setting the SCHED_ENABLE parameter to OFF temporarily disables the Task Center.

Question 21

The correct answer is **C**. The EXEC_ESP_TASK DAS configuration parameter is used to identify whether or not expired tasks are to be executed when the Scheduler is turned on. (The Scheduler only detects expired tasks when it is started.) For example, if you have a job scheduled to run every Saturday, and the Scheduler is turned off on Friday and then restarted on Monday, the job scheduled for Saturday is now an expired task. If EXEC_EXP_TASK DAS configuration parameter is set to YES, the Saturday job will run immediately when the Scheduler is restarted. JOURNAL_TASKS and SCHED_RESTART are not valid DAS configuration parameters; the SCHED_ENABLE DAS configuration parameter is used to identify whether or not the Scheduler is running.

Question 22

The correct answer is **B**. Automatic maintenance can be used to perform the following maintenance operations:

- **Create a backup image of the database.** Automatic database backup provides users with a solution to help ensure their database is being backed up both properly and regularly, without having to worry about when to back up, or having any knowledge of the syntax for the BACKUP command.

- **Data defragmentation (table or index reorganization).** This maintenance activity can increase the efficiency with which the DB2 Database Manager accesses tables. Automatic reorganization manages offline table and index reorganization without users having to worry about when and how to reorganize their data.

- **Data access optimization (running** RUNSTATS**).** The DB2 Database Manager updates the system catalog statistics on the data in a table, the data in a table's indexes, or the data in both a table and its indexes. The DB2 Optimizer uses these statistics to determine which path to use to access data in response to a query. Automatic statistics collection attempts to improve the performance of the database by maintaining up-to-date table statistics. The goal is to allow the DB2 Optimizer to always choose an access plan based on accurate statistics.

- **Statistics profiling.** Automatic statistics profiling advises when and how to collect table statistics by detecting outdated, missing, and incorrectly specified statistics and by generating statistical profiles based on query feedback.

Question 23

The correct answer is **A**. When a DB2 9 database is created, automatic maintenance is enabled by default. Enablement of the automatic maintenance features available for a database that is not using automatic maintenance is controlled via the automatic maintenance-specific database configuration parameters that are available (AUTO_MAINT, AUTO_DB_BACKUP, AUTO_TBL_MAINT, AUTO_RUNSTATS, AUTO_STATS_PROF, AUTO_PROF_UPD, and AUTO_REORG). These parameters represent a hierarchical set of switches that can be set to ON or OFF.

Question 24

The correct answer is **C**. To control utility throttling, you must establish an impact policy. The impact policy refers to the instance-wide limit that all throttled utilities can cumulatively have on the production workload; once such a policy is established, it's the system's responsibility to ensure that the policy is obeyed. The impact policy for all throttling-enabled utilities running within an instance is controlled through the *util_impact_lim* DB2 Database Manager configuration parameter. (This parameter is dynamic, so it can be changed without stopping and restarting the instance; it can even be set while throttling-enabled utilities are running.) To define the impact policy for *all* throttled utilities, you simply assign a value between 1 and 100 to the *util_impact_lim* configuration parameter.

Thus, to set the instance-wide limit that all throttled utilities can cumulatively have on a production workloads to 20 percent (or in other words, to ensure performance degradation from all throttled utilities will not impact the system workload by more than 20 percent), you would assign the *util_impact_lim* configuration parameter the value 20 by executing an UPDATE DATABASE MANAGER CONFIGURATION command that looks like this:

```
UPDATE DATABASE MANAGER CONFIGURATION USING UTIL_IMPACT_LIM 20
```

Question 25

The correct answer is **A**. If you want to change the impact priority (level of throttling) of a utility that is already running, you can do so by executing the SET UTIL_IMPACT_PRIORITY command. With this command, you can:

- throttle a running utility that was started in unthrottled mode

- unthrottle a running throttled utility (disable throttling)

- reprioritize a running throttled utility (this is useful if multiple simultaneous throttled utilities are running and one is more important than the others)

The syntax for the SET UTIL_IMPACT_PRIORITY command is:

```
SET UTIL_IMPACT_PRIORITY [UtilityID]
TO [Priority]
```

where:

UtilityID   Identifies the running utility, by ID, whose priority is to be changed. (The ID assigned to a running utility can be obtained by executing the LIST UTILITIES command.)

Priority   Specifies an instance-level limit on the impact associated with running the utility specified. A value of 100 represents the highest priority; a value of 1 represents the lowest. Setting *Priority* to 0 will force a throttled utility to continue running unthrottled; setting *Priority* to a non-zero value will force an unthrottled utility to continue running in throttled mode.

Thus, if you wanted force a throttled backup operation that has been assigned a utility ID of 1 to continue running unthrottled, you could do so by executing a SET UTIL_IMPACT_PRIORITY command that looks like this:

```
SET UTIL_IMPACT_PRIORITY 1 TO 0
```

Question 26

The correct answer is **C**. When a database has been enabled for self tuning, the memory tuner responds to significant changes in database workload characteristics, adjusting the values of memory configuration parameters and buffer pool sizes to optimize performance. The following memory consumers can be enabled for self tuning:

- Buffer pools (controlled by the ALTER BUFFERPOOL and CREATE BUFFERPOOL statements)

- Package cache (controlled by the PCKCACHESZ configuration parameter)

- Locking memory (controlled by the LOCKLIST and MAXLOCKS configuration parameters)

- Sort memory (controlled by the SHEAPTHRES_SHR and the SORTHEAP configuration parameters)

- Database shared memory (controlled by the DATABASE_MEMORY configuration parameter)

Question 27

The correct answer is **A**. Changes made by the Self Tuning Memory Manager are recorded in memory tuning log files, which reside in the *stmmlog* subdirectory of the instance. (The first file created will be assigned the name *stmm.0.log*, the second will be assigned the name *stmm.1.log*, and so on.) Each memory tuning log file contains summaries of the resource demands for each memory consumer at the time a tuning operation was performed. Tuning intervals can be determined by examining the timestamps for the entries made in the memory tuning log files.

Question 28

The correct answer is **C**. To find out more about the type of activity being performed by the function that produced an entry in the administration notification log, look at the fourth letter of its name. The following shows some of the letters used in the fourth position of DB2 function names, along with the type of activity each function performs:

b: Buffer pool management and manipulation.

c: Communications between clients and servers.

d: Data management.

e: Database engine processes.

o: Operating system calls (such as opening and closing files).

p: Data protection (such as locking and logging).

r: Relational database services.

s: Sorting operations.

x: Indexing operations.

Question 29

The correct answer is **D**. Once created, the DB2 Diagnostics Log File (db2diag.log) grows continuously. As a result, the most recent entries are always found near the end of the file. If storage space for this file becomes an issue, the existing file can be deleted — a new db2diag.log file will be created automatically the next time one is needed. To aid in problem determination, DB2 9 provides a utility that can be used to filter and format the information available in the db2diag.log file. This utility is known as the db2diag utility and it is activated by executing the db2diag command.

There is no DB2DIAG_RESTART DB2 Database Manager configuration parameter.

Question 30

The correct answer is **C**. Every entry in the administration notification log file and the DB2 diagnostic log file begins with a specific set of values that are intended to help identify the particular event the entry corresponds to. Because this block of information is recorded for all entries and because it is always recorded in a specific format, it is referred to as the *entry header*. Figure 2–1 illustrates how a typical administration notification log entry header looks.

```
❶ 2007-04-27-13.59.03.745000-240  ❷ I1907855H435   ❸ LEVEL: Info
❹ PID     : 3072              ❺ TID  : 3512      ❻ PROC : db2syscs.exe
❼ INSTANCE: DB2               ❽ NODE : 000        ❾ DB   : SAMPLE
❿ APPHDL  : 0-514             ⓫ APPID: *LOCAL.DB2.070427175900
⓬ AUTHID  : RSANDERS
⓭ FUNCTION: DB2 UDB, buffer pool services, sqlbAlterBufferPoolAct, probe:90
⓮ MESSAGE : Altering bufferpool "IBMDEFAULTBP" From: "250" To: "350" <automatic>
```

Figure 2–1: Individual components of an administration notification log/DB2 diagnostic log entry header.

All entry headers consist of the following components (refer to the numbered bullets in Figure 2–1):

1. A timestamp that identifies when the entry was made.

2. The db2diag.log file's record ID. This ID specifies the file offset at which the current message is being logged (for example, "907855") and the message length (for example, "435") for the platform where the DB2 diagnostic log was created.

3. The diagnostic level associated with the error message. Valid values are: Info, Warning, Error, Severe, and Event.

4. The unique identifier that has been assigned (by the operating system) to the process that generated the entry. This value is more applicable in a UNIX environment where DB2 operates using multiple processes. In a Windows environment, DB2 operates with multiple threads rather than multiple processes; therefore, the process ID provided is usually that of the main DB2 executable. (If the application is operating in a Distributed Unit Of Work (DUOW) environment, the Process ID shown will be the DUOW correlation token.)

5. The unique identifier that has been assigned (by the operating system) to the thread that generated the entry.

6. The name of the process that generated the entry.

7. The name of the instance that generated the entry.

8. The number that corresponds to the node that generated the entry. If a non-partitioned database is being used, the node number will always be 000.

9. The name of the database for which the entry was generated.

10. The application handle that has been assigned to the application for which the process that generated the event is working. This value consists of the coordinator partition number followed by the coordinator index number, separated by a dash.

11. The unique identifier that has been assigned to the application for which the process that generated the event is working. To find out more about a particular application ID:

   - Use the LIST APPLICATIONS command on a DB2 server or the LIST DCS APPLICATIONS command on a DB2 Connect gateway to obtain a list of application IDs. Search this list for the application ID; once found, you can obtain information about the client experiencing the error, such as its node name and its TCP/IP address.

   - Use the GET SNAPSHOT FOR APPLICATION command to view a list of application IDs.

   - Execute the command db2pd -applications -db [*DatabaseName*].

12. The authorization ID of the user who was working with the instance/database when the entry was generated

13. The product name ("DB2 UDB"), component name ("buffer pool services"), and function name ("sqlbAlterBufferPoolAct") that generated the message (as well as the probe point (90) within the function). If the entry was generated by a user application that executed the db2AdminMsgWrite() API, this component of the entry header will read "User Application." (Applications can write messages to the administration notification log file and the DB2 diagnostic log file by invoking the db2AdminMsgWrite() API.)

14. A message that describes the event that was logged.

CHAPTER 3

Data Placement

Seventeen and one-half percent (17.5%) of the DB2 9 for Linux, UNIX, and Windows Database Administration exam (Exam 731) is designed to test your ability to create a DB2 database, as well as to test your knowledge of the methods used to create and manage table spaces and store the data associated with different DB2 objects in them. The questions that make up this portion of the exam are intended to evaluate the following:

- Your ability to create a DB2 database

- Your ability to discuss the differences between System Managed Space (SMS) and Database Managed Space (DMS) table spaces

- Your knowledge of the characteristics of SMS, DMS, and Automatic Storage table spaces

- Your ability to construct and alter table spaces

- Your knowledge of table space states

- Your ability to describe how schemas are used

- Your ability to create range-clustered and range-partitioned tables

- Your ability to work with XML data and construct XML indexes

- Your knowledge of data row compression

This chapter is designed to introduce you to instances and databases, to walk you through the database creation process, and to provide you with an overview of the various types of table spaces that can be constructed once a database exists. This chapter is also designed to show you how to construct schemas, range-clustered tables, range-partitioned tables, and XML indexes, as well as use data row compression to reduce storage space requirements for a table.

Servers, Instances, and Databases

In Chapter 2, "Server Management," we learned that DB2 sees the world as a hierarchy of objects. Workstations (or servers) on which DB2 has been installed occupy the highest level of this hierarchy. Instances occupy the second level in the hierarchy and are responsible for managing system resources and databases that fall under their control. Databases make up the third level in the hierarchy and are responsible for managing the storage, modification, and retrieval of data. Each database has its own environment (controlled by a set of configuration parameters), as well as its own set of grantable authorities and privileges to govern how users interact with the data and database objects it controls. From a user's perspective, a database is a collection of tables (preferably related in some way) that are used to store data. However, from a database administrator's viewpoint, a DB2 database is much more; a database is an entity composed of many physical and logical components. Some of these components help determine how data is organized while others determine how and where data is physically stored.

Creating a DB2 9 Database

There are two ways to create a DB2 9 database: by using the Create Database Wizard or by using the CREATE DATABASE command. Because the Create Database Wizard is essentially a graphical user interface (GUI) for the CREATE DATABASE command, we will look at the command method first.

In its simplest form, the syntax for the CREATE DATABASE command is:

```
CREATE [DATABASE | DB] [DatabaseName]
```

where:

DatabaseName   Identifies a unique name that is to be assigned to the database
                  once it is created.

The only value you must provide when executing this command is a name to assign to the new database. This name

- can consist of only the characters **a** through **z**, **A** through **Z**, **0** through **9**, **@**, **#**, **$**, and **_** (underscore);

- cannot begin with a number;

- cannot begin with the letter sequences "SYS," "DBM," or "IBM"; and

- cannot be the same as the name already assigned to another database within the same instance.

Of course, a more complex form of the CREATE DATABASE command that provides you with much more control over database parameters is available, and we will examine it shortly. But for now, let's look at what happens when this form of the CREATE DATABASE command is executed.

What Happens When a DB2 9 Database Is Created

Regardless of how the process is initiated, whenever a new DB2 9 database is created, the following tasks are performed, in the order shown:

1. All directories and subdirectories needed are created in the appropriate location.

   Information about every DB2 9 database created is stored in a special hierarchical directory tree. Where this directory tree is actually created is determined by information provided with the CREATE DATABASE command—if no location information is provided, this directory tree is created in the location specified by the *dftdbpath* DB2 Database Manager configuration parameter associated with the instance under which the database is being created. The root directory of this hierarchical tree is assigned the name of the instance with which the database is associated. This directory will contain a subdirectory that has been assigned a name corresponding to the partition's node. If the database is a partitioned database, this directory will be named NODExxxx, where xxxx is the unique node number that has been assigned to the partition; if the database is a nonpartitioned database, this directory will be named NODE0000. The node-name directory, in turn, will contain one subdirectory for each database that has been created, along with one subdirectory that includes the containers that are used to hold the database's data.

The name assigned to the subdirectory that holds the containers used to house the database's data is the same as that specified for the database; the name assigned to the subdirectory that contains the base files for the database corresponds to the database token that is assigned to the database during the creation process (the subdirectory for the first database created will be named SQL00001, the subdirectory for the second database will be named SQL00002, and so on). Figure 3–1 illustrates how this directory hierarchy typically looks in a nonpartitioned database environment.

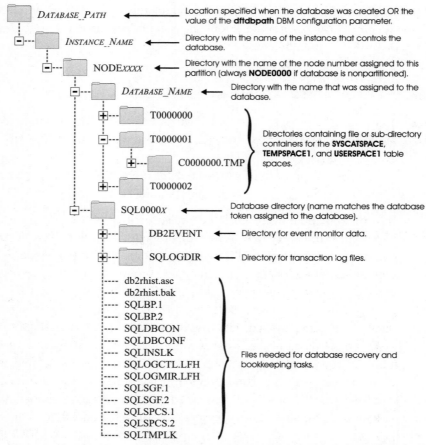

Figure 3–1: Typical directory hierarchy tree for a nonpartitioned database.

> Never attempt to modify this directory structure or any of the files stored in it. Such actions could destroy one or more databases or make them unusable.

2. Files needed for management, monitoring, and database recovery are created.

   After the subdirectory that was assigned the name of the database's token is created, the following files are created in it:

   db2rhist.asc This file contains historical information about backup operations, restore operations, table load operations, table reorganization operations, table space alterations, and similar database changes (i.e., the recovery history file).

   db2rhist.bak This file is a backup copy of db2rhist.asc.

   SQLBP.1 This file contains buffer pool information.

   SQLBP.2 This file is a backup copy of SQLBP.1.

   SQLDBCON This file contains database configuration information.

   SQLDBCONF This file is a backup copy of SQLDBCON.

   SQLINSLK This file contains information that is used to ensure that the database is assigned to only one instance of the DB2 Database Manager.

   SQLOGCTL.LFH This file contains information about active transaction log files. Recovery operations use information stored in this file to determine how far back in the logs to begin the recovery process.

   SQLOGMIR.LFH This file is a mirrored copy of SQLOGCTL.LFH.

   SQLSGF.1 This file contains storage path information associated with automatic storage.

   SQLSGF.2 This file is a backup copy of SQLSGF.1.

   SQLSPCS.1 This file contains table space information.

   SQLSPCS.2 This file is a backup copy of SQLSPCS.1.

   SQLTMPLK This file contains information about temporary table spaces.

Two subdirectories named DB2EVENT and SQLOGDIR are also created; a detailed deadlocks event monitor is created and stored in the DB2EVENT subdirectory, and three files named S0000000.LOG, S0000001.LOG, and S0000002.LOG are created and stored in the SQLLOGDIR subdirectory. These three files are used to store transaction log records as SQL operations are performed against the database.

3. A buffer pool is created for the database.

    During the database creation process, a buffer pool is created and assigned the name IBMDEFAULTBP. By default, on Linux and UNIX platforms, this buffer pool is 1,000 4K (kilobyte) pages in size; on Windows platforms, this buffer pool is 250 4K pages in size. The actual memory used by this buffer pool (and for that matter, by any other buffer pools that may exist) is allocated when the first connection to the database is established and freed when all connections to the database have been terminated.

4. Two regular table spaces and one system temporary table space are created.

    Immediately after the buffer pool IBMDEFAULTBP is created, three table spaces are created and associated with this buffer pool. These three table spaces are as follows:

    -   A regular table space named SYSCATSPACE, which is used to store the system catalog tables and views associated with the database

    -   A regular table space named USERSPACE1, which is used to store all user-defined objects (such as tables, indexes, and so on) along with user data, index data, and long value data

    -   A system temporary table space named TEMPSPACE1, which is used as a temporary storage area for operations such as sorting data, reorganizing tables, and creating indexes

    Unless otherwise specified, SYSCATSPACE and USERSPACE1 will be DMS File table spaces, and TEMPSPACE1 will be an SMS table space; characteristics for each of these table spaces can be provided as input to the CREATE DATABASE command or the Create Database Wizard.

5. The system catalog tables and views are created.

    After the table space SYSCATSPACE is created, a special set of tables, known as the system catalog tables, are constructed within that table space. The DB2 Database Manager uses the system catalog tables to keep track of such information as database object definitions, database object dependencies, database object privileges, column data types, table constraints, and object relationships. A set of system catalog views is created along with the system catalog tables, and these views are typically used when accessing data stored in the system catalog tables. The system catalog tables and views cannot be modified with DDL SQL statements (however, their contents can be viewed). Instead, they are modified by the DB2 Database Manager whenever one of the following events occurs:

    -   A database object (such as a table, view, or index) is created, altered, or dropped.

    -   Authorizations or privileges are granted or revoked.

    -   Statistical information is collected for a table.

    -   Packages are bound to the database.

    In most cases, the complete characteristics of a database object are stored in one or more system catalog tables when the object is created. However, in some cases, such as when triggers and constraints are defined, the actual SQL used to create the object is stored instead.

6. The database is cataloged in the system and local database directory (a system or local database directory is created first if it does not already exist.)

    DB2 uses a set of special files to keep track of where databases are stored and to provide access to those databases. Because the information stored in these files is used like the information stored in an office-building directory is used, they are referred to as directory files. Whenever a database is created, these directories are updated with the database's name and alias. If specified, a comment and code set values are also stored in these directories.

7. The database configuration file for the database is initialized.

   Some of the parameters in the database configuration file (such as code set, territory, and collating sequence) will be set using values that were specified as input for the CREATE DATABASE command or the Create Database Wizard; others are assigned system default values.

8. Four schemas are created.

   Once the system catalog tables and views are created, the following schemas are created: SYSIBM, SYSCAT, SYSSTAT, and SYSFUN. A special user named SYSIBM is made the owner of each.

9. A set of utility programs is bound to the database.

   Before some of the DB2 9 utilities available can work with a database, the packages needed to run those utilities must be created. Such packages are created by binding a set of predefined DB2 Database Manager bind files to the database (the bind files used are stored in the utilities bind list file *db2ubind.lst*).

10. Authorities and privileges are granted to the appropriate users.

    To connect to and work with a particular database, a user must have the authorities and privileges needed to use that database. Therefore, whenever a new database is created, unless otherwise specified, the following authorities and privileges are granted:

    - Database Administrator (DBADM) authority as well as CONNECT, CREATETAB, BINDADD, CREATE_NOT_FENCED, IMPLICIT_SCHEMA, and LOAD privileges are granted to the user who created the database.

    - USE privilege on the table space USERSPACE1 is granted to the group PUBLIC.

    - CONNECT, CREATETAB, BINDADD, and IMPLICIT_SCHEMA privileges are granted to the group PUBLIC.

    - SELECT privilege on each system catalog table is granted to the group PUBLIC.

    - EXECUTE privilege on all procedures found in the SYSIBM schema is granted to the group PUBLIC.

- EXECUTE WITH GRANT privilege on all functions found in the SYSFUN schema is granted to the group PUBLIC.

- BIND and EXECUTE privileges for each successfully bound utility are granted to the group PUBLIC.

11. Several autonomic features are enabled.

To help make management easy, whenever a new database is created, the following features are enabled:

- Automatic Maintenance (database backups, table and index reorganization, data access optimization, and statistics profiling)

- Self-Tuning Memory Manager (package cache, locking memory, sort memory, database shared memory, and buffer pool memory)

- Utility throttling

- The Health Monitor

12. The Configuration Advisor is launched.

The Configuration Advisor is a tool designed to help you tune performance and balance memory requirements for a database by suggesting which configuration parameters to modify based on information you provide about the database. In DB2 9, the Configuration Advisor is automatically invoked whenever you create a database, unless the default behavior is changed by assigning the value NO to the DB2_ENABLE_AUTOCONFIG_DEFAULT registry variable.

The Complete CREATE DATABASE Command

When the simplest form of the CREATE DATABASE command is executed, the characteristics of the database created, such as the storage and transaction logging method used, are determined by several predefined defaults. If you wish to change any of the default characteristics, you must specify one or more options available when executing the CREATE DATABASE command. The complete syntax for this command is:

```
CREATE [DATABASE | DB] [DatabaseName] <AT DBPARTITIONNUM>
```

or

```
CREATE [DATABASE | DB] [DatabaseName]
<AUTOMATIC STORAGE [YES | NO]>
<ON [StoragePath ,...] <DBPATH [DBPath]>>
<ALIAS [Alias]>
<USING CODESET [CodeSet] TERRITORY [Territory]>
<COLLATE USING [CollateType]>
<PAGESIZE [4096 | Pagesize <K>]>
<NUMSEGS [NumSegments]>
<DFT_EXTENT_SZ [DefaultExtSize]>
<RESTRICTIVE>
<CATALOG TABLESPACE [TS_Definition]>
<USER TABLESPACE [TS_Definition]>
<TEMPORARY TABLESPACE [TS_Definition]>
<WITH "[Description]">
<AUTOCONFIGURE <USING [Keyword] [Value] ,...>
    <APPLY [DB ONLY | DB AND DBM | NONE>>
```

where:

DatabaseName   Identifies the unique name that is to be assigned to the database to be created.

StoragePath   If AUTOMATIC STORAGE YES is specified (the default), identifies one or more storage paths that are to be used to hold table space containers used by automatic storage. Otherwise, identifies the location (drive or directory) where the directory hierarchy and files associated with the database to be created are to be physically stored.

DBPath   If AUTOMATIC STORAGE YES is specified (the default), identifies the location (drive or directory) where the directory hierarchy and metadata files associated with the database to be created are to be physically stored. (If this parameter is not specified, and automatic storage is used, the metadata files will be stored in the first storage path specified in the *StoragePath* parameter.)

Alias   Identifies the alias to be assigned to the database to be created.

CodeSet   Identifies the code set to be used for storing data in the database to
                   be created. (In a DB2 9 database, each single-byte character is
                   represented internally as a unique number between 0 and 255. This
                   number is referred to as the code point of the character; the
                   assignments of code points to every character in a particular
                   character set are called the code page; and the International
                   Organization for Standardization term for a code page is code set.)

Territory   Identifies the territory to be used for storing data in the database
                   to be created.

CollateType   Specifies the collating sequence (i.e., the sequence in which
                   characters are ordered for the purpose of sorting, merging, and
                   making comparisons) that is to be used by the database to be
                   created. The following values are valid for this parameter:
                   COMPATABILITY, IDENTITY, IDENTITY_16BIT, UCA400_NO,
                   UCA400_LSK, UCA400_LTH, NLSCHAR, and SYSTEM.

NumSegments   Specifies the number of directories that are to be created and
                   used to store files for the default SMS table space used by the
                   database to be created (TEMPSPACE1).

DefaultExtSize   Specifies the default extent size to be used whenever a table
                   space is created and no extent size is specified during the
                   creation process.

Description   A comment used to describe the database entry that will be
                   made in the database directory for the database to be created.
                   The description must be enclosed by double quotation marks.

Keyword   One or more keywords recognized by the AUTOCONFIGURE
                   command. Valid values include mem_percent, workload_type,
                   num_stmts, tpm, admin_priority, is_populated, num_local_apps,
                   num_remote_apps, isolation, and bp_resizable. Refer to the *DB2
                   9 Command Reference* for more information on how the
                   AUTOCONFIGURE command is used.

Value   Identifies the value that is to be associated with the *Keyword* specified.

TS_Definition   Specifies the definition that is to be used to create the table space that will be used to hold the system catalog tables (SYSCATSPACE), user-defined objects (USERSPACE1), and/or temporary objects (TEMPSPACE1).

The syntax used to define a system managed (SMS) table space is:

```
MANAGED BY SYSTEM
USING ('[Container]' ,...)
<EXTENTSIZE [ExtentSize]>
<PREFETCHSIZE [PrefetchSize]>
<OVERHEAD [Overhead]>
<TRANSFERRATE [TransferRate]>
```

The syntax used to define a database managed (DMS) table space is:

```
MANAGED BY DATABASE
USING ([FILE | DEVICE] '[Container]' NumberOfPages ,...)
<EXTENTSIZE [ExtentSize]>
<PREFETCHSIZE [PrefetchSize]>
<OVERHEAD [Overhead]>
<TRANSFERRATE [TransferRate]>
<AUTORESIZE [NO | YES]>
<INCREASESIZE [Increment] <PERCENT | K | M | G>>
<MAXSIZE [NONE | MaxSize <K | M | G>]>
```

And the syntax used to define an automatic storage table space is:

```
MANAGED BY AUTOMATIC STORAGE
<EXTENTSIZE [ExtentSize]>
<PREFETCHSIZE [PrefetchSize]>
<OVERHEAD [Overhead]>
<TRANSFERRATE [TransferRate]>
<AUTORESIZE [NO | YES]>
<INITIALSIZE [InitialSize] <K | M | G>>
<INCREASESIZE [Increment] <PERCENT | K | M | G>>
<MAXSIZE [NONE | MaxSize <K | M | G>]>
```

where:

Container	Identifies one or more containers to be used to store data that will be assigned to the table space specified. For SMS table spaces, each container specified must identify a valid directory; for DMS FILE containers, each container specified must identify a valid file; and for DMS DEVICE containers, each container specified must identify an existing device.
NumberOfPages	Specifies the number of pages to be used by the table space container.
ExtentSize	Specifies the number of pages of data that will be written in a round-robin fashion to each table space container used.
PrefetchSize	Specifies the number of pages of data that will be read from the specified table space when data prefetching is performed.
Overhead	Identifies the input/output (I/O) controller overhead and disk-seek latency time (in number of milliseconds) associated with the containers that belong to the specified table space.
TransferRate	Identifies the time, in number of milliseconds, that it takes to read one page of data from a table space container and store it in memory.
InitialSize	Specifies the initial size an autoresize DMS or an automatic storage table space should be.
Increment	Specifies the amount by which a table space that has been enabled for automatic resizing will be increased when the table space becomes full and a request for space is made.
MaxSize	Specifies the maximum size to which a table space that has been enabled for automatic resizing can be increased to.

If the RESTRICTIVE clause is specified, the RESTRICT_ACCESS database configuration parameter for the database being created will be set to YES, and no privileges will be granted to the group PUBLIC.

Suppose you wanted to create a DB2 database that has the following characteristics:

- Will be physically located on drive E:.

- Will not use automatic storage.

- Will be assigned the name SAMPLEDB.

- Will recognize the United States/Canada code set. (The code page, along with the territory, is used to convert alphanumeric data to binary data that is stored in the database.)

- Will use a collating sequence that is based on the territory used (which in this case is United States/Canada).

- Will not automatically be accessible to the group PUBLIC.

- Will store the system catalog in a DMS table space that uses the file SYSCATSPACE.DAT as its container. (This file is stored on drive E: and is capable of holding up to 5,000 pages that are 4K in size.)

In this case, you would execute a CREATE DATABASE command that looks something like this:

```
CREATE DATABASE sampledb
AUTOMATIC STORAGE NO
ON E:
USING CODESET 1252 TERRITORY US
COLLATE USING SYSTEM
PAGESIZE 4096
RESTRICTIVE
CATALOG TABLESPACE MANAGED BY DATABASE
  (FILE 'E:\syscatspace.dat', 5000)
```

Creating a DB2 9 Database with the Create Database Wizard

If you prefer using graphical user interfaces to typing long commands, you can use the Create Database Wizard to construct a DB2 9 database. (The Create Database

Wizard is designed to collect information that defines the characteristics of a
database—and then create a database that has those characteristics. These same
characteristics can be specified through the various options that are available with
the CREATE DATABASE command.) The Create Database Wizard is invoked by
selecting the appropriate action from the Databases menu found in the Control
Center. Figure 3–2 shows the Control Center menu items that must be selected to
activate the Create Database Wizard; Figure 3–3 shows what the first page of the
Create Database Wizard looks like when it is first initiated.

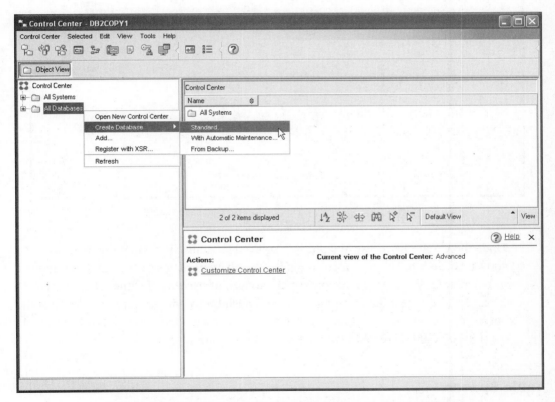

Figure 3–2: Invoking the Create Database Wizard from the Control Center.

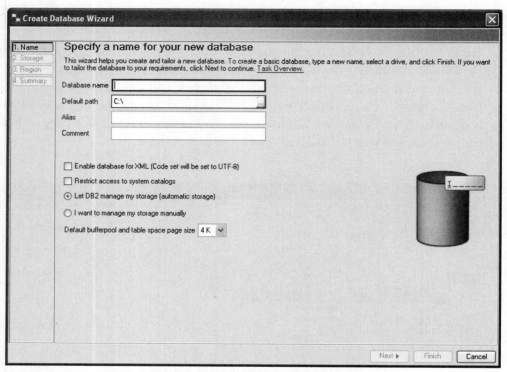

Figure 3–3: The first page of the Create Database Wizard.

Once the Create Database Wizard is displayed, you simply follow the directions shown on each panel presented to define the characteristics of the database that is to be created. When you have provided enough information for the DB2 Database Manager to create a database, the "Finish" push button displayed in the lower right corner of the wizard (see Figure 3–3) will be enabled. Once this button is selected, a database will be created using the information provided.

Table Spaces

Table spaces are used to control where data is physically stored and to provide a layer of indirection between database objects (such as tables, indexes, and MQTs) and one or more containers (i.e., directories, files, or raw devices) in which the object's data actually resides. A single table space can span many containers, but each container can belong to only one table space. When a table space spans multiple containers, data is written in a round-robin fashion (in groups of pages called extents) to each container assigned to that table space; this helps balance data across all containers that belong to a given table space. Figure 3–4 shows the relationship between pages, extents, and table space containers.

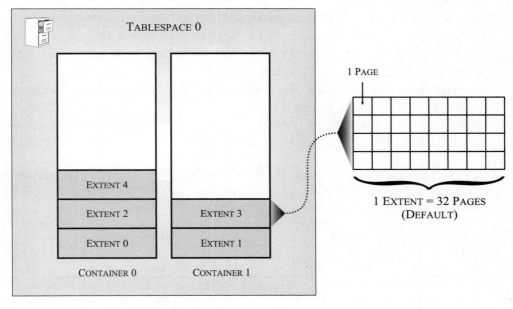

DATA WRITTEN IN
ROUND-ROBIN MANNER

Figure 3–4: How data is written to table space containers.

When multiple containers are used with SMS or DMS table spaces, the maximum amount of data that each container can hold is determined by the smallest container used. For example, if a table space uses one container that is 10M in size and a second container that is 12M in size, 2M of the second container will not be useable; the maximum amount of storage available to the table space will be 20M. Therefore, container sizes should be equal whenever possible.

Two types of table spaces can exist: system managed space (SMS) table spaces and database managed space (DMS) table spaces. With SMS table spaces, only directory containers can be used for storage, and the operating system's file manager is responsible for controlling how that space is used. The SMS storage model consists of many files (each representing a table, index, or long data object) that reside within the file system space—the user decides on the location of the files, the DB2 Database Manager assigns the files their names, and the file system is responsible for managing their growth. With DMS table spaces, only file and/or device containers can be used for storage, and the DB2 Database Manager is responsible for controlling how the space is used. In DB2 9, the initial allocation of space for an object in a DMS table space is two extents; the initial allocation of space for an object in an SMS table space is one extent. Other differences between SMS and DMS table spaces can be seen in Table 3.1.

Table 3.1 Differences Between SMS and DMS Table Spaces	
SMS Table Spaces	**DMS Table Spaces**
Storage space is allocated and managed by the operating system's file manager.	Storage space is allocated, if so specified, and managed by the DB2 Database Manager.
Only directory containers can be used for storage; file and device containers cannot be used.	File or device containers can be used as storage; directory containers cannot be used.
No additional containers can be added to a table space (using the ALTER TABLESPACE SQL statement) once it has been created.	Additional containers can be added to a table space after it has been created. When new containers are added, existing data can automatically be rebalanced across the new set of containers to retain optimal I/O efficiency.
Storage space is allocated as it is needed.	Storage space is preallocated.
A container's size cannot be changed once a table space has been created.	A container's size can be increased or decreased after a table space has been created.
Regular data and long data are stored in the same table space.	Regular data and long data can be split across multiple table spaces (regular data can reside in one table space while long data resides in another).
Table spaces are easier to create and manage.	Table access is slightly faster, so overall performance is better.

Both SMS and DMS table spaces are classified according to the type of data they are intended to store; three classifications exist: regular, large, and temporary. Regular data and index data reside in regular table spaces, whereas long field data and large object data can reside in large table spaces—but only if DMS table spaces are used. (The use of large table spaces is optional given that large data can reside in regular table spaces as well.) Temporary table spaces are further classified as being either system or user—system temporary table spaces are used to store internal temporary data generated when some types of operations are performed (for example, sorting data, reorganizing tables, creating indexes, and joining tables), whereas user temporary table spaces are used to store declared global temporary tables, which in turn are used to store application-specific data for a brief period of time.

If a database is enabled for automatic storage, one other type of table space—an automatic storage table space—can exist. Although at first glance, automatic storage table spaces appear to be a third type of table space, they are really just an extension of SMS and DMS table spaces: regular and large table spaces are created as DMS table spaces with one or more file containers; system and user temporary table spaces are created as SMS table spaces with one or more directory containers. Unlike when SMS and DMS table spaces are defined, no container definitions are needed for automatic storage table spaces; the DB2 Database Manager assigns containers to automatic storage table spaces automatically.

Obtaining Information About Existing Table Spaces

As with other objects, whenever a table space object is created, information about that table space is recorded in the system catalog. As a result, you can obtain specific information about any table space in a database by querying the appropriate system catalog tables or system catalog views. You can also obtain information about all table spaces that have been created for a particular database by executing the LIST TABLESPACES command. The syntax for this command is:

```
LIST TABLESPACES
<SHOW DETAIL>
```

If this command is executed without the SHOW DETAIL option specified, the following information will be displayed for every table space that has been created for a database:

- The internal ID that was assigned to the table space when it was created.

- The name that has been assigned to the table space.

- Table space type (SMS table space or DMS table space).

- The type of data the table space is designed to hold (i.e., regular data, large data, or temporary data).

- The current state of the table space. (Table 3.2 contains a list of the table space states available.)

Table 3.2 Table Space States and Their Corresponding Hexadecimal Values	
Table Space State	**Hexadecimal Value**
Normal	0x0
Quiesced: SHARE	0x1
Quiesced: UPDATE	0x2
Quiesced: EXCLUSIVE	0x4
Load pending	0x8
Delete pending	0x10
Backup pending	0x20
Roll-forward recovery in progress	0x40
Roll-forward recovery pending	0x80
Restore pending	0x100
Recovery pending (no longer used)	0x100
Disable pending	0x200
Reorg in progress	0x400
Backup in progress	0x800
Storage must be defined	0x1000
Restore in progress	0x2000
Offline and not accessible	0x4000
Drop pending	0x8000
Storage may be defined	0x2000000
StorDef is in "Final" state	0x4000000
StorDef was changed prior to roll-forward recovery	0x8000000
DMS rebalancer is active	0x10000000
Table space deletion in progress	0x20000000
Table space creation in progress	0x40000000
Load in progress*	
A single table space can be in more than one state at a given point in time. If this is the case, multiple table space state hexadecimal values will be ANDed together to keep track of the multiple states. The Get Table Space State command (db2tbst) can be used to obtain the table space state associated with any given hexadecimal value.	
*The Load utility will place a table space in the "Load in progress" state if the COPY NO option is specified when data is being loaded into a recoverable database. The table space remains in this state for the duration of the load operation and is returned to normal state when the load operation completes. This state does not have a hexadecimal value.	

If the LIST TABLESPACES command is executed with the SHOW DETAIL option specified, the following additional information about each table space is provided:

- **Total number of pages.** The total number of pages the table space is designed to hold. For DMS table spaces, this is the sum of all pages available from all containers associated with the table space. For SMS table spaces, this is the total amount of file space currently being used.

- **Number of usable pages.** The number of pages in the table space in which user data can be stored. For DMS table spaces, this number is calculated by subtracting the number of pages required for overhead from the total number of pages available. For SMS table spaces, this number is equal to the total number of pages the table space is designed to hold.

- **Number of used pages.** The number of pages in the table space that already contain data. (For SMS table spaces, this value is equal to the total number of pages the table space is designed to hold.)

- **Number of free pages.** The number of pages in the table space that are currently empty. (This information is applicable only for DMS table spaces.)

- **High water mark.** The number of pages that mark the current "high water mark" or "end" of the table space's address space (i.e., the page number of the first free page following the last allocated extent of the table space). (This information is applicable only to DMS table spaces.)

- **Page size.** The size, in bytes, that one page of data in the table space will occupy.

- **Extent size.** The number of pages that are contained in one extent of the table space.

- **Prefetch size.** The number of pages of data that will be read from the table space in advance of those pages currently being referenced by a query, in anticipation that they will be needed to resolve the query (prefetched).

- **Number of containers.** The number of containers used by the table space.

- **Minimum recovery time.** The earliest point in time that may be specified if a point-in-time roll-forward recovery operation is to be performed on the table space.

- **State change table space ID.** The ID of the table space that caused the table space being queried to be placed in the "Load Pending" or "Delete Pending" state. (This information is displayed only if the table space being queried has been placed in the "Load Pending" or "Delete Pending" state.)

- **State change object ID.** The ID of the object that caused the table space being queried to be placed in the "Load Pending" or "Delete Pending" state. (This information is displayed only if the table space being queried has been placed in the "Load Pending" or "Delete Pending" state.)

- **Number of quiescers.** The number of users and/or applications that have placed the table space in a "Quiesced" (restricted access) state. (This information is displayed only if the table space being queried has been placed in the "Quiesced:SHARE," "Quiesced:UPDATE," or "Quiesced:EXCLUSIVE" state.)

- **Table space ID and object ID for each quiescer.** The ID of the table spaces and objects that caused the table space being queried to be placed in a "Quiesced" state. (This information is displayed only if the number of users or applications that have placed the table space in a. "Quiesced" state is greater than zero.)

So if you wanted to obtain detailed information about all table spaces that have been created for a database named SALES, you could do so by connecting to the database and executing a LIST TABLESPACES command that looks like this:

```
LIST TABLESPACES SHOW DETAIL
```

And when this command is executed, the output produced should look something like this:

```
                    Tablespaces for Current Database
     Tablespace ID              = 0
     Name                       = SYSCATSPACE
     Type                       = Database managed space
     Contents                   = All permanent data. Regular table space.
     State                      = 0x0000
       Detailed explanation:
         Normal
     Total pages                = 8192
     Useable pages              = 8188
     Used pages                 = 7940
     Free pages                 = 248
```

```
High water mark (pages)        = 7940
Page size (bytes)              = 4096
Extent size (pages)            = 4
Prefetch size (pages)          = 4
Number of containers           = 1

Tablespace ID                  = 1
Name                           = TEMPSPACE1
Type                           = System managed space
Contents                       = System Temporary data
State                          = 0x0000
   Detailed explanation:
      Normal
Total pages                    = 1
Useable pages                  = 1
Used pages                     = 1
Free pages                     = Not applicable
High water mark (pages)        = Not applicable
Page size (bytes)              = 4096
Extent size (pages)            = 32
Prefetch size (pages)          = 32
Number of containers           = 1

Tablespace ID                  = 2
Name                           = USERSPACE1
Type                           = Database managed space
Contents                       = All permanent data. Large table space.
State                          = 0x0000
   Detailed explanation:
      Normal
Total pages                    = 8192
Useable pages                  = 8160
Used pages                     = 416
Free pages                     = 7744
High water mark (pages)        = 416
Page size (bytes)              = 4096
Extent size (pages)            = 32
Prefetch size (pages)          = 32
Number of containers           = 1

Tablespace ID                  = 3
Name                           = SYSTOOLSPACE
Type                           = Database managed space
Contents                       = All permanent data. Large table space.
State                          = 0x0000
   Detailed explanation:
      Normal
Total pages                    = 8192
Useable pages                  = 8188
Used pages                     = 20
Free pages                     = 8168
High water mark (pages)        = 20
```

```
Page size (bytes)           = 4096
Extent size (pages)         = 4
Prefetch size (pages)       = 4
Number of containers        = 1
```

You can also obtain detailed information about all table spaces that have been created for a particular database by capturing and displaying snapshot monitor data. The command that is used to capture table space–specific snapshot monitor information is:

```
GET SNAPSHOT FOR TABLESPACES ON [DatabaseAlias]
```

(We will take a close look at the snapshot monitor in Chapter 5, "Analyzing DB2 Activity.")

Obtaining Information About the Containers Used by a Table Space

Just as you can obtain information about the table spaces that have been created for a particular database, you can obtain information about the containers that are used to physically hold table space data. You obtain information about the containers that are associated with a particular table space by executing the LIST TABLESPACE CONTAINERS command. The syntax for this command is:

```
LIST TABLESPACE CONTAINERS FOR [TablespaceID]
<SHOW DETAIL>
```

where:

TablespaceID   Identifies the internal ID assigned to the table space for which container information is to be obtained.

If this command is executed without the SHOW DETAIL option specified, the following information will be displayed for every table space that has been created for a database:

- The internal ID that was assigned to the container when it was associated with the table space specified

- The name that was used to reference the container when it was assigned to the table space specified

- Indication that the container is a directory (path) container, a file container, or a device container

On the other hand, if this command is executed with the SHOW DETAIL option specified, the following additional information about each table space container is provided:

- **Total number of pages.** The total number of pages the table space container is designed to hold. (For SMS table spaces, this is the total amount of storage space that is currently being used by the container.)

- **Number of usable pages.** The number of pages in the table space container in which user data can be stored. For DMS table spaces, this number is calculated by subtracting the number of pages needed for overhead from the total number of pages available. For SMS table spaces, this value is equal to the total number of pages the table space container is designed to hold.

- **Accessibility.** An indication of whether the container is accessible.

So if you wanted to obtain detailed information about the containers that are associated with the table space whose internal ID is 0 (in a database named SALES), you could do so by executing a LIST TABLESPACE CONTAINERS command that looks like this:

```
LIST TABLESPACE CONTAINERS FOR 0 SHOW DETAIL
```

And when this command is executed, you might see output that looks something like this:

```
                Tablespace Containers for Tablespace 0
    Container ID          = 0
    Name                  = C:\DB2\NODE0000\TEST\T0000000\C0000000.CAT
    Type                  = File
    Total pages           = 16384
    Useable pages         = 16380
    Accessible            = Yes
```

It is important to note that if for some reason a particular table space container becomes inaccessible (Accessible = No), the table space associated with that container will automatically be placed in the "Offline" state. When the issue that made the container inaccessible is resolved, the associated table space can be returned to the "Normal" state by executing the ALTER TABLESPACE SQL statement with the SWITCH ONLINE option specified.

Creating New Table Spaces

Earlier, we saw that when a DB2 database is created, one buffer pool named IBMDEFAULTBP is created, and three table spaces are created and associated with this buffer pool as part of the database initialization process. These three table spaces are sufficient for small databases; however, large databases are usually composed of many different buffer pool and table space objects.

Additional table spaces can be created by executing the CREATE TABLESPACE SQL statement. The basic syntax for this statement is:

```
CREATE
<REGULAR | LARGE | SYSTEM TEMPORARY | USER TEMPORARY>
TABLESPACE [TablespaceName]
<PAGESIZE [PageSize] <K>>
MANAGED BY SYSTEM USING ('[Container]' ,...)
<EXTENTSIZE [ExtentPages | ExtentSize <K | M | G>]>
<PREFETCHSIZE [AUTOMATIC | PrefetchPages |
     PrefetchSize <K | M | G>]>
<BUFFERPOOL [BufferPoolName]>
<<NO> FILE SYSTEM CACHING>
<DROPPED TABLE RECOVERY <ON | OFF>>
```

or

```
CREATE
<REGULAR | LARGE | SYSTEM TEMPORARY | USER TEMPORARY>
TABLESPACE [TablespaceName]
<PAGESIZE [PageSize] <K>>
MANAGED BY DATABASE USING ([FILE | DEVICE] '[Container]'
   [ContainerPages | ContainerSize <K | M | G>] ,...)
<AUTORESIZE [YES | NO]>
<INCREASESIZE [IncSize <PERCENT | K | M | G>]>
<MAXSIZE [NONE | MaxSize <K | M | G>]>
<EXTENTSIZE [ExtentPages | ExtentSize <K | M | G>]>
<PREFETCHSIZE [AUTOMATIC | PrefetchPages |
   PrefetchSize <K | M | G>]>
<BUFFERPOOL [BufferPoolName]>
<<NO> FILE SYSTEM CACHING>
<DROPPED TABLE RECOVERY <ON | OFF>>
```

or

```
CREATE
<REGULAR | LARGE | SYSTEM TEMPORARY | USER TEMPORARY>
TABLESPACE [TablespaceName]
<PAGESIZE [PageSize] <K>>
MANAGED BY AUTOMATIC STORAGE
<AUTORESIZE [YES | NO]>
<INITIALSIZE [InitSize <K | M | G>]>
<INCREASESIZE [IncSize <PERCENT | K | M | G>]>
<MAXSIZE [NONE | MaxSize <K | M | G>]>
<EXTENTSIZE [ExtentPages | ExtentSize <K | M | G>]>
<PREFETCHSIZE [AUTOMATIC | PrefetchPages |
    PrefetchSize <K | M | G>]>
<BUFFERPOOL [BufferPoolName]>
<<NO> FILE SYSTEM CACHING>
<DROPPED TABLE RECOVERY <ON | OFF>>
```

where:

TablespaceName   Identifies the name that is to be assigned to the table space to be created.

PageSize   Specifies the size of each page used by the table space being created. The following values are valid for this parameter: 4,096; 8,192; 16,384 or 32,768 bytes—if the suffix K (for kilobytes) is provided, this parameter must be set to 4, 8, 16, or 32. Unless otherwise specified, pages used by table spaces are 4K in size.

Container   Identifies, by name, one or more containers that are to be used to store the data associated with the table space to be created.

ContainerPages   Identifies the amount of storage, by number of pages, that is to be preallocated for the container(s) identified in the *Container* parameter.

ContainerSize   Identifies the amount of storage that is to be preallocated for the container(s) identified in the *Container* parameter. The value specified for this parameter is treated as the total number of bytes, unless the letter K (for kilobytes), M (for megabytes), or

G (for gigabytes) is also specified. (If a *ContainerSize* value is specified, it is converted to a *ContainerPages* value using the *PageSize* value provided.)

InitSize   Identifies the amount of storage that is to be preallocated for an autoresize DMS or automatic storage table space.

IncSize   Identifies the amount by which a table space enabled for automatic resizing will automatically be increased when the table space is full and a request for more space is made.

MaxSize   Identifies the maximum size to which a table space enabled for automatic resizing can automatically be increased.

ExtentPages   Identifies the number of pages of data that are to be written to a single table space container before another container will be used.

ExtentSize   Identifies the amount of data that is to be written to a single table space container before another container will be used. The value specified for this parameter is treated as the total number of bytes, unless the letter K (for kilobytes), M (for megabytes), or G (for gigabytes) is also specified. (If an *ExtentSize* value is specified, it is converted to an *ExtentPages* value using the *PageSize* value provided.)

PrefetchPages   Identifies the number of pages of data that are to be read from the table space when data prefetching is performed (prefetching allows data needed by a query to be read before it is referenced so that the query spends less time waiting for I/O).

PrefetchSize   Identifies the amount of data that is to be read from the table space when data prefetching is performed. The value specified for this parameter is treated as the total number of bytes, unless the letter K (for kilobytes), M (for megabytes), or G (for gigabytes) is also specified. (If a *PrefetchSize* value is specified, it is converted to a *PrefetchPages* value using the *PageSize* value provided.)

BufferPoolName Identifies the name of the buffer pool to be used by the table space to be created. (The page size of the buffer pool specified must match the page size of the table space to be created, or the CREATE TABLESPACE statement will fail.)

If the MANAGED BY SYSTEM version of this statement is executed, the resulting table space will be an SMS table space. On the other hand, if the MANAGED BY DATABASE version is executed, the resulting table space will be a DMS table space. Furthermore, if an SMS table space is to be created, only directories can be used as that table space's storage containers; if a DMS table space is to be created, only fixed-size preallocated files or physical raw devices can be used as that table space's storage containers.

Thus, if you wanted to create an SMS table space that has the name SALES_TS; consists of pages that are 4 kilobytes in size; uses the directories C:\TBSP1, C:\TBSP2, and C:\TBSP3 as its storage containers; and uses the buffer pool IBMDEFAULTBP, you could do so by executing a CREATE TABLESPACE SQL statement that looks something like this:

```
CREATE REGULAR TABLESPACE sales_ts
PAGESIZE 4096
MANAGED BY SYSTEM USING
    ('C:\tbsp1', C:\tbsp2', 'C:\tbsp3')
EXTENTSIZE 32
PREFETCHSIZE 96
BUFFERPOOL ibmdefaultbp
```

On the other hand, if you wanted to create a DMS table space that has the name PAYROLL_TS, consists of pages that are 8 kilobytes in size, uses the file DMS_TBSP.TSF, (which is 1,000 megabytes in size and resides in the directory C:\TABLESPACES) as its storage container, and uses the buffer pool PAYROLL_BP, you could do so by executing a CREATE TABLESPACE SQL statement that looks something like this:

```
CREATE REGULAR TABLESPACE payroll_ts
PAGESIZE 8K
MANAGED BY DATABASE USING
```

```
        (FILE 'C:\TABLESPACES\dms_tbsp.tsf' 1000 M)
    BUFFERPOOL payroll_bp
```

And finally, if you wanted to create an automatic storage table space that has the name HR_TS and uses the buffer pool IBMDEFAULTBP, you could do so by executing a CREATE TABLESPACE SQL statement that looks something like this:

> If a database is enabled for automatic storage, the MANAGED BY AUTOMATIC STORAGE clause can be left out completely—its absence implies automatic storage. No container definitions are provided in this case because the DB2 Database Manager assigns containers automatically.

```
CREATE REGULAR TABLESPACE hr_ts
MANAGED BY AUTOMATIC STORAGE
```

Table spaces can also be created using the Create Table Space Wizard, which can be activated by selecting the appropriate action from the Table Spaces menu found in the Control Center. Figure 3–5 shows the Control Center menu items that must be selected to activate the Create Table Space Wizard; Figure 3–6 shows how the first page of the Create Table Space Wizard might look after its input fields have been populated.

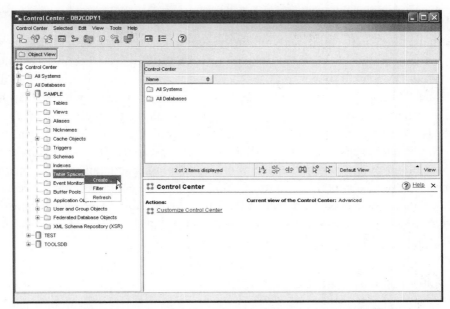

Figure 3–5: Invoking the Create Table Space Wizard from the Control Center.

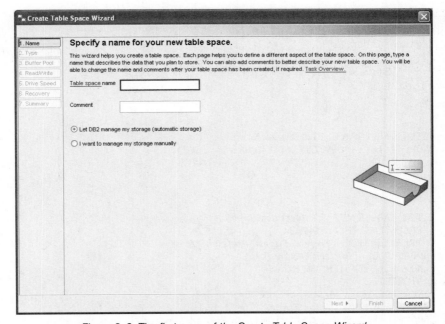

Figure 3–6: The first page of the Create Table Space Wizard.

Modifying Existing Table Spaces

Because SMS table spaces rely on the operating system for physical storage space management, they rarely need to be modified after they have been successfully created. DMS table spaces, on the other hand, have to be monitored closely to ensure that the fixed-size preallocated file(s) or physical raw device(s) that they use for storage always have enough free space available to meet the database's needs. When the amount of free storage space available to a DMS table space becomes dangerously low (typically less than 10 percent), you can add more free space either by increasing the size of one or more of its containers or by adding one or more new containers to it. Existing table space containers can be resized, new containers can be made available to an existing table space, and an existing table space's properties can be changed by executing the ALTER TABLESPACE SQL statement. The basic syntax for this statement is:

```
ALTER TABLESPACE [TablespaceName]
[ADD | EXTEND | REDUCE | RESIZE]
    ([FILE | DEVICE] '[Container]'
    [ContainerPages | ContainerSize <K | M | G>] ,...)
```

or

```
ALTER TABLESPACE [TablespaceName]
[EXTEND | REDUCE | RESIZE]
    (ALL <CONTAINERS>
       [ContainerPages | ContainerSize <K | M | G>])
```

or

```
ALTER TABLESPACE [TablespaceName]
DROP ([FILE | DEVICE] '[Container]' ,...)
```

or

```
ALTER TABLESPACE [TablespaceName]
< PREFETCHSIZE AUTOMATIC |
  PREFETCHSIZE [PrefetchPages | PrefetchSize <K | M | G>]>
<BUFFERPOOL [BufferPoolName]>
<<NO> FILE SYSTEM CACHING>
<AUTORESIZE [NO | YES]>
<INCREASESIZE [IncSize <PERCENT | K | M | G>]>
<MAXSIZE [NONE | MaxSize <K | M | G>]>
<DROPPED TABLE RECOVERY [ON | OFF]>
<CONVERT TO LARGE>
```

where:

TablespaceName   Identifies the name assigned to the table space that is to be altered.

Container   Identifies one or more containers that are to be added to, resized, or removed from the table space specified.

ContainerPages   Identifies the amount of storage, by number of pages, that is to be added to, removed from, or allocated for all containers or the container(s) identified in the *Container* parameter.

ContainerSize   Identifies the amount of storage that is to be added to, removed from, or allocated for all containers or the container(s) identified in the *Container* parameter. The value specified for this parameter is treated as the total number of bytes, unless the letter K (for kilobytes), M (for megabytes), or G (for gigabytes) is also specified. (If a *ContainerSize* value is specified, it is converted to a *ContainerPages* value using the *PageSize* value provided.)

PrefetchPages   Identifies the number of pages of data to be read from the table space when data prefetching is performed.

PrefetchSize   Identifies the amount of data to be read from the table space when data prefetching is performed. The value specified for this parameter is treated as the total number of bytes, unless the letter K (for kilobytes), M (for megabytes), or G (for gigabytes) is also specified. (If a *PrefetchSize* value is specified, it is converted to a *PrefetchPages* value using the page size of the table space being altered.)

BufferPoolName   Identifies the name of the buffer pool to be used by the table space to be altered. (The page size of the buffer pool specified must match the page size used by the table space to be altered.)

IncSize   Identifies the amount by which a table space enabled for automatic resizing will automatically be increased when the table space is full and a request for more space is made.

MaxSize   Identifies the maximum size to which a table space enabled for automatic resizing can automatically be increased.

Thus, if you wanted a fixed-size preallocated file named NEWFILE.TSF that is 1,000 megabytes in size and resides in the directory C:\TABLESPACES, to be used as a new storage container for an existing DMS table space named PAYROLL_TS, you could do so by executing an ALTER TABLESPACE SQL statement that looks like this:

```
ALTER TABLESPACE payroll_ts
ADD (FILE 'C:\tablespaces\newfile.tsf' 1000 M)
```

On the other hand, if you wanted to expand the size of all containers associated with an existing DMS table space named PAYROLL_TS by 200 megabytes, you could do so by executing an ALTER TABLESPACE SQL statement that looks like this:

```
ALTER TABLESPACE payroll_ts
EXTEND (ALL CONTAINERS 200 M)
```

Table spaces can also be altered using the Alter Table Space dialog, which can be activated by selecting the appropriate action from the Table Spaces menu found in the Control Center. Figure 3–7 shows the Control Center menu items that must be selected in order to activate the Alter Table Space dialog; Figure 3–8 shows how the first page of the Alter Table Space dialog looks when it is first activated.

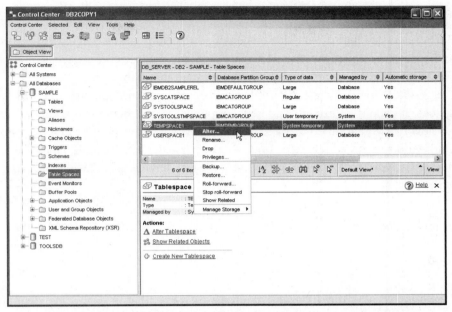

Figure 3–7: Invoking the Alter Table Space dialog from the Control Center.

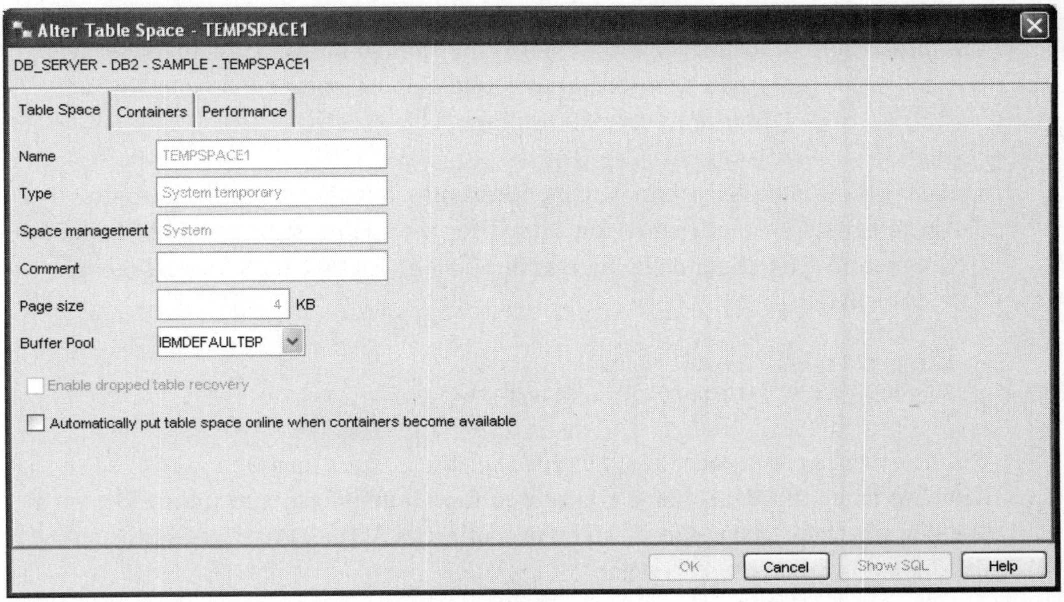

Figure 3–8: The first page of the Alter Table Space dialog.

Adding new containers to existing automatic storage table spaces

Earlier, we saw that if a database is enabled for automatic storage, the container- and space- management characteristics of its table spaces are determined by the DB2 Database Manager. And we have just seen that although the ALTER TABLESPACE command can be used to add new containers to existing DMS table spaces, it cannot be used to add new containers to automatic storage table spaces. So how can you add new storage paths to the collection of paths that are used for automatic storage table spaces once a database has been created? To perform this operation, you must use the ALTER DATABASE statement. The basic syntax for this statement is:

```
ALTER DATABASE [DatabaseName]
ADD STORAGE ON '[Container]' ,...)
```

where:

DatabaseName   Identifies the database, by name, that is to have new containers added to its pool of containers that are used for automatic storage.

Container   Identifies one or more new storage locations (containers) that are to be added to the collection of storage locations that are used for automatic storage table spaces.

Thus, if you wanted to add the storage locations /data/path1 and /data/path2 to a database named SAMPLE that is configured for automatic storage and resides on a UNIX system, you could do so by executing an ALTER DATABASE SQL statement that looks like this:

```
ALTER DATABASE sample
ADD STORAGE '/data/path1', '/data/path2'
```

On the other hand, if you wanted to add the storage locations D: and E: to a database named SAMPLE that is configured for automatic storage and resides on a Windows system, you could do so by executing an ALTER DATABASE SQL statement that looks like this:

```
ALTER DATABASE sample ADD STORAGE ON 'D:', 'E:'
```

A Word About Declared Temporary Tables and User Temporary Table Spaces

A declared temporary table is a special table that is used to hold temporary data on behalf of a single application. Like base tables, indexes can be created on and statistics can be collected for declared temporary tables. Unlike base tables, whose descriptions and constraints are stored in the system catalog tables of the database to which they belong, declared temporary tables are not persistent and can be used only by the application that creates them—and only for the life of the application. When the application that creates a declared temporary table terminates, the rows of the table are deleted, and the description of the table is dropped. (However, data stored in a temporary table can exist across transaction boundaries.) Another significant difference focuses on where the data for each type of table is stored. Before an application can create and use a declared temporary table, at least one user temporary table space must be created for the database the application will be working with, and the privileges needed to use that table space must be granted to the appropriate users. (User temporary table spaces are not created by default when a database is created.) Base tables, on the other hand, are created in regular table spaces; if no table space is specified when a base table is created, its data is stored in the table space USERSPACE1, which is created by default when a database is created.

Schemas

Whereas table spaces are used to physically store objects in a database, schemas are used to logically classify and group other objects in the database, regardless of where they are physically stored. And because schemas are objects themselves, they have privileges associated with them that allow the schema owner to control which users can create, alter, and drop objects within them.

Most objects in a database are named using a two-part naming convention. The first (leftmost) part of the name is called the schema name or qualifier, and the second (rightmost) part is called the object name. Syntactically, these two parts are concatenated and delimited with a period (for example, HR.EMPLOYEE). When any object that can be qualified by a schema name (such as a table, view, index, user-defined data type, user-defined function, nickname, package, or trigger) is first created, it is assigned to a particular schema based on the qualifier in its name.

Figure 3–9 illustrates how a table named STAFF would be assigned to the PAYROLL schema during the table creation process.

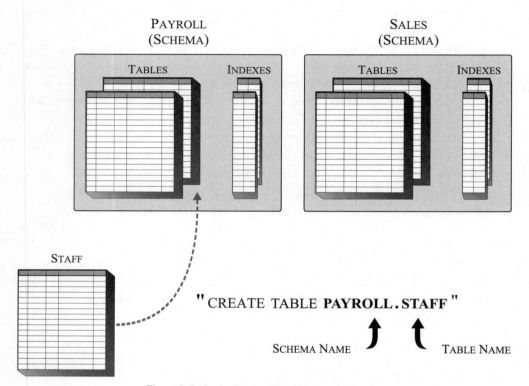

Figure 3–9: Assigning a table object to a schema.

Some schema names are reserved and cannot be used. An example includes the names assigned to the four schemas that are automatically created when a database is created—SYSIBM, SYSCAT, SYSSTAT, and SYSFUN.

If no schema/qualifier name is specified when an object is created, that object is assigned to the default schema, which is usually the user ID of the individual who is currently connected to the database and creating the object.

Schemas are implicitly created whenever a data object that has been assigned a qualifier that is different from existing schema names is created—provided the user creating the object holds IMPLICIT_SCHEMA authority. (Unless otherwise specified, when a new database is created, the group PUBLIC is given IMPLICIT_SCHEMA privilege. This privilege allows any user that can successfully connect to the database to implicitly create new schemas if they do not already exist.) Schemas can be explicitly created by executing the CREATE SCHEMA SQL statement. The basic syntax for this statement is:

```
CREATE SCHEMA [SchemaName]
<SQLStatement ,...>
```

or

```
CREATE SCHEMA
AUTHORIZATION [AuthorizationName]
<SQLStatement ,...>
```

or

```
CREATE SCHEMA [SchemaName]
AUTHORIZATION [AuthorizationName]
<SQLStatement ,...>
```

where:

SchemaName   Identifies the name that is to be assigned to the schema to be created.

AuthorizationName   Identifies the user who is to be given ownership of the schema once it is created.

SQLStatement   Specifies one or more SQL statements that are to be executed together with the CREATE SCHEMA statement. (Only the following SQL statements are valid: CREATE TABLE, CREATE VIEW, CREATE INDEX, COMMENT ON, and GRANT).

If a schema name is specified, but no authorization name is provided, the authorization ID of the user who issued the CREATE SCHEMA statement is given ownership of the newly created schema; if an authorization name is specified but no schema name is provided, the new schema is assigned the same name as the authorization name used.

So if you wanted to explicitly create a schema named PAYROLL and give ownership of the schema to the user DB2ADMIN, you could do so by executing a CREATE SCHEMA SQL statement that looks something like this:

```
CREATE SCHEMA payroll
AUTHORIZATION db2admin
```

On the other hand, if you wanted to explicitly create a schema named INVENTORY, along with a table named PARTS inside the schema named INVENTORY, you could do so by executing a CREATE SCHEMA statement that looks something like this:

```
CREATE SCHEMA inventory
CREATE TABLE PARTS (partno        INTEGER NOT NULL,
                    description   VARCHAR(50),
                    quantity      SMALLINT)
```

Schemas can also be created using the Create Schema dialog, which can be activated by selecting the appropriate action from the Schemas menu found in the Control Center. Figure 3–10 shows the Control Center menu items that must be selected to activate the Create Schema dialog; Figure 3–11 shows how the Create Schema dialog looks when it is first activated.

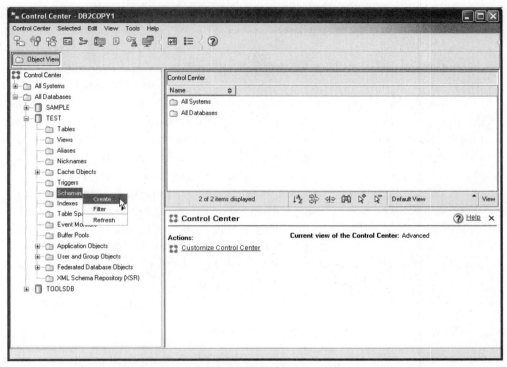

Figure 3–10: Invoking the Create Schema dialog from the Control Center.

Figure 3–11: The Create Schema dialog.

Given that schemas can be implicitly created by creating an object and assigning it a new schema name, you may be wondering why anyone would want to explicitly create a schema using the CREATE SCHEMA statement (or the Create Schema dialog). The primary reason for explicitly creating a schema has to do with access control. An explicitly created schema has an owner, who is identified either by the authorization ID of the user who executed the CREATE SCHEMA statement or by the authorization ID of the user to whom ownership was passed when the schema was created. A schema owner has the privileges needed to create, alter, and drop any object stored in the schema, as well as to drop the schema itself; the schema owner also has the right to grant the privileges needed to create, alter, and drop objects in the schema (CREATEIN, ALTERIN, and DROPIN privileges) to other users and groups. (We'll take a closer look at schema privileges in Chapter 8, "Security.") On the other hand, implicitly created schemas are considered to be owned by the user SYSIBM. Any user can create an object in an implicitly created schema, and each object in the schema is controlled by the user who created it. Furthermore, only users with System Administrator (SYSADM) or Database Administrator (DBADM) authority are allowed to drop implicitly created schemas. Thus, in order for users other than System Administrators and Database Administrators to have complete control over a schema, as well as all data objects stored in that schema, the schema must be created explicitly.

Range Clustering and Range Partitioning

Earlier, we saw that table spaces are used to control where data is physically stored and to provide a layer of indirection between database objects (such as tables, indexes, and views) and one or more containers (i.e., directories, files, or raw devices) in which the object's data actually resides. Consequently, how database objects are assigned to table spaces when they are created determines how data is physically stored on disk. The physical storage of table data can be controlled even further by creating range-clustered tables or by taking advantage of a new feature introduced in DB2 9 known as range partitioning.

Range-Clustered Tables

A range-clustered table (RCT) is a table whose data is organized in ascending key sequence with a fixed size based on the specified range of key sequence values. Range-clustered tables are useful when data is tightly clustered across one or more columns in a table—the smallest and largest values in select columns define the range of possible values. Each possible key value in the defined range has a predetermined location in the physical table. Thus, the storage required for a range-clustered table must be preallocated and available when the table is created, and it must be sufficient to store the number of rows found in the specified range multiplied by the row size.

Range-clustered tables can result in significant performance advantages during query processing because fewer input/output (I/O) operations are required. Additionally, range-clustered tables require less cache buffer allocation because there are no secondary objects to maintain; indexes are not required nor are they supported.

Range-clustered tables are created by specifying the ORGANIZE BY KEY SEQUENCE clause of the CREATE TABLE SQL statement when a table is created. The syntax for this optional clause is:

```
ORGANIZE BY KEY SEQUENCE
([ColumnName]
   <STARTING <FROM> [Start]>
   ENDING <AT> [End] ,...)
<ALLOW OVERFLOW | DISALLOW OVERFLOW>
<PCTFREE [PercentFree]>
```

where:

ColumnName Identifies one or more columns, by name, whose values are to be used to determine the sequence of the range-clustered table.

Start Specifies the low end of the range of values allowed. (Values less than the starting value specified are allowed only if the ALLOW OVERFLOW option is specified.)

End Specifies the high end of the range of values allowed. (Values greater than the ending value specified are allowed only if the ALLOW OVERFLOW option is specified.)

PercentFree Specifies the percentage of each page that is to be left as free space. (The first row on each page is added without restriction; when additional rows are added to a page, a check is performed to ensure the specified percentage of the page is left free.)

If the DISALLOW OVERFLOW clause is specified, key values will not be allowed to exceed the defined range. On the other hand, if the ALLOW OVERFLOW clause is specified, key values will be allowed to exceed the defined range, in which case overflow data will be placed in an overflow area, which is dynamically allocated. A range-clustered table that overflows data that falls outside the predefined range will suffer from poor performance.

Thus, if you wanted to create a range-clustered table named CUSTOMERS that has two columns named CUSTOMER_ID and CUSTOMER_NAME, where the CUSTOMER_ID column will become the unique key that determines how records are physically stored and where only unique values between 1 and 100 can be assigned to the CUSTOMER_ID column, you could do so by executing a CREATE TABLE SQL statement that looks something like this:

```
CREATE TABLE customers
   (customer_id    INTEGER NOT NULL,
    customer_name VARCHAR(80))
 ORGANIZE BY KEY SEQUENCE (customer_id
    STARTING FROM 1 ENDING AT 100)
    DISALLOW OVERFLOW
```

Once this table is created and populated, if an application needs to access the row for the customer whose ID is 2, the DB2 Database Manager will look for the second row in the CUSTOMERS table, using a predetermined offset from the logical start of the table. If a row is updated such that the key column values are modified, the updated row is copied to the new location, and the old copy of the row is deleted, maintaining the clustering of data in the table.

The ORGANIZE BY KEY SEQUENCE clause of the CREATE TABLE SQL statement cannot be used in conjunction with any other clause that controls how table data is to be organized (for example, ORGANIZE BY DIMENSIONS and PARTITION BY RANGE).

Range-Partitioned Tables

Table partitioning (also referred to as range partitioning) is a data organization scheme in which table data is divided across multiple storage objects called data partitions or ranges based on values in one or more columns. Each data partition is stored separately, and the storage objects used can be in different table spaces, in the same table space, or a combination of the two. Table partitioning improves performance and eliminates the need to create a partitioned database using the Data Partitioning Feature.

Other advantages of using table partitioning include:

Easy roll-in and roll-out of data. Rolling in partitioned table data allows a new range to be easily incorporated into a partitioned table as an additional data partition. Rolling out partitioned table data allows you to easily separate ranges of data from a partitioned table for subsequent purging or archiving. Data can be quickly rolled in and out by using the ATTACH PARTITION and DETACH PARTITION clauses of the ALTER TABLE statement.

Easier administration of large tables. Table-level administration becomes more flexible because administrative tasks can be performed on individual data partitions. Such tasks include detaching and reattaching of a data partition, backing up and restoring individual data partitions, and reorganizing individual indexes. In addition, time-consuming maintenance operations can be shortened by breaking them down into a series of smaller operations. For example, backup operations can be performed at the data-partition level when each data partition is placed in a separate table space. Thus, it is possible to back up one data partition of a partitioned table at a time.

Flexible index placement. With table partitioning, indexes can be placed in different table spaces, allowing for more granular control of index placement.

Better query processing. In the process of resolving queries, one or more data partitions may be automatically eliminated based on the query predicates used. This functionality, known as Data Partition Elimination, improves the performance of many decision support queries because less data has to be analyzed before a result data set can be returned.

Data from a given table is partitioned into multiple storage objects based on the specifications provided in the PARTITION BY clause of the CREATE TABLE statement. The syntax for this optional clause is:

```
PARTITION BY <RANGE>
  ([ColumnName] <NULLS LAST | NULLS FIRST> ,...)
  (STARTING <FROM>
       <(> [Start | MINVALUE | MAXVALUE] < ,...)>
       <INCLUSIVE | EXCLUSIVE>
    ENDING <AT>
       <(> [End | MINVALUE | MAXVALUE] < ,...)>
       <INCLUSIVE | EXCLUSIVE>
    EVERY <(>[Constant] <DurationLabel><)>
  )
```

or

```
PARTITION BY <RANGE>
  ([ColumnName] <NULLS LAST | NULLS FIRST> ,...)
  (<PARTITION [PartitionName]>
   STARTING <FROM>
       <(> [Start | MINVALUE | MAXVALUE] < ,...)>
       <INCLUSIVE | EXCLUSIVE>
    ENDING <AT>
       <(> [End | MINVALUE | MAXVALUE] < ,...)>
       <INCLUSIVE | EXCLUSIVE>
    <IN [TableSpaceName]>
  )
```

where:

ColumnName   Identifies one or more columns, by name, whose values are to be used to determine which data partition a particular row is to be stored in. (The group of columns specified make up the partitioning key for the table.)

PartitionName   Identifies the unique name that is to be assigned to the data partition to be created.

Start   Specifies the low end of the range for each data partition.

End   Specifies the high end of the range for each data partition.

Constant Specifies the width of each data-partition range when the automatically generated form of the syntax is used. Data partitions will be created starting at the STARTING FROM value and will contain this number of values in the range. This form of the syntax is supported only if the partitioning key is made up of a single column that has been assigned a numeric, date, time, or timestamp data type.

DurationLabel Identifies the duration that is associated with the *Constant* value specified if the partitioning key column has been assigned a date, time, or timestamp data type. The following values are valid for this parameter: YEAR, YEARS, MONTH, MONTHS, DAY, DAYS, HOUR, HOURS, MINUTE, MINUTES, SECOND, SECONDS, MICROSECOND, and MICROSECONDS.

TableSpaceName Identifies the table space in which each data partition is to be stored.

Thus, if you wanted to create a table named SALES that is partitioned such that each quarter's data is stored in a different data partition, and each partition resides in a different table space, you could do so by executing a CREATE TABLE SQL statement that looks something like this:

```
CREATE TABLE sales
    (sales_date      DATE,
     sales_amt       NUMERIC(5,2))
    IN tbsp0, tbsp1, tbsp2, tbsp3
    PARTITION BY RANGE (sales_date NULLS FIRST)
        (STARTING '1/1/2007' ENDING '12/31/2007'
         EVERY 3 MONTHS)
```

On the other hand, if you wanted to create a table named DEPARTMENTS that is partitioned such that rows with numerical values that fall in the range of 0 to 9 are stored in one partition that resides in one table space, rows with numerical values that fall in the range of 10 to 19 are stored in another partition that resides in another table space, and so on, you could do so by executing a CREATE TABLE SQL statement that looks something like this:

```
CREATE TABLE departments
    (dept_no    INT
     desc       CHAR(3))
    PARTITION BY (dept_no NULLS FIRST)
        (STARTING   0 ENDING  9 IN tbsp0,
         STARTING  10 ENDING 19 IN tbsp1,
         STARTING  20 ENDING 29 IN tbsp2,
         STARTING  30 ENDING 39 IN tbsp3)
```

It is important to note that when an index is created for a range-partitioned table, the data for that index will be stored in the table space that is used to hold the first partition's data, unless otherwise specified. For example, suppose the following CREATE INDEX SQL statement is used to create an index for the DEPARTMENTS table just created:

```
CREATE INDEX dept_idx ON departments (dept_no)
```

After this statement is executed, data for the index named DEPT_IDX will be stored in the table space named TBSP0. If you wanted the index data to be stored in the table space that is used to hold the last partition's data (the table space named TBSP3), the following CREATE INDEX SQL statement would have to be executed instead:

```
CREATE INDEX dept_idx ON departments (dept_no) IN tbsp3
```

Working with XML Data

DB2 9's pureXML technology unlocks the latent potential of XML by providing simple efficient access to XML data with the same levels of security, integrity, and resiliency taken for granted with relational data. DB2's pureXML technology is available as an add-on feature to DB2 Express Edition, DB2 Workgroup Server Edition, and DB2 Enterprise Server Edition; however, it is part of DB2 Express-C, and the use of pureXML is included in the base DB2 Express-C license. With pureXML, XML data is stored in a hierarchical structure that naturally reflects the structure of XML documents. This structure, along with innovative indexing techniques, allows DB2 to efficiently manage XML data while eliminating the complex and time-consuming parsing that is typically required to store XML data in a relational database. However, there are some restrictions when it comes to using pureXML:

- pureXML can be used only with single-partition databases.

- The use of any pureXML feature will prevent future use of the database-partitioning feature (DPF) that is available with DB2 Enterprise Server Edition (ESE).

- pureXML cannot be used with DB2 Data Warehouse Edition (DWE) because DWE uses DB2 ESE and DPF.

In order to make use of the pureXML feature, a database must be created using the UTF-8 codeset. The UTF-8 codeset is specified through the USING CODESET option of the CREATE DATABASE command; to create a database named XML_DB with a UTF-8 code set, you would execute a CREATE DATABASE command that looks something like this:

```
CREATE DATABASE xml_db USING CODESET UTF-8 TERRITORY US
```

The XML Data Type and XML Columns

To support pureXML, a new data type called XML was introduced with DB2 9. This data type is used to define columns that will be used to store XML values. Each XML value stored must be a well-formed XML document; a well-formed XML document looks something like this:

```
<?xml version="1.0" encoding="UTF-8" ?>
<customerinfo xmlns="http://crecord.dat" id="1000">
   <name>John Doe</name>
   <addr country="United States">
     <street>25 East Creek Drive</street>
     <city>Raleigh</city>
     <state-prov>North Carolina</state-prov>
     <zip-pcode>27603</zip-pcode>
   </addr>
   <phone type="work">919-555-1212</phone>
   <email>john.doe@xyz.com</email>
</customerinfo>
```

Most XML documents begin with an XML declaration; an XML declaration looks something like this:

```
<?xml version="1.0" encoding="UTF-8" ?>
```

or

```
<?xml version="1.0"?>
```

The XML declaration is followed by one or more attributes and elements. All XML elements are enclosed with opening and closing tags; XML elements look something like this:

```
<p>This is a paragraph</p>
<p>This is another paragraph</p>
```

It is important to note that the opening and closing tags used are case sensitive—the tag <Letter> is different from the tag <letter>. Therefore, opening and closing tags must be written with the same case.

XML attributes are normally used to describe XML elements or to provide additional information about an element. Attributes are always contained within the start tag of an element, and attribute values must always be quoted. Here are some examples:

```
<file type="gif">
```

```
<person id="3344">
```

Attributes are handy in HTML, but in XML you should try to avoid them whenever the same information can be expressed using elements. The following examples convey the same information:

```
<person sex="female">
    <firstname>Anna</firstname>
    <lastname>Smith</lastname>
</person>

<person>
    <sex>female</sex>
    <firstname>Anna</firstname>
    <lastname>Smith</lastname>
</person>
```

In the first example, SEX is an attribute. In the last example SEX is an element.

To create tables with XML columns, you specify columns with the XML data type in the CREATE TABLE statement. (A table can have one or more XML columns.) Like an LOB column, an XML column holds only a descriptor of the column. The data itself is stored separately. Unlike a LOB column, you do not specify a length when you define an XML column. So to create a table named CUSTOMER that contains an XML column named CUSTINFO, you would execute a CREATE TABLE statement that looks like this:

```
CREATE TABLE customer
    (custid    INTEGER NOT NULL,
     custinfo XML)
```

XML columns have the following restrictions:

- They cannot have a default value specified by the WITH DEFAULT clause; if the column is nullable, the default for the column is NULL.

- They cannot be referenced in CHECK constraints (except when a VALIDATED predicate is used).

- They cannot be referenced in generated columns.

- They cannot be included in typed tables and typed views.

- They cannot be used in a range-clustered table (RCT).

- They cannot be used in a range-partitioned table.

- They cannot be used in a multidimensional clustering (MDC) table.

- They cannot be added to tables that have Type-1 indexes defined on them (note that Type-1 indexes are deprecated indexes; indexes created since DB2 UDB Version 8.1 are Type-2 indexes).

- They cannot be specified in the select-list of scrollable cursors.

- They cannot be referenced in the triggered action of a CREATE TRIGGER statement.

- They cannot be included as columns of keys, including primary, foreign, and unique keys; dimension keys of multidimensional clustering (MDC) tables; sequence keys of range-clustered tables; distribution keys; and data-partitioning keys.

- They cannot be used in a table with a distribution key.

- They cannot be part of any index except an index over XML data.

- They cause data blocking to be disabled when retrieving XML data.

- They cannot be compressed using data row compression.

Manipulating XML Data

Like traditional data, XML documents can be added to a database table, altered, removed, and retrieved using SQL Data Manipulation Language statements (INSERT, UPDATE, DELETE, and SELECT statements). Typically, XML documents (as defined in the XML 1.0 specification) are manipulated by application programs; when DML operations from an application program are performed, IBM recommends that XML data be manipulated through host variables, rather than literals, so that DB2 can use the host variable data type to determine some of the encoding information needed for processing. And although you can manipulate XML data using XML, binary, or character types, IBM recommends that you use XML or binary types to avoid code page conversion issues.

XML data used in an application is often stored in a serialized string format—when this data is inserted into an XML column or when data in an XML column is updated, it must be converted to its XML hierarchical format. If the application data type used is an XML data type, DB2 performs this operation implicitly. However, if the application data type is a character or binary data type, the XMLPARSE() function must be used to explicitly convert the data from its serialized string format to the XML hierarchical format during insert and update operations. A simple INSERT statement that uses the XMLPARSE() function to insert a string value into an XML column named CUSTINFO in a table named CUSTOMERS might look something like this:

```
INSERT INTO customers (custinfo) VALUES
    (XMLPARSE(DOCUMENT '<name>John Doe</name>'
     PRESERVE WHITESPACE))
```

When the Command Line Processor is used to manipulate XML documents stored in XML columns, string data can be directly assigned to XML columns without an explicit call to the XMLPARSE() function when insert, update, and delete operations are performed. For example, let's say you want to add a record containing XML data to a table named CUSTOMER that has the following characteristics:

Column Name	Data Type
CUSTID	INTEGER
INFO	XML

You could do so by executing an INSERT statement from the Command Line Processor that looks something like this:

```
INSERT INTO customer VALUES (1000,
'<customerinfo xmlns="http://custrecord.dat"custid="1000">
  <name>John Doe</name>
  <addr country="United States">
    <street>25 East Creek Drive</street>
    <city>Raleigh</city>
    <state-prov>North Carolina</state-prov>
    <zip-pcode>27603</zip-pcode>
  </addr>
  <phone type="work">919-555-1212</phone>
  <email>john.doe@xyz.com</email>
</customerinfo>')
```

And if you wanted to update the XML data portion of this record from the Command Line Processor, you could do so by executing an UPDATE statement that looks something like this:

```
UPDATE customer SET custinfo =
'<customerinfo xmlns="http://custrecord.dat" custid="1000">
  <name>Jane Doe</name>
  <addr country="Canada">
    <street>25 East Creek Drive</street>
    <city>Raleigh</city>
    <state-prov>North Carolina</state-prov>
    <zip-pcode>27603</zip-pcode>
  </addr>
  <phone type="work">919-555-1212</phone>
  <email>jane.doe@xyz.com</email>
</customerinfo>'
WHERE XMLEXISTS ('declare default element namespace "http://custrecord.dat";
$info/customerinfo[name/text()="John Doe"]' PASSING custinfo as "info")
```

Finally, if you wanted to delete the record from the CUSTOMER table, you could do so by executing a DELETE statement from the Command Line Processor that looks something like this:

```
DELETE FROM customer
WHERE XMLEXISTS ('declare default element namespace "http://custrecord.dat";
$info/customerinfo[name/text()="John Doe"]' PASSING custinfo as "info")
```

So how do you retrieve XML data once it has been stored in a table? With DB2 9, XML data can be retrieved using an SQL query or one of the SQL/XML query functions available. When querying XML data using SQL, you can retrieve data only at the column level—in other words, an entire XML document must be retrieved. It is not possible to return fragments of a document using SQL; to query within XML documents, you need to use XQuery.

XQuery is a functional programming language that was designed by the World Wide Web Consortium (W3C) to meet specific requirements for querying XML data. Unlike relational data, which is predictable and has a regular structure, XML data is often unpredictable, highly variable, sparse, and self-describing. Because the structure of XML data is unpredictable, the queries that are performed on XML data often differ from typical relational queries. For example, you might need to create XML queries that perform the following operations:

- Search XML data for objects that are at unknown levels of the hierarchy.

- Perform structural transformations on the data (for example, you might want to invert a hierarchy).

- Return results that have mixed types.

In XQuery, expressions are the main building blocks of a query. Expressions can be nested, and they form the body of a query. A query can also have a prolog that contains a series of declarations that define the processing environment for the query. Thus, if you wanted to retrieve customer names for all customers who reside in North Carolina from XML documents stored in the CUSTINFO column of a table named CUSTOMER (assuming this table has been populated with the INSERT statement we looked at earlier), you could do so by executing an XQuery expression that looks something like this:

```
XQUERY declare default element namespace "http://custrecord.dat"; for
$info in db2-fn:xmlcolumn('CUSTOMER.CUSTINFO')/customerinfo where
$info/addr/state-prov="North Carolina" return $info/name
```

And when this XQuery expression is executed from the Command Line Processor, it should return information that looks like this (again, assuming this table has been populated with the INSERT statement we looked at earlier):

```
1
---------------------------------------------------------------------
<name xmlns="http://custrecord.dat">John Doe</name>
```

If you wanted to remove the XML tags and just return the customer name, you could do so by executing an XQuery expression that looks like this instead:

```
XQUERY declare default element namespace "http://custrecord.dat"; for
$info in db2-fn:xmlcolumn('CUSTOMER.CUSTINFO')/customerinfo where
$info/addr/state-prov="North Carolina" return $info/name/text()
```

Now when the XQuery expression is executed from the Command Line Processor, it should return information that looks like this:

```
1
---------------------------------------------------------------------
John Doe
```

As mentioned previously, XQuery expressions can be invoked from SQL using any of the following SQL/XML functions or predicates:

XMLQUERY(). XMLQUERY() is an SQL scalar function that enables you to execute an XQuery expression from within an SQL context. XMLQUERY() returns an XML value, which is an XML sequence. This sequence can be empty, or it can contain one or more items. You can also pass variables to the XQuery expression specified in XMLQUERY().

XMLTABLE(). XMLTABLE() is an SQL table function that returns a table from the evaluation of XQuery expressions. XQuery expressions normally return values as a sequence; however, XMLTABLE() allows you to execute an XQuery expression and return values as a table instead. The table that is returned can contain columns of any SQL data type, including XML. The structure of the resulting table is defined by the COLUMNS clause of XMLTABLE().

XMLEXISTS. The XMLEXISTS predicate determines whether an XQuery expression returns a sequence of one or more items. If the XQuery expression specified in this predicate returns an empty sequence, XMLEXISTS returns FALSE; otherwise, TRUE is returned. The XMLEXISTS predicate can be used in the WHERE clauses of UPDATE, DELETE, and SELECT statements. This usage means that values from stored XML documents can be used to restrict the set of rows that a DML statement operates on.

By executing XQuery expressions from within the SQL context, you can

- operate on parts of stored XML documents, instead of entire XML documents (only XQuery can query within an XML document; SQL alone queries at the whole document level);

- enable XML data to participate in SQL queries;

- operate on both relational and XML data; and

- apply further SQL processing to the returned XML values (for example, ordering results with the ORDER BY clause of a subselect).

Suppose you wanted to retrieve customer IDs and customer names for a table named CUSTOMER that has the following characteristics:

Column Name	Data Type
CUSTID	INTEGER
INFO	XML

You could do so (assuming this table has been populated with the INSERT statement we looked at earlier) by executing a SELECT statement from the Command Line Processor that looks something like this:

```
SELECT custid, XMLQUERY ('declare default element namespace
"http://custrecord.dat"; $d/customerinfo/name' passing CUSTINFO as "d") AS
address
FROM customer;
```

And when this query is executed, it should return information that looks something like this:

```
CUSTID ADDRESS
------ -----------------------------------------------------
1000   <name xmlns="http://custrecord.dat">John Doe</name>
```

XML Indexes

Just as an index over relational data can be used to improve query performance, an index over XML data can be used to improve the efficiency of queries on XML documents that are stored in an XML column. In contrast to traditional relational indexes, where index keys are composed of one or more columns that you specify, an index over XML data uses a particular XML pattern expression to index paths and values found in XML documents stored in a single column. The data type of that column must be XML.

To identify those parts of the document that will be indexed, an XML pattern is used to specify a set of nodes within the XML document. This pattern expression is similar to the path expression defined in the XQuery language, but it differs in that only a subset of the XQuery language is supported. Path expression steps are separated by the forward slash (/). The double forward slash (//)—which is the abbreviated syntax for /descendant-or-self::node()—may also be specified. In each step, a forward axis (child::, @, attribute::, descendant::, self::, and descendant-or-self::) is chosen, followed by an XML name or XML kind test. If no forward axis is specified, the child axis is used as the default. Figure 3–12 shows a simple XML pattern and how it is used to identify a specific value within an XML document.

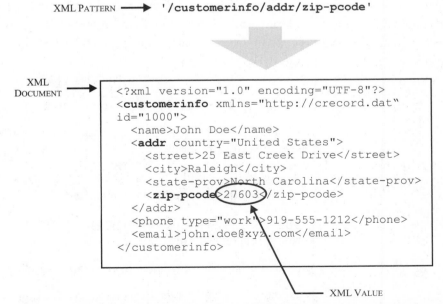

Figure 3–12: How an XML pattern is used to identify a specific value within an XML document.

Instead of providing access to the beginning of a document, index entries in an index over XML data provide access to nodes within the document by creating index keys based on XML pattern expressions. And because multiple parts of an XML document can satisfy an XML pattern, multiple index keys may be inserted into the index for a single document.

XML indexes are created by specifying the GENERATE KEY USING XMLPATTERN clause of the CREATE INDEX SQL statement. The basic syntax for this optional clause is:

```
GENERATE KEY USING XMLPATTERN
<Namespace>
[XMLPattern]
AS  [SQLDataType]
```

where:

Namespace   Identifies a valid namespace declaration that is used to identify namespace prefixes when qualified names are used in the pattern expression specified.

XMLPattern   Specifies a pattern expression that identifies the nodes that are to be indexed. The pattern expression provided can contain any of the following XQuery components:

- * (asterisk)—Specifies a pattern-matching character.

- / (forward slash)—Separates path expression steps.

- // (double forward slash)—The abbreviated syntax for /descendant-or-self::node()/..

- child::—Specifies children of the context node. This is the default if no other forward axis is specified.

- @—Specifies attributes of the context node. This is the abbreviated syntax for attribute::.

- attribute::—Specifies attributes of the context node.

- descendant::—Specifies the descendants of the context node.

- self::—Specifies just the context node itself.

- descendant-or-self::—Specifies the context node and the descendants of the context node.

SQLDataType   Specifies the SQL data type to which indexed values are converted before they are stored. The following values are valid for this parameter: VARCHAR(*Size*), DOUBLE, DATE, and TIMESTAMP.

Thus, if you wanted to create an XML index using postal/zip code values found in an XML column named CUSTINFO in a table named CUSTOMER and to store those values as DOUBLE values, you could do so by executing a CREATE INDEX statement that looks something like this:

```
CREATE INDEX custindex ON customer(custinfo)
GENERATE KEY
USING XMLPATTERN '/customerinfo/addr/zip-pcode'
AS SQL DOUBLE;
```

On the other hand, if you wanted to create an XML index using address information found in an XML column named CUSTINFO in a table named CUSTOMER and to store those values as VARCHAR values, you could do so by executing a CREATE INDEX statement that looks something like this:

```
CREATE INDEX custindex ON customer(custinfo)
GENERATE KEY
USING XMLPATTERN /customerinfo/@addr'
AS SQL VARCHAR(100);
```

In the first example, the index is created for an element; in the second, it is created for an attribute. Although it is possible to create XML indexes on attributes (or on the entire document, for that matter), performance can suffer. Therefore, it is usually better to create XML indexes on individual elements within an XML document.

Data Row Compression

Along with table partitioning and pureXML, one of the most prominent features introduced in DB2 9 is the ability to reduce the amount of storage needed to store table data using what is known as data row compression. Although the primary purpose of data row compression is to save storage space, it can lead to significant disk I/O savings and higher buffer pool hit ratios as well. (More data can be cached in memory.) All of this can lead to an increase in performance, but not without some cost—extra CPU cycles are needed to compress and decompress the data. The storage savings and performance impact of data row compression are tied directly to the characteristics of the data within the database, the design of the database itself, how well the database has been tuned, and application workloads.

As the volume of data increases, the cardinality of that data tends to drop. As it turns out, there just are not that many truly "unique" things in the world. They may be unique when used in combination, but the basic elements themselves are not all that varied. Consider the periodic table of elements—everything in our world is made up of combinations of this rather small set of elements. Apply the concept to data, and you find the same is true. For instance, according to the last U.S. census, there are about 300 million people in living in the United States of America. But there are only approximately 78,800 unique last names, resulting in very low cardinality with huge "clumps" in certain name sets. First names are even worse, coming in at around 6,600 (4,400 unique first names for females and 2,200 for males). The names of cities, streets, and addresses, as well as product names, descriptions, and attributes, also tend to be highly redundant with low cardinality.

Data row compression works by searching for repeating patterns in the data and replacing the patterns with 12-bit symbols, which are stored along with the pattern they represent in a static dictionary. (Once this dictionary is created, it is stored in the table along with the compressed data and is loaded into memory whenever data in the table is accessed to aid in decompression.) This is done by scanning an entire table and looking for repeating column values, as well as repeating patterns that span multiple columns in a row. DB2 also looks for repeating patterns that are substrings of a given column. However, just because a repeating pattern is found does not mean that the data is automatically compressed—data is compressed only where storage savings will be realized. Figure 3–13 illustrates how data row compression works.

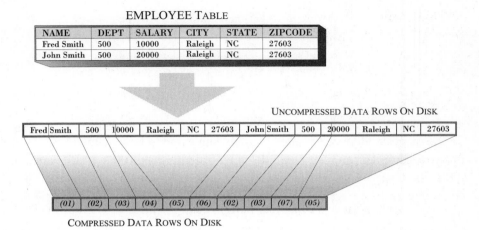

EMPLOYEE TABLE

NAME	DEPT	SALARY	CITY	STATE	ZIPCODE
Fred Smith	500	10000	Raleigh	NC	27603
John Smith	500	20000	Raleigh	NC	27603

UNCOMPRESSED DATA ROWS ON DISK

| Fred | Smith | 500 | 10000 | Raleigh | NC | 27603 | John | Smith | 500 | 20000 | Raleigh | NC | 27603 |

| (01) | (02) | (03) | (04) | (05) | (06) | (02) | (03) | (07) | (05) |

COMPRESSED DATA ROWS ON DISK

COMPRESSION DICTIONARY

SYMBOL	PATTERN
01	Fred
02	Smith
03	500
04	1
05	0000 Raleigh NC 27603
06	John
07	2

Figure 3–13: How data row compression works.

In order to use data row compression with a table, two prerequisites must be satisfied:

1. Compression must be enabled at the table level.

2. A compression dictionary for the table must be built.

Enabling a Table for Data Row Compression

Compression is enabled at the table level by executing either the CREATE TABLE SQL statement or the ALTER TABLE statement with the COMPRESS YES option specified. For example, if you wanted to create a new table named EMPLOYEE and enable it for data row compression, you could do so by executing a CREATE TABLE statement that looks something like this:

```
CREATE TABLE   employee
   (name        VARCHAR(60),
    dept        CHAR(3),
    salary      DECIMAL(7,2),
    city        VARCHAR(25),
    state       CHAR(2),
    zipcode     VARCHAR(10))
COMPRESS YES
```

On the other hand, if you wanted to enable an existing table named EMPLOYEE for data row compression, you could do so by executing an ALTER TABLE statement that looks like this:

```
ALTER TABLE employee COMPRESS YES
```

Building a Compression Dictionary

Although you can enable a table for data row compression at any time by setting its COMPRESS attribute to YES, data stored in the table will not be compressed until a compression dictionary has been built. A compression dictionary is built (and data in a table is compressed) through an offline table reorganization operation; such an operation is initiated by executing the REORG command with either the KEEPDICTIONARY or the RESETDICTIONARY option specified. If the REORG command is executed with either option specified, and a compression dictionary does not exist, a new dictionary will be built; if the REORG command is executed with either option specified, and a dictionary already exists, data in the table will be reorganized/compressed, and the existing dictionary will either be recreated (RESETDICTIONARY) or left as it is (KEEPDICTIONARY).

Thus, if you wanted to create a new compression dictionary (and compress the existing data) for a table named EMPLOYEE that has been enabled for data row compression, you could do so by executing a REORG command that looks like this:

```
REORG TABLE employee RESETDICTIONARY
```

When this command is executed, data stored in the EMPLOYEE table will be analyzed, a compression dictionary will be constructed and stored at the beginning of the table, and the data will be compressed and written to the table directly behind the compression dictionary. Figure 3–14 illustrates how the EMPLOYEE table would look before and after data row compression is applied.

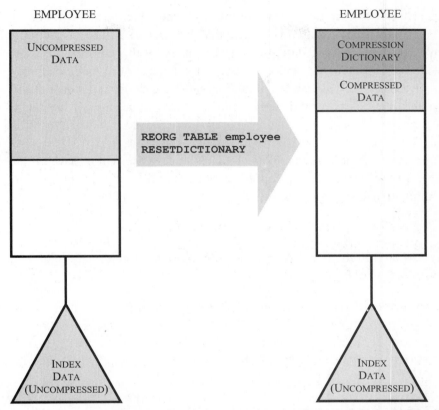

Figure 3–14: How data in a table is altered when a compression dictionary is built and data row compression is applied.

It is important to note that index data is not affected by data row compression; only data stored on a page in a base table can be compressed. However, because records in a compressed table are moved between storage and memory in compressed form (the compression dictionary is moved into memory as well so that decompression can take place), records for compressed tables that are written to transaction log files will be compressed as well.

Estimating Storage Savings from Data Row Compression

Because an offline reorganization operation is needed to construct a compression dictionary and perform data compression, the initial overhead required to compress data can be quite high. Therefore, it can be beneficial to know which tables will benefit the most from data row compression and which tables will not. In DB2 9, the Inspect utility can help you make that determination. The Inspect utility is invoked by executing the INSPECT command, and if this command is executed with the ROWCOMPESTIMATE option specified, the Inspect utility will examine each row in the table specified, build a compression dictionary from the data found, and then use this dictionary to estimate how much space will be saved if the data in the table is compressed.

Thus, if you want to estimate how much storage space will be saved if the data in a table named EMPLOYEE is compressed, you could do so by executing an INSPECT command that looks something like this:

```
INSPECT ROWCOMPESTIMATE TABLE NAME employee
```

And when this command is executed, the information returned might look something like this:

```
DATABASE: TEST
VERSION: SQL09000
2007-06-06-12.35.58.14.296000

Action: ROWCOMPESTIMATE TABLE
Schema name: PAYROLL
Table name: EMPLOYEE
Tablespace ID: 4 Object ID: 6
Result file name: emp
   Table phase start (ID Signed: 6, Unsigned: 6; Tablespace
      ID:4) PAYROLL.EMPLOYEE
   Data phase start. Object: 6 Tablespace : 4
   Row compression estimate results:
   Percentage of pages saved from compression: 46
   Percentage of bytes saved from compression: 46
   Percentage of rows ineligible for compression due to
      smallrow size: 0
   Compression dictionary size: 13312 bytes.
   Expansion dictionary size: 10240 bytes.
   Data phase end.
   Table phase end.
```

If a table is enabled for data row compression (i.e., the COMPRESS attribute is set to YES) before the INSPECT command is executed, the compression dictionary that is built and used to estimate space savings will be written to the table, at the end of the existing data. Figure 3–15 illustrates how a table would look before and after the Inspect utility was used to estimate storage savings if it was enabled for data row compression before the estimate was acquired.

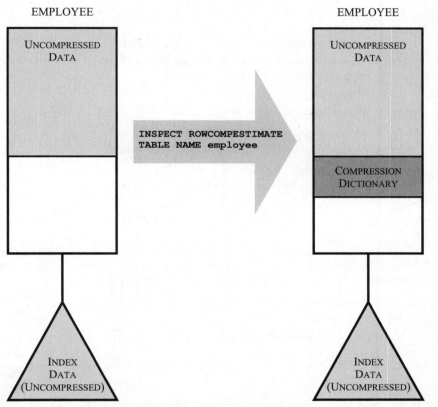

Figure 3–15: How data in a table is altered when a table that has been enabled for data row compression is evaluated by the Inspect utility.

Once a data compression dictionary has been created and written to a table that has been enabled for data row compression, new records added to that table will automatically be compressed. The same is true for existing records that are modified. However, if the compression dictionary for a table was created by the Inspect utility, preexisting data in the table will remain uncompressed until an offline reorganization operation is performed.

Practice Questions

Question 1

An instance named DB2INST1 exists on a server and the DFTDBPATH Database Manager configuration parameter for that instance contains the value "/home". If no databases exist on the server and the following command is executed:

    CREATE DATABASE my_db

Where will the metadata files for the database reside?

- ○ A. In the /home/NODE0000/SQL00001 subdirectory
- ⊘ B. In the /home/db2inst1/NODE0000/SQL00001 subdirectory
- ○ C. In the /home/NODE0000/MY_DB subdirectory
- ○ D. In the /home/db2inst1/NODE0000/MY_DB subdirectory

Question 2

Which of the following features is NOT automatically enabled when a new DB2 9 database is created?

- ○ A. Automatic maintenance
- ○ B. Self tuning memory manager
- ⊘ C. Data row compression
- ○ D. Utility throttling

Question 3

If the following CREATE DATABASE command is executed:

    CREATE DATABASE sales ON C: USING CODESET UTF-8 TERRITORY US
    RESTRICTIVE

Which of the following privileges will be automatically granted to the group PUBLIC?

- ⊘ A. No privileges are granted
- ○ B. CONNECT, CREATETAB, BINDADD, and IMPLICIT_SCHEMA privileges on the database
- ○ C. SELECT privilege on each system catalog table
- ○ D. EXECUTE privilege on all procedures found in the SYSIBM schema

Question 4

If the following CREATE DATABASE command is executed:

```
CREATE DATABASE sales ON /mnt/data1, /mnt/data2
COLLATE USING IDENTITY
CATALOG TABLESPACE MANAGED BY SYSTEM USING ('mnt/syscat');
```

Which of the following statements is NOT true about the resulting database?

- ○ A. Automatic storage is enabled for the database
- ○ B. An SMS table space will be used to hold the system catalog
- ○ C. User data will be stored on /mnt/data1 and /mnt/data2
- ☑ D. Metadata for the database will be stored on /mnt/data2

Question 5

If the following CREATE TABLESPACE statement is executed:

```
CREATE REGULAR TABLESPACE sales_ts
PAGESIZE 4096
MANAGED BY DATABASE USING
    (FILE 'D:\tbsp1.tsf' 10 G, FILE 'D:\tbsp2.tsf' 6 G,
FILE 'D:\tbsp3.tsf' 4 G)
EXTENTSIZE 32
PREFETCHSIZE 96
```

What is the maximum amount of data that can be stored in the SALES_TS table space?

- ○ A. 10 GB
- ☑ B. 12 GB
- ○ C. 16 GB
- ○ D. 20 GB

Question 6

Which of the following is NOT a true statement about SMS table spaces?

- ○ A. Regular data and long data cannot be split across multiple table spaces.
- ○ B. Storage space is allocated by the operating system as it is needed.
- ☑ C. Containers can be added to or deleted from existing table spaces using the ALTER TABLESPACE command.
- ○ D. Only directory containers can be used for storage; file and device containers cannot be used.

Question 7

If the following CREATE TABLESPACE statement is executed:

```
CREATE REGULAR TABLESPACE sales_ts
PAGESIZE 8 K
MANAGED BY SYSTEM USING
    ('/mnt/data1','/mnt/data2', '/mnt/data3')
EXTENTSIZE 32
PREFETCHSIZE 128
```

How much space does DB2 allocate for the SALES_TS table space when all existing pages in the table space become full?

- ○ A.   8 KB
- ○ B.   32 KB
- ○ C.   128 KB
- ○ D.   256 KB   _SnS = 1 EXTENT = 32 × 8_

Question 8

Which two of the following commands can be used to obtain detailed information, including status, about all table spaces that have been created for a database named SALES?

- ❑ A.   SELECT * FROM syscat.tablespaces
- ☑ B.   LIST TABLESPACES SHOW DETAIL
- ❑ C.   LIST TABLESPACE CONTAINERS SHOW DETAIL
- ☑ D.   GET SNAPSHOT FOR TABLESPACES ON sales
- ❑ E.   GET SNAPSHOT FOR TABLESPACE CONTAINERS ON sales

Question 9

Which of the following is NOT a valid table space state?

- ○ A.   Load pending
- ◉ B.   Online and not accessible
- ○ C.   Load in progress
- ○ D.   Offline and not accessible

Question 10

If the following CREATE DATABASE command is executed:

    CREATE DATABASE payroll ON C:

Which of the following commands will add new storage containers to the PAYROLL database?

- ○ A. ALTER TABLESPACE ADD STORAGE D:\data1, D:\data2
- ◉ B. ALTER DATABASE ADD STORAGE D:\data1, D:\data2
- ○ C. ALTER TABLESPACE ADD CONTAINERS D:\data1, D:\data2
- ○ D. ALTER DATABASE ADD CONTAINERS D:\data1, D:\data2

Question 11

Which of the following options can be specified with the CREATE TABLESPACE statement to create a DMS table space that can automatically expand beyond its original storage definition?

- ◉ A. AUTORESIZE YES
- ○ B. RESIZE YES
- ○ C. EXTEND YES
- ○ D. EXPAND YES

Question 12

Given the following CREATE TABLESPACE statement:

    CREATE REGULAR TABLESPACE payroll_ts
    MANAGED BY AUTOMATIC STORAGE
    EXTENTSIZE 32
    PREFETCHSIZE 128

Which of the following statements is NOT true?

- ○ A. When created, the PAYROLL_TS table space will be a DMS table space with file containers.
- ○ B. The database the PAYROLL_TS table space is to be created for must be enabled for automatic storage.
- ◉ C. When created, the PAYROLL_TS table space will be an SMS table space with directory containers.
- ○ D. The MANAGED BY AUTOMATIC STORAGE clause is unnecessary and could have been left out of the CREATE TABLESPACE command.

Question 13

Which of the following is NOT true about Global Temporary Tables?

- ○ A. Indexes can be created on Global Temporary Tables
- ○ B. Global Temporary Tables reside in user temporary table spaces
- ○ C. Statistics can be collected on Global Temporary Tables
- ◉ D. Global Temporary Tables are visible to all users connected to a database

Question 14

A user named USER1 logs on to an AIX server and connects to a database named SALES that belongs to an instance named DB2INST1 by executing the following command:

    CONNECT TO sales USER db2admin USING ibmdb2;

After connecting to the database, user USER1 creates a table by executing the following statement:

    CREATE TABLE test_tab (col1 INTEGER, col2 CHAR(12));

Assuming the CREATE TABLE statement executed successfully, what schema was the table TEST_TAB created in?

- ○ A. ROOT
- ○ B. DB2INST1
- ○ C. USER1
- ◉ D. DB2ADMIN

Question 15

Which of the following statements about schema objects is NOT true?

- ○ A. After connecting to a new database, all users who have successfully authenticated with the server have the ability to create a new schema.
- ◉ B. Like table spaces, schemas are used to physically group and store objects in a database.
- ○ C. If a schema is explicitly created with the CREATE SCHEMA statement, the schema owner is granted CREATEIN, DROPIN, and ALTERIN privileges on the schema, as well as the ability to grant these privileges to other users.
- ○ D. Ownership of a schema that is explicitly created can be assigned during the creation process.

Question 16

Which of the following is NOT a true statement about range-clustered tables?

☑ A.   Range-clustered tables require less buffer cache because they rely on a special index for organizing data.

◯ B.   Storage for a range-clustered table must be pre-allocated and available when the table is created.

◯ C.   Range-clustered tables can result in significant performance advantages during query processing because fewer input/output (I/O) operations are needed.

◯ D.   Range-clustered tables are created by specifying the ORGANIZE BY KEY SEQUENCE clause with a CREATE TABLE statement.

Question 17

Which of the following statements will create a table named PARTS that is partitioned such that rows with part numbers that fall in the range of 0 to 33 are stored in one partition that resides in one table space, rows with part numbers in the range of 34 to 66 are stored in another partition that resides in another table space, and rows with part numbers in the range of 67 to 99 are stored in a third partition that resides in a third table space?

◯ A.   CREATE TABLE parts (partno INT, desc VARCHAR(25))
        IN tbsp0, tbsp1, tbsp2
        PARTITION BY (partno NULLS FIRST)
            (STARTING 0 ENDING 33,
            STARTING 34 ENDING 66,
            STARTING 67 ENDING 99)

◯ B.   CREATE TABLE parts (partno INT, desc VARCHAR(25))
        PARTITION BY (partno NULLS FIRST)
            (PART part0 STARTING   0 ENDING 33,
            PART part1 STARTING 34 ENDING 66,
            PART part2 STARTING 67 ENDING 99)

◯ C.   CREATE TABLE parts (partno INT, desc VARCHAR(25))
        PARTITION BY (partno NULLS FIRST
            (STARTING   0 ENDING 33,
            STARTING 34 ENDING 66,
            STARTING 67 ENDING 99)
            IN tbsp0, tbsp1, tbsp2)

☑ D.   CREATE TABLE parts (partno INT, desc VARCHAR(25))
        PARTITION BY (partno NULLS FIRST)
            (STARTING 0 ENDING 33 IN tbsp0,
            STARTING 34 ENDING 66 IN tbsp1,
            STARTING 67 ENDING 99 IN tbsp2)

Question 18

If the following statements are executed in the order shown:

```
CREATE TABLE sales
    (invoice_no      INTEGER,
     sales_date      DATE,
     sales_amt       NUMERIC(5,2))
    IN tbsp0, tbsp1, tbsp2, tbsp3
    PARTITION BY RANGE (sales_date NULLS FIRST)
        (STARTING '1/1/2006' ENDING '12/31/2006'
          EVERY 3 MONTHS);
CREATE INDEX sales_idx ON sales (invoice_no);
```

Which of the following table spaces will contain the data for the SALES_IDX index?

☑ A. TBSP0

○ B. TBSP1

○ C. TBSP2

○ D. TBSP3

Question 19

Which of the following statements about XML indexes is true?

○ A. XML indexes can contain relational data columns.

☑ B. An index over XML data can be used to improve the efficiency of XQuery expressions performed against XML columns.

○ C. Unique XML indexes can be created by combining multiple XML columns.

○ D. The entire contents of an XML document stored in an XML column are indexed.

Question 20

If the following CREATE INDEX statements are executed:

```
CREATE INDEX cust_zip_idx ON customer(custinfo)
GENERATE KEY
USING XMLPATTERN '/customerinfo/addr/zip-pcode'
AS SQL DOUBLE;

CREATE INDEX cust_city_idx ON customer(custinfo)
GENERATE KEY
USING XMLPATTERN '/customerinfo/addr/city'
AS SQL VARCHAR(40);
```

And the following XML documents are inserted into the CUSTOMER table:

```
<?xml version="1.0" encoding="UTF-8" ?>
   <customerinfo xmlns="http://crecord.dat" id="1000">
    <name>John Doe</name>
    <addr country="United States">
       <street>25 East Creek Drive</street>
       <city>Raleigh</city>
       <state-prov>North Carolina</state-prov>
       <zip-pcode>27603</zip-pcode>
    </addr>
    <phone type="work">919-555-1212</phone>
    <email>john.doe@yahoo.com</email>
</customerinfo>

<?xml version="1.0" encoding="UTF-8" ?>
   <customerinfo xmlns="http://crecord.dat" id="1010">
    <name>Jane Smith</name>
    <addr country="United States">
       <street>2120 Stewart Street</street>
       <city></city>
       <state-prov>South Carolina</state-prov>
       <zip-pcode>29501</zip-pcode>
    </addr>
    <phone type="work">843-555-3434</phone>
    <email>jane.smith@aol.com</email>
</customerinfo>
```

How many index keys will be generated?

○ A. 1

○ B. 2

◉ C. 3

○ D. 4

Question 21

In order to use data row compression with a table, which of the following must exist?

○ A.   A compression index

◉ B.   A compression dictionary

○ C.   A user-defined compression algorithm

○ D.   A table that only contains character data type columns

Question 22

Which of the following statements is NOT valid when discussing data row compression?

○ A.   Data row compression can lead to disk I/O savings and improved buffer pool hit ratios.

○ B.   Compressing data at the row level is advantageous because it allows repeating patterns that span multiple columns within a row to be replaced with shorter symbols.

○ C.   Data row compression for a table can be enabled by executing the ALTER TABLE statement with the COMPRESS YES option specified.

◉ D.   Only data in a table enabled for data row compression is compressed; data in corresponding indexes and transaction logs is not compressed.

Question 23

Which two of the following utilities can be used to create a compression dictionary?

☑ A.   reorg

☐ B.   db2pd

☑ C.   inspect

☐ D.   runstats

☐ E.   db2buildcd

Question 24

Which of the following options can be used with the REORG command to construct a new compression dictionary before compressing data stored in a table?

○ A.   KEEPDICTIONARY

◉ B.   RESETDICTIONARY

○ C.   GENERATEDICTIONARY

○ D.   NEWDICTIONARY

Answers

Question 1

The correct answer is **B**. Information about every DB2 9 database created is stored in a special hierarchical directory tree. Where this directory tree is actually created is determined by information provided with the CREATE DATABASE command - if no location information is provided, this directory tree is created in the location specified by the DFTDBPATH DB2 Database Manager configuration parameter associated with the instance the database is being created under. The root directory of this hierarchical tree is assigned the name of the instance the database is associated with. This directory will contain a subdirectory that has been assigned a name corresponding to the partition's node. If the database is a partitioned database, this directory will be named NODExxxx, where xxxx is the unique node number that has been assigned to the partition; if the database is a non-partitioned database, this directory will be named NODE0000. The node-name directory, in turn, will contain one subdirectory for each database that has been created, along with one subdirectory that contains the containers that are used to hold the database's data.

The name assigned to the subdirectory that holds the containers that are used to house the database's data is the same as that specified for the database; the name assigned to the subdirectory that contains the base files for the database corresponds to the database token that is assigned to the database during the creation process (the subdirectory for the first database created will be named SQL00001, the subdirectory for the second database will be named SQL00002, and so on).

Question 2

The correct answer is **C**. Whenever a new DB2 9 database is created, the following features are enabled by default:

- Automatic intenance (database backups, table and index reorganization, data access optimization, and statistics profiling).

- Self tuning memory manager (package cache, locking memory, sort memory, database shared memory, and buffer pool memory)

- Utility throttling

- The Health Monitor

Question 3

The correct answer is **A**. Whenever a new database is created, by default, the following authorities and privileges are granted automatically:

- Database Administrator (DBADM) authority, along with CONNECT, CREATETAB, BINDADD, CREATE_NOT_FENCED, IMPLICIT_SCHEMA, and LOAD privileges, are granted to the user who created the database.

- USE privilege on the table space USERSPACE1 is granted to the group PUBLIC.

- CONNECT, CREATETAB, BINDADD, and IMPLICIT_SCHEMA privileges are granted to the group PUBLIC.

- SELECT privilege on each system catalog table is granted to the group PUBLIC.

- EXECUTE privilege on all procedures found in the SYSIBM schema is granted to the group PUBLIC.

- EXECUTE WITH GRANT privilege on all functions found in the SYSFUN schema is granted to the group PUBLIC.

- BIND and EXECUTE privileges for each successfully bound utility are granted to the group PUBLIC.

However, if the RESTRICTIVE clause is specified with the CREATE DATABASE command, privileges are only granted to the database creator—no privileges are granted to the group PUBLIC.

Question 4

The correct answer is **D**. The syntax for the CREATE DATABASE command used is this example can be broken down into something that looks like this:

```
CREATE [DATABASE | DB] [DatabaseName]
<AUTOMATIC STORAGE [YES | NO]>
<ON [StoragePath ,...] <DBPATH [DBPath]>>
<COLLATE USING [CollateType]>
<CATALOG TABLESPACE [TS_Definition]>
```

where:

DatabaseName	Identifies the unique name that is to be assigned to the database to be created.
StoragePath	If AUTOMATIC STORAGE YES is specified (the default), identifies one or more storage paths that are to be used to hold table space containers used by automatic storage. Otherwise, identifies the location (drive and/or directory) where the directory hierarchy and files associated with the database to be created are to be physically stored.
DBPath	If AUTOMATIC STORAGE YES is specified (the default), identifies the location (drive and/or directory) where the directory hierarchy and metadata files associated with the database to be created are to be physically stored. (If this parameter is not specified and automatic storage is used, the metadata files will be stored in the first storage path specified in the *StoragePath* parameter.)
CollateType	Specifies the collating sequence (i.e., the sequence in which characters are ordered for the purpose of sorting, merging, and making comparisons) that is to be used by the database to be created. The following values are valid for this parameter: COMPATABILITY, IDENTITY, IDENTITY_16BIT, UCA400_NO, UCA400_LSK, UCA400_LTH, NLSCHAR, and SYSTEM.
TS_Definition	Specifies the definition that is to be used to create the table space that will be used to hold the system catalog tables (SYSCATSPACE).

So in this case, automatic storage is enabled by default, and the storage paths /mnt/data1 and /mnt/data2 will be used to hold table space containers used by automatic storage. And since no database path was specified, the metadata files associated with the database will be stored in the first storage path specified (/mnt/data1).

Question 5

The correct answer is **B**. When multiple containers are used with SMS or DMS table spaces, the maximum amount of data that each container can hold is determined by the smallest container used. For example, if a table space uses one container that is 10M in size and a second container that is 12M in size, 2M of the second container will not be useable; the maximum amount of storage available to the table space will be 20M.

In this example, the smallest container used is 4 GB in size so the table space and 3 containers are used so the maximum size is: 3×4 GB = 12 GB.

Question 6

The correct answer is **C**. Additional containers cannot be added to an SMS table space (using the ALTER TABLESPACE SQL statement) once the table space has been created. (Additional containers can be added to a DMS table space after it has been created; when new containers are added, existing data can automatically be rebalanced across the new set of containers to retain optimal I/O efficiency.)

Question 7

The correct answer is **D**. In DB2 9, the initial allocation of space for an object in a DMS table space is two extents; the initial allocation of space for an object in an SMS table space is one extent. In this example, one extent is comprised of thirty-two 8 K pages or 256 KB (8 KB $\times$ 32 = 256 KB).

Question 8

The correct answers are **B** and **D**. Information about all table spaces that have been created for a particular database can be obtained by executing the LIST TABLESPACES command. The syntax for this command is:

```
LIST TABLESPACES
<SHOW DETAIL>
```

If this command is executed without the SHOW DETAIL option specified, the following information will be displayed for every table space that has been created for a database:

- The internal ID that was assigned to the table space when it was created.

- The name that has been assigned to the table space.

- Table space type (SMS table space or DMS table space).

- The type of data the table space is designed to hold (i.e., regular data, large data, or temporary data).

- The current state of the table space.

On the other hand, if the LIST TABLESPACES command is executed with the SHOW DETAIL option specified, the following additional information about each table space is provided:

- **Total number of pages.** The total number of pages the table space is designed to hold. For DMS table spaces, this is the sum of all pages available from all containers associated with the table space. For SMS table spaces, this is the total amount of file space currently being used.

- **Number of useable pages.** The number of pages in the table space that user data can be stored in. For DMS table spaces, this number is calculated by subtracting the number of pages required for overhead from the total number of pages available. For SMS table spaces, this number is equal to the total number of pages the table space is designed to hold.

- **Number of used pages.** The number of pages in the table space that already contain data. (For SMS table spaces, this value is equal to the total number of pages the table space is designed to hold.)

- **Number of free pages.** The number of pages in the table space that are currently empty. (This information is only applicable for DMS table spaces.)

- **High water mark.** The number of pages that mark the current "high water mark" or "end" of the table space's address space (i.e., the page number of the first free page following the last allocated extent of the table space). (This information is only applicable to DMS table spaces.)

- **Page size.** The size, in bytes, that one page of data in the table space will occupy.

- **Extent size.** The number of pages that are contained in one extent of the table space.

- **Prefetch size.** The number of pages of data that will be read from the table space in advance of those pages currently being referenced by a query, in anticipation that they will be needed to resolve the query (prefetched).

- **Number of containers.** The number of containers used by the table space.

- **Minimum recovery time.** The earliest point in time that may be specified if a point-in-time roll-forward recovery operation is to be performed on the table space.

- **State change table space ID.** The ID of the table space that caused the table space being queried to be placed in the "Load Pending" or "Delete Pending" state. (This information is only displayed if the table space being queried has been placed in the "Load Pending" or "Delete Pending" state.)

- **State change object ID.** The ID of the object that caused the table space being queried to be placed in the "Load Pending" or "Delete Pending" state. (This information is only displayed if the table space being queried has been placed in the "Load Pending" or "Delete Pending" state.)

- **Number of quiescers.** The number of users and/or applications that have placed the table space in a "Quiesced" (restricted access) state. (This information is only displayed if the table space being queried has been placed in the "Quiesced:SHARE", "Quiesced:UPDATE" or "Quiesced:EXCLUSIVE" state.)

- **Table space ID and object ID for each quiescer.** The ID of the table spaces and objects that caused the table space being queried to be placed in a "Quiesced" state. (This information is only displayed if the number of users and/or applications that have placed the table space in a "Quiesced" state is greater than zero.)

You can also obtain detailed information about all table spaces that have been created for a particular database by capturing and displaying snapshot monitor data. The command that is used to capture table space-specific snapshot monitor information is:

```
GET SNAPSHOT FOR TABLESPACES ON [DatabaseAlias]
```

Question 9

The correct answer is **B**. The table space states available are shown in Table 1.

Table 1 Table Space States and Their Corresponding Hexadecimal Values	
Table space State	**Hexadecimal Value**
Normal	0x0
Quiesced:SHARE	0x1
Quiesced:UPDATE	0x2
Quiesced:EXCLUSIVE	0x4
Load pending	0x8
Delete pending	0x10
Backup pending	0x20
Roll forward recovery in progress	0x40
Roll forward recovery pending	0x80
Restore pending	0x100
Recovery pending (no longer used)	0x100
Disable pending	0x200
Reorg in progress	0x400
Backup in progress	0x800
Storage must be defined	0x1000
Restore in progress	0x2000
Offline and not accessible	0x4000
Drop pending	0x8000
Storage may be defined	0x2000000
StorDef is in 'Final 'state	0x4000000
StorDef was changed prior to roll forward recovery	0x8000000
DMS rebalancer is active	0x10000000
Table space deletion in progress	0x20000000
Table space creation in progress	0x40000000
Load in progress*	
A single table space can be in more than one state at a given point in time. If this is the case, multiple table space state hexadecimal values will be ANDed together to keep track of the multiple states. The Get Table Space State command (db2tbst) can be used to obtain the table space state associated with any given hexadecimal value. *The Load utility will place a table space in the "Load in progress" state if the COPY NO option is specified when data is being loaded into a recoverable database. The table space remains in this state for the duration of the load operation and is returned to normal state when the load operation completes. This state does not have a hexadecimal value.	

Question 10

The correct answer is **B**. If a database is enabled for automatic storage (which is the default behavior in DB2 9), container and space management characteristics of its table spaces are determined by the DB2 Database Manager. And, although the ALTER TABLESPACE command can be used to add new containers to existing DMS table spaces, it cannot be used to add new containers to automatic storage stable spaces. To perform this type of operation, you must use the ALTER DATABASE statement instead. The basic syntax for this statement is:

```
ALTER DATABASE [DatabaseName]
ADD STORAGE ON '[Container]' ,... )
```

where:

DatabaseName   Identifies the database, by name that is to have new containers added to its pool of containers that are used for automatic storage.

Container   Identifies one or more new storage locations (containers) that are to be added to the collection of storage locations that are used for automatic storage table spaces.

Thus, if you wanted to add the storage locations D:\data1 and D:\data2 to a database named SAMPLE that is configured for automatic storage and resides on a Windows system, you could do so by executing an ALTER DATABASE SQL statement that looks like this:

```
ALTER DATABASE sample ADD STORAGE ON 'D:\data1', 'D:\data2'
```

Question 11

The correct answer is **A**. DMS table spaces are made up of file containers or raw device containers, and their sizes are set when the containers are assigned to the table space. A table space is considered full when all of the space within the containers has been used. However, with DMS table spaces, you can add or extend containers using the ALTER TABLESPACE statement to provide more storage space to a given table space.

DMS table spaces also have a feature called "auto-resize." As space is consumed in a DMS table space that can be automatically resized, the DB2 Database Manager can automatically extend one or more file containers associated with the table space. (SMS table spaces have similar capabilities for growing automatically but the term "auto-resize" is used exclusively for DMS.) The auto-resize feature of a DMS table space is enabled by specifying the AUTORESIZE YES option with the CREATE TABLESPACE statement that is used to create the table space. For example, the following CREATE TABLESPACE statement could be used to create an auto-resize DMS table space:

```
CREATE TABLESPACE tbsp1 MANAGED BY DATABASE
      USING (FILE '/db2files/data1.dat' 10 M) AUTORESIZE YES
```

You can also enable the auto-resize feature after a DMS table space has been created by executing the ALTER TABLESPACE statement with the AUTORESIZE YES option specified. For example:

```
ALTER TABLESPACE tbsp1 AUTORESIZE YES
```

Question 12

The correct answer is **C**. If a database is enabled for automatic storage, the MANAGED BY AUTOMATIC STORAGE clause can be specified with the CREATE TABLESPACE command to create an automatic storage table space (or this clause can be left out completely; in which case automatic storage is implied). No container definitions are provided in this case because the DB2 Database Manager assigns the containers automatically.

Although automatic storage table spaces appear to be a different table space type, they are really just an extension of the existing SMS and DMS types. If the table space being created is a REGULAR or LARGE table space, it is created as a DMS with file containers. If the table space being created is a USER or SYSTEM TEMPORARY table space, it is created as a SMS with directory containers.

Question 13

The correct answer is **D**. A declared temporary table is a special table that is used to hold temporary data on behalf of a single application. Like base tables, indexes can be created on and statistics can be collected for declared temporary tables. Unlike base tables, whose descriptions and constraints are stored in the system catalog tables of the database to which they belong, declared temporary tables are not persistent and can only be used by the application that creates them—and only for the life of the application. When the application that creates a declared temporary table terminates, the rows of the table are deleted, and the description of the table is dropped. (However, data stored in a temporary table can exist across transaction boundaries.) Another significant difference focuses on where the data for each type of table is stored. Before an application can create and use a declared temporary table, at least one user temporary table space must be created for the database the application will be working with and the privileges needed to use that table space must be granted to the appropriate users. (User temporary table spaces are not created by default when a database is created.) Base tables, on the other hand are created in regular table spaces; if no table space is specified when a base table is created, its data is stored in the table space USERSPACE1, which is created by default when a database is created.

Question 14

The correct answer is **D**. If no schema/qualifier name is specified when an object is created, that object is assigned to the default schema, which is usually the user ID of the individual who is currently connected to the database and is creating the object. In this example, the default schema is DB2ADMIN because the user ID was used to establish the database connection and create the TEST_TAB table object.

Question 15

The correct answer is **B**. While table spaces are used to physically store objects in a database, schemas are used to logically classify and group other objects in the database, regardless of where they are physically stored.

Question 16

The correct answer is **A**. Range-clustered tables require less cache buffer allocation because there are no secondary objects to maintain; indexes are not required nor are they supported.

Question 17

The correct answer is **D**. Data from a given table is partitioned into multiple storage objects based on the specifications provided in the PARTITION BY clause of the CREATE TABLE statement. The syntax for this optional clause is:

```
PARTITION BY <RANGE>
   ([ColumnName] <NULLS LAST | NULLS FIRST> ,...)
   (STARTING <FROM>
          <(> [Start | MINVALUE | MAXVALUE] < ,...)>
          <INCLUSIVE | EXCLUSIVE>
      ENDING <AT>
          <(> [End | MINVALUE | MAXVALUE] < ,...)>
          <INCLUSIVE | EXCLUSIVE>
      EVERY <(>[Constant] <DurationLabel><)>
   )
```

or

```
PARTITION BY <RANGE>
   ([ColumnName] <NULLS LAST | NULLS FIRST> ,...)
   (<PARTITION [PartitionName]>
    STARTING <FROM>
          <(> [Start | MINVALUE | MAXVALUE] < ,...)>
          <INCLUSIVE | EXCLUSIVE>
      ENDING <AT>
          <(> [End | MINVALUE | MAXVALUE] < ,...)>
          <INCLUSIVE | EXCLUSIVE>
      <IN [TableSpaceName]>
   )
```

where:

ColumnName	Identifies one or more columns, by name, whose values are to be used to determine which data partition a particular row is to be stored in. (The group of columns specified make up the partitioning key for the table.)
PartitionName	Identifies the unique name that is to be assigned to the data partition to be created.
Start	Specifies the low end of the range for each data partition.
End	Specifies the high end of the range for each data partition.
Constant	Specifies the width of each data partition range when the automatically generated form of the syntax is used. Data partitions will be created

starting at the STARTING FROM value and will contain this number of values in the range. This form of the syntax is only supported if the partitioning key is comprised of a single column that has been assigned a numeric, date, time, or timestamp data type.

DurationLabel Identifies the duration that is associated with the *Constant* value specified if the partitioning key column has been assigned a date, time, or timestamp data type. The following values are valid for this parameter: YEAR, YEARS, MONTH, MONTHS, DAY, DAYS, HOUR, HOURS, MINUTE, MINUTES, SECOND, SECONDS, MICROSECOND, and MICROSECONDS.

TableSpaceName Identifies the table space that each data partition is to be stored in.

Thus, if you wanted to create a table named DEPARTMENTS that is partitioned such that rows with numerical values that fall in the range of 0 to 9 are stored in one partition that resides in one table space, rows with numerical values that fall in the range of 10 to 19 are stored in another partition that resides in another table space, and so on, you could do so by executing a CREATE TABLE SQL statement that looks something like this:

```
CREATE TABLE departments
    (dept_no   INT,
     desc      CHAR(3))
    PARTITION BY (dept_no NULLS FIRST)
        (STARTING  0 ENDING  9 IN tbsp0,
         STARTING 10 ENDING 19 IN tbsp1,
         STARTING 20 ENDING 29 IN tbsp2,
         STARTING 30 ENDING 39 IN tbsp3)
```

Question 18

The correct answer is **A**. When an index is created for a range partitioned table, the data for that index will be stored in the table space that is used to hold the first partition's data, unless otherwise specified. Since, in the example, the following CREATE INDEX SQL statement was used to create an index for the SALES table:

```
CREATE INDEX sales_idx ON sales (invoice_no);)
```

Data for the index named SALES_IDX will be stored in the table space named TBSP0. If you wanted the index data to be stored in the table space that is used to hold the last partition's data (the table space named TBSP3), the following CREATE INDEX SQL statement would have to be executed instead:

```
CREATE INDEX sales_idx ON sales (invoice_no) IN tbsp3
```

Question 19

The correct answer is **B**. Just as an index over relational data can be used to improve query performance, an index over XML data can be used to improve the efficiency of queries on XML documents that are stored in an XML column. In contrast to traditional relational indexes, where index keys are composed of one or more columns you specify, an index over XML data uses a particular XML pattern expression to index paths and values found in XML documents stored in a single column—the data type of that column must be XML. All or part of the contents of an XML column can be indexed.

Question 20

The correct answer is **C**. When the documents specified are inserted into the CUSTINFO column of the CUSTOMER table, the values 27603 and 29501 will be added to the CUST_ZIP_IDX index and the value "Raleigh" will be added to the CUST_CITY_IDX index.

Question 21

The correct answer is **B**. In order to use data row compression with a table, two prerequisites must be satisfied:

1. Compression must be enabled at the table level.
2. A compression dictionary for the table must be built

Question 22

The correct answer is **D**. Index data is not affected by data row compression; only data stored on a page in a base table can be compressed. However, because records in a compressed table are moved between storage and memory in compressed form (the compression dictionary is moved into memory as well so decompression can take place), records for compressed tables that are written to transaction log files will be compressed as well.

Question 23

The correct answers are **A** and **C**. Although a table can be enabled for data row compression at any time by setting its COMPRESS attribute to YES, data stored in the table will not be compressed until a compression dictionary has been built. A compression dictionary is built (and data in a table is compressed) by performing an offline table reorganization operation; such an operation is initiated by executing the REORG command with either the KEEPDICTIONARY or the RESETDICTIONARY option specified.

Because an offline reorganization operation is needed to construct a compression dictionary and perform data compression, the initial overhead required to compress data can be quite high. Therefore, it can be beneficial to know which tables will benefit most from data row compression and which tables will not. In DB2 9, the Inspect utility can help you make that determination. The Inspect utility is invoked by executing the INSPECT command and if this command is executed with the ROWCOMPESTIMATE option specified, the Inspect utility will examine each row in the table specified, build a compression dictionary from the data found, and then use this dictionary to estimate how much space will be saved if the data in the table is compressed.

Question 24

The correct answer is **B**. A compression dictionary is built (and data in a table is compressed) by performing an offline table reorganization operation; such an operation is initiated by executing the REORG command with either the KEEPDICTIONARY or the RESETDICTIONARY option specified. If the REORG command is executed with either option specified and a compression dictionary does not exist, a new dictionary will be built; if the REORG command is executed with either option specified and a dictionary already exists, data in the table will be reorganized/compressed and the existing dictionary will either be recreated (RESETDICTIONARY) or left as it is (KEEPDICTIONARY).

CHAPTER 4

Database Access

Eleven and one-half percent (11.5%) of the DB2 9 for Linux, UNIX, and Windows Database Administration exam (Exam 731) is designed to test your ability to create tables, indexes, and views as well as your knowledge of when and how the different constraints that are available with DB2 should be used in a table definition. The questions that make up this portion of the exam are intended to evaluate the following:

- Your knowledge of the basic objects that are used to manage data in a database: tables, indexes, and views

- Your knowledge of the various constraints available and your ability to identify when and how NOT NULL constraints, default constraints, check constraints, unique constraints, referential integrity constraints, and informational constraints should be used

- Your ability to create base tables that contain one or more constraints

- Your ability to identify how operations performed on the parent table of a referential integrity constraint are reflected in the child table of the constraint

- Your ability to create views

- Your ability to create and manage indexes

- Your ability to examine the contents of the System Catalog tables

- Your ability to use the DB2 GUI tools available to administer a database

This chapter is designed to introduce you to the various constraints that are available with DB2 and to show you how to construct base tables, views, and indexes. This chapter is also designed to introduce you to the GUI tools that are available with DB2.

Tables

If you have had the opportunity to work with a relational database in the past, you are probably already aware that a table is a logical database object that acts as the main repository in a database. Tables present data as a collection of unordered rows with a fixed number of columns. Each column contains values of the same data type or one of its subtypes, and each row contains a set of values for every column available. Usually, the columns in a table are logically related, and additional relationships can be defined between two or more tables. The storage representation of a row is called a record, the storage representation of a column is called a field, and each intersection of a row and column is called a value. Figure 4–1 shows the structure of a simple database table.

DEPARTMENT TABLE

DEPTID	DEPTNAME	COSTCENTER
A000	ADMINISTRATION	10250
B001	PLANNING	10820
C001	ACCOUNTING	20450
D001	HUMAN RESOURCES	30200
E001	R & D	50120
E002	MANUFACTURING	50220
E003	OPERATIONS	50230
F001	MARKETING	42100
F002	SALES	42200
F003	CUSTOMER SUPPORT	42300
G010	LEGAL	60680

RECORD (ROW)

FIELD (COLUMN)

VALUE

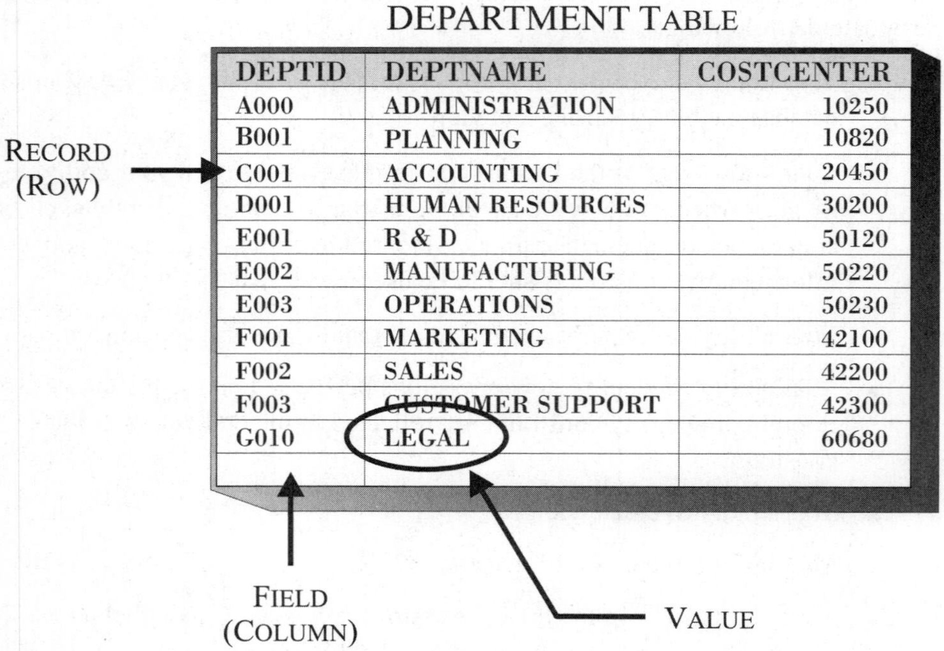

Figure 4-1: A simple database table.

With DB2 9, five types of tables are available:

Base tables. User-defined tables designed to hold persistent user data.

Result tables. DB2 Database Manager–defined tables populated with rows retrieved from one or more base tables in response to a query.

Materialized query tables. User-defined tables whose definition is based on the result of a query and whose data is in the form of precomputed results that are taken from one or more tables upon which the materialized query table definition is based. Materialized query tables (MQTs) are used during query optimization to improve the performance of a subset of queries.

Declared temporary tables. User-defined tables used to hold nonpersistent data temporarily, on behalf of a single application. Declared temporary tables are explicitly created by an application when they are needed and implicitly destroyed when the application that created them terminates its last database connection.

Typed tables. User-defined tables whose column definitions are based on the attributes of a user-defined structured data type.

Because tables are the basic data objects used to store information, many are often created for a single database.

Constraints

Within most businesses, data often must adhere to a certain set of rules and restrictions. For example, companies typically have a specific format and numbering sequence they use when generating purchase orders. Constraints allow you to place the logic needed to enforce such business rules directly in the database rather than in applications that work with the database. Essentially, constraints are rules that govern how data values can be added to a table, as well as how those values can be modified once they have been added. The following types of constraints are available:

- NOT NULL constraints

- Default constraints

- Check constraints

- Unique constraints

- Referential integrity constraints

- Informational constraints

Constraints are usually defined during table creation; however, constraints can also be added to existing tables using the ALTER TABLE SQL statement.

NOT NULL Constraints

With DB2, null values (not to be confused with empty strings) are used to represent missing or unknown data or states. And by default, every column in a table will accept a null value. This allows you to add records to a table when not all of the values that pertain to the record are known. However, there may be times when this behavior is unacceptable (for example, a tax identification number might be required for every employee who works for a company). When such a situation arises, the NOT NULL constraint can be used to ensure that a particular column in a base table is never assigned a null value; once the NOT NULL constraint has been defined for a column, any operation that attempts to place a null value in that column will fail. Figure 4–2 illustrates how the NOT NULL constraint is used.

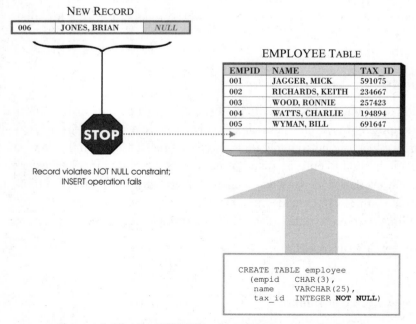

Figure 4-2: How the NOT NULL constraint prevents null values.

Because NOT NULL constraints are associated with a specific column in a base table, they are usually defined during the table creation process.

Default Constraints

Just as there are times when it is objectionable to accept a null value, there may be times when it is desirable to have the system provide a specific value for you (for example, you might want to automatically assign the current date to a particular column whenever a new record is added to a table). In these situations, the default constraint can be used to ensure that a particular column in a base table is assigned a predefined value (unless that value is overridden) each time a record is added to the table. The predefined value provided could be null (if the NOT NULL constraint has not been defined for the column), could be a user-supplied value compatible with the column's data type, or could be a value furnished by the DB2 Database Manager. Table 4.1 shows the default values that can be provided by the DB2 Database Manager for the various DB2 9 data types available.

Table 4.1: DB2 Database Manager–Supplied Default Values	
Column Data Type	**Default Value Provided**
Small integer (SMALLINT)	0
Integer (INTEGER or INT)	0
Decimal (DECIMAL, DEC, NUMERIC, or NUM)	0
Single-precision floating-point (REAL or FLOAT)	0
Double-precision floating-point (DOUBLE, DOUBLE PRECISION, or FLOAT)	0
Fixed-length character string (CHARACTER or CHAR)	A string of blank characters
Varying-length character string (CHARACTER VARYING, CHAR VARYING, or VARCHAR)	A zero-length string
Long varying-length character string (LONG VARCHAR)	A zero-length string

Table 4.1: DB2 Database Manager–Supplied Default Values (continued)	
Column Data Type	**Default Value Provided**
Fixed-length double-byte character string (GRAPHIC)	A string of blank characters
Varying-length double-byte character string (VARGRAPHIC)	A zero-length string
Long varying-length double-byte character string (LONG VARGRAPHIC)	A zero-length string
Date (DATE)	The system date at the time the record is added to the table. (When a date column is added to an existing table, existing rows are assigned the date January 01, 0001.)
Time (TIME)	The system time at the time the record is added to the table. (When a time column is added to an existing table, existing rows are assigned the time 00:00:00.)
Timestamp (TIMESTAMP)	The system date and time (including microseconds) at the time the record is added to the table. (When a timestamp column is added to an existing table, existing rows are assigned a timestamp that corresponds to January 01, 0001–00:00:00.000000)
Binary large object (BLOB)	A zero-length string
Character large object (CLOB)	A zero-length string
Double-byte character large object (DBCLOB)	A zero-length string
XML document (XML)	Not applicable
Any distinct user-defined data type	The default value provided for the built-in data type that the distinct user-defined data type is based on (typecast to the distinct user-defined data type).
Adapted from Table 11 on page 67 of the DB2 SQL Reference, Volume 2 manual	

Figure 4–3 illustrates how the default constraint is used.

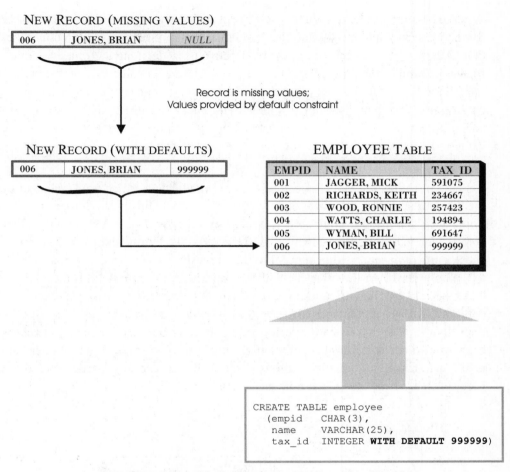

Figure 4-3: How the default constraint is used to provide data values.

Like NOT NULL constraints, default constraints are associated with a specific column in a base table and are usually defined during the table creation process.

Check Constraints

Sometimes, it is desirable to control what values will be accepted for a particular item and what values will not (for example, a company might decide that all nonexempt employees must be paid, at a minimum, the federal minimum wage).

When this is the case, the logic needed to determine whether a value is acceptable can be incorporated directly into the data-entry program being used to collect the data. A better way to achieve the same objective is by defining a check constraint for the column in the base table that is to receive the data value. A check constraint (also known as a table check constraint) can be used to ensure that a particular column in a base table is never assigned an unacceptable value—once a check constraint has been defined for a column, any operation that attempts to place a value in that column that does not meet specific criteria will fail.

Check constraints are made up of one or more predicates (which are connected by the keywords AND or OR) that collectively are known as the check condition. This check condition is compared with data values provided, and the result of this comparison is returned as the value "TRUE," "FALSE," or "Unknown." If the check constraint returns the value "TRUE," the value is acceptable, so it is added to the column. If, on the other hand, the check constraint returns the value "FALSE" or "Unknown," the operation attempting to place the value in the column fails, and all changes made by that operation are backed out. However, it is important to note that when the results of a particular operation are rolled back because of a check constraint violation, the transaction that invoked that operation is not terminated, and other operations within that transaction are unaffected. Figure 4–4 illustrates how a simple check constraint is used.

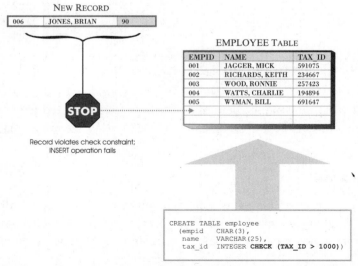

Figure 4–4: How a check constraint is used to control what values are accepted by a column.

Like NOT NULL constraints and default constraints, check constraints are associated with a specific column in a base table and are usually defined during the table creation process.

Unique Constraints

By default, records that are added to a base table can have the same values assigned to any of the columns available any number of times. As long as the records stored in the table do not contain information that should not be duplicated, this kind of behavior is acceptable. However, there are times when certain pieces of information that make up a record should be unique (for example, if an employee identification number is assigned to each individual that works for a particular company, each number used should be unique—two employees should never be assigned the same employee identification number). In these situations, the unique constraint can be used to ensure that the value(s) assigned to one or more columns when a record is added to a base table are always unique; once a unique constraint has been defined for one or more columns, any operation that attempts to place duplicate values in those columns will fail. Figure 4–5 illustrates how the unique constraint is used.

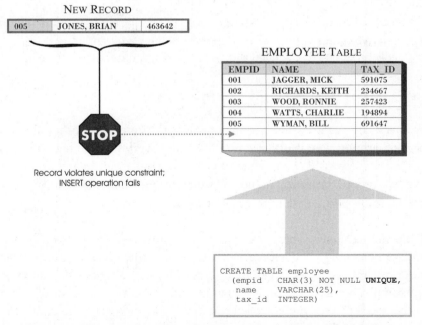

Figure 4–5: How the unique constraint prevents the duplication of data values.

Unlike NOT NULL constraints, default constraints, and check constraints, which can be associated with only a single column in a base table, unique constraints can be associated with either an individual column or a group of columns. However, each column in a base table can participate in only one unique constraint, regardless of how the columns are grouped. Like the other constraints, unique constraints are usually defined during the table creation process.

Regardless of when a unique constraint is defined, when it is created, the DB2 Database Manager looks to see if an index for the columns the unique constraint refers to already exists. If so, that index is marked as being unique and system-required. If not, an appropriate index is created and marked as being unique and system-required. This index is then used to enforce uniqueness whenever new records are added to the column(s) for which the unique constraint was defined.

Although a unique, system-required index is used to enforce a unique constraint, there is a distinction between defining a unique constraint and creating a unique index. Even though both enforce uniqueness, a unique index allows NULL values and generally cannot be used in a referential constraint. A unique constraint, on the other hand, does not allow NULL values and can be referenced in a foreign key specification. (The value "NULL" means a column's value is undefined and distinct from any other value, including other NULL values.)

A primary key, which we will look at next, is a special form of a unique constraint. Only one primary key is allowed per table, and every column that is used to define a primary key must be assigned the NOT NULL constraint. In addition to ensuring that every record added to a table has some unique characteristic, primary keys allow tables to participate in referential constraints.

A table can have any number of unique constraints; however, a table cannot have more than one unique constraint defined on the same set of columns. And because unique constraints are enforced by indexes, all the limitations that apply to indexes (for example, a maximum of 16 columns with a combined length of 255 bytes is allowed; none of the columns used can have a large object, long character string data type, etc.) apply to unique constraints.

Referential Integrity Constraints

If you've worked with a relational database management system for any length of time, you are probably aware that data normalization is a technique used to ensure that there is only one way to get to a single fact. Data normalization is possible because two or more individual base tables can have some type of relationship with one another, and information stored in related base tables can be combined if necessary, through a join operation. This is where referential integrity constraints come into play; referential integrity constraints (also known as *referential constraints* and *foreign key constraints*) are used to define required relationships between two base tables.

To understand how referential constraints work, it helps to look at an example. Suppose you own a small auto parts store, and you use a database to keep track of the inventory you have on hand. Many of the parts you stock will work only with a specific make and model of an automobile; therefore, your database has one table named MAKE to hold make information and another table named MODEL to hold model information. Because these two tables are related (every model must belong to a make), a referential constraint can be used to ensure that every record that is stored in the MODEL table has a corresponding record in the MAKE table. The relationship between these two tables is established by comparing values that are to be added to the "MAKE" column of the MODEL table (known as the foreign key of the child table) with the values that currently exist for the set of columns that make up the primary key of the MAKE table (known as the parent key of the parent table). To create the referential constraint just described, you would define a primary key, using one or more columns in the MAKE table, and you would define a foreign key for one or more corresponding columns in the MODEL table that reference the MAKE table's primary key. Assuming a column named MAKEID is used to create the primary key for the MAKE table and a column also named MAKEID is used to create the foreign key for the MODEL table, the referential constraint created would look something like the one shown in Figure 4–6.

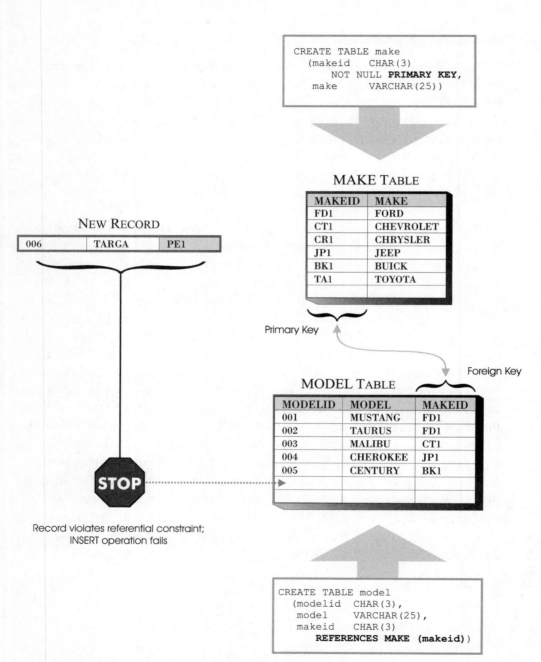

```
CREATE TABLE make
  (makeid   CHAR(3)
       NOT NULL PRIMARY KEY,
   make     VARCHAR(25))
```

MAKE TABLE

MAKEID	MAKE
FD1	FORD
CT1	CHEVROLET
CR1	CHRYSLER
JP1	JEEP
BK1	BUICK
TA1	TOYOTA

Primary Key

Foreign Key

NEW RECORD

006	TARGA	PE1

MODEL TABLE

MODELID	MODEL	MAKEID
001	MUSTANG	FD1
002	TAURUS	FD1
003	MALIBU	CT1
004	CHEROKEE	JP1
005	CENTURY	BK1

STOP

Record violates referential constraint;
INSERT operation fails

```
CREATE TABLE model
  (modelid  CHAR(3),
   model    VARCHAR(25),
   makeid   CHAR(3)
       REFERENCES MAKE (makeid))
```

Figure 4–6: How a referential constraint is used to define a relationship between two tables.

In this example, a single column is used to define the parent key and the foreign key of the referential constraint. However, as with unique constraints, multiple columns can be used to define both the parent and the foreign key of a referential constraint.

> The names of the columns used to create the foreign key of a referential constraint do not have to be the same as the names of the columns used to create the primary key of the constraint (as was the case in the previous example). However, the data types used for the column or columns that make up the primary key and the foreign key of a referential constraint must be identical.

As you can see, referential constraints are much more complex than NOT NULL constraints, default constraints, check constraints, and unique constraints. In fact, they can be so complex that a set of special terms is used to identify the individual components that can make up a single referential constraint. You may already be familiar with some of them; the complete list of terms used can be seen in Table 4.2.

Table 4.2: Referential Integrity Constraint Terminology	
Term	**Meaning**
Unique key	A column or set of columns in which every row of values is different from the values of all other rows.
Primary key	A special unique key that does not accept null values.
Foreign key	A column or set of columns in a child table whose values must match those of a parent key in a parent table.
Parent key	A primary key or unique key in a parent table that is referenced by a foreign key in a referential constraint.
Parent table	A table that contains a parent key of a referential constraint. (A table can be both a parent table and a dependent table of any number of referential constraints.)
Parent row	A row in a parent table that has at least one matching row in a dependent table.
Dependent or child table	A table that contains at least one foreign key that references a parent key in a referential constraint. (A table can be both a dependent table and a parent table of any number of referential constraints.)

Table 4.2: Referential Integrity Constraint Terminology (continued)	
Term	**Meaning**
Dependent or child row	A row in a dependent table that has at least one matching row in a parent table.
Descendent table	A dependent table or a descendent of a dependent table.
Descendent row	A dependent row or a descendent of a dependent row.
Referential cycle	A set of referential constraints defined in such a way that each table in the set is a descendent of itself.
Self-referencing table	A table that is both a parent table and a dependent table in the same referential constraint. (The constraint is known as a self-referencing constraint.)
Self-referencing row	A row that is a parent of itself.

The primary reason referential constraints are created is to guarantee that data integrity is maintained whenever one table object references another. As long as a referential constraint is in effect, the DB2 Database Manager guarantees that for every row in a child table that has a value in any column that is part of a foreign key, there is a corresponding row in the parent table. So what happens when an SQL operation attempts to manipulate data in a way that would violate a referential constraint? To answer this question, let's look at what could compromise data integrity if the checks and balances provided by a referential constraint were not in place:

- An insert operation could add a row of data to a child table that does not have a matching value in the corresponding parent table. (For example, using our MAKE/MODEL scenario, a record could be added to the MODEL table that does not have a corresponding value in the MAKE table.)

- An update operation could change an existing value in a child table such that it no longer has a matching value in the corresponding parent table. (For example, a record could be changed in the MODEL table so that it no longer has a corresponding value in the MAKE table.)

- An update operation could change an existing value in a parent table, leaving rows in a child table with values that no longer match those in the parent table. (For example, a record could be changed in the MAKE table, leaving records in the MODEL table that no longer have a corresponding MAKE value.)

- A delete operation could remove a value from a parent table, leaving rows in a child table with values that no longer match those in the parent table. (For example, a record could be removed from the MAKE table, leaving records in the MODEL table that no longer have a corresponding MAKE value.)

The DB2 Database Manager can either prohibit ("restrict") these types of operations from being performed on tables that are part of a referential constraint, or it can attempt to carry out these actions in a way that will safeguard data integrity. In either case, DB2 uses a set of rules to control the operation's behavior. Each referential constraint has its own set of rules (which consist of an Insert Rule, an Update Rule, and a Delete Rule), and the way each rule is to be enforced is specified as part of the referential constraint creation process.

The Insert Rule for referential constraints

The Insert Rule guarantees that a value can never be inserted into the foreign key of a child table unless a matching value can be found in the corresponding parent key of the associated parent table. Any attempt to insert records into a child table that violates this rule will result in an error, and the insert operation will fail. In contrast, no checking is performed when records are added to the parent key of the parent table.

The Insert Rule for a referential constraint is implicitly created when the referential constraint itself is created. Figure 4–7 illustrates how a row that conforms to the Insert Rule for a referential constraint is successfully added to a child table; Figure 4–8 illustrates how a row that violates the Insert Rule causes an insert operation to fail.

```
CREATE TABLE color
   (c_id    INTEGER
        NOT NULL PRIMARY KEY,
   c_desc  CHAR(20))
```

```
CREATE TABLE object
   (o_id   CHAR(2),
    o_desc CHAR(20),
    c_id   INTEGER
        REFERENCES COLOR (c_id))
```

COLOR TABLE

C_ID	C_DESC
1	RED/ROJO
2	BLUE/AZUL
3	YELLOW/AMARILLO
4	BLACK/NEGRO
5	WHITE/BLANCO

OBJECT TABLE

O_ID	O_DESC	C_ID
01	STOP SIGN	1
02	SKY	2
03	SCHOOL BUS	3
04	COAL	4

Primary Key   Foreign Key

INSERT OPERATION (CHILD TABLE)

```
INSERT INTO object VALUES('05', 'SNOW', 5)
```

INSERT operation successful

COLOR TABLE

C_ID	C_DESC
1	RED/ROJO
2	BLUE/AZUL
3	YELLOW/AMARILLO
4	BLACK/NEGRO
5	WHITE/BLANCO

OBJECT TABLE

O_ID	O_DESC	C_ID
01	STOP SIGN	1
02	SKY	2
03	SCHOOL BUS	3
04	COAL	4
05	SNOW	5

Figure 4–7: An insert operation that conforms to the Insert Rule of a referential constraint.

```
CREATE TABLE color
  (c_id    INTEGER
       NOT NULL PRIMARY KEY,
   c_desc  CHAR(20))
```

```
CREATE TABLE object
  (o_id   CHAR(2),
   o_desc CHAR(20),
   c_id   INTEGER
       REFERENCES COLOR (c_id))
```

COLOR Table

C_ID	C_DESC
1	RED/ROJO
2	BLUE/AZUL
3	YELLOW/AMARILLO
4	BLACK/NEGRO
5	WHITE/BLANCO

OBJECT Table

O_ID	O_DESC	C_ID
01	STOP SIGN	1
02	SKY	2
03	SCHOOL BUS	3
04	COAL	4

Primary Key   Foreign Key

INSERT Operation (CHILD TABLE)

```
INSERT INTO object VALUES('05', 'SNOW', 8)
```

The value **8** does not exist in the primary key;
INSERT operation fails

COLOR Table

C_ID	C_DESC
1	RED/ROJO
2	BLUE/AZUL
3	YELLOW/AMARILLO
4	BLACK/NEGRO
5	WHITE/BLANCO

OBJECT Table

O_ID	O_DESC	C_ID
01	STOP SIGN	1
02	SKY	2
03	SCHOOL BUS	3
04	COAL	4

Figure 4–8: An insert operation that violates the Insert Rule of a referential constraint.

It is important to note that because the Insert Rule exists, records must be inserted in the parent key of the parent table before corresponding records can be inserted into the child table. (Going back to our MAKE/MODEL example, this means that a record for a new MAKE must be added to the MAKE table *before* a record that references the new MAKE can be added to the MODEL table.)

The Update Rule for referential constraints

The Update Rule controls how update operations performed against either table (child or parent) participating in a referential constraint are to be processed. The following two types of behaviors are possible, depending on how the Update Rule is defined:

ON UPDATE RESTRICT. This definition ensures that whenever an update operation is performed on the parent table of a referential constraint, the value for the foreign key of each row in the child table will have the same matching value in the parent key of the parent table that it had before the update operation was performed.

ON UPDATE NO ACTION. This definition ensures that whenever an update operation is performed on either table in a referential constraint, the value for the foreign key of each row in the child table will have a matching value in the parent key of the corresponding parent table; however, the value may not be the same as it was before the update operation occurred.

Figure 4–9 illustrates how the Update Rule is enforced when the ON UPDATE RESTRICT definition is used; Figure 4–10 illustrates how the Update Rule is enforced when the ON UPDATE NO ACTION definition is used.

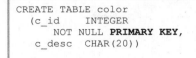

```
CREATE TABLE color
   (c_id    INTEGER
        NOT NULL PRIMARY KEY,
    c_desc  CHAR(20))
```

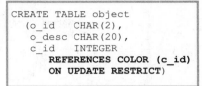

```
CREATE TABLE object
   (o_id   CHAR(2),
    o_desc CHAR(20),
    c_id   INTEGER
         REFERENCES COLOR (c_id)
         ON UPDATE RESTRICT)
```

COLOR TABLE

C_ID	C_DESC
1	RED/ROJO
2	BLUE/AZUL
3	YELLOW/AMARILLO
4	BLACK/NEGRO
5	WHITE/BLANCO

OBJECT TABLE

O_ID	O_DESC	C_ID
01	STOP SIGN	1
02	SKY	2
03	SCHOOL BUS	3
04	COAL	4

Primary Key   Foreign Key

UPDATE OPERATION (PARENT TABLE)

```
UPDATE color SET c_id = c_id - 1
```

Operation violates ON UPDATE RESTRICT rule;
UPDATE operation fails

COLOR TABLE

C_ID	C_DESC
1	RED/ROJO
2	BLUE/AZUL
3	YELLOW/AMARILLO
4	BLACK/NEGRO
5	WHITE/BLANCO

OBJECT TABLE

O_ID	O_DESC	C_ID
01	STOP SIGN	1
02	SKY	2
03	SCHOOL BUS	3
04	COAL	4

Figure 4–9: How the ON UPDATE RESTRICT Update Rule of a referential constraint is enforced.

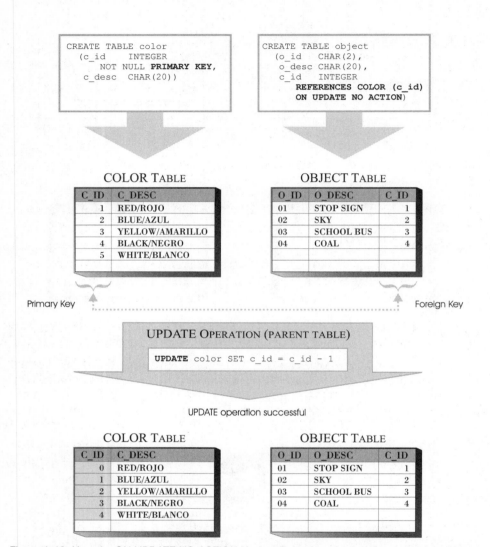

Figure 4–10: How the ON UPDATE NO ACTION Update Rule of a referential constraint is enforced.

Like the Insert Rule, the Update Rule for a referential constraint is implicitly created when the referential constraint itself is created. If no Update Rule definition is provided, the ON UPDATE NO ACTION definition is used by default. Regardless of which Update Rule definition is used, if the condition of the rule is not met, the update operation will fail, an error message will be displayed, and any changes made to the data in either table participating in the referential constraint will be backed out.

The Delete Rule for referential constraints

The Delete Rule controls how delete operations performed against the parent table of a referential constraint are to be processed. The following four types of behaviors are possible, depending on how the Delete Rule is defined:

ON DELETE CASCADE. This definition ensures that when a parent row is deleted from the parent table of a referential constraint, all dependent rows in the child table that have matching primary key values in their foreign key are deleted as well.

ON DELETE SET NULL. This definition ensures that when a parent row is deleted from the parent table of a referential constraint, all dependent rows in the child table that have matching primary key values in their foreign key are located and their foreign key values are changed to NULL (provided the foreign key columns are nullable). Other values for the dependent row are not affected.

ON DELETE RESTRICT. This definition ensures that whenever a delete operation is performed on the parent table of a referential constraint, the value for the foreign key of each row in the child table will have the same matching value in the parent key of the parent table that it had before the delete operation was performed.

ON DELETE NO ACTION. This definition ensures that whenever a delete operation is performed on the parent table of a referential constraint, the value for the foreign key of each row in the child table will have a matching value in the parent key of the parent table after the other referential constraints have been enforced.

Figure 4–11 illustrates how the Delete Rule is enforced when the ON DELETE CASCADE definition is used; Figure 4–12 illustrates how the Delete Rule is enforced when the ON DELETE SET NULL definition is used; Figure 4–13 illustrates how the Delete Rule is enforced when the ON DELETE RESTRICT definition is used; and Figure 4–14 illustrates how the Delete Rule is enforced when the ON DELETE NO ACTION definition is used.

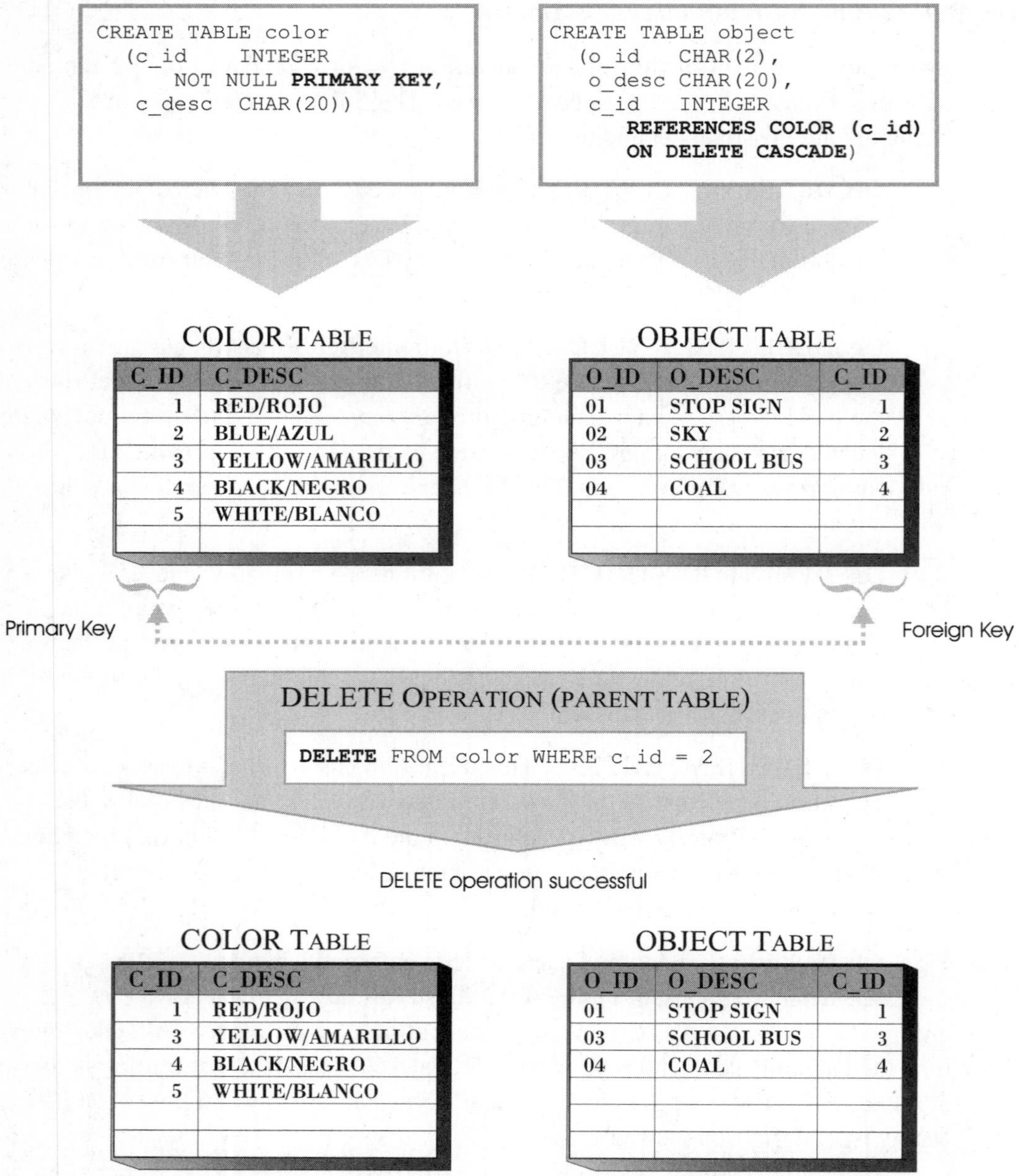

```
CREATE TABLE color
  (c_id    INTEGER
      NOT NULL PRIMARY KEY,
  c_desc  CHAR(20))
```

```
CREATE TABLE object
  (o_id   CHAR(2),
  o_desc CHAR(20),
  c_id   INTEGER
      REFERENCES COLOR (c_id)
      ON DELETE CASCADE)
```

COLOR Table

C_ID	C_DESC
1	RED/ROJO
2	BLUE/AZUL
3	YELLOW/AMARILLO
4	BLACK/NEGRO
5	WHITE/BLANCO

OBJECT Table

O_ID	O_DESC	C_ID
01	STOP SIGN	1
02	SKY	2
03	SCHOOL BUS	3
04	COAL	4

Primary Key   Foreign Key

DELETE Operation (PARENT TABLE)

```
DELETE FROM color WHERE c_id = 2
```

DELETE operation successful

COLOR Table

C_ID	C_DESC
1	RED/ROJO
3	YELLOW/AMARILLO
4	BLACK/NEGRO
5	WHITE/BLANCO

OBJECT Table

O_ID	O_DESC	C_ID
01	STOP SIGN	1
03	SCHOOL BUS	3
04	COAL	4

Figure 4–11: How the ON DELETE CASCADE Delete Rule of a referential constraint is enforced.

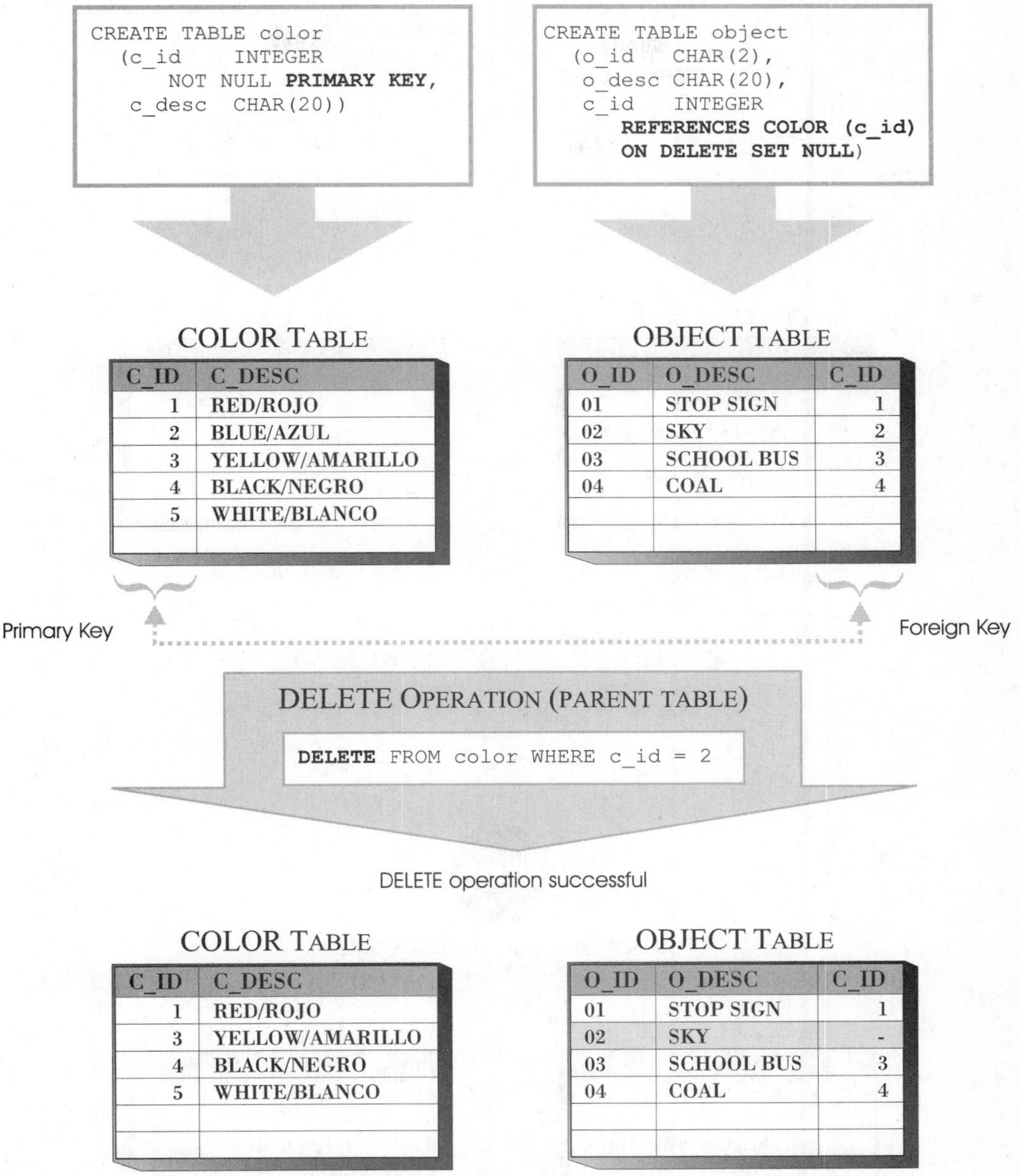

```
CREATE TABLE color
  (c_id    INTEGER
     NOT NULL PRIMARY KEY,
   c_desc  CHAR(20))
```

```
CREATE TABLE object
  (o_id   CHAR(2),
   o_desc CHAR(20),
   c_id   INTEGER
     REFERENCES COLOR (c_id)
     ON DELETE SET NULL)
```

COLOR Table

C_ID	C_DESC
1	RED/ROJO
2	BLUE/AZUL
3	YELLOW/AMARILLO
4	BLACK/NEGRO
5	WHITE/BLANCO

OBJECT Table

O_ID	O_DESC	C_ID
01	STOP SIGN	1
02	SKY	2
03	SCHOOL BUS	3
04	COAL	4

Primary Key

Foreign Key

DELETE Operation (parent table)

```
DELETE FROM color WHERE c_id = 2
```

DELETE operation successful

COLOR Table

C_ID	C_DESC
1	RED/ROJO
3	YELLOW/AMARILLO
4	BLACK/NEGRO
5	WHITE/BLANCO

OBJECT Table

O_ID	O_DESC	C_ID
01	STOP SIGN	1
02	SKY	-
03	SCHOOL BUS	3
04	COAL	4

Figure 4–12: How the ON DELETE SET NULL Delete Rule of a referential constraint is enforced.

```
CREATE TABLE color
   (c_id    INTEGER
        NOT NULL PRIMARY KEY,
    c_desc  CHAR(20))
```

```
CREATE TABLE object
   (O_id    CHAR(2),
    o_desc  CHAR(20),
    c_id    INTEGER
        REFERENCES COLOR (c_id)
        ON DELETE RESTRICT)
```

COLOR Table

C_ID	C_DESC
1	RED/ROJO
2	BLUE/AZUL
3	YELLOW/AMARILLO
4	BLACK/NEGRO
5	WHITE/BLANCO

OBJECT Table

O_ID	O_DESC	C_ID
01	STOP SIGN	1
02	SKY	2
03	SCHOOL BUS	3
04	COAL	4

Primary Key   Foreign Key

DELETE Operation (PARENT TABLE)

```
DELETE FROM color WHERE c_id = 2
```

Operation violates ON DELETE RESTRICT rule;
DELETE operation fails

COLOR Table

C_ID	C_DESC
1	RED/ROJO
2	BLUE/AZUL
3	YELLOW/AMARILLO
4	BLACK/NEGRO
5	WHITE/BLANCO

OBJECT Table

O_ID	O_DESC	C_ID
01	STOP SIGN	1
02	SKY	2
03	SCHOOL BUS	3
04	COAL	4

Figure 4–13: How the ON DELETE RESTRICT Delete Rule of a referential constraint is enforced.

```
CREATE TABLE color
  (c_id    INTEGER
      NOT NULL PRIMARY KEY,
   c_desc  CHAR(20))
```

```
CREATE TABLE object
  (o_id    CHAR(2),
   o_desc  CHAR(20),
   c_id    INTEGER
      REFERENCES COLOR (c_id)
      ON DELETE NO ACTION)
```

COLOR Table

C_ID	C_DESC
1	RED/ROJO
2	BLUE/AZUL
3	YELLOW/AMARILLO
4	BLACK/NEGRO
5	WHITE/BLANCO

OBJECT Table

O_ID	O_DESC	C_ID
01	STOP SIGN	1
02	SKY	2
03	SCHOOL BUS	3
04	COAL	4

Primary Key

Foreign Key

DELETE Operation (PARENT TABLE)

```
DELETE FROM color WHERE c_id = 2
```

STOP

Operation violates ON DELETE NO ACTION rule;
DELETE operation fails

COLOR Table

C_ID	C_DESC
1	RED/ROJO
2	BLUE/AZUL
3	YELLOW/AMARILLO
4	BLACK/NEGRO
5	WHITE/BLANCO

OBJECT Table

O_ID	O_DESC	C_ID
01	STOP SIGN	1
02	SKY	2
03	SCHOOL BUS	3
04	COAL	4

Figure 4–14: How the ON DELETE NO ACTION Delete Rule of a referential constraint is enforced.

Like the Insert Rule and the Update Rule, the Delete Rule for a referential constraint is implicitly created when the referential constraint itself is created. If no Delete Rule definition is provided, the ON DELETE NO ACTION definition is used by default. No matter which form of the Delete Rule is used, if the condition of the rule is not met, an error message will be displayed, and the delete operation will fail.

If the ON DELETE CASCADE Delete Rule is used, and the deletion of a parent row in a parent table causes one or more dependent rows to be deleted from the corresponding child table, the delete operation is said to have been propagated to the child table. In such a situation, the child table is said to be delete-connected to the parent table. Because a delete-connected child table can also be the parent table in another referential constraint, a delete operation that is propagated to one child table can, in turn, be propagated to another child table, and so on. Thus, the deletion of one parent row from a single parent table can result in the deletion of several hundred rows from any number of tables, depending on how tables are delete-connected. Therefore, the ON DELETE CASCADE Delete Rule should be used with extreme caution when a hierarchy of referential constraints permeates a database.

Informational Constraints

The DB2 Database Manager automatically enforces all of the constraints that we have looked at so far whenever new data values are added to a table or existing data values are modified or deleted. As you might imagine, if a large number of constraints have been defined, a large amount of system overhead can be required to enforce those constraints—particularly when large amounts of data are loaded into a table.

If an application is coded in such a way that it validates data before inserting it into a DB2 database, it may be more efficient to create one or more informational constraints, as opposed to creating any of the other constraints available. Unlike other constraints, informational constraints are not enforced during insert and update processing. However, the DB2 SQL optimizer will evaluate information provided by an informational constraint when considering the best access plan to use to resolve a query. (Informational constraints are defined by appending the keywords NOT ENFORCED ENABLE QUERY OPTIMIZATION to a normal constraint definition.) As a result, an informational constraint may result in better query performance even though the constraint itself will not be used to validate data entry/modification. Figure 4–15 illustrates the behavior of a simple informational constraint.

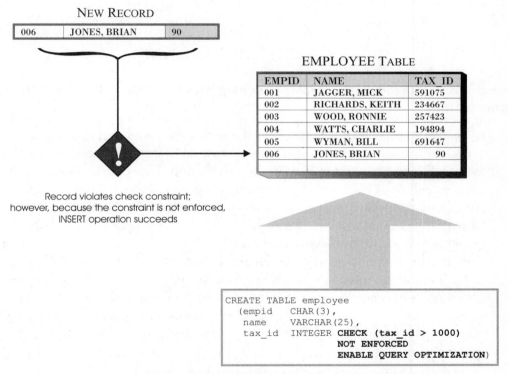

Figure 4–15: Behavior of a simple informational constraint.

It is important to note that because the DB2 Optimizer evaluates informational constraints when selecting the best data access plan to use to resolve a query, records that have been inserted into a table that violate one or more informational constraints may not be returned by some queries. For example, if the query "SELECT * FROM employee WHERE tax_id = 90" were to be executed against the EMPLOYEE table shown in Figure 4–15, no records would be returned because the access plan chosen would assume that no records with a TAX_ID value that is less than 1,000 exist in the table.

To tell the DB2 Optimizer to ignore an informational constraint when selecting the best data access plan to use to resolve a query, you simply disable query optimization for the constraint. You can do this at the time the constraint is created, or you can do this later by executing an ALTER TABLE statement, identifying the constraint to be altered, and specifying the DISABLE QUERY OPTIMIZATION option.

Temporarily Suspending Constraint Checking with the SET INTEGRITY SQL Statement

Although constraints provide a means of ensuring that some level of integrity is maintained as data is manipulated within a base table, their enforcement can prevent some types of operations from executing successfully. For example, suppose you want to bulk-load 10,000 rows of data into a base table using the Load utility (which we will look at in more detail in Chapter 6, "DB2 Utilities"). If the data contains values that will violate a constraint that has been defined for the table into which the data is to be loaded, the operation will fail. Or suppose you wish to add a new constraint to an existing table that already contains several hundred rows of data. If one or more rows in the table contain data values that violate the constraint you wish to add, any attempt to add the constraint will fail. In situations like these, it can be advantageous to suspend constraint checking just long enough to perform the desired operation. However, when constraint checking is suspended, at some point it must be resumed, and at that time, rows in the table that cause a constraint to be violated must be located and dealt with.

Constraint checking for a table can be suspended temporarily by executing the SET INTEGRITY SQL statement. When used to suspend constraint checking, the syntax for the simplest form of this statement is:

```
SET INTEGRITY FOR [TableName , . . .] OFF <AccessMode>
```

where:

TableName   Identifies the name of one or more base tables for which constraint checking is to be temporarily suspended.

AccessMode   Identifies whether the table(s) specified can be accessed in read-only mode while constraint checking is suspended. The following values are valid for this parameter: NO ACCESS and READ ACCESS—if no access mode is specified, NO ACCESS is used as the default.

Thus, if you wanted to temporarily suspend constraint checking for a table named EMPLOYEE and deny read-only access to that table while constraint checking is turned off, you could do so by executing a SET INTEGRITY statement that looks something like this:

```
SET INTEGRITY FOR employee OFF
```

When constraint checking is suspended for a particular table, that table is placed in "Check Pending" state to indicate that it contains data that has not been checked (and that it may not be free of constraint violations). While a table is in "Check Pending" state, it cannot be used in insert, update, or delete operations, nor can it be used by any DB2 utility that needs to perform these types of operations. Indexes cannot be created for a table while it is in "Check Pending" state, and data stored in the table can be retrieved only if the access mode specified when the SET INTEGRITY statement was used to place the table in "Check Pending" state allows read-only access.

Just as one form of the SET INTEGRITY statement is used to temporarily suspend constraint checking, another form is used to resume it. In this case, the syntax for the simplest form of the SET INTEGRITY statement is:

```
SET INTEGRITY FOR [TableName] IMMEDIATE CHECKED FOR EXCEPTION [IN
    [TableName] USE [ExceptionTable] , . . .]
```

or

```
SET INTEGRITY FOR [[TableName] [ConstraintType] , . . .] IMMEDIATE UNCHECKED
```

where:

TableName   Identifies the name of one or more base tables for which suspended constraint checking is to be resumed. These are also the base tables from which all rows that are in violation of a referential constraint or a check constraint are to be copied.

ExceptionTable Identifies the name of a base table to which all rows that are in violation of a referential constraint or a check constraint are to be copied.

ConstraintType Identifies the type of constraint checking that is to be resumed. The following values are valid for this parameter: FOREIGN KEY, CHECK, MATERILIZED QUERY, GENERATED COLUMN, STAGING, and ALL.

Thus, if you wanted to resume constraint checking for the EMPLOYEE table for which constraint checking was suspended in the previous example, you could do so by executing a SET INTEGRITY statement that looks something like this:

```
SET INTEGRITY FOR employee
IMMEDIATE CHECKED
```

When this particular form of the SET INTEGRITY statement is executed, the table named EMPLOYEE is taken out of the "Check Pending" state, and each row of data stored in the table is checked for constraint violations. If an offensive row is found, constraint checking is stopped, and the EMPLOYEE table is returned to the "Check Pending" state. However, consider the following form of the SET INTEGRITY statement:

```
SET INTEGRITY FOR employee
IMMEDIATE CHECKED
FOR EXCEPTION IN employee USE bad_rows
```

If this statement is executed, each row found that violates one or more of the constraints that have been defined for the EMPLOYEE table will be copied to a table named BAD_ROWS, where it can be corrected and copied back to the EMPLOYEE table if so desired. On the other hand, if the following form of the SET INTEGRITY statement is executed, the table named EMPLOYEE is taken out of the "Check Pending" state, and no constraint checking is performed:

```
SET INTEGRITY FOR employee ALL
IMMEDIATE UNCHECKED
```

However, this is a very hazardous thing to do and should only be done if you have some independent means of ensuring that the EMPLOYEE table does not contain data that violates one or more constraints defined for the EMPLOYEE table.

> You can determine whether constraint checking has been performed for a table (and if so, how) by examining the CONST_CHECKED column of the SYSCAT.TABLES system catalog table. This column contains encoded constraint checking information for each table that has been defined for the database.

Creating Tables and Defining Constraints

Although constraints can be added to an existing table by executing the ALTER TABLE SQL statement, they are usually defined as part of the table creation process. Like many of the database objects available, tables can be created using a GUI tool that is accessible from the Control Center. In this case, the tool is the Create Table Wizard, and it can be activated by selecting the appropriate action from the Tables menu. Figure 4–16 shows the Control Center menu items that must be selected to activate the Create Table Wizard; Figure 4–17 shows how the first page of the Create Table Wizard looks when it is first activated.

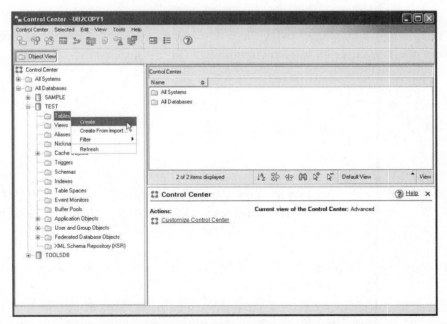

Figure 4–16: Invoking the Create Table Wizard from the Control Center.

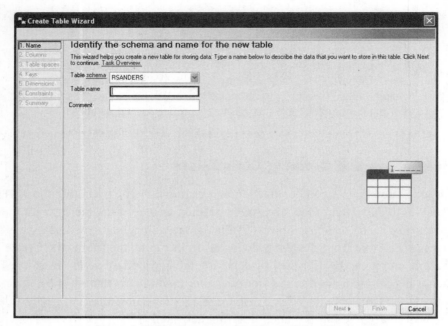

Figure 4–17: The first page of the Create Table Wizard.

Tables can also be created using the CREATE TABLE SQL statement. In its simplest form, the syntax for this statement is:

```
CREATE TABLE [TableName] ([Element] , . . .)
<IN [TablespaceName]>
<INDEX IN [TablespaceName]>
<LONG IN [TablespaceName]>
```

where:

TableName   Identifies the name that is to be assigned to the table to be created. (A table name must be unique within the schema in which the table is to be defined.)

Element   Identifies one or more columns, unique/primary key constraints, referential constraints, check constraints, and/or informational constraints to be included in the table definition. The syntax used for defining each of these elements varies according to the element being defined.

TablespaceName   Identifies the table spaces in which the table and its regular data, indexes, or long/large object data are to be stored.

The basic syntax used to define a column is:

```
[ColumnName] [DataType]
<NOT NULL>
<WITH DEFAULT <[DefaultValue] | CURRENT DATE |  CURRENT TIME | CURRENT
    TIMESTAMP | NULL>>
<UniqueConstraint>
<CheckConstraint>
<ReferentialConstraint>
```

where:

ColumnName   Identifies the unique name to be assigned to the column that is to be created.

DataType   Identifies the data type (built-in or user-defined) that is to be assigned to the column to be created; the data type specified determines the kind of data values that can be stored in the column. Table 4.3 contains a list of the data type definitions that are valid.

DefaultValue   Identifies the value that is to be provided for the column in the event no value is supplied when an insert or update operation is performed against the table.

UniqueConstraint   Identifies a unique or primary key constraint that is to be associated with the column.

CheckConstraint   Identifies a check constraint that is to be associated with the column.

ReferentialConstraint   Identifies a referential constraint that is to be associated with the column.

Table 4.3: Data Type Definitions That Can Be Used with the *CREATE TABLE* Statement	
Data Type	**Definition(s)**
Small integer	SMALLINT
Integer	INTEGER INT
Big integer	BIGINT
Decimal	DECIMAL(*Precision, Scale*) DEC(*Precision, Scale*) NUMERIC(*Precision, Scale*) NUM(*Precision, Scale*) where *Precision* is any number between 1 and 31; *Scale* is any number between 0 and *Precision*
Single-precision floating-point	REAL FLOAT(*Precision*) where *Precision* is any number between 1 and 24
Double-precision floating-point	DOUBLE FLOAT(*Precision*) where *Precision* is any number between 25 and 53
Fixed-length character string	CHARACTER(*Length*) <FOR BIT DATA>* CHAR(*Length*) <FOR BIT DATA>* where *Length* is any number between 1 and 254
Varying-length character string	CHARACTER VARYING(*MaxLength*) <FOR BIT DATA>* CHAR VARYING(*MaxLength*) <FOR BIT DATA>* VARCHAR(*MaxLength*) <FOR BIT DATA>* where *MaxLength* is any number between 1 and 32,672
Long varying-length character string	LONG VARCHAR
Fixed-length double-byte character string	GRAPHIC(*Length*) where *Length* is any number between 1 and 127
Varying-length double-byte character string	VARGRAPHIC(*MaxLength*) where *MaxLength* is any number between 1 and 16,336
Long varying-length double-byte character string	LONG VARGRAPHIC
Date	DATE
Time	TIME
Timestamp	TIMESTAMP

Data Type	Definition(s)
Table 4.3: Data Type Definitions That Can Be Used with the *CREATE TABLE* Statement (continued)	
Binary large object	BINARY LARGE OBJECT(*Size* <K | M | G>) BLOB(*Size* <K | M | G>) where *Length* is any number between 1 and 2,147,483,647; if K (for kilobyte) is specified, *Length* is any number between 1 and 2,097,152; if M (for megabyte) is specified, *Length* is any number between 1 and 2,048; if G (for gigabyte) is specified, *Length* is any number between 1 and 2.
Character large object	CHARACTER LARGE OBJECT(*Size* <K | M | G>) CHAR LARGE OBJECT(*Size* <K | M | G>) CLOB(*Size* <K | M | G>) where *Length* is any number between 1 and 2,147,483,647; if K (for kilobyte) is specified, *Length* is any number between 1 and 2,097,152; if M (for megabyte) is specified, *Length* is any number between 1 and 2,048; if G (for gigabyte) is specified, *Length* is any number between 1 and 2.
Double-byte character large object	DBCLOB(*Size* <K | M | G>) where *Length* is any number between 1 and 1,073,741,823; if K (for kilobyte) is specified, *Length* is any number between 1 and 1,048,576; if M (for megabyte) is specified, *Length* is any number between 1 and 1,024; if G (for gigabyte) is specified, *Length* must be 1.
XML document	XML
Label-based access control (LBAC) security label	DB2SECURITYLABEL
*If the FOR BIT DATA option is used with any character string data type definition, the contents of the column to which the data type is assigned are treated as binary data. As a result, code page conversions are not performed if data is exchanged between other systems, and all comparisons made are done in binary, regardless of the collating sequence used by the database.	

```
<CONSTRAINT [ConstraintName]> [UNIQUE | PRIMARY KEY]
```

where:

ConstraintName   Identifies the unique name that is to be assigned to the constraint to be created.

The syntax used to create a check constraint as part of a column definition is:

```
<CONSTRAINT [ConstraintName]> CHECK ([CheckCondition])
<ENFORCED | NOT ENFORCED>
<ENABLE QUERY OPTIMIZATION | DISABLE QUERY OPTIMIZATION>
```

where:

ConstraintName   Identifies the unique name that is to be assigned to the constraint to be created.

CheckCondition   Identifies a condition or test that must evaluate to TRUE before a value can be stored in the column.

And finally, the syntax used to create a referential constraint as part of a column definition is:

```
<CONSTRAINT [ConstraintName]>
REFERENCES [PKTableName] <([PKColumnName] , . . .)>
<ON UPDATE [RESTRICT | NO ACTION]>
<ON DELETE [CASCADE | SET NULL | RESTRICT | NO ACTION]>
<ENFORCED | NOT ENFORCED>
<ENABLE QUERY OPTIMIZATION | DISABLE QUERY OPTIMIZATION>
```

where:

ConstraintName   Identifies the unique name that is to be assigned to the constraint to be created.

PKTableName   Identifies the name of the parent table that is to participate in the referential constraint.

PKColumnName   Identifies the column or columns that make up the parent key of the parent table that is to participate in the referential constraint.

If the NOT ENFORCED clause is specified as part of a constraint's definition, an informational constraint will be created, and the constraint will not be enforced during insert and update processing. If the ENABLE QUERY OPTIMIZATION clause is specified, the DB2 Optimizer will evaluate the information provided about the constraint when generating an access plan in response to a query. (When the ENABLE QUERY OPTIMIZATION is used, the constraint will be imposed when SELECT statements are issued against the table and records stored in the table that do not conform to the constraint are not returned.)

Therefore, if you wanted to create a table that had three columns in it, two of which use an integer data type and one of which uses a fixed-length character string data type, you could do so by executing a CREATE TABLE SQL statement that looks something like this:

```
CREATE TABLE employee
    (empid    INTEGER,
     name     CHAR(50)
     dept     INTEGER)
```

If you wanted to create the same table such that the EMPID column had both the NOT NULL constraint and a primary key constraint associated with it, you could do so by executing a CREATE TABLE statement that looks something like this:

```
CREATE TABLE employee
    (empid    INTEGER NOT NULL PRIMARY KEY,
     name     CHAR(50)
     dept     INTEGER)
```

If you wanted to create the same table such that the DEPT column participates in a referential constraint with a column named DEPTID that resides in a table named DEPARTMENT, you could do so by executing a CREATE TABLE statement that looks something like this:

```
CREATE TABLE employee
    (empid    INTEGER,
     name     CHAR(50)
     dept     INTEGER REFERENCES department (deptid))
```

And finally, if you wanted to create the same table such that the EMPID column has an informational constraint associated with it, you could do so by executing a CREATE TABLE statement that looks something like this:

```
CREATE TABLE employee
    (empid    INTEGER NOT NULL
         CONSTRAINT inf_cs CHECK (empid BETWEEN 1 AND 100)
         NOT ENFORCED
         ENABLE QUERY OPTIMIZATION,
     name     CHAR(50)
     dept     INTEGER)
```

As you can see from these examples, a unique constraint, a check constraint, a referential constraint, or an informational constraint that involves a single column can be defined as part of that particular column's definition. But what if you needed to define a constraint that encompasses multiple columns in the table? Or what if you want to separate the constraint definitions from the column definitions? You do this by defining a constraint as another element, rather than as an extension to a single column's definition. The basic syntax used to define a unique constraint as an individual element is:

```
<CONSTRAINT [ConstraintName]> [UNIQUE | PRIMARY KEY]
    ([ColumnName] , . . .)
```

where:

ConstraintName   Identifies the unique name that is to be assigned to the constraint to be created.

ColumnName   Identifies one or more columns that are to be part of the unique or primary key constraint to be created.

The syntax used to create a check constraint as an individual element is the same as the syntax used to create a check constraint as part of a column definition:

```
<CONSTRAINT [ConstraintName]> CHECK ([CheckCondition])
<ENFORCED | NOT ENFORCED>
<ENABLE QUERY OPTIMIZATION | DISABLE QUERY OPTIMIZATION>
```

where:

ConstraintName   Identifies the unique name that is to be assigned to the constraint to be created.

CheckCondition   Identifies a condition or test that must evaluate to TRUE before a value can be stored in the column.

And finally, the syntax used to create a referential constraint as an individual element is:

```
<CONSTRAINT [ConstraintName]>
FOREIGN KEY ([ColumnName] , . . .)
REFERENCES [PKTableName] < ([PKColumnName] , . . .)>
<ON UPDATE [NO ACTION | RESTRICT]>
<ON DELETE [CASCADE | SET NULL | NO ACTION | RESTRICT]>
<ENFORCED | NOT ENFORCED>
<ENABLE QUERY OPTIMIZATION | DISABLE QUERY OPTIMIZATION>
```

where:

ConstraintName   Identifies the unique name that is to be assigned to the constraint to be created.

ColumnName   Identifies one or more columns that are to be part of the referential constraint to be created.

PKTableName   Identifies the name of the parent table that is to participate in the referential constraint.

PKColumnName   Identifies the column or columns that make up the parent key of the parent table that is to participate in the referential constraint.

Thus, a table that was created by executing a CREATE TABLE statement that looks something like this:

```
CREATE TABLE employee
    (empid   INTEGER NOT NULL PRIMARY KEY,
     name    CHAR(50)
     dept    INTEGER REFERENCES department(deptid))
```

could also be created by executing a CREATE TABLE statement that looks something like this:

```
CREATE TABLE employee
    (empid   INTEGER NOT NULL,
     name    CHAR(50)
     dept    INTEGER,
     PRIMARY KEY (empid),
     FOREIGN KEY (dept) REFERENCES department(deptid))
```

Views

Views are used to provide a different way of looking at the data stored in one or more base tables. Essentially, a view is a named specification of a result table that is populated whenever the view is referenced in an SQL statement. (Each time a view is referenced, a query is executed, and the results are returned in a table-like format.) Like base tables, views can be thought of as having columns and rows. And in most cases, data can be retrieved from a view the same way it can be retrieved from a table. However, whether a view can be used in insert, update, and delete operations depends on how it was defined—views can be defined as being insertable, updatable, deletable, and read-only.

Although views look (and often behave) like base tables, they do not have their own physical storage; therefore, they do not contain real data. Instead, views refer to data that is physically stored in other base tables. Only the view definition itself is actually stored in the database. (In fact, when changes are made to the data presented in a view, the changes are actually made to the data stored in the base table(s) that the view references.) Figure 4–18 shows the structure of a simple view, along with its relationship to two base tables.

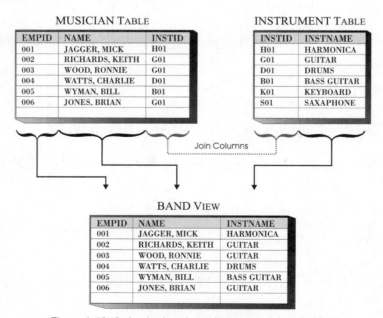

MUSICIAN Table

EMPID	NAME	INSTID
001	JAGGER, MICK	H01
002	RICHARDS, KEITH	G01
003	WOOD, RONNIE	G01
004	WATTS, CHARLIE	D01
005	WYMAN, BILL	B01
006	JONES, BRIAN	G01

INSTRUMENT Table

INSTID	INSTNAME
H01	HARMONICA
G01	GUITAR
D01	DRUMS
B01	BASS GUITAR
K01	KEYBOARD
S01	SAXAPHONE

Join Columns

BAND View

EMPID	NAME	INSTNAME
001	JAGGER, MICK	HARMONICA
002	RICHARDS, KEITH	GUITAR
003	WOOD, RONNIE	GUITAR
004	WATTS, CHARLIE	DRUMS
005	WYMAN, BILL	BASS GUITAR
006	JONES, BRIAN	GUITAR

Figure 4–18: A simple view that references two base tables.

Because views allow different users to see different presentations of the same data, they are often used, together with view privileges, to control data access. For example, suppose you had a table that contained information about all employees who worked for a particular company. Department managers could be given access to this table using a view that allows them to see information only about the employees who work in their department. Members of the payroll department, on the other hand, could be given access to the table using a view that allows them to see only the information needed to generate employee paychecks. Both sets of users are given access to the same table; however, because each user works with a different view, it appears that they are working with their own tables. By creating views and coupling them with the view privileges available, a database administrator can have greater control over how individual users access specific pieces of data.

••

Because there is no way to grant SELECT privileges on specific columns within a table, the only way to prevent users from accessing every column in a table is by creating a result, summary, or declared temporary table that holds only the data a particular user needs—or by creating a view that contains only the table columns a user is allowed to access. Of the two options, a view is easier to implement and manage.

••

Views can be created by executing the CREATE VIEW SQL statement. The basic syntax for this statement is:

```
CREATE VIEW [ViewName]
<( [ColumnName] ,... )>
AS [SELECTStatement]
<WITH <LOCAL | CASCADED> CHECK OPTION>
```

where:

ViewName	Identifies the name that is to be assigned to the view to be created.
ColumnName	Identifies the names of one or more columns that are to be included in the view to be created. If a list of column names is specified, the number of column names

provided must match the number of columns that will be returned by the SELECT statement used to create the view. (If a list of column names is not provided, the columns of the view will inherit the names that are assigned to the columns returned by the SELECT statement used to create the view.)

SELECTStatement   Identifies a SELECT SQL statement that, when executed, will produce data that will populate the view.

Thus, if you wanted to create a view that references all data stored in a table named DEPARTMENT and assign it the name DEPT_VIEW, you could do so by executing a CREATE VIEW SQL statement that looks something like this:

```
CREATE VIEW dept_view
AS SELECT * FROM department
```

On the other hand, if you wanted to create a view that references specific data values stored in a table named DEPARTMENT and assign it the name ADV_DEPT_VIEW, you could do so by executing a CREATE VIEW SQL statement that looks something like this:

```
CREATE VIEW adv_dept_view
AS SELECT (dept_no, dept_name, dept_size)
    FROM department
    WHERE dept_size > 25
```

The view created by this statement would contain only department number, department name, and department size information for each department that has more than 25 people in it.

Views can also be created using the Create View dialog, which can be activated by selecting the appropriate action from the Views menu found in the Control Center. Figure 4–19 shows the Control Center menu items that must be selected to activate the Create View dialog; Figure 4–20 shows how the Create View dialog looks when it is first activated.

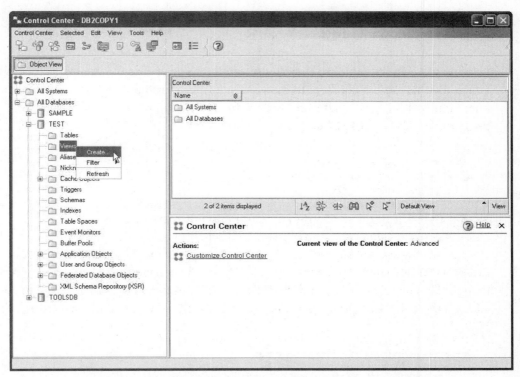

Figure 4–19: Invoking the Create View dialog from the Control Center.

Figure 4–20: The Create View dialog.

If the WITH LOCAL CHECK OPTION clause of the CREATE VIEW SQL statement is specified (or if the Local Check option is selected on the Create View dialog), insert and update operations performed against the view that is created are validated to ensure that all rows being inserted into or updated in the base table to which the view refers conform to the view's definition (otherwise, the insert/update operation will fail). So what exactly does this mean? Suppose a view was created using the following CREATE VIEW statement:

```
CREATE VIEW priority_orders
AS SELECT * FROM orders WHERE response_time < 4
WITH LOCAL CHECK OPTION
```

Now, suppose a user tries to insert a record into this view that has a RESPONSE_TIME value of 6. The insert operation will fail because the record violates the view's definition. Had the view not been created with the WITH LOCAL CHECK OPTION clause, the insert operation would have been successful, even though the new record would not have been visible to the view that was used to add it. Figure 4–21 illustrates how the WITH LOCAL CHECK OPTION clause works.

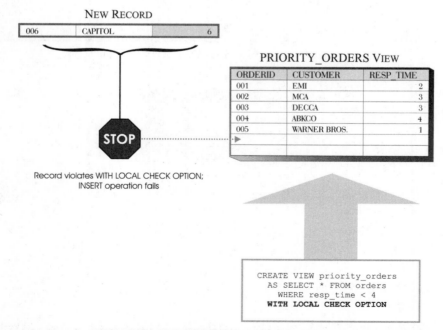

Figure 4–21: How the WITH LOCAL CHECK OPTION clause is used to ensure that insert and update operations conform to a view's definition.

Views created with the WITH LOCAL CHECK OPTION clause specified are referred to as *symmetric views* because every record that can be inserted into them can also be retrieved from them.

If the WITH CASCADED CHECK OPTION clause of the CREATE VIEW SQL statement is specified (or if the Cascaded Check option is selected on the Create View dialog), the view created will inherit the search conditions of the parent view on which the view is based and will treat those conditions as one or more constraints that are used to validate insert and update operations that are performed against the view. Additionally, every view created that is a child of the view that was created with the WITH CASCADED CHECK OPTION clause specified will inherit those constraints; the search conditions of both parent and child views are ANDed together to form the constraints. To better understand what this means, let's look at an example. Suppose a view was created using the following CREATE VIEW statement:

```
CREATE VIEW priority_orders
AS SELECT * FROM orders WHERE response_time < 4
```

Now, suppose a second view was created using the following CREATE VIEW statement:

```
CREATE VIEW special_orders
AS SELECT * FROM priority_orders
WITH CASCADED CHECK OPTION
```

If a user tries to insert a record into the SPECIAL_ORDERS view that has a RESPONSE_TIME value of 6, the insert operation will fail because the record violates the search condition of the PRIORITY_ORDERS view's definition (which is a constraint for the SPECIAL_ORDERS view). Figure 4–22 illustrates how the WITH CASCADED CHECK OPTION clause works.

```
CREATE VIEW priority_orders
  AS SELECT * FROM orders
    WHERE resp_time < 4
```

PRIORITY_ORDERS View

ORDERID	CUSTOMER	RESP_TIME
001	EMI	2
002	MCA	3
003	DECCA	3
004	ABKCO	4
005	WARNER BROS.	1

New Record

006	CAPITOL	6

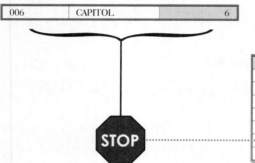

Record violates WITH CASCADED CHECK OPTION;
INSERT operation fails

SPECIAL_ORDERS View

ORDERID	CUSTOMER	RESP_TIME
001	EMI	2
002	MCA	3
003	DECCA	3
004	ABKCO	4
005	WARNER BROS.	1

```
CREATE VIEW special_orders
  AS SELECT * FROM primary_orders
  WITH CASCADED CHECK OPTION
```

Figure 4–22: How the WITH CASCADED CHECK OPTION clause is used to ensure that insert and update operations conform to a parent view's definition.

A Word About Inoperative Views

An inoperative view is a view that is no longer available and accessible to users and applications. A view can become inoperative when any of the following occur:

- A privilege on which the view definition is dependent is revoked, preventing access to one or more underlying base tables.

- An underlying view, table, alias, or function on which the view definition is dependent is dropped.

- A view on which the view definition is dependent becomes inoperative.

- The view's *superview* becomes inoperative (a superview is a typed view on which another typed view, known as a *subview*, is based).

Once a view becomes inoperative, the following steps can be used to recover it:

- Obtain the SQL statement initially used to create the view by querying the TEXT column of the SYSCAT.VIEW catalog view.

- Re-create the view by re-executing the CREATE VIEW statement (using the same view name and definition).

- Use the GRANT statement to re-grant all privileges that were previously granted on the view. (Privileges granted on a view are revoked when the view is marked inoperative.)

If you do not wish to recover an inoperative view, you can explicitly drop it with the DROP VIEW statement. Alternately, you can create a new view and assign it the same name as that of the inoperative view, but give it a different definition.

Indexes

An index is an object that contains an ordered set of pointers that refer to rows in a base table. Each index is based on one or more columns in the base table to which it refers (known as *keys*), however, indexes are stored as separate entities. Figure 4–23 shows the structure of a simple index, along with its relationship to a base table.

DEPARTMENT TABLE

DEPTID INDEX

KEY	ROW
A000	5
B001	2
C001	8
D001	11
E001	3
E002	6
E003	4
F001	1
F002	9
F003	7
G010	10

	DEPTID	DEPTNAME	COSTCENTER
Row 1 →	F001	ADMINISTRATION	10250
Row 2 →	B001	PLANNING	10820
Row 3 →	E001	ACCOUNTING	20450
Row 4 →	E003	HUMAN RESOURCES	30200
Row 5 →	A000	R & D	50120
Row 6 →	E002	MANUFACTURING	50220
Row 7 →	F003	OPERATIONS	50230
Row 8 →	C001	MARKETING	42100
Row 9 →	F002	SALES	42200
Row 10 →	G010	CUSTOMER SUPPORT	42300
Row 11 →	D001	LEGAL	60680

Figure 4–23: A simple index.

With DB2 9, several types of indexes are available:

Relational indexes. Indexes that are optimized for a single dimension.

Spatial Grid indexes. Indexes that are optimized for two-dimensional data. (Each spatial grid index is created on the X and Y dimensions of a geometry; the DB2 Spatial Extender generates a spatial grid index using the minimum bounding rectangle (MBR) of a geometry.)

Dynamic Bitmap indexes. Indexes that are produced by ANDing the results of multiple index scans using Dynamic Bitmap techniques. (ANDed predicates can be applied to multiple indexes to keep underlying table accesses to a minimum.)

Block Based indexes. Indexes that contain pointers to rows in a single dimension of a multidimensional clustering (MDC) table.

XML indexes. User-defined indexes over XML data that use a particular XML pattern (which is a limited XPath expression) to index paths and values in XML documents stored within a single column.

Indexes are important because they do the following:

- Provide a fast, efficient method for locating specific rows of data in very large tables. (In some cases, all the information needed to resolve a query may be found in the index itself, in which case the actual table data does not have to be accessed.)

- Provide a logical ordering of the rows of a table. (Data is stored in a table in no particular order; when indexes are used, the values of one or more columns can be sorted in ascending or descending order. This is very beneficial when processing queries that contain ORDER BY and GROUP BY clauses.)

- Improve overall query performance. (If no index exists on a table, a table scan must be performed for each table referenced in a query. The larger the table, the longer a table scan takes because a table scan requires each table row to be accessed sequentially.)

- Can be used to enforce the uniqueness of records stored in a table.

- Can require a table to use clustering storage, which causes the rows of a table to be physically arranged according to the ordering of their index column values. (Although all indexes provide a logical ordering of data, only a clustering index provides a physical ordering of data.)

- Can provide greater concurrency in multi-user environments. (Because records can be located faster, acquired locks do not have to be held as long.)

However, there is a price to pay for these benefits:

- Each index created requires additional storage or disk space. The exact amount of space needed is dependent on the size of the associated table, along with the size and number of columns contained in the index.

- Every insert and update operation performed on a table requires additional updating of the indexes associated with that table. This is also true when data is bulk-loaded into a table using DB2's LOAD utility.

- Each index potentially adds an alternative access path that the DB2 Optimizer must consider when generating the optimum access plan to use to resolve a query. This in turn increases compilation time when static queries are embedded in an application program.

Although some indexes are created implicitly to provide support for a table's definition (for example, to provide support for a primary key), indexes are typically created explicitly, using tools available with DB2. One way to explicitly create an index is by executing the CREATE INDEX SQL statement. The basic syntax for this statement is:

```
CREATE <UNIQUE> INDEX [IndexName]
ON [TableName] ([PriColumnName] <ASC | DESC> , . . .)
<INCLUDE ([SecColumnName] , . . .)>
<CLUSTER>
<PCTFREE 10 | PCTFREE [PercentFree]>
<ALLOW REVERSE SCANS | DISALLOW REVERSE SCANS>
```

where:

IndexName   Identifies the name that is to be assigned to the index to be created.

TableName   Identifies the name assigned to the base table with which the index to be created is to be associated.

PriColumnName Identifies one or more primary columns that are to be part of the index's key. (The combined values of each primary column specified will be used to enforce data uniqueness in the associated base table.)

SecColumnName Identifies one or more secondary columns whose values are to be stored with the values of the primary columns specified, but are not to be used to enforce data uniqueness.

PercentFree   Specifies a percentage of each index page to leave as free space when building the index.

If the UNIQUE clause is specified when the CREATE INDEX statement is executed, rows in the table associated with the index to be created must not have two or more occurrences of the same values in the set of columns that make up the index key. If the base table for which the index is to be created contains data, this uniqueness is checked when the DB2 Database Manager attempts to create the index specified— if records with duplicate values for the index key are found, the index will not be created; if no duplicates are found, the index is created, and uniqueness is enforced each time an insert or update operation is performed against the table. Any time the uniqueness of the index key is compromised, the insert or update operation will fail, and an error will be generated. It is important to keep in mind that when the UNIQUE clause is used, it is possible to have an index key that contains one (and only one) NULL value.

So if you wanted to create an index for a base table named EMPLOYEE such that the index key consists of a column named EMPNO and employee numbers are stored in descending order, you could do so by executing a CREATE INDEX statement that looks something like this:

```
CREATE INDEX empno_indx
ON employee (empno DESC)
```

On the other hand, if you wanted to create an index for a base table named EMPLOYEE that will store employee names in ascending order and ensure that no two employees can have the same first name, middle initial, and last name combination, you could do so by executing a CREATE INDEX statement that looks something like this:

```
CREATE UNIQUE INDEX empname_indx
ON employee (firstname, midinit, lastname)
```

And finally, if you wanted to create an index for a base table named EMPLOYEE to improve the performance of a query that retrieves employee number, salary, and bonus information (from columns named EMPNO, SALARY, and BONUS, respectively) while ensuring that all employee numbers entered into the EMPNO column are unique, you could do so by executing a CREATE INDEX statement that looks something like this:

```
CREATE UNIQUE INDEX empno_indx
ON employee (empno)
INCLUDE (salary, bonus)
```

Indexes can also be created using the Create Index wizard, which can be activated by selecting the appropriate action from the Indexes menu found in the Control Center. Figure 4–24 shows the Control Center menu items that must be selected to activate the Create Indexes dialog; Figure 4–25 shows how the Create Index wizard might look when it is first activated.

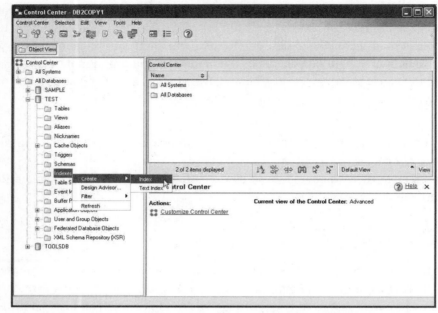

Figure 4–24: Invoking the Create Index dialog from the Control Center.

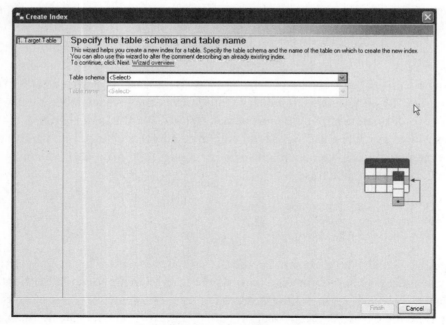

Figure 4-25: The Create Index wizard.

If an index is created for an empty table, that index will not have any entries stored in it until the table with which the index is associated is populated. On the other hand, if an index is created for a table that already contains data, index entries will be generated for the existing data and added to the index upon its creation.

Any number of indexes can be created for a table, using a wide variety of combinations of columns. However, as was pointed out earlier, each index comes at a price in both storage requirements and performance: each index replicates its key values, and this replication requires additional storage space. And because each modification to a table results in a similar modification to all indexes defined on the table, performance can decrease when insert, update, and delete operations are performed. In fact, if a large number of indexes are created for a table that is modified frequently, overall performance will decrease rather than increase for all operations *except* data retrieval. Tables that are used for data mining, business intelligence, business warehousing, and other applications that execute many (and often complex) queries while rarely modifying data are prime targets for multiple indexes. On the other hand, tables that are used in On-Line Transactional Processing (OLTP) environments or other environments where data throughput is high should use indexes sparingly.

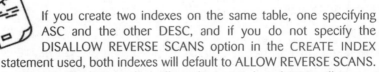

If you create two indexes on the same table, one specifying ASC and the other DESC, and if you do not specify the DISALLOW REVERSE SCANS option in the CREATE INDEX statement used, both indexes will default to ALLOW REVERSE SCANS. As a result, the latter index will not be created, and DB2 will issue a duplicate index warning message. (The ALLOW REVERSE SCANS option allows the same index to be used in two different queries that require the data to be in ascending *and* descending order.)

Clustering Indexes

A clustering index is a special index that, when used, informs the DB2 Database Manager to always try to store records on a page that contains other records that have similar index key values. (If no space is available on that page, the DB2 Database Manager will attempt to store the record in a page that is nearby.)

A clustering index usually increases performance by decreasing the amount of I/O required to access data: this results in fewer page fetches, given that like data values are stored on the same physical page. (Only one index in a table can be a clustering index.)

When rows in a logical set are physically stored close together, a read operation on the set of rows will require less I/O because adjacent rows are more likely to be found within the same extent (remember, data pages are written in batches called extents) instead of being widely distributed across multiple extents. And because similar key values are placed on the same data page whenever possible, often only a portion of a table will need to be read in response to a query. A clustering index is most useful for columns that have range predicates because it allows better sequential access of data in the base table.

A clustering index is created by specifying the CLUSTER option with the CREATE INDEX SQL statement. Thus, if you wanted to create a clustering index for a base table named EMPLOYEE such that the index key consists of a column named EMPNO, and all employee numbers entered into the EMPNO column are guaranteed to be unique, you could do so by executing a CREATE INDEX statement that looks something like this:

```
CREATE UNIQUE INDEX empno_cindx
ON employee (empno)
CLUSTER
```

When creating a clustering index, the PCTFREE option of the CREATE INDEX SQL statement can be used to control how much space is reserved for future insert and update operations. Specify a higher PCTFREE value (the default is 10 percent) at index creation time to reduce the likelihood that index page splits will occur when records are inserted into the index.

Over time, update operations can cause rows to change page locations, thereby reducing the degree of clustering that exists between an index and its data pages. Reorganizing a table (with the REORG utility) using the appropriate index will return the index specified to its original level of clustering.

Multidimensional Clustering (MDC) Indexes

Multidimensional clustering (MDC) provides a way to automatically cluster data along multiple dimensions. Such clustering results in significant improvement in query performance, as well as significant reduction in the overhead of data maintenance operations such as table/index reorganization and index maintenance operations during insert, update, and delete operations. Multidimensional clustering is primarily intended for data warehousing, online transaction processing (OLTP), and large database environments.

We just saw that when a clustering index is used, the DB2 Database Manager maintains the physical order of data on pages in the key order of the index, as records are inserted and updated in the table. With good clustering, only a portion of the table needs to be accessed in response to a query, and when the pages are stored sequentially, more efficient prefetching can be performed. With MDC, these benefits are extended to multiple keys (or dimensions); MDC allows a table to be physically clustered on more than one key (or dimension) simultaneously. Not only will queries access only those pages that contain records with the correct dimension values, but additionally, these qualifying pages will be grouped by extents. Furthermore, although a table with a clustering index can become unclustered over time as space fills up in the table, an MDC table is able to maintain its clustering over all dimensions automatically and continuously, thus eliminating the need to reorganize a table in order to restore the original level of clustering used.

When you create a multidimensional clustering index, you can specify one or more keys as dimensions that are to be used to cluster data; each dimension can consist of one or more columns, just like regular index keys. A dimension block index will be then be created automatically for each dimension specified, and the DB2 Optimizer will use this index to quickly and efficiently access data across each dimension. A composite block index that contains all dimension key columns will also be created, and this index will be used to maintain the clustering of data during insert and update operations. (A composite block index will be created only if a single dimension block index does not already contain all the dimension key columns specified for the table.) The composite block index can also be used by the DB2 Optimizer to efficiently access data. Every unique combination of dimension values forms a logical cell, which is physically composed of blocks of pages, where a block is a set of consecutive pages on disk. The set of blocks that contain pages with data having a certain key value of one of the dimension block indexes is called a *slice*. Every page of the table is part of exactly one block, and all blocks of the table consist of the same number of pages: the *blocking factor*. The blocking factor is equal to extent size, so that block boundaries line up with extent boundaries. Figure 4–26 shows a simple MDC table and its associated MDC indexes.

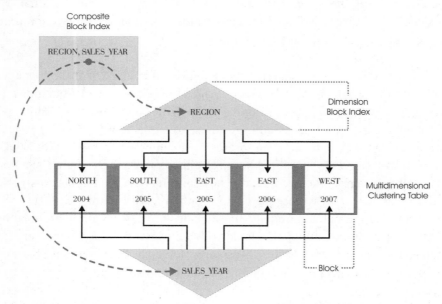

Figure 4–26: A simple multidimensional clustering table and its associated indexes.

Type-1 Versus Type-2 Indexes

In DB2 Version 8.1, the structure used to store index records was modified to help eliminate a phenomenon known as *Next-key locking*. Next-key locking occurs during index insert and delete operations and during index scans; when a row is inserted into, updated in, or deleted from a table, an Exclusive (X) lock is acquired for that row. When a corresponding key is inserted into or deleted from the table's index, the table row that corresponds to the key that follows the deleted or inserted key in the index is locked as well, with a Next-key Exclusive (NX) lock. (For update operations that affect the value of the key, the original key value is first deleted and the new value is inserted, so two Next-key Exclusive (NX) locks are acquired.) Thus, Next-key locking for Type-1 (older style) indexes during key value insertions and deletions could sometimes result in a deadlock cycle. With Type-2 indexes, such deadlocks do not occur because deleted keys are marked as being deleted and are not physically removed from the index. (Keys that have been marked as being deleted are overwritten by subsequent insert and update operations.)

By default, all new indexes created in DB2 9 use the Type-2 index structure, whereas existing indexes will continue to use the Type-1 index structure until they are manually converted. To convert a Type-1 index to a Type-2 index, you can either reorganize it with the REORG...CONVERT command (which we will look at in Chapter 6, "DB2 Utilities") or drop and recreate it.

A Word About the System Catalog

The system catalog is comprised of a set of special tables (and views) that contain information about all the objects within a database. These tables contain information about the definitions of the database objects (for example, tables, views, indexes, and packages) and security information about the type of access that users have to these objects. In Chapter 3, "Data Placement," we saw that the system catalog tables are created automatically when a new database is created. You cannot explicitly create or drop these tables, but you can control who has access to them.

Whenever an object is created, altered, or dropped, DB2 inserts, updates, or deletes records in the catalog that describe the object and how that object relates to other objects. Thus, if you want to obtain information about a particular database, often you can do so by connecting to that database and querying the system catalog. For example, suppose you wanted to find out whether a table named EMPLOYEE needed to be reorganized to eliminate fragmentation. You could do so by executing a query against a system catalog table named SYSCAT.TABLES that looks something like this:

```
SELECT TABNAME, OVERFLOW FROM
FROM SYSCAT.TABLES
WHERE TABNAME = 'EMPLOYEE'
```

If the results of this query indicate that a high number of overflow records exist for the EMPLOYEE table, the data is fragmented and the table probably needs to be reorganized. (We'll look at how to reorganize a table in Chapter 6, "DB2 Utilities.")

On the other hand, if you wanted to know whether statistics have been collected for the EMPLOYEE table, you could find this out by executing a query against the system catalog that looks something like this:

```
SELECT CARD AS num_rows
FROM SYSCAT.TABLES
WHERE TABNAME = 'EMPLOYEE'
```

In this case, if the query returns a value of -1 instead of the number of rows stored in the EMPLOYEE table, statistics have not been collected. (We'll look at how to collect statistics for a table in Chapter 6.)

The possibilities are almost endless. To find out more about the tables found in the system catalog and the information each table holds, refer to Appendix D, "Catalog Views," in the *IBM DB2 9 SQL Reference, Volume 1* product documentation.

The system catalog can be used only to obtain information about a specific database. If you want to obtain information at the system level, you must resort to executing administrative system commands or querying the administrative views available. For example, to obtain information about the DB2 products that have been installed on a particular server, you would have to execute the system command db2ls –q –a (if you are on a Linux or UNIX server) or issue a query against the SYSIBMADM.ENV_PROD_INFO administrative view that looks something like this: SELECT * FROM SYSIBMADM.ENV_PROD_INFO.

DB2 9's Comprehensive Tool Set

With the exception of DB2 Everyplace, DB2 for i5/OS, and DB2 for z/OS, each edition of DB2 and the DB2 Client comes with a comprehensive set of tools designed to assist in administering and managing DB2 instances, databases, and database objects. The majority of these tools have a graphical user interface (GUI); however, most of the tasks that can be performed with the GUI tools provided can also be performed by issuing equivalent DB2 commands from the operating system prompt or the DB2 Command Line Processor (another tool that we'll look at shortly). The following sections describe the most commonly used GUI tools available.

The Control Center

Of all the DB2 GUI tools available, the Control Center is the most important and versatile one provided. The Control Center presents a clear, concise view of an entire system and serves as the central point for managing DB2 systems and performing common administration tasks. With the Control Center, users can do the following:

- Create and delete instances

- Create and delete (drop) DB2 databases

- Catalog and uncatalog databases

- Configure instances and databases

- Create, alter, and drop buffer pools, table spaces, tables, views, indexes, aliases, triggers, schemas, and user-defined data types (UDTs)

- Grant and revoke authorities and privileges

- Export, import, or load data

- Reorganize tables and collect table statistics

- Back up and restore databases and table spaces

- Replicate data between systems

- Manage database connections

- Monitor resources and track events as they take place

- Analyze queries

- Schedule jobs to run unattended

The Control Center interface presents itself using one of three different views:

Basic. The basic view displays essential objects such as databases, tables, views, and stored procedures and limits the actions you can perform on those objects. This is the view you should use if you want to perform only core DB2 database operations.

Advanced. The advanced view displays all objects available in the Control Center and allows you to perform all actions available. This is the view you should use if you are working in an enterprise environment or if you want to connect to DB2 for i5/OS or DB2 for z/OS.

Custom. The custom view gives you the ability to tailor the object tree and actions allowed to meet your specific needs.

Figure 4–27 shows how the Control Center looks on a Windows XP server when the advanced view is used.

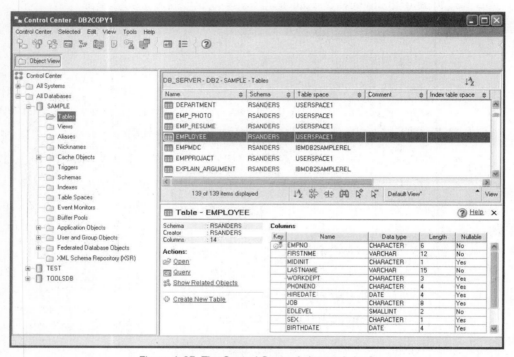

Figure 4–27: The Control Center (advanced view).

If you look closely at Figure 4–27, you will notice that the Control Center is made up of the following elements:

- A menu bar, which allows users to perform any of the Control Center functions available.

- A toolbar, which can be used to launch the other DB2 GUI tools available. Figure 4–28 identifies the tools that can be invoked directly from the Control Center toolbar.

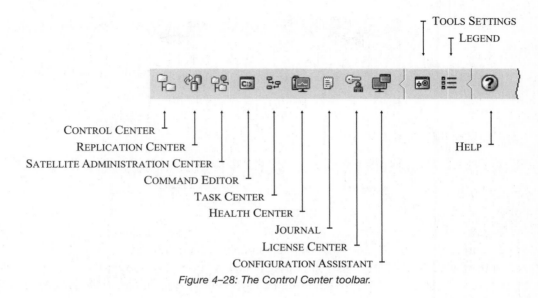

Figure 4–28: The Control Center toolbar.

It is important to note that every tool that can be invoked from the Control Center toolbar can also be invoked from the Control Center's menu bar.

- An objects pane (located on the left-hand side of the Control Center), which contains a hierarchical representation of every object type that can be managed from the Control Center.

- A contents pane (located on the upper right-hand side of the Control Center), which contains a listing of existing objects that correspond to the object type selected in the objects pane. (For example, if the Tables object type were selected in the objects pane, a list of all tables available would be listed in the contents pane.)

- An objects details pane (located on the lower right-hand side of the Control Center), which contains detailed information about the object selected in the object tree or contents pane.

As you can see in Figure 4–27, every object listed in the contents pane is preceded by an icon intended to identify the type of object being described in the list. A wide variety of icons are used, and users can see a list of all icons available, along with their corresponding object type, by viewing the Legend dialog, which can be accessed from the Control Center's menu and toolbar. Figure 4–29 shows what the Legend dialog looks like on a Windows XP server.

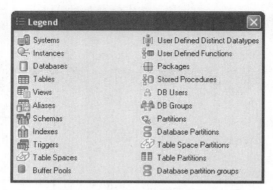

Figure 4–29: The Legend dialog.

Users can perform specific tasks on an object by selecting it from the list provided (in either the objects pane or the contents pane) and clicking the right mouse button; when the right mouse button is clicked, a pop-up menu that lists every action available for that particular object will be displayed, and the user simply selects the desired action from the menu.

The Replication Center

The Replication Center is an interactive GUI application that allows users to administer data replication between a DB2 database and any other relational database—whether that database is a DB2 database or not. From the Replication Center, users can perform the following actions:

- Define replication environments

- Create replication control tables

- Register replication sources

- Create subscription sets

- Add members to a subscription set

- Apply designated changes from one location to another

- Synchronize data in two locations

- Monitor the replication process

- Perform basic troubleshooting for replication operations

Figure 4–30 shows how the Replication Center looks when it is first invoked on a Windows XP server.

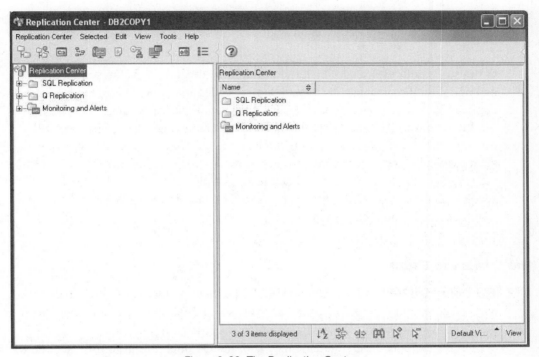

Figure 2–30: The Replication Center.

The Satellite Administration Center

The Satellite Administration Center is a GUI application that allows users to set up and administer a group of DB2 servers that perform the same business function. These servers, known as satellites, all run the same application and have the same DB2 database definition needed to support a particular application. With the Satellite Administration Center, users create a group and then define satellites as members of this group. You can then administer this group of satellites as a single entity, as opposed to having to administer each satellite separately. If additional DB2 servers that perform the same business function are acquired later, you simply add them to the group as additional satellites.

Information about a satellite environment is stored in a central database referred to as the satellite control database. This database records, among other things, which satellites are in the environment, the group to which each satellite belongs, and which version of an end-user business application a satellite is currently running. This database resides on a DB2 server known as the DB2 control server, and must be cataloged and accessible to the Control Center before the Satellite Administration Center can interact with it.

Groups of satellites are administered through the creation of batch scripts to set up and maintain the database definition that is needed to support the same business application on each satellite in a group. Each satellite then regularly connects to its satellite control server and downloads any scripts that apply to it. The satellite executes these scripts locally and uploads the results back to the satellite control database. This process of downloading batch scripts, executing them, and reporting the results of the batch execution back to the satellite control database is known as *synchronization*. A satellite synchronizes to maintain its consistency with the other satellites that belong to its group.

The Command Editor

The Command Editor is an interactive GUI application that is used to generate, edit, execute, and manipulate SQL statements and DB2 commands; to work with the resulting output; and to view a graphical representation of the access plan chosen for explained SQL statements. From the Command Editor, users can do the following:

- Execute SQL statements, DB2 commands, and operating system commands—operating system commands must be preceded by an exclamation mark (!).

- View the results of the execution of SQL statements and DB2 commands and see the result data set produced in response to a query.

- Save the results of the execution of SQL statements and DB2 commands to an external file.

- Create and save a sequence of SQL statements and DB2 commands to a script file that can be invoked by the Task Center. (Such a script file can then be scheduled to run at a specific time or frequency.)

- Use the SQL Assist tool to build complex queries.

- Examine the execution plan and statistics associated with a SQL statement before (or after) it is executed.

Figure 4–31 shows how the Command Editor looks on a Windows XP server after a database connection has been established.

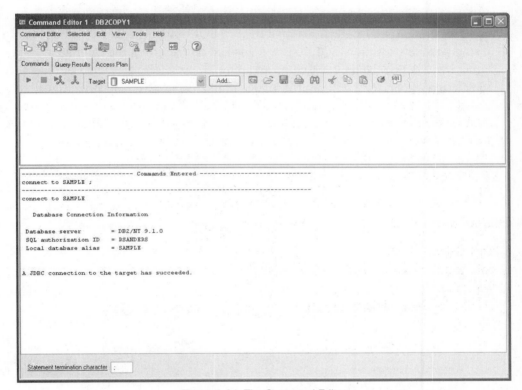

Figure 4–31: The Command Editor.

As you can see in Figure 4–31, the Command Editor is comprised of three different individual pages (which are accessed by tabs): the Commands page, the Query Results page, and the Access Plan page. Users can enter and execute an SQL statement or a DB2 command, create and save a script, run an existing script, or schedule a task from the Commands page. Once a query has been executed, users can see the results, if any, on the Query Results page. And on the Access Plan page, users can see the access plan for any explainable statement that was specified on the

Commands page. (If more than one SQL statement is specified on the Commands page, an access plan will be created for only the first statement encountered.)

SQL Assist

SQL Assist is an interactive GUI application that allows users to visually construct complex SELECT, INSERT, UPDATE, and DELETE SQL statements and examine the results of their execution. SQL Assist is invoked directly from the Command Editor, either by selecting the appropriate menu option or by selecting the appropriate toolbar icon (this icon will not be available until a database connection is established). Figure 4–32 identifies the Command Editor toolbar icon that is used to activate the SQL Assist dialog; Figure 4–33 shows how the SQL Assist dialog might look on a Windows XP server after it has been used to build a complex query.

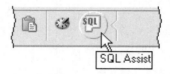

Figure 4-32: The SQL Assist icon on the Command Editor toolbar

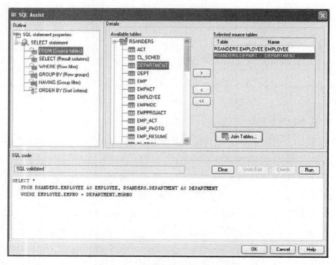

Figure 4–33: SQL Assist.

Once the desired SQL statement has been constructed inside SQL Assist, it can be written back to the Command Editor, where it can then be executed immediately or saved to a script file where it can be executed later using the Task Center.

Visual Explain

Visual Explain is a GUI tool that provides database administrators and application developers with the ability to view a graphical representation of the access plan that has been chosen by the DB2 Optimizer for a particular SQL statement. In addition, Visual Explain allows you to do the following:

- See the database statistics that were used to optimize the SQL statement.

- Determine whether an index was used to access table data. (If an index was not used, Visual Explain can help you determine which columns might benefit from being indexed.)

- View the effects of performance tuning by allowing you to make "before" and "after" comparisons.

- Obtain detailed information about each operation that is performed by the access plan, including the estimated cost of each.

Figure 4–34 shows how the Visual Explain tool might look like on a Windows XP server when it is displayed through selection of the Access Plan page from the Command Editor.

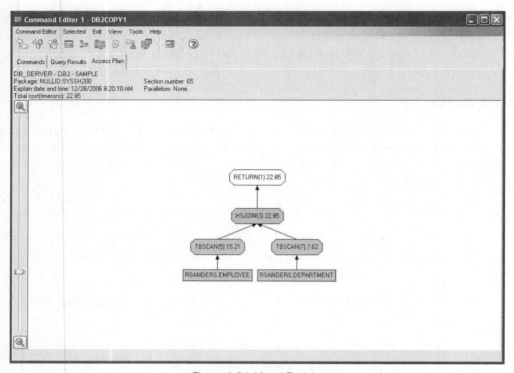

Figure 4–34: Visual Explain.

The output provided by Visual Explain consists of a hierarchical graph that represents the various components that are needed to process the access plan that has been chosen for a particular SQL statement. Each component is represented as a graphical object known as a node, and two types of nodes can exist:

> **Operator.** An operator node is used to identify either an action that must be performed on data or an output produced from a table or index.

> **Operand.** An operand node is used to identify an entity on which an operation is performed (for example, a table would be the operand of a table scan operator).

Typically, operand nodes are used to identify tables, indexes, and table queues (table queues are used when intrapartition parallelism is used), which are symbolized in the hierarchical graph by rectangles (tables), diamonds (indexes), and parallelograms (table queues). Operator nodes, on the other hand, are used to identify anything from an insert operation to an index or table scan. Operator nodes, which are symbolized in the hierarchical graph by ovals, indicate how data is accessed, how tables are joined, and other factors such as whether a sort operation is to be performed. Arrows that illustrate how data flows from one node to the next connect all nodes shown in the hierarchical graph, and a RETURN operator normally terminates this path.

Visual Explain can be invoked directly from the Command Editor by selecting the Access Plan page. However, before Explain information can be displayed, an access plan must exist; access plans can be generated for SQL statements entered on the Commands page of the Command Editor through selection of either the Execute and Access plan or the Access Plan icon from the Command Editor toolbar. Figure 4–35 identifies the Command Editor toolbar icon that is used to generate an access plan for an SQL statement.

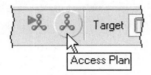

Figure 4–35: The Access Plan icon on the Command Editor toolbar

We'll take a closer look at Visual Explain in Chapter 5, "Analyzing DB2 Activity."

The Task Center

The Task Center is an interactive GUI application that allows users to schedule tasks, run tasks, and send notifications about completed tasks to other users. A task is a script together with any associated success conditions, schedules, and notifications. Users can create a task within the Task Center, generate a task by saving the results from a DB2 dialog or wizard, create a script within another tool and save it to the Task Center, or import an existing script. Such scripts can contain DB2 commands, SQL statements, operating system commands, or any combination of the three.

The Task Center uses *success code sets* (the return codes or range of return codes that, if received, indicate the task was executed successfully) to evaluate the success or failure of any task it executes—codes that fall outside the range specified indicate failure. In addition, the Task Center evaluates the SQLCA return code of every SQL statement executed in a DB2 script, and if any statement fails, the entire task fails. As well as evaluating the success or failure of a particular task, the Task Center can perform one or more actions if a particular task succeeds and perform other actions if the task fails. The Task Center can also be configured to perform one or more actions each time a scheduled task completes, regardless of the outcome of that task (success or failure).

Figure 4–36 shows how the Task Center might look on a Windows XP server after a Database Backup task has been created.

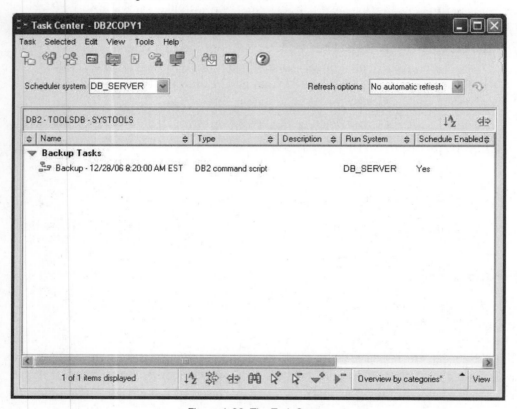

Figure 4–36: The Task Center.

If you run a script from the Task Center, instead of from the Command Editor or a command prompt, the results will be logged in the Journal. By viewing the Journal, you can see a list of jobs that use a particular script, along with the status of all jobs that either already have been executed or are scheduled to be executed.

The Health Center

Database monitoring is such an integral part of database administration that DB2 comes equipped with a monitoring utility known as the Database System Monitor. Although the name "Database System Monitor" suggests that only one monitoring tool is provided, in reality the Database System Monitor is composed of two distinct tools—a *snapshot monitor* and one or more *event monitors*—that can be used to capture and return system monitor information. The snapshot monitor allows you to capture a picture of the state of a database (along with all database activity) at a specific point in time, whereas event monitors capture and log data as specific database events occur. Along with the Database System Monitor, DB2 provides two additional tools that are designed to help database administrators monitor DB2 systems under their control. These tools are known as the Health Monitor and the Health Center. Together, these tools provide a management by exception capability that enables administrators to address system health issues before they become real problems.

The Health Monitor is a server-side tool that constantly monitors the health of a DB2 Database Manager instance without a need for user interaction; the Health Monitor uses several health indicators to evaluate specific aspects of instance and database performance. A *health indicator* is a system characteristic that the Health Monitor monitors continuously to determine whether an object is operating normally; each health indicator has a corresponding set of predefined threshold values, and the Health Monitor compares the state of the system against these health-indicator thresholds to see if they have been exceeded. If the Health Monitor finds that a predefined threshold has been surpassed (for example, if the amount of log space available is insufficient), or if it detects an abnormal state for an object (for example, if the instance is down), it will automatically raise an alert.

The Health Center is a GUI tool designed to interact with the Health Monitor. Using the Health Center, you can select the instance and database objects that you want to monitor, customize the threshold settings of any health indicator, and specify where notifications are to be sent and what actions are to be taken if an alert is issued. The Health Center also allows you to start and stop the Health Monitor, as well as access details about current alerts and obtain a list of recommended actions that describe how to resolve the situation that caused an alert to be generated. Figure 4–37 shows how the Health Center looks on a

Windows XP server (in this case, after two warning type alerts have been generated).

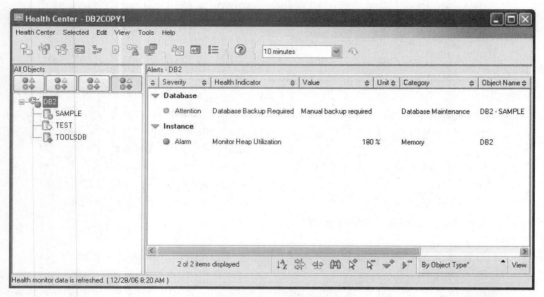

Figure 4–37: The Health Center.

We'll take a closer look at the database system monitor, the Health Monitor, and the Health Center in Chapter 5, "Analyzing DB2 Activity."

The Journal

The Journal is an interactive GUI application that tracks historical information about tasks, database actions and operations, Control Center actions, messages, and alerts. To present this information in an organized manner, the Journal uses several different views:

- Task History
- Database History
- Messages
- Notification Log

The Task History view shows the results of tasks that have already been executed. This view contains one entry for each individual task (regardless of how many times the task was executed) and allows users to do the following:

- View details of any task that has been executed
- View the results any task that has been executed
- Edit any task that has been executed
- View execution statistics associated with any task that has been executed
- Remove any task execution record from the Journal

The Database History view shows information stored in a database's recovery history file. The recovery history file is automatically updated whenever any of the following operations are performed:

- Database or table space backup
- Database or table space restore
- Roll-forward recovery
- Load
- Table reorganization

The Messages view shows a running history of messages that were issued from the Control Center and any other GUI tool, and the Notification Log view shows information from the administration notification log.

Figure 4–38 shows how the Messages view of the Journal might look on a Windows XP server.

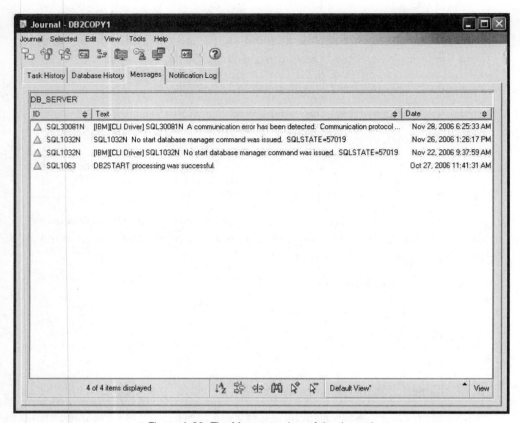

Figure 4–38: The Messages view of the Journal.

The License Center

The License Center is an interactive GUI application that allows users to view information about the license associated with each DB2 product installed on a particular system. Such information includes processor status information, concurrent users policy information, license information, and user statistics or details. This tool can also be used to add or remove licenses or registered users, change license type policies, change the number of concurrent users, change the number of licensed processors, change the number of Internet processor licenses, and configure a particular system for proper license monitoring. Figure 4–39 shows how the License Center might look on a Windows XP server.

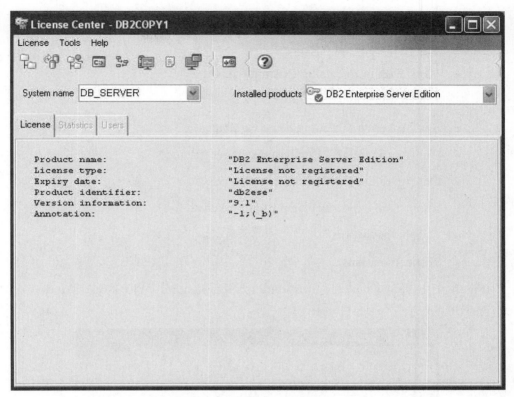

Figure 4–39: The License Center.

The Configuration Assistant

The Configuration Assistant is an interactive GUI application that allows users to configure clients so that they can access databases stored on remote DB2 servers. In order to access an instance or database on another server/system, that system must first be cataloged in the node directory of the client workstation, and information about the remote database must be cataloged in the database directory (and on the client workstation). The Configuration Assistant provides a way to quickly catalog nodes and databases without having to know the inherent complexities involved with performing these tasks. And because the Configuration Assistant maintains a list of databases to which users and applications can connect, it can act as a lightweight alternative to the Control Center in situations where the complete set of GUI tools available has not been installed.

From the Configuration Assistant, users can do the following:

- Catalog new databases

- Work with or uncatalog existing databases

- Bind applications

- Set DB2 environment/registry variables

- Configure the DB2 Database Manager instance

- Configure ODBC/CLI parameters

- Import and export configuration information

- Change passwords

- Test connections

Figure 4–40 shows how the Configuration Assistant might look on a Windows XP server.

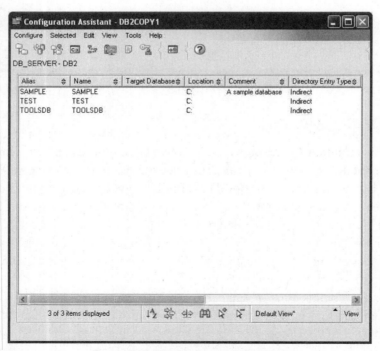

Figure 4–40: The Configuration Assistant.

The Tools Settings Notebook

The Tools Settings notebook is an interactive GUI application used to customize settings and set properties for the various DB2 administration tools available. To present and collect this information in an organized manner, the Tools Settings notebook uses several different pages/tabs—some pages/tabs will be displayed only after the tools for which they apply have been installed. The pages available with the Tools Settings notebook are as follows:

General page. This page is used to specify whether the local DB2 instance should be started automatically when the DB2 tools are started, whether to use a statement termination character, and whether to use filtering when the maximum number of rows returned for a display sample contents request is exceeded.

Documentation page. This page is used to specify whether hover help and infopop help features in the DB2 administration tools should display automatically and also to specify the location from which the contextual help is accessed at the instance level.

Fonts page. This page is used to change the font in which text and menus appear in the DB2 administration tools.

OS/390 and z/OS page. This page is used to set column headings and define the online and batch utility execution options for OS/390 and z/OS objects.

Health Center Status Beacon page. This page is used to specify the type of notification you will receive when an alert is generated in the Health Monitor. You can be notified through a pop-up message, with the graphical beacon that displays on the lower-right portion of the status line for each DB2 center, or through both methods of notification.

Scheduler Settings page. This page is used to set the default scheduling scheme. Select Server Scheduling if you want task scheduling to be handled by the scheduler that is local to the database server; select Centralized Scheduling if you want the storage and scheduling of tasks to be handled by a centralized system, in which case you need to select the centralized system from the Centralized Scheduler list. (To enable another scheduler, select a system and click Create New to open a window in which you can create a database for the DB2 Tools Catalog on a cataloged system. If the system you want is not cataloged, you must catalog it first.)

Command Editor page. This page is used to specify how you will generate, edit, execute, and manipulate SQL and XQuery statements, IMS commands, and DB2 commands. This page is also used to specify how you want to work with the resulting output.

IMS page. This page is used to set your preferences when working with IMS. From this page, you can set preferences for using wizards, for syntax support, and for returning results.

Figure 4–41 shows how the Tools Settings notebook looks on a Windows XP server when it is first activated.

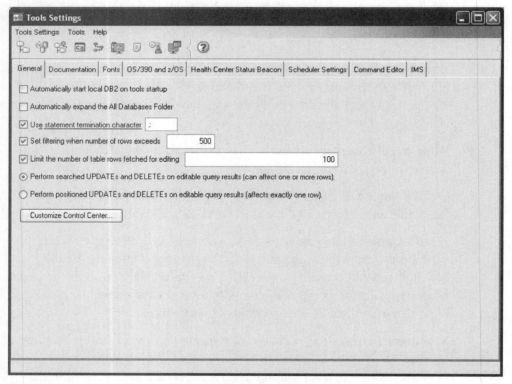

Figure 4–41: The Tools Settings dialog.

The Design Advisor

Earlier, we saw that the primary purpose of an index in a DB2 database is to help the database engine quickly locate records stored in a table; if a table is referenced in a query, and no corresponding index exists, the entire table must be scanned sequentially to locate the desired data. And if the table contains a large amount of data, such a scan can take a significant amount of time. In most cases, if an index is created for frequently used columns in a table, performance can often be greatly improved for data access operations. That's because index files are generally smaller and require less time to read than their corresponding table files, particularly as tables grow in size. Furthermore, the entire index may not need to be scanned; predicates can be applied to an index to reduce the number of rows that must actually be read.

So how do you decide when having an index would be beneficial, and how do you determine what indexes should exist? And how do you decide whether to use materialized query tables (MQTs) or partitioning to help improve index performance? Even if you have a lot of experience with database and database application design, the task of selecting which indexes, MQTs, clustering dimensions, or database partitions to create for a complex workload can be quite daunting. That's where the Design Advisor comes in.

The Design Advisor is a special tool that is designed to capture specific information about typical workloads (queries or sets of SQL operations) performed against your database and to recommend changes based on the information provided. When given a set of SQL statements in a workload, the Design Advisor will make recommendations for the following:

- New indexes
- New materialized query tables (MQTs)
- Conversions of base tables to multidimensional clustering (MDC) tables
- Redistribution of table data
- Deletion of indexes and MQTs that are not being used by the specified workload

You can have the Design Advisor implement some or all of these recommendations immediately or arrange for them to be applied at a later time. Furthermore, the Design Advisor can be used to aid in the design of a new database or to improve performance of a database that is already in operation. For example, while designing a database, the Design Advisor can do the following:

- Generate design alternatives for a partitioned database environment and for indexes, MQTs, and MDC tables

- For partitioned database environments, determine the best database partitioning strategy to use

- For partitioned database environments, assist in migrating from another database product to a multiple-partition DB2 database

Once a database is in production, the Design Advisor can be used to do the following:

- Improve performance of a particular SQL statement or workload

- Improve general database performance, using the performance of a sample workload as a gauge

- Improve performance of the most frequently executed queries, for example, as identified by the Activity Monitor

- Determine how to optimize the performance of a new key query

- Respond to Health Center recommendations regarding shared memory utility or sort heap problems encountered by a sort-intensive workload

- Find objects such as indexes and MQTs that are not used in a workload

- Assist in migrating from a single-partition DB2 database to a multiple-partition DB2 database

- Evaluate indexes, MQTs, MDC tables, or database partitioning strategies that have been generated manually

Figure 4–42 shows how the second page of the Design Advisor looks on a Windows XP server.

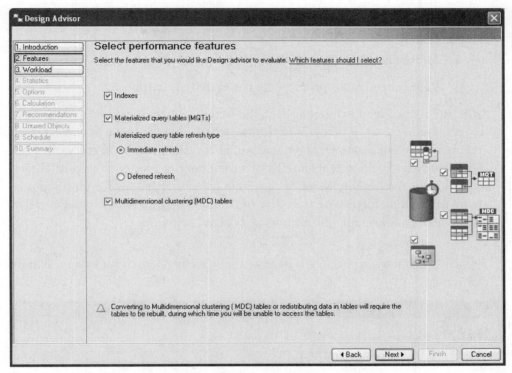

Figure 4–42: The second page of the Design Advisor wizard.

The Activity Monitor

The Activity Monitor is an interactive GUI application that allows users to monitor application performance, application concurrency, resource consumption, and SQL statement usage on a database or a database partition. With the Activity Monitor, you can view the following:

- Transactions running on a selected application

- SQL statements running on a selected application

- The text of SQL statements running on a selected application

- Locks and lock-waiting situations that currently affect a selected application

- Information about a selected application for which you are viewing lock information

- Information about the locks held and the locks waited on by a selected application in your database

- Information to help you interpret report data

- Recommendations provided by the Activity Monitor

In addition to collecting monitor data, the Activity Monitor can present the data collected using a set of predefined reports, which are based on a specific subset of monitor data. (For example, one report might contain a graphical representation that identifies a locking problem that's causing poor concurrency on a database.) Additionally, the Activity Monitor can make recommendations for most reports that will assist in diagnosing the cause of database performance problems and in tuning queries for optimal utilization of database resources.

Figure 4–43 shows how the first page of the Activity Monitor looks on a Windows XP server.

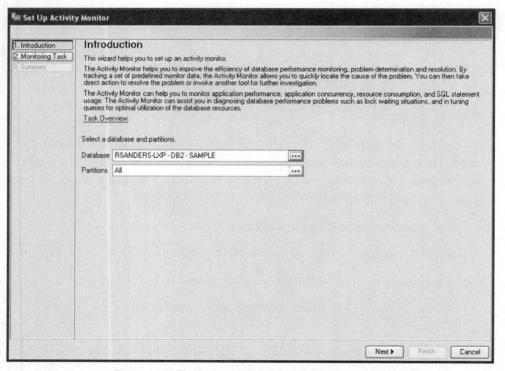

Figure 4–43: The first page of the Activity Monitor wizard.

The Command Line Processor

The Command Line Processor (CLP) is a text-oriented application that allows users to issue DB2 commands, system commands, and SQL statements, as well as view the results of the statements/commands executed. The Command Line Processor can be run in three different modes:

Command mode. When the Command Line Processor is run in command mode, the user simply enters a DB2 command or SQL statement—preceded by the characters "db2"—at the system prompt. (For example, the command "CONNECT TO sample" would be entered as "db2 CONNECT TO sample"). If the command contains characters that have a special meaning to the operating system being used, it must be enclosed in quotation marks to ensure that it will be properly executed (for example, db2 "SELECT COUNT(*) FROM employee"). If the command to be executed is too long to fit on a single line, a space followed by the line continuation character (\) can be placed at the end of the line that is to be continued, and the rest of the command can follow on a new line.

Interactive Input mode. When the Command Line Processor is run in interactive input mode, the "db2" prefix is automatically provided (as characterized by the **db2** => input prompt) for each command/SQL statement entered. To run the Command Line Processor in interactive input mode, you simply enter the command "db2" at the system prompt. To exit out of interactive mode, you enter the command "quit" at the Command Line Processor prompt. Aside from that, the rules that apply to using the command mode of the Command Line Processor also apply to using the interactive input mode.

Batch mode. When the Command Line Processor is run in batch mode, it is assumed that all commands and/or SQL statements to be executed have been stored in an ASCII-format text file. (The characters "db2" should not precede the commands/statements stored in this file.) To run the Command Line Processor in batch mode, you simply enter the command "db2-f *xxxxxxxx*" (where *xxxxxxxx* is the name of the file that contains the set of commands that are to be executed) at the system prompt.

Figure 4–44 shows how the Command Line Processor looks on a Windows XP server when it is run in interactive input mode.

Figure 4–44: The Command Line Processor (in interactive input mode).

Various command-line options can be specified when the Command Line
Processor is invoked; a list of all options available can be obtained by executing the
command LIST COMMAND OPTIONS, from either the system prompt or the
Command Line Processor prompt (when the Command Line Processor is run in
interactive input mode).

Practice Questions

Question 1

What are informational constraints used for?

- ✓ A. To influence DB2 Optimizer data access plan selection without slowing down DML operations
- ○ B. To provide information to an application about any constraints that have been defined
- ○ C. To define non-checked primary keys
- ○ D. To influence DB2 Optimizer data access plans for foreign key-primary key relationships

Question 2

Given the following CREATE TABLE statement:

```
CREATE TABLE department
    (deptid    INTEGER,
    deptname   CHAR(25),
    budget     NUMERIC(12,2))
```

Which of the following statements prevents two departments from being assigned the same DEPTID, but allows null values?

- ○ A. ALTER TABLE department ADD CONSTRAINT dpt_cst PRIMARY KEY (deptid)
- ○ B. CREATE INDEX dpt_idx ON department(deptid)
- ○ C. ALTER TABLE department ADD CONSTRAINT dpt_cst UNIQUE (deptid)
- ✓ D. CREATE UNIQUE INDEX dpt_idx ON department(deptid)

Question 3

Given the following CREATE TABLE statement:

```
CREATE TABLE products
    (prodid        INTEGER NOT NULL PRIMARY KEY,
     category      CHAR(3) CHECK(category IN ('323', '441',
        '615', '832', '934')),
     description   VARCHAR(200),
     quantity      INTEGER CHECK (quantity > 0),
     sellprice     NUMERIC(7,2) WITH DEFAULT,
     buyprice      NUMERIC(7,2) WITH DEFAULT,
 CONSTRAINT zeroloss CHECK (sellprice > buyprice))
```

Assuming the table is empty, which of the following INSERT statements will succeed?

- ○ A. INSERT INTO products (prodid, category, description, buyprice) VALUES (1, '832', 'medium white shirt', 6.99)

- ○ B. INSERT INTO products (prodid, category, quantity, sellprice, buyprice) VALUES (2, '323', 5, 28.99, 26.99)

- ○ C. INSERT INTO products (prodid, category, description, quantity) VALUES (1, '934', 'black shoe', 10)

- ○ D. INSERT INTO products (prodid, category, description, quantity, sellprice, buyprice) VALUES (2, '615', 'dark blue socks', 3, 20.00, 25.65)

Question 4

Given the following CREATE TABLE statement:

```
CREATE TABLE employee
    (empid    INTEGER NOT NULL,
     name     VARVHAR(25),
     gender   CHAR(1) NOT NULL,
  CONSTRAINT gender_ok CHECK(gender IN ('M', 'F'))
      NOT ENFORCED
    ENABLE QUERY OPTIMIZATION)
```

What effect, if any, will the following command have when it is executed?

```
ALTER TABLE employee ALTER CHECK gender_ok DISABLE QUERY
OPTIMIZATION
```

○ A. The GENDER_OK constraint will become an enforced check constraint and will be used to check the validity of insert and update operations.

○ B. The GENDER_OK constraint will become an enforced check constraint and any data that resides in the EMPLOYEE table will be checked immediately for constraint violations.

◉ C. The ability for the DB2 Optimizer to use the GENDER_OK constraint for query optimization will be disabled.

○ D. All data access plans that used the GENDER_OK constraint for query optimization will be marked inoperative.

Question 5

Given the following CREATE TABLE statement:

```
CREATE TABLE employee
   (empid    INTEGER NOT NULL,
    lname    VARVHAR(20),
    gender   CHAR(1) NOT NULL,
  CONSTRAINT gender_ok CHECK(gender IN ('M', 'F'))
    NOT ENFORCED
    ENABLE QUERY OPTIMIZATION)
```

And the following INSERT statement:

```
INSERT INTO employee VALUES (1, 'Smith', 'M'),
    (2, 'Doe', 'F'), (3, 'Jones', 'U')
```

Which of the following queries will return an empty result set?

○ A. SELECT COUNT(gender) FROM employee

○ B. SELECT * FROM employee WHERE gender = 'M'

○ C. SELECT * FROM employee WHERE gender = 'F'

◉ D. SELECT * FROM employee WHERE gender = 'U'

Question 6

Which of the following CREATE VIEW statements will ensure that every attempt to insert or update a record in table T1 via the view V1 must pass some criteria before the row can be inserted/updated?

- ○ A.   CREATE VIEW v1 AS SELECT c1, c2 FROM t1 WHERE c1 < 100
- ○ B.   CREATE VIEW v1 AS SELECT c1, c2 FROM t1 WHERE c1 < 100 ENFORCED
- ○ C.   CREATE VIEW v1 AS SELECT c1, c2 FROM t1 WHERE c1 < 100 WITH VALIDATION
- ☑ D.   CREATE VIEW v1 AS SELECT c1, c2 FROM t1 WHERE c1 < 100 WITH LOCAL CHECK OPTION

Question 7

Which of the following statements is NOT true concerning inoperative views?

- ○ A.   A view can become inoperative when a privilege the view definition is dependent upon is revoked.
- ○ B.   Privileges granted on a view are revoked when the view is marked inoperative.
- ☑ C.   An inoperative must be recovered before it can be dropped.
- ○ D.   An inoperative view can be recreated by re-executing the statement initially used to create it (found in the TEXT column of the SYSCAT.VIEW catalog view.)

Question 8

Which two of the following are valid indexes that are supported by DB2?

- ☑ A.   Spatial grid indexes
- ☐ B.   Static bitmap indexes
- ☑ C.   Dynamic bitmap indexes
- ☐ D.   Page-based indexes
- ☐ E.   Multidimensional range-clustered indexes

Question 9

Given the following CREATE TABLE statement:

```
CREATE TABLE tab1
    (c1    SMALLINT,
     c2    SMALLINT,
     c3    SMALLINT,
     c4    CHAR(4))
```

If the column C1 must be unique and the following queries are frequently issued against table TAB1:

```
SELECT c1, c2 FROM tab1 ORDER BY c1;
SELECT c1, c2, c3 FROM tab1 ORDER BY c1;
```

Which of the following statements will improve performance by providing index-only access?

○ A. CREATE INDEX indx1 ON tab1 (c1)

○ B. CREATE UNIQUE INDEX indx1 ON tab1 (c1) INCLUDE (c2)

○ C. CREATE INDEX indx1 ON tab1 (c1, c2, c3)

✓ D. CREATE UNIQUE INDEX indx1 ON tab1 (c1) INCLUDE (c2, c3)

Question 10

Given the following CREATE TABLE statement:

```
CREATE TABLE tab1
    (c1    SMALLINT,
     c2    CHAR(4))
```

Table TAB1 is accessed frequently by two applications; one application returns the data in column C1 in ascending order, the other application returns the data in column C1 in descending order. To improve performance, a database administrator executes the following commands:

```
CREATE INDEX indx1 ON tab1(c1 ASC);
CREATE INDEX indx2 ON tab1(c1 DESC);
```

Which of the following will occur?

○ A. Index INDX1 will be created and the first application will use it when retrieving data; the index INDX2 will be created and the second application will use it when retrieving data.

○ B. Index INDX1 will be created. When an attempt is made to create index INDX2, DB2 will alter index INDX1 to allow reverse scans and index INDX1 be used by both applications when retrieving data.

○ C. Index INDX1 will be created. When an attempt is made to create index INDX2, DB2 will alter index INDX2 to allow reverse scans and drop index INDX1; index INDX2 will be used by both applications when retrieving data.

◉ D. Index INDX1 will be created and allow reverse scans by default. When an attempt is made to create index INDX2, DB2 will issue a duplicate index warning message. Index INDX1 will be used by both applications when retrieving data.

Question 11

Given the following table:

SALES

REGION	SALES_REP_ID	AMOUNT
East	1200	24000
East	1420	32000
West	1200	29000
South	2120	34000

If the following SQL statements are executed:

```
CREATE UNIQUE INDEX indx1 ON sales(sales_rep_id);
INSERT INTO sales VALUES ('North', 1420, 27500);
SELECT * FROM sales;
```

How many rows will be returned by the last query?

○ A. 3

○ B. 4

○ C. 5

○ D. 6

Question 12

Which of the following best describes the function of the db2ls command?

○ A. It retrieves information about the DB2 products that have been installed on a particular server.

○ B. It locks a DB2 system and limits access to users who hold System Administrator authority.

○ C. It generates a list of all remote servers that have been cataloged on a client workstation.

○ D. It returns the location of the system catalog for a particular database.

Question 13

If the following query is executed:

```
SELECT TABNAME, OVERFLOW
FROM SYSCAT,TABLES
WHERE TABNAME = 'SALES'
```

Which of the following can be determined based on the results?

○ A. Whether or not the SALES table needs to be reorganized to reduce data fragmentation.

○ B. Whether or not the amount of memory available for sort operations needs to be increased.

○ C. Whether or not statistics for the SALES table need to be updated.

○ D. Whether or not the size of the lock list should be increased to reduce the amount of lock escalations seen.

Question 14

If the following query is executed:

```
SELECT TABNAME, CARD
FROM SYSCAT, TABLES
WHERE TABNAME = 'EMPLOYEES'
```

Which of the following can be determined based on the results?

- ○ A. Whether or not the EMPLOYEES table needs to be reorganized to reduce data fragmentation.
- ○ B. Whether or not the amount of storage available for the table space where the EMPLOYEES table resides needs to be increased.
- ◉ C. Whether or not statistics for the EMPLOYEES table have been collected.
- ○ D. Whether or not storage space can be saved by enabling the EMPLOYEES table for data row compression.

Question 15

Which of the following is NOT a valid Control Center view?

- ○ A. Basic
- ◉ B. Intermediate
- ○ C. Advanced
- ○ D. Custom

Question 16

Which of the following objects can NOT be created from the Control Center?

- ○ A. Buffer pool
- ○ B. Event monitor
- ○ C. Trigger
- ◉ D. User-defined function

Question 17

Which of the following best describes the function of the Activity Monitor?

- ○ A. Captures specific information about typical workloads (queries or sets of SQL operations) performed against a database and recommends changes based upon the information provided.

- ○ B. Constantly monitors the health of a DB2 Database Manager instance using several health indicators to evaluate specific aspects of instance and database performance.

- ☑ C. Monitors application performance, application concurrency, resource consumption, and SQL statement usage on a database or a database partition.

- ○ D. Configures clients so they can access databases stored on remote DB2 servers.

Question 18

Which of the following operations can NOT be performed using the Tools Settings notebook?

- ☑ A. Define replication environments.
- ○ B. Change the font used to display text and menu options.
- ○ C. Set the default scheduling scheme.
- ○ D. Configure Health Status Beacons.

Question 19

Which of the following tools is NOT accessible through the Control Center?

- ○ A. The Health Center
- ○ B. The Command Editor
- ☑ C. The Command Line Processor
- ○ D. The License Center

Question 20

Which of the following can NOT be used to set DB2 environment/registry variables?

- ○ A. Configuration Assistant
- ◉ B. Design Advisor
- ○ C. Command Editor
- ○ D. Command Line Processor

Answers

Question 1

The correct answer is **A**. Unlike other constraints, informational constraints are not enforced during insert and update processing. However, the DB2 SQL optimizer will evaluate information provided by an informational constraint when considering the best access plan to use to resolve a query. As a result, an informational constraint may result in better query performance even though the constraint itself will not be used to validate data entry/modification. (Informational constraints are defined by appending the keywords NOT ENFORCED ENABLE QUERY OPTIMIZATION to a normal constraint definition.)

Question 2

The correct answer is **D**. By default, records that are added to a base table can have the same values assigned to any of the columns available any number of times. DB2. The unique constraint can be used to ensure that the value(s) assigned to one or more columns when a record is added to a base table are always unique; once a unique constraint has been defined for one or more columns, any operation that attempts to place duplicate values in those columns will fail. Unique constraints are usually defined during the table creation process, but can be added later with the ALTER TABLE SQL statement.

When a unique constraint is defined the DB2 Database Manager looks to see if an index for the columns the unique constraint refers to already exists. If so, that index is marked as being unique and system-required. If not, an appropriate index is created and marked as being unique and system-required. This index is then used to enforce uniqueness whenever new records are added to the column(s) the unique constraint was defined for.

Although a unique, system-required index is used to enforce a unique constraint, there is a distinction between defining a unique constraint and creating a unique index. Even though both enforce uniqueness, a unique index allows NULL values and generally cannot be used in a referential constraint. A unique constraint on the other hand, does not allow NULL values and can be referenced in a foreign key specification.

Question 3

The correct answer is **B**. The first INSERT statement will fail because the resulting SELLPRICE will be 0 (since no value was provided) and a SELLPRICE of 0 is less than a BUYPRICE of 6.99 which violates the ZEROLOSS check constraint. The third INSERT statement will fail because the CATEGORY '423' is not in the set of values that are allowed for the CATEGORY column. Also, the resulting SELLPRICE and BUYPRICE will be 0 (since no value was provided) and a SELLPRICE of 0 is not greater than a BUYPRICE of 0 which violates the ZEROLOSS check constraint. And finally, the last INSERT statement will fail because a SELLPRICE of 20.00 is less than a BUYPRICE of 25.65 which violates the ZEROLOSS check constraint.

Question 4

The correct answer is **C**. To tell the DB2 Optimizer to ignore an informational constraint when selecting the best data access plan to use to resolve a query, you simply disable query optimization for the constraint. This can be done at the time the constraint is created, or it can be done later by executing an ALTER TABLE statement, identifying the constraint to be altered, and specifying the DISABLE QUERY OPTIMIZATION option.

Question 5

The correct answer is **D**. Because the DB2 Optimizer evaluates informational constraints when selecting the best data access plan to use to resolve a query, records that have been inserted into a table that violate one or more informational constraints may not be returned by some queries. Thus, if the query "SELECT * FROM employee WHERE gender = 'U'" were to be executed against the EMPLOYEE table shown, no records would be returned because the access plan chosen would assume that no records with a GENDER value of anything other than 'M' or 'F' exists in the table.

Question 6

The correct answer is **D**. If the WITH LOCAL CHECK OPTION clause of with the CREATE VIEW SQL statement is specified (or if the Local Check option is selected on the Create View dialog), insert and update operations performed against the view that is created are validated to ensure that all rows being inserted into or updated in the base table the view refers to conform to the view's definition (otherwise, the insert/update operation will fail).

So what exactly does this mean? Suppose a view was created using the following CREATE VIEW statement:

```
CREATE VIEW prority_orders
AS SELECT * FROM oirders WHERE response_time < 4
WITH LOCAL CHECK OPTION
```

Now, suppose a user tries to insert a record into this view that has a RESPONSE_TIME value of 6. The insert operation will fail because the record violates the view's definition. Had the view not been created with the WITH LOCAL CHECK OPTION clause, the insert operation would have been successful, even though the new record would not be visible to the view that was used to add it.

Question 7

The correct answer is **C**. If you do not wish to recover an inoperative view, you can explicitly drop it with the DROP VIEW statement. Alternately, you can create a new view and assign it the same name as that of the inoperative view, but give it a different definition.

Question 8

The correct answers are **A** and **C**. With DB2 9, several types of indexes are available:

Relational indexes. Indexes that are optimized for a single dimension.

Spatial Grid indexes. Indexes that are optimized for two dimensional data. (Each spatial grid index is created on the X and Y dimensions of a geometry; used by the DB2 Spatial Extender.)

Dynamic Bitmap indexes. Indexes that are produced by ANDing the results of multiple index scans using Dynamic Bitmap techniques. (ANDed predicates can be applied to multiple indexes to keep underlying table accesses to a minimum.)

Block Based indexes. Indexes that contain pointers to rows in a single dimension of a Multidimensional Clustering (MDC) table.

XML indexes. User-defined indexes over XML data that use a particular XML pattern (which is a limited XPath expression) to index paths and values in XML documents stored within a single column.

Question 9

The correct answer is **D**. If the UNIQUE clause is specified when the CREATE INDEX statement is executed, rows in the table associated with the index to be created must not have two or more occurrences of the same values in the set of columns that make up the index key. The INCLUDE clause is used to identify one or more secondary columns whose values are to be stored with the values of the primary columns specified, but are not to be used to enforce data uniqueness.

Thus, if you wanted to create an index for a base table named TAB1 to improve the performance of a query that retrieves information from columns named C1, C2, and C3 while ensuring that all values entered into the C1 column are unique, you could do so by executing a CREATE INDEX statement that looks something like this:

```
CREATE UNIQUE INDEX indx1
ON tab1 (c1)
INCLUDE (c2, c3)
```

Question 10

The correct answer is **D**. If you create two indexes on the same table, one specifying ASC and the other DESC, and if you do not specify the DISALLOW REVERSE SCANS option in the CREATE INDEX statement used, both indexes will default to ALLOW REVERSE SCANS. As a result, the latter index will not be created and DB2 will issue a duplicate index warning message. (The ALLOW REVERSE SCANS option allows the same index to be used in two different queries that require the data to be in ascending and descending order.)

Question 11

The correct answer is **C**. If the UNIQUE clause is specified when the CREATE INDEX statement is executed, rows in the table associated with the index to be created must not have two or more occurrences of the same values in the set of columns that make up the index key. If the base table the index is to be created for contains data, this uniqueness is checked when the DB2 Database Manager attempts to create the index specified – if records with duplicate values for the index key are found, the index will not be created; if no duplicates are found, the index is created and uniqueness is enforced each time an insert or update operation is performed against the table.

In this example, records with duplicate SALES_REP_ID numbers were found when the CREATE INDEX statement was executed so the statement failed and the next insert operation was successful, bringing the total number of rows in the SALES table to 5.

Question 12

The correct answer is **A**. The system catalog can only be used to obtain information about a specific database. If you want to obtain information at the system level, you must resort to executing administrative system commands or querying the administrative views available. For example, to obtain information about the DB2 products that have been installed on a particular server, you would have to execute the system command db2ls –q -a (if you are on a Linux or UNIX server).

When executed, the db2ls command lists the DB2 products and features installed on your system, including the DB2 Version 9 HTML documentation. You can use the db2ls command to find out where DB2 products are installed on a system, what DB2 product levels are installed, and what specific DB2 products and features were installed using a particular installation path.

Question 13

The correct answer is **A**. Whenever an object is created, altered, or dropped, DB2 inserts, updates, or deletes records in the catalog that describe the object and how that object relates to other objects. Thus, if you want to obtain information about a particular database, often, you can do so by connecting to that database and querying the system catalog. For example, suppose you wanted to find out whether a table named EMPLOYEES needed to be reorganized to eliminate fragmentation. You could do so by executing a query against a system catalog table named SYSCAT.TABLES that looks something like this:

```
SELECT TABNAME, OVERFLOW FROM
FROM SYSCAT.TABLES
WHERE TABNAME = 'EMPLOYEES'
```

If the results of this query indicate that a high number of overflow records exist for the EMPLOYEES table, the data is fragmented and the table probably needs to be reorganized.

Question 14

The correct answer is **C**. The CARD column of the SYSCAT.TABLES system catalog table contains the number of rows found in each table the last time statistics were collected for the table. If this column contains the value -1 instead of the number of rows stored in the table, statistics have not been collected. Thus, if you wanted to know whether or not statistics have been collected for the EMPLOYEES table, you could find this out by executing a query against the system catalog that looks something like this:

```
SELECT TABNAME, CARD AS num_rows
FROM SYSCAT.TABLES
WHERE TABNAME = 'EMPLOYEES'
```

Question 15

The correct answer is **B**. The Control Center interface presents itself using one of three different views:

Basic. The basic view displays essential objects such as databases, tables, views, and stored procedures and limits the actions you can perform to those objects. This is the view you should use if you only want to perform core DB2 database operations.

Advanced. The advanced view displays all objects available in the Control Center and allows you to perform all actions available. This is the view you should use if you are working in an enterprise environment and/or if you want to connect to DB2 for i5/OS or DB2 for z/OS.

Custom. The custom view gives you the ability to tailor the object tree and actions allowed to meet your specific needs.

Question 16

The correct answer is **D**. While most objects can be created from the Control Center, if you have paid attention to the Control Center screen shots presented in this Chapter, you may have noticed that user-defined functions (UDFs) cannot. User-defined functions must be created by executing the CREATE FUNCTION SQL statement from the Command Line Processor or the Command Editor, or by using the DB2 Developer Workbench.

Question 17

The correct answer is **C**. The Activity Monitor is an interactive GUI application that allows users to monitor application performance, application concurrency, resource consumption, and SQL statement usage on a database or a database partition. With the Activity Monitor, you can:

- View transactions running on a selected application.
- View SQL statements running on a selected application.
- View the text of SQL statements running on a selected application.
- View locks and lock-waiting situations that currently affect a selected application.
- View information about a selected application for which you are viewing lock information.
- View information about the locks held and the locks waited on by a selected application in your database.
- View information to help you interpret report data.
- View recommendations provided by the Activity Monitor.

In addition to collecting monitor data, the Activity Monitor can present the data collected using a set of predefined reports, which are based on a specific subset of monitor data. (For example, one report might contain a graphical representation that identifies a locking problem that's causing poor concurrency on a database.) Additionally, the Activity Monitor can make recommendations for most reports that will assist in diagnosing the cause of database performance problems, and in tuning queries for optimal utilization of database resources.

The Design Advisor captures specific information about typical workloads (queries or sets of SQL operations) performed against a database and recommends changes based upon the information provided; The Health Monitor constantly monitors the health of a DB2 Database Manager instance using several health indicators to evaluate specific aspects of instance and database performance; and the Configuration Assistant is an interactive GUI application that allows users to configure clients so they can access databases stored on remote DB2 servers.

Question 18

The correct answer is **A**. Tools Settings notebook is an interactive GUI application that is used to customize settings and set properties for the various DB2 administration tools available. To present and collect this information in an organized manner, the Tools Settings notebook uses several different pages/tabs—some pages/tabs will only be displayed after the tools for which they apply have been installed. The pages available with the Tools Settings notebook are:

General page. This page is used to specify whether the local DB2 instance should be started automatically when the DB2 tools are started, whether to use a statement termination character, and whether to use filtering when the maximum number of rows returned for a display sample contents request is exceeded.

Documentation page. This page is used to specify whether hover help and infopop help features in the DB2 administration tools should display automatically, and also to specify the location from which the contextual help is accessed at the instance level.

Fonts page. This page is used to change the font in which text and menus appear in the DB2 administration tools.

OS/390 and z/OS page. This page is used to set column headings and define the online and batch utility execution options for OS/390 and z/OS objects.

Health Center Status Beacon page. This page is used to specify the type of notification you will receive when an alert is generated in the Health Monitor. You can be notified through a pop-up message or with the graphical beacon that displays on the lower-right portion of the status line for each DB2 center, or using both methods of notification.

Scheduler Settings page. This page is used to set the default scheduling scheme. Select Server Scheduling if you want task scheduling to be handled by the scheduler that is local to the database server; select Centralized Scheduling if you want the storage and scheduling of tasks to be handled by a centralized system, in which case you need to select the centralized system from the Centralized Scheduler list. (To enable another scheduler, select a system and click Create New to open a window in which you can create a database for the DB2 Tools Catalog on a cataloged system. If the system you want is not cataloged, you must catalog it first.)

Command Editor page. This page is used to specify how you will generate, edit, execute, and manipulate SQL and XQuery statements, IMS commands, and DB2 commands. This page is also used to specify how you want to work with the resulting output.

IMS page. This page is used to set your preferences when working with IMS. From this page, you can set preferences for using wizards, for syntax support, and for returning results.

The Replication Center is used to define replication environments.

Question 19

The correct answer is **C**. The Command Line Processor (CLP) is a text-oriented application that allows users to issue DB2 commands, system commands, and SQL statements, as well as view the results of the statements/commands executed. Unlike most other Graphical User Interface tools available, the Command Line Processor cannot be invoked from the Control Center.

Question 20

The correct answer is **B**. The Design Advisor is a special tool that is designed to capture specific information about typical workloads (queries or sets of SQL operations) performed against your database and recommend changes based upon the information provided. When given a set of SQL statements in a workload, the Design Advisor will make recommendations for:

- New indexes.
- New materialized query tables (MQTs).
- Conversions of base tables to multidimensional clustering (MDC) tables.
- Redistribution of table data.
- Deletion of indexes and MQTs that are not being used by the specified workload.

Because the Configuration Assistant maintains a list of databases to which users/applications can connect, it can act as a lightweight alternative to the Control Center in situations where the complete set of GUI tools available has not been installed. Therefore, it can be used to set DB2 environment/registry variables. The db2set command can also be used to set DB2 environment/registry variables and this command can be executed from the Command Editor or the Command Line Processor.

CHAPTER 5

Analyzing DB2 Activity

Thirteen percent (13%) of the DB2 9 for Linux, UNIX, and Windows Database Administration exam (Exam 731) is designed to test your ability to use each of the database monitoring tools that are available with DB2. The questions that make up this portion of the exam are intended to evaluate the following:

- Your knowledge of the various monitoring tools available with DB2

- Your ability to use the snapshot monitor, including capturing and analyzing snapshot data with the GET SNAPSHOT command or the snapshot monitor functions

- Your ability to create and activate event monitors, including capturing and analyzing event monitor data

- Your ability to use the Health Center

- Your ability to use the Explain Facility to capture and analyze both comprehensive Explain information and Explain snapshot data

- Your ability to identify the basic functionality of the troubleshooting tools available with DB2 9

This chapter is designed to introduce you to the set of monitoring tools that are available with DB2 and to show you how each is used to monitor how well (or how poorly) your database system is operating. This chapter is also designed to introduce you to some of the troubleshooting tools available with DB2 9.

The Database System Monitor

Database monitoring is a vital activity that, when performed on a regular basis, provides continuous feedback on the health of a database system. And because database monitoring is such an integral part of database administration, DB2 comes equipped with a built-in monitoring utility known as the Database System Monitor. Although the name "Database System Monitor" suggests that only one monitoring tool is available, in reality the Database System Monitor is composed of two distinct tools (a snapshot monitor and one or more event monitors) that can be used to capture and return system monitor information. The snapshot monitor allows you to capture a picture of the state of a database (along with all database activity) at a specific point in time whereas event monitors capture and log data as specific database events occur. Information collected by both tools is stored in entities that are referred to as *monitor elements* (or data elements), and each monitor element used is (1) identified by a unique name and (2) designed to store a certain type of information. The following are the element types that monitor elements use to store data:

Counter. Keeps an accurate count of the number of times an activity or event has occurred. Counter values increase throughout the life of the monitor; often a counter monitor element is resettable.

Gauge. Indicates the current value for an item. Unlike counters, gauge values can go up or down, depending on the amount of database activity (for example, the number of applications currently connected to the database).

Water mark. Indicates the highest (maximum) or lowest (minimum) value an item has seen since monitoring began (for example, the largest number of agents associated with a particular application).

Information. Provides reference-type details of all monitoring activities performed (for example, buffer pool names, database names and aliases, path details, etc.).

Timestamp. Indicates the date and time an activity or event took place (for example, the date and time the first database connection was established).

Timestamp values are provided as the number of seconds and microseconds that have elapsed since January 1, 1970.

Time. Indicates the amount of time that was spent performing an activity or event (for example, the amount of time spent performing a sort operation). Time values are provided as the number of seconds and microseconds that have elapsed since the activity or event was started. Some time elements are resettable.

The Database System Monitor employs several methods for presenting the data collected. For both snapshot and event monitors, you have the option of storing all collected data in files or database tables, viewing it on screen, or processing it using a custom application. (The Database System Monitor returns monitor data to a client application using a self-describing data stream; with a snapshot monitoring application, you call the appropriate snapshot APIs to capture a snapshot and then process the data stream returned. With an event monitoring application, you prepare to receive the data produced via a file or a named pipe, activate the appropriate event monitor, and process the data stream as it is received.)

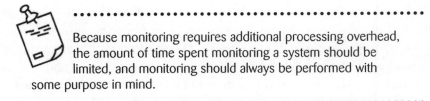

Because monitoring requires additional processing overhead, the amount of time spent monitoring a system should be limited, and monitoring should always be performed with some purpose in mind.

The Snapshot Monitor

The snapshot monitor is designed to collect information about the state of a DB2 instance and the databases it controls at a specific point in time (i.e., at the time the snapshot is taken). Additionally, the snapshot monitor can be tailored to retrieve specific types of monitoring data (for example, it could be configured to collect just information about buffer pools). Snapshots can be taken by executing the GET SNAPSHOT command from the DB2 Command Line Processor (CLP), by using the snapshot administrative views and/or snapshot table functions, or by embedding the snapshot monitor APIs in a C or C++ application. Snapshots are useful for determining the status of a database system and, when taken at regular intervals, can provide valuable information that can be used to observe trends and identify potential problem areas.

Snapshot monitor switches

Often, the collection of database system monitor data introduces additional processing overhead. For example, in order to calculate the execution time of SQL statements, the DB2 Database Manager must make a call to the operating system to obtain timestamps before and after every SQL statement is executed; these types of system calls are normally expensive. Another side effect of using the database system monitor is an increase in memory consumption—the DB2 Database Manager uses memory to store data collected for every monitor element tracked.

To help minimize the overhead involved in collecting database system monitor information, a group of switches known as the snapshot monitor switches can be used to control what information is collected when a snapshot is taken; the type and amount of information collected is determined by the way these snapshot monitor switches have been set. Each snapshot monitor switch has two settings: ON and OFF. When a snapshot monitor switch is set to OFF, monitor elements that fall under that switch's control do not collect information. The opposite is true if the switch is set to ON. (Keep in mind that a considerable amount of monitoring information is not under switch control and will always be collected regardless of how the snapshot monitor switches have been set.) The snapshot monitor switches available, along with a description of the type of information that is collected when each has been set to ON, can be seen in Table 5.1.

Table 5.1 Snapshot Monitor Switches			
Monitor Group	**Monitor Switch**	**DB2 Database Manager Configuration Parameter**	**Information Provided**
Buffer Pools	BUFFERPOOL	*dft_mon_bufferpool*	Amount of buffer pool activity (i.e., number of read and write operations performed and the amount of time taken, for each read/write operation)
Locks	LOCK	*dft_mon_lock*	Number of locks held and number of deadlock cycles encountered
Sorts	SORT	*dft_mon_sort*	Number of sort operations performed, number of heaps used, number of overflows encountered, and the amount of time taken for each sort operation performed
SQL Statements	STATEMENT	*dft_mon_stmt*	SQL statement processing start time, SQL statement processing end time, and SQL statement identification
Tables	TABLE	*dft_mon_table*	Amount of table activity performed, such as number of rows read, number of rows written, and so on
Timestamps	TIMESTAMP	*dft_mon_timestamp*	Times and timestamp information
Transactions (units of work)	UOW	*dft_mon_uow*	Transaction start times, transaction completion times, and transaction completion status
Adapted from Table 2 on page 14 of the *DB2 System Monitor Guide and Reference* manual			

By default, all of the switches shown in Table 5.1 are set to OFF, with the exception of the TIMESTAMP switch, which is set to ON.

Viewing current snapshot monitor switch settings

Because the type and amount of information collected when a snapshot is taken are controlled, to some extent, by the way the snapshot monitor switches have been set, before you take a snapshot, it is important that you know which snapshot monitor switches have been turned on and which snapshot monitor switches remain off. So how can you find out what the current setting of each snapshot monitor switch available is? The easiest way is by executing the GET MONITOR SWITCHES command from the DB2 Command Line Processor (CLP). The basic syntax for this command is:

```
GET MONITOR SWITCHES
<AT DBPARTITIONNUM [PartitionNum] | GLOBAL>
```

where:

PartitionNum   Identifies the database partition (in a multi-partitioned database environment) for which the status of the snapshot monitor switches available is to be obtained and displayed.

So if you wanted to obtain and display the status of the snapshot monitor switches for a single-partition database, you could do so by executing a GET MONITOR SWITCHES command that looks something like this:

```
GET MONITOR SWITCHES
```

And when this command is executed, you will most likely see output that looks something like this:

```
                    Monitor Recording Switches

Switch list for db partition number 0
Buffer Pool Activity Information (BUFFERPOOL) = OFF
Lock Information                      (LOCK) = OFF
Sorting Information                   (SORT) = OFF
SQL Statement Information        (STATEMENT) = OFF
Table Activity Information           (TABLE) = OFF
Take Timestamp Information        (TIMESTAMP) = ON 05/14/2007 11:35.00.186250
Unit of Work Information              (UOW) = OFF
```

On close examination of this output, you will notice that the TIMESTAMP snapshot monitoring switch has been turned on and that all other switches are off. The timestamp value that follows the TIMESTAMP monitoring switch's state tells you the exact date and time the TIMESTAMP monitoring switch was turned on (which in this case is May 14, 2007, at 11:35 AM—the date and time the instance was started).

Changing the state of a snapshot monitor switch

Once you know which snapshot monitor switches have been turned on and which snapshot monitor switches have been turned off, you may find it necessary to change one or more switch settings before you start the monitoring process. Snapshot monitor switch settings can be changed at the instance level by modifying the appropriate DB2 Database Manager configuration parameters (see Table 5.1) with the UPDATE DATABASE MANAGER CONFIGURATION command. (Snapshot monitor switch settings made at the instance level remain persistent across instance restarts.) Snapshot monitor switch settings can be changed at the application level by calling the db2MonitorSwitches() API or by executing the UPDATE MONITOR SWITCHES command. The basic syntax for this command is:

```
UPDATE MONITOR SWITCHES USING [[SwitchID] ON | OFF ,...]
```

where:

SwitchID   Identifies one or more snapshot monitor switches whose state is to be changed. The following values are valid for this parameter: BUFFERPOOL, LOCK, SORT, STATEMENT, TABLE, TIMESTAMP, and UOW.

Thus, if you wanted to change the state of the LOCK snapshot monitor switch to ON at the application level, you could do so by executing an UPDATE MONITOR SWITCHES command that looks like this:

```
UPDATE MONITOR SWITCHES USING LOCKS ON
```

Likewise, if you wanted to change the state of the BUFFERPOOL snapshot monitor switch to OFF, you could do so by executing an UPDATE MONITOR SWITCHES command that looks like this:

```
UPDATE MONITOR SWITCHES USING BUFFERPOOL OFF
```

On the other hand, if you wanted to change the state of the LOCK snapshot monitor switch to ON at the instance level, you would do so by executing an UPDATE DATABASE MANAGER CONFIGURATION command that looks like this:

```
UPDATE DBM CFG USING DFT_MON_LOCK ON
```

Setting snapshot monitor switches at the instance level affects all databases under the instance's control (i.e., every application that establishes a connection to a database under the instance's control will inherit the switch settings made in the instance's configuration), whereas setting monitor switches at the application level affects only the database with which a single application is interacting.

Capturing snapshot data

As soon as a database is activated or a connection to a database is established, the snapshot monitor begins collecting monitor data. And before the data collected can be viewed, a snapshot must be taken. Snapshots can be taken by embedding the db2GetSnapshot() API in an application program or by executing the GET SNAPSHOT command. The basic syntax for this command is:

```
GET SNAPSHOT FOR
[[DATABASE MANAGER | DB MANAGER | DBM] |
 ALL <DCS> DATABASES |
 ALL <DCS> APPLICATIONS |
 ALL BUFFERPOOLS |
 ALL REMOTE_DATABASES |
 ALL REMOTE_APPLICATIONS |
 ALL ON [DatabaseAlias] |
 <DCS> [DATABASE | DB] ON [DatabaseAlias] |
 <DCS> APPLICATIONS ON [DatabaseAlias] |
 <DCS> APPLICATION [APPLID AppID | AGENTID AgentID] |
 TABLES ON [DatabaseAlias] |
 TABLESPACES ON [DatabaseAlias] |
 LOCKS ON [DatabaseAlias] |
 BUFFERPOOLS ON [DatabaseAlias] |
 REMOTE DATABASES ON [DatabaseAlias] |
 REMOTE APPLICATIONS ON [DatabaseAlias]
 DYNAMIC SQL ON [DatabaseAlias] <WRITE TO FILE>]
```

where:

DatabaseAlias   Identifies the alias assigned to the database that snapshot monitor information is to be collected for.

AppID   Identifies the application, by ID, for which snapshot monitor information is to be collected.

AgentID   Identifies the application, by application handle agent ID, for which snapshot monitor information is to be collected for.

So if you wanted to take a snapshot that contained only data collected on locks being held by applications interacting with a database named SAMPLE, you could do so by executing a GET SNAPSHOT command that looks like this:

```
GET SNAPSHOT FOR LOCKS ON sample
```

And when this command is executed, you might see output that looks something like this:

```
                    Database Lock Snapshot

Database name                     = SAMPLE
Database path                     = C:\DB2\NODE0000\SQL00002\
Input database alias              = SAMPLE
Locks held                        = 0
Applications currently connected  = 1
Agents currently waiting on locks = 0
Snapshot timestamp                = 05/14/2007 14:57:04.559027

Application handle                = 110
Application ID                    = *LOCAL.DB2.070514185703
Sequence number                   = 00001
Application name                  = db2taskd
CONNECT Authorization ID          = RSANDERS
Application status                = Connect Completed
Status change time                = Not Collected
Application code page             = 1252
Locks held                        = 0
Total wait time (ms)              = Not Collected

Application handle                = 109
Application ID                    = *LOCAL.DB2.070514185702
Sequence number                   = 00001
Application name                  = db2stmm
CONNECT Authorization ID          = RSANDERS
Application status                = Connect Completed
Status change time                = Not Collected
Application code page             = 1252
Locks held                        = 0
Total wait time (ms)              = Not Collected

Application handle                = 108
Application ID                    = *LOCAL.DB2.070514185659
```

```
Sequence number                 = 00001
Application name                = db2bp.exe
CONNECT Authorization ID        = RSANDERS
Application status              = Connect Completed
Status change time              = Not Collected
Application code page           = 1252
Locks held                      = 0
Total wait time (ms)            = Not Collected
```

While examining the syntax used by the GET SNAPSHOT command, you may have noticed that different types of monitoring data can be captured when a snapshot is taken. This data includes the following:

DB2 Database Manager data. Information for an active instance.

Database data. Information about one or more remote or local databases.

Application data. Information about one or more applications.

Buffer pool data. Information about buffer pool activity.

Table space data. Information about one or more table spaces within a database.

Table data. Information about one or more tables within a database.

Lock data. Information about locks being held by applications.

Dynamic SQL data. Point-in-time information about SQL statements being held in the SQL statement cache.

The snapshot monitor switches, together with the options available with the GET SNAPSHOT command, determine the type and volume of data that will be returned when a snapshot is taken. In fact, if a particular snapshot monitor switch has not been turned on, and a snapshot of the monitoring data that is associated with that switch is taken, the monitoring data captured may not contain any values at all. (If you look closely at the previous example, you will see that some values were "Not Collected." That's because when the snapshot of LOCK information was taken, the LOCK snapshot monitor switch was turned off.)

In order to execute the GET SNAPSHOT command, you must be attached to an instance; if no instance attachment exists, an attachment to the default instance is made automatically. To obtain a snapshot of a remote instance, you must first attach to that instance.

Capturing snapshot monitor data using SQL

With earlier versions of DB2, the only way to capture snapshot monitor data was by executing the GET SNAPSHOT command or by calling its corresponding API from an application program. With DB2 UDB version 8.1, the ability to capture snapshot monitor data by constructing a query that referenced one of 20 snapshot monitor table functions available was introduced. Table 5.2 lists these functions, along with the snapshot information they were designed to capture.

Table 5.2 DB2 8.1 Snapshot Monitor SQL Table Functions

Monitor Level	Table Function Name	Information Returned
Database Manager	SNAPSHOT_DBM()	Information about the DB2 Database Manager instance.
Database Manager	SNAPSHOT_FCM()	Information about the DB2 Database Manager instance regarding the fast communication manager (FCM).
Database Manager	SNAPSHOT_FCMNODE()	Information about the DB2 Database Manager instance regarding the fast communication manager (FCM) for a specific partition.
Database Manager	SNAPSHOT_SWITCHES()	The current settings of the DB2 Database Manager instance's snapshot monitor switches.
Database	SNAPSHOT_DATABASE()	Information about a particular database. (For this information to be obtained, at least one application must be connected to the database.)
Application	SNAPSHOT_APPL()	General application-level identification information for each application that is connected to a particular database (on the specified partition). This includes cumulative counters, status information, and information about the most recent SQL statement executed (provided the STATEMENT snapshot monitor switch has been set).

Table 5.2 DB2 8.1 Snapshot Monitor SQL Table Functions (continued)		
Monitor Level	**Table Function Name**	**Information Returned**
Application	SNAPSHOT_APPL_INFO()	General application-level identification information for each application that is connected to a particular database (on the specified partition). This includes details about the client on which the application is running, the authorization ID of the person running the application, and the database to which the application is connected.
Application	SNAPSHOT_LOCKWAIT()	Information regarding lock waits for each application that is connected to a particular database (on the specified partition).
Application	SNAPSHOT_STATEMENT()	Information regarding SQL statements for each application connected to a particular database (on the specified partition), including information for the most recent SQL statement executed (provided the STATEMENT snapshot monitor switch has been set).
Application	SNAPSHOT_AGENT()	Information regarding the agents associated with each application that is connected to a particular database (on the specified partition).
Application	SNAPSHOT_SUBSECT()	Information regarding the subsections of access plans for each application that is connected to a particular database (on the specified partition).
Table	SNAPSHOT_TABLE()	Information about table activity at the database and application level for each application connected to the database, including table activity information for each table that was accessed by an application connected to the database (provided the TABLE snapshot monitor switch has been set).
Lock	SNAPSHOT_LOCK()	Information about locks acquired at the database and application level for each application connected to the database (provided the LOCK snapshot monitor switch has been set).
Table Space	SNAPSHOT_TBS()	Information about table space activity at the database and application level for each application connected to the database, including information about table space activity at the table space level for each table space that has been accessed by an application connected to the database (provided the BUFFERPOOL snapshot monitor switch has been set).
Table Space	SNAPSHOT_TBS_CFG()	Information about the table space configuration used by a particular database (on the specified partition).
Table Space	SNAPSHOT_QUIESCER()	Information about quiescers at the table space level.

Table 5.2 DB2 8.1 Snapshot Monitor SQL Table Functions (continued)		
Monitor Level	**Table Function Name**	**Information Returned**
Table Space	SNAPSHOT_CONTAINER()	Information about the table space container configuration used (at the table space level) used by a particular database (on the specified partition).
Table Space	SNAPSHOT_RANGES()	Information about the ranges used by a table space map.
Buffer Pool	SNAPSHOT_BP()	Information about buffer pool activity for a particular database (on the specified partition), provided the BUFFERPOOL snapshot monitor switch has been set.
Dynamic SQL	SNAPSHOT_DYNSQL()	Point-in-time statement information collected from the SQL statement cache for the database.

The syntax used to construct a query that references a non-Database Manager–level snapshot monitor table function looks something like this:

```
SELECT * FROM TABLE ([FunctionName]
('[DBName]', [PartitionNum]) AS
[CorrelationName]
```

where:

FunctionName   Identifies the snapshot monitor table function to be used (i.e., one of the functions listed in Table 5.2).

DBName   Identifies the database for which snapshot monitor data is to be collected.

PartitionNum   Identifies the database partition for which snapshot monitor data is to be collected.

CorrelationName   Identifies the name that is to be assigned to the result data set produced by the query.

The syntax used to construct a query that references a Database Manager level snapshot monitor table function is identical, with one exception: the *DBName* parameter is not used.

In either case, if you wanted to capture snapshot monitor data for the current partition in a partitioned database environment, you could do so by specifying the value -1 for the *PartitionNum* parameter; if you wanted to capture snapshot monitor data for all partitions, you specify the value -2. Similarly, if you wanted to capture snapshot monitor data for the current connected database, you could do so by specifying a null value for the *DBName* parameter, either by using empty single quotation marks (' ') or by using a cast operation—for example, CAST (NULL AS CHAR).

Thus, if you wanted to take a snapshot that contains data collected on locks held by applications interacting with the current connected database using the DB2 V8.1 SNAPSHOT_LOCK() snapshot monitor table function, you could do so by executing the following query:

```
SELECT * FROM TABLE (SNAPSHOT_LOCK
    (CAST (NULL AS CHAR), -1) AS snap_info
```

Although these functions are still available and can be used in DB2 9, they have been depreciated. Now snapshot monitor data can be obtained by querying special administrative views or by using a new set of SQL table functions. These routines and views are described in detail in Table 5.3.

Table 5.3 DB2 9 Snapshot Monitor Administrative Tables and SQL Table Functions		
Administrative View	**Table Function**	**Description**
SYSIBMADM.APPLICATIONS	N/A	This administrative view contains information about connected database applications.
SYSIBMADM.APPL_ PERFORMANCE	N/A	This administrative view contains information about the rate of rows selected versus rows read per application.
SYSIBMADM.BP_HITRATIO	N/A	This administrative view contains buffer pool hit ratios, including total, data, and index.
SYSIBMADM.BP_READ_IO	N/A	This administrative view contains buffer pool read performance information.
SYSIBMADM.BP_WRITE_IO	N/A	This administrative view contains buffer pool write performance information.
SYSIBMADM.CONTAINER_ UTILIZATION	N/A	This administrative view contains information about table space containers and utilization rates.
SYSIBMADM.LOCKS_HELD	N/A	This administrative view contains information on current locks held.

Table 5.3 DB2 9 Snapshot Monitor Administrative Tables and SQL Table Functions (continued)		
Administrative View	**Table Function**	**Description**
SYSIBMADM.LOCKWAITS	N/A	This administrative view contains information on locks that are waiting to be granted.
SYSIBMADM.LOG_ UTILIZATION	N/A	This administrative view contains information about log utilization for the currently connected database.
SYSIBMADM.LONG_ RUNNING_SQL	N/A	This administrative view contains information about the longest-running SQL statements in the currently connected database.
SYSIBMADM.QUERY_PREP_ COST	N/A	This administrative view contains a list of SQL statements, along with information about the time required to prepare each statement.
N/A	SNAP_WRITE_FILE()	This procedure writes system snapshot data to a file in the *tmp* subdirectory of the instance directory.
SYSIBMADM.SNAPAGENT	SNAP_GET_AGENT()	The administrative view and table function returns information about agents from an application snapshot—in particular, the agent logical data group.
SYSIBMADM.SNAPAGENT_ MEMORY_POOL	SNAP_GET_AGENT _MEMORY_POOL()	This administrative view and table function returns information about memory usage at the agent level.
SYSIBMADM.SNAPAPPL	SNAP_GET_APPL()	This administrative view and table function returns information about applications from an application snapshot—in particular, the appl logical data group.
SYSIBMADM.SNAPAPPL_ INFO	SNAP_GET_APPL_ INFO()	This administrative view and table function returns information about applications from an application snapshot—in particular, the appl_info logical data group.
SYSIBMADM.SNAPBP	SNAP_GET_BP()	This administrative view and table function returns information about buffer pools from a bufferpool snapshot—in particular, the bufferpool logical data group.
SYSIBMADM.SNAPBP_PART	SNAP_GET_BP_ PART()	This administrative view and table function returns information about buffer pools from a bufferpool snapshot—in particular, the bufferpool_nodeinfo logical data group.
SYSIBMADM. SNAPCONTAINER	SNAP_GET_ CONTAINER_V91()	This administrative view and table function returns table space snapshot information from the tablespace_container logical data group.

Table 5.3 DB2 9 Snapshot Monitor Administrative Tables and SQL Table Functions (continued)

Administrative View	Table Function	Description
SYSIBMADM.SNAPDB	SNAP_GET_DB_V91()	This administrative view and table function returns snapshot information from the database (dbase) and database storage (db_storage_group) logical groupings.
SYSIBMADM.SNAPDB_MEMORY_POOL	SNAP_GET_DB_MEMORY_POOL()	This administrative view and table function returns information about memory usage at the database level for UNIX(R) platforms only.
SYSIBMADM.SNAPDBM	SNAP_GET_DBM()	This administrative view and table function returns the snapshot monitor DB2 database manager (dbm) logical grouping information.
SYSIBMADM.SNAPDBM_MEMORY_POOL	SNAP_GET_DBM_MEMORY_POOL()	This administrative view and table function returns information about memory usage at the database manager level.
SYSIBMADM.SNAPDETAILLOG	SNAP_GET_DETAILLOG_V91()	This administrative view and table function returns snapshot information from the detail_log logical data group.
SYSIBMADM.SNAPDYN_SQL	SNAP_GET_DYN_SQL_V91()	This administrative view and table function returns snapshot information from the dynsql logical data group.
SYSIBMADM.SNAPFCM	SNAP_GET_FCM()	This administrative view and table function returns information about the fast communication manager (FCM) from a database manager snapshot—in particular, the fcm logical data group.
SYSIBMADM.SNAPFCM_PART	SNAP_GET_FCM_PART()	This administrative view and table function returns information about the fast communication manager (FCM) from a database manager snapshot, in particular, the fcm_node logical data group.
SYSIBMADM.SNAPHADR	SNAP_GET_HADR()	This administrative view and table function returns information about high availability disaster recovery (HADR) from a database snapshot—in particular, the HADR logical data group.
SYSIBMADM.SNAPLOCK	SNAP_GET_LOCK()	This administrative view and table function returns snapshot information about locks—in particular, the lock logical data group.
SYSIBMADM.SNAPLOCKWAIT	SNAP_GET_LOCKWAIT()	This administrative view and table function returns snapshot information about lock waits—in particular, the lockwait logical data group.

Table 5.3 DB2 9 Snapshot Monitor Administrative Tables and SQL Table Functions (continued)		
Administrative View	**Table Function**	**Description**
SYSIBMADM.SNAPSTMT	SNAP_GET_STMT()	This administrative view and table function returns information about statements from an application snapshot.
SYSIBMADM. SNAPSTORAGE_PATHS	SNAP_GET_ STORAGE_PATHS()	This administrative view and table function returns a list of automatic storage paths for the database, including file system information for each storage path—specifically, from the db_storage_group logical data group.
SYSIBMADM. SNAPSUBSECTION	SNAP_GET_ SUBSECTION()	This administrative view and table function returns information about application subsections, namely the subsection logical monitor grouping.
SYSIBMADM. SNAPSWITCHES	SNAP_GET_ SWITCHES()	This administrative view and table function returns information about the database snapshot switch state.
SYSIBMADM.SNAPTAB	SNAP_GET_TAB_ V91()	This administrative view and table function returns snapshot information from the table logical data group.
SYSIBMADM.SNAPTAB_ REORG	SNAP_GET_TAB_ REORG()	This administrative view and table function returns table reorganization information.
SYSIBMADM.SNAPTBSP	SNAP_GET_TBSP_ V91()	This administrative view and table function returns snapshot information from the table space logical data group.
SYSIBMADM.SNAPTBSP_ PART	SNAP_GET_TBSP_ PART_V91()	This administrative view and table function returns snapshot information from the tablespace_nodeinfo logical data group.
SYSIBMADM.SNAPTBSP_ QUIESCER	SNAP_GET_TBSP_ QUIESCER()	This administrative view and table function returns information about quiescers from a table space snapshot.
SYSIBMADM.SNAPTBSP_ RANGE	SNAP_GET_TBSP_ RANGE()	This administrative view and table function returns information from a range snapshot.
SYSIBMADM.SNAPUTIL	SNAP_GET_UTIL()	This administrative view and table function returns snapshot information on utilities from the utility_info logical data group.
SYSIBMADM.SNAPUTIL_ PROGRESS	SNAP_GET_UTIL_ PROGRESS()	This administrative view and table function returns information about utility progress—in particular, the progress logical data group.
SYSIBMADM.TBSP_ UTILIZATION	N/A	This administrative view contains table space configuration and utilization information.
SYSIBMADM.TOP_DYNAMIC _SQL	N/A	This administrative view contains the top dynamic SQL statements, sortable by number of executions, average execution time, number of sorts, or sorts per statement.

Thus, if you wanted to obtain snapshot monitor lock information for the currently connected database, you could do so by executing a query that looks something like this:

```
SELECT AGENT_ID, LOCK_OBJECT_TYPE, LOCK_MODE, LOCK_STATUS
FROM SYSIBMADM.SNAPLOCK
```

Each DB2 9 snapshot monitor table function returns the same information as the corresponding administrative view, but the function allows you to retrieve information for a specific database instead of the current connected database. (If no database is specified when a snapshot monitor table function is used, you must be connected to the appropriate database.) The syntax used to construct a query that references a DB2 9 snapshot monitor table function is the same as that used to reference a DB2 8.1 function—only the function names have changed. Therefore, if you wanted to obtain snapshot monitor lock information for a database named SAMPLE using the SNAP_GET_LOCK() table function (instead of querying the SYSIBMADM.SNAPLOCK administrative view), you could do so by constructing a query that looks something like this:

```
SELECT AGENT_ID, LOCK_OBJECT_TYPE, LOCK_MODE, LOCK_STATUS
FROM TABLE(SNAP_GET_LOCK('sample',-1)) AS snap_info
```

Resetting snapshot monitor counters

Earlier, we saw that one of the element types that monitor elements use to store data is a counter and that counters keep running totals of the number of times an activity or event occurs. Thus, counter values increase throughout the life of the monitor. So when exactly does counting begin? Counting typically begins as soon as a snapshot monitor switch is turned on or when connection to a database is established (if instance level monitoring is used, counting begins the first time an application establishes a connection to a database under the instance's control). There may be times, however, when it is desirable to reset all counters to zero without turning snapshot monitor switches off and back on and without terminating and reestablishing database connections. By far, the easiest way to quickly reset all snapshot monitor counters to zero is by executing the RESET MONITOR command. The basic syntax for this command is:

```
RESET MONITOR ALL
```

or

```
RESET MONITOR FOR <DCS> [DATABASE | DB] [DatabaseAlias]
```

where:

DatabaseAlias　　Identifies the alias assigned to the database for which snapshot monitor counters are to be reset.

Thus, if you wanted to reset the snapshot monitor counters for all databases under an instance's control to zero, you could do so by attaching to that instance and executing a RESET MONITOR command that looks like this:

```
RESET MONITOR ALL
```

On the other hand, if you wanted to reset just the snapshot monitor counters associated with a database named SAMPLE to zero, you could do so by executing a RESET MONITOR command that looks like this:

```
RESET MONITOR FOR DATABASE sample
```

You cannot selectively reset counters for a particular monitoring group that is controlled by a snapshot monitor switch using the RESET MONITOR command. To perform this type of operation, you must turn the appropriate snapshot monitor switch off and back on or terminate and reestablish connections to the database.

Event Monitors

Whereas the snapshot monitor provides a method for recording information about the state of database activity at a given point in time, an event monitor can be used to record information about database activity *when an event or transition occurs*. Therefore, event monitors provide a way to collect monitor data when events or activities that cannot be monitored using the snapshot monitor occur. For example, suppose you want to capture monitor data whenever a deadlock cycle occurs. If you are familiar with the concept of deadlocks, you may recall that a special process known as the deadlock detector runs quietly in the background and "wakes up" at predefined intervals to scan the locking system in search of a deadlock cycle. If a deadlock cycle exists, the deadlock detector randomly selects one of the transactions involved in the cycle to roll back and terminate. (The transaction that is rolled back and terminated receives an SQL error code, all locks it had acquired are released, and the remaining transaction or transactions are then allowed to proceed.) Information about such a series of events cannot be captured by the snapshot monitor because, in all likelihood, the deadlock cycle will have been broken long before a snapshot can be taken. An event monitor, on the other hand, could be used to capture such information because it would be activated the moment the deadlock cycle was detected.

•••
By default, whenever a DB2 9 database is created, a deadlock event monitor is defined for that database, and this event monitor is activated when a connection to the database is first established, or whenever the database is activated.
•••

Unlike the snapshot monitor, which resides in the background and is always available, event monitors are special objects that must be created. You create event monitors by executing the CREATE EVENT MONITOR SQL statement. The basic syntax for this statement is:

```
CREATE EVENT MONITOR [EventMonName]
FOR [DATABASE |
     BUFFERPOOLS |
     TABLESPACES |
     TABLES |
     DEADLOCKS <WITH DETAILS> |
     CONNECTIONS <WHERE [EventCondition]> |
     STATEMENTS <WHERE [EventCondition]>  |
     TRANSACTIONS <WHERE [EventCondition]> , ...]
WRITE TO [PIPE [PipeName] |
         TABLE (TABLE [TableName]) <BLOCKED | NONBLOCKED>|
         FILE [DirectoryName] <BLOCKED | NONBLOCKED>]
[MANUALSTART | AUTOSTART]
```

where:

EventMonName   Identifies the name to be assigned to the event monitor that is to be created.

EventCondition   Identifies a condition that is used to determine for which CONNECTION, STATEMENT, or TRANSACTION events monitor data is to be collected.

TableName   Identifies the name assigned to the database table to which all event monitor data collected is to be written.

PipeName   Identifies the name assigned to the named pipe to which all event monitor data collected is to be written.

DirectoryName   Identifies the name assigned to the directory to which one or more files containing event monitor data are to be written.

As you can see by examining the syntax of the CREATE EVENT MONITOR statement, when an event monitor is created, the type of event to be monitored must be specified; Table 5.4 lists the event types available, along with the type of information that is collected for each type and details on when the data is actually collected.

Table 5.4 Event Monitor Types		
Event Type	**Data Collected**	**When Data Is Collected**
DATABASE	The values of all database level counters.	When the database is deactivated or when the last application connected to the database disconnects.
BUFFERPOOLS	The values of all buffer pool counters, prefetchers, and page cleaners, as well as direct I/Os for each buffer pool used.	When the database is deactivated or when the last application connected to the database disconnects.
TABLESPACES	The values of all buffer pool counters, prefetchers, page cleaners, and direct I/Os for each table space used.	When the database is deactivated or when the last application connected to the database disconnects.
TABLES	The number of rows read and the number of rows written for each table.	When the database is deactivated or when the last application connected to the database disconnects.
DEADLOCKS	Comprehensive information regarding applications involved, including the identification of participating SQL statements (along with statement text) and a list of locks being held.	When a deadlock cycle is detected.

Table 5.4 Event Monitor Types (continued)		
Event Type	Data Collected	When Data Is Collected
CONNECTIONS	The values of all application level counters.	When an application that is connected to the database disconnects.
STATEMENTS	Statement start/stop time, amount of CPU used, text of dynamic SQL statements, SQLCA (the return code of the SQL statement), and other metrics such as fetch count. For partitioned databases: amount of CPU used, execution time, table information, and table queue information.	When an SQL statement finishes executing. For partitioned databases: when a subsection of an SQL statement finishes executing.
TRANSACTIONS	Transaction start/stop time, previous transaction time, and amount of CPU consumed, along with locking and logging metrics. (Transaction records are not generated if database is using two-phase commit processing and an X/Open XA Interface.)	When a transaction is terminated (by a COMMIT or a ROLLBACK statement).

Adapted from Table 9 on pages 60–61 of the *DB2 System Monitor Guide and Reference* manual.

The location to which all monitor data collected is to be written must be specified as well; output from an event monitor can be written to one or more database tables, one or more external files, or a named pipe. Table event monitors and pipe event monitors stream event records directly to the table or named pipe specified. File event monitors, on the other hand, stream event records to a series of eight-character numbered files that have the extension ".evt" (for example, 00000000.evt, 00000001.evt, 00000002.evt, etc.). The monitor data collected and stored in these files should be considered to be stored as one logical file even though the data is broken up into smaller pieces. In other words, the start of the data stream is the first byte in the file named 00000000.evt; the end of the data stream is the last byte in the file named *nnnnnnnn*.evt.

Data collected by event monitors is streamed to buffers before it is externalized to disk (i.e., written to a table or file). If the BLOCKED option is specified, agents that generate an event that is being monitored will wait for an event buffer to be written to disk before continuing if it determines that both event buffers are full. As a result, although BLOCKED event monitors guarantee that no event monitor data will be lost, their behavior can increase application response time because any suspended agents (along with any dependent agents) will be allowed to run only when the event monitor buffers are clear. If the NONBLOCKED option is specified instead, an agent that generates an event that is being monitored will not wait for an event buffer to be written to disk before continuing if it determines that both event buffers are full. Thus, NONBLOCKED event monitors perform faster than BLOCKED event monitors but are subject to data loss on highly active systems. (If neither option is specified, the event monitor created will be a BLOCKED event monitor.)

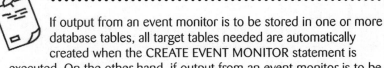

If output from an event monitor is to be stored in one or more database tables, all target tables needed are automatically created when the CREATE EVENT MONITOR statement is executed. On the other hand, if output from an event monitor is to be written to one or more external files or a named pipe, the output directory/named pipe specified as the target location for the event monitor does not have to exist when the CREATE EVENT MONITOR statement is executed; however, it must exist and the DB2 Database Manager instance owner must be able to write to it at the time the event monitor is activated. (The application monitoring the named pipe must also have opened the pipe for reading before the event monitor is activated.)

So if you wanted to create an event monitor that captures the values of all application-level counters and writes them to a database table named CONN_DATA every time an application that is connected to a database terminates its connection, you could do so by executing a CREATE EVENT MONITOR statement that looks something like this:

```
CREATE EVENT MONITOR conn_events
FOR CONNECTIONS
WRITE TO TABLE TABLE(conn_data)
```

On the other hand, if you wanted to create an event monitor that captures monitor data for both buffer pool and table space events and writes all data collected to a directory named /export/home/BPTS_DATA, you could do so by executing a CREATE EVENT MONITOR statement that looks something like this:

```
CREATE EVENT MONITOR bpts_events
FOR BUFFERPOOLS, TABLESPACES
WRITE TO FILE '/export/home/BPTS_DATA'
```

Event monitors can also be created using the Create Event Monitor dialog, which can be activated by selecting the appropriate action from the Event Monitors menu found in the Control Center. Figure 5–1 shows the Control Center menu items that must be selected to activate the Create Event Monitor dialog; Figure 5–2 shows how the Create Event Monitor dialog looks when it is first activated.

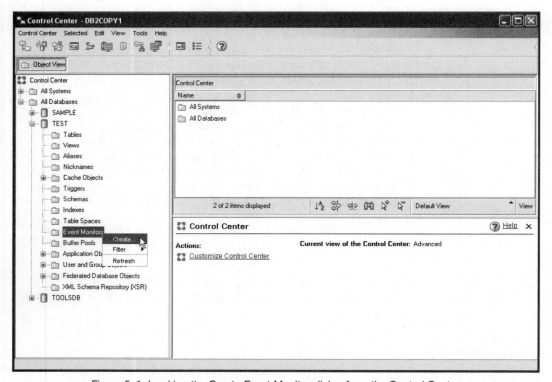

Figure 5–1: Invoking the Create Event Monitor dialog from the Control Center.

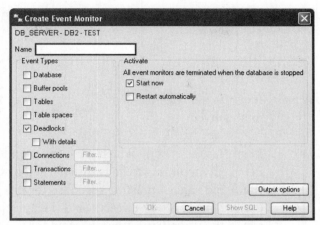

Figure 5–2: The Create Event Monitor dialog.

Only users with System Administrator (SYSADM) authority, System Control (SYSCTRL) authority, System Maintenance (SYSMAINT) authority, or Database Administrator (DBADM) authority are allowed to create and use event monitors.

It is important to note that because event monitors are special database objects that must be created by users who hold the appropriate authorization, they can be used only to collect information for the database in which they have been defined; event monitors cannot be used to collect information at the DB2 Database Manager instance level.

Activating and deactivating event monitors

Like the snapshot monitor, event monitors will begin collecting monitor data as soon as the database with which they are associated is activated or a connection to the database is established—provided the AUTOSTART option was specified when the event monitor was created. If the MANUALSTART option was used instead, or if neither option was specified (in which case the MANUALSTART option is used by default), an event monitor must be activated before it will begin collecting data. Event monitors are activated (and deactivated) by executing the SET EVENT MONITOR SQL statement. The basic syntax for this statement is:

```
SET EVENT MONITOR [EventMonName]
STATE <=> [MonitorState]
```

where:

EventMonName   Identifies the name assigned to the event monitor whose state is to be altered.

MonitorState   Identifies the state in which the event monitor is to be placed. If the event monitor is to be activated (i.e., placed in the active state), the value 1 must be specified for this parameter; if the event monitor is to be deactivated (i.e., placed in the inactive state), the value 0 must be specified for this parameter.

Therefore, if you wanted to activate an event monitor named CONN_EVENTS that was created with the MANUALSTART option specified, you could do so by executing a SET EVENT MONITOR statement that looks like this:

```
SET EVENT MONITOR conn_events STATE 1
```

On the other hand, if you wanted to deactivate the CONN_EVENTS event monitor, you could do so by executing a SET EVENT MONITOR statement that looks like this:

```
SET EVENT MONITOR conn_events STATE 0
```

Event monitors can also be activated and deactivated by highlighting the appropriate event monitor name shown in the Control Center and selecting the appropriate action from the Event Monitors menu. Figure 5–3 shows the Control Center menu item that must be selected to activate (start) an inactive event monitor; Figure 5–4 shows the Control Center menu item that must be selected to deactivate (stop) an active event monitor.

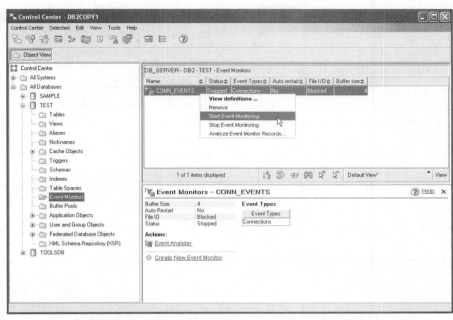

Figure 5–3: Starting an event monitor from the Control Center.

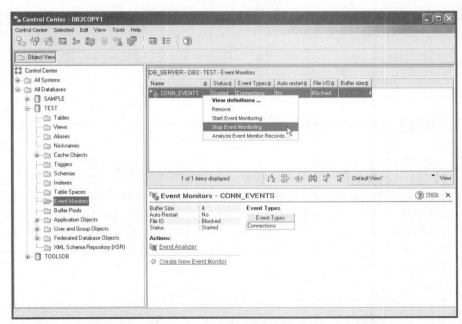

Figure 5–4: Stopping an event monitor from the Control Center

When an event monitor is activated (started), it sits quietly in the background and waits for one of the events it is associated with to occur. Immediately after an event being monitored takes place, the event monitor collects monitor data associated with the event that triggered it and writes all data collected to the event monitor's target location. Thus, the event itself controls when monitor data is collected—unlike with the snapshot monitor, no special steps are required to capture the monitor data.

Although there is no limit to the number of event monitors that can be defined for a single database, no more than 32 event monitors can be active at one time.

Forcing an event monitor to generate output prematurely

Because some events do not activate event monitors as frequently as others, it may be desirable to force an event monitor to collect monitor data and write it to its target location *before* a monitor-triggering event takes place. In such situations, you can make an event monitor collect information early by executing the FLUSH EVENT MONITOR SQL statement. The basic syntax for this statement is:

```
FLUSH EVENT MONITOR [EventMonName] <BUFFER>
```

where:

EventMonName   Identifies the name assigned to the event monitor that is to be forced to collect monitor data.

By default, records that are written to an event monitor's target location prematurely are logged in the event monitor log and assigned a "partial record" identifier. However, if the BUFFER option is specified when the FLUSH EVENT MONITOR statement is executed, only monitor data that is present in the event monitor's active internal buffers is written to the event monitor's target location; partial records are not generated.

Thus, if you wanted to force an event monitor named CONN_EVENTS to collect monitor data and write it to its target location immediately, you could do so by executing a FLUSH EVENT MONITOR statement that looks like this:

```
FLUSH EVENT MONITOR conn_events
```

It is important to note that when event monitors are flushed, counters are not reset. This means that the event monitor record that would have been generated if the FLUSH EVENT MONITOR statement had not been used to force event monitor data to be written will still be generated when the event monitor is triggered normally.

Deleting an event monitor

Just as there may be times when you need to create an event monitor, you may also want to delete existing event monitors when they are no longer needed. Previously defined event monitors can be removed from a database by executing a special form of the DROP SQL statement. The basic syntax for this form of the DROP statement is:

```
DROP EVENT MONITOR [MonitorName]
```

where:

MonitorName   Identifies the name that has been assigned to the event monitor that is to be deleted.

Thus, if you wanted to delete an event monitor that has been assigned the name CONN_EVENTS and resides in a schema named CORP, you could do so by executing a DROP SQL statement that looks something like this:

```
DROP EVENT MONITOR corp.conn_events
```

Event monitors can also be dropped from the Control Center by highlighting the appropriate object and selecting the appropriate action from any object menu found. Figure 5–5 shows the Control Center menu items that must be selected in order to drop an event monitor (in this case, an event monitor named CONN_EVENTS).

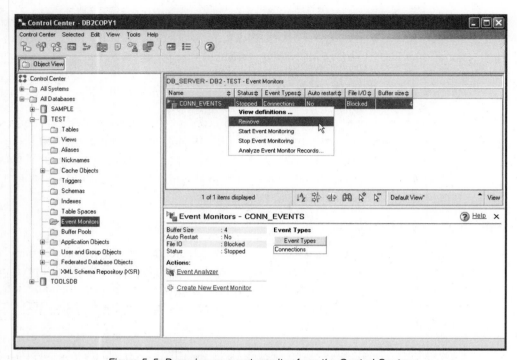

Figure 5–5: Dropping an event monitor from the Control Center.

It is important to note that an active event monitor cannot be deleted; active event monitors must be deactivated (stopped) before they can be deleted.

Viewing event monitor data

Data that has been collected by an event monitor can be viewed in one of two ways: by using a special utility known as the Event Analyzer or by using the Event Monitor Productivity Tool. The Event Analyzer is a Graphical User Interface (GUI) tool that can be activated by highlighting the desired event monitor shown in the Control Center and selecting the appropriate action from the Event Monitors menu. Figure 5–6 shows the Control Center menu items that must be selected to activate the Event Analyzer utility; Figure 5–7 shows how the "Monitored Periods" view of the Event Analyzer might look after an event monitor has been activated for two different monitoring sessions.

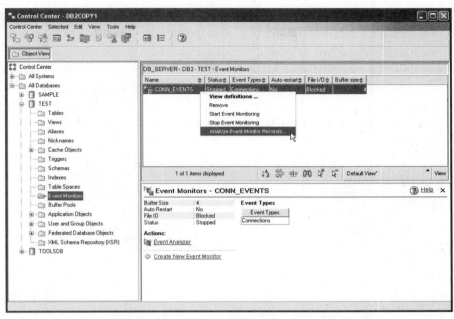

Figure 5–6: Starting the Event Analyzer from the Control Center.

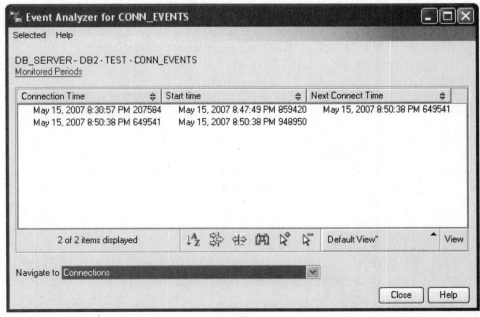

Figure 5–7: The Event Analyzer utility.

Once the Event Analyzer is activated, you can view/analyze the information that was captured for each event that was monitored by selecting the appropriate event from the "Drill down to" menu, which can be displayed by selecting the Selected menu item from the Event Analyzer's main menu. Figure 5–8 shows how the "Drill down to" menu would be used to drill down to monitor data that was collected for connection events that took place during one or more monitoring periods; Figure 5–9 shows how the Event Analyzer will display all connection events that were detected.

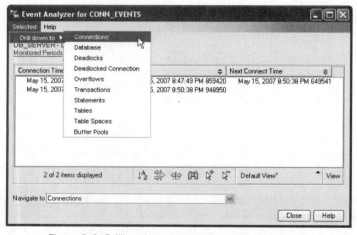

Figure 5–8: Drilling down to specific monitoring events.

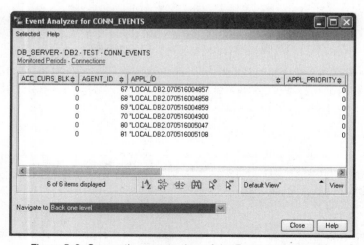

Figure 5–9: Connection events view of the Event Analyzer utility.

Unfortunately, the Event Analyzer can be used only to view event monitor data that was collected and stored in database tables. To view event monitor data that was written to files and named pipes, the Event Monitor Productivity Tool must be used instead. Unlike the Event Analyzer, the Event Monitor Productivity Tool is a text-based tool that is designed to retrieve information from an event monitor data file or named pipe and produce a formatted report. (Event monitor files and named pipes contain a binary stream of logical data groupings that must be formatted before they can be displayed.) The Event Monitor Productivity Tool is activated by executing the db2evmon command. The basic syntax for this command is:

```
db2evmon -db [DatabaseAlias] -evm [EventMonName]
```

or

```
db2evmon -path [EventMonTarget]
```

where:

DatabaseAlias Identifies the alias assigned to the database where the event monitor whose data is to be displayed has been defined.

EventMonName Identifies the name assigned to the event monitor whose data is to be displayed.

EventMonTarget Identifies the location (directory or named pipe) where data that has been collected by an event monitor is stored.

Thus, if you wanted to format and display all data collected by an event monitor named CONN_EVENTS that resides in a database named SAMPLE, you could do so by executing a db2evmon command statement that looks like this:

```
db2evmon -db sample -evm conn_events
```

Assume that the event monitor CONN_EVENTS was created using the following CREATE EVENT MONITOR statement:

```
CREATE EVENT MONITOR conn_events
FOR CONNECTIONS
WRITE TO FILE 'C:\MONDATA'
```

Also assuming that the event monitor was activated immediately after it was created and that one connection to the database was established after the event monitor was activated, the beginning of the output returned by the command

```
db2evmon -db sample -evm conn_events
```

should look something like this:

```
Reading C:\MONDATA\00000000.EVT ...
--------------------------------------------------------
                              EVENT LOG HEADER
  Event Monitor name: CONN_EVENTS
  Server Product ID: SQL09010
  Version of event monitor data: 8
  Byte order: LITTLE ENDIAN
  Number of nodes in db2 instance: 1
  Codepage of database: 1208
  Territory code of database: 1
  Server instance name: DB2
  ------------------------------


  ------------------------------

  Database Name: TEST
  Database Path: C:\DB2\NODE0000\SQL00003\
  First connection timestamp: 05/17/2007 16:15:41.818326
  Event Monitor Start time:   05/17/2007 16:20:49.434330
  ------------------------------

3) Connection Header Event...
  Appl Handle: 11
  Appl Id: *LOCAL.DB2.070517201539
  Appl Seq number: 00004
  DRDA AS Correlation Token: *LOCAL.DB2.070517201539
  Program Name     : db2bp.exe
  Authorization Id: RSANDERS
  Execution Id    : RSANDERS
  Codepage Id: 1252
  Territory code: 1
  Client Process Id: 2028
  Client Database Alias: TEST
  Client Product Id: SQL09010
  Client Platform: Unknown
  Client Communication Protocol: Local
  Client Network Name: rsanders-1xp
  Connect timestamp: 05/17/2007 16:15:41.818326
...
```

The Health Monitor and the Health Center

Along with the snapshot monitor and event monitors, DB2 9 provides two additional tools that are designed to help database administrators monitor DB2 systems under their control: the Health Monitor and the Health Center. Together, these tools provide management-by-exception capability that enables administrators to address health issues before they become real problems that adversely affect a system's performance.

The Health Monitor is a server-side tool that constantly monitors the health of a DB2 Database Manager instance without a need for user interaction. Instead, the Health Monitor uses several health indicators to evaluate specific aspects of instance and database performance. (Health indicators exist at the instance, database, table space, and table space container level.) A health indicator is a system characteristic that the Health Monitor scrutinizes continuously to determine whether an object is operating normally; each health indicator has a corresponding set of predefined threshold values, and the Health Monitor compares the state of the system against these health-indicator thresholds to see if they have been exceeded. If the Health Monitor finds that a predefined threshold has been exceeded (for example, if the amount of log space available is insufficient), or if it detects an abnormal state for an object (for example, if the instance is down), it will automatically raise an alert.

In most cases, the threshold values provided for a health indicator define boundaries or zones for three different operating states: normal (or attention), warning, and alarm. Thus, three types of alerts can be generated; regardless of the level, three things can happen whenever an alert is raised:

- Alert information can be recorded in the Journal. (All alarm alerts are written to the Journal.)

- Alert notifications can be sent via email or pager address to whoever is responsible for the system.

- One or more preconfigured actions can be taken. (For example, a task can be run.)

Next, the Health Center is a GUI tool that is designed to interact with the Health
Monitor. Using the Health Center, you can select the instance and database objects
that you want to monitor, customize the threshold settings of any health indicator,
specify where notifications are to be sent, and specify what actions are to be taken
if an alert is raised. The Health Center also allows you to start and stop the Health
Monitor, view the current status of the database environment, access details about
current alerts, obtain a list of recommended actions for resolving any alerts that
have been raised, and view a history of alerts that have been generated for an
instance or a database. Like other GUI tools, the Health Center can be activated by
selecting the appropriate action from the Tools menu of the Control Center. Figure
5–10 shows the Control Center menu items that must be selected in order to
activate the Health Center; Figure 5–11 shows how the Health Center looks on a
Windows XP system when it is first activated.

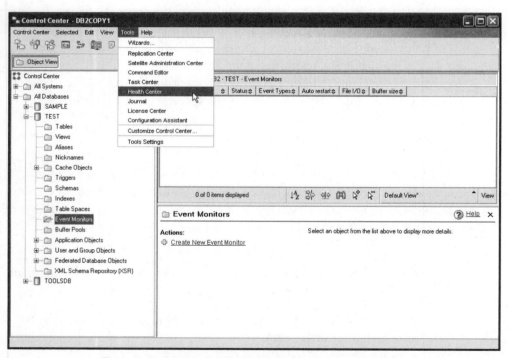

Figure 5–10: Starting the Health Center from the Control Center.

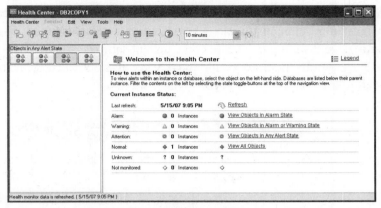

Figure 5–11: The Health Center.

One of the most common tasks performed using the Health Center is customization of the threshold settings of the health indicators that get evaluated by the Event Monitor. The customization of health indicator threshold values is performed by activating the Health Indicator Configuration Launchpad, selecting the desired level (instance, global, or object), selecting the desired health indicator variable, and changing the health indicator settings for that variable when the Configure Health Indicator dialog is displayed. Figure 5–12 shows the Health Center menu items that must be selected to activate the Health Indicator

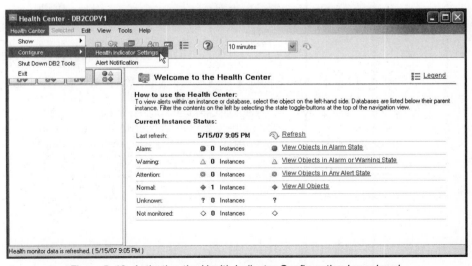

Figure 5–12: Activating the Health Indicator Configuration Launchpad.

Configuration Launchpad; Figure 5–13 shows how the Health Indicator Configuration Launchpad looks when it is first activated; Figure 5–14 shows the instance-level health indicator list and current settings; Figure 5–15 shows how the Configure Health Indicator dialog looks when it is activated for a specific health indicator variable.

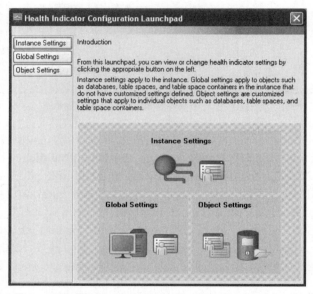

Figure 5–13: The Health Indicator Configuration Launchpad.

Changes made at the instance level apply to the entire instance, whereas changes made at the global level and object level apply only to databases, table spaces, and table space containers. Changes made at the object level override changes made at the global level; changes made at the global level override changes made at the instance level.

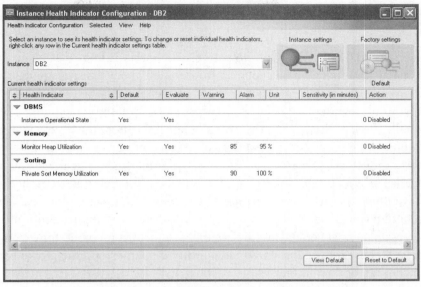

Figure 5–14: The Instance Health Indicator Configuration dialog.

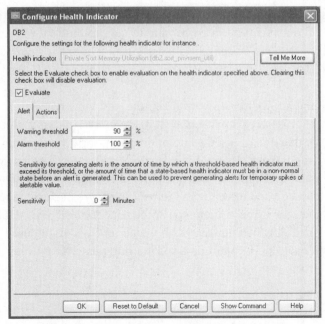

Figure 5–15: The Configure Health Indicator dialog.

Monitoring SQL with the Explain Facility

When an SQL statement is submitted to the DB2 database engine for processing, it is analyzed by the DB2 Optimizer to produce what is known as an access plan. Each access plan contains detailed information about the strategy that will be used to execute the statement (such as whether indexes will be used; what sort methods, if any, are required; what locks are needed; and what join methods, if any, will be used). If the SQL statement is coded in an application, the access plan is generated at precompile time (or at bind time if deferred binding is used), and an executable form of the access plan produced is stored in the system catalog as an object known as a *package*. If, however, the statement is submitted from the Command Line Processor, or if the statement is a dynamic SQL statement in an application program (i.e., an SQL statement that is constructed at application run time), the access plan is generated at the time the statement is prepared for execution, and the access plan produced is stored temporarily in memory (in the global package cache) rather than in the system catalog.

Although the Database System Monitor and the Health Monitor can be used to obtain information about how well (or poorly) some SQL operations perform, they cannot be used to analyze how an SQL statement was optimized. To perform this type of analysis, you must be able to capture and view the information stored in an SQL statement's access plan, and that's where the DB2 Explain Facility comes in.

The Explain Facility allows you to capture and view detailed information about the access plan chosen for a particular SQL statement, along with performance information that can be used to help identify poorly written statements or a weakness in database design. Specifically, Explain data helps you understand how the DB2 Database Manager accesses tables and indexes to satisfy a query. Explain data can also be used to evaluate the results of any performance-tuning action taken. In fact, any time you change some aspect of the DB2 Database Manager, an SQL statement, or the database with which an SQL statement interacts, you should collect and examine Explain data to find out what effect, if any, your changes have had on performance.

The Explain Tables

Before Explain information can be captured, a special set of tables, known as the Explain tables, must be created. Each Explain table used, along with the information it is designed to hold, can be seen in Table 5.5.

Table 5.5 Explain Tables	
Table Name	**Contents**
EXPLAIN_ARGUMENT	Contains the unique characteristics for each individual operator used, if there are any.
EXPLAIN_INSTANCE	Contains basic information about the source of the SQL statements being explained as well as information about the environment in which the explanation took place. (The EXPLAIN_INSTANCE table is the main control table for all Explain information. Each row of data in the other Explain tables is explicitly linked to one unique row in this table.)
EXPLAIN_OBJECT	Contains information about the data objects that are required by the access plan generated for an SQL statement.
EXPLAIN_OPERATOR	Contains all the operators that are needed by the SQL compiler to satisfy the SQL statement.
EXPLAIN_PREDICATE	Contains information that identifies which predicates are applied by a specific operator.
EXPLAIN_STATEMENT	Contains the text of the SQL statement as it exists for the different levels of Explain information. The original SQL statement as entered by the user is stored in this table along with the version used by the DB2 Optimizer to choose an access plan to satisfy the SQL statement. (The latter version may bear little resemblance to the original because it may have been rewritten or enhanced with additional predicates by the SQL Precompiler.)
EXPLAIN_STREAM	Contains information about the input and output data streams that exist between individual operators and data objects. (The data objects themselves are represented in the EXPLAIN_OBJECT table, and the operators involved in a data stream can be found in the EXPLAIN_OPERATOR table.)

Typically, Explain tables are used in a development database to aid in application design, but not in production databases, where application code remains fairly static. Because of this, they are not created along with the system catalog tables as part of the database creation process. Instead, Explain tables must be created manually in the database with which the Explain Facility will be used. Fortunately, the process used to create the Explain tables is pretty straightforward: using the Command Line Processor, you establish a connection to the appropriate database and execute a script named EXPLAIN.DDL, which can be found in the misc subdirectory of the sqllib directory where the DB2 software was initially installed. (Comments in the header of this file provide information on how it is to be executed.) On the other hand, if you attempt to invoke the Explain Facility from within the Control Center, and the Explain tables have not been created for the database with which you are interacting, they will be created for you automatically.

Collecting Explain Data

The Explain Facility is comprised of several individual tools, and not all tools require the same kind of Explain data. Therefore, two different types of Explain data can be collected:

Comprehensive Explain Data. Contains detailed information about an SQL statement's access plan. This information is stored across several different Explain tables.

Explain Snapshot Data. Contains the current internal representation of an SQL statement, along with any related information. This information is stored in the SNAPSHOT column of the EXPLAIN_STATEMENT Explain table.

And as you might imagine, there are a variety of ways in which both types of Explain data can be collected. The methods available for collecting Explain data include the following:

- Executing the EXPLAIN SQL statement

- Setting the CURRENT EXPLAIN MODE special register

- Setting the CURRENT EXPLAIN SNAPSHOT special register

- Using the EXPLAIN bind option with the PRECOMPILE or BIND command

- Using the EXPLSNAP bind option with the PRECOMPILE or BIND command

The EXPLAIN SQL statement

One way to collect both comprehensive Explain information and Explain snapshot data for a single, dynamic SQL statement is by executing the EXPLAIN SQL statement. The basic syntax for this statement is:

```
EXPLAIN [ALL | PLAN | PLAN SELECTION]
<FOR SNAPSHOT | WITH SNAPSHOT>
FOR [SQLStatement]
```

where:

SQLStatement   Identifies the SQL statement for which Explain data or Explain snapshot data is to be collected. (The statement specified must be a valid INSERT, UPDATE, DELETE, SELECT, SELECT INTO, VALUES, or VALUES INTO SQL statement.)

If the FOR SNAPSHOT option is specified with the EXPLAIN statement, only Explain snapshot information will be collected for the dynamic SQL statement specified. On the other hand, if the WITH SNAPSHOT option is specified instead, both comprehensive Explain information and Explain snapshot data will be collected for the dynamic SQL statement specified. However, if neither option is used, only comprehensive Explain data will be collected; no Explain snapshot data will be produced.

Thus, if you wanted to collect only comprehensive Explain data for the SQL statement "SELECT * FROM department," you could do so by executing an EXPLAIN statement that looks like this:

```
EXPLAIN ALL FOR SELECT * FROM department
```

On the other hand, if you wanted to collect only Explain snapshot data for the same SQL statement, you could do so by executing an EXPLAIN statement that looks like this:

```
EXPLAIN ALL FOR SNAPSHOT FOR SELECT * FROM department
```

And finally, if you wanted to collect both comprehensive Explain data and Explain snapshot information for the SQL statement "SELECT * FROM department," you could do so by executing an EXPLAIN statement that looks like this:

```
EXPLAIN ALL WITH SNAPSHOT FOR SELECT * FROM department
```

It is important to note that the EXPLAIN statement does not execute the SQL statement specified, nor does it display the Explain information collected—other Explain Facility tools must be used to view the information collected. (We'll look at those tools shortly.)

The CURRENT EXPLAIN MODE and the CURRENT EXPLAIN SNAPSHOT special registers

Although the EXPLAIN SQL statement is useful when you want to collect Explain and/or Explain snapshot information for a single dynamic SQL statement, it can become very time-consuming to use if a large number of SQL statements need to be analyzed. A better way to collect the same information for several dynamic SQL statements is setting one or both of the special Explain Facility registers provided before a group of dynamic SQL statements are executed. Then, as the statements are prepared for execution, Explain or Explain snapshot information is collected for each statement processed. The statements themselves, however, may or may not be executed.

The two Explain Facility special registers that are used in this manner are the CURRENT EXPLAIN MODE special register and the CURRENT EXPLAIN SNAPSHOT special register. The CURRENT EXPLAIN MODE special register is set using the SET CURRENT EXPLAIN MODE SQL statement, and the CURRENT EXPLAIN SNAPSHOT special register is set using the SET CURRENT EXPLAIN SNAPSHOT SQL statement. The basic syntax for the SET CURRENT EXPLAIN MODE statement is:

```
SET CURRENT EXPLAIN MODE <=> [YES | NO | EXPLAIN]
```

And the basic syntax for the SET CURRENT EXPLAIN SNAPSHOT statement is:

```
SET CURRENT EXPLAIN SNAPSHOT <=> [YES | NO | EXPLAIN]
```

As you might imagine, if both the CURRENT EXPLAIN MODE and the CURRENT EXPLAIN SNAPSHOT special register are set to NO, the Explain Facility is disabled, and no Explain data is captured. On the other hand, if either special register is set to EXPLAIN, the Explain Facility is activated, and comprehensive Explain information or Explain snapshot data (or both if both special registers have been set) is collected each time a dynamic SQL statement is prepared for execution. However, the statements themselves are not executed. If either special register is set to YES, the behavior is the same as when the corresponding register is set to EXPLAIN, with one significant difference: the dynamic SQL statements for which Explain information is collected are executed as soon as the appropriate Explain/Explain snapshot data has been collected. Table 5.6 summarizes the behavior each Explain special register setting has on the Explain Facility and dynamic SQL statement processing.

Table 5.6 Interaction of Explain Facility Special Register Settings			
	EXPLAIN MODE Values		
	NO	YES	EXPLAIN
NO	• Explain Facility is disabled. • No Explain data is captured. • Dynamic SQL statements are executed.	• Explain Facility is enabled. • Comprehensive Explain data is collected and written to the Explain tables. • Dynamic SQL statements are executed.	• Explain Facility is enabled • Comprehensive Explain data is collected and written to the Explain tables. • Dynamic SQL statements are executed.
YES	• Explain Facility is enabled. • Explain snapshot data is collected and written to the SNAPSHOT column of the EXPLAIN_STATEMENT Explain table. • Dynamic SQL statements are executed.	• Explain Facility is enabled. • Comprehensive Explain data is collected and written to the Explain tables. • Explain snapshot data is collected and written to the SNAPSHOT column of the EXPLAIN_STATEMENT Explain table. • Dynamic SQL statements are executed.	• Explain Facility is enabled. • Comprehensive Explain data is collected and written to the Explain tables. • Explain snapshot data is collected and written to the SNAPSHOT column of the EXPLAIN_STATEMENT Explain table. • Dynamic SQL statements are not executed.
EXPLAIN	• Explain Facility is enabled. • Explain snapshot data is collected and written to the SNAPSHOT column of the EXPLAIN_STATEMENT Explain table. • Dynamic SQL statements are not executed.	• Explain Facility is enabled. • Comprehensive Explain data is collected and written to the Explain tables. • Explain snapshot data is collected and written to the SNAPSHOT column of the EXPLAIN_STATEMENT Explain table. • Dynamic SQL statements are not executed	• Explain Facility is enabled. • Comprehensive Explain data is collected and written to the Explain tables. • Explain snapshot data is collected and written to the SNAPSHOT column of the EXPLAIN_STATEMENT Explain table. • Dynamic SQL statements are not executed

(Left axis label: EXPLAIN SNAPSHOT Values)

Adapted from Table 200 on pages 821–822 of volume 1 of the *DB2 9 SQL Reference, Volume 1* manual.

The EXPLAIN and EXPLSNAP bind options

So far, we have looked at ways in which comprehensive Explain information and Explain snapshot data can be collected for dynamic SQL statements. But often, database applications contain static SQL statements that need to be analyzed as well. So how can you use the Explain Facility to analyze static SQL statements coded in an Embedded SQL application? To collect comprehensive Explain information and/or Explain snapshot data for both static and dynamic SQL statements that have been coded in an Embedded SQL application, you must use the EXPLAIN and EXPLSNAP bind options.

The EXPLAIN bind option is used to control whether comprehensive Explain data is collected for SQL statements that have been coded in an Embedded SQL application; the EXPLSNAP bind option controls whether Explain snapshot data is collected. One or both of these options can be specified as part of the PRECOMPILE command used to precompile the source code file that contains Embedded SQL statements—if deferred binding is used, these options can be provided with the BIND command that is used to bind the Embedded SQL application's bind file to a database.

Both the EXPLAIN option and the EXPLSNAP option can be assigned the value NO, YES, or ALL. If both options are assigned the value NO (for example, EXPLAIN NO EXPLSNAP NO), the Explain Facility is disabled, and no Explain data is captured. On the other hand, if either option is assigned the value YES, the Explain Facility is activated, and comprehensive Explain information or Explain snapshot data (or both if both options are set to YES) is collected for each static SQL statement encountered in the source code file; dynamic SQL statements are ignored. If either option is assigned the value ALL, the Explain Facility is activated, and comprehensive Explain information or Explain snapshot data (or both if both options are set) is collected for every static and dynamic SQL statement found, even if the CURRENT EXPLAIN MODE and/or the CURRENT EXPLAIN SNAPSHOT special registers have been set to NO. Table 5.7 summarizes the behavior the EXPLAIN bind option has on the Explain Facility and on static and dynamic SQL statement processing when used in conjunction with the EXPLAIN MODE special register; Table 5.8 summarizes the behavior that the EXPLSNAP bind option has on the Explain Facility and on static and dynamic SQL statement processing when used in conjunction with the EXPLAIN SNAPSHOT special register.

Table 5.7 Interaction of the EXPLAIN Bind Option and the EXPLAIN MODE Special Register			
	EXPLAIN Bind Option Values		
	NO	YES	ALL
NO	• Explain Facility is disabled. • No Explain data is captured.	• Explain Facility is enabled. • Comprehensive Explain data is collected and written to the Explain tables for static SQL statements.	• Explain Facility is enabled. • Comprehensive Explain data is collected and written to the Explain tables for both static and dynamic SQL statements.
YES	• Explain Facility is enabled. • Comprehensive Explain data is collected and written to the Explain tables for dynamic SQL statements.	• Explain Facility is enabled. • Comprehensive Explain data is collected and written to the Explain tables for both static and dynamic SQL statements	• Explain Facility is enabled. • Comprehensive Explain data is collected and written to the Explain tables for both static and dynamic SQL statements.
EXPLAIN	• Explain Facility is enabled. • Comprehensive Explain data is collected and written to the Explain tables for dynamic SQL statements. • Dynamic SQL statements are not executed.	• Explain Facility is enabled. • Comprehensive Explain data is collected and written to the Explain tables for both static and dynamic SQL statements. • Dynamic SQL statements are not executed.	• Explain Facility is enabled. • Comprehensive Explain data is collected and written to the Explain tables for both static and dynamic SQL statements. • Dynamic SQL statements are not executed.

(Left vertical axis label: EXPLAIN MODE Special Register Values)

Adapted from Table 201 on pages 823–824 of the *DB2 9 SQL Reference, Volume 1* manual.

Evaluating Explain Data

So far, we have concentrated on the various ways in which comprehensive Explain and Explain snapshot data can be collected. We have also seen that once collected, this data is stored in one or more Explain tables. We could construct a query to retrieve the data collected, but a better way to view Explain information collected is by using one of the Explain Facility tools that have been designed specifically for presenting Explain information in a meaningful format. This set of tools consists of:

Table 5.8 Interaction of the EXPLAIN Bind Option and the EXPLAIN MODE Special Register

EXPLAIN SNAPSHOT Special Register Values	EXPLSNAP Bind Option Values: NO	EXPLSNAP Bind Option Values: YES	EXPLSNAP Bind Option Values: ALL
NO	• Explain Facility is disabled. • No Explain data is captured.	• Explain Facility is enabled. • Explain snapshot data is collected and written to the SNAPSHOT column of the EXPLAIN_STATEMENT Explain table for static SQL statements.	• Explain Facility is enabled. • Explain snapshot data is collected and written to the SNAPSHOT column of the EXPLAIN_STATEMENT Explain table for both static and dynamic SQL statements.
YES	• Explain Facility is enabled. • Explain snapshot data is collected and written to the SNAPSHOT column of the EXPLAIN_STATEMENT Explain table for dynamic SQL statements.	• Explain Facility is enabled. • Explain snapshot data is collected and written to the SNAPSHOT column of the EXPLAIN_STATEMENT Explain table for both static and dynamic SQL statements.	• Explain Facility is enabled. • Explain snapshot data is collected and written to the SNAPSHOT column of the EXPLAIN_STATEMENT Explain table for both static and dynamic SQL statements.
EXPLAIN	• Explain Facility is enabled. • Explain snapshot data is collected and written to the SNAPSHOT column of the EXPLAIN_STATEMENT Explain table for dynamic SQL statements. • Dynamic SQL statements are not executed.	• Explain Facility is enabled. • Explain snapshot data is collected and written to the SNAPSHOT column of the EXPLAIN_STATEMENT Explain table for both static and dynamic SQL statements. • Dynamic SQL statements are not executed.	• Explain Facility is enabled. • Explain snapshot data is collected and written to the SNAPSHOT column of the EXPLAIN_STATEMENT Explain table for both static and dynamic SQL statements. • Dynamic SQL statements are not executed.

Adapted from Table 202 on pages 824–825 of the *DB2 9 SQL Reference, Volume 1* manual.

- The db2expln tool
- The db2exfmt tool
- Visual Explain

db2expln

Earlier, we saw that when a source code file containing Embedded SQL statements is bound to a database (either as part of the precompile process or during deferred binding), the DB2 Optimizer analyzes each static SQL statement encountered and generates a corresponding access plan, which is then stored in the database in the form of a package. Given the name of the database, the name of the package, the ID of the package creator, and a section number (if the section number 0 is specified, all sections of the package will be processed), the db2expln tool will interpret and describe the access plan information for any package that is stored in a database's system catalog. Because the db2expln tool works directly with a package and not with comprehensive Explain or Explain snapshot data, it is typically used to produce information about the access plans that have been chosen for packages for which Explain data has not been captured. However, because the db2expln tool can only access information that has been stored in a package, it can only describe the implementation of the final access plan chosen; it cannot provide information on how a particular SQL statement was optimized.

The db2expln tool can also be used to Explain—and optionally, produce a graph of the access plan chosen by the DB2 Optimizer for—a dynamic SQL statement. For example, suppose you wanted to view the access plan the Optimizer would select for the query "SELECT * FROM department." You could do so by executing a db2expln command that looks something like this:

```
db2expln -d sample -t -g -statement "SELECT * FROM department"
```

And if you executed this command using the SAMPLE database provided with DB2, you would see a report that looks something like this:

```
DB2 Universal Database Version 9.1, 5622-044 (c) Copyright IBM
Corp. 1991, 2006
Licensed Material - Program Property of IBM
IBM DB2 Universal Database SQL and XQUERY Explain Tool

********************** DYNAMIC *******************************

===================== STATEMENT =============================
    Isolation Level          = Cursor Stability
    Blocking                 = Block Unambiguous Cursors
    Query Optimization Class  = 5
```

```
        Partition Parallel        = No
        Intra-Partition Parallel  = No
        SQL Path                  = "SYSIBM", "SYSFUN", "SYSPROC",
                                    SYSIBMADM", "RSANDERS"

    Statement:

      SELECT * FROM department

    Section Code Page = 1252

    Estimated Cost = 7.596399
    Estimated Cardinality = 14.000000

    Access Table Name = RSANDERS.DEPARTMENT   ID = 2,5
    |   #Columns = 5
    |   Relation Scan
    |   |   Prefetch: Eligible
    |   Lock Intents
    |   |   Table: Intent Share
    |   |   Row  : Next Key Share
    |   Sargable Predicate(s)
    |   |   Return Data to Application
    |   |   |   #Columns = 5
    Return Data Completion

    End of section

    Optimizer Plan:

      RETURN
      (   1)
        |
      TBSCAN
      (   2)
        |
     Table:
     RSANDERS
     DEPARTMENT
```

db2exfmt

Unlike the db2expln tool, the db2exfmt tool is designed to work directly with comprehensive Explain or Explain snapshot data that has been collected and stored in the Explain tables. Given a database name and other qualifying information, the db2exfmt tool will query the Explain tables for information, format the results, and produce a text-based report that can be displayed directly on the terminal or written to an ASCII-formatted file.

For example, if you wanted to generate a detailed report consisting of all Explain data that has been collected and stored in the SAMPLE database provided with DB2, you could do so by executing a db2exfmt command that looks something like this:

```
db2exfmt -d sample -1 -o F:/db2exfmt.out
```

When this command is executed, a report will be produced and written to a file named db2exfmt.out (that resides on the F: drive), and you should see a message that looks something like this:

```
DB2 Universal Database Version 9.1, 5622-044 (c) Copyright IBM
Corp. 1991, 2006
Licensed Material - Program Property of IBM
IBM DATABASE 2 Explain Table Format Tool

Connecting to the Database.
Connect to Database Successful.
Output is in F:/db2exfmt.out.
Executing Connect Reset -- Connect Reset was Successful.
```

The beginning of the output file created (db2exfmt.out) should look something like this:

```
DB2 Universal Database Version 9.1, 5622-044 (c) Copyright IBM
Corp. 1991, 2006
Licensed Material - Program Property of IBM
IBM DATABASE 2 Explain Table Format Tool

******************** EXPLAIN INSTANCE ********************

DB2_VERSION:            09.01.0
SOURCE_NAME:            SYSSH200
SOURCE_SCHEMA:          NULLID
SOURCE_VERSION:
EXPLAIN_TIME:           2007-05-17-16.40.32.188000
EXPLAIN_REQUESTER:      RSANDERS
Database Context:
-------------------
     Parallelism:           None
     CPU Speed:             4.762805e-007
     Comm Speed:            100
     Buffer Pool size:      250
     Sort Heap size:        256
     Database Heap size:    600
     Lock List size:        50
     Maximum Lock List:     22
```

```
      Average Applications:     1
      Locks Available:          935

Package Context:
----------------
      SQL Type:                 Dynamic
      Optimization Level:       5
      Blocking:                 Block All Cursors
      Isolation Level:          Cursor Stability

   ...
```

Visual Explain

Visual Explain is a GUI tool that provides database administrators and application developers with the ability to view a graphical representation of the access plan that has been chosen for a particular SQL statement. In addition, Visual Explain allows you to do the following:

- See the database statistics that were used to optimize the SQL statement.

- Determine whether an index was used to access table data. (If an index was not used, Visual Explain can help you determine which columns might benefit from being indexed.)

- View the effects of performance tuning by allowing you to make "before" and "after" comparisons.

- Obtain detailed information about each operation that is performed by the access plan, including the estimated cost of each.

However, Visual Explain can be used to view only Explain snapshot data; to view Explain data that has been collected and written to the Explain tables, the db2exfmt tool must be used instead.

Activating Visual Explain. One of the more common ways to activate Visual Explain is by generating Explain data for a dynamic SQL statement using the Explain Query Statement dialog. (Another is by choosing a query for which Explain data has already been generated from the Explained Statement History dialog.) Figure 5–16 shows the Control Center menu items that must be selected to activate Explain Query Statement dialog; Figure 5–17 shows how the Explain Query Statement dialog might look when it has been populated with a simple query.

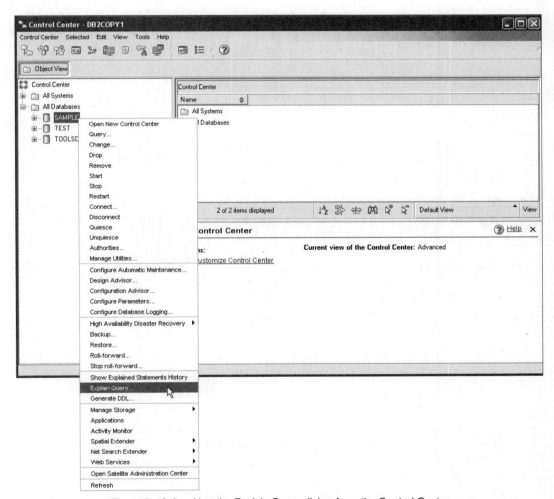

Figure 5–16: Invoking the Explain Query dialog from the Control Center.

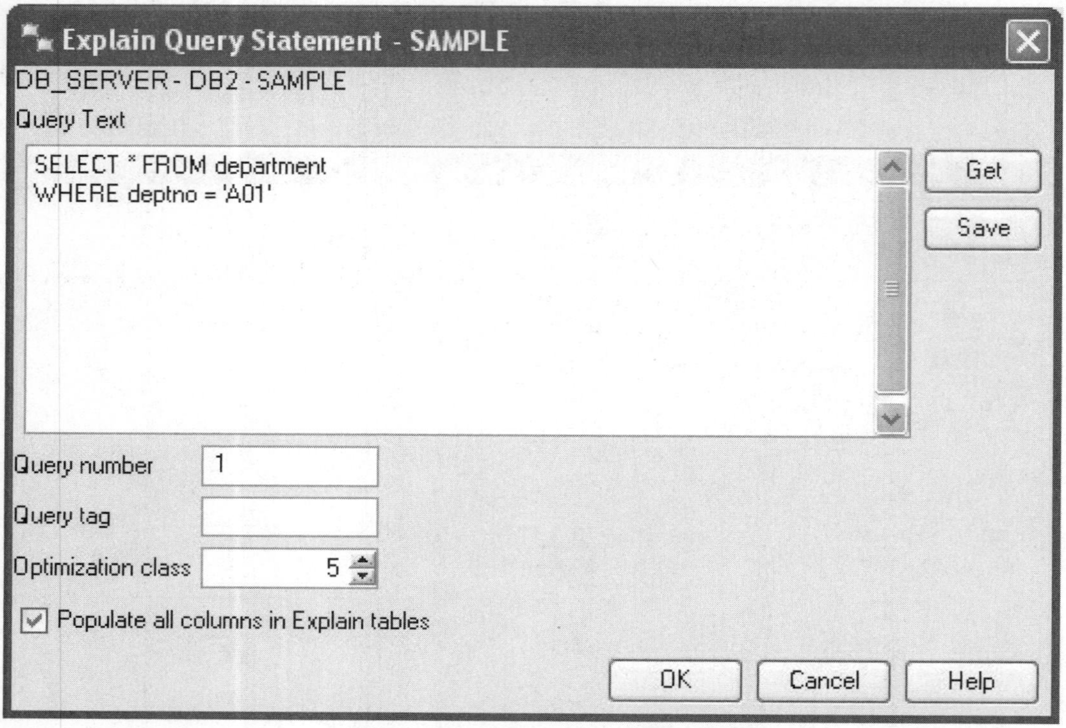

Figure 5–17: The Explain Query Statement dialog.

After the Explain Query Statement dialog is opened, any dynamic SQL statement can be entered into the "Query text" entry field. Then, when the "OK" push button located at the bottom of the dialog is selected, Explain snapshot data will be collected for the SQL statement specified. And after all processing is complete, control will be transferred to the Access Plan Graph dialog of Visual Explain, where a graphical view of the access plan chosen for the SQL statement specified will be presented.

Figure 5–18 shows how the Access Plan Graph dialog of Visual Explain might look when it first activated.

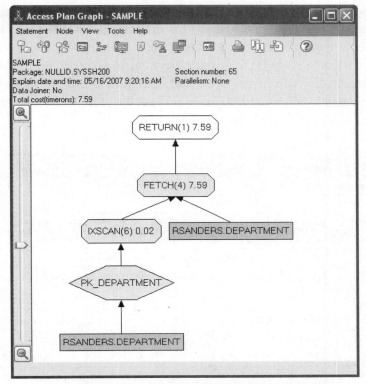

Figure 5–18: The Access Plan Graph dialog of Visual Explain.

Visual Explain output. As you can see in Figure 5–18, the output provided by Visual Explain consists of a hierarchical graph that represents the various components needed to process the access plan that has been chosen for a particular SQL statement. Each component is represented as a graphical object that is known as a node, and two types of nodes can exist:

> **Operator.** An operator node is used to identify either an action that must be performed on data or output produced from a table or index.
>
> **Operand.** An operand node is used to identify an entity on which an operation is performed (for example, a table would be the operand of a table scan operator).

Typically, operand nodes are used to identify tables, indexes, and table queues (table queues are used when intrapartition parallelism is used), which are symbolized in the hierarchical graph by rectangles (tables), diamonds (indexes), and parallelograms (table queues). Operator nodes, on the other hand, are used to identify anything from an insert operation to an index or table scan. Operator nodes, which are symbolized in the hierarchical graph by ovals, indicate how data is accessed, how tables are joined, and other factors such as whether a sort operation is to be performed. Table 5.8 lists the more common operators that can appear in an access plan hierarchical graph.

Table 5.8 Common Operators	
Definition	**Description**
DELETE	Deletes rows from a table.
EISCAN	Scans a user-defined index to produce a reduced stream of rows.
FETCH	Fetches columns from a table using a specific record identifier.
FILTER	Filters data by applying one or more predicates to it.
GRPBY	Groups rows by common values of designated columns or functions and evaluates set functions.
HSJOIN	Represents a hash join, where two or more tables are hashed on the join columns. (Preferred method for joins performed in a decision support environment.)
INSERT	Inserts rows into a table.
IXAND	ANDs together the row identifiers (RIDs) from two or more index scans.
IXSCAN	Scans an index of a table with optional start/stop conditions, producing an ordered stream of rows.
MSJOIN	Represents a merge join, where both outer and inner tables must be in join-predicate order.
NLJOIN	Represents a nested loop join that accesses an inner table once for each row of the outer table. (Preferred method for joins performed in an OLTP environment.)
RETURN	Represents the return of data from the query to the user.
RIDSCN	Scans a list of row identifiers (RIDs) obtained from one or more indexes.
SHIP	Retrieves data from a remote database source. Used in the federated system.
SORT	Sorts rows in the order of specified columns and optionally eliminates duplicate entries.
TBSCAN	Retrieves rows by reading all required data directly from the data pages.
TEMP	Stores data in a temporary table to be read back out (possibly multiple times).
TQUEUE	Transfers table data between database agents.
UNION	Concatenates streams of rows from multiple tables.
UNIQUE	Eliminates rows with duplicate values, for specified columns.
UPDATE	Updates rows in a table.

Arrows that illustrate how data flows from one node to the next connect all nodes shown in the hierarchical graph, and a RETURN operator normally terminates this path. Figure 5–18 shows how the hierarchical graph for an access plan that contains three different operator nodes (IXSCAN, FETCH, and RETURN) and two different operand nodes (a table named RSANDERS.DEPARTMENT and an index named PK_DEPARTMENT) might be displayed in Visual Explain.

Detailed information about each operator node shown in an access plan hierarchical graph is also available, and this information can be accessed by placing the mouse pointer over any operator node, right-clicking the mouse button, and selecting the Show Details action from the pop-up menu displayed. Figure 5–19 shows the menu items that must be selected to view detailed information about a particular operator node; Figure 5–20 shows how the Operator details dialog might look after it has been activated.

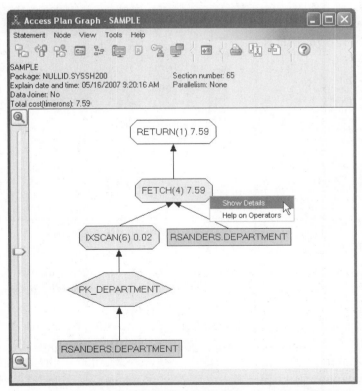

Figure 5–19: Invoking the Operator details dialog from Visual Explain.

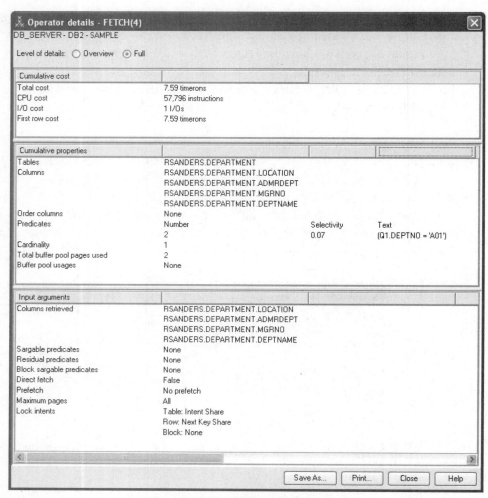

Figure 5–20: The Operator details dialog.

Likewise, detailed information about the table or index statistics that were used to select the access plan chosen are available for each operand node shown in an access plan hierarchical graph. This information can be accessed by placing the mouse pointer over any operand node, right-clicking the mouse button, and selecting the Show Statistics action from the menu displayed. Figure 5–21 shows the menu items that must be selected to view detailed information about a particular operand node; Figure 5–22 shows how the Table/Index Statistics dialog might look after it has been activated.

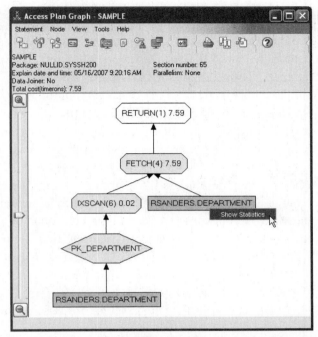

Figure 5–21: Invoking the Table/Index Statistics dialog from Visual Explain.

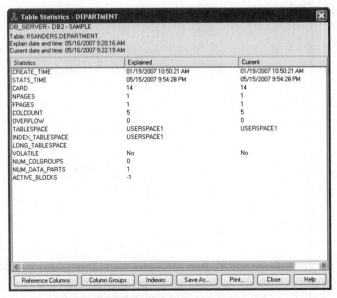

Figure 5–22: The Table/Index Statistics dialog.

A word about optimization classes

When you compile an SQL or XQuery query, you can specify an optimization class that determines how the DB2 Optimizer will choose the most efficient access plan for that query. The optimization classes are differentiated by the number and type of optimization strategies that are considered in the compilation of the query. The possible values range from 0 to 9; in general, the higher classes cause the Optimizer to use more time and memory when selecting optimal access plans, which potentially results in better access plans and improved runtime performance.

The QUERYOPT precompile/bind option is used to specify the class of optimization techniques that is to be used when preparing static SQL statements. If this option is not provided when an application is precompiled or bound to a database, the current value of the *dft_queryopt* database configuration file parameter is used as the default. The CURRENT QUERY OPTIMIZATION special register is used to control the class of optimization techniques used when binding dynamic SQL statements; the value of the parameter can be changed by executing the SET CURRENT QUERY OPTIMIZATION SQL statement. The basic syntax for this statement is:

```
SET CURRENT QUERY OPTIMIZATION <=> [OptimizationLevel]
```

where:

OptimizationLevel   Specifies the optimization level (class) to use when preparing dynamic SQL statements. This parameter must be set to one of the following values.

- **0**
  Specifies that a minimal amount of optimization techniques is to be used when the Optimizer generates an access plan. This optimization class level is most suitable for simple dynamic SQL statements that access well-indexed tables.

- **1**
  Specifies that the amount of optimization techniques to be used when the Optimizer generates an access plan should be roughly equal to that provided by DB2 Version 1.

- **2**

  Specifies that the amount of optimization techniques to be used when the Optimizer generates an access plan should be higher than that provided by DB2 Version 1, but significantly less than the amount used by level 3 and higher.

- **3**

  Specifies that a moderate amount of optimization techniques is to be used when the Optimizer generates an access plan.

- **5**

  Specifies that a significant amount of optimization techniques is to be used when the Optimizer generates an access plan. For complex queries, heuristic rules are used to limit the amount of time spent selecting an access plan. Whenever possible, queries will use summary tables instead of underlying base tables. This is the default optimization class used by DB2.

- **7**

  Specifies that a significant amount of optimization techniques is to be used when the Optimizer generates an access plan. This level is similar to level 5; however, no heuristic rules are used to limit the amount of time spent selecting access plans for complex queries.

- **9**

  Specifies that the maximum amount of optimization techniques is to be used when the Optimizer generates an access plan. This optimization class can greatly expand the number of possible access paths that are evaluated before an access plan is chosen. For this reason, this class is typically used to process SQL statements that contain very complex and very long-running queries that are executed against very large tables.

Therefore, if you wanted to tell the DB2 Optimizer to use more optimization techniques than are normally used by default when generating access plans for dynamic SQL statements, you could do so by executing a SET CURRENT QUERY OPTIMIZATION statement that looks like this:

```
SET CURRENT QUERY OPTIMIZATION = 7
```

When the CURRENT QUERY OPTIMIZATION special register is assigned a new value, a new class of query rewrite rules is enabled, and certain optimization variables are assigned appropriate values for the class. These query rewrite rules and optimization variables are then used during the preparation of dynamic SQL statements so that the optimum access plan for the statement is chosen.

It is important to note that the QUERYOPT precompile/bind can be assigned the same values as the CURRENT QUERY OPTIMIZATION special register.

Other Troubleshooting Tools

Along with the database system monitor and the Explain Facility, several other tools are available to help a database administrator isolate and identify problems with a system, database, or application. Some of the more popular problem determination tools are the Bind File Description tool, the DB2 memory tracker utility, and the DB2 Problem Determination tool. In this section, we'll take a closer look at each.

The DB2 Bind File Description Tool

The DB2 Bind File Description Tool can be used to examine and verify the SQL statements within a bind file, as well as to display the precompile options used to create the bind file. The DB2 Bind File Description Tool is invoked by executing the db2bfd command. The syntax for this command is:

```
db2bfd <-b> <-s> <-v> <-h> [BindFileName]
```

where:

BindFileName   Identifies, by name, the bind file whose contents are to be retrieved and displayed.

All options shown with this command are described in Table 5.8.

Table 5.8 db2bfd Command Options	
Option	Meaning
-b	Specifies that the bind file header is to be displayed.
-s	Specifies that the SQL statements in the bind file are to be displayed.
-v	Specifies that host variable declarations in the bind file are to be displayed.
-h	Displays help information. When this option is specified, all other options are ignored, and only the help information is displayed.

Thus, if you wanted to see the contents of a bind file named DB29TEST.BND, you could do so by executing a db2bfd command that looks something like this:

```
db2bfd -b -s -v db29test.bnd
```

And when this command is executed, the information returned might look something like this:

```
db29test.bnd: Header Contents

Header Fields:

Field                   Value
_____                   _____
releaseNum              0x800
Endian                  0x4c
numHvars                4
maxSect                 1
numStmt                 6
optInternalCnt          5
optCount                11

Name                    Value
____                    _____
Isolation Level         Cursor Stability
Creator                 "RSANDERS"
Collection              "RSANDERS"
App Name                "DB29TEST"
Timestamp               "QAmtMVFX:2007/05/21 12:45:38:16"
Cnulreqd                Yes
Sql Error               No package
Qualifier               "RSANDERS"
Validate                Bind
```

```
Date                    Default/local
Time                    Default/local
```

*** All other options are using default settings as specified by the
server ***

db29test.bnd: SQL Statements = 6

Line	Sec	Typ	Var	Len	SQL statement text
46	0	5	0	21	BEGIN DECLARE SECTION
51	0	2	0	19	END DECLARE SECTION
68	0	19	3	47	CONNECT TO :H00001 USER :H00002 USING :H00003
77	1	0	1	55	SELECT COUNT(*) INTO :H00004 FROM
					RSANDERS.DEPARTMENT
90	0	8	0	6	COMMIT
96	0	19	0	13	CONNECT RESET

db29test.bnd: Host Variables = 4

Type	SQL Data Type	Length	Alias	Name_Len	Name	UDT Name
460	C STRING	9	H00001	6	DBName	
460	C STRING	9	H00002	6	UserID	
460	C STRING	19	H00003	8	Password	
480	FLOAT	4	H00004	8	RowCount	

The DB2 Memory Tracker

The DB2 memory tracker utility is used to produce a complete report of memory status for instances, databases, and agents. This utility provides the following information about memory pool allocation:

- Current size

- Maximum size (hard limit)

- Largest size (high water mark)

- Type (identifier indicating function for which memory will be used)

- Agent who allocated pool (only if the pool is private)

(This information is also available from the snapshot monitor.)

The DB2 memory tracker utility is invoked by executing the db2mtrk command. The syntax for this command is:

```
db2mtrk
<-i>
```

```
<-d>
<-p
<-m | -w>
<-r [Interval] <Count>>
<-v>
<-h>
```

where:

Interval   Identifies the number of seconds to wait between subsequent calls to the DB2 memory tracker.

Count   Identifies the number of times to repeat calls to the DB2 memory tracker.

All other options shown with this command are described in Table 5.9.

Option	Meaning
Table 5.9 db2mtrk Command Options	
-i	Specifies that information about instance level memory is to be collected and displayed.
-d	Specifies that information about database level memory is to be collected and displayed.
-p	Specifies that information about private memory is to be collected and displayed
-m	Specifies that maximum values for each memory pool are to be collected and displayed.
-w	Specifies that high watermark values for each memory pool are to be collected and displayed.
-v	Indicates that verbose output is to be returned.
-h	Displays help information. When this option is specified, all other options are ignored, and only the help information is displayed.

Thus, if you wanted to see how memory is utilized by the active databases on a system, you could do so by executing a db2mtrk command that looks something like this:

```
db2mtrk -d
```

Assuming a database named SAMPLE is active at the time the db2mtrk command is issued, the results produced should look something like this:

```
Tracking Memory on: 2007/05/21 at 14:00:38
Memory for database: SAMPLE
```

```
utilh        pckcacheh  catcacheh  bph (1)   bph (S32K)  bph (S16K)  bph (S8K)
64.0K        128.0K     64.0K      1.2M      704.0K      448.0K      320.0K

bph (S4K)    shsorth    lockh      dbh       other
256.0K       0          320.0K     4.3M      128.0K
```

The DB2 Problem Determination Tool

The DB2 Problem Determination tool is used to obtain quick and immediate information from the DB2 database system memory sets, without acquiring any latches. Two benefits to collecting information without latching include faster data retrieval and no competition for engine resources. However, because the DB2 Problem Determination tool works directly with memory, it is possible to retrieve information that is changing as it is being collected; hence, the data retrieved might not be completely accurate. (A signal handler is used to prevent the DB2 Problem Determination tool from aborting abnormally when changing memory pointers are encountered. However, this can result in messages such as "Changing data structure forced command termination" to appear in the output produced.) Nonetheless, this tool can be extremely helpful for problem determination.

The DB2 Problem Determination tool is invoked by executing the db2pd command. The basic syntax for this command is:

```
db2pd
<- version | -v >
<-inst>
<[-database | -db] [DatabaseName] ,...>
<-alldatabases | -alldbs>
<-full>
<-everything>
<-hadr [-db [DatabaseName] | -alldbs]>
<-utilities>
<-applications [-db [DatabaseName] | -alldbs]>
<-agents>
<-transactions [-db [DatabaseName] | -alldbs]>
<-bufferpools [-db [DatabaseName] | -alldbs]>
<-logs [-db [DatabaseName] | -alldbs]>
<-tablespaces [-db [DatabaseName] | -alldbs]>
<-dynamic [-db [DatabaseName] | -alldbs]>
<-static [-db [DatabaseName] | -alldbs]>
<-fcm>
<-memsets>
<-mempools>
<-memblocks>
<-dbmcfg>
```

```
<-dbcfg [-db [DatabaseName] | -alldbs]>
<-catalogcache [-db [DatabaseName] | -alldbs]>
<-tcbstats [-db [DatabaseName] | -alldbs]>
<-reorg [-db [DatabaseName] | -alldbs]>
<-recovery [-db [DatabaseName] | -alldbs]>
<-reopt [-db [DatabaseName] | -alldbs]>
<-osinfo>
<-storagepaths [-db [DatabaseName] | -alldbs]>
<-pages [-db [DatabaseName] | -alldbs]>
<-stack [all | [ProcessID]]>
<-repeat [Interval] <[Count]>>
<-command [CmdFileName]>
<-file [OutFileName]>
<-interactive>
<-h | -help>
```

where:

DatabaseName Identifies, by name, the database with which the DB2 Problem Determination tool is to interact.

ProcessID Identifies the process, by ID, for which a stack trace file is to be produced.

Interval Identifies the number of seconds to wait between subsequent calls to the DB2 Problem Determination tool.

Count Identifies the number of time to repeat calls to the DB2 Problem Determination tool.

CmdFileName Identifies the name assigned to an ASCII format file that contains DB2 Problem Determination tool command options that are to be used.

OutFile Identifies the name of the file to which information returned by the DB2 Problem Determination tool is to be written.

All other options shown with this command are described in Table 5.10.

Table 5.10 db2pd Command Options	
Option	**Meaning**
-version | -v	Specifies that the current version and service level of the installed DB2 product is to be collected and displayed.
-inst	Specifies that all instance level information available is to be collected and displayed.
-alldatabases | -alldbs	Specifies that the utility is to attach to all memory sets of all available databases.
-full	Specifies that all output is to be expanded to its maximum length. (If this option is not specified, output is truncated to save space on the display.)
-everything	Specifies that all options are to be used and that information is to be collected and displayed for all databases on all database partition servers that are local to the server.
-hadr	Specifies that information about high availability disaster recovery (HADR) is to be collected and displayed.
-utilities	Specifies that information about utilities is to be collected and displayed.
-applications	Specifies that information about applications is to be collected and displayed.
-agents	Specifies that information about agents is to be collected and displayed.
-transactions	Specifies that information about active transactions is to be collected and displayed.
-bufferpools	Specifies that information about buffer pools is to be collected and displayed.
-logs	Specifies that information about transaction log files is to be collected and displayed.
-locks	Specifies that information about locks is to be collected and displayed.
-tablespaces	Specifies that information about table spaces is to be collected and displayed.
-dynamic	Specifies that information about the execution of dynamic SQL statements is to be collected and displayed.
-static	Specifies that information about the execution of static SQL and packages is to be collected and displayed.
-fcm	Specifies that information about the fast communication manager is to be collected and displayed.
-memsets	Specifies that information about memory sets is to be collected and displayed.
-mempools	Specifies that information about memory pools is to be collected and displayed.
-memblocks	Specifies that information about memory blocks is to be collected and displayed.

Table 5.10 db2pd Command Options (continued)	
Option	**Meaning**
-dbmcfg	Specifies that information about current DB2 Database Manager configuration parameter settings is to be collected and displayed.
-dbcfg	Specifies that information about current database configuration parameter settings is to be collected and displayed.
-catalogcache	Specifies that information about the catalog cache is to be collected and displayed.
-tcbstats	Specifies that information about tables and indexes is to be collected and displayed.
-reorg	Specifies that information about table and data partition reorganization is to be collected and displayed.
-recovery	Specifies that information about recovery activity is to be collected and displayed.
-reopt	Specifies that information about cached SQL statements that were reoptimized using the REOPT ONCE option is to be collected and displayed.
-osinfo	Specifies that operating system information is to be collected and displayed.
-storagepaths	Specifies that information about the automatic storage paths defined for the database is to be collected and displayed.
-pages	Specifies that information about buffer pool pages is to be collected and displayed.
-stack	Specifies that stack trace information is to be collected and displayed.
-repeat	Specifies that the command is to be repeated after the specified number of seconds for the specified number of times.
-command	Specifies that db2pd commands that are stored in the specified in the file are to be executed.
-file	Specifies that all information collected is to be written to the specified file.
-interactive	Indicates that values specified for the DB2PDOPT environment variable are to be overridden when running the db2pd command.
-help | -h	Displays help information. When this option is specified, all other options are ignored, and only the help information is displayed.

So if you wanted to determine which indexes are actually being used for accessing data in a database named SAMPLE, you could do so by executing a db2pd command that looks something like this:

```
db2pd -tcbstats -db sample
```

On the other hand, if you wanted to find out how many pages have been written to the transaction log files associated with a database named SAMPLE, you could do so by executing a db2pd command that looks something like this:

```
db2pd -logs -db sample
```

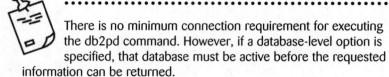

There is no minimum connection requirement for executing the db2pd command. However, if a database-level option is specified, that database must be active before the requested information can be returned.

Practice Questions

Question 1

A user issues the following commands:

```
UPDATE DBM CFG USING DFT_MON_SORT ON;
UPDATE MONITOR SWITCHES USING UOW ON;
UPDATE DBM CFG USING DFT_MON_TIMESTAMP ON;
UPDATE MONITOR SWITCHES USING BUFFERPOOL ON;
```

Assuming no other monitor switches have been set, if the DB2 instance is stopped and restarted, which of the following database monitor switches will be set?

- ○ A. SORT, UOW
- ○ B. UOW, BUFFERPOOL
- ✓ C. SORT, TIMESTAMP
- ○ D   TIMESTAMP, BUFFERPOOL

Question 2

Which of the following queries can be used to obtain information about how buffer pools defined for a DB2 database named SAMPLE are being utilized?

- ○ A. SELECT * FROM SNAPSHOT_INFO ('sample', BUFFERPOOL)
- ○ B. SELECT * FROM SNAPSHOT_BP ('sample', -1)
- ○ C. SELECT * FROM TABLE(SNAPSHOT_INFO('sample', BUFFERPOOL)) AS snap_info
- ✓ D. SELECT * FROM TABLE(SNAP_GET_BP('sample', -1)) AS snap_info

Question 3

What is the RESET MONITOR command used for?

- ✓ A. To reset all snapshot monitor counters to zero.
- ○ B. To reset individual snapshot monitor counters to zero.
- ○ C. To turn all snapshot monitor switches off.
- ○ D. To turn all snapshot monitor switches except the TIMESTAMP switch off.

Question 4

A database administrator executed the following command while several applications were interacting with a database named SAMPLE:

```
GET SNAPSHOT FOR LOCKS ON sample
```

And received the following output:

```
Database name                      = SAMPLE
Database path                      = C:\DB2\NODE0000\SQL00002\
Input database alias               = SAMPLE
Locks held                         = 0
Applications currently connected   = 1
Agents currently waiting on locks  = 0
Snapshot timestamp                 = 05/14/2007 14:57:04.559027

Application handle                 = 110
Application ID                     = *LOCAL.DB2.070514185703
Sequence number                    = 00001
Application name                   = db2taskd
CONNECT Authorization ID           = DBUSER
Application status                 = Connect Completed
Status change time                 = Not Collected
Application code page              = 1252
Locks held                         = 0
Total wait time (ms)               = Not Collected
```

Why was the value "Not Collected" returned for the total lock wait time?

- ○ A. The RESET MONITOR command was executed just before the snapshot was taken.
- ✓ B. The LOCK snapshot monitor switch was off when the snapshot was taken.
- ○ C. No locks were held at the time the snapshot was taken.
- ○ D. The UOW snapshot monitor switch was off when the snapshot was taken.

Question 5

Which of the following is NOT a true statement about DEADLOCKS event monitors?

- ○ A. By default, a DEADLOCKS event monitor is automatically created when a DB2 9 database is created.
- ✓ B. Once created, the default DEADLOCKS event monitor cannot be deleted.
- ○ C. The default DEADLOCKS event monitor is activated when a connection to the database is first established.
- ○ D. Event monitor data is collected at the time a deadlock cycle is detected.

Question 6

Which of the following options can be specified with the CREATE EVENT MONITOR statement to indicate that each agent that generates an event that is being monitored will not wait for an event buffer to be externalized to disk before continuing if it determines that both event buffers are full?

○ A. BLOCKED

◉ B. NONBLOCKED

○ C. BUFFERED

○ D. NONBUFFERED

Question 7

Which of the following is NOT a true statement about event monitors?

○ A. An unlimited number of event monitors may be defined.

○ B. An event monitor must be activated before it will start collecting data.

◉ C. Up to, but no more than 16 event monitors can be active at the same time.

○ D. An active event monitor must be stopped before it can be dropped.

Question 8

Which two of the following are key tasks that can be performed using the Health Center?

☑ A. View alerts for an instance or a database.

☐ B. Clear all previous alert entries recorded in the Journal

☐ C. View the history of threshold settings for a database.

☐ D. Quiesce the Health Monitor.

☑ E. View the history of alerts for an instance or a database.

Question 9

Which of the following is NOT a valid level that health indicator settings can be defined for?

◉ A. Server

○ B. Global

○ C. Instance

○ D. Object

Question 10

A database named SAMPLE contains a DMS table space that spans five files.
Three of the files are 4 GB in size and two of the files are 3 GB in size. A
database administrator wants an alert to be generated whenever the 3 GB files
are 80% full and the 4GB files are 85% full. What is the best way to accomplish
this using the Health Center?

- ○ A. Change the Global level settings for all table space containers; change the
  Instance level settings for the 3 GB table space containers.
- ○ B. Change the Instance level settings for all table space containers; change
  the Global level settings for the 3 GB table space containers.
- ⊘ C. Change the Global level settings for all table space containers; change the
  Object level settings for the 4 GB table space containers.
- ○ D. Change the Instance level settings for all table space containers; change
  the Object level settings for the 4 GB table space containers.

Question 11

Which two of the following utilities can be used to present Explain information in a
meaningful format?

- ❏ A. db2bfd
- ☑ B. db2expln
- ❏ C. db2look
- ☑ D. db2exfmt
- ❏ E. db2advis

Question 12

If a query used in an OLTP environment joins two tables on their primary key,
which of the following operators will most likely represent this join in an access
plan graph produced by Visual Explain?

- ○ A. HSJOIN
- ○ B. MSJOIN
- ⊘ C. NLJOIN
- ○ D. SJOIN

Question 13

If a query used in a decision support environment joins two tables, which of the following operators will most likely be used to represent this join in an access plan graph produced by Visual Explain?

- ◉ A. HSJOIN
- ○ B. MSJOIN
- ○ C. NLJOIN
- ○ D. SJOIN

Question 14

Which of the following commands instructs the DB2 Optimizer to use the maximum amount of optimization techniques available when generating data access plans for dynamic SQL statements that will interact with a database named SAMPLE?

- ○ A. db2set –g DB2_QUERYOPT=9
- ○ B. UPDATE DBM CFG USING QUERYOPT 9
- ○ C. UPDATE DB CFG FOR sample USING QUERYOPT 9
- ◉ D. SET CURRENT QUERY OPTIMIZATION = 9

Question 15

Which of the following can be used to display the precompile options that were used to create a bind file?

- ○ A. db2advis
- ◉ B. db2bfd
- ○ C. db2mtrk
- ○ D. db2rbind

Question 16

Which of the following best describes the functionality of db2mtrk?

○ A. It reports how memory is being managed by the Self Tuning Memory Manager.

○ B. It estimates the memory requirements for a database, based on values assigned to the memory-related Database Manager configuration parameters.

✓ C. It produces a report of memory status for instances, databases and agents.

○ D. It recommends memory-related Database Manager configuration parameter values that will improve memory utilization.

Question 17

Which of the following can be used to determine how many pages have been written to the transaction log files associated with a particular database?

✓ A. db2pd

○ B. db2advis

○ C. db2look

○ D. db2mtrk

Question 18

Which of the following statements is NOT true about the DB2 Problem Determination tool (db2pd)?

○ A. db2pd is used to obtain quick and immediate information from the DB2 database system memory sets.

○ B. db2pd does not require a connection to an active database in order to obtain information about it.

✓ C. db2pd can be used to obtain information about an instance that has stopped prematurely.

○ D. Because db2pd works directly with memory, it is possible to retrieve information that will change as it is being collected.

Answers

Question 1

The correct answer is **C**. Snapshot monitor switch settings can be changed at the instance level by modifying the appropriate DB2 Database Manager configuration parameters with the UPDATE DATABASE MANAGER CONFIGURATION command. Snapshot monitor switch settings made at the instance level remain persistent across instance restarts.

Snapshot monitor switch settings can be changed at the application level by executing the UPDATE MONITOR SWITCHES command. Switch settings made at the application level are not persistent across instance restarts.

Question 2

The correct answer is **D**. With earlier versions of DB2, the only way to capture snapshot monitor data was by executing the GET SNAPSHOT command or by calling its corresponding API from an application program. With DB2 UDB version 8.1, the ability to capture snapshot monitor data by constructing a query that referenced one of 20 snapshot monitor table functions available was introduced. If you wanted to take a snapshot that contains data collected on buffer pools associated with the current connected database using the DB2 V8.1 SNAPSHOT_BP() snapshot monitor table function, you could do so by executing the following query:

```
SELECT * FROM TABLE (SNAPSHOT_BP
    (CAST (NULL AS CHAR), -1) AS snap_info
```

Although these functions are still available and can be used in DB2 9, they have been depreciated. Now, snapshot monitor data can be obtained by querying special administrative views or by using a new set of SQL table functions. Each DB2 9 snapshot monitor table function returns the same information as the corresponding administrative view, but the function allows you to retrieve information for a specific database instead of the current connected database. (If no database is specified when a snapshot monitor table function is used, you must be connected to the appropriate database.) The syntax used to construct a query that references a DB2 9 snapshot monitor table function is the same as that used to reference a DB2 8.1 function—only the function names have changed. Therefore, if you wanted to obtain snapshot monitor buffer pool information for a database named SAMPLE using the SNAP_GET_BP() table function you could do so by constructing a query that looks something like this:

```
SELECT * FROM TABLE(SNAP_GET_BP('sample', -1)) AS snap_info
```

Question 3

The correct answer is **A**. There may be times when it is desirable to reset all counters to zero without turning snapshot monitor switches off and back on and without terminating and reestablishing database connections. The easiest way to quickly reset all snapshot monitor counters to zero is by executing the RESET MONITOR command. The basic syntax for this command is:

```
RESET MONITOR ALL
```
or
```
RESET MONITOR FOR <DCS> [DATABASE | DB] [DatabaseAlias]
```

where:

DatabaseAlias   Identifies the alias assigned to the database that snapshot monitor counters are to be reset for.

Thus, if you wanted to reset the snapshot monitor counters for all databases under an instance's control to zero, you could do so by attaching to that instance and executing a RESET MONITOR command that looks like this:

```
RESET MONITOR ALL
```

On the other hand, if you wanted to reset just the snapshot monitor counters associated with a database named SAMPLE to zero, you could do so by executing a RESET MONITOR command that looks like this:

```
RESET MONITOR FOR DATABASE sample
```

Question 4

The correct answer is **B**. The snapshot monitor switches, together with the options available with the GET SNAPSHOT command, determine the type and volume of data that will be returned when a snapshot is taken. If a particular snapshot monitor switch has not been turned on and a snapshot of the monitoring data that is associated with that switch is taken, the monitoring data captured may not contain any values at all. (If you look closely at the snapshot monitoring data collected and notice that some values were "Not Collected", chances are the corresponding snapshot monitor switch was turned off when the snapshot was taken. In this example, when the snapshot of LOCK information was taken, the LOCK snapshot monitor switch was turned off.

Question 5

The correct answer is **B**. If you are familiar with the concept of deadlocks, you may recall that a special process known as the deadlock detector runs quietly in the background and "wakes up" at predefined intervals to scan the locking system in search of a deadlock cycle. If a deadlock cycle exists, the deadlock detector randomly selects one of the transactions involved in the cycle to roll back and terminate. (The transaction that is rolled back and terminated receives an SQL error code, all locks it had acquired are released, and the remaining transaction(s) are then allowed to proceed.) Information about such a series of events can be captured the moment the deadlock cycle is detected.

By default, whenever a DB2 9 database is created, a deadlock event monitor is defined for that database and this event monitor is activated when a connection to the database is first established, or whenever the database is activated.

Question 6

The correct answer is **B**. Data collected by event monitors is streamed to buffers before it is externalized to disk (i.e. written to a table or file). If the BLOCKED option is specified with the CREATE EVENT MONITOR command, agents that generate an event that is being monitored will wait for an event buffer to be written to disk before continuing if it determines that both event buffers are full. As a result, although BLOCKED event monitors guarantee that no event monitor data will be lost, their behavior can increase application response time since any suspended agents (along with any dependent agents) will only be allowed to run when the event monitor buffers are clear. If the NONBLOCKED option is specified instead, agents that generate an event that is being monitored will not wait for an event buffer to be written to disk before continuing if they determine that both event buffers are full. Thus, NONBLOCKED event monitors perform faster than BLOCKED event monitors, but are subject to data loss on highly active systems. (If neither option is specified, the event monitor created will be a BLOCKED event monitor.)

Question 7

The correct answer is **C**. While there is no limit to the number of event monitors that can be defined for a single database, no more than 32 event monitors can be active at one time.

Question 8

The correct answers are **A** and **E**. The Health Center is a GUI tool that is designed to interact with the Health Monitor. Using the Health Center, you can select the instance and database objects that you want to monitor, customize the threshold settings of any health indicator, specify where notifications are to be sent, and specify what actions are to be taken if an alert is raised. The Health Center also allows you to start and stop the Health Monitor, view the current status of the database environment, access details about current alerts, obtain a list of recommended actions for resolving any alerts that have been raised, and view a history of alerts that have been generated for an instance or a database.

Question 9

The correct answer is **A**. Health indicator settings can be set at the instance level, global level, or object level. Instance level settings apply to the instance. Global settings apply to objects such as databases, table spaces, and table space containers in the instance that do not have customized settings defined. Object settings are customized settings that apply to individual objects such as databases, table spaces, and table space containers.

Question 10

The correct answer is **C**. Health indicator settings can be set at the instance level, global level, or object level. Instance level settings apply to the instance. Global settings apply to objects such as databases, table spaces, and table space containers in the instance that do not have customized settings defined. Object settings are customized settings that apply to individual objects such as databases, table spaces, and table space containers. Therefore, to generate an alert whenever the 3 GB files are 80% full and the 4 GB files are 85% full, you would change the Global level settings for all table space containers (80% full) and then change the Object level settings for the 4 GB table space containers (85% full).

Question 11

The correct answers are **B** and **D**. When Explain information is collected, the resulting data is stored in one or more Explain tables. You could construct a query to retrieve this data, but a better way to view the Explain information collected is by using one of the Explain Facility tools that have been designed specifically for presenting explain information in a meaningful format. This set of tools is comprised of:

- The db2expln tool
- The db2exfmt tool
- Visual Explain

Question 12

The correct answer is **C**. The NLJOIN operator in a Visual Explain access plan graph represents a nested-loop join that accesses an inner table once for each row of the outer table. Nested-loop joins are preferred for join operations performed in an OLTP environment.

Question 13

The correct answer is **A**. The HSJOIN operator in a Visual Explain access plan graph represents a hash join, where two or more tables are hashed on the join columns. Hash joins are preferred for join operations performed in a decision support environment.

Question 14

The correct answer is **D**. The CURRENT QUERY OPTIMIZATION special register is used to control the class of optimization techniques used when binding dynamic SQL statements; the value of the register can be changed by executing the SET CURRENT QUERY OPTIMIZATION SQL statement. The basic syntax for this statement is:

```
SET CURRENT QUERY OPTIMIZATION <=> [OptimizationLevel]
```

where:

OptimizationLevel   Specifies the optimization level (class) to use when preparing dynamic SQL statements. This parameter must be set to one of the following values.

- **0**

  Specifies that a minimal amount of optimization techniques are to be used when the optimizer generates an access plan. This optimization class level is most suitable for simple dynamic SQL statements that access well-indexed tables.

- **1**

  Specifies that the amount of optimization techniques to be used when the optimizer generates an access plan should be roughly equal to that provided by DB2 Version 1.

- **2**

  Specifies that the amount of optimization techniques to be used when the optimizer generates an access plan should be higher than that provided by DB2 Version 1, but significantly less than those used by level 3 and higher.

- **3**
  Specifies that a moderate amount of optimization techniques are to be used when the optimizer generates an access plan.

- **5**
  Specifies that a significant amount of optimization techniques are to be used when the optimizer generates an access plan. For complex queries, heuristic rules are used to limit the amount of time spent selecting an access plan. Whenever possible, queries will use summary tables instead of underlying base tables. This is the default optimization class used by DB2.

- **7**
  Specifies that a significant amount of optimization techniques are to be used when the optimizer generates an access plan. This level is similar to level 5; however, no heuristic rules are used to limit the amount of time spent selecting access plans for complex queries.

- **9**
  Specifies that the maximum amount of optimization techniques are to be used when the optimizer generates an access plan. This optimization class can greatly expand the number of possible access paths that are evaluated before an access plan is chosen. For this reason, this class is typically used to process SQL statements that contain very complex and very long running queries that are executed against very large tables.

Therefore, if you wanted to tell the DB2 optimizer to use the maximum amount of optimization techniques available when generating access plans for dynamic SQL statements, you could do so by executing a SET CURRENT QUERY OPTIMIZATION statement that looks like this:

```
SET CURRENT QUERY OPTIMIZATION = 9
```

Question 15

The correct answer is **B**. The DB2 Bind File Description Tool can be used to examine and to verify the SQL statements within a bind file, as well as to display the precompile options used to create the bind file. The DB2 Bind File Description Tool is invoked by executing the db2bfd command.

Question 16

The correct answer is **C**. The DB2 memory tracker utility is used to produce a complete report of memory status for instances, databases and agents. This utility provides the following information about memory pool allocation:

- Current size
- Maximum size (hard limit)
- Largest size (high water mark)
- Type (identifier indicating function for which memory will be used)
- Agent who allocated pool (only if the pool is private)

(This information is also available from the Snapshot monitor.)

The DB2 memory tracker is invoked by executing the db2mtrk command.

Question 17

The correct answer is **A**. The DB2 Problem Determination tool is used to obtain quick and immediate information from the DB2 database system memory sets, without acquiring any latches. The DB2 Problem Determination tool is invoked by executing the db2pd command. The basic syntax for this command is:

```
db2pd
<- version | -v >
<-inst>
<[-database | -db] [DatabaseName] ,...>
<-alldatabases | -alldbs>
<-full>
<-everything>
<-hadr [-db [DatabaseName] | -alldbs]>
<-utilities>
<-applications [-db [DatabaseName] | -alldbs]>
<-agents>
<-transactions [-db [DatabaseName] | -alldbs]>
<-bufferpools [-db [DatabaseName] | -alldbs]>
<-logs [-db [DatabaseName] | -alldbs]>
```

```
<-tablespaces [-db [DatabaseName] | -alldbs]>
<-dynamic [-db [DatabaseName] | -alldbs]>
<-static [-db [DatabaseName] | -alldbs]>
<-fcm>
<-memsets>
<-mempools>
<-memblocks>
<-dbmcfg>
<-dbcfg [-db [DatabaseName] | -alldbs]>
<-catalogcache [-db [DatabaseName] | -alldbs]>
<-tcbstats [-db [DatabaseName] | -alldbs]>
<-reorg [-db [DatabaseName] | -alldbs]>
<-recovery [-db [DatabaseName] | -alldbs]>
<-reopt [-db [DatabaseName] | -alldbs]>
<-osinfo>
<-storagepaths [-db [DatabaseName] | -alldbs]>
<-pages [-db [DatabaseName] | -alldbs]>
<-stack [all | [ProcessID]]>
<-repeat [Interval] <[Count]>>
<-command [CmdFileName]>
<-file [OutFileName]>
<-interactive>
<-h | -help>
```

where:

DatabaseName	Identifies, by name, the database the DB2 Problem Determination tool is to interact with.
ProcessID	Identifies the process, by ID, that a stack trace file is to be produced for.
Interval	Identifies the number of seconds to wait between subsequent calls to the DB2 Problem Determination tool.
Count	Identifies the number of time to repeat calls to the DB2 Problem Determination tool.
CmdFileName	Identifies the name assigned to an ASCII format file that contains DB2 Problem Determination tool command options that are to be used.
OutFile	Identifies the name of the file that information returned by the DB2 Problem Determination tool is to be written to.

So, if you wanted to find out how many pages have been written to the transaction log files associated with a database named SAMPLE, you could do so by executing a db2pd command that looks something like this:

```
db2pd -logs -db sample
```

Question 18

The correct answer is **C**. The DB2 Problem Determination tool (db2pd) is used to obtain quick and immediate information from the DB2 database system memory sets, without acquiring any latches. Two benefits to collecting information without latching include faster data retrieval and no competition for engine resources. However, because the DB2 Problem Determination tool works directly with memory, it is possible to retrieve information that is changing as it is being collected; hence the data retrieved might not be completely accurate. (A signal handler is used to prevent the DB2 Problem Determination tool from aborting abnormally when changing memory pointers are encountered. However, this can result in messages such as "Changing data structure forced command termination" to appear in the output produced.) Nonetheless, this tool can be extremely helpful for problem determination.

There is no minimum connection requirement for executing the db2pd command; if a database-level option is specified, that database must be active before the requested information can be returned. The db2pd command cannot be used to obtain information about a stopped instance.

DB2 Utilities

Fourteen and one-half percent (14.5%) of the DB2 9 for Linux, UNIX, and Windows Database Administration exam (Exam 731) is designed to test your ability to perform common database administration tasks using some of the utilities provided with DB2. The questions that make up this portion of the exam are intended to evaluate the following:

- Your ability to use the Export utility to extract data from a database and store it in an external file

- Your ability to use the Import utility to transfer data from an external file to a database table

- Your ability to use the Load utility to bulk-load data into a database table

- Your knowledge of when to use the Import utility versus the Load utility

- Your ability to use the REORGCHK and REORG commands to locate and remove fragmentation in table space containers

- Your ability to use the RUNSTATS, REBIND, and FLUSH PACKAGE CACHE commands to ensure that the DB2 Optimizer will always generate the best access plan for a given query and that applications will take advantage of new access plans when they are generated

- Your ability to use the db2look, db2move, and db2batch commands

- Your knowledge of the purpose and functionality of the Design Advisor

- Your ability to use the Control Center

This chapter is designed to introduce you to the various database administration utilities that are available with DB2.

DB2's Data Movement Utilities and the File Formats They Support

Although a database usually functions as a self-contained entity, there are times when it becomes necessary to exchange data with "the outside world." That's the purpose of DB2's data movement utilities. However, for data to be transferred between databases and external files, any external file used must be formatted in such a way that it can be processed by the DB2 data movement utilities available. (A file's format determines how data is physically stored in the file.) The data movement utilities provided by DB2 (which we will look at shortly) recognize and support up to four different file formats:

- Delimited ASCII (DEL)

- Non-delimited or fixed-length ASCII (ASC)

- Worksheet Format (WSF)

- PC Integrated Exchange Format (IXF)

But just what are these formats, how are they similar, and how do they differ? To answer these questions, we need to take a closer look at each format supported.

Delimited ASCII (DEL)

The delimited ASCII file format is used extensively in many relational database management systems and software applications to exchange data with a wide variety of application products. With this format, data values typically vary in length, and a delimiter, which is a unique character not found in the data values themselves, is used to separate individual values and rows. Actually, delimited ASCII format files typically use three distinct delimiters:

> **Column delimiters.** Column delimiters are characters used to mark the beginning or end of a data value. (Usually, each value is associated with a particular column, based on its position in the file.) Commas (,) are typically used as the column delimiter for delimited ASCII format files (in fact, such files are sometimes referred to as Comma Separated Variable/Value or CSV

files and are often given a .csv extension). Vertical bars (|) are also commonly used as column delimiters.

Row delimiters. Row delimiters are characters used to mark the end of a single record or row. On UNIX systems, the new line character (0x0A) is normally used as the row delimiter for a delimited ASCII format file; on Windows systems, the carriage return/linefeed characters (0x0D–0x0A) are typically used instead.

Character delimiters. Character delimiters are characters used to mark the beginning and end of character data values. Double quotes (") are typically used as character delimiters for a delimited ASCII format files.

Typically, when data is written to a delimited ASCII file, rows are streamed into the file, one after another. The appropriate column delimiter is used to separate each column's data values, the appropriate row delimiter is used to separate each individual record (row), and all character and character string values are enclosed with the appropriate character delimiters. Numeric values are represented by their ASCII equivalent—the period character (.) is used to denote the decimal point (if appropriate); real values are represented with scientific notation (E); negative values are preceded by the minus character (-); and positive values may or may not be preceded by the plus character (+). And because delimited ASCII files are written in ASCII, their contents can be edited with any simple text editor.

Thus, if the comma character was used as the column delimiter, the carriage return/line feed character was used as the row delimiter, and the double quote character was used as the character delimiter, the contents of a delimited ASCII file might look something like this:

```
10,"Headquarters",860,"Corporate","New York"
15,"Research",150,"Eastern","Boston"
20,"Legal",40,"Eastern","Washington"
38,"Support Center 1",80,"Eastern","Atlanta"
42,"Manufacturing",100,"Midwest","Chicago"
51,"Training Center",34,"Midwest","Dallas"
66,"Support Center 2",112,"Western","San Francisco"
84,"Distribution",290,"Western","Denver"
```

Non-Delimited ASCII (ASC)

The non-delimited ASCII file format is also used by a wide variety of software and database applications to exchange data with application products. With this format, data values have a fixed length, and the position of each value in the file determines to which column and row a particular value belongs. (For this reason, non-delimited ASCII files are sometimes referred to as fixed-length ASCII files.)

Typically, when data is written to a non-delimited ASCII file, rows are streamed into the file, one after another; each column's data values are written using a fixed number of bytes, and an appropriate row delimiter is used to separate each individual record (row). On UNIX systems, the new line character (0x0A) typically acts as the row delimiter for non-delimited ASCII format files; on Windows systems, the carriage return/linefeed characters (0x0D–0x0A) act as the row delimiter instead. If a data value is smaller that the fixed length allotted for a particular column, it is padded with blanks until its length matches the length specified for the column.

As with delimited ASCII format files, numeric values are represented by their ASCII equivalent—the period character (.) is used to denote the decimal point (if appropriate); real values are represented with scientific notation (E); negative values are preceded by the minus character (-); and positive values may or may not be preceded by the plus character (+).

Thus, a simple non-delimited ASCII file might look something like this:

```
10Headquarters     860CorporateNew York
15Research         150Eastern  Boston
20Legal            40 Eastern  Washington
38Support Center 180Eastern  Atlanta
42Manufacturing    100Midwest  Chicago
51Training Center34 Midwest  Dallas
66Support Center 211Western   San Francisco
84Distribution     290Western   Denver
```

Like delimited ASCII files, the contents of non-delimited ASCII files can be edited with a simple text editor.

Worksheet Format (WSF)

The worksheet format file format is a special file format that is used exclusively by the Lotus 1-2-3 and Lotus Symphony spreadsheet products. Different releases of each of these products incorporate different features into the file formats they use for data storage; however, all releases use a common subset of features, and it is this subset that is recognized and supported by some of DB2's data movement utilities. Worksheet format files cannot be edited with a simple text editor.

PC Integrated Exchange Format (IXF)

The PC Integrated Exchange Format file format is a special file format used almost exclusively to move data between different DB2 databases. Typically, when data is written to a PC Integrated Exchange Format file, rows are streamed into the file, one after another, as an unbroken sequence of variable-length records. With this format, character data values are stored in their original ASCII representation (without additional padding), and numeric values are stored either as packed decimal values or as binary values, depending on the data type used to store them in the database. In addition to data, table definitions and associated index definitions are also stored in PC Integrated Exchange Format files. Thus, tables (along with any corresponding indexes) can be both defined and populated when this file format is used. Like worksheet format files, PC Integrated Exchange Format files cannot be edited with a simple text editor.

Extracting Columnar Data from External Files

As you can see, the file format used determines how data is physically stored in an external file. And the way data physically resides in a file determines the method that must be used to extract that data and map it to one or more columns of a table. With DB2, three mapping methods are used:

- The position method (METHOD P)
- The location method (METHOD L)
- The name method (METHOD N)

The position method

When the position method is used to extract data from an external file, columnar data values are identified by their indexed position within a single row; the first data value found is assigned the index position 1, the second data value found is assigned the index position 2, and so on. Figure 6–1 illustrates how the position method is used to map data values found in an external file to columns in a table.

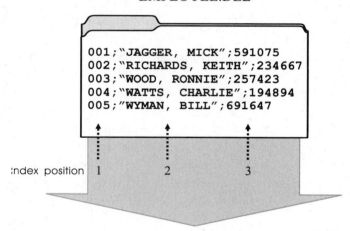

Figure 6–1: Mapping columnar data using the position method.

Only data values found in external files that use either the delimited ASCII (DEL) format or the PC Integrated Exchange Format (IXF) format can be mapped using the position method.

The location method

When the location method is used to extract data from an external file, columnar data values are identified by a series of beginning and ending byte positions that, when used together, identify the location of a specific data value within a single row. Each byte position specified is treated as an offset from the beginning of the row (which is byte position 1), and two byte positions are required to extract a single value. Figure 6–2 illustrates how the location method is used to map data values found in an external file to columns in a table.

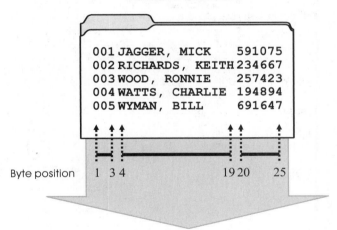

Figure 6–2: Mapping columnar data using the location method.

Only data values found in external files that use the non-delimited ASCII (ASC) format can be mapped using the location method.

The name method

When the name method is used to extract data from an external file, it is assumed that column names are stored in the file, and columnar data values are identified by the name of the column with which they are associated. Figure 6–3 illustrates how the name method is used to map data values found in an external file to columns in a table.

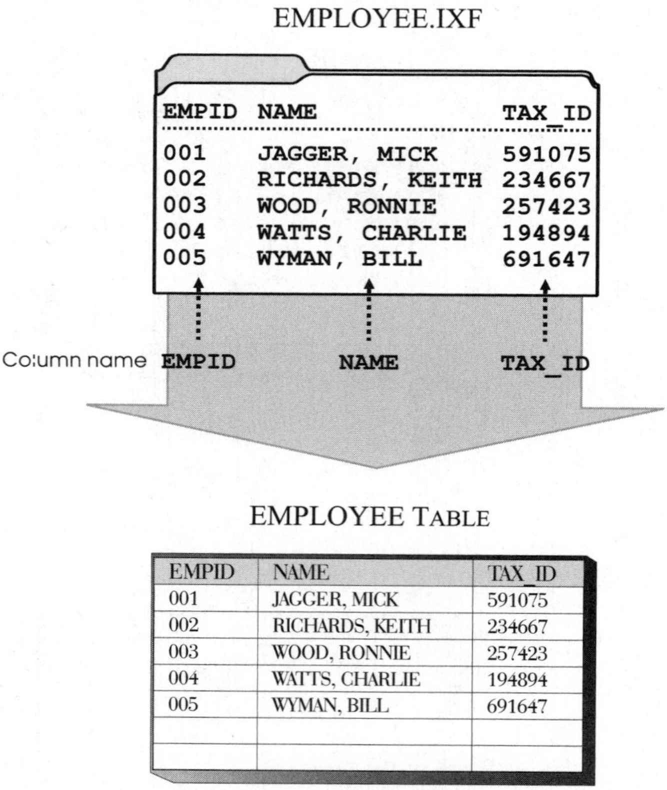

EMPLOYEE.IXF

EMPID	NAME	TAX_ID
001	JAGGER, MICK	591075
002	RICHARDS, KEITH	234667
003	WOOD, RONNIE	257423
004	WATTS, CHARLIE	194894
005	WYMAN, BILL	691647

Column name **EMPID   NAME   TAX_ID**

EMPLOYEE TABLE

EMPID	NAME	TAX_ID
001	JAGGER, MICK	591075
002	RICHARDS, KEITH	234667
003	WOOD, RONNIE	257423
004	WATTS, CHARLIE	194894
005	WYMAN, BILL	691647

Figure 6–3: Mapping columnar data using the name method.

Because DB2 expects column names to be stored in the external file along with the data values themselves when the name method is used, only data values found in external files that use the PC Integrated Exchange Format (IXF) format can be mapped with the name method.

The DB2 Export Utility

The Export utility is designed to extract data from a DB2 database table or view and externalize it to a file, using the delimited ASCII (DEL) format, the worksheet format (WSF), or the PC Information Exchange Format (IXF) format. Such files can then be used to provide data values to other databases (including the database from which the data was extracted) and software applications such as spreadsheets and word processors.

One way to invoke the Export utility is by executing the EXPORT command. The basic syntax for this command is:

```
EXPORT TO [FileName] OF [DEL | WSF | IXF]
<LOBS TO [LOBPath ,...]>
<LOBFILE [LOBFileName ,...]>
<XML TO [XMLPath ,...]>
<XMLFILE [XMLFileName ,...]>
<MODIFIED BY [Modifier ,...]>
<METHOD N ([ColumnName ,...])>
<MESSAGES [MsgFileName]>
[SELECTStatement | XQueryExpression]
```

where:

FileName   Identifies the name and location of the external file data to which data is to be exported (copied).

LOBPath   Identifies one or more locations where large object (LOB) data values are to be stored. (If this option is specified, each LOB value found will be stored in its own file at the location specified.)

LOBFileName   Identifies one or more base names that are to be used to name the files to which large object (LOB) data values are to be written. During an export operation, file names are constructed by appending a period (.) and a three-digit sequence number to the current base file name in this list, and then appending the generated file name to the large object data path specified (in *LOBPath*). For example, if the current LOB path is the directory "C:\LOBData" and the current LOB file name is "Value," the LOB files created will be C:\LOBData\Value.001.lob, C:\LOBData\Value.002.lob, and so on.

XMLPath	Identifies one or more locations where Extensible Markup Language (XML) documents are to be stored. (If this option is specified, each XML value found will be stored in its own file at the location specified.)
XMLFileName	Identifies one or more base names that are to be used to name the files to which Extensible Markup Language (XML) documents are to be written. During an export operation, file names are constructed by appending a period (.) and a three-digit sequence number to the current base file name in this list and then appending the generated file name to the XML data path specified (in *XMLPath*). For example, if the current XML path is the directory "C:\XMLData", and the current XML file name is "Value," the XML files created will be C:\XMLData\Value.001.xml, C:\XMLData\Value.002.xml, and so on.
Modifier	Identifies one or more options that are used to override the default behavior of the Export utility. (Table 6.1 contains a list of valid modifiers.)
ColumnName	Identifies one or more column names that are to be written to the external file to which data is to be exported.
MsgFileName	Identifies the name and location of an external file to which messages produced by the Export utility are to be written as the export operation is performed.

SELECTStatement   Identifies a SELECT SQL statement that, when executed, will retrieve data that is to be copied to an external file.

XQueryExpression   Identifies an XQuery expression that, when executed, will retrieve data that is to be copied to an external file.

Table 6.1 File Type Modifiers Recognized by the EXPORT Command		
Modifier	**Description**	**File Format**
lobsinfile	Indicates that large object (LOB) data values are to be written to the location(s) specified by the LOBS TO clause. Otherwise, LOB data is sent to the same location as the data file produced.	Delimited ASCII (DEL), Worksheet Format (WSF), and PC Integrated Exchange Format (IXF)
lobsinsepfiles	Indicates that each LOB value is to be written to a separate file. By default, multiple values are concatenated together in the same file.	Delimited ASCII (DEL), Worksheet Format (WSF), and PC Integrated Exchange Format (IXF)
xmlinsepfiles	Indicates that each XML document (XQuery Data Model, or QDM instance) is to be written to a separate file. By default, multiple values are concatenated together in the same file.	Delimited ASCII (DEL), Worksheet Format (WSF), and PC Integrated Exchange Format (IXF)
xmlnodeclaration	Indicates that XML documents are to be written without an XML declaration tag. By default, XML documents are exported with an XML declaration tag at the beginning that includes an encoding attribute.	Delimited ASCII (DEL), Worksheet Format (WSF), and PC Integrated Exchange Format (IXF)
xmlchar	Indicates that XML documents are to be written using the character code page. (The character code page is the value specified by the *codepage* modifier, or the application code page if this modifier is not specified.) By default, XML documents are written in Unicode.	Delimited ASCII (DEL), Worksheet Format (WSF), and PC Integrated Exchange Format (IXF)
xmlgraphic	Indicates that XML documents are to be encoded and written in the UTF-16 code page, regardless of the application code page or character code page specified with the *codepage* modifier.	Delimited ASCII (DEL), Worksheet Format (WSF), and PC Integrated Exchange Format (IXF)

Modifier	Description	Format
chardel*x* where *x* is any valid delimiter character	Identifies a specific character that is to be used as a character delimiter. The default character delimiter is a double quotation mark (") character. The character specified is used in place of the double quotation mark to enclose a character string.	Delimited ASCII (DEL)
codepage=*x* where *x* is any valid code page identifier	Identifies the code page of the data contained in the output data set produced. Character data is converted from the application code page to the code page specified during the export operation.	Delimited ASCII (DEL) and PC Integrated Exchange Format (IXF)
coldel*x* where *x* is any valid delimiter character	Identifies a specific character that is to be used as a column delimiter. The default column delimiter is a comma (,) character. The character specified is used in place of a comma to signal the end of a column.	Delimited ASCII (DEL)
decplusblank	Indicates that positive decimal values are to be prefixed with a blank space instead of a plus sign (+). The default action is to prefix positive decimal values with a plus sign.	Delimited ASCII (DEL)
decpt*x* where *x* is any valid delimiter character	Identifies a specific character that is to be used as a decimal point character. The default decimal point character is a period (.) character. The character specified is used in place of a period as a decimal point character.	Delimited ASCII (DEL)
nochardel	Indicates that column data will not be surrounded by character delimiters. This option should not be specified if the data is intended to be imported or loaded using DB2; it is provided to support vendor data files that do not have character delimiters. Improper usage might result in data loss or corruption. This option cannot be specified with the *chardelx* or *nodoubledel* modifiers. These are mutually exclusive options.	Delimited ASCII (DEL)
nodoubledel	Indicates that double character delimiters are not recognized.	Delimited ASCII (DEL)

Table 6.1 File Type Modifiers Recognized by the EXPORT Command (continued)

Table 6.1 File Type Modifiers Recognized by the EXPORT Command (continued)		
Modifier	**Description**	**File Format**
striplzeros	Indicates that leading zeros are to be removed from all exported decimal columns.	Delimited ASCII (DEL)
timestampformat="*x*" where *x* is any valid combination of date and time format elements	Identifies how date, time, and timestamp values are to be formatted before they are written to an external file. The following date and time elements can be used to create the format string provided with this modifier: • YYYY—Year (four digits ranging from 0000 to 9999) • M—Month (one or two digits ranging from 1 to 12) • MM—Month (two digits ranging from 1 to 12; mutually exclusive with M) • D—Day (one or two digits ranging from 1 to 31) • DD—Day (two digits ranging from 1 to 31; mutually exclusive with D) • DDD—Day of the year (three digits ranging from 001 to 366; mutually exclusive with other day or month elements) • H—Hour (one or two digits ranging from 0 to 12 for a 12-hour system, and 0 to 24 for a 24-hour system) • HH—Hour (two digits ranging from 0 to 12 for a 12-hour system, and 0 to 24 for a 24-hour system; mutually exclusive with H) • M—Minute (one or two digits ranging from 0 to 59) • MM—Minute (two digits ranging from 0 to 59; mutually exclusive with M) • S—Second (one or two digits ranging from 0 to 59) • SS—Second (two digits ranging from 0 to 59; mutually exclusive with S) • SSSSS—Second of the day after midnight (5 digits ranging from 00000 to 86399; mutually exclusive with other time elements)	Delimited ASCII (DEL)

Table 6.1 File Type Modifiers Recognized by the EXPORT Command (continued)		
Modifier	Description	File Format
	• UUUUUU—Microsecond (6 digits ranging from 000000 to 999999) • TT—Meridian indicator (AM or PM) An example of a valid timestamp format string is: "YYYY/MM/DD HH:MM:SS.UUUUUU"	
nodoubledel	Indicates that double character delimiters are not to be recognized.	Delimited ASCII (DEL)
1	Indicates that a WSF file that is compatible with Lotus 1-2-3 Release 1 or Lotus 1-2-3 Release 1a is to be created. By default, WSF files that are compatible with Lotus 1-2-3 Release 1 or Lotus 1-2-3 Release 1a are generated unless otherwise specified.	Worksheet Format (WSF)
2	Indicates that a WSF file that is compatible with Lotus Symphony Release 1.0 is to be created.	Worksheet Format (WSF)
3	Indicates that a WSF file that is compatible with Lotus 1-2-3 Version 2 or Lotus Symphony Release 1.1 is to be created.	Worksheet Format (WSF)
4	Indicates that a WSF file containing DBCS characters is to be created.	Worksheet Format (WSF)
Adapted from Tables 28, 29, 30, and 31 on pages 821–824 of the *IBM DB2 9 Command Reference* manual.		

If a table whose data is to be exported contains packed character data, that data must be unpacked before it can be written to a PC Integrated Exchange Format (IXF) formatted file. The easiest way to unpack packed character data is to create a view on the table that contains the packed data and to export the data using the view—a view will form character data from packed character data automatically.

So if you wanted to export data stored in a table named DEPARTMENT to a PC Integrated Exchange Format (IXF)–format external file named DEPT.IXF, you could do so by executing an EXPORT command that looks something like this:

```
EXPORT TO dept.ixf OF IXF
MESSAGES exp_msgs.txt
SELECT * FROM department
```

When data to be exported contains large object (LOB) values, by default only the first 32 K (kilobytes) of each LOB value are actually written to the file containing the exported data—LOB values that are greater than 32 K in size will be truncated. As you might imagine, this presents quite a problem if LOB values are greater than 32 K in size. By overriding this default behavior (using the *lobsinfile* or the *lobsinsepfiles* modifier) and providing the Export utility with one or more locations to which LOB data values are to be written, each LOB value encountered will be stored, in its entirety, in its own individual file (which is assigned a name that either the user or the Export utility provides).

Thus, if you wanted to export data stored in a table named EMPLOYEE to a delimited ASCII (DEL)–format external file named EMPLOYEE.DEL, and have all large object values stored in the PHOTO column of this table written to individual files, you could do so by executing an EXPORT command that looks something like this:

```
EXPORT TO C:\employee.del OF DEL
LOBS TO C:\lob_data
LOBFILE e_photo
MODIFIED BY lobsinsepfiles coldel;
MESSAGES exp_msgs.txt
SELECT * FROM employee
```

When executed, this command would do the following:

- Retrieve all data values stored in the table named EMPLOYEE.

- Copy all non-LOB values retrieved from the EMPLOYEE table to a delimited ASCII (DEL)–format external file named EMPLOYEE.DEL. (This file will reside in the root directory on drive C:.)

- Copy each LOB value retrieved from the PHOTO column to its own individual file. (Each file created will reside in a directory named LOB_DATA that is located on drive C:.)

- Record all messages produced by the Export utility to a file named EXP_MSGS.TXT (which will reside in the current working directory).

Figure 6–4 illustrates this export operation.

EMPLOYEE

EMPID	NAME	PHOTO
001	JAGGER, MICK	
002	RICHARDS, KEITH	
003	WOOD, RONNIE	
004	WATTS, CHARLIE	
005	WYMAN, BILL	

EXPORT OPERATION

```
EXPORT TO C:\employee.del OF DEL
LOBS TO C:\lobfiles
LOBFILE e_photo
MODIFIED BY lobsinsepfiles coldel;
SELECT * FROM employee
```

```
1;"JAGGER, MICK";"e_photo.001.lob"
2;"RICHARDS, KEITH";"e_photo.002.lob"
3;"WOOD, RONNIE";"e_photo.003.lob"
4;"WATTS, CHARLIE";"e_photo.004.lob"
5;"WYMAN, BILL";"e_photo.005.lob"
```

EMPLOYEE.DEL

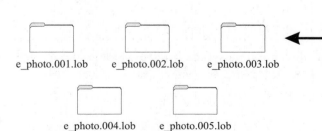

e_photo.001.lob   e_photo.002.lob   e_photo.003.lob

e_photo.004.lob   e_photo.005.lob

Figure 6–4: An export operation in which LOB values are stored in individual files.

As with LOB data, XML data can be written to a file along with other exported data, or each XML document stored in a table can be copied to its own individual file (which is assigned a name that either the user or the Export utility provides). Figure 6–5 illustrates a simple export operation in which XML documents are processed in this manner.

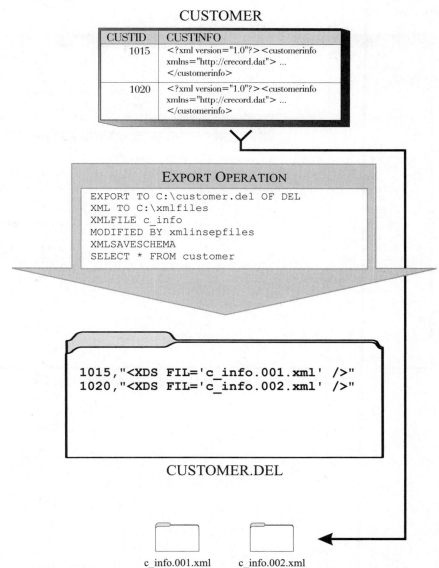

Figure 6–5: An export operation in which XML values are stored in individual files.

Data stored in a DB2 database can also be exported to an external file using the Export Table dialog, which can be activated by selecting the appropriate action from the Tables or Views menu found in the Control Center. Figure 6–6 shows the Control Center menu items that must be selected to activate the Export Table dialog; Figure 6–7 shows how the Export Table dialog typically looks when it is first activated.

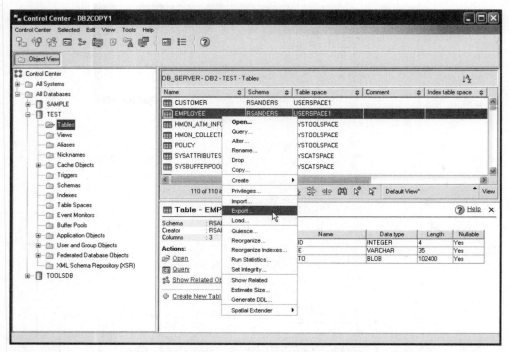

Figure 6–6: Invoking the Export Table dialog from the Control Center.

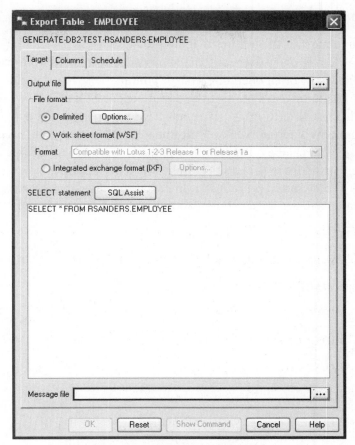

Figure 6–7: The first page of the Export Table dialog.

It is important to note that regardless of whether you use the EXPORT command or the Export Table dialog to export data, a database connection must be established before the Export utility is invoked. Additionally, the Export utility is bound to a database using the Cursor Stability isolation level so that its use does not prohibit other applications and users from accessing a table while data is being exported.

Only users with System Administrator (SYSADM) authority or Database Administrator (DBADMN) authority are allowed to export data using the EXPORT utility.

A Word About the ADMIN_CMD() Stored Procedure

Although most of the utilities that are provided with DB2 can be invoked from the Control Center or by executing the appropriate command from the DB2 Command Line Processor or an operating system prompt, there may be times when you would like to invoke a utility from an Embedded SQL, CLI, or Java application. For this reason, most DB2 commands have a corresponding application programming interface (API). Unfortunately, the source code needed to use some of these APIs can be quite complex, and all of the APIs available are designed to be used primarily in C and C++ applications. A simpler approach is to use the ADMIN_CMD() stored procedure, which is a special stored procedure that allows applications to run select administrative commands by using the CALL SQL statement.

The following commands can be invoked with the ADMIN_CMD() stored procedure:

- ADD CONTACT

- ADD CONTACTGROUP

- AUTOCONFIGURE

- BACKUP (Online only)

- DESCRIBE

- DROP CONTACT

- DROP CONTACTGROUP

- EXPORT

- FORCE APPLICATION

- IMPORT

- INITIALIZE TAPE

- LOAD

- PRUNE HISTORY/LOGFILE

- QUIESCE DATABASE

- QUIESCE TABLESPACES FOR TABLE

- REDISTRIBUTE

- REORG INDEXES/TABLE

- RESET ALERT CONFIGURATION

- RESET DATABASE CONFIGURATION

- RESET DATABASE MANAGER CONFIGURATION

- REWIND TAPE

- RUNSTATS

- SET TAPE POSITION

- UNQUIESCE DATABASE

- UPDATE ALERT CONFIGURATION

- UPDATE CONTACT

- UPDATE CONTACTGROUP

- UPDATE DATABASE CONFIGURATION

- UPDATE DATABASE MANAGER CONFIGURATION

- UPDATE HEALTH NOTIFICATION CONTACT LIST

- UPDATE HISTORY

Thus, if you wanted to use the ADMIN_CMD() stored procedure to export data stored in a table named STAFF to a PC Integrated Exchange Format (IXF) format, external file named STAFF.IXF, you could do so by connecting to the database that contains the STAFF table and executing a CALL SQL statement that looks something like this:

```
CALL SYSPROC.ADMIN_CMD ('EXPORT TO staff.ixf OF IXF
MESSAGES ON SERVER SELECT * FROM staff')
```

Because the ADMIN_CMD() stored procedure runs on the server, messages produced by the utility being executed are generated on the server; the MESSAGES ON SERVER option available with some commands is used to indicate that any message file used is to be created on the server. Additionally, command execution status is returned in the SQL Communications Area (SQLCA) data structure associated with the CALL statement used.

If the execution of the administrative command is successful, and the command returns more than execution status, the additional information is returned in the form of one or more result data sets. For example, if the EXPORT command executes successfully, a result data set is returned that contains information about the number of rows that were successfully exported. (The actual result set information returned is documented with each command.) It is important to note that result set information can be retrieved using the Command Line Processor or with JDBC and DB2 CLI applications, but not with Embedded SQL applications.

If the execution of an administrative command is not successful, an SQL20397W warning message is returned by the ADMIN_CMD( ) stored procedure, along with a result set containing details about the reason for the failure. Therefore, any application that uses the ADMIN_CMD( ) procedure should check the SQLCA return code generated by the procedure call. If the return code is greater than or equal to 0, a result set was produced and should be retrieved for evaluation.

••

The user ID that was used to establish the connection to a database is the user ID that is used for authentication of any command that is executed using the ADMIN_CMD() stored procedure.

••

The DB2 Import Utility

Just as there are times when it is beneficial to copy data stored in a table or view to an external file, there can be times when it is advantageous to copy data stored in an external file to a database table or updatable view. One way to copy data from an external file to a database is by using DB2's Import utility; the Import utility is designed to read data directly from an external file (provided the file is written in a format that is supported by DB2) and insert it in a specific table or updatable view.

The Import utility can be invoked by executing the IMPORT command. The basic syntax for this command is:

```
IMPORT FROM [FileName] OF [DEL | ASC | WSF | IXF]
<LOBS FROM [LOBPath ,...]>
<XML FROM [XMLPath ,...]>
<MODIFIED BY [Modifier ,...]>
```

```
<Method>
<XML PARSE [STRIP | PRESERVE] WHITESPACE>
<XMLVALIDATE USING [XDS | SCHEMA [SchemaID]]>
<ALLOW NO ACCESS | ALLOW WRITE ACCESS>
<COMMITCOUNT [CommitCount] | COMMITCOUNT AUTOMATIC>
<RESTARTCOUNT | SKIPCOUNT [RestartCount]>
<NOTIMEOUT>
<WARNINGCOUNT [WarningCount]>
<MESSAGES [MsgFileName]>
[CREATE | INSERT | INSERT_UPDATE | REPLACE |
 REPLACE_CREATE]
    INTO [TableName] <([ColumnName ,...])>
    <IN [TSName] <INDEX IN [TSName]> <LONG IN [TSName]>>
```

where:

FileName   Identifies the name and location of the external file from which data is to be imported (copied).

LOBPath   Identifies one or more locations where large object (LOB) data values that are to be imported are stored.

XMLPath   Identifies one or more locations where XML documents that are to be imported are stored.

Modifier   Identifies one or more options that are used to override the default behavior of the Import utility. (Table 6.2 contains a list of valid modifiers.)

Method   Identifies the method (location, name, or position) that is to be used to extract data values from the source external file(s) specified and map them to one or more columns of the target table/updatable view specified. The syntax used to specify each method varies. (We will look at this syntax a little later.)

SchemaID   Identifies the XML schema/SQL identifier against which XML documents being imported are to be validated. When XML documents are validated in this manner, the SCH attribute of the XML Data Specifier (XDS) is ignored.

CommitCount   Identifies the number of rows of data (records) that are to be copied to the table/updatable view specified before a commit operation is to be performed. (COMMITCOUNT AUTOMATIC should be used instead for import operations that fail because transaction logs become full.)

RestartCount   Identifies the number of rows of data in the external file specified that are to be skipped. This option is typically used when an earlier import operation failed—by skipping rows that have already been successfully imported into a table/updatable view, one import operation can essentially continue where another import operation left off.

WarningCount   Identifies the number of warnings that are allowed before the import operation is to be stopped. (If the file to be imported or the target table is specified incorrectly, the Import utility will generate a warning for each row that it attempts to import.) If this parameter is set to 0 or not specified, the import operation will continue regardless of the number of warnings issued.

MsgFileName   Identifies the name and location of an external file to which messages produced by the Import utility are to be written as the import operation is performed.

TableName   Identifies the name assigned to the table or updatable view to which data is to be imported (copied). (This cannot be the name of a system catalog table or view.)

ColumnName   Identifies one or more specific columns (by name) to which data is to be imported.

TSName   Identifies the table space in which the table and its regular data, indexes, and/or long data/large object data are to be stored if the table specified is to be created.

Table 6.2 File Type Modifiers Recognized by the IMPORT Command		
Modifier	**Description**	**File Format**
compound=*x* where *x* is any number between 1 and 100	Indicates that non-atomic compound SQL should be used to insert the data read from a file into a table/updatable view and that a specific number of statements (between 1 and 100) are to be included in the compound SQL block. This modifier cannot be used when INSERT_UPDATE mode is used and is incompatible with the following modifiers: *usedefaults*, *identitymissing*, *identityignore*, *generatedmissing*, and *generatedignore*.	Delimited ASCII (DEL), non-delimited ASCII (ASC), Worksheet Format (WSF), and PC Integrated Exchange Format (IXF)
generatedignore	Indicates that although data for all generated columns is present in the file being imported, this data should be ignored. Instead, the Import utility should replace all generated data values found with its own generated values. This modifier is incompatible with the *generatedmissing* modifier.	Delimited ASCII (DEL), non-delimited ASCII (ASC), Worksheet Format (WSF), and PC Integrated Exchange Format (IXF)
generatedmissing	Indicates that data for generated columns is missing from the file being imported and that the Import utility should generate an appropriate value for each missing value encountered. This modifier is incompatible with the *generatedignore* modifier.	Delimited ASCII (DEL), non-delimited ASCII (ASC), Worksheet Format (WSF), and PC Integrated Exchange Format (IXF)
identityignore	Indicates that although data for all identity columns is present in the file being imported, this data should be ignored. Instead, the Import utility should replace all identity column data found with its own generated values. This modifier is incompatible with the *identitymissing* modifier.	Delimited ASCII (DEL), non-delimited ASCII (ASC), Worksheet Format (WSF), and PC Integrated Exchange Format (IXF)
identitymissing	Indicates that data for identity columns is missing from the file being imported and that the Import utility should generate an appropriate value for each missing value encountered. This modifier is incompatible with the *identityignore* modifier.	Delimited ASCII (DEL), non-delimited ASCII (ASC), Worksheet Format (WSF), and PC Integrated Exchange Format (IXF)
lobsinfile	Indicates that large object (LOB) data values are stored in their own individual files.	Delimited ASCII (DEL), non-delimited ASCII (ASC), Worksheet Format (WSF), and PC Integrated Exchange Format (IXF)

Table 6.2 File Type Modifiers Recognized by the IMPORT Command (continued)		
Modifier	**Description**	**File Format**
no_type_id	Indicates that data for typed tables should be converted to a single nontyped sub-table. This modifier is valid only when importing data into a single sub-table of a table hierarchy.	Delimited ASCII (DEL), non-delimited ASCII (ASC), Worksheet Format (WSF), and PC Integrated Exchange Format (IXF)
nodefaults	Indicates that if the source column data for a target table column is not provided, and if the target table column is not nullable, default values are not to be imported. If this modifier is not used, and a source column data value for one of the target table columns is not provided, one of the following will occur: • If a default value can be found for the column, the default value will be imported. • If the column is nullable, and a default value cannot be found for that column, a NULL value is stored in the column. • If the column is not nullable, and a default value cannot be found, an error is returned, and the Import utility stops processing.	Delimited ASCII (DEL), non-delimited ASCII (ASC), Worksheet Format (WSF), and PC Integrated Exchange Format (IXF)
norowwarnings	Indicates that all warning messages about rejected rows are to be suppressed.	Delimited ASCII (DEL), non-delimited ASCII (ASC), Worksheet Format (WSF), and PC Integrated Exchange Format (IXF)
seclabelchar	Indicates that security labels in the input source file are stored in the string format for security label values rather than in the default encoded numeric format. (The Import utility converts each security label found into the internal format as it is loaded. If a string is not in the proper format, the row is not imported, and a warning is returned. If the string does not represent a valid security label that is part of the security policy protecting the table, then the row is not imported, and a warning is returned.) This modifier cannot be used if the *seclabelname* modifier is specified.	Delimited ASCII (DEL), non-delimited ASCII (ASC), Worksheet Format (WSF), and PC Integrated Exchange Format (IXF)

Table 6.2 File Type Modifiers Recognized by the IMPORT Command (continued)		
Modifier	**Description**	**File Format**
seclabelname	Indicates that security labels in the input source file are indicated by their name rather than the default encoded numeric format. (The Import utility will convert the name to the appropriate security label if it exists. If no security label exists with the indicated name for the security policy protecting the table, the row is not imported and a warning is returned.) This modifier cannot be used if the *seclabelchar* modifier is specified.	Delimited ASCII (DEL), non-delimited ASCII (ASC), Worksheet Format (WSF), and PC Integrated Exchange Format (IXF)
usedefaults	Indicates that if the source column data for a target table column is not provided, and if the target table column has a defaults constraint, default values are to be generated for the column. If this modifier is not used, and a source column data value for one of the target table columns is not provided, one of the following will occur: • If the column is nullable, a NULL value is stored in the column. • If the column is not nullable, and a default value cannot be generated, the row is rejected.	Delimited ASCII (DEL), non-delimited ASCII (ASC), Worksheet Format (WSF), and PC Integrated Exchange Format (IXF)
codepage=*x* where *x* is any valid code page identifier	Identifies the code page of the data contained in the output data set produced. Character data is converted from the application code page to the code page specified during the import operation.	Delimited ASCII (DEL), non-delimited ASCII (ASC), Worksheet Format (WSF), and PC Integrated Exchange Format (IXF)
dateformat="*x*" where *x* is any valid combination of date format elements	Identifies how date values stored in the source file are formatted. The following date elements can be used to create the format string provided with this modifier: • YYYY—Year (four digits ranging from 0000 to 9999) • M—Month (one or two digits ranging from 1 to 12) • MM—Month (two digits ranging from 1 to 12; mutually exclusive with M) • D—Day (one or two digits ranging from 1 to 31) • DD—Day (two digits ranging from 1 to 31; mutually exclusive with D)	Delimited ASCII (DEL) and non-delimited ASCII (ASC)

Table 6.2 File Type Modifiers Recognized by the IMPORT Command (continued)		
Modifier	Description	File Format
	• DDD—Day of the year (three digits ranging from 001 to 366; mutually exclusive with other day or month elements) Examples of valid date format strings include the following: "D-M-YYYY" "MM.DD.YYYY" "YYYYDDD"	
implieddecimal	Indicates that the location of an implied decimal point is to be determined by the column definition—the Import utility is not to assume that the decimal point is at the end of the value (default behavior). For example, if this modifier is specified, the value 12345 would be loaded into a DECIMAL(8,2) column as 123.45 , *not* as 12345.00.	Delimited ASCII (DEL) and non-delimited ASCII (ASC)
timeformat="*x*" where *x* is any valid combination of time format elements	Identifies how time values stored in the source file are formatted. The following time elements can be used to create the format string provided with this modifier: • H—Hour (one or two digits ranging from 0 to 12 for a 12-hour system, and 0 to 24 for a 24-hour system) • HH—Hour (two digits ranging from 0 to 12 for a 12-hour system, and 0 to 24 for a 24-hour system; mutually exclusive with H) • M—Minute (one or two digits ranging from 0 to 59) • MM—Minute (two digits ranging from 0 to 59; mutually exclusive with M) • S—Second (one or two digits ranging from 0 to 59) • SS—Second (two digits ranging from 0 to 59; mutually exclusive with S) • SSSSS—Second of the day after midnight (5 digits ranging from 00000 to 86399; mutually exclusive with other time elements)	Delimited ASCII (DEL) and non-delimited ASCII (ASC)

Table 6.2 File Type Modifiers Recognized by the IMPORT Command (continued)		
Modifier	**Description**	**File Format**
	• TT—Meridian indicator (AM or PM) Examples of valid time format strings include: "HH:MM:SS" "HH.MM TT" "SSSSS"	
timestampformat="*x*" where *x* is any valid combination of date and time format elements	Identifies how timestamp values stored in the source file are formatted. The following date and time elements can be used to create the format string provided with this modifier: • YYYY—Year (four digits ranging from 0000 to 9999) • M—Month (one or two digits ranging from 1 to 12) • MM—Month (two digits ranging from 1 to 12; mutually exclusive with M) • D—Day (one or two digits ranging from 1 to 31) • DD—Day (two digits ranging from 1 to 31; mutually exclusive with D) • DDD—Day of the year (three digits ranging from 001 to 366; mutually exclusive with other day or month elements) • H—Hour (one or two digits ranging from 0 to 12 for a 12-hour system, and 0 to 24 for a 24-hour system) • HH—Hour (two digits ranging from 0 to 12 for a 12-hour system, and 0 to 24 for a 24-hour system; mutually exclusive with H) • M—Minute (one or two digits ranging from 0 to 59) • MM—Minute (two digits ranging from 0 to 59; mutually exclusive with M) • S—Second (one or two digits ranging from 0 to 59) • SS—Second (two digits ranging from 0 to 59; mutually exclusive with S) • SSSSS—Second of the day after midnight (5 digits ranging from 00000 to 86399; mutually exclusive with other time elements) • UUUUUU—Microsecond (6 digits ranging from 000000 to 999999)	Delimited ASCII (DEL) and non-delimited ASCII (ASC)

Table 6.2 File Type Modifiers Recognized by the IMPORT Command (continued)		
Modifier	**Description**	**File Format**
	• TT—Meridian indicator (AM or PM) An example of a valid timestamp format string is: "YYYY/MM/DD HH:MM:SS.UUUUUU"	
usegraphiccodepage	Indicates that data being imported into graphic or double-byte character large object (DBCLOB) columns is stored in the graphic code page. The rest of the data is assumed to be stored in the character code page. The Import utility determines the character code page either through the *codepage* modifier, if it is specified, or through the code page of the application if the *codepage* modifier is not specified. This modifier must not be specified with delimited ASCII (DEL) files created by the Export utility—those files contain data encoded in only one code page.	Delimited ASCII (DEL) and non-delimited ASCII (ASC)
xmlchar	Specifies that XML documents are encoded in the character code page. This modifier is useful for processing XML documents that are encoded in the specified character code page but do not contain an encoding declaration.	Delimited ASCII (DEL) and non-delimited ASCII (ASC)
xmlgraphic	Specifies that XML documents are encoded in the graphic code page specified. This modifier is useful for processing XML documents that are encoded in a specific graphic code page but do not contain an encoding declaration.	Delimited ASCII (DEL) and non-delimited ASCII (ASC)
chardel*x* where *x* is any valid delimiter character	Identifies a specific character that is to be used as a character delimiter. The default character delimiter is a double quotation mark (") character. The character specified is used in place of the double quotation mark to enclose a character string.	Delimited ASCII (DEL)
coldel*x* where *x* is any valid delimiter character	Identifies a specific character that is to be used as a column delimiter. The default column delimiter is a comma (,) character. The character specified is used in place of a comma to signal the end of a column.	Delimited ASCII (DEL)

Table 6.2 File Type Modifiers Recognized by the IMPORT Command (continued)		
Modifier	**Description**	**File Format**
decplusblank	Indicates that positive decimal values are to be prefixed with a blank space instead of a plus sign (+). The default action is to prefix positive decimal values with a plus sign.	Delimited ASCII (DEL)
decpt*x* where *x* is any valid delimiter character	Identifies a specific character that is to be used as a decimal point character. The default decimal point character is a period (.) character. The character specified is used in place of a period as a decimal point character.	Delimited ASCII (DEL)
delprioritychar	Indicates that the priority for evaluating delimiters is to be *character delimiter, record delimiter, column delimiter* rather than *record delimiter, character delimiter, column delimiter* (which is the default). This modifier is typically used with older applications that depend on the other priority.	Delimited ASCII (DEL)
keepblanks	Indicates that all leading and trailing blanks found for each column that has a data type of CHAR, VARCHAR, LONG VARCHAR, or CLOB are to be retained. If this modifier is not specified, all leading and trailing blanks that reside outside character delimiters are removed, and a NULL is inserted into the table for all missing data values found.	Delimited ASCII (DEL)
nochardel	Indicates that the Import utility is to assume all bytes found between the column delimiters to be part of the column's data. (Character delimiters will be parsed as part of column data.) This modifier should not be specified if the data was exported by DB2 (unless the *nochardel* modifier was specified at export time). It is provided to support vendor data files that do not have character delimiters. Improper usage might result in data loss or corruption. This modifier cannot be specified with *chardelx, delprioritychar,* or *nodoubledel.* These are mutually exclusive options.	Delimited ASCII (DEL)

Modifier	Description	File Format
nodoubledel	Indicates that double character delimiters are not to be recognized.	Delimited ASCII (DEL)
nochecklengths	Indicates that the Import utility is to attempt to import every row in the source file, even if the source data has a column value that exceeds the size of the target column's definition. Such rows can be successfully imported if code page conversion causes the source data to shrink in size. For example, 4-byte EUC data found in a source file could shrink to 2-byte DBCS data in the target table and require half the space. This option is particularly useful if it is known in advance that the source data will always fit in a column despite mismatched column definitions/sizes.	Non-delimited ASCII (ASC) and PC Integrated Exchange Format (IXF)
nullindchar=*x* where *x* is any valid character	Identifies a specific character that is to be used as a null indicator value. The default null indicator is the letter *Y*. This modifier is case sensitive for EBCDIC data files, except when the character is an English letter. For example, if the null indicator character is specified to be the letter *N*, then the letter *n* is also recognized as a null indicator.	Non-delimited ASCII (ASC)
reclen=*x* where *x* is any number between 1 and 32,767	Indicates that a specific number of characters are to be read from the source file for each row found; new-line characters are to be ignored instead of being used to indicate the end of a row.	Non-delimited ASCII (ASC)
striptblanks	Indicates that all leading and trailing blanks found for each column that has a data type of VARCHAR, LONG VARCHAR, VARGRAPHIC, or LONG VARGRAPHIC are to be truncated. This modifier is incompatible with the *striptnulls* modifier.	Non-delimited ASCII (ASC)
striptnulls	Indicates that all leading and trailing nulls (0x00 characters) found for each column that has a data type of VARCHAR, LONG VARCHAR, VARGRAPHIC, or LONG VARGRAPHIC are to be truncated. This modifier is incompatible with the *striptblanks* modifier.	Non-delimited ASCII (ASC)

Table 6.2 File Type Modifiers Recognized by the IMPORT Command (continued)

Table 6.2 File Type Modifiers Recognized by the IMPORT Command (continued)		
Modifier	**Description**	**File Format**
forcein	Indicates that the Import utility is to accept data despite code page mismatches (in other words, to suppress translation between code pages). Fixed-length target columns are checked to verify that they are large enough to hold the data unless the *nochecklengths* modifier has been specified	PC Integrated Exchange Format (IXF)
indexixf	Indicates that the Import utility is to drop all indexes currently defined on the existing table and is to create new indexes using the index definitions stored in the IXF formatted source file. This modifier can be used only when the contents of a table are being replaced, and it cannot be used with a view.	PC Integrated Exchange Format (IXF)
indexschema=*x* where *x* is a valid schema name	Indicates that the Import utility is to assign all indexes created to the schema specified. If this modifier is used, and no schema name is provided, all indexes created will be assigned to the default schema for the user ID that is associated with the current database connection. If this modifier is not used, all indexes created will be assigned to the schema identified in the IXF formatted source file.	PC Integrated Exchange Format (IXF)
forcecreate	Specifies that a table should be created with possible missing or limited information after an import operation returns the error code SQL3311N.	PC Integrated Exchange Format (IXF)
Adapted from Tables 22, 23, 24, 25, and 26 on pages 810–819 of the *IBM DB2 9 Command Reference* manual.		

Earlier we saw that three methods are used to map data values found in external files to columns in a table: the location method, the name method, and the position method. The syntax used to indicate that the location method is to be used to extract data values from the external file specified is:

```
METHOD L ( [ColumnStart] [ColumnEnd] ,... )
    <NULL INDICATORS ( [NullIndColNumber] ,...] )>
```

where:

ColumnStart   Identifies the starting position of one or more data
                   values in the non-delimited ASCII (ASC) formatted file
                   from which values are to be retrieved.

ColumnEnd   Identifies the ending position of one or more data values
                   in the non-delimited ASCII (ASC) formatted file from
                   which values are to be retrieved.

NullIndColNumber   Identifies the position of one or more data values that
                   are to be treated as null indicator variables for column
                   data values in the non-delimited ASCII (ASC) formatted
                   file from which values are to be retrieved.

The syntax used to indicate that the name method is to be used to extract data
values from the external file specified is:

    METHOD N ([ColumnName ,...])

where:

ColumnName   Identifies one or more unique names assigned to columns in the
             PC Integrated Exchange Format (IXF) formatted file from
             which values are to be retrieved.

And the syntax used to indicate that the position method is to be used to extract
data values from the external file specified is:

    METHOD P ([ColumnPosition ,...])

where:

ColumnPosition   Identifies the indexed position of one or more columns in the
                 delimited ASCII (DEL) or PC Integrated Exchange Format
                 (IXF) formatted file from which values are to be retrieved.

You may also have noticed that there are five different options available with the
IMPORT command that are used to control how the target table data to be copied to
will be altered by the import operation. These options include the following:

CREATE. When the CREATE option is used, the target table is created along with all of its associated indexes, and then data is imported into the new table. This option also allows you to control in what table space the new table will be created. However, this option can be used only when importing data from PC Integrated Exchange Format (IXF) formatted files.

INSERT. When the INSERT option is used, data is inserted into the target table (which must already exist). Imported data is appended to any data that already exists.

INSERT_UPDATE. When the INSERT_UPDATE option is used, data is either inserted into the target table (which must already exist) or used to update existing rows (if the row being imported has a primary key value that matches that of an existing record). Existing records will be updated only if the target table specified has a primary key defined.

REPLACE. When the REPLACE option is used, any existing data is deleted from the target table (which must already exist); then the new data is inserted. (This option cannot be used if the target table contains a primary key that is referenced by a foreign key in another table.)

REPLACE_CREATE. When the REPLACE_CREATE option is used, any existing data is deleted from the target table if it already exists; then the new data is inserted. On the other hand, if the target table does not exist, it is created along with all of its associated indexes, and then data is imported into the new table. As you might imagine, this option can be used only when importing data from PC Integrated Exchange Format (IXF) formatted files. (This option cannot be used if the target table contains a primary key that is referenced by a foreign key in another table.)

Thus, if you wanted to import data stored in a PC Integrated Exchange Format (IXF)–format external file named DEPT.IXF to a new table named DEPARTMENT, you could do so by executing an IMPORT command that looks something like this:

```
IMPORT FROM C:\dept.ixf OF IXF
MESSAGES imp_msgs.txt
CREATE INTO department IN hr_space1
```

Earlier, we saw that when data that is to be exported contains large object (LOB) values, by default only the first 32 K (kilobytes) of each LOB value are actually written to the file containing the exported data. We also saw that this behavior can be overridden by using the *lobsinfile* or *lobsinsepfiles* modifier and providing the Export utility with one or more locations to which LOB data values are to be written. In this case, each LOB value found will be stored, in its entirety, in its own individual file that is assigned a name that either the user or the Export utility provides. LOB values that reside in individual files can also be imported if the appropriate modifier (*lobsinfile*) is used. And because the names and locations of files containing LOB data values are stored in the source data file (assuming the source data file was produced by the Export utility) along with other data, this information does not have to be provided to the Import utility in order for the LOB data values to be retrieved.

Thus, if you wanted to import data stored in a delimited ASCII (DEL)–format external file named EMPLOYEE.DEL, along with LOB data values stored in individual files, to a table named EMPLOYEE, you could do so by executing an IMPORT command that looks something like this:

```
IMPORT FROM C:\employee.del OF DEL
LOBS FROM C:\lob_data
MODIFIED BY lobsinfile coldel;
MESSAGES imp_msgs.txt
INSERT INTO employee
```

When executed, this command would do the following:

- Retrieve all data values stored in a delimited ASCII (DEL)–format external file named EMPLOYEE.DEL. (This file resides in the root directory on drive C:.)

- Locate all LOB values referenced in the file named EMPLOYEE.DEL and retrieve each value from its own individual file. (Each file is expected to reside in a directory named "LOB_DATA" located on drive C:.)

- Insert all data values retrieved from both the file named EMPLOYEE.DEL and the individual LOB data files into a table named EMPLOYEE (which already exists).

- Record all messages produced by the Import utility to a file named IMP_MSGS.TXT (which will reside in the current working directory).

Figure 6–8 illustrates this import operation.

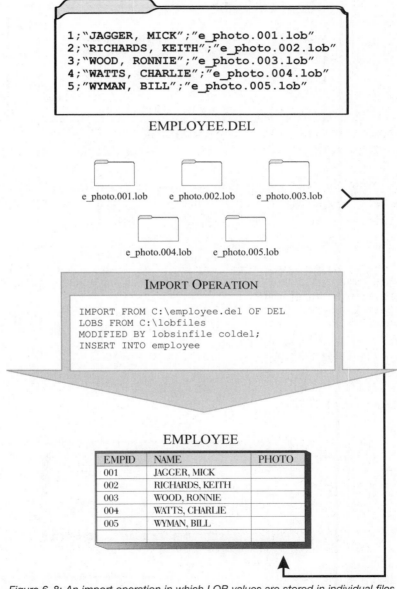

Figure 6–8: An import operation in which LOB values are stored in individual files.

XML documents stored in individual files can be retrieved and copied to a table in a similar manner. Figure 6–9 illustrates a simple import operation in which XML documents are processed this way.

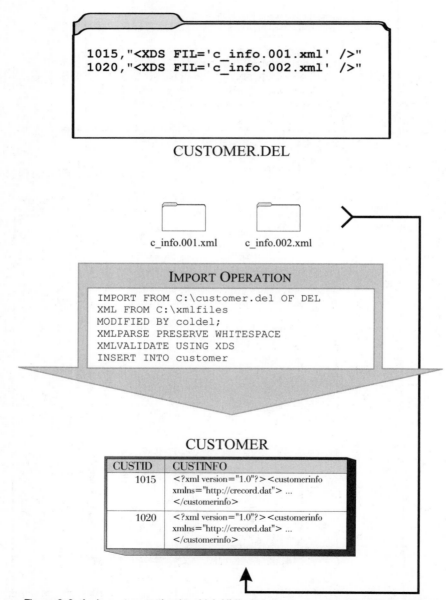

Figure 6–9: An import operation in which XML documents are stored in individual files.

Data stored in external files can also be imported using the Import Table dialog, which can be activated by selecting the appropriate action from the Tables or Views menu found in the Control Center. Figure 6–10 shows the Control Center menu items that must be selected to activate the Import Table dialog; Figure 6–11 shows how the Import Table dialog typically looks when it is first activated.

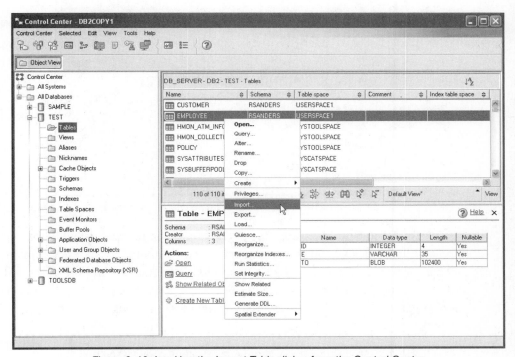

Figure 6–10: Invoking the Import Table dialog from the Control Center.

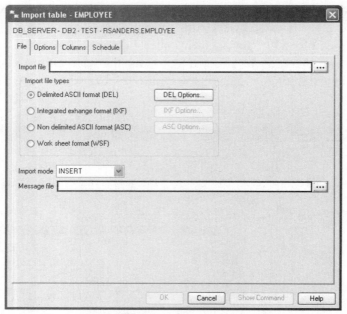

Figure 6–11: The first page of the Import Table dialog.

As with the Export utility, a database connection must be established before the Import utility is invoked. It is also important to note that if the IMPORT command is executed with the ALLOW WRITE ACCESS option specified, the Import utility will request a table lock after every commit operation is performed. This can cause an import operation to run slowly in environments that have high concurrency.

> Only users with System Administrator (SYSADM) authority, Database Administrator (DBADMN) authority, or CREATETAB authority on the database and either IMPLICIT_SCHEMA privilege on the database or CREATEIN privilege on the schema referenced are allowed to create a new table and import data into it using the CREATE or the REPLACE_CREATE option. Only users with SYSADM authority, DBADMN authority, CONTROL privilege on all tables and/or views referenced, or INSERT and SELECT privilege on all tables and/or views referenced are allowed to import data into existing tables using the INSERT option. And only users with SYSADM authority, DBADMN authority, or CONTROL privilege on all tables and/or views referenced are allowed to import data into existing tables using the INSERT_UPDATE, REPLACE, or REPLACE_CREATE option.

The DB2 Load Utility

Like the Import utility, the Load utility is designed to read data directly from an external file (provided the file is written in a format that is supported by DB2) and store it in a specific table. However, unlike when the Import utility is used, when the Load utility is used, the table to which data is to be copied must already exist in the database before the load operation is initiated. Other differences between the Import utility and the Load utility can be seen in Table 6.3.

Table 6.3 Differences Between the Import Utility and the Load Utility	
Import Utility	**Load Utility**
Slow when processing large amounts of data.	Significantly faster than the Import utility when processing large amounts of data because the Load utility writes formatted pages directly into the database's storage containers.
Tables and indexes can be created from IXF format files.	Tables and indexes must exist before data can be loaded into them.
Limited exploitation of intrapartition parallelism.	Exploitation of intrapartition parallelism on symmetric multiprocessor (SMP) machines.
Worksheet Format (WSF) formatted files are supported.	Worksheet Format (WSF) formatted files are not supported.
Data can be imported into tables, views, or aliases that refer to tables or views.	Data can be loaded only into tables or aliases that refer to tables—data cannot be loaded into views or aliases that refer to views.
Table spaces in which the table and its indexes reside remain online during the import operation.	Table spaces in which the table and its indexes reside are taken off-line during the load operation.
Row transactions are recorded in the database's transaction log files.	Minimal logging is performed—row transactions are not recorded in the database's transaction log files.
Triggers can be fired during processing.	Triggers are not fired during processing.
If an import operation is interrupted, and a commit frequency value was specified, the table will remain usable, and it will contain all rows that were inserted up to the moment the last commit operation was performed. The user has the option of restarting the import operation or leaving the table as it is.	If a load operation was interrupted, and a consistency point (commit frequency) value was specified, the table remains in the "Load pending" state and cannot be used until (1) the load process is restarted, and the load operation is completed, or (2) the table space in which the table resides is restored from a backup image that was created before the load operation was initiated.
The amount of free disk space needed to import data is approximately the size of the largest index being imported plus about 10 percent. This space is allocated from system temporary table spaces that have been defined for the database.	The amount of free disk space needed to load data is approximately the size of the sum of all indexes for the table being loaded. This space is temporarily allocated outside the database environment.

Table 6.3 Differences Between the Import Utility and the Load Utility (continued)	
Import Utility	**Load Utility**
All constraint checking is performed during processing.	Only uniqueness checking is performed during processing. All other constraint checking (check constraints, referential integrity constraints, etc.) must be performed after the load operation has completed using the SET INTEGRITY SQL statement.
The keys of each row are inserted into the appropriate index during an import operation.	All keys are sorted during a load operation, and the indexes are rebuilt when the load phase of the load operation has completed.
Statistics for the affected table must be manually collected (by issuing the RUNSTATS command) after an import operation is performed.	Statistics for the affected table can be collected and updated during a load operation.
Data can be imported into a host database through DB2 Connect.	Data cannot be loaded into a host database.
Data files to be imported must reside on the workstation from which the Import facility is invoked.	Data files and named pipes that will provide the data to be loaded must reside on the same workstation where the database receiving the data resides.
A backup image is not created during an import operation. (Because the Import utility uses SQL inserts, the DB2 Database Manager logs all processing, and no backup images are required to reproduce the import operation in the event a failure occurs.)	A backup image (copy) can be created during a load operation.
Supports hierarchical data.	Does not support hierarchical data.
Numeric data must be stored as character representations.	Numeric data (other than DECIMAL data) can be stored and loaded either in binary form or as character representations. DECIMAL data can be stored and loaded in packed decimal or zoned decimal form or as character representations.
Data conversion between code pages is not performed.	Character data (and numeric data expressed as characters) can be converted from one code page to another during processing.
No FASTPARSE support provided.	FASTPARSE support provided. (FASTPARSE provides reduced data checking of user-supplied data.)
No BINARYNUMERICS support provided.	BINARYNUMERICS support provided.
No PACKEDDECIMAL support provided.	PACKEDDECIMAL support provided.
No ZONEDDECIMAL support provided.	ZONEDDECIMAL support provided.
Cannot override columns defined as GENERATED ALWAYS.	Can override columns defined as GENERATED ALWAYS by using the GENERATEDIGNORE and IDENTITYIGNORE file type modifiers.

Table 6.3. Differences Between the Import Utility and the Load Utility (continued)	
Import Utility	**Load Utility**
No support for importing into materialized query tables.	Support for loading into materialized query tables.
XML documents can be imported into XML columns.	XML documents cannot be loaded.
Adapted from Appendix B on pages 281–282 of the *IBM DB2 9 Data Movement Utilities Guide and Reference* manual.	

The most important difference between the Import utility and the Load utility is the way in which each utility moves data between an external file and a database table. The Import utility copies data using SQL insert or update operations. As a result, each row processed must be checked for constraint compliance, and all activity performed by the Import utility is recorded in the database's transaction log files.

The Load utility, on the other hand, inserts data into a table by building data pages consisting of several individual rows of data and writing those pages directly to the table space container(s) the target table uses for data storage. Once all data pages have been constructed and written to the appropriate table space container(s), all existing primary and/or unique indexes associated with the target table are rebuilt and all rows that violate primary or unique key constraints defined for the table are deleted (and copied to an exception table, if appropriate). Because pages of data are written instead of individual rows, changes made to the target table are not recorded in the database's transaction log files. As a result, overall performance is typically faster. However, because changes made to a table by the Load utility are not logged, if a database failure occurs, the loaded data cannot be reloaded by performing a roll-forward recovery operation. To get around this limitation, the Load utility can generate a backup copy of all data loaded so that it can be quickly reloaded if necessary.

It is a good idea to restrict access to all table spaces associated with the target table of a load operation by executing the QUIESCE TABLESPACES FOR TABLE command just before a load operation is initiated and immediately after a load operation completes.

The four phases of a load operation

A complete load operation consists of four distinct phases:

- The load phase
- The build phase
- The delete phase
- The index copy phase

The load phase. Four things happen during the load phase: data is read from the source file specified and loaded into the appropriate target table, index key values and table statistics are collected, point of consistency information is recorded, and invalid data is placed into dump files. Point of consistency information serves as a checkpoint for the Load utility—in the event the load operation is interrupted during execution of the load phase and restarted, the operation will continue from the last consistency point established. As part of updating point of consistency information, the Load utility writes a message to the appropriate message file identifying the current number of records that have been successfully loaded. This information can then be used to pick up where the load operation left off if a failure occurs or to monitor the load operation's progress. (The LOAD QUERY command is used to monitor the progress/status of a load operation.)

The build phase. During the build phase, indexes associated with primary and/or unique keys that have been defined for the table that was loaded are updated with the index key values that were collected and sorted during the load phase. This is also when statistical information about the table and its indexes is updated, if appropriate.

Because the beginning of the build phase is recorded as a point of consistency, if the load operation is interrupted during execution of the build phase and restarted, the operation will be restarted at the beginning of the build phase—the load phase will not have to be repeated.

The delete phase. During the delete phase, all rows that violated primary and/or unique key constraints defined on the target table are removed and copied to an exception table (if appropriate), and a message about each offending row is written to the appropriate message file so that it can be modified and manually moved to the target table at some point in the future. These are the only table constraints that are checked. To check loaded data for additional constraint violations, constraint checking should be turned off (with the SET INTEGRITY SQL statement) before the load operation is started and then turned back on and performed immediately (again, with the SET INTEGRITY statement) after the load operation has completed.

The beginning of the delete phase is also recorded as a point of consistency. Thus, if a load operation is interrupted during execution of the delete phase and restarted, the operation will be restarted at the beginning of the delete phase—the load phase and the build phase do not have to be repeated.

The index copy phase. During the index copy phase, index data is copied from the system temporary table space used to the table space where the index data associated with the table that was loaded is to reside. It is important to note that this phase is executed only if the LOAD command is executed with the ALLOW READ ACCESS and USE [*TablespaceName*] options specified.

Performing a load operation

Now that we have seen how the Load utility differs from the Import utility, and how the Load utility copies data stored in an external file to a database table, let's look at how the Load utility is invoked. The Load utility can be invoked by executing the LOAD command. The basic syntax for this command is:

```
LOAD <CLIENT> FROM [FileName OF [DEL | ASC | IXF] |
    PipeName | Device | CursorName OF CURSOR ,...]
<LOBS FROM [LOBPath ,...]>
<MODIFIED BY [Modifier ,...]>
<Method>
<SAVECOUNT [SaveCount]>
<ROWCOUNT [RowCount]>
<WARNINGCOUNT [WarningCount]>
<MESSAGES [MsgFileName]>
<TEMPFILES PATH [TempFilesPath]>
[INSERT | REPLACE | RESTART | TERMINATE]
INTO [TableName] < ([ColumnName ,...])>
<FOR EXCEPTION [ExTableName]>
<STATISTICS [NO | USE PROFILE]>
<NONRECOVERABLE | COPY YES TO [CopyLocation ,...]>
<WITHOUT PROMPTING>
<DATA BUFFER [Size]>
<INDEXING MODE [AUTOSELECT | REBUILD | INCREMENTAL |
    DEFERRED]>
```

```
<ALLOW NO ACCESS | ALLOW READ ACCESS <USE [TmpTSName]>>
<SET INTEGRITY PENDING CASCADE [IMMEDIATE | DEFERRED]>
```

where:

FileName   Identifies the name and location of one or more external files from which data is to be loaded (copied).

PipeName   Identifies the name of one or more named pipes from which data is to be loaded.

Device   Identifies the name of one or more devices from which data is to be loaded.

CursorName   Identifies the name of one or more cursors from which data is to be loaded.

LOBPath   Identifies one or more locations where large object (LOB) data values to be loaded are stored.

Modifier   Identifies one or more options that are used to override the default behavior of the Load utility. (Table 6.4 contains a list of valid modifiers.)

Method   Identifies the method (location, name, or position) that is to be used to extract data values from the source external file(s) specified and map them to one or more columns of the target table specified. The syntax used to specify each method varies.

SaveCount   Identifies the number of rows of data (records) that are to be copied to the target table specified before the Load utility will establish a new point of consistency.

RowCount   Identifies the actual number of rows of data in the specified external file(s), named pipe(s), device(s), and/or cursor(s) that are to be loaded.

WarningCount   Identifies the number of warning conditions the Load utility should ignore before terminating the load operation.

MsgFileName   Identifies the name and location of an external file to which messages produced by the Load utility are to be written as the load operation is performed.

TempFilesPath   Identifies the location where temporary files that might be needed by the Load utility are stored.

TableName   Identifies the name assigned to the table into which data is to be loaded. (This cannot be the name of a system catalog table.)

ColumnName   Identifies one or more specific columns (by name) into which data is to be loaded.

ExTableName   Identifies the name assigned to the table to which all rows that violate unique index or primary key constraints defined for the target table specified are to be copied.

CopyLocation   Identifies the directory or device where a backup copy of all data loaded into the target table is to be stored.

Size   Identifies the number of 4 K (kilobyte) pages that are to be used as buffered storage space for the purpose of transferring data within the Load utility.

TmpTSName   Identifies the system temporary table space in which shadow copies of indexes are to be built before they are copied to the appropriate regular table space for final storage during the Index Copy phase of a load operation.

Table 6.4 File Type Modifiers Recognized by the LOAD Command		
Modifier	Description	File Format
anyorder	Indicates that the preservation of source data order is not required. (This will yield significant performance increases on SMP systems). This modifier is not supported if SAVECOUNT > 0 because data must be loaded in sequence in order for crash recovery (after a consistency point has been taken) to work properly.	Delimited ASCII (DEL), non-delimited ASCII (ASC), and PC Integrated Exchange Format (IXF)
generatedignore	Indicates that although data for all generated columns is present in the file being loaded, this data should be ignored. Instead, the Load utility should replace all generated data values found with its own generated values. This modifier is incompatible with the *generatedmissing* modifier.	Delimited ASCII (DEL), non-delimited ASCII (ASC), and PC Integrated Exchange Format (IXF)
generatedmissing	Indicates that data for generated columns is missing from the file being loaded and that the Load utility should generate an appropriate value for each missing value encountered. This modifier is incompatible with the *generatedignore* modifier.	Delimited ASCII (DEL), non-delimited ASCII (ASC), and PC Integrated Exchange Format (IXF)
generatedoverride	Indicates that the Load utility is to accept explicit, non-NULL data values for all generated columns in the table (contrary to the normal rules for these types of columns). This modifier is useful when migrating data from another database system or when loading a table from data that was recovered using the DROPPED TABLE RECOVERY option of the ROLLFORWARD DATABASE command. This modifier is incompatible with the *generatedignore* and *generatedmissing* modifiers.	Delimited ASCII (DEL), non-delimited ASCII (ASC), and PC Integrated Exchange Format (IXF)
identityignore	Indicates that although data for all identity columns is present in the file being loaded, this data should be ignored. Instead, the Load utility should replace all identity column data found with its own generated values. This modifier is incompatible with the *identitymissing* modifier.	Delimited ASCII (DEL), non-delimited ASCII (ASC), and PC Integrated Exchange Format (IXF)
identitymissing	Indicates that data for identity columns is missing from the file being loaded and that the Load utility should generate an appropriate value for each missing value encountered. This modifier is incompatible with the *identityignore* modifier.	Delimited ASCII (DEL), non-delimited ASCII (ASC), and PC Integrated Exchange Format (IXF)

Table 6.4 File Type Modifiers Recognized by the LOAD Command (continued)

Modifier	Description	File Format
identityoverride	Indicates that the Load utility is to accept explicit, non-NULL data values for all identity columns in the table (contrary to the normal rules for these types of columns). This modifier is useful when migrating data from another database system or when loading a table from data that was recovered using the DROPPED TABLE RECOVERY option of the ROLLFORWARD DATABASE command. This modifier should be used only when an identity column that was defined as GENERATED ALWAYS is present in the table that is to be loaded. This modifier is incompatible with the *identityignore* and *identitymissing* modifiers.	Delimited ASCII (DEL), non-delimited ASCII (ASC), and PC Integrated Exchange Format (IXF)
indexfreespace=*x* where *x* is a number between 0 and 99 (percent)	Indicates that a percentage of each index page is to be left as free space when loading indexes that are associated with the table being loaded.	Delimited ASCII (DEL), non-delimited ASCII (ASC), and PC Integrated Exchange Format (IXF)
lobsinfile	Indicates that large object (LOB) data values are stored in their own individual files.	Delimited ASCII (DEL), non-delimited ASCII (ASC), and PC Integrated Exchange Format (IXF)
noheader	Indicates that the Load utility is to skip the header verification code (applicable only to load operations performed on tables that reside in a single-node nodegroup) when processing the source data file.	Delimited ASCII (DEL), non-delimited ASCII (ASC), and PC Integrated Exchange Format (IXF)
norowwarnings	Indicates that warning messages about rejected rows are to be suppressed.	Delimited ASCII (DEL), non-delimited ASCII (ASC), and PC Integrated Exchange Format (IXF)
pagefreespace=*x* where *x* is a number between 0 and 100 (percent)	Indicates that a percentage of each data page associated with the table being loaded is to be left as free space.	Delimited ASCII (DEL), non-delimited ASCII (ASC), and PC Integrated Exchange Format (IXF)

Table 6.4 File Type Modifiers Recognized by the LOAD Command (continued)		
Modifier	**Description**	**File Format**
seclabelchar	Indicates that security labels in the input source file are stored in the string format for security label values rather than in the default encoded numeric format. (The Load utility converts each security label found into the internal format as it is loaded. If a string is not in the proper format, the row is not loaded, and a warning is returned. If the string does not represent a valid security label that is part of the security policy protecting the table, then the row is not loaded, and a warning is returned.) This modifier cannot be used if the *seclabelname* modifier is specified.	Delimited ASCII (DEL), non-delimited ASCII (ASC), and PC Integrated Exchange Format (IXF)
seclabelname	Indicates that security labels in the input source file are indicated by their name rather than the default encoded numeric format. (The Load utility will convert the name to the appropriate security label if it exists. If no security label exists with the indicated name for the security policy protecting the table, the row is not loaded, and a warning is returned.) This modifier cannot be used if the *seclabelchar* modifier is specified.	Delimited ASCII (DEL), non-delimited ASCII (ASC), and PC Integrated Exchange Format (IXF)
totalfreespace=*x* where *x* is a number between 0 and 100 (percent)	Indicates that a percentage of the total number of data pages used by the table being loaded are to be appended to the end of the table and treated as free space.	Delimited ASCII (DEL), non-delimited ASCII (ASC), and PC Integrated Exchange Format (IXF)
usedefaults	Indicates that if the source column data for a target table column is not provided, and if the target table column has a defaults constraint, default values are to be generated for the column. If this modifier is not used, and a source column data value for one of the target table columns is not provided, one of the following will occur: • If the column is nullable, a NULL value is stored in the column. • If the column is not nullable, and a default value cannot be generated, the row is rejected.	Delimited ASCII (DEL), non-delimited ASCII (ASC), and PC Integrated Exchange Format (IXF)
codepage=*x* where *x* is any valid code page identifier	Identifies the code page of the data contained in the output data set produced. Character data is converted from the application code page to the code page specified during the load operation.	Delimited ASCII (DEL) and non-delimited ASCII (ASC)

	Table 6.4 File Type Modifiers Recognized by the LOAD Command (continued)	
Modifier	**Description**	**File Format**
dateformat="*x*" where *x* is any valid combination of date format elements	Identifies how date values stored in the source file are formatted. The following date elements can be used to create the format string provided with this modifier: • YYYY—Year (four digits ranging from 0000 to 9999) • M—Month (one or two digits ranging from 1 to 12) • MM—Month (two digits ranging from 1 to 12; mutually exclusive with M) • D—Day (one or two digits ranging from 1 to 31) • DD—Day (two digits ranging from 1 to 31; mutually exclusive with D) • DDD—Day of the year (three digits ranging from 001 to 366; mutually exclusive with other day or month elements) Examples of valid date format strings include the following: "D-M-YYYY" "MM.DD.YYYY" "YYYYDDD"	Delimited ASCII (DEL) and non-delimited ASCII (ASC)
dumpfile=*x* where *x* is a fully qualified name of a file	Identifies the name and location of an exception file to which rejected rows are to be written. The contents of a dump file are written to disk in an asynchronous buffered mode. In the event a load operation fails or is interrupted, the number of records committed to disk cannot be known with certainty, and consistency cannot be guaranteed after a LOAD RESTART. A dump file can only be assumed to be complete for load operations that start and complete in a single pass. This modifier does not support file names with multiple file extensions. For example, dumpfile=/home/DUMP.FILE is acceptable; dumpfile=/home/DUMP.LOAD.FILE is not.	Delimited ASCII (DEL) and non-delimited ASCII (ASC)
dumpfileaccessall	Grants read access to "OTHERS" when a dump file is created. This modifier is only valid when • it is used in conjunction with the *dumpfile* modifier, • the user has SELECT privilege on the target table specified, and • it is used on a DB2 server database partition that resides on a UNIX operating system.	Delimited ASCII (DEL) and non-delimited ASCII (ASC)
fastparse	Indicates that reduced syntax checking is to be performed on user-supplied column values. (This can yield significant performance increases.) When this modifier is used, tables are guaranteed to be architecturally correct, and the Load utility only performs sufficient data checking to prevent a segmentation violation or trap from occurring.	Delimited ASCII (DEL) and non-delimited ASCII (ASC)

Table 6.4 File Type Modifiers Recognized by the LOAD Command (continued)		
Modifier	**Description**	**File Format**
implieddecimal	Indicates that the location of an implied decimal point is to be determined by the column definition—the Load utility is not to assume that the decimal point is at the end of the value (default behavior). For example, if this modifier is specified, the value 12345 would be loaded into a DECIMAL(8,2) column as 123.45, *not* as 12345.00.	Delimited ASCII (DEL) and non-delimited ASCII (ASC)
timeformat="*x*" where *x* is any valid combination of time format elements	Identifies how time values stored in the source file are formatted. The following time elements can be used to create the format string provided with this modifier: • H—Hour (one or two digits ranging from 0 to 12 for a 12-hour system, and 0 to 24 for a 24-hour system) • HH—Hour (two digits ranging from 0 to 12 for a 12-hour system, and 0 to 24 for a 24-hour system; mutually exclusive with H) • M—Minute (one or two digits ranging from 0 to 59) • MM—Minute (two digits ranging from 0 to 59; mutually exclusive with M) • S—Second (one or two digits ranging from 0 to 59) • SS—Second (two digits ranging from 0 to 59; mutually exclusive with S) • SSSSS—Second of the day after midnight (5 digits ranging from 00000 to 86399; mutually exclusive with other time elements) • TT—Meridian indicator (AM or PM) Examples of valid time format strings include the following: "HH:MM:SS" "HH.MM TT" "SSSSS"	Delimited ASCII (DEL) and non-delimited ASCII (ASC)
timestampformat="*x*" where *x* is any valid combination of date and time format elements	Identifies how timestamp values stored in the source file are formatted. The following date and time elements can be used to create the format string provided with this modifier: • YYYY—Year (four digits ranging from 0000 to 9999) • M—Month (one or two digits ranging from 1 to 12) • MM—Month (two digits ranging from 1 to 12; mutually exclusive with M) • D—Day (one or two digits ranging from 1 to 31) • DD—Day (two digits ranging from 1 to 31; mutually exclusive with D) • DDD—Day of the year (three digits ranging from 001 to 366; mutually exclusive with other day or month elements) • H—Hour (one or two digits ranging from 0 to 12 for a 12-hour system, and 0 to 24 for a 24-hour system)	Delimited ASCII (DEL) and non-delimited ASCII (ASC)

Table 6.4 File Type Modifiers Recognized by the LOAD Command (continued)		
Modifier	**Description**	**File Format**
	• HH—Hour (two digits ranging from 0 to 12 for a 12-hour system, and 0 to 24 for a 24-hour system; mutually exclusive with H) • M—Minute (one or two digits ranging from 0 to 59) • MM—Minute (two digits ranging from 0 to 59; mutually exclusive with M) • S—Second (one or two digits ranging from 0 to 59) • SS—Second (two digits ranging from 0 to 59; mutually exclusive with S) • SSSSS—Second of the day after midnight (5 digits ranging from 00000 to 86399; mutually exclusive with other time elements) • UUUUUU—Microsecond (6 digits ranging from 000000 to 999999) • TT—Meridian indicator (AM or PM) An example of a valid timestamp format string is: "YYYY/MM/DD HH:MM:SS.UUUUUU"	
usegraphiccodepage	Indicates that data being loaded into graphic or double-byte character large object (DBCLOB) columns is stored in the graphic code page. The rest of the data is assumed to be stored in the character code page. The Load utility determines the character code page either through the *codepage* modifier, if it is specified, or through the code page of the application if the *codepage* modifier is not specified. This modifier must not be specified with delimited ASCII (DEL) files created by the Export utility—those files contain data encoded in only one code page.	Delimited ASCII (DEL) and non-delimited ASCII (ASC)
chardel*x* where *x* is any valid delimiter character	Identifies a specific character that is to be used as a character delimiter. The default character delimiter is a double quotation mark (") character. The character specified is used in place of the double quotation mark to enclose a character string.	Delimited ASCII (DEL)
coldel*x* where *x* is any valid delimiter character	Identifies a specific character that is to be used as a column delimiter. The default column delimiter is a comma (,) character. The character specified is used in place of a comma to signal the end of a column.	Delimited ASCII (DEL)
decplusblank	Indicates that positive decimal values are to be prefixed with a blank space instead of a plus sign (+). The default action is to prefix positive decimal values with a plus sign.	Delimited ASCII (DEL)
decpt*x* where *x* is any valid delimiter character	Identifies a specific character that is to be used as a decimal point character. The default decimal point character is a period (.) character. The character specified is used in place of a period as a decimal point character.	Delimited ASCII (DEL)

Table 6.4 File Type Modifiers Recognized by the LOAD Command (continued)		
Modifier	**Description**	**File Format**
delprioritychar	Indicates that the priority for evaluating delimiters is to be *character delimiter, record delimiter, column delimiter* rather than *record delimiter, character delimiter, column delimiter* (which is the default). This modifier is typically used with older applications that depend on the first priority.	Delimited ASCII (DEL)
keepblanks	Indicates that all leading and trailing blanks found for each column that has a data type of CHAR, VARCHAR, LONG VARCHAR, or CLOB are to be retained. If this modifier is not specified, all leading and trailing blanks that reside outside character delimiters are removed, and a NULL is inserted into the table for all missing data values found.	Delimited ASCII (DEL)
nochardel	Indicates that the Load utility is to assume all bytes found between the column delimiters to be part of the column's data. (Character delimiters will be parsed as part of column data.) This modifier should not be specified if the data was exported by DB2 (unless the *nochardel* modifier was specified at export time). It is provided to support vendor data files that do not have character delimiters. Improper usage might result in data loss or corruption. This modifier cannot be specified with *chardelx*, *delprioritychar*, or *nodoubledel*. These are mutually exclusive options.	Delimited ASCII (DEL)
nodoubledel	Indicates that double character delimiters are to be ignored.	Delimited ASCII (DEL)
binarynumerics	Indicates that numeric (but not DECIMAL) data is stored in binary format rather than as character representations. When this modifier is used, the following conditions apply: • No conversion between data types is performed, with the exception of BIGINT, INTEGER, and SMALLINT. • Data lengths must match their target column definitions. • FLOAT values must be in IEEE Floating Point format. • The byte order of the binary data stored in the source file is assumed to be big-endian, regardless of the server platform used. (Little-endian computers—Intel-based PCs, VAX workstations, and so on—store the least significant byte (LSB) of a multi-byte word at the lowest address in a word and the most significant byte (MSB) at the highest address. Big-endian computers — machines based on the Motorola 68000a series of CPUs, such as Sun, Macintosh, and so on—do the opposite: the MSB is stored at the lowest address and the LSB is stored at the highest address.)	Non-delimited ASCII (ASC)

Table 6.4 File Type Modifiers Recognized by the LOAD Command (continued)		
Modifier	**Description**	**File Format**
	• NULLs cannot be present in the data for columns that are affected by this modifier. Blanks (normally interpreted as NULL) are interpreted as a binary value when this modifier is used.	
nochecklengths	Indicates that the Load utility is to attempt to load every row found in the source, even if the source data has a column value that exceeds the size of the target column's definition. Such rows can be successfully loaded if code page conversion causes the source data to shrink in size. For example, 4-byte EUC data found in a source file could shrink to 2-byte DBCS data in the target table and require half the space. This option is particularly useful if it is known in advance that the source data will always fit in a column despite mismatched column definitions/sizes.	Non-delimited ASCII (ASC) and PC Integrated Exchange Format (IXF)
nullindchar=*x* where *x* is any valid character	Identifies a specific character that is to be used as a null indicator value. The default null indicator is the letter *Y*. This modifier is case sensitive for EBCDIC data files, except when the character is an English letter. For example, if the null indicator character is specified to be the letter *N*, then the letter *n* is also recognized as a null indicator.	Non-delimited ASCII (ASC)
packeddecimal	Indicates that numeric DECIMAL data is stored in packed decimal format rather than as character representations. When this modifier is used, the following apply: • The byte order of the binary data stored in the source file is assumed to be big-endian, regardless of the server platform used. • NULLs cannot be present in the data for columns that are affected by this modifier. Blanks (normally interpreted as NULL) are interpreted as a binary value when this modifier is used.	Non-delimited ASCII (ASC)
reclen=*x* where *x* is any number between 1 and 32,767	Indicates that a specific number of characters are to be read from the source file for each row found; new-line characters are to be ignored instead of being used to indicate the end of a row.	Non-delimited ASCII (ASC)
striptblanks	Indicates that all leading and trailing blanks found for each column that has a data type of VARCHAR, LONG VARCHAR, VARGRAPHIC, or LONG VARGRAPHIC are to be truncated. This modifier is incompatible with the *striptnulls* modifier.	Non-delimited ASCII (ASC)
striptnulls	Indicates that all leading and trailing nulls (0x00 characters) found for each column that has a data type of VARCHAR, LONG VARCHAR, VARGRAPHIC, or LONG VARGRAPHIC are to be truncated. This modifier is incompatible with the *striptblanks* modifier.	Non-delimited ASCII (ASC)

Table 6.4 File Type Modifiers Recognized by the LOAD Command (continued)		
Modifier	Description	File Format
zoneddecimal	Indicates that numeric DECIMAL data is stored in zoned decimal format rather than as character representations. When this modifier is used, the following conditions apply: • Half-byte sign values can be one of the following: "+" = 0xC 0xA 0xE 0xF "-" = 0xD 0xB • Supported values for digits are 0x0 to 0x9. • Supported values for zones are 0x3 and 0xF.	Non-delimited ASCII (ASC)
forcein	Indicates that the Load utility is to accept data despite code page mismatches (in other words, to suppress translation between code pages). Fixed-length target columns are checked to verify that they are large enough to hold the data unless the *nochecklengths* modifier has been specified.	PC Integrated Exchange Format (IXF)
Adapted from Tables 16, 17, 18, 19, and 20 on pages 799–809 of the *IBM DB2 9 Command Reference* manual.		

As with the Import utility, one of three methods can be used to map data values found in external files to columns in a table: the location method, the name method, and the position method. The syntax used to indicate that the location method is to be used to extract data values from the external file specified is:

```
METHOD L ( [ColumnStart] [ColumnEnd] ,... )
    <NULL INDICATORS ( [NullIndColNumber ,...] )>
```

where:

ColumnStart   Identifies the starting position of one or more data values in the non-delimited ASCII (ASC) formatted file from which values are to be retrieved.

ColumnEnd   Identifies the ending position of one or more data values in the non-delimited ASCII (ASC) formatted file from which values are to be retrieved.

NullIndColNumber   Identifies the position of one or more data values that are to be treated as null indicator variables for column data values in the non-delimited ASCII (ASC) formatted file from which values are to be retrieved.

The syntax used to indicate that the name method is to be used to extract data values from the external file specified is:

```
METHOD  N  ( [ColumnName , ...] )
```

where:

ColumnName   Identifies one or more unique names assigned to columns in the PC Integrated Exchange Format (IXF) formatted file from which values are to be retrieved.

And the syntax used to indicate that the position method is to be used to extract data values from the external file specified is:

```
METHOD  P  ( [ColumnPosition , ...] )
```

where:

ColumnPosition   Identifies the indexed position of one or more columns in the delimited ASCII (DEL) or PC Integrated Exchange Format (IXF) formatted file from which values are to be retrieved.

As you can see, there are four different options available with the LOAD command that control how the table data to be copied to will be affected by the load operation. These options include the following:

INSERT. When the INSERT option is used, data is appended to the target table (which must already exist).

REPLACE. When the REPLACE option is used, any existing data is deleted from the target table (which must already exist); then the new data is loaded.

RESTART. When the RESTART option is used, any previous load operation that failed or was terminated is continued, starting from the last recorded point of consistency. If this option is used, the LOAD command specified must be identical to the LOAD command used to initiate the previous load operation (with the exception of the RESTART option specification).

TERMINATE. When the TERMINATE option is used, the current load operation is terminated, and any changes made are backed out if the load operation being terminated was started with the INSERT option. If the load operation being terminated was started with the REPLACE option specified, data in the target table is truncated.

So if you wanted to load data stored in a PC Integrated Exchange Format (IXF)–format external file named DEPT.IXF into an existing table named DEPARTMENT, you could do so by executing a LOAD command that looks something like this:

```
LOAD FROM C:\dept.ixf OF IXF
MESSAGES load_msgs.txt
INSERT INTO department
```

On the other hand, if you wanted to load data stored in a PC Integrated Exchange Format (IXF)–format external file named EMP_PHOTO.IXF, along with LOB data values stored in individual files, into a table named EMP_PHOTO and then update the statistics for the EMP_PHOTO table and its associated indexes, you could do so by executing a LOAD command that looks something like this:

```
LOAD FROM C:\emp_photo.ixf OF IXF
LOBS FROM C:\lob_data
MODIFIED BY lobsinfile
MESSAGES load_msgs.txt
REPLACE INTO emp_photo
STATISTICS USE PROFILE
```

In this case, you would have to execute the LOAD command with the REPLACE option specified; statistics cannot be collected if the LOAD command is executed with any option other than the REPLACE option specified. Additionally, a statistics profile for the EMP_PHOTO table must already exist (statistics profiles are created by executing the RUNSTATS command, which we will look at shortly). If a profile does not exist, and the Load utility is instructed to collect statistics, a warning is returned, and statistics are not collected.

Now, suppose you wanted to load data stored in a delimited ASCII (DEL)–format external file named DEPT.DEL into an existing table named DEPARTMENT, while allowing other transactions to read data that existed in the

DEPARTMENT table before the load operation was initiated. You could do so by executing a LOAD command that looks something like this:

```
LOAD FROM C:\dept.del OF DEL
MESSAGES load_msgs.txt
INSERT INTO department
ALLOW READ ACCESS
```

It is important to note that while this load operation is in process, the data residing in the table before the load operation was started will be accessible to other transactions. If, for some reason, the load operation fails, the original data in the table will remain available for read access.

And finally, if you wanted to load data stored in a delimited ASCII (DEL)–format external file named EMP.DEL into an existing table named EMPLOYEE, in such a way that records that violate constraints that have been defined for the EMPLOYEE table are written to a table named EMP_EXP, you could do so by executing a LOAD command that looks something like this:

```
LOAD FROM C:\emp.del OF DEL
MESSAGES load_msgs.txt
INSERT INTO employee
FOR EXCEPTION emp_exp
```

In this case, any record found that violates a constraint that has been defined for the EMPLOYEE table will be loaded into the EMP_EXP table, rather than the EMPLOYEE table.

> The Load utility can also be used to delete all records in a table without generating corresponding log records. Simply specify the null device (on UNIX this is /dev/null; on Windows it is nul) as the input file. For example,
>
> LOAD FROM /dev/null OF DEL REPLACE INTO department (UNIX)
>
> LOAD FROM nul OF DEL REPLACE INTO department (Windows)

Data can also be loaded into existing tables using the Load Wizard, which can be activated by selecting the appropriate action from the Tables menu found in the Control Center. (The Load Wizard cannot be used to load data from named pipes and devices.) Figure 6–12 shows the Control Center menu items that must be selected to activate the Load Wizard; Figure 6–13 shows how the first page of the Load Wizard typically looks when it is first activated.

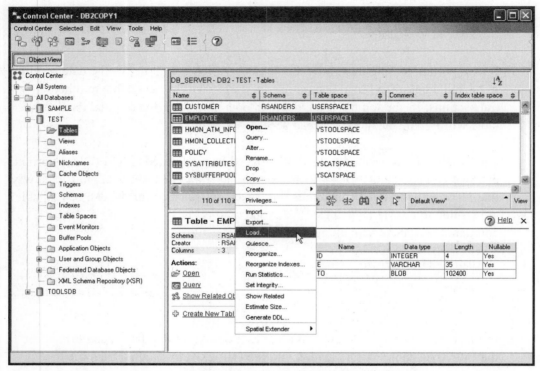

Figure 6–12: Invoking the Load Wizard from the Control Center.

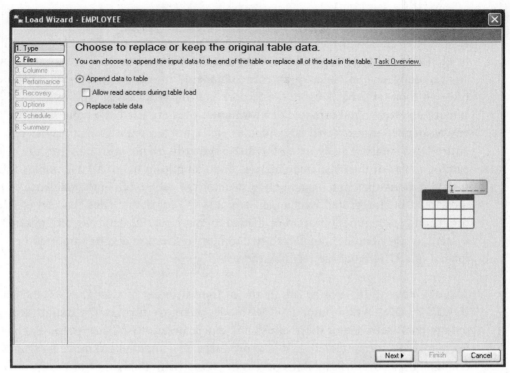

Figure 6–13: The first page of the Load Wizard.

Whether you use the LOAD command or the Load Wizard to perform a load operation, a database connection must be established before the Load utility is invoked.

Only users with System Administrator (SYSADM) authority, Database Administrator (DBADMN) authority, or Load (LOAD) authority and INSERT privilege on all tables referenced are allowed to load data using the INSERT option (or restart or terminate INSERT load operations). Only users with SYSADM authority, DBADMN authority, or LOAD authority and INSERT *and* DELETE privilege on all tables referenced are allowed to load data using the REPLACE option (or restart or terminate REPLACE load operations). And only users with SYSADM authority, DBADMN authority, or INSERT privilege on the exception table used are allowed to perform load operations in which invalid rows are written to an exception table.

db2move and db2look

It's easy to see how the Export utility can be used together with the Import utility or the Load utility to copy a table from one database to another. But what if you want to copy several tables or an entire database? In this case, data can be copied on a table-by-table basis using the Export and Import or Load utilities (if PC Integrated Exchange Format (IXF) formatted files are used, the table structure and any associated indexes will be copied as well), but a more efficient way to copy an entire DB2 database is by using the db2move utility. This utility queries the system catalog tables of the specified database and compiles a list of all user tables found. It then exports the contents and table structure of each table in the database to individual PC Integrated Exchange Format (IXF) formatted files. The set of files produced can then be imported or loaded to another DB2 database on the same system, or they can be transferred to another workstation and be imported or loaded to a DB2 database residing there.

The db2move utility can be run in one of four different modes: EXPORT, IMPORT, LOAD, or COPY. When run in EXPORT mode, db2move invokes the Export utility to extract data from one or more tables and externalize it to PC Integrated Exchange Format (IXF) formatted files. It also produces a file named db2move.lst that contains the names of all tables processed, along with the names of the files to which each table's data was written. Additionally, the db2move utility may also produce one or more message files that contain warning or error messages that were generated as a result of the Export operation.

When run in IMPORT mode, db2move invokes the Import utility to recreate each table and their associated indexes using information stored in PC Integrated Exchange Format (IXF) formatted files. When run in this mode, the file db2move.lst is used to establish a link between the PC Integrated Exchange Format (IXF) formatted files needed and the tables into which data is to be imported.

When run in LOAD mode, db2move invokes the Load utility to populate tables that already exist with data stored in PC Integrated Exchange Format (IXF) formatted files. (LOAD mode should never be used to populate an empty database that does not contain table definitions.) Again, the file db2move.lst is used to establish a link between the PC Integrated Exchange Format (IXF) formatted files needed and the tables into which data is to be loaded.

Unfortunately, the db2move utility can be used to migrate only table and index objects. If the database to be migrated contains other objects such as aliases, views, triggers, user-defined data types (UDTs), user-defined functions (UDFs), and so on, you must to duplicate those objects in the target database as well if you want to have an identical copy of the source database. That is where the db2look utility comes in. When invoked, db2look can reverse-engineer an existing database and produce a set of Data Definition Language (DDL) SQL statements, which can then be used to recreate all of the data objects found in the database that was analyzed. The db2look utility can also collect environment registry variable settings, configuration parameter settings, and statistical (RUNSTATS) information on the source system, which can be used to duplicate those settings on the target system.

To obtain more information about the db2move and db2look utilities, or to see the syntax used to invoke each of these commands, refer to the *IBM DB2, Version 9 Command Reference* product documentation.

Maintenance Utilities

Along with moving data between a database and external files, a database administrator often has to perform routine maintenance on a database in order to keep it running at optimum performance. In this section, we'll take a look at some of the utilities that are provided with DB2 for this purpose and at the functions they are designed to perform.

The REORGCHK Utility

The way in which data is physically distributed across table space containers can have a significant impact on how applications that access the data perform. And the way data gets distributed is controlled primarily by the insert, update, and delete operations that are executed against tables. For example, a series of insert operations will try to distribute data pages contiguously across table space containers. However, a subsequent delete operation may leave empty pages in storage that, for some reason, never get refilled. Or an update operation performed on a variable-length column may cause an entire row to be written to another page because a larger column value no longer allows the record to fit on the original page. In both cases, internal gaps are created in the underlying table space containers. As a consequence, the DB2 Database Manager may have to read more physical pages into memory in order to retrieve the data needed to satisfy a query.

So how do you know how much storage space is currently being utilized by data and how much is free, but part of an unusable gap? You can obtain this information by taking advantage of DB2's REORGCHK utility. When executed, this utility generates statistics on a database and analyzes the statistics produced to determine whether one or more tables need to be reorganized (which will cause any existing internal gaps to be removed).

The REORGCHK utility is invoked by executing the REORGCHK command, usually from the DB2 Command Line Processor. The basic syntax for this command is:

```
REORGCHK
<UPDATE STATISTICS | CURRENT STATISTICS>
<ON TABLE USER |
    ON SCHEMA [SchemaName] |
    ON TABLE [USER | SYSTEM | ALL | [TableName]>
```

where:

SchemaName Identifies the name assigned to a schema whose objects are to be analyzed to determine whether they need to be reorganized.

TableName Identifies the name assigned to a specific table that is to be analyzed to determine whether it needs to be reorganized.

So if you wanted to generate statistics for all tables that reside in the PAYROLL schema and have those statistics analyzed to determine whether one or more tables need to be reorganized, you could do so by executing a REORGCHK command that looks something like this:

```
REORGCHK UPDATE STATISTICS ON SCHEMA payroll
```

And when such a REORGCHK command is executed, output that looks something like the following will be produced:

Doing RUNSTATS ....

Table statistics:

F1: 100 * OVERFLOW / CARD < 5
F2: 100 * (Effective Space Utilization of Data Pages) > 70
F3: 100 * (Required Pages / Total Pages) > 80

SCHEMA	NAME	CARD	OV	NP	FP	ACTBLK	TSIZE	F1	F2	F3	REORG
PAYROLL	EMPLOYEE	32	0	2	2	-	2784	0	68	100	-*-
PAYROLL	DEPARTMENT	9	0	1	1	-	549	0	-	100	---

Index statistics:

F4: CLUSTERRATIO or normalized CLUSTERFACTOR > 80
F5: 100 * (Space used on leaf pages / Space available on non-empty
    leaf pages) > MIN(50, (100 - PCTFREE))
F6: (100 - PCTFREE) * (Amount of space available in an index with
    one less level / Amount of space required for all keys) < 100
F7: 100 * (Number of pseudo-deleted RIDs / Total number of RIDs) < 20
F8: 100 * (Number of pseudo-empty leaf pages / Total number of leaf
    pages) < 20

| SCHEMA.NAME | INDCARD | LEAF | ELEAF | LVLS | NDEL | KEYS | LEAF_RECSIZE |
| NLEAF_RECSIZE | LEAF_PAGE_OVERHEAD | NLEAF_PAGE_OVERHEAD | F4 | F5 | F6 | F7 | F8 |
REORG							

Table: PAYROLL.EMPLOYEE
Index: PAYROLL.PK_EMP

| | | 8 | 1 | 0 | 1 | 0 | 18 | 2 |
| 2 | 822 | | | | 822 | 100 | - - 0 | 0 |

CLUSTERRATIO or normalized CLUSTERFACTOR (F4) will indicate REORG is
necessary for indexes that are not in the same sequence as the base
table. When multiple indexes are defined on a table, one or more
indexes may be flagged as needing REORG. Specify the most important
index for REORG sequencing.

Tables defined using the ORGANIZE BY clause and the corresponding
dimension indexes have a '*' suffix to their names. The cardinality of a
dimension index is equal to the Active blocks statistic of the table.

Interpreting REORGCHK output

As you can see, the output generated by the REORGCHK utility is divided into two sections: one for table statistics and one for index statistics. The table statistics section shows the table statistics produced, along with the formulas that are used to determine whether table reorganization is necessary. If you examine the preceding sample output, the first things you will see listed after the "Table statistics" heading are three formulas named F1, F2, and F3.

- Formula F1 works with the number of overflow rows encountered. It will recommend that a table be reorganized if 5 percent or more of the total number of rows in the table are overflow rows. (Overflow rows are rows that have been moved to new pages because an update operation made them too large to be stored in the page they were written to originally or because new columns were added to an existing table.)

- Formula F2 works with free/unused space. It will recommend that a table be reorganized if the table size (TSIZE) is less than or equal to 70 percent of the size of the total storage space allocated for that table. In other words, if more than 30 percent of the total storage space allocated for the table is unused.

- Formula F3 works with free pages. It will recommend that a table be reorganized if 20 percent or more of the pages for that table are free. (A page is considered free when it does not contain any rows.)

Immediately below these three formulas is a table containing information about the values that were used to solve the formula equations for each table processed, along with the results. This table contains the following information:

SCHEMA.NAME. The fully qualified name of the table that was evaluated to determine whether reorganization is necessary.

CARD. The number of rows found in the table.

OV (OVERHEAD). The number of overflow rows found in the table.

NP (NUMBER OF USED PAGES). The number of pages that currently contain data.

FP (TOTAL NUMBER OF PAGES). The total number of pages that have been allocated for the table.

ACTBLK (ACTIVE BLOCKS). The total number of active blocks for a multidimensional clustering (MDC) table (the number of blocks of the table that contain data). This field is applicable only to tables that were defined using the ORGANIZE BY clause.

TSIZE (TABLE SIZE). The size of the table, in bytes. This value is calculated by multiplying the number of rows found in the table (CARD) by the average row length. The average row length is computed as the sum of the average column lengths (the AVGCOLLEN column in the system catalog table SYSCAT.SYSCOLUMNS) of all columns defined for the table plus 10 bytes for row overhead. For long data and LOB data columns, only the approximate length of the descriptor is used—the actual size of long data and LOB data columns is not included in TSIZE.

F1. The results of Formula F1.

F2. The results of Formula F2.

F3. The results of Formula F3.

REORG. A set of indicators that point out whether the table needs to be reorganized. Each hyphen (-) displayed in this column indicates that the calculated results were within the set bounds of the corresponding formula, and each asterisk (*) indicates that the calculated results exceeded the set bounds of the corresponding formula. The first - or * corresponds to Formula 1, the second - or * corresponds to Formula 2, and the third - or * corresponds to Formula 3. Table reorganization is suggested when the results of the calculations exceed the bounds set for the formula. For example, the value --- indicates that because the results of F1, F2, and F3 are within the set bounds of each formula, no table reorganization is necessary. The notation -*- indicates that the results of F2 suggest that the table be reorganized, even though the results of F2 and F3 are within their set bounds.

The index statistics section shows information about the index statistics produced, along with the formulas used to determine whether index reorganization is necessary. This section is marked by the heading "Index statistics," which is followed by the formulas F4, F5, and F6.

- Formula F4 works with the cluster ratio or normalized cluster factor of an index. This ratio identifies the percentage of table data rows that are stored in the same physical sequence as the indexed data for the table. It will recommend that a table be reorganized if the cluster ratio for the index is less than 80 percent. (Often, the cluster ratio is not optimal for indexes that contain several duplicate keys and a large number of entries.)

- Formula F5 works with storage space that has been reserved for index entries. It will recommend that a table be reorganized if 50 percent or more of the storage space allocated for an index is empty.

- Formula F6 measures the usage of the index's pages. It will recommend that a table be reorganized if the actual number of entries found in the index is less than 90 percent of the number of entries (NLEVELS) the index tree can handle.

- Formula F7 measures the number of pseudo-deleted record IDs (RIDs) on non-pseudo-empty pages. It will recommend that a table be reorganized if the actual number of pseudo-deleted record IDs (RIDs) found on non-pseudo-empty pages is more than 20 percent.

- Formula F8 measures the number of pseudo-empty leaf pages found. It will recommend that a table be reorganized if the actual number of pseudo-empty leaf pages found in the index is more than 20 percent of the total number of leaf pages available.

Immediately below these three formulas is a table that contains information about the values that were used to solve the formula equations for each index processed, along with the results. This table contains the following information:

SCHEMA.NAME. The fully qualified name of the index that was evaluated to determine whether reorganization is necessary.

INDCARD (INDEX CARDINALITY). The number of rows found in the index. (This could be different than table cardinality for some indexes. For example, for indexes on XML columns, the index cardinality is likely greater than the table cardinality.)

LEAF. The total number of index leafs (pages) that have been allocated for the index.

ELEAF (EMPTY LEAFS). The number of pseudo-empty index leaf pages found. A pseudo-empty index leaf page is a page on which all the record IDs are marked as deleted, even though they have not yet been physically removed.

LVLS (LEVELS). The total number of levels the index has.

NDEL (NUMBER OF DELETED RECORDS). Number of pseudo-deleted record IDs. A pseudo-deleted record ID (RID) is a RID that is marked deleted. This statistic reports pseudo-deleted RIDs on leaf pages that are not pseudo-empty. It does not include RIDs marked as deleted on leaf pages where all the RIDs are marked deleted.

KEYS. The number of unique entries found in the index.

LEAF_RECSIZE (LEAF RECORD SIZE). Record size of the index entry on a leaf page. This is the average size of the index entry excluding any overhead, and it is calculated from the average column length of all columns participating in the index.

NLEAF_RECSIZE (NON-LEAF RECORD SIZE). Record size of the index entry on a non-leaf page. This is the average size of the index entry excluding any overhead, and it is calculated from the average column length of all columns participating in the index except any INCLUDE columns.

LEAF_PAGE_OVERHEAD. Space on each index leaf page that is reserved for internal use.

NLEAF_PAGE_OVERHEAD. Space on each non-index leaf page that is reserved for internal use.

F4. The results of Formula F4.

F5. The results of Formula F5. (The notation +++ indicates that the result exceeds 999 and is invalid, in which case the REORGCHK utility should be run again with the UPDATE STATISTICS option specified.)

F6. The results of Formula F6. (The notation +++ indicates that the result exceeds 999 and is invalid, in which case the REORGCHK utility should be run again with the UPDATE STATISTICS option specified.)

F7. The results of Formula 7.

F8. The results of Formula 8.

REORG. A set of indicators that point out whether the index needs to be reorganized. Each hyphen (-) displayed in this column indicates that the calculated results were within the set bounds of the corresponding formula, and each asterisk (*) indicates that the calculated results exceeded the set bounds of the corresponding formula. The first - or * corresponds to Formula 4, the second - or * corresponds to Formula 5, and so on. Index reorganization is suggested when the results of the calculations exceed the bounds set for the formula. For example, the value ----- indicates that because the results of F4, F5, F6, F7, and F8 are within the set bounds of each formula, no index reorganization is necessary. The notation -*--- indicates that the results of F5 suggest that the index be reorganized, even though the results of F4, F6, F7, and F8 are within their set bounds.

The REORG Utility

Upon careful evaluation of the output produced by the REORGCHK utility, you may discover that one or more tables or indexes need to be reorganized. If that's the case, you can reorganize them using DB2's REORG utility. The REORG utility eliminates gaps in table space containers by retrieving the data stored in a table and one or more of its associated indexes and rewriting it onto unfragmented, physically contiguous pages in storage. (The REORG utility works much like the way a disk defragmenter works). The REORG utility can also physically order the data rows of the table to mirror the logical order presented by a particular index, thereby increasing the cluster ratio of the specified index. This behavior has an attractive side effect—if the DB2 Database Manager finds that the data needed to resolve a query is stored in contiguous storage space and already ordered, the overall performance of the query will be improved because the seek time needed to retrieve the data will be shorter. The REORG utility can also be used to convert Type-1 indexes to Type-2 indexes.

The REORG utility can be invoked by executing the REORG command. The basic syntax for this command is:

```
REORG TABLE [TableName]
<INDEX [IndexName]>
<ALLOW READ ACCESS | ALLOW NO ACCESS>
<USE [TmpTSName]>
<INDEXSCAN>
<LONGLOBDATA <USE [LongTSName]>>
<KEEPDICTIONARY | RESETDICTIONARY>
```

or

```
REORG TABLE [TableName]
<INDEX [IndexName]>
INPLACE
[ALLOW READ ACCESS | ALLOW NO ACCESS]
<NOTRUNCATE TABLE>
[START | RESUME]
```

or

```
REORG TABLE [TableName]
<INDEX [IndexName]>
INPLACE
[STOP | PAUSE]
```

or

```
REORG [INDEXES ALL FOR TABLE [SrcTableName] |
        INDEX [SrcIndexName] <FOR TABLE [SrcTableName]>]
<ALLOW READ ACCESS | ALLOW WRITE ACCESS | ALLOW NO ACCESS>
<CLEANUP ONLY ALL | CLEANUP ONLY PAGES | CONVERT>
```

where:

TableName	Identifies the name assigned to the table whose physical layout is to be reorganized.
IndexName	Identifies the name assigned to the associated index that is to be used to order the data stored in the table that is to be reorganized. (If no index name is specified, the data in the table is reorganized without any regard to order.)
TmpTSName	Identifies the system temporary table space in which the DB2 Database Manager is to temporarily store a copy of the table to be reorganized. (If no table space name is specified, the DB2 Database Manager will store a working copy of the table to be reorganized in the same table space the table resides in.)
LongTSName	Identifies the temporary table space that the DB2 Database Manager is to use for rebuilding long data. (If no table space name is specified, the DB2 Database Manager will rebuild long data objects in the table space where they reside.)
SrcTableName	Identifies the name assigned to the table whose associated indexes are to be reorganized.
SrcIndexName	Identifies the name assigned to the index whose physical layout is to be reorganized.

If the CLEANUP ONLY option is specified, a cleanup operation rather than a full reorganization will be performed. As a result, indexes will not be rebuilt, and any pages freed up will be available only for reuse by the indexes defined on the table specified.

Thus, if you wanted to reorganize the data for a table named EMPLOYEE and physically order the data to match the order presented by an index named EMPNO_PK, you could do so by executing a REORG command that looks something like this:

```
REORG TABLE employee INDEX empno_pk
```

On the other hand, if you wanted to reorganize a table named MKT_VALUE and cluster its rows based on index MKT_INDX, you could do so by executing the following command:

```
REORG TABLE mkt_value INDEX mkt_indx USE tbspace1
```

Tables and indexes can also be reorganized using the Reorganize Table and Reorganize Index dialogs, which can be activated by selecting the appropriate action from the Tables menu found in the Control Center. Figure 6–14 shows the Control Center menu items that must be selected in order to activate the Reorganize Table dialog; Figure 6–15 shows how the Reorganize Table dialog typically looks when it is first activated; Figure 6–16 shows the Control Center menu items that must be selected in order to activate the Reorganize Index dialog; Figure 6–17 shows how the Reorganize Index dialog normally looks when it is first activated.

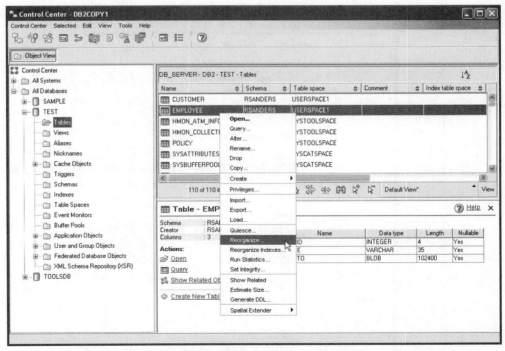

Figure 6–14: Invoking the Reorganize Table dialog from the Control Center.

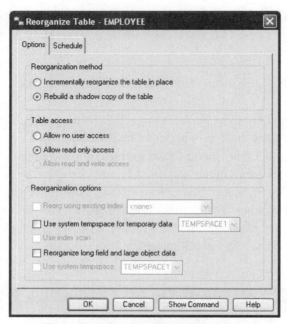

Figure 6–15: The Reorganize Table dialog.

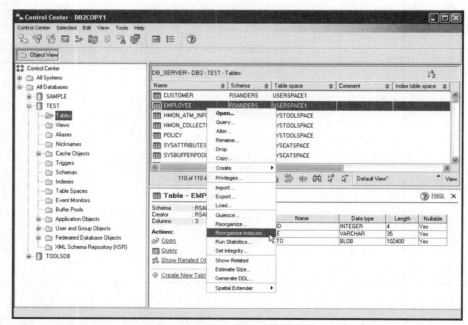

Figure 6–16: Invoking the Reorganize Index dialog from the Control Center.

Figure 6–17: The Reorganize Index dialog.

The RUNSTATS Utility

Among other things, the system catalog tables for a database can contain statistical information such as the number of rows stored in a table, the way tables and indexes utilize storage space, and a count of the number of unique values found in a particular column. Such information is used by the DB2 Optimizer when deciding on the best access plan to use to obtain data in response to a query. (Whenever an SQL statement is sent to the DB2 Database Manager for processing, the DB2 Optimizer reads the system catalog tables to determine the size of each table referenced, the characteristics of each column referenced, whether indexes have been defined for the tables/columns referenced, and to obtain other similar information. Using this information, the DB2 Optimizer then determines the best access path to take to satisfy the needs of the SQL statement.) Therefore, if the information needed by the DB2 Optimizer is missing or out of date, the access plan chosen may cause the SQL statement to take longer to execute than necessary. Having valid information available becomes more crucial as the complexity of the SQL statement increases—with simple statements, there are usually a limited number of choices available; with complex statements, the number of choices available increases dramatically.

Prior to DB2 Version 9, the information used by the DB2 Optimizer was not automatically updated as changes were made to a database. Instead, this information had to be updated periodically by manually running DB2's RUNSTATS utility. Starting with DB2 Version 9, automatic statistics collection (part of DB2's Automated Table Maintenance feature) is enabled by default when a new database is created. As long as automatic statistics collection remains enabled, DB2 will automatically execute the RUNSTATS utility in the background to ensure that the most current database statistics are available.

If automatic statistics collection is disabled, the RUNSTATS utility can be invoked by executing the RUNSTATS command. The basic syntax for this command is:

```
RUNSTATS ON TABLE [TableName]
USE PROFILE
<UTIL_IMPACT_PRIORITY [Priority]>
```

or

```
RUNSTATS ON TABLE [TableName] FOR
<<SAMPLED> DETAILED>
[INDEXES | INDEX]
[[IndexName,...] | ALL]
<EXCLUDING XML COLUMNS>
<ALLOW READ ACCESS | ALLOW WRITE ACCESS>
<SET PROFILE NONE | SET PROFILE <ONLY> | UPDATE PROFILE
    <ONLY>>
<UTIL_IMPACT_PRIORITY [Priority]>
```

or

```
RUNSTATS ON TABLE [TableName]
<ON ALL COLUMNS |
    ON KEY COLUMNS> |
    ON COLUMNS [ColumnName ,...] |
    ON ALL COLUMNS AND COLUMNS [ColumnName ,...] |
    ON KEY COLUMNS AND COLUMNS [ColumnName ,...]>
<WITH DISTRIBUTION>
<EXCLUDING XML COLUMNS>
<AND <<SAMPLED> DETAILED>
    [INDEXES | INDEX]
    [[IndexName,...] | ALL]>
<EXCLUDING XML COLUMNS>
<ALLOW READ ACCESS | ALLOW WRITE ACCESS>
<SET PROFILE NONE | SET PROFILE <ONLY> | UPDATE PROFILE
    <ONLY>>
<UTIL_IMPACT_PRIORITY [Priority]>
```

where:

TableName	Identifies the name assigned to the table for which statistical information is to be collected. This can be any base table including a VOLATILE table.
IndexName	Identifies the name assigned to one or more associated indexes for which statistical information is to be collected.
ColumnName	Identifies the name assigned to one or more columns for which statistical information is to be collected.
Priority	Indicates that the RUNSTATS utility is to be throttled such that it executes at a specific rate so that its effect on concurrent database activity can be controlled. This parameter can be assigned a numerical value within the range of 1 to 100, with 100 representing the highest priority and 1 representing the lowest.

Thus, if you wanted to collect statistics for a table named EMPLOYEE (which resides in a schema named PAYROLL) along with all of its associated indexes and allow read-only access to the table while statistics are being gathered, you could do so by executing a RUNSTATS command that looks something like this:

```
RUNSTATS ON TABLE payroll.employee
FOR INDEXES ALL
ALLOW READ ACCESS
```

On the other hand, if you only wanted to collect basic statistics, and distribution statistics for all eligible columns of a table named DEPARTMENT (which resides in a schema named PAYROLL), you could do so by executing a RUNSTATS command that looks something like this:

```
RUNSTATS ON TABLE payroll.department
ON ALL COLUMNS
WITH DISTRIBUTION DEFAULT
```

(Statistics collection can be done on some columns and not on others. For example, columns with data types such as LONG VARCHAR and CLOB are ineligible.)

The RUNSTATS utility does not provide output information other than a success or failure message. To view the results of a RUNSTATS operation, you must examine the contents of the CARD, OVERFLOW, NPAGES, and FPAGES columns of the system catalog table named SYSCAT.TABLES. (If the value of any of these columns is −1, statistical information has not been produced for the object that is identified by that particular row.)

Statistical information for tables and indexes can also be collected using the Run Statistics dialog, which can be activated by selecting the appropriate action from the Tables menu found in the Control Center. Figure 6–18 shows the Control Center menu items that must be selected in order to activate the Run Statistics dialog; Figure 6–19 shows how the Run Statistics dialog typically looks when it is first activated.

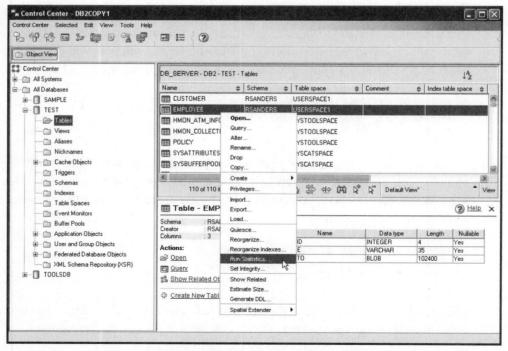

Figure 6–18: Invoking the Run Statistics dialog from the Control Center.

Figure 6–19: The Run Statistics dialog.

So just how often should the RUNSTATS utility be used? Ideally, the RUNSTATS utility should be run immediately after any of the following occur:

- A large number of insert, update, or delete operations are performed against a specific table.

- An import operation is performed.

- A load operation is performed.

- One or more columns are added to an existing table.

- A new index is created.

- A table or index is reorganized.

It is also a good idea to run the RUNSTATS utility before running the REORGCHK utility; if query response is slow because of fragmentation and statistics are not up to date, the REORGCHK utility may report that a table/index reorganization operation is unnecessary when it really is.

A word about rebinding

Earlier, we saw that the DB2 Optimizer uses the statistical information produced by the RUNSTATS utility to select the best access plan to use to obtain data in response to a query. Because the DB2 Optimizer generates an access plan each time a dynamic SQL statement is prepared for execution, applications using dynamic SQL may see performance improvements immediately after new statistical information has been produced. Unfortunately, that is not the case for applications that use static SQL. That's because the DB2 Optimizer generates access plans for static SQL statements only when the package that contains those statement is bound to the database. Therefore, in order for existing packages to take advantage of new statistical information produced by the RUNSTATS utility, they must be rebound to the database so that the DB2 Optimizer will evaluate the new information and formulate new access plans (which may or may not perform better that the original access plan used).

The easiest way to rebind an existing package—provided the application source code used to produce the package has not changed—is by executing the REBIND command. The basic syntax for this command is:

```
REBIND <PACKAGE> [PackageName]
<VERSION [Version]>
RESOLVE [ANY | CONSERVATIVE]
<REOPT NONE | REOPT ONCE | REOPT ALWAYS>
```

where:

PackageName   Identifies the name assigned to the package that is to be rebound.

IndexName   Identifies a specific version of the package that is to be rebound.

If the REOPT NONE option is specified, the access path for SQL statements containing host variables, parameter markers, or special registers will not be optimized using real values—default estimates for these variables/markers/registers will be used instead. If the REOPT ONCE option is specified, the access path for SQL statements containing host variables, parameter markers, or special registers will be optimized using real values when the statement is first executed. And finally, if the REOPT ALWAYS option is specified, the access path for SQL statements containing host variables, parameter markers, or special registers will be optimized using real values each time the statement is executed.

Thus, if you wanted to rebind a package named EMP_MGMT, you could do so by executing a REBIND command that looks something like this:

```
REBIND PACKAGE emp_mgmt
```

Any time statistics are collected for a table with the RUNSTATS utility, packages that contain access plans for retrieving data from the table should be rebound with the REBIND utility.

Flushing the package cache

If a dynamic SQL statement is prepared, and its corresponding access plan is placed in memory *before* new statistical information is collected, and if the application that uses the statement is coded such that the statement is prepared once and executed multiple times, that particular statement will not be able to take advantage of the new statistical information produced by the RUNSTATS utility until it is re-prepared. In most cases, this behavior is acceptable. However, if the new statistical information could result in significant performance gains, you may wish to take advantage of the new information immediately, as opposed to waiting for the cached package to get rebuilt.

The FLUSH PACKAGE CACHE SQL statement provides database administrators with the ability to remove cached dynamic SQL statement packages from memory (the package cache) by invalidating them. The invalidation of a cached dynamic SQL statement package has no affect on current users of the statement; however, once a package is invalidated, any new requests for the statement with which the invalidated package was associated will cause the statement to be reprocessed by the DB2 Optimizer, which in turn will produce a new cached package (which may or may not contain a more efficient access plan). The basic syntax for the FLUSH PACKAGE CACHE statement is:

```
FLUSH PACKAGE CACHE DYNAMIC
```

Once this statement is executed, any cached packages associated with dynamic SQL statements that are currently in use will be allowed to continue to exist in the package cache until they are no longer needed by their current user; the next new user of the same statement will force the DB2 Database manager to implicitly prepare the statement, and the new user will then execute the new version of the cached dynamic SQL statement.

Other Utilities

Along with data movement utilities and maintenance utilities, DB2 provides additional tools that can be used to help pinpoint performance bottlenecks and make recommendations for additional data objects that can improve overall performance. In this section, we'll take a look at some of those utilities and the functions they are designed to perform.

The db2batch Utility

Benchmark testing is a normal part of the application development life cycle; ideally, it is a team effort that involves both application developers and database administrators. Typically, two different types of benchmark tests are run to obtain two different kinds of information:

- A transaction-per-second benchmark determines the throughput capabilities of the DB2 Database Manager under certain limited laboratory conditions.

- An application benchmark tests throughput capabilities under conditions that mirror production conditions.

Benchmarking can also be helpful in understanding how the DB2 Database Manager responds under varying conditions. For example, you can create scenarios that test deadlock handling, utility performance, different methods of loading data, transaction rate characteristics as more users are added, and the effect of using a new release of DB2 software, just to name a few.

Benchmarking is performed by developing a test scenario and then running the scenario several times, capturing key information during each run. You can develop an elaborate application specifically for this purpose, or a simpler approach is to take advantage of DB2's db2batch utility. The db2batch utility is a simple benchmark tool that reads SQL statements and/or XQuery expressions from either an ASCII format file or standard input; dynamically prepares, describes, and executes the statements/expressions found; and returns a result set that includes, among other things, the timing for the execution.

The db2batch utility is invoked by executing the db2batch command. The basic syntax for this command is:

```
db2batch
<-d [DatabaseAlias]>
<-f [InFile]>
<-a [Authorization]>
<-m [ParametersFile]>
<-t [Delimiter]>
<-r [OutFile] <,SummaryFile>>
<-c [on | off]>
<-i [short | long | complete]>
<-g [on | off]>
<-w [32768 | ColumnWidth]>
<-time [on | off]>
<-msw MonSwitch [hold | on | off]>
<-mss Snapshot>
<-iso [RR | RS | CS | UR]>
<-v [on | off]>
<-s [on | off]>
<-q [off | on | del]>
<-l TermDelimiter>
<-h>
```

where:

DatabaseAlias   Identifies, by alias, the database against which SQL statements and XQuery statements are to be applied. If this option is not specified, the value of the DB2DBDFT environment variable is used.

InFile   Identifies the name assigned to an ASCII format file that contains SQL statements and XQuery expressions that constitute the benchmark workload.

Authorization   Specifies the authentication ID (or user ID) and password, separated by a forward slash (/), that are to be used to establish a connection to the database specified.

ParametersFile   Identifies an input file containing parameter values that are to be bound to any SQL statement parameter markers used before executing a statement.

Delimiter   Specifies a single character that is to act as a column separator. (Specify "–t TAB" for a tab column delimiter or "–t SPACE" for a space column delimiter. By default, a space is used when the "-q on" option is set, and a comma is used when the "-q del" option is set.)

OutFile   Identifies an output file to which query results are to be written.

SummaryFile   Identifies an output file to which summary information is to be written.

ColumnWidth   Specifies the maximum column width of the result data set produced, with an allowable range of 0 to 2G. Data is truncated to this width when displayed, unless the data cannot be truncated.

MonSwitch   Identifies a specific snapshot monitor switch that is to be set. Valid values for this parameter are uow, statement, table, bufferpool, lock, sort, timestamp, and all.

Snapshot   Identifies the type of snapshot(s) that should be taken after each statement or block is executed (depending on the value of the -g option). Valid values for this parameter are applinfo_all, dbase_applinfo, dcs_applinfo_all, db2, dbase, dbase_all, dcs_dbase, dcs_dbase_all, dbase_remote, dbase_remote_all, agent_id, dbase_appls, appl_all, dcs_appl_all, dcs_appl_handle, dcs_dbase_appls, dbase_appls_remote, appl_remote_all, dbase_tables, appl_locks_agent_id, dbase_locks, dbase_tablespaces, bufferpools_all, dbase_bufferpools, dynamic_sql, and all.

TermDelimiter   Specifies 1 or 2 characters that are to serve as a termination character (delimiter). The default is a semi-colon (;).

All other options shown with this command are described in Table 6.5.

Table 6.5 db2bench Command Options	
Option	**Meaning**
-c	Indicates whether changes resulting from each SQL statement/XQuery expression executed are to be automatically committed.
-i	Indicates which time intervals are to be measured. SHORT indicates that db2batch is to measure the elapsed time required to run each statement. LONG indicates that db2batch is to measure the elapsed time required to run each statement including any overhead between statements. COMPLETE indicates that db2batch is to measure the elapsed time required to run each statement and report the times needed to prepare, execute, and fetch data separately.
-g	Specifies whether timing is to be reported by block or by statement. ON indicates that a snapshot is taken for the entire block, and only block timing is reported in the summary table. OFF indicates that a snapshot is taken, and summary table timing is reported for each statement executed in the block.
-iso	Specifies the isolation level to use, which determines how transactions are locked and isolated from other processes while the data is being accessed. By default, db2batch uses the Repeatable Read (RR) isolation level.
-v	Indicates that db2batch is to be run in verbose mode. (Information is sent to standard error during query processing.)
-s	Specifies whether db2batch should stop running when a noncritical error occurs.
-q	Specifies how query results are to be returned. OFF indicates query results and all associated information are to be returned to standard output (stdout). ON indicates that only query results are to be returned in non-delimited ASCII format. DEL indicates that only query results are to be returned in delimited ASCII format.
-h | -u | -?	Displays help information. When this option is specified, all other options are ignored, and only the help information is displayed.

The easiest way to conduct benchmark testing with the db2batch utility is by constructing a file that contains one or more queries that represent a typical workload and providing that file's contents as input to the db2batch command. Such a file might look something like this:

```
-- File Name: wkload.sql
-- Execution Command:
--        db2batch -d sample -f test.sql -r results.txt
---------------------------------------------------------

--#SET PERF_DETAIL 1
--#SET ROWS_OUT 5
-- This query lists employees, the name of their department
-- and the number of activities to which they are assigned
-- for employees who are assigned to more than one activity
-- less than full-time.
```

```
--#COMMENT Query 1
SELECT lastname, firstnme,
       deptname, count(*) AS num_act
FROM employee, department, emp_act
WHERE employee.workdept = department.deptno AND
      employee.empno = emp_act.empno AND
      emp_act.emptime < 1
GROUP BY lastname, firstnme, deptname
HAVING count(*) > 2;
```

Once such a file is created, benchmark testing can be conducted by executing a db2batch command that looks something like this (assuming the file containing the workload is named WKLOAD.SQL and the workload is to be run against a database named SAMPLE):

```
db2batch -d sample -f test.sql -r results.txt
```

When this command is executed, results collected by db2batch will be recorded in a file named RESULTS.TXT and can be reviewed after each benchmark run.

The Design Advisor

Earlier, we saw how the RUNSTATS utility can be used to update system catalog statistics and force the DB2 Optimizer to use those statistics to provide optimum access plans in response to a query or XQuery expression. Another factor that can have great influence on access plan selection is the existence (or nonexistence) of appropriate indexes.

So how do you decide when having an index would be beneficial, and how do you determine what indexes should exist? If you have a lot of experience with database and database application design, these decisions may be easy to make. On the other hand, if you have relatively little experience in this area, or if you want to validate the decisions you have already made, you can turn to DB2's Design Advisor.

The Design Advisor is a special tool that is designed to identify indexes, materialized query tables (MQTs), and multidimensional clustering tables (MDCs) that could help improve query performance in your database environment. Using current database statistics, the DB2 Optimizer, snapshot monitor information, and/or a specific query or set of SQL statements (known as a workload) you provide, the Design Advisor recommends one or more indexes that would improve query/workload performance. In addition, the indexes/MQTs/MDCs recommended, the statistics derived for them, and the data definition language (DDL) statements required to create them can be written to a user-created table named ADVISE_INDEX, if so desired.

The Design Advisor is invoked by executing the db2advis command. The basic syntax for this command is:

```
db2advis [-d | -db] [DatabaseName]
<-w [WorkloadName]>
<-s "[SQLStatement]">
<-i [InFile]>
<-g>
<-qp>
<-a [UserID] </[Password]>
<-m [AdviseType ,...]>
<-l [DiskLimit]>
<-t "[MaxAdviseTime]">
<-k [high | med | low | off]>
<-h>
<-p>
<-o [OutFile]>
```

where:

DatabaseName	Identifies, by name, the database with which the Design Advisor is to interact.
WorkloadName	Identifies the name of a workload that is to be analyzed to determine whether new indexes/MQTs/MDCs should be created.
SQLStatement	Identifies a single SQL statement that is to be analyzed to determine whether new indexes/MQTs/MDCs should be created.
InFile	Identifies the name assigned to an ASCII format file that contains a set of SQL statements that are to be analyzed to determine whether new indexes/MQTs/MDCs should be created.
UserID	Identifies the authentication ID (or user ID) that is to be used to establish a connection to the database specified.
Password	Identifies the password that is to be used to establish a connection to the database specified.

AdviseType   Specifies one or more types of recommendations for which the Design Advisor is to analyze. Valid values for this parameter include the following: I (index), M (materialized query tables [MQTs] and indexes on the MQTs), C (convert standard tables to multidimensional clustering [MDC] tables), and P (repartitioning of existing tables).

DiskLimit   Identifies the maximum amount of storage space, in megabytes, that is available for all indexes/MQTs/MDCs in the existing schema.

MaxAdviseTime   Identifies the maximum amount of time, in minutes, in which the Design Advisor will be allowed to conduct an analysis. When this time limit is reached, the Design Advisor will stop all processing.

OutFile   Identifies the name of the file to which the DDL that is needed to create the indexes/MQTs/MDCs recommended is to be written.

All other options shown with this command are described in Table 6.6.

Table 6.6 db2advis Command Options	
Option	**Meaning**
-g	Specifies that the SQL statements that make up the workload are to be retrieved from a dynamic SQL snapshot. If combined with the -p parameter, the SQL statements are kept in the ADVISE_WORKLOAD table.
-qp	Specifies that the workload is coming from the DB2 Query Patroller.
-k	Specifies to what degree the workload will be compressed. Compression is done to allow the advisor to reduce the complexity of the advisor's execution while achieving similar results to those the advisor could provide when the full workload is considered. HIGH indicates that the advisor will concentrate on a small subset of the workload. MED indicates that the advisor will concentrate on a medium-sized subset of the workload. LOW indicates that the advisor will concentrate on a larger subset of the workload. OFF indicates that no compression will occur, and every query is considered.
-p	Specifies that the plans that were generated while running the Design Advisor are to be kept in the explain tables. This option causes the workload for -qp and -g to be saved in the ADVISE_WORKLOAD table and the workload query plans that use the final recommendation to be saved in the Explain tables.
-h	Displays help information. When this option is specified, all other options are ignored, and only the help information is displayed.

The easiest way to determine whether an index, MQT, and/or MDC would improve the performance of a workload is by constructing a file that contains one or more queries that represent a typical workload and providing that file's contents as input to the db2advis command. Such a file might look something like this:

```
-- File Name: wkload.sql
-- Execution Command:
--        db2advis -d sample -i db2advis.sql -t 5

-- Evaluate the following set of statements 100 times
--#SET FREQUENCY 100
SELECT COUNT(*) FROM employee;
SELECT * FROM employee WHERE lastname='HAAS';

-- Evaluate the following statement once
--#SET FREQUENCY 1
SELECT AVG(bonus), AVG(salary) FROM employee
    GROUP BY workdept ORDER BY workdept;
```

Once such a file is created, analysis can be conducted by executing a db2advis command that looks something like this (assuming the file containing the workload is named WKLOAD.SQL, and the workload is to be run against a database named SAMPLE):

```
db2advis -d sample -i db2advis.sql -t 5
```

When this command is executed, the results produced might look something like this:

```
Using user id as default schema name. Use -n option to specify schema
execution started at timestamp 2007-05-13-10.27.28.134000
found [3] SQL statements from the input file
Recommending indexes...
total disk space needed for initial set [   0.017] MB
total disk space constrained to        [  11.439] MB
Trying variations of the solution set.
Optimization finished.
  1  indexes in current solution
 [1520.9002] timerons  (without recommendations)
 [820.9002] timerons  (with current solution)
 [46.03%] improvement

--
-- LIST OF RECOMMENDED INDEXES
-- ===========================
-- index[1],    0.017MB
   CREATE INDEX "RSANDERS"."IDX705131427300000" ON "RSANDERS"."EMPLOYEE"
```

```
        ("LASTNAME" ASC, "COMM" ASC, "BONUS" ASC, "SALARY"
        ASC, "BIRTHDATE" ASC, "SEX" ASC, "EDLEVEL" ASC, "JOB"
        ASC, "HIREDATE" ASC, "PHONENO" ASC, "WORKDEPT" ASC,
        "MIDINIT" ASC, "FIRSTNME" ASC, "EMPNO" ASC) ALLOW
        REVERSE SCANS ;
        COMMIT WORK ;
        RUNSTATS ON TABLE "RSANDERS"."EMPLOYEE" FOR INDEX
"RSANDERS"."IDX705131427300000" ;
        COMMIT WORK ;

    --
    -- RECOMMENDED EXISTING INDEXES
    -- ==============================
    -- RUNSTATS ON TABLE "RSANDERS"."EMPLOYEE" FOR INDEX "RSANDERS"."XEMP2" ;
    -- COMMIT WORK ;

    --
    -- UNUSED EXISTING INDEXES
    -- ==============================
    -- ==============================
    --

    31 solutions were evaluated by the advisor
    DB2 Workload Performance Advisor tool is finished.
```

A GUI version of the Design Advisor (known as the Design Advisor Wizard) is also available. The Design Advisor Wizard can be activated by selecting the appropriate action from the Databases menu found in the Control Center. Figure 6–20 shows the Control Center menu items that must be selected in order to activate the Design Advisor Wizard; Figure 6–21 shows how the first page of the Design Advisor Wizard typically looks after it has been activated.

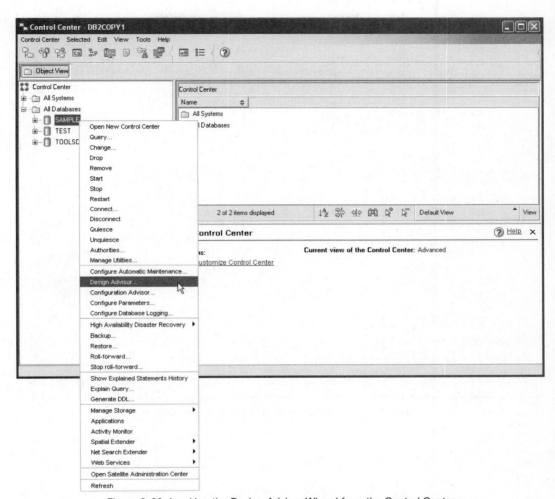

Figure 6–20: Invoking the Design Advisor Wizard from the Control Center.

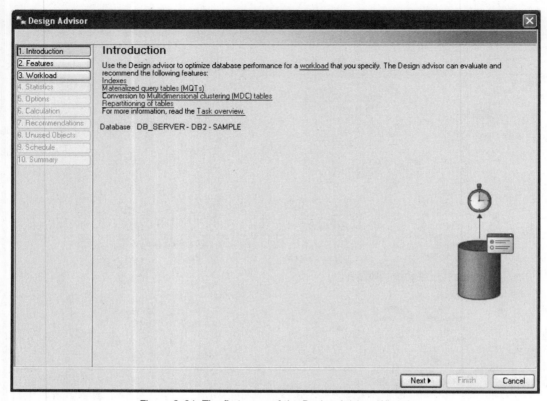

Figure 6–21: The first page of the Design Advisor Wizard.

Practice Questions

Question 1

Which of the following is NOT a method by which the Export utility can be invoked?

○ A. Control Center

○ B. Command Line Processor

○ C. ADMIN_CMD stored procedure

○ D. Replication Center

Question 2

Which of the following IMPORT command options will cause the Import utility to acquire a table-level lock after every commit?

○ A. ALLOW NO ACCESS

○ B. ALLOW READ ACCESS

○ C. ALLOW WRITE ACCESS

○ D. ALLOW FULL ACCESS

Question 3

Which of the following operations can NOT be performed on a table that contains a primary key that is referenced by a foreign key in another table?

○ A. IMPORT ... INSERT

○ B. IMPORT ... REPLACE

○ C. IMPORT ... INSERT_UPDATE

○ D. IMPORT ... CREATE

Question 4

Which of the following IMPORT command options can be used to prevent an import operation from filling up a database's transaction log files and failing?

○ A. ALLOW NO ACCESS

○ B. NOTIMEOUT

○ C. COMMITCOUNT AUTOMATIC

○ D. ALLOW WRITE ACCESS

Question 5

Which of the following LOAD command modifiers can be used when working with identity column data?

○ A.   IDENTITYRESET

○ B.   IDENTITYOVERRIDE

○ C.   IDENTITYSUPRESS

○ D.   IDENTITYRETAIN

Question 6

A database administrator wants to delete all records found in a table named DEPARTMENT. If the DEPARTMENT table resides in a database that is stored on an AIX server, which of the following commands can be used to accomplish this objective?

○ A.   LOAD FROM null OF DEL INSERT INTO department

○ B.   LOAD FROM null OF DEL REPLACE INTO department

○ C.   LOAD FROM /dev/null OF DEL INSERT INTO department

○ D.   LOAD FROM /dev/null OF DEL REPLACE INTO department

Question 7

Given the following command:

```
LOAD FROM salesdata.del OF DEL INSERT INTO sales
MODIFIED BY DELPRIORITYCHAR
ALLOW READ ACCESS
STATISTICS USE PROFILE
```

Which of the following is NOT true?

○ A.   During the load operation, statistics will be collected and the statistics profile for the SALES table and its associated indexes will be updated; if a statistics profile does not exist one will be created.

○ B.   Only data in the SALES table that existed prior to the invocation of the LOAD command can be read by other applications while the load operation is in progress.

○ C.   The priority for evaluating delimiters is character delimiter, record delimiter, column delimiter rather than record delimiter, character delimiter, column delimiter.

○ D.   If the load operation aborts, the original data stored in the SALES table will be accessible for read access.

Question 8

Which of the following commands can be used to display the status of a load operation?

- O A. LOAD STATUS
- O B. LOAD MESSAGES
- O C. LOAD QUERY
- O D. LOAD STATISTICS

Question 9

The table EMPLOYEES was created by executing the following command:

```
CREATE TABLE employees (empid  INTEGER NOT NULL PRIMARY KEY,
                        name    VARCHAR(25))
```

Assuming the file EMPDATA.DEL contains the following data:

100, "Kim Moutsos"
100, "Dwaine Snow"
200, "Rebecca Bond"
300, "Phil Gunning"
400, "Paul Zikopoulos"

If the following commands are executed:

```
CREATE TABLE emp_exp LIKE EMPLOYEES;
LOAD FROM empdata.del OF DEL
     INSERT INTO EMPLOYEE
     FOR EXECPTION emp_exp;
```

Which of the following statements is true?

- O A. The table EMPLOYEES will contain four rows; the table EMP_EXP will be empty.
- O B. The table EMPLOYEES will contain five rows; the table EMP_EXP will contain five rows.
- O C. The table EMPLOYEES will contain four rows; the table EMP_EXP will contain one row.
- O D. The table EMPLOYEES will contain five rows; the table EMP_EXP will contain one row.

Question 10

In which of the following scenarios should the load utility be used instead of the Import utility?

○ A. Data needs to be added to a table and any associated triggers need to be fired.

○ B. A large amount of data needs to be added to a table quickly without incurring a significant amount of transaction logging.

○ C. Data stored in a Worksheet (WSF) formatted file needs to be added to a table.

○ D. A large amount of data needs to be added to a table and constraint checking needs to be enforced during population.

Question 11

Which of the following set of steps could be used to build a test database that has the same structure and statisics of a production database, but contains less data?

○ A. 1) Extract the data from the production database using the db2move utility (EXPORT mode).

2) Create a test database and populate it using the db2move utility (IMPORT mode).

○ B. 1) Generate the SQL needed to create the objects in the production database using the db2look utility.

2) Create a test database and run the script produced by db2look to create the database objects.

3) Extract the data from the production database using the db2move utility (EXPORT mode)

4) Populate the test database using the db2move utility (IMPORT mode).

5) Run the RUNSTATS utility on each table in the test database.

○ C. 1) Run the RUNSTATS utility on each table in the production database.

2) Generate the SQL needed to create the objects in the production database and reproduce the statistics profile using the db2look utility.

3) Create a test database and run the script produced by db2look to create the database objects and duplicate the statistics.

4) Insert, Import, or Load test data into the database.

○ D. 1) Generate the SQL needed to create the objects in the production database using the db2look utility.

2) Create a test database and run the script produced by db2look to create the database objects.

3) Load test data into the database using the LOAD command with the STATISTICS USE PROFILE option specified so that statistics will be collected.

Question 12

Which of the following tasks is the db2batch utility best suited for?

○ A. Benchmarking SQL and XQuery operations.

○ B. Copying 50 tables created under a single schema from one database to another.

○ C. Reorganizing table data and clustering its rows.

○ D. Updating access plan information stored in packages.

Question 13

In an attempt to improve query performance, a database administrator created an index for a table named EMPLOYEE, which contains 500,000 records. Performance of ad-hoc queries ran against the EMPLOYEE table has improved, but performance of a batch application that runs at night has not improved. Which of the following operations should correct this problem?

○ A. REORGCHK

○ B. REORG

○ C. FLUSH PACKAGE CACHE

○ D. REBIND

Question 14

Which of the following illustrates the proper order in which the DB2 data management utilities available should be used?

○ A. RUNSTATS, REORG table, REORG indexes, REORGCHK, REBIND

○ B. RUNSTATS, REORGCHK, REORG table, REORG indexes, RUNSTATS, REBIND

○ C. REORGCHK, REORG indexes, REORG table, RUNSTATS, REBIND

○ D. RUNSTATS, REBIND, REORGCHK, REORG table, REORG indexes, RUNSTATS

Question 15

Which of the following commands invokes the Design Advisor and instructs it to make recommendations for a database named SAMPLE, based on information collected by the snapshot monitor?

○ A. db2advis –d SAMPLE –k

○ B. db2advis –d SAMPLE –qp

○ C. db2advis –d SAMPLE –g

○ D. db2advis –d SAMPLE –h

Question 16

The Design Advisor can be used to analyze SQL from which two of the following?

- ○ A. The EXPLAIN_STATEMENT table
- ○ B. A file containing a workload
- ○ C. The SYSIBM.SYSPLANS system catalog table
- ○ D. The EXPLAIN_STREAM table
- ○ E. The ADVISE_WORKLOAD table

Answers

Question 1

The correct answer is **D**. Most of the utilities that are provided with DB2 can be invoked from the Control Center or by executing the appropriate command from the DB2 Command Line Processor or an operating system prompt. And because most DB2 commands have a corresponding application programming interface (API), they can be invoked from an Embedded SQL, or CLI application as well. However, the source code needed to use some of these APIs can be quite complex and all of the APIs available are designed to be used primarily in C and C++ applications. Another approach is to use the ADMIN_CMD() stored procedure, which is a special stored procedure that allows applications to run select administrative commands by using the CALL SQL statement. The ADMIN_CMD() stored procedure also allows you to invoke utilities from Java applications—something that cannot be done easily with the APIs.

Question 2

The correct answer is **C**. If the IMPORT command is executed with the ALLOW WRITE ACCESS option specified, the Import utility will request a table lock after every commit operation is performed. This can cause an import operation to run slowly in environments that have high concurrency. That is not the case if the ALLOW NO ACCESS option is specified. (There is no ALLOW READ ACCESS or ALLOW FULL ACCESS option.)

Question 3

The correct answer is **B**. When the REPLACE option of the Import utility is used, any existing data is deleted from the target table (which must already exist); then, the new data is inserted. This option cannot be used if the target table contains a primary key that is referenced by a foreign key in another table.

When the INSERT option is used, data is inserted into the target table (which must already exist). Imported data is appended to any data that already exists. When the INSERT_UPDATE option is used, data is either inserted into the target table (which must already exist), or used to update existing rows (if the row being imported has a primary key value that matches that of an existing record). Existing records will only be updated if the target table specified has a primary key defined. When the CREATE option is used, the target table is created along with all of its associated indexes, then data is imported into the new table.

Question 4

The correct answer is **C**. The COMMITCOUNT option of the IMPORT command is used to specify the number of rows of data (records) that are to be copied to the table/updatable view specified before a commit operation is to be performed. The COMMITCOUNT AUTOMATIC option should be used for Import operations that fail because transaction logs become full. This guarantees that transaction logs do not become full of uncommitted data.

Question 5

The correct answer is **B**. The LOAD command modifiers can be used when loading identity column data are IDENTITYIGNORE, IDENTITYMISSING, and IDENTITYOVERRIDE.

The IDENTITYIGNORE modifier indicates that although data for all identity columns is present in the file being loaded, this data should be ignored and the Load utility should replace all identity column data found with its own generated values.

The IDENTITYMISSING modifier indicates that data for identity columns is missing from the file being loaded and that the Load utility should generate an appropriate value for each missing value encountered.

The IDENTITYOVERRIDE modifier indicates that the Load utility is to accept explicit, non-NULL data values for all identity columns in the table. This modifier is useful when migrating data from another database system, or when loading a table from data that was recovered using the DROPPED TABLE RECOVERY option of the ROLLFORWARD DATABASE command. (This modifier should be used only when an identity column that was defined as GENERATED ALWAYS is present in the table that is to be loaded.)

Question 6

The correct answer is **D**. The Load utility can be used to delete all records in a table without generating corresponding log records by specifying the null device as the input file and invoking the LOAD with the REPLACE option specified. On UNIX the null device is */dev/null*, on Windows it is *nul*). Thus, the following commands could be used to delete all records found in a table named DEPARTMENT:

```
LOAD FROM /dev/null OF DEL REPLACE INTO department (UNIX)
LOAD FROM nul OF DEL REPLACE INTO department (Windows)
```

Question 7

The correct answer is **A**. Statistics cannot be collected if the LOAD command is executed with any option other than the REPLACE option specified. Additionally, a statistics profile for the SALES table must already exist (statistics profiles are created by executing the RUNSTATS command); the Load utility will not create one. If a profile does not exist and the Load utility is instructed to collect statistics, a warning is returned that statistics are not collected.

Question 8

The correct answer is **C**. The LOAD QUERY command is used to monitor the progress/status of a load operation. (There are no LOAD STATUS, LOAD MESSAGES, or LOAD STATISTICS commands.)

Question 9

The correct answer is **C**. During the delete phase of a load operation, any rows that violated primary and/or unique key constraints defined on the target table are removed and copied to an exception table (if appropriate) and a message about each offending row is written to the appropriate message file so it can be modified and manually moved to the target table at some point in the future. Since the data in this example contains two records that have an employee ID value of 100, and because the EMPID column in the EMPLOYEES is a primary key, the first record will be loaded into the EMPLOYEES table and the second will be moved to the EMP_EXP table.

Question 10

The correct answer is **B**. The Load utility is significantly faster than the Import utility when processing large amounts of data, because the load utility writes formatted pages directly into the database's storage containers. Additionally, when the Load utility is used, a minimal amount of logging is performed—individual row transactions are not recorded in the database's transaction log files.

Worksheet Format (WSF) formatted files are not supported by the Load utility, triggers are not fired during load processing, and only uniqueness checking is performed during processing. All other constraint checking (check constraints, referential integrity constraints, etc.) must be performed after the load operation has completed using the SET INTEGRITY SQL statement.

Question 11

The correct answer is **C**. The db2move utility queries the system catalog tables of the specified database and compiles a list of all user tables found. It then exports the contents and table structure of each table in the database to individual PC Integrated Exchange Format (IXF) formatted files. The set of files produced can then be imported or loaded to another DB2 database on the same system, or they can be transferred to another workstation and be imported or loaded to a DB2 database residing there. Thus the db2move can be used to copy the entire contents of a database from one location to another.

One limitation of the db2move utility is that it can only be used to duplicate table and index objects. If the database to be duplicated contains other objects such as aliases, views, triggers, user-defined data types (UDTs), user-defined functions (UDFs), etc., you must to duplicate those objects in the target database as well if you want to have an identical copy of the source database. That is where the db2look utility comes in. When invoked, db2look can reverse engineer an existing database and produce a set of Data Definition Language (DDL) SQL statements, which can then be used to recreate all of the data objects found in the database that was analyzed. The db2look utility can also collect environment registry variable settings, configuration parameter settings, and statistical (RUNSTATS) information on the source system, which can be used to duplicate those settings on the target system.

In this scenario we only want to copy a portion of the data and we want the statistics from the production database to be copied to the test database. Therefore, db2move cannot be used to move the date; instead, db2look must be used to duplicate the objects and statistics found in the production database and then the appropriate amount of data must be added to the tables.

Question 12

The correct answer is **A**. The db2batch utility is a simple benchmark tool that reads SQL statements and/or XQuery expressions from either an ASCII format file or standard input, dynamically prepares, describes, and executes the statements/expressions found, and returns a result set that includes among other things, the timing of the execution. (db2move is best suited for copying 50 tables from one database to another; REORG is best suited for reorganizing table data and clustering its rows, and REBIND is best suited for updating access plan information stored in packages.)

Question 13

The correct answer is **D**. Because the DB2 Optimizer generates an access plan each time a dynamic SQL statement is prepared for execution, applications using dynamic SQL may see performance improvements immediately after new statistical information has been produced. Unfortunately, that is not the case for applications that use static SQL. That's because the DB2 Optimizer only generates access plans for static SQL statements when the package that contains those statement is bound to the database. Therefore, in order for existing packages to take advantage of new statistical information produced by the RUNSTATS utility, they must be rebound to the database so the DB2 Optimizer will evaluate the new information and formulate new access plans (which may or may not perform better than the original access plan used). The easiest way to rebind an existing package—provided the application source code used to produce the package has not changed—is by executing the REBIND command.

Question 14

The correct answer is **B**. The RUNSTATS utility should be run immediately after any of the following occur:

- A large number of insert, update, or delete operations are performed against a specific table.

- An import operation is performed

- A load operation is performed

- One or more columns are added to an existing table

- A new index is created

- A table or index is reorganized

It is also a good idea to run the RUNSTATS utility before running the REORGCHK utility; if query response is slow because of fragmentation and statistics are not up to date, the REORGCHK utility may report that a table/index reorganization operation is unnecessary when it really is. Upon careful evaluation of the output produced by the REORGCHK utility, you may discover that one or more tables and/or indexes need to be reorganized. If that's the case, you can reorganize the tables, followed by the indexes, using DB2's REORG utility. After reorganizing data, statistics should be collected again and any packages that are associated with the table should be rebound (using the REBIND utility) so the DB2 Optimizer can generate new data access plans using the new statistics information collected.

Question 15

The correct answer is **C**. The Design Advisor is a special tool that is designed to identify indexes, Materialized Query Tables (MQTs), and Multidimensional Clustering Tables (MDCs) that could help improve query performance in your database environment. The Design Advisor is invoked by executing the db2advis command; the –g option of the db2advis command specifies that the SQL statements that make up the workload to be analyzed are to be retrieved from a dynamic SQL snapshot.

The –k option specifies to what degree the workload will be compressed. (Compression is done to allow the advisor to reduce the complexity of the advisor's execution while achieving similar results to those the advisor could provide when the full workload is considered.) The –qp option specifies that the workload is coming from the DB2 Query Patroller, and the –h option displays help information.

Question 16

The correct answers are **B** and **E**. The Design Advisor recommends one or more indexes that would improve query/workload performance using current database statistics, the DB2 Optimizer, snapshot monitor information, and/or a specific query or set of SQL statements (known as a workload) you provide. The indexes/MQTs/MDCs recommended, the statistics derived for them, and the data definition language (DDL) statements required to create them can be written to a user-created table named ADVISE_INDEX, if so desired.

(If the db2advis command is executed with the –p option specified, the plans that were generated while running the Design Advisor will be saved in the ADVISE_WORKLOAD table and the workload query plans that use the final recommendation to be written to the Explain tables. However, input for the Design Advisor does not come from the Explain tables.)

CHAPTER 7

High Availability

Fourteen and one-half percent (14.5%) of the DB2 9 for Linux, UNIX, and Windows Database Administration exam (Exam 731) is designed to evaluate your knowledge of transactions and transaction logging and to test your ability to back up and restore a database using the various methods of backup and recovery available. The questions that make up this portion of the exam are intended to evaluate the following:

- Your knowledge of the various transaction logging features available

- Your ability to configure a database for log mirroring

- Your knowledge of the types of database recovery available (crash, version, and roll-forward) and your ability to demonstrate when and how each is used.

- Your ability to create and use database-level and table space-level backup images

- Your ability to create and use full, incremental, and delta backup images

- Your ability to return a damaged or corrupt database to the state it was in at any given point in time

- Your knowledge of how and when invalid indexes are recreated

- Your knowledge of high availability disaster recovery (HADR)

- Your ability to suspend and resume database I/O and your ability to initialize a split mirror copy of a database

This chapter is designed to introduce you to the backup and recovery tools that are available with DB2 and to show you how to both back up a database on a regular basis and restore a database if it becomes damaged or corrupted.

Transactions

A transaction (also known as a *unit of work*) is a sequence of one or more SQL operations grouped together as a single unit, usually within an application process. A given transaction can perform any number of SQL operations—from a single operation to many hundreds or even thousands, depending on what is considered a "single step" within your business logic.

The initiation and termination of a single transaction defines points of data consistency within a database; either the effects of all operations performed within a transaction are applied to the database and made permanent (committed), or the effects of all operations performed are backed out (rolled back), and the database is returned to the state it was in before the transaction was initiated.

In most cases, transactions are initiated the first time an executable SQL statement is executed after a connection to a database has been made or immediately after a preexisting transaction has been terminated. Once initiated, transactions can be implicitly terminated using a feature known as "automatic commit" (in which case, each executable SQL statement is treated as a single transaction, and any changes made by that statement are applied to the database if the statement executes successfully or are discarded if the statement fails), or they can be explicitly terminated by executing the COMMIT or the ROLLBACK SQL statement. The basic syntax for these two statements is:

```
COMMIT <WORK>
```

and

```
ROLLBACK <WORK>
```

When the COMMIT statement is used to terminate a transaction, all changes made to the database since the transaction began are made permanent. On the other hand, when the ROLLBACK statement is used, all changes made are backed out, and the database is returned to the state it was in just before the transaction began. Figure

7–1 shows the effects of a transaction that was terminated with a COMMIT statement; Figure 7–2 shows the effects of a transaction that was terminated with a ROLLBACK statement.

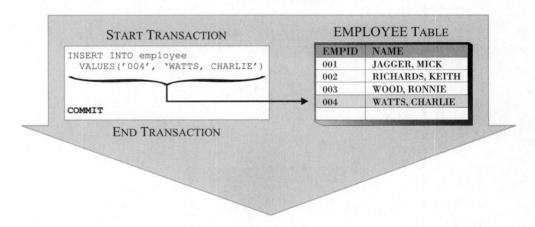

EMPLOYEE TABLE
(BEFORE TRANSACTION)

EMPID	NAME
001	JAGGER, MICK
002	RICHARDS, KEITH
003	WOOD, RONNIE

START TRANSACTION

```
INSERT INTO employee
  VALUES('004', 'WATTS, CHARLIE')
```

COMMIT

END TRANSACTION

EMPLOYEE TABLE

EMPID	NAME
001	JAGGER, MICK
002	RICHARDS, KEITH
003	WOOD, RONNIE
004	WATTS, CHARLIE

EMPLOYEE TABLE
(AFTER TRANSACTION)

EMPID	NAME
001	JAGGER, MICK
002	RICHARDS, KEITH
003	WOOD, RONNIE
004	WATTS, CHARLIE

Figure 7–1: Terminating a transaction with the COMMIT SQL statement.

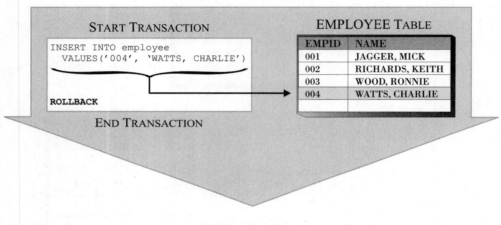

EMPLOYEE TABLE
(BEFORE TRANSACTION)

EMPID	NAME
001	JAGGER, MICK
002	RICHARDS, KEITH
003	WOOD, RONNIE

START TRANSACTION

```
INSERT INTO employee
  VALUES('004', 'WATTS, CHARLIE')

ROLLBACK
```

END TRANSACTION

EMPLOYEE TABLE

EMPID	NAME
001	JAGGER, MICK
002	RICHARDS, KEITH
003	WOOD, RONNIE
004	WATTS, CHARLIE

EMPLOYEE TABLE
(AFTER TRANSACTION)

EMPID	NAME
001	JAGGER, MICK
002	RICHARDS, KEITH
003	WOOD, RONNIE

Figure 7–2: Terminating a transaction with the ROLLBACK SQL statement.

It is important to remember that commit and rollback operations only have an effect on changes that have been made within the transaction they terminate. So in order to evaluate the effects of a series of transactions, you must be able to identify where each transaction begins, as well as when and how each transaction is terminated. Figure 7–3 shows how the effects of a series of transactions can be evaluated.

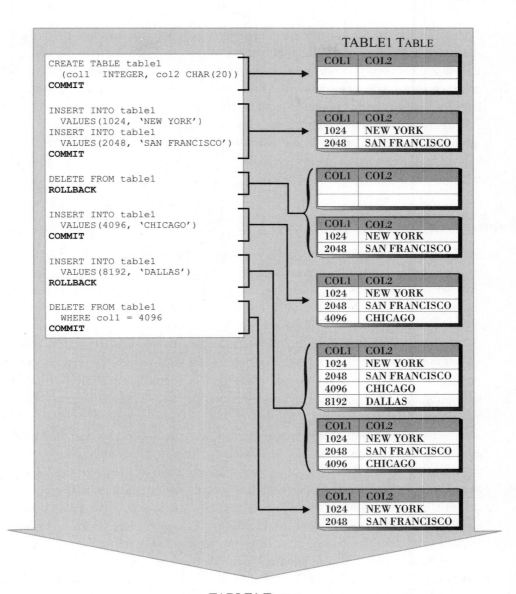

TABLE1 TABLE

COL1	COL2

```
CREATE TABLE table1
   (col1  INTEGER, col2 CHAR(20))
COMMIT


INSERT INTO table1
   VALUES(1024, 'NEW YORK')
INSERT INTO table1
   VALUES(2048, 'SAN FRANCISCO')
COMMIT

DELETE FROM table1
ROLLBACK


INSERT INTO table1
   VALUES(4096, 'CHICAGO')
COMMIT


INSERT INTO table1
   VALUES(8192, 'DALLAS')
ROLLBACK

DELETE FROM table1
   WHERE col1 = 4096
COMMIT
```

COL1	COL2
1024	NEW YORK
2048	SAN FRANCISCO

COL1	COL2

COL1	COL2
1024	NEW YORK
2048	SAN FRANCISCO

COL1	COL2
1024	NEW YORK
2048	SAN FRANCISCO
4096	CHICAGO

COL1	COL2
1024	NEW YORK
2048	SAN FRANCISCO
4096	CHICAGO
8192	DALLAS

COL1	COL2
1024	NEW YORK
2048	SAN FRANCISCO
4096	CHICAGO

COL1	COL2
1024	NEW YORK
2048	SAN FRANCISCO

TABLE1 TABLE

COL1	COL2
1024	NEW YORK
2048	SAN FRANCISCO

Figure 7–3: Evaluating the effects of a series of transactions.

Changes made by a transaction that have not been committed are usually inaccessible to other users and applications (unless the Uncommitted Read isolation level is used) and can be backed out with a rollback operation. However, once changes made by a transaction have been committed, they become accessible to all other users and applications and can be removed only by executing new SQL statements (within a new transaction). So what happens if a system failure occurs or an application abends before a transaction's changes can be committed? To answer that question, we must first look at how data changes are made and how transactions are logged.

Transaction Logging

So just what is transaction logging and how does it work? Transaction logging is simply a process used to keep track of changes made to a database (by a transaction), *as they occur*. Each time an update or a delete operation is performed, the page containing the record to be updated/deleted is retrieved from storage and copied to the appropriate buffer pool, where it is then modified by the update/delete operation. (If a new record is created by an insert operation, that record is created directly in the appropriate buffer pool.) Once the record has been modified (or inserted), a record reflecting the modification/insertion is written to the log buffer, which is simply another designated storage area in memory. (The actual amount of memory reserved for the log buffer is controlled by the *logbufsiz* database configuration parameter.) If an insert operation is performed, a record containing the new row is written to the log buffer; if a delete operation is performed, a record containing the row's original values is written to the log buffer; and if an update operation is performed, a record containing the row's original values, combined with the row's new values, is written to the log buffer. (If replication has not been enabled, an Exclusive OR operation is performed using the "before" and "after" rows and the results are written to the log buffer.) These kinds of records, along with records that indicate whether the transactions that were responsible for making changes were committed or rolled back, make up the majority of the records stored in the log buffer.

Whenever buffer pool I/O page cleaners are activated, the log buffer becomes full, or a transaction is terminated (by being committed or rolled back), all records stored in the log buffer are immediately written to one or more log files stored on disk. This is done to minimize the number of log records that might get lost in the

event a system failure occurs. As soon as all log records associated with a
particular transaction have been externalized to one or more log files, the effects of
the transaction itself are recorded in the database (i.e., written to the appropriate
table space containers for permanent storage). The modified data pages remain in
memory, where they can be quickly accessed if necessary—eventually, they will be
overwritten as newer pages are retrieved from storage. The transaction logging
process can be seen in Figure 7–4.

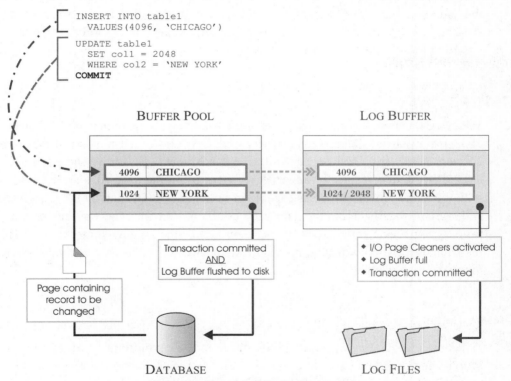

Figure 7–4: The transaction logging process.

Because multiple transactions may be working with a database at any given point
in time, a single log file may contain log records that belong to several different
transactions. Therefore, to keep track of which log records belong to which
transactions, every log record is assigned a special "transaction identifier" that ties
it to the transaction that created it. By using transaction IDs, log records associated
with a particular transaction can be written to one or more log files at any time,

without impacting data consistency—eventually, the execution of the COMMIT or ROLLBACK statement that terminates the transaction will be logged as well.

Because log records are externalized frequently and because changes made by a particular transaction are only externalized to the database when the transaction itself is successfully terminated, the ability to return a database to a consistent state after a failure occurs is guaranteed—when the database is restarted, log records are analyzed, and each record that has a corresponding COMMIT record is reapplied to the database; every record that does not have a corresponding COMMIT record is either ignored or backed out (which is why "before" and "after" information is recorded for all update operations).

Logging Strategies

When a database is first created, three log files, known as *primary log files*, are allocated as part of the creation process. On Linux and UNIX platforms, these log files are 1,000 4K (kilobyte) pages in size; on Windows platforms, these log files are 250 4K pages in size. However, the number of primary log files used, along with the amount of data each is capable of holding, is controlled by the *logprimary* and *logfilsiz* parameters in the database's configuration file. The way in which all primary log files created are used is determined by the logging strategy chosen for the database. Two very different strategies, known as *circular logging* and *archival logging*, are available.

Circular logging

When circular logging is used, records stored in the log buffer are written to primary log files in a circular sequence. Log records are written to the current "active" log file, and when that log file becomes full, it is marked as "unavailable." At that point, DB2 makes the next log file in the sequence the active log file and begins writing log records to it; when that log file becomes full, the process is repeated. In the meantime, as transactions are terminated and their effects are externalized to the database, their corresponding log records are released because they are no longer needed. When all records stored in an individual log file are released, that file is marked as being "reusable," and the next time it becomes the active log file, its contents are overwritten with new log records.

Although primary log files are not marked reusable in any particular order (they are marked reusable when they are no longer needed), they must be written to in sequence. So what happens when the logging process cycles back to a primary log file that is marked as being "unavailable"? When this occurs, the DB2 Database Manager will allocate what is known as a *secondary log file* and begin writing log records to it. As soon as the secondary log file becomes full, the DB2 Database Manager will poll the primary log file again, and if its status is still "unavailable," another secondary log file is allocated and filled. This process will continue until either the desired primary log file becomes "reusable" or the number of secondary log files created matches the number of secondary log files allowed (designated by the *logsecond* database configuration parameter). If the former occurs, the DB2 Database Manager will begin writing log records to the appropriate primary log file, and logging will pick up where it left off in the logging sequence. In the meantime, log records stored in the secondary log files are eventually released, and when all connections to the database have been terminated, any secondary log files created are destroyed. On the other hand, if the maximum number of secondary log files allowed have been allocated, and the desired primary log file is still unavailable, all database activity will stop, and the following message will be generated:

SQL0964C The transaction log for the database is full.

By default, up to two secondary log files will be created if necessary, and their size will be the same as that of each primary log file used. Circular logging is illustrated in Figure 7–5.

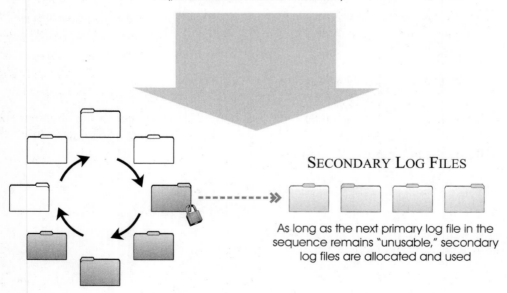

PRIMARY LOG FILES

When a primary log file becomes full,
the next file in the sequence is used
(provided it is marked "reusable")

SECONDARY LOG FILES

As long as the next primary log file in the
sequence remains "unusable," secondary
log files are allocated and used

Figure 7–5: Circular logging.

By default, when a new database is first created, circular logging is the logging
strategy used.

Archival logging

Like circular logging, when archival logging (also known as *log retention logging*) is used, log records stored in the log buffer are written to the primary log files that have been preallocated. However, unlike with circular logging, these log files are never reused. Instead, when all records stored in an individual log file are released, that file is marked as being "archived" rather than as being "reusable," and the only time it is used again is if it is needed for a roll-forward recovery operation. When all of the primary log files available become full, the DB2 Database Manager allocates a new set of primary log files. This process continues as long as there is sufficient disk space available.

Because any number of primary log files can exist when archival logging is used, they are classified according to their current state and storage location. Log files containing records associated with transactions that have not yet been committed or rolled back are known as *active log files* and reside in the active log directory (or device); log files containing records associated with completed transactions (i.e., transactions that have been externalized to the database) that reside in the active log directory are known as online archive log files; and log files containing records that are associated with completed transactions that have been moved to a storage location other than the active log directory are known as offline archive log files. Offline archive files can be moved to their storage location automatically by assigning the appropriate value (USEREXIT, DISK, TSM, or VENDOR) to the *logarcmeth1* or *logarcmeth2* database configuration parameter. Archival logging is illustrated in Figure 7–6.

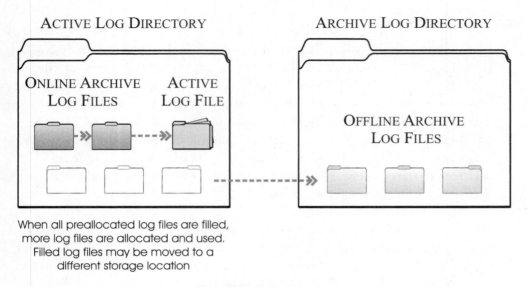

Figure 7–6: Archival logging.

Other Logging Considerations

Along with specifying the logging strategy to employ, several database configuration parameters can be used to control a database's logging behavior. The following items should be taken into consideration when configuring a database for transaction log management.

Infinite logging

You would think that you could avoid running out of log space simply by configuring a database to use a large number of secondary log files if needed. However, the maximum number of primary and secondary log files allowed (*logprimary* + *logsecond*) is 256, and if the size of your log files is relatively small, you can still run out of log space quickly when transaction workloads become heavy. Furthermore, you want to avoid allocating a large number of secondary log files if possible because performance is impacted each time a log file has to be allocated. Ideally, you want to allocate enough primary log files to handle most situations, and you want to use just enough secondary log files to handle peaks in transaction workloads.

If you are concerned about running out of log space, and you want to avoid allocating a large number of secondary log files, you can configure a database to use what is known as *infinite logging*. To enable infinite logging, you simply set the *logsecond* database configuration parameter to -1.

> In order to use infinite logging, a database must be configured to use archival logging; infinite logging can have a huge impact on performance if one or more long running transactions must be rolled back and the log files needed have already been archived.

Dual logging

With DB2 Version 8.1 and later, you have the ability to configure a database such that the DB2 Database Manager will simultaneously create and update active log files in two different locations. If you store active log files in one location and mirror them in another, separate location, database activity can continue if a disk failure or human error causes log files in one location to become inaccessible. (Mirroring log files may also aid in database recovery.) To enable log file mirroring, you simply assign the fully qualified name of the mirror log location (path) to the *mirrorlogpath* database configuration parameter. Alternately, on UNIX systems, you can assign the value 1 to the DB2_NEWLOGPATH registry variable—in this case, the name of the mirror log location is generated by appending the character "2" to the current value of the *logpath* database configuration parameter. Ideally, the mirror log path used should refer to a physical location (disk) that does not see a large amount of disk I/O and that is separate from the physical location used to store primary log files.

If an error is encountered during attempts to write to either the active log path or the mirror log path, the DB2 Database Manager will mark the failing path as "bad," write a message to the administration notification log, and write subsequent log records to the remaining "good" log path only. When DB2 allocates storage for its next primary log file, the DB2 Database Manager will make a second attempt to write to both log paths. If successful, dual logging will continue. If not, DB2 will not attempt to use the "bad" path again until the next log file is accessed for the first time. There is no attempt to synchronize the log paths, but DB2 keeps track of each access error that occurs, so that the correct paths will be used when log files are archived. If a failure occurs while writing to the remaining "good" path, the database shuts down.

> The DB2_NEWLOGPATH registry variable is a temporary registry variable and should be used with caution. The preferred method for enabling dual logging is by assigning the fully qualified name of the mirror log location to the *mirrorlogpath* database configuration parameter.

Controlling how "disk full" errors are handled

When archival logging is used and archived log files are not moved from the active log directory to another location, the disk where the active log directory resides can quickly become full. By default, when this happens, transactions will receive a disk full error and be rolled back. But what if, instead of the current transaction being terminated, you were given the chance to manually move or delete files to make more room available? That's the purpose behind the *blk_log_dsk_ful* database configuration parameter; if this parameter is set to YES, applications will hang if the DB2 Database Manager receives a disk full error when it attempts to create a new log file in the active log directory. The DB2 Database Manager will then attempt to create the log file every five minutes until it succeeds—after each attempt, a message is written to the Administration Notification Log. (The only way that you can confirm that an application is hung because of a disk full condition is to monitor this log.) Until the log file is successfully created, applications attempting to insert or update data will not be permitted to commit their transactions. Read-only queries may not be directly affected; however, if a query needs to access data that is locked by an update request or a data page that has been changed in the buffer pool by the updating application, read-only queries will also appear to hang.

To resolve a disk full situation, you simply move old log files to another location or enlarge the current file system. As soon as the needed space becomes available, new log files can be created, and all hung applications will be able to continue processing.

Database Recovery Concepts

Over time, a database can encounter any number of problems, including power interruptions, storage media failure, and application abends. All of these can result in database failure, and each failure scenario requires a different recovery action.

The concept of backing up a database is the same as that of backing up any other set of data files: you make a copy of the data and store it on a different medium where it can be accessed in the event the original becomes damaged or destroyed. The simplest way to back up a database is to shut it down to ensure that no further transactions are processed and then back it up using the Backup utility provided with DB2. Once a backup image has been created, you can use it to rebuild the database if for some reason it becomes damaged or corrupted.

The process of rebuilding a database is known as recovery, and three types of recovery are available with DB2:

- Crash recovery

- Version recovery

- Roll-forward recovery

Crash Recovery

When an event or condition that causes a database or the DB2 Database Manager to end abnormally takes place, one or more transaction failures may result. Conditions that can cause transaction failure include the following:

- A power failure at the workstation where the DB2 Database Manager is running

- A serious operating system error

- A hardware failure such as memory corruption, disk failure, CPU failure, or network failure

When a transaction failure takes place, all work done by partially completed transactions that had not yet been externalized to the database is lost. As a result, the database may be left in an inconsistent state (and therefore will be unusable). Crash recovery is the process used to return such a database to a consistent and usable state. Crash recovery is performed by using information stored in the transaction log files to complete any committed transactions that were in memory (but had not yet been externalized to storage) when the transaction failure occurred, roll back any incomplete transactions found, and purge any uncommitted transactions from memory. Once a database is returned to a consistent and usable state, it has attained what is known as a "point of consistency." Crash recovery is illustrated in Figure 7–7.

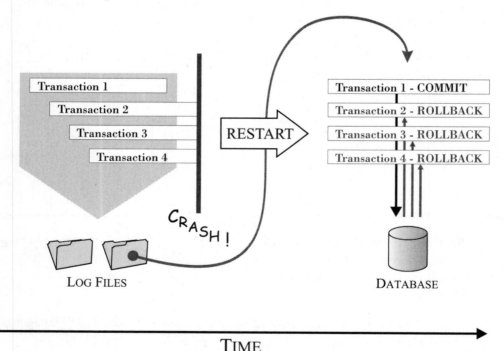

Figure 7–7: Crash recovery.

Version Recovery

Version recovery is the process used to return a database to the state it was in at the time a particular backup image was made. Version recovery is performed by replacing the current version of a database with a previous version, using a copy that was made with a backup operation—the entire database is rebuilt using a backup image that was created earlier. Unfortunately, when a version recovery is performed, all changes made to the database since the backup image used was created are lost. Version recovery is illustrated in Figure 7–8.

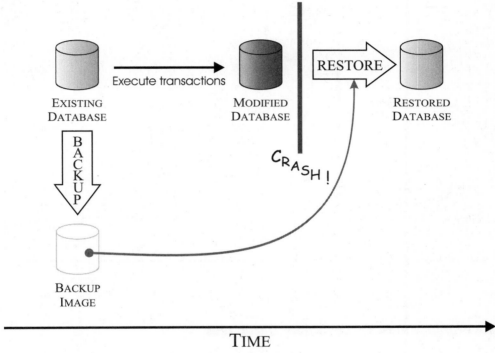

Figure 7–8: Version recovery.

Roll-Forward Recovery

Roll-forward recovery takes version recovery one step farther by rebuilding a database or one or more individual table spaces using a backup image and replaying information stored in transaction log files to return the database/table spaces to the state they were in at an exact point in time. In order to perform a roll-forward recovery operation, you must have archival logging enabled, you must have either a full backup image of the database or a complete set of table space backup images available, and you must have access to all archived log files that have been created since the backup image(s) were made. Roll-forward recovery is illustrated in Figure 7–9.

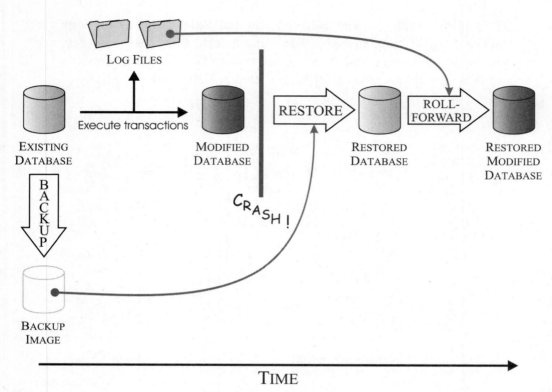

LOG FILES

Execute transactions

EXISTING DATABASE

MODIFIED DATABASE

RESTORE

RESTORED DATABASE

ROLL-FORWARD

RESTORED MODIFIED DATABASE

BACKUP

CRASH!

BACKUP IMAGE

TIME

Figure 7–9: Roll-forward recovery.

Recoverable and Nonrecoverable Databases

Although any DB2 database can be recovered from a backup image, whether a database is considered recoverable is determined by the values of the database's *logarchmeth1* and *logarchmeth2* configuration parameters; when both of these configuration parameters are set to OFF—which is the default—circular logging is used, and the database is considered nonrecoverable. A database is considered recoverable when crash recovery, version recovery, *and* roll-forward recovery are possible. Other differences between recoverable and nonrecoverable databases can be seen in Table 7.1.

Table 7.1 *Differences Between Recoverable and Nonrecoverable Databases*

Recoverable Database	Nonrecoverable Database
Archive logging is used.	Circular logging is used.
The database can be backed up at any time, regardless of whether applications are connected to it and transactions are in progress.	The database can be backed up only when all connections to it have been terminated.
The entire database can be backed up, or individual table spaces can be backed up. Table spaces can also be restored independently.	The entire database must be backed up; table space–level backups are not supported.
A damaged database can be returned to the state it was in at any point in time; crash recovery, version recovery, and roll-forward recovery are supported.	A damaged database can be returned only to the state it was in at the time the last backup image was taken; only crash recovery and version recovery are supported.

The decision of whether a database should be recoverable or nonrecoverable is based on several factors:

- If a database is used to support read-only operations, it can be nonrecoverable; because no transactions will be logged, roll-forward recovery is not necessary.

- If relatively few changes will be made to a database, and if all changes made can be easily re-created, it may be desirable to leave the database nonrecoverable.

- If a large amount of changes will be made to a database, or if it would be difficult and time-consuming to re-create all changes made, the database should be recoverable.

Online Versus Offline Backup and Recovery

From a backup and recovery perspective, a database is considered to be either online or offline: when a database is offline, other applications and users cannot gain access to it; when a database is online, just the opposite is true. Backup and recovery operations can be performed against a nonrecoverable database only while it is offline. Recoverable databases, on the other hand, can be backed up at any time, regardless of whether the database is offline or online. However, before any database (recoverable or nonrecoverable) can be restored, it must first be taken offline.

When an online backup operation is performed, archival logging ensures that *all* changes made while the backup image is being made are captured and can be recreated with a roll-forward recovery operation. Additionally, online backup operations can be performed against individual table spaces as well as entire databases. And, unlike when full database version recovery operations are performed, table space version recovery operations and table space roll-forward recovery operations can be performed while a database remains online—provided the table space that contains the system catalog is not the table space being recovered. While an online table space backup operation is performed, the table space being backed up remains available for use, and all modifications to the data stored in that table space are recorded in the transaction log files. However, when an online restore or online roll-forward recovery operation is performed against a table space, the table space itself is taken offline and is not available for use until the restore/roll-forward recovery operation is complete.

Incremental and Delta Backup and Recovery

As the size of a database grows, the time and hardware needed to back up and recover the databases also grows substantially. Thus, creating full database and table space backup images is not always the best approach when dealing with large databases because the storage requirements for multiple copies of such backup images can be enormous. A better alternative is to create a full backup image periodically and one or more incremental backup images on a more frequent basis. An incremental backup is a backup image that contains only pages that have been updated since the previous backup image was made. Along with updated data and index pages, each incremental backup image also contains all of the initial database meta-data (such as database configuration, table space definitions, recovery history file, etc.) that is normally found in a full database backup image.

Two types of incremental backup images can be produced: incremental and delta. An incremental backup image is a copy of all database data that has changed since the most recent, successful, full backup image was created. An incremental backup image is also known as a *cumulative backup image* because the last incremental backup image in a series of incremental backup images made over a period of time will contain the contents of all of the previous incremental backup images. The predecessor of an incremental backup image is always the most recent successful full backup image of the same object.

A delta backup image, on the other hand, is a copy of all database data that has changed since the last successful backup (full, incremental, or delta) of the database or table space in question. For this reason, a delta backup image is also known as a differential, or noncumulative, backup image. The predecessor of a delta backup image is the most recent successful backup image that contains a copy of each of the objects found in the delta backup image.

The one thing that incremental and delta backup images have in common is that before either type of backup image can be created, a full backup image must already exist. Where they differ can be seen both in their creation (usually, delta backup images are smaller and can be created faster than incremental backup images) and in how they are used for recovery. When incremental backup images are taken, database recovery involves restoring the database using the most recent full backup image available and applying the most recent incremental backup image produced. On the other hand, when delta backup images are taken, database recovery involves restoring the database using the most recent full backup image available and applying each delta backup image produced since the full backup image used was made, in the order in which they were created.

Performing a Crash Recovery Operation

Earlier, we saw that whenever transaction processing is interrupted by an unexpected event (such as a power failure), the database with which the transaction was interacting at the time is placed in an inconsistent state. Such a database will remain in an inconsistent state and will be unusable until a crash recovery operation returns it to some point of consistency. (An inconsistent database will notify users and applications that it is unusable via a return code and error message that is generated each time an attempt to activate it or establish a connection to it is made.)

So just how is a crash recovery operation initiated? One way is by executing the RESTART DATABASE command from the DB2 Command Line Processor (CLP). The basic syntax for this command is:

```
RESTART [DATABASE | DB] [DatabaseAlias]
<USER [UserName] <USING [Password]>>
<DROP PENDING TABLESPACES ([TS_Name], ... )>
<WRITE RESUME>
```

where:

DatabaseAlias   Identifies the alias assigned to the database that is to be returned to a consistent and usable state.

UserName   Identifies the name assigned to a specific user under whose authority the crash recovery operation is to be performed.

Password   Identifies the password that corresponds to the name of the user under whom the crash recovery operation is to be performed.

TS_Name   Identifies the name assigned to one or more table spaces that are to be disabled and placed in "Drop Pending" state during the crash recovery process.

If a problem occurs with a table space container during the restart process, the DROP PENDING TABLESPACES ([*TS_Name*]) option can be used to place one or more table spaces in "Drop Pending" state. This allows the database to be successfully restarted, after which the offending table space can be dropped and, if necessary, recreated. A list of troubled table space names can be found in the administration notification log if a database restart operation fails because of table space container problems.

> If there is only one system temporary table space in the database, and if it is placed in "Drop Pending" state, a new system temporary table space must be created immediately following a successful database restart operation.

If all database I/O happened to be suspended at the time a crash occurred, the WRITE RESUME option of the RESTART command could be used to resume database I/O as part of the crash recovery process.

Thus, if you wanted to perform a crash recovery operation on an unusable database named SAMPLE, you could do so by executing a RESTART command that looks something like this:

```
RESTART DATABASE sample
```

On the other hand, if you wanted to perform a crash recovery operation on a database named SAMPLE and place a table space named TEMPSPACE1 in "Drop Pending" state, you could do so by executing a RESTART command that looks something like this:

```
RESTART DATABASE sample
DROP PENDING TABLESPACES (TEMPSPACE1)
```

You can also initiate a crash recovery operation for a particular database by selecting the Restart action from the Databases menu found in the Control Center. Figure 7–10 shows the Control Center menu items that must be selected in order to perform a crash recovery operation on an unusable database.

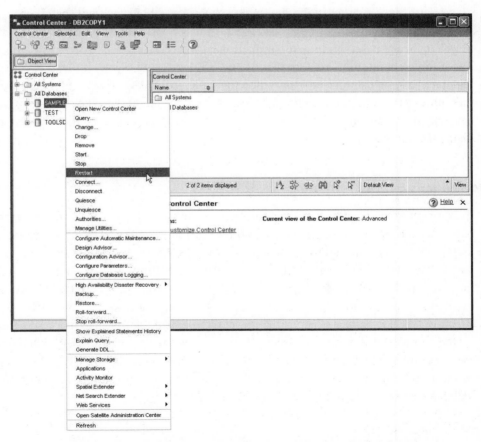

Figure 7–10: Initiating a crash recovery operation from the Control Center.

It is possible to configure a database in such a way that crash recovery will automatically be performed, if necessary, when an application or user attempts to establish a connection to it. This is done by assigning the value ON to the *autorestart* database configuration parameter. (The DB2 Database Manager checks the state of a database the first time an attempt to establish a connection to the database is made, and if it determines that the database is in an inconsistent state, it executes the RESTART command automatically if the *autorestart* database configuration parameter is set to ON.)

It is important to note that if a crash recovery operation is performed on a recoverable database (i.e., a database that has been configured to support roll-forward recovery operations), and an error occurs during the recovery process that is attributable to an individual table space, that table space will be taken offline and will no longer be accessible until it is repaired. This has no effect on crash recovery itself, and upon completion of the crash recovery operation, all other table spaces in the database will be accessible, and connections to the database can be established—provided the table space that is taken offline is not the table space that contains the system catalogs. If the table space containing the system catalogs is taken offline, it must be repaired before any connections to the database will be permitted.

A Word About Soft Checkpoints

It was mentioned earlier that crash recovery is performed by using information stored in the transaction log files to roll back all incomplete transactions found and complete any committed transactions that were still in memory (but had not yet been externalized to storage) when the transaction failure occurred. As you might imagine, if the transaction log files for a database are large, it could take quite a while to scan the entire log and check for corresponding rows in the database. However, it is usually not necessary to scan the entire log because records recorded at the beginning of a log file are usually associated with transactions that have been completed and have already been externalized to the database. Furthermore, if these records can be skipped, the amount of time required to recover a crashed database can be greatly reduced.

That's where a mechanism known as the *soft checkpoint* comes in. The DB2 Database Manager uses a log control file to determine which records from a specific log file need to be applied to the database. This log control file is written to disk periodically, and the frequency at which this file is updated is determined by the value of the *softmax* database configuration parameter. Once the log control file is updated, the soft checkpoint information stored in it establishes where in a transaction log file crash recovery should begin; all records in a log file that precede the soft checkpoint are assumed to be associated with transactions that have already been written to the database and are ignored.

Backup and Recovery

Although crash recovery can be used to resolve inconsistency problems that result from power interruptions or application failures, it cannot be used to handle problems that arise when the storage media being used to hold a database's files becomes corrupted or fails. In order to handle these types of problems, some kind of backup (and recovery) program must be put in place.

A database recovery strategy should include a regular schedule for making database backup images and, in the case of partitioned database systems, include making backup images whenever the system is scaled (i.e., whenever database partition servers are added or dropped). Additionally, the strategy used should ensure that all information needed is available when database recovery is necessary, and it should include procedures for restoring command scripts, applications, user-defined functions (UDFs), stored procedure code in operating system libraries, and load copies as well as database data. To help with such a strategy, DB2 provides four utilities that are used to facilitate backing up and restoring a database:

- The Backup utility
- The Restore utility
- The Roll-forward utility
- The Recover utility

The DB2 Backup Utility

The single most important item you can possess that will prevent catastrophic data losses in the event storage media becomes corrupted or fails is a database backup image. A database backup image is essentially a copy of an entire database that includes its metadata, its objects, its data, and optionally, its transaction logs. Once created, a backup image can be used at any time to return a database to the exact state it was in at the time the backup image was made (version recovery). A good database recovery strategy should ensure that backup images are created on a regular basis and that backup copies of critical data are retained in a secure location and on different storage media from that used to house the database. Depending on the logging method used (circular or archival), database backup images can be made when a database is offline or while other users and applications are connected to it. (In order to backup a database while it is online, archival logging must be enabled.)

A backup image of a DB2 database, or a table space within a DB2 database, can be created by executing the BACKUP DATABASE command. The basic syntax for this command is:

```
BACKUP [DATABASE | DB] [DatabaseAlias]
<USER [UserName] <USING [Password]>>
<TABLESPACE ([TS_Name],...)
<ONLINE>
<INCREMENTAL <DELTA>>
<TO [Location] | USE TSM <OPTIONS [TSMOptions]>>
<WITH [NumBuffers] BUFFERS>
<BUFFER [BufferSize]>
<PARALLELISM [ParallelNum]>
<UTIL_IMPACT_PRIORITY [Priority]>
<WITHOUT PROMPTING>
```

where:

DatabaseAlias   Identifies the alias assigned to the database for which a backup image is to be created.

UserName   Identifies the name assigned to a specific user under whose authority the backup operation is to be performed.

Password   Identifies the password that corresponds to the name of the user under whom the backup operation is to be performed.

TS_Name   Identifies the name assigned to one or more specific table spaces for which backup images are to be created.

Location   Identifies the directory or device where the backup image created is to be stored.

TSMOptions   Identifies options that are to be used by Tivoli Storage Manager (TSM) during the backup operation.

NumBuffers   Identifies the number of buffers that are to be used to perform the backup operation. (By default, two buffers are used if this option is not specified.)

BufferSize   Identifies the size, in pages, that each buffer used to perform the backup operation will be. (By default, the size of each buffer used by the Backup utility is determined by the value of the *backbufsz* DB2 Database Manager configuration parameter.)

ParallelNum   Identifies the number of table spaces that can be read in parallel during the backup operation.

Priority   Indicates that the Backup utility is to be throttled such that it executes at a specific rate so that its effect on concurrent database activity can be controlled. This parameter can be assigned a numerical value within the range of 1 to 100, with 100 representing the highest priority and 1 representing the lowest.

If the INCREMENTAL option is specified, an incremental backup image will be produced—an incremental backup image is a copy of all data that has changed since the last successful, full backup image was produced. If the INCREMENTAL DELTA option is specified, a delta backup image will be produced—a delta backup image is a copy of all data that has changed since the last successful backup image of any type (full, incremental, or delta) was produced.

Thus, if you wanted to create a full backup image of a database named SAMPLE that is currently offline and store the image created in a directory named BACKUPS on logical disk drive E:, you could do so by executing a BACKUP DATABASE command that looks something like this:

```
BACKUP DATABASE sample
USER db2admin USING ibmdb2
TO E:\backups
```

On the other hand, if you wanted to create an incremental backup image of a table space named TBSP1 and store the image created in a directory named BACKUPS on logical disk drive E: while the database it is associated with (named SAMPLE) remains online, you could do so by executing a BACKUP DATABASE command that looks something like this:

```
BACKUP DATABASE sample
USER db2admin USING ibmdb2
TABLESPACE (tbsp1) ONLINE INCREMENTAL TO E:\backups
```

Keep in mind that table space backup images can be created only if archival logging is being used; if circular logging is used instead, table space backups are not supported.

You can also create a backup image of a database or one or more table spaces using the Backup Wizard, which can be activated by selecting the Backup action from the Databases menu found in the Control Center. Figure 7–11 shows the Control Center menu items that must be selected to activate the Backup Wizard; Figure 7–12 shows how the first page of the Backup Wizard might look immediately after it is activated.

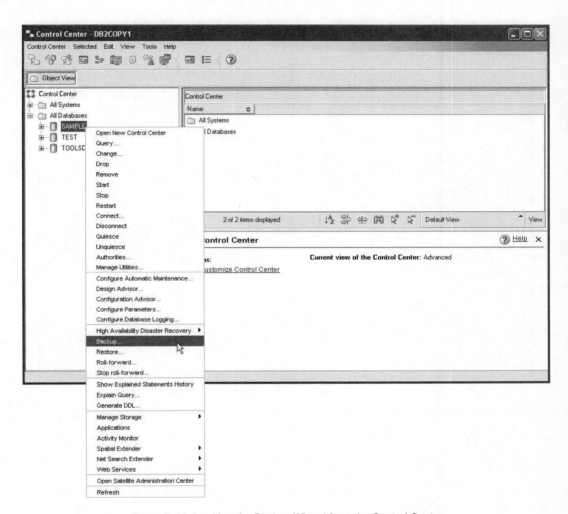

Figure 7–11: Invoking the Backup Wizard from the Control Center.

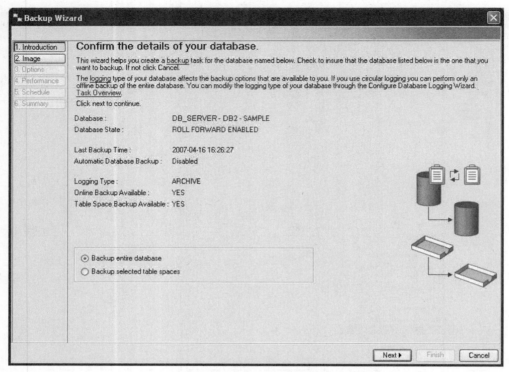

Figure 7–12: The first page of the Backup Wizard.

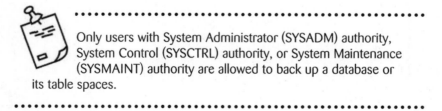

Only users with System Administrator (SYSADM) authority, System Control (SYSCTRL) authority, or System Maintenance (SYSMAINT) authority are allowed to back up a database or its table spaces.

The DB2 Restore Utility

Earlier, we saw that version recovery is the process that returns a database to the state it was in at the time a backup image was made. This means that in order to perform a version recovery operation, at least one backup image must exist and be available. So just how is a version recovery operation initiated? The most common way is by executing the RESTORE DATABASE command. The basic syntax for this command is:

```
RESTORE [DATABASE | DB] [DatabaseAlias]
<USER [UserName] <USING [Password]>>
[TABLESPACE ([TS_Name] ,... ) <ONLINE> |
    HISTORY FILE <ONLINE>> |
    COMPRESSION LIBRARY <ONLINE>> |
    LOGS <ONLINE>]
<INCREMENTAL <AUTO | AUTOMATIC | ABORT>>
<FROM [SourceLocation] | USE TSM <OPTIONS [TSMOptions]>>
<TAKEN AT [Timestamp]>
<TO [TargetLocation]>
<DBPATH ON [TargetPath]>
<INTO [TargetAlias]> <LOGTARGET [LogsLocation]>
<NEWLOGPATH [LogsLocation]>
<WITH [NumBuffers] BUFFERS>
<BUFFER [BufferSize]>
<REPLACE HISTORY FILE>
<REPLACE EXISTING>
<REDIRECT <GENERATE SCRIPT [ScriptFile]>>
<PARALLELISM [ParallelNum]>
<WITHOUT ROLLING FORWARD>
<WITHOUT PROMPTING>
```

or

```
RESTORE [DATABASE | DB] [DatabaseAlias]
<USER [UserName] <USING [Password]>>
<REBUILD WITH [TABLESPACE ([TS_Name] ,... )] |
    [ALL TABLESPACES IN [DATABASE | IMAGE]]
        <EXCEPT TABLESPACE ([TS_Name] ,... )>>
<INCREMENTAL <AUTO | AUTOMATIC | ABORT>>
<FROM [SourceLocation] | USE TSM <OPTIONS [TSMOptions]>>
<TAKEN AT [Timestamp]>
<TO [TargetLocation]>
<DBPATH ON [TargetPath]>
<INTO [TargetAlias]> <LOGTARGET [LogsLocation]>
<NEWLOGPATH [LogsLocation]>
<WITH [NumBuffers] BUFFERS>
<BUFFER [BufferSize]>
<REPLACE HISTORY FILE>
<REPLACE EXISTING>
<REDIRECT <GENERATE SCRIPT [ScriptFile]>>
<PARALLELISM [ParallelNum]>
<WITHOUT ROLLING FORWARD>
<WITHOUT PROMPTING>
```

or

```
RESTORE [DATABASE | DB] [DatabaseName]
[CONTINUE | ABORT]
```

where:

DatabaseAlias   Identifies the alias assigned to the database that a version recovery operation is to be performed for.

UserName   Identifies the name assigned to a specific user under whom the version recovery operation is to be performed.

Password   Identifies the password that corresponds to the name of the user under whom the version recovery operation is to be performed.

TS_Name   Identifies the name assigned to one or more specific table spaces that are to be restored from a backup image. (If the table space name has changed since the backup image was made, the new name should be specified.)

SourceLocation   Identifies the directory or device where the backup image to be used for version recovery is stored.

TSMOptions   Identifies options that are to be used by Tivoli Storage Manager (TSM) during the version recovery operation.

Timestamp   Identifies a timestamp that is to be used as search criterion when looking for a particular backup image to use for version recovery. (If no timestamp is specified, it is assumed that there is only one backup image stored at the source location specified.)

TargetLocation   Identifies the directory where the storage containers for the database that will be created are to be stored—if the backup image is to be used to create a new database and automatic storage is used.

TargetPath   Identifies the directory where the metadata for the database that will be created is to be stored—if the backup image is to be used to create a new database and automatic storage is used.

TargetAlias   Identifies the alias to be assigned to the new database to be
                       created.

LogsLocation   Identifies the directory or device where log files for the new
                       database are to be stored.

NumBuffers   Identifies the number of buffers that are to be used to perform
                       the version recovery operation. (By default, two buffers are used
                       if this option is not specified.)

BufferSize   Identifies the size, in pages, that each buffer used to perform the
                       backup operation will be. (By default, the size of each buffer
                       used by the RESTORE utility is determined by the value of the
                       restbufsz DB2 Database Manager configuration parameter.)

ScriptFile   Identifies the name of a file to which all commands needed to
                       perform a redirected restore operation are to be written.

ParallelNum   Identifies the number of table spaces that can be read in parallel
                       during the version recovery operation.

Thus, if you wanted to restore a database named SAMPLE (which already exists),
using a full backup image stored in a directory named BACKUPS on logical disk
drive E:, you could do so by executing a RESTORE DATABASE command that looks
something like this:

```
RESTORE DATABASE sample
USER db2admin USING ibmdb2
FROM E:\backups
REPLACE EXISTING
WITHOUT PROMPTING
```

On the other hand, if you wanted to restore a table space named TBSP1 from an
incremental backup image stored in a directory named BACKUPS on logical disk
drive E: while the database it is associated with (named SAMPLE) remains online,
you could do so by executing a RESTORE DATABASE command that looks something
like this:

```
RESTORE DATABASE sample
USER db2admin USING ibmdb2
TABLESPACE (tbsp1) ONLINE
INCREMENTAL
FROM E:\backups
```

Each full database backup image contains, among other things, a copy of the database's recovery history file. However, when an existing database is restored from a full database backup image, the existing recovery history file is not overwritten. But what if the recovery history file for the database happens to be corrupted? Can the recovery history file be restored as well given that a copy exists in the database backup image? The answer is yes. A special form of the RESTORE DATABASE command can be used to restore *just* the recovery history file from a database backup image. Such a RESTORE DATABASE command looks something like this:

```
RESTORE DATABASE sample
HISTORY FILE
FROM E:\backups
```

It is also possible to create an entirely new database from a full database backup image, effectively cloning an existing database. Thus, you could create a new database named SAMPLE_2 that is an exact duplicate of a database named SAMPLE, using a backup image stored in a directory named BACKUPS on logical disk drive E: by executing a RESTORE DATABASE command that looks something like this:

```
RESTORE DATABASE sample
USER db2admin USING ibmdb2
FROM E:\backups
INTO sample_2
```

It is important to note that if a backup image is used to create a new database, the recovery history file stored in the backup image will become the recovery history file for the new database.

You can also perform any of the restore/recovery operations just described (along with many others) using the Restore Data Wizard, which can be activated by selecting the Restore action from the Databases menu found in the Control Center. Figure 7–13 shows the Control Center menu items that must be selected to activate the Restore Data Wizard; Figure 7–14 shows how the first page of the Restore Data Wizard might look immediately after it is activated.

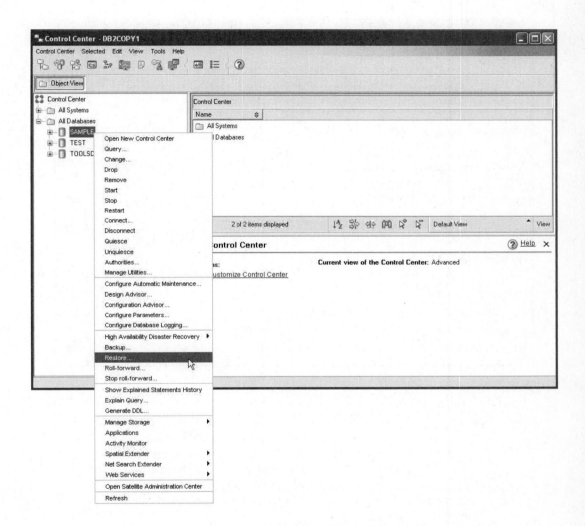

Figure 7–13: Invoking the Restore Data Wizard from the Control Center.

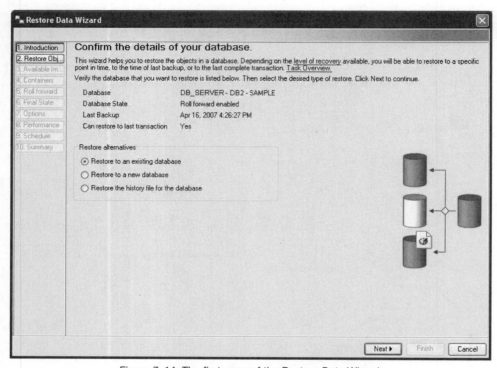

Figure 7–14: The first page of the Restore Data Wizard.

Only users with System Administrator (SYSADM) authority, System Control (SYSCTRL) authority, or System Maintenance (SYSMAINT) authority are allowed to restore a database or any of its table spaces from a backup image; only users with SYSADM authority or SYSCTRL authority are allowed to create a new database from a backup image.

Redirected restore

As you might imagine, a full backup image of a database contains, among other things, information about all table spaces that have been defined for the database, including specific information about each table space container being used at the time the backup image was made. During a version recovery operation, a check is performed to verify that all table space containers referenced by the backup image exist and are accessible. If this check determines that one or more of the table space containers needed is no longer available/accessible, the recovery operation will fail, and the database will not be restored. When this happens, any invalid table space containers encountered can be redefined at the beginning of the recovery process by performing what is known as a *redirected restore*. (A redirected restore operation can also be used to restore a backup image to a target machine that is different from the source machine or to store table space data in a different physical location.)

Unavailable/inaccessible table space containers are redefined by executing the SET TABLESPACE CONTAINERS command. The basic syntax for this command is:

```
SET TABLESPACE CONTAINERS FOR [TS_ID] USING
[(PATH '[Container]' ,...) |
  ([FILE | DEVICE] '[Container]' [ContainerSize] ,...)]
```

where:

TS_ID   Identifies the identification number assigned to the table space for which new storage containers are to be provided.

Container   Identifies one or more containers that are to be used to store the data associated with the table space specified.

ContainerSize   Identifies the number of pages to be stored in the table space container specified.

The steps used to perform a redirected restore operation are as follows:

1. Start the redirected restore operation by executing the RESTORE DATABASE command with the REDIRECT option specified. (When this option is specified, each invalid table space container encountered is flagged, and all table spaces that reference invalid table space containers are placed in the "Restore Pending" state. A list of all table spaces affected can be obtained by executing the LIST TABLESPACES command.) At some point, you should see a message that looks something like this:

```
SQL1277N Restore has detected that one or more table space
containers are inaccessible, or has set their state to
'storage must be defined'.
DB20000I The RESTORE DATABASE command completed successfully.
```

2. Specify new table space containers for each table space placed in "Restore Pending" state by executing a SET TABLESPACE CONTAINERS command for each appropriate table space. (Keep in mind that SMS table spaces can use only PATH containers, whereas DMS table spaces can use only FILE or DEVICE containers.)

3. Complete the redirected restore operation by executing the RESTORE DATABASE command again with the CONTINUE option specified.

To simplify things, all of these steps can be coded in a UNIX shell script or Windows batch file, which can then be executed from a system prompt. Such a file would look something like this:

```
db2 "RESTORE DATABASE sample FROM C:\backups TO D:\DB_DIR INTO
sample_2 REDIRECT"

db2 "SET TABLESPACE CONTAINERS FOR 0 USING
(PATH 'D:\DB_DIR\SYSTEM')"

db2 "SET TABLESPACE CONTAINERS FOR 1 USING
(PATH 'D:\DB_DIR\TEMP')"

db2 "SET TABLESPACE CONTAINERS FOR 2 USING
(PATH 'D:\DB_DIR\USER')"

db2 "RESTORE DATABASE sample CONTINUE"
```

With DB2 9, the RESTORE DATABASE command can be used to take a lot of the work out of creating such a script file. You simply execute the RESTORE DATABASE command with the REDIRECT GENERATE SCRIPT option specified, modify the script produced, and then run the script to perform the redirected restore operation. For example, to generate a redirected restore script based on an existing backup image of a database named SAMPLE that resides on a AIX server, you would execute a RESTORE DATABASE command that looks something like this:

```
RESTORE DATABASE sample FROM /home/db2inst1/backups
TAKEN AT 20070514093000
REDIRECT GENERATE SCRIPT redir_rest.sh
```

You can also perform a redirected restore by assigning new table space containers to existing table spaces on the Containers page of the Restore Data Wizard. Figure 7–15 shows how this page looks.

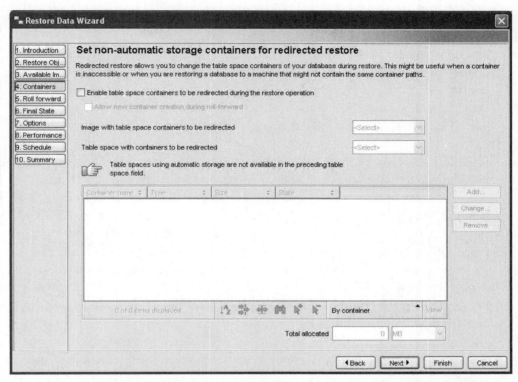

Figure 7–15: The Containers page of the Restore Data Wizard (used when performing a redirected restore operation).

In addition to providing new storage containers for table spaces when older table space containers are inaccessible or are no longer present, a redirected restore can also be used to add new containers to existing SMS table spaces. (The ALTER TABLESPACE command does not allow you to add new storage containers to existing SMS table spaces; a redirected restore provides a workaround to this limitation.)

The DB2 Roll-Forward Utility

When a backup image is used to restore a damaged or corrupted database, the database can be returned only to the state it was in at the time the backup image was made. Therefore, all changes that were made to the database after the backup image was created will be lost when a version recovery operation is performed. To return a database to the state it was in at any given point in time, roll-forward recovery must be used instead. And in order to perform a roll-forward recovery operation, the database must be recoverable (that is, the database must be configured to use archival logging), you must have a full backup image of the database available, and you must have access to all archived log files that have been created since the last backup image (full, incremental, or delta) was made.

Roll-forward recovery starts out as a version recovery operation. However, where a version recovery operation will leave a nonrecoverable database in a "Normal" state, the same operation will leave a recoverable database in "Roll-forward pending" state (unless the WITHOUT ROLLING FORWARD option was specified with the RESTORE DATABASE command that was used to recover the database). At that point, either the database can be taken out of "Roll-forward pending" state (in which case all changes made to the database since the backup image used for version recovery was made will be lost), or information stored in the database's transaction log files can be replayed to return the database to the state it was in at any given point in time.

The process of replaying transactions stored in archived log files is known as "rolling the database forward," and one way to roll a database forward is by executing the ROLLFORWARD DATABASE command. The basic syntax for this command is:

```
ROLLFORWARD [DATABASE | DB] [DatabaseAlias]
<USER [UserName] <USING [Password]>>
<TO [PointInTime] <USING [UTC | LOCAL] TIME>
    <AND [COMPLETE | STOP]> |
          END OF LOGS <AND [COMPLETE | STOP]> |
          COMPLETE |
          STOP |
          CANCEL |
          QUERY STATUS <USING [UTC | LOCAL] TIME>>
<TABLESPACE ONLINE |
    TABLESPACE <( [TS_Name] ,... )> <ONLINE>>
<OVERFLOW LOG PATH ([LogDirectory] ,...)>
<RECOVER DROPPED TABLE [TableID] TO [Location]>
```

where:

DatabaseAlias   Identifies the alias assigned to the database that is to be rolled forward.

UserName   Identifies the name assigned to a specific user under whom the roll-forward operation is to be performed.

Password   Identifies the password that corresponds to the name of the user under whom the roll-forward operation is to be performed.

PointInTime   Identifies a specific point in time, identified by a timestamp value in the form *yyyy-mm-dd-hh.mm.ss.nnnnnn* (year, month, day, hour, minutes, seconds, microseconds), to which that the database is to be rolled forward. (Only transactions that took place before and up to the date and time specified will be reapplied to the database.)

TS_Name   Identifies the name assigned to one or more specific table spaces that are to be rolled forward. (If the table space name has changed since the backup image used to restore the database was made, the new name should be specified.)

LogDirectory   Identifies the directory that contains offline archived log files that are to be used to perform the roll-forward operation.

TableID   Identifies a specific table (by ID) that was dropped earlier that is to be restored as part of the roll-forward operation. (The table ID can be obtained by examining the database's recovery history file.)

Location   Identifies the directory to which files containing dropped table data are to be written when the table is restored as part of the roll-forward operation.

If the AND COMPLETE, AND STOP, COMPLETE, or STOP option is specified, the database will be returned to "Normal" state when the roll-forward operation has completed. Otherwise, the database will remain in "Roll-forward pending state." (When a recoverable database is restored from a backup image, it is automatically placed in "Roll-forward pending" state unless the WITHOUT ROLLING FORWARD option is used with the RESTORE DATABASE command; while a database is in "Roll-forward pending" state, it cannot be accessed by users and applications.)

If the QUERY STATUS option is specified, a list of the log files that have been used to perform the roll-forward recovery operation, along with the next archive file required, and the time stamp (in UTC) of the last committed transaction since roll-forward processing began is returned.

Thus, if you wanted to perform a roll-forward recovery operation on a database named SAMPLE that was just restored from a backup image, you could do so by executing a ROLLFORWARD DATABASE command that looks something like this:

```
ROLLFORWARD DATABASE sample TO END OF LOGS AND STOP
```

On the other hand, if you wanted to perform a roll-forward recovery operation on a table space named DATA_TBSP in a database named SAMPLE by reapplying transactions that were performed against the table space on or before April 1, 2007 (04/01/2007), you could do so by executing a ROLLFORWARD DATABASE command that looks something like this:

```
ROLLFORWARD DATABASE sample TO 2007-04-01-00.00.00.0000
AND STOP TABLESPACE (data_tbsp)
```

It is important to note that the time value specified is interpreted as a Coordinated Universal Time (UTC)—otherwise known as Greenwich Mean Time (GMT)—value. If a ROLLFORWARD DATABASE command that looks something like the following had been executed instead, the time value specified would have been interpreted as a local time value:

```
ROLLFORWARD DATABASE SAMPLE TO 2007-04-01-00.00.00.0000 USING
LOCAL TIME AND STOP TABLESPACE (data_tbsp)
```

When rolling a table space forward to a specific point in time, the time specified must be greater than the minimum recovery time recorded for the table space. This time can be obtained by executing the command LIST TABLESPACES SHOW DETAIL; among other things, this command returns the earliest point in time to which each table space can be rolled forward. (The minimum recovery time is updated when data definition language (DDL) statements are run against a table space or against tables stored in a table space.) A table space must be rolled forward to at least the minimum recovery time so that it becomes synchronized with the information in the system catalog tables. If recovering more than one table space, each table space must be rolled forward to at least the highest minimum recovery time of all the table spaces being recovered.

If you want to roll a table space forward to a specific point in time, and a table in the table space participates in a referential integrity constraint with another table that resides in another table space, you should roll both table spaces forward simultaneously to the same point in time. If you do not, the child table in the referential integrity relationship will be placed in "Set integrity pending" state at the end of the roll-forward recovery operation, and constraint checking will have to be performed on the table before it can be used.

You can also initiate a roll-forward recovery operation using the Roll-forward Wizard, which can be activated by selecting the Roll-forward action from the Databases menu found in the Control Center. Figure 7–16 shows the Control Center menu items that must be selected to activate the Roll-forward Wizard; Figure 7–17 shows how the first page of the Roll-forward Wizard might look immediately after it is activated.

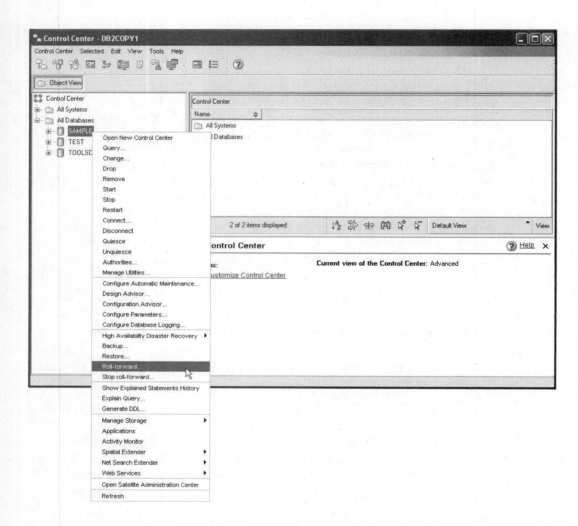

Figure 7–16: Invoking the Roll-forward Wizard from the Control Center.

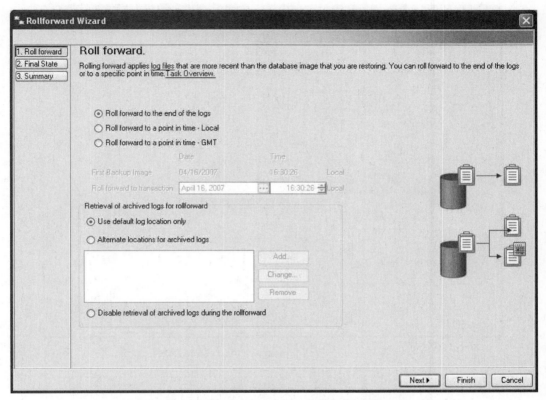

Figure 7–17: The first page of the Roll-forward Wizard.

Because a roll-forward recovery operation is typically performed immediately after a database is restored from a backup image, a roll-forward recovery operation can also be initiated by providing the appropriate information on the Roll-forward page of the Restore Data Wizard. Figure 7–18 shows how the Roll forward page of the Restore Data Wizard normally looks.

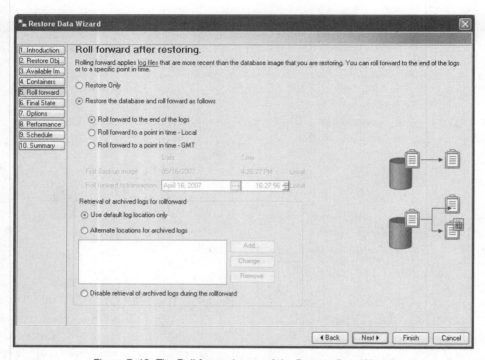

Figure 7–18: The Roll forward page of the Restore Data Wizard.

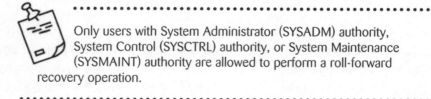

Only users with System Administrator (SYSADM) authority, System Control (SYSCTRL) authority, or System Maintenance (SYSMAINT) authority are allowed to perform a roll-forward recovery operation.

A Word About the Recovery History File

In chapter 3, "Data Placement," we saw that a special file, known as the recovery history file, is created as part of the database creation process. This file is used to log historical information about specific actions that are performed against the database with which the file is associated. Specifically, records are written to the recovery history file whenever any of the following actions are performed:

- A backup image of any type is created.

- A version recovery operation is performed either on the database or on one of its table spaces.

- A table is loaded, using the Load utility.

- A roll-forward recovery operation is performed either on the database or on one of its table spaces.

- A table space is altered.

- A table space is quiesced.

- Data in a table is reorganized, using the REORG utility.

- Statistics for a table are updated, using the RUNSTATS utility.

- A table is deleted (dropped).

In addition to identifying the event that was performed, each entry in the recovery history file identifies the date and time the event took place, how the event took place, the table spaces and tables that were affected and, if the action was a backup operation, the location where the backup image produced was stored, along with information on how to access this image. And because the recovery history file contains image location information for each backup image available, it acts as a tracking and verification mechanism during version recovery operations.

Because the recovery history file sits quietly in the background and the DB2 Database Manager is responsible for managing its contents, a database administrator rarely has to interact with it. However, two commands—LIST HISTORY and PRUNE HISTORY—provide a way to both view the contents of a database's recovery history file and remove one or more entries stored in it. Additionally, if the recovery history file for a database becomes corrupt, it is possible to restore just the recovery history file from a database backup image.

The DB2 Recover Utility

Earlier, we saw how the RESTORE DATABASE command can be used to return a database to the state it was in at the time a backup image was made and how the ROLLFORWARD DATABASE command can be used to replay information recorded in a database's transaction log files to return a database to the state it was in at a specific point in time. If you are restoring the database from a full database backup image, this process is pretty straightforward. However, if you have a full database backup image and several incremental backup images, delta backup images, or table space backup images, the process can be a little complicated. That's where DB2's Recover utility comes in.

Introduced in DB2 9, the Recover utility performs the necessary restore and roll-forward operations to recover a database to a specific point in time, based on information found in the recovery history file. The Recovery utility is invoked by executing the RECOVER DATABASE command. The basic syntax for this command is:

```
RECOVER [DATABASE | DB] [DatabaseAlias]
<TO [PointInTime] <USING [UTC | LOCAL] TIME> |
    END OF LOGS>
<USER [UserName] <USING [Password]>>
<USING HISTORY FILE ([HistoryFile])>
<OVERFLOW LOG PATH ([LogDirectory] ,...)>
<RESTART>
```

where:

DatabaseAlias   Identifies the alias assigned to the database that is to be restored and rolled forward.

PointInTime   Identifies a specific point in time, identified by a timestamp value in the form *yyyy-mm-dd-hh.mm.ss.nnnnnn* (year, month, day, hour, minutes, seconds, microseconds), to which the database is to be rolled forward. (Only transactions that took place before and up to the date and time specified will be reapplied to the database.)

UserName   Identifies the name assigned to a specific user under whom the recovery operation is to be performed.

Password   Identifies the password that corresponds to the name of the user under whom the recovery operation is to be performed.

HistoryFile   Identifies the name assigned to the recovery history log file that
                        is to be used by the Recovery utility.

LogDirectory   Identifies the directory that contains offline archived log files
                        that are to be used to perform the roll-forward portion of the
                        recovery operation.

Thus, if you wanted to perform a full recovery operation on a database named
SAMPLE (which already exists) using information stored in the recovery history file,
you could do so by executing a RECOVER DATABASE command that looks something
like this:

```
RECOVER DATABASE sample
TO END OF LOGS
```

On the other hand, if you wanted to restore a database named SAMPLE and roll it
forward to an extremely old point in time that is no longer contained in the current
recovery history file, you could do so by executing a RECOVER DATABASE
command that looks something like this (assuming you have a copy of an older
recovery history file available):

```
RECOVER DATABASE sample
TO 2005-01-31-04.00.00
USING HISTORY FILE (/home/user/old2005files/db2rhist.asc)
```

It is important to note that if the Recover utility successfully restores a database,
but for some reason fails while attempting to roll it forward, the Recover utility
will attempt to continue the previous recover operation, without redoing the restore
phase. If you want to force the Recover utility to redo the restore phase, you need
to execute the RECOVER DATABASE command with the RESTART option specified.
There is no way to explicitly restart a recovery operation from a point of failure.

Rebuilding Invalid Indexes

So far we have looked at ways that data can be recovered in the event the storage
media being used to hold a database's files becomes corrupted or fails. But what if
only indexes are damaged, and a database's data is unaffected (which could be the
case if data and indexes are stored in separate table spaces and only the physical

device where index data is stored fails)? In this case, the affected indexes are invalidated and can be recovered by being re-created once the faulty media has been replaced.

Whenever the DB2 Database Manager detects that an index is no longer valid, it automatically attempts to rebuild it. However, the point in time at which the DB2 Database Manager attempts to rebuild an invalid index is controlled by the *indexrec* parameter of the database or the DB2 Database Manager configuration file. There are three possible settings for this parameter:

SYSTEM. Invalid indexes are to be rebuilt at the time specified in the *indexrec* parameter of the DB2 Database Manager configuration file. (This setting is valid only for database configuration files.)

RESTART. Invalid indexes are to be rebuilt, either explicitly or implicitly, when the database is restarted (i.e., when crash recovery is performed on the database).

ACCESS. Invalid indexes are to be rebuilt the first time they are accessed after they have been marked as being invalid.

So when is the best time to rebuild invalid indexes? If the time needed to perform a crash recovery operation on a database is not a concern, it is better to let the DB2 Database Manager rebuild invalid indexes while it is in the process of returning the database to a consistent state; the time needed to restart a database will be longer because of the index recreation process, but once the database has been restored, query processing will not be impacted. On the other hand, if indexes are rebuilt as they are accessed, crash recovery will be performed faster, but users may experience a decrease in performance—queries against tables that contain associated invalid indexes will have to wait for the invalid indexes to be rebuilt before they can be processed. Furthermore, unexpected locks may be acquired and held long after an invalid index has been recreated, especially if the transaction that caused the index recreation to occur is not committed (or rolled back) for some time.

Although the *indexrec* parameter of the database or the DB2 Database Manager configuration file can be used to control when indexes are rebuilt as part of a crash recovery operation, it has no effect on how indexes are rebuilt during roll-forward recovery operations. To control that behavior, you must assign the appropriate value to the *logindexbuild* database configuration parameter. There are two possible settings for this parameter:

ON. Index creation, re-creation, and reorganization operations are to be recorded in the database's transaction log files so that indexes can be reconstructed during roll-forward recovery operations or high availability disaster recovery (HADR) log replay operations.

OFF. Index creation, re-creation, and reorganization operations will not be recorded in the database's transaction log files.

If the LOG INDEX BUILD table attribute is set to its default value of NULL, DB2 will use the value specified for the *logindexbuild* database configuration parameter. If the LOG INDEX BUILD table attribute is set to ON or OFF, the value specified for the *logindexbuild* database configuration parameter will be ignored.

Backing Up a Database with Split Mirroring

It was mentioned earlier that as databases increase in size and as heavy usage demands require databases to be available 24 hours a day, 7 days a week, the time and hardware needed to back up and restore a database can increase substantially. Backing up an entire database or several table spaces of a large database can put a strain on system resources, require a considerable amount of additional storage space (to hold the backup images), and reduce the availability of the database system (particularly if the system has to be taken offline in order to be backed up). Therefore, a popular alternative to creating and maintaining backup images of high-availability databases is to use what is known as a *split mirror*.

A split mirror is an "instantaneous" copy of a database that is made by mirroring the disk or disks that contain the database's data and splitting the mirror when a backup copy of the database is required. Mirroring is the process of writing all database data to two separate disks (or disk subsystems) simultaneously; one disk/subsystem holds the database data while the other holds an exact copy (known as a mirror) of the primary disk/subsystem being used. Splitting a mirror simply involves separating the primary and secondary copies of the database from each other. Split mirroring provides the following advantages:

- The overhead required to create backup images of the database is eliminated.

- Entire systems can be cloned very quickly.

- It provides a fast implementation of idle standby failover.

To further enhance split mirroring, DB2 provides a way to temporarily suspend (and later resume) all database I/O so that a mirror can be split without having to take a database offline. The command that provides this functionality is the SET WRITE command, and the syntax for this command is:

```
SET WRITE [SUSPEND | RESUME] FOR [DATABASE | DB]
```

Therefore, if you wanted to temporarily suspend all I/O for a database, you would do so by establishing a connection to that database and executing a SET WRITE command that looks like this:

```
SET WRITE SUSPEND FOR DATABASE
```

When executed, the SET WRITE SUSPEND FOR DATABASE command causes the DB2 Database Manager to suspend all write operations to table space containers and log files that are associated with the current database. (The suspension of writes to table spaces and log files is intended to prevent partial page writes from occurring until the suspension is removed.) All operations, apart from online backup and restore operations, will function normally while database writes are suspended. That's because read-only transactions are not suspended and are able to continue working with a write-suspended database provided they do not require I/O processing; applications can continue to perform insert, update, and delete operations with data that has been cached in the database's buffer pool(s), but new pages cannot be read from disk. Additionally, new database connections can be established to a write-suspended database provided the system catalog pages required to authenticate the connections already reside in a buffer pool.

I/O for a write-suspended database can be resumed at any time by executing a SET WRITE command that looks like this:

```
SET WRITE RESUME FOR DATABASE
```

When executed, the SET WRITE RESUME FOR DATABASE command causes the DB2 Database Manager to lift all write suspensions and to allow write operations to table space containers and log files that are associated with the current database to continue.

 The SET WRITE RESUME FOR DATABASE command must be executed from the same connection from which the SET WRITE SUSPEND FOR DATABASE command was issued.

Initializing a Split Mirror with db2inidb

Before a split mirror copy of a DB2 database can be used, it must first be initialized; a split mirror database copy is initialized by executing the system command db2inidb. The syntax for this command is:

```
db2inidb [DatabaseAlias]
AS [SNAPSHOT | MIRROR | STANDBY]
<RELOCATE USING [ConfigFile]>
```

where:

DatabaseAlias   Identifies the alias assigned to the database that the split mirror copy to be initialized references.

ConfigFile   Indicates that the database files contained in the split mirror copy are to be relocated according to information stored in the configuration file specified.

As you can see, a split mirror database copy can be initialized in one of three ways:

SNAPSHOT. The split mirror copy of the database will be initialized as a read-only clone of the primary database.

MIRROR. The split mirror copy of the database will be initialized as a backup image that can be used to restore the primary database.

STANDBY. The split mirror copy of the database will be initialized and placed in roll-forward pending state so that it can be continuously synchronized with the primary database. (New logs from the primary database can be retrieved and applied to the copy of the database at any time.) The standby copy of the database can then be used in place of the primary database if, for some reason, the primary database goes down.

Thus, if you wanted to initialize a split mirror copy of a database named SAMPLE and make it a backup image that can be used to restore the primary database, you could do so by executing a db2inidb command that looks like this:

```
db2inidb SAMPLE AS MIRROR
```

High Availability Disaster Recovery (HADR)

High availability disaster recovery (HADR) is a DB2 database replication feature that provides a high availability solution for both partial and complete site failures. HADR protects against data loss by replicating data changes from a source database, called the *primary*, to a target database, called the *standby*. In an HADR environment, applications can access the current primary database— synchronization with the standby database occurs by rolling forward transaction log data that is generated on the primary database and shipped to the standby database. And with HADR, you can choose the level of protection you want from potential loss of data by specifying one of three synchronization modes: synchronous, near synchronous, or asynchronous.

HADR is designed to minimize the impact to a database system when a partial or a complete site failure occurs. A partial site failure can be caused by a hardware, network, or software (DB2 or operating system) malfunction. Without HADR, a partial site failure requires restarting the server and the instance where one or more DB2 databases reside. The length of time it takes to restart the server and the instance is unpredictable; if the transaction load was heavy at the time of the partial site failure, it can take several minutes before a database is returned to a consistent state and made available for use. With HADR, the standby database can take over in seconds. Furthermore, you can redirect the clients that were using the original primary database to the standby database (which is now the new primary database) by using automatic client reroute or retry logic in the applications that interact with the database. After the failed original primary server is repaired, it can rejoin the HADR pair as a standby database if both copies of the database can be made consistent. And once the original primary database is reintegrated into the HADR pair as the standby database, you can switch the roles so that the original primary database once again functions as the primary database. (This is known as *failback operation*).

A complete site failure can occur when a disaster, such as a fire, causes the entire site to be destroyed. Because HADR uses TCP/IP to communicate between a primary and a standby database, the databases can reside in two different locations. For example, your primary database might be located at your head office in one city, whereas your standby database is located at your sales office in another city. If a disaster occurs at the primary site, data availability is maintained by having the remote standby database take over as the primary database.

Requirements for HADR Environments

To achieve optimal performance with HADR, the system hosting the standby database should consist of the same hardware and software as the system where the primary database resides. If the system hosting the standby database has fewer resources than the system hosting the primary database, the standby database may not be able to keep up with the transaction load generated by the primary database. This can cause the standby database to fall behind or the performance of the primary database to suffer. But more importantly, if a failover situation occurs, the new primary database may not have the resources needed to adequately service the client applications. And because buffer pool operations performed on the primary database are replayed on the standby database, it is important that the primary and standby database servers have the same amount of memory.

IBM recommends that you use identical host computers for the HADR primary and standby databases. (If possible, they should be manufactured by the same vendor and have the same architecture.) Furthermore, the operating system on the primary and standby database servers should be the same version, including patch level. You can violate this rule for a short time during a rolling upgrade, but use extreme caution when doing so. A TCP/IP interface must also be available between the HADR host machines, and a high-speed, high-capacity network should be used to connect the two.

The DB2 software installed on both the primary and the standby database server must have the same bit size (32 or 64), and the version of DB2 used for the primary and standby databases must be identical; for example, both must be either version 8 or version 9. During rolling upgrades, the modification level (for example, the fix pack level) of the database system for the standby database can be later than that of the primary database for a short while. However, you should not keep this configuration for an extended period of time. The primary and standby databases will not connect to each other if the modification level of the database system for the primary database is later than that of the standby database. Therefore, fix packs must always be applied to the standby database system first.

Both the primary and the standby database must be a single-partition database, and they both must have the same database name; however, they do not have to be stored on the same database path. The amount of storage space allocated for transaction log files should also be the same on both the primary and the standby database server; the use of raw devices for transaction logging is not supported. (Archival logging is performed only by the current primary database.)

Table space properties such as table space name, table space type (DMS, SMS, or Automatic Storage), table space page size, table space size, container path, container size, and container type (raw device, file, or directory) must be identical on the primary and standby databases. When you issue a table space statement such as CREATE TABLESPACE, ALTER TABLESPACE, or DROP TABLESPACE on the primary database, it is replayed on the standby database. Therefore, you must ensure that the table space containers involved with such statements exist on both systems before you issue the table space statement on the primary database. (If you create a table space on the primary database, and log replay fails on the standby database because the containers are not available, the primary database does not receive an error message stating that the log replay failed.) Automatic storage databases are fully supported, including replication of ALTER DATABASE statements. Similar to table space containers, the storage paths specified must exist on both the primary and the standby server.

Additionally, once an HADR environment has been established, the following restrictions apply:

- Reads on the standby database are not supported; clients cannot connect to the standby database.

- Self Tuning Memory Manager (STMM) can be run only on the current primary database.

- Backup operations cannot be performed on the standby database.

- Redirected restore is not supported. That is, HADR does not support redirecting table space containers. However, database directory and log directory changes are supported.

- Load operations with the COPY NO option specified are not supported.

Setting Up an HADR Environment

The process of setting up an HADR environment is fairly straightforward. After ensuring that the systems to be used as primary and secondary server are identical and that a TCP/IP connection exists between them, you simply perform the following tasks, in the order shown:

1. Determine the host name, host IP address, and the service name or port number for both the primary and the secondary database server.

   If a server has multiple network interfaces, ensure that the HADR host name or IP address maps to the intended interface. You will need to allocate separate HADR ports for each protected database—these cannot be the same as the ports that have been allocated to the instance. The host name can map to only one IP address.

2. Create the standby database by restoring a backup image or initializing a split mirror copy of the database that is to serve as the primary database.

   It is recommended that you do not issue the ROLLFORWARD DATABASE command on the standby database after the restore operation or split mirror initialization. The results of performing a roll-forward recovery operation might differ slightly from replaying the logs on the standby database using HADR. If the primary and standby databases are not identical when HADR is started, an error will occur.

   When setting up the standby database using the RESTORE DATABASE command, it is recommended that the REPLACE HISTORY FILE option be used; use of the following options should be avoided: TABLESPACE, INTO, REDIRECT, and WITHOUT ROLLING FORWARD.

When setting up the standby database using the db2inidb utility, do not use the SNAPSHOT or MIRROR options. You can specify the RELOCATE USING option to change one or more of the following configuration attributes: instance name, log path, and database path. However, you must not change the database name or the table space container paths.

3. Set the HADR configuration parameters on both the primary and the standby databases.

   After the standby database has been created, but before HADR is started, the HADR configuration parameters shown in Table 7.2 need to be set.

Table 7.2 HADR-Specific Database Configuration Parameters	
Parameter	**Description**
HADR_LOCAL_HOST	Specifies the local host for high availability disaster recovery (HADR) TCP communication.
HADR_LOCAL_SVC	Specifies the TCP service name or port number for which the local high availability disaster recovery (HADR) process accepts connections.
HADR_REMOTE_HOST	Specifies the TCP/IP host name or IP address of the remote high availability disaster recovery (HADR) node.
HADR_REMOTE_INST	Specifies the instance name of the remote high availability disaster recovery (HADR) server.
HADR_REMOTE_SVC	Specifies the TCP service name or port number that will be used by the remote high availability disaster recovery (HADR) node.
HADR_SYNCMODE	Specifies the synchronization mode to use for high availability disaster recovery (HADR). This determines how primary log writes are synchronized with the standby database when the systems are in peer state. Valid values for this configuration parameter are SYNC (this mode provides the greatest protection against transaction loss, but at a higher cost of transaction response time), NEARSYNC (this mode provides somewhat less protection against transaction loss, in exchange for a shorter transaction response time than that of SYNC mode), and ASYNC (this mode has the highest probability of transaction loss in the event of primary failure, in exchange for the shortest transaction response time among the three modes).
HADR_TIMEOUT	Specifies the time (in seconds) that the high availability disaster recovery (HADR) process waits before considering a communication attempt to have failed.

4.   Connect to the standby instance and start HADR on the standby database.

HADR is started by executing the START HADR command. The basic syntax for this command is:

```
START HADR ON [DATABASE | DB] [DatabaseAlias]
<USER [UserName] <USING [Password]>>
AS [PRIMARY <BY FORCE> | SECONDARY]
```

where:

DatabaseAlias   Identifies the alias assigned to the database for which HADR is to be started.

UserName   Identifies the name assigned to a specific user under whom HADR is to be started.

Password   Identifies the password that corresponds to the name of the user under whom HADR is to be started.

Thus, if you wanted to start HADR on a database named SAMPLE and indicate that it is to act as a standby database, you could do so by executing a START HADR command that looks something like this:

```
START HADR ON DATABASE sample AS STANDBY
```

5.   Connect to the primary instance and start HADR on the primary database.

In this case, you would execute a START HADR command that looks something like this:

```
START HADR ON DATABASE sample AS PRIMARY
```

You can also set up an HADR environment using the Set Up HADR Databases Wizard, which can be activated by selecting the High Availability Disaster Recovery action from the Databases menu found in the Control Center. Figure 7–19 shows the Control Center menu items that must be selected to activate the Set Up HADR Databases Wizard; Figure 7–20 shows how the first page of the Set Up HADR Databases Wizard might look immediately after it is activated.

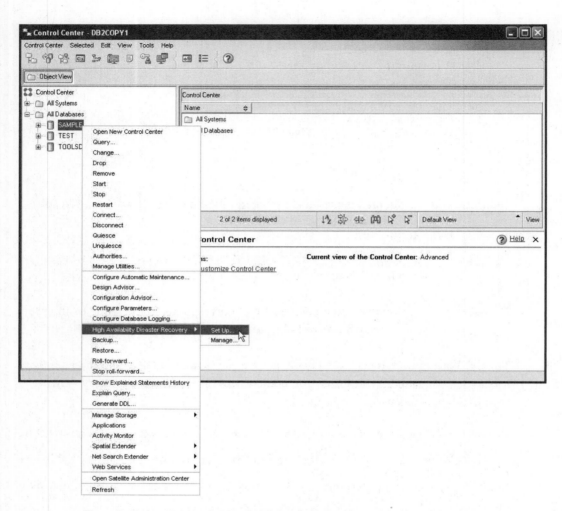

Figure 7–19: Invoking the Set Up HADR Databases Wizard from the Control Center.

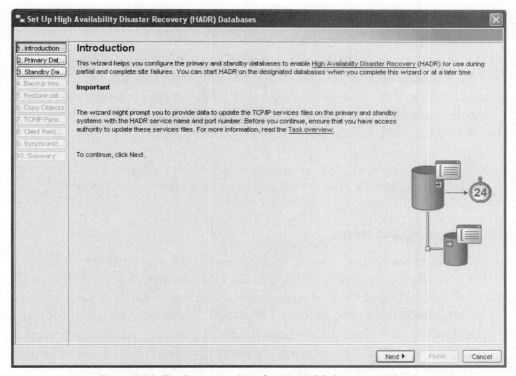

Figure 7–20: The first page of the Set Up HADR Databases Wizard.

Once an HADR environment has been established, the following operations will be replicated automatically in the standby database whenever they are performed on the primary database:

- Execution of Data Definition Language (DDL) statements (CREATE, ALTER, DROP)

- Execution of Data Manipulation Language (DML) statements (INSERT, UPDATE, DELETE)

- Buffer pool operations

- Table space operations

- Online reorganization

- Offline reorganization

- Changes to metadata for stored procedures and user-defined functions (UDFs)

HADR does not replicate stored procedure and UDF object and library files. If this type of replication is needed, you must physically create the files on identical paths on both the primary and standby databases. (If the standby database cannot find the referenced object or library file, the stored procedure or UDF invocation will fail on the standby database.)

Non-logged operations, such as changes to database configuration parameters and to the recovery history file, are not replicated to the standby database.

Load Operations and HADR

Load operations present a special problem for HADR. Because load operations are not recorded in a database's transaction log files, whether a load operation can be duplicated is dependent on whether a copy of the loaded data was saved as part of the load process (which is the case if the COPY YES option of the LOAD command is specified). If a load operation is performed on the primary database with the COPY YES option specified, the command will execute on the primary database, and the data will be replicated to the standby database—provided the load copy image created can be accessed by the standby database via the path or device provided with the LOAD command. If the standby database cannot access the load copy image, the table space in which the table is stored is marked invalid on the standby database, and the standby database will stop replaying log records that pertain to this table space. To ensure that the load operation can access the copy on the standby database, it is recommended that you use a shared location for the load copy image output file location specified with the COPY YES option. Alternatively, you can deactivate the standby database while the load operation is performed, perform the load operation on the primary database, place a copy of the output file produced in the standby path, and then activate the standby database.

If a load operation is executed on the primary database with the NONRECOVERABLE option specified, data will be loaded into the appropriate table in the primary database, the corresponding table on the standby database will be marked invalid, and the standby database will stop replaying log records that pertain to this table. You can reissue the LOAD command with the COPY YES and REPLACE options specified to restore the table on the standby database, or you can drop the table and recover the space.

Because executing a load operation with the COPY NO option specified is not supported by HADR, an attempt to perform such an operation is automatically converted to a load operation that behaves as if the NONRECOVERABLE option was specified. To prevent this behavior, you can set the DB2_LOAD_COPY_NO_OVERRIDE registry variable on the primary database to COPY YES, in which case all load operations performed will behave as if the COPY YES option were specified. When setting this variable, make sure that the device or directory specified on the primary database can be accessed by the standby database using the same path, device, or load library.

Load operations against primary databases in an HADR environment can have an impact on indexes as well as tables and table spaces. If a load operation is performed on the primary database with the COPY YES option specified, affected indexes will be replicated as follows:

- If the indexing mode is set to REBUILD, and the table being loaded has been assigned the LOG INDEX BUILD attribute, or if the table being loaded has been assigned the DEFAULT attribute, and the *logindexbuild* database configuration parameter on the primary database is set to ON, the primary database will include the rebuilt index object in the copy file so that the standby database can replicate the index object. If the index object on the standby database is marked invalid before the load operation is performed, it will become usable again after the load operation as a result of the index rebuild.

- If the indexing mode is set to INCREMENTAL, and the table being loaded has been assigned the LOG INDEX BUILD attribute, or if the table being loaded has been assigned the NULL attribute, and the *logindexbuild* database configuration parameter on the primary database is set to ON, the index object on the standby database is updated only if it is not marked invalid before the load operation. Otherwise, the index is marked invalid on the standby database.

IBM recommends you set the *logindexbuild* database configuration parameter to ON for HADR databases to ensure that complete information is logged for index creation, recreation, and reorganization. Although this means that index builds might take longer on the primary system and that more log space may be required, the indexes will be rebuilt on the standby system during HADR log replay and will be available when a failover takes place. If index operations on the primary system are not logged, and a failover occurs, any invalid indexes that remain after the failover is complete will have to be rebuilt before they can be accessed—while indexes are being recreated, they cannot be accessed by any application.

Practice Questions

Question 1

Which two of the following commands can be used to enable dual logging for a database named SAMPLE?

- ❑ A. db2set DB2_NEWLOGPATH=D:\logs_copy
- ☑ B. db2set DB2_NEWLOGPATH=1
- ❑ C. UPDATE DB CFG FOR sample USING failarchpath D:\ logs_copy
- ☑ D. UPDATE DB CFG FOR sample USING mirrorlogpath D:\ logs_copy
- ❑ E. UPDATE DB CFG FOR sample USING logarchmeth2 MIRRORPATH: D:\ logs_copy

Question 2

If the following SQL statement is executed:

```
UPDATE DB CFG FOR sample USING BLK_LOG_DSK_FUL YES
```

What will happen?

- ○ A. The SAMPLE database will be configured to use infinite logging.
- ○ B. The SAMPLE database will not automatically allocate additional storage space when the active log directory becomes full.
- ○ C. Log files for the SAMPLE database will be backed up automatically whenever a full backup image of the SAMPLE database is made.
- ◉ D. Transactions running against the SAMPLE database will not be rolled back if they receive a disk full error.

Question 3

What type of recovery operation is used to reapply transactions that were committed but not externalized to storage, roll back transactions that were externalized to storage but not committed, and purge transactions from memory that were neither committed nor externalized to storage?

- ○ A. Quick recovery
- ◉ B. Crash recovery
- ○ C. Version recovery
- ○ D. Roll-forward recovery

Question 4

A power failure occurred while several applications were interacting with a database named SAMPLE. When power was restored, the database could not be restarted because a user temporary table space named USER_TMPTS is damaged. What must be done to successfully recover the database?

☑ A. Restart the database by executing the command RESTART DATABASE sample DROP PENDING TABLESPACES (USER_TMPTS); drop and recreate the USER_TMPTS table space

○ B. Restart the database by executing the command RESTART DATABASE sample DROP PENDING TABLESPACES; recreate the USER_TMPTS table space

○ C. Restart the database by executing the command RESTART DATABASE sample DROP TABLESPACE (USER_TMPTS); recreate the USER_TMPTS table space

○ D. Restart the database by executing the command RESTART DATABASE sample RECREATE TABLESPACES (USER_TMPTS)

Question 5

Which of the following commands will restore a database using information found in the recovery history log file?

○ A. RESTART DATABASE

○ B. RESTORE DATABASE

☑ C. RECOVER DATABASE

○ D. REBUILD DATABASE

Question 6

While cleaning up files stored on an older AIX server, a database administrator found a shell script that contained the following commands:

```
db2 "RESTORE DATABASE sample FROM C:\backups TO D:\DB_DIR INTO
sample_2 REDIRECT"

db2 "SET TABLESPACE CONTAINERS FOR 0 USING
(PATH 'D:\DB_DIR\SYSTEM')"

db2 "SET TABLESPACE CONTAINERS FOR 1 USING
(PATH 'D:\DB_DIR\TEMP')"

db2 "SET TABLESPACE CONTAINERS FOR 2 USING
(PATH 'D:\DB_DIR\USER')"

db2 "RESTORE DATABASE sample CONTINUE"
```

What was this file designed to perform?

○ A. A multiple table space recovery operation

○ B. A reverted restore operation

○ C. A partial table space reconstruction operation

◉ D. A redirected restore operation

Question 7

If a database named SAMPLE was backed up on Sunday, which of the
following commands will produce a backup image on Wednesday that contains
a copy of just the data that has changed since the backup image on Sunday
was created?

○ A. BACKUP DATABASE sample INCREMENTAL TO C:\backups

○ B. BACKUP DATABASE sample DELTA TO C:\backups

○ C. BACKUP DATABASE sample DELTA INCREMENTAL TO C:\backups

◉ D. BACKUP DATABASE sample INCREMENTAL DELTA TO C:\backups

Question 8

Which of the following commands can be used to backup a database named
PAYROLL, in such a way that workloads against the database are not impacted
by more than 25%?

◉ A. BACKUP DATABASE payroll ONLINE TO D:\backups
       UTIL_IMPACT_PRIORITY 25

○ B. BACKUP DATABASE payroll ONLINE TO D:\backups
       UTIL_IMPACT_LIM 25

○ C. BACKUP DATABASE payroll ONLINE TO D:\backups
       UTIL_IMPACT_PRIORITY 75

○ D. BACKUP DATABASE payroll ONLINE TO D:\backups
       UTIL_IMPACT_LIM 75

Question 9

Which of the following statements about incremental backups is NOT true?

○ A. The predecessor of an incremental backup image is always the most recent successful full backup image of the same object (database or table space).

⊘ B. Database recovery involves restoring the database using the most recent full backup image available and applying each incremental backup image produced since the last full backup, in the order in which they were created.

○ C. Before an incremental backup image can be created, a full backup image must already exist.

○ D. Along with updated data and index pages, each incremental backup image also contains all of the initial database metadata that is normally found in a full database backup image.

Question 10

Which of the following is NOT needed to recover a database to a specific point in time?

○ A. Access to a full database backup image

⊘ B. Access to a backup copy of the recovery history file

○ C. Access to archive log files produced since a backup image was made

○ D. Access to all delta backup images produced since the last full backup image was made

Question 11

Which of the following statements about roll-forward recovery is NOT true?

⊘ A. Roll-forward recovery cannot be accomplished while users are connected to the database.

○ B. Recovery must be to a point in time that is greater than the minimum recovery time obtained with the LIST TABLESPACES command.

○ C. Recovery to a specific point in time can only be done on a database that is using archival logging.

○ D. By default, all recovery times specified are interpreted as Coordinated Universal Time (UTC) – otherwise known as Greenwich Mean Time (GMT) values.

Question 12

The following command was executed in an attempt to return a database named SAMPLE to the state it was in at 9:30 AM on July 1, 2007:

```
ROLLFORWARD DB sample TO 2007-07-01-09.30.00.000000 AND STOP
```

During execution, the following error was returned:

SQL4970N Roll-forward recovery on database SAMPLE cannot reach the specified stop point (end-of-log or point-in-time) because of missing or corrupted log file(s) on database partition(s) "0". Roll-forward recovery processing has halted on log file S0000007.LOG.

Which of the following options can be added to the ROLLFORWARD command to resolve the problem?

○ A. END OF LOGS
◉ B. OVERFLOW LOG PATH
○ C. ALTERNATE LOG PATH
○ D. MIRROR LOG PATH

Question 13

A database named COMPANY was backed up on June 1 and on June 15 the following SQL statement was executed:

```
RENAME TABLESPACE emp_info TO hr_info
```

On July 1, a failed operation made recovery of the HR_INFO table space necessary.

Which of the following commands must be used to roll forward the table space?

○ A. ROLLFORWARD DATABASE company TO END OF LOGS AND STOP
         TABLESPACE (emp_info)
◉ B. ROLLFORWARD DATABASE company TO END OF LOGS AND STOP
         TABLESPACE (hr_info)
○ C. ROLLFORWARD DATABASE company TO END OF LOGS AND STOP
         TABLESPACE (emp_info TO hr_info)
○ D. ROLLFORWARD DATABASE company TO END OF LOGS AND STOP
         TABLESPACE (RENAME emp_info TO hr_info)

Question 14

Which of the following commands can cause queries against a database named SAMPLE that utilize indexes to run slower than usual the first time they are executed after a crash recovery operation has been performed?

- ✓ A. UPDATE DBM CFG USING INDEXREC ACCESS;
       UPDATE DB CFG FOR sample USING INDEXREC ACCESS;

- ○ B. UPDATE DBM CFG USING INDEXREC SYSTEM;
       UPDATE DB CFG FOR sample USING INDEXREC FIRSTEXEC;

- ○ C. UPDATE DBM CFG USING INDEXREC RESTART;
       UPDATE DB CFG FOR sample USING INDEXREC RESTART;

- ○ D. UPDATE DBM CFG USING INDEXREC FIRSTEXEC;
       UPDATE DB CFG FOR sample USING INDEXREC SYSTEM;

Question 15

Which of the following commands will ensure that index creation, recreation, and reorganization operations against a database named SAMPLE will be logged so that indexes can be reconstructed during roll-forward recovery operations or high availability disaster recovery (HADR) log replay procedures?

- ○ A. UPDATE DB CFG FOR sample USING INDEXREC ON
- ○ B. UPDATE DB CFG FOR sample USING LOGINDEXMAINT ON
- ○ C. UPDATE DB CFG FOR sample USING INDEXOPS ON
- ✓ D. UPDATE DB CFG FOR sample USING LOGINDEXBUILD ON

Question 16

In a split mirror environment, which of the following commands is used to initialize a mirrored copy of a database named MYDB as a read-only clone of the primary database?

- ✓ A. db2inidb mydb AS SNAPSHOT
- ○ B. db2inidb mydb AS MIRROR
- ○ C. db2inidb mydb AS DUPLICATE
- ○ D. db2inidb mydb AS STANDBY

Question 17

Given two servers named SVR1 and SVR2 with a database named SALES on SRV1, in what order should the following steps be performed to set up an HADR environment using SRV2 as a standby server?

- a) Backup the SALES database on SVR1.
- b) Determine the host name, host IP address, and the service name or port number for SVR1 and SVR2.
- c) Start HADR on SVR2.
- d) Set the HADR configuration parameters on SVR1 and SVR2.
- e) Restore the SALES database on SVR2.
- f) Start HADR on SVR1.

- ○ A. b, a, e, d, f, c
- ○ B. b, d, f, c, a, e
- ◉ C. b, a, e, d, c, f
- ○ D. f, c, b, d, a, e

Question 18

Which of the following is NOT a requirement for an HADR environment?

- ○ A. The operating system on the primary server and the standby server must be the same (including fix pack level).
- ◉ B. The database path on the primary server and the standby server must be the same.
- ○ C. The DB2 software version and bit size (32 or 64) used on the primary server and the standby server must be the same.
- ○ D. Table spaces and table space containers on the primary server and the standby server must be identical.

Question 19

The LOG INDEX BUILD attribute for a table named EMPLOYEES was set to ON just before the table was populated with a load operation. If the database the EMPLOYEES table resides in has been configured for HADR, what will happen when the database fails over to the standby server?

- ✓ A.   Indexes defined for the EMPLOYEES table may be rebuilt.
- ○ B.   Insert operations on the standby server (after the failover to the standby server) will take longer.
- ○ C.   Indexes defined for the EMPLOYEES table will not be rebuilt.
- ○ D.   An attempt to create a unique index on the EMPLOYEES table (after the failover to the standby server) will fail.

Question 20

A database administrator has HADR enabled and wants to do a load operation on the primary server. If the LOAD command is executed with the COPY YES option specified and the copy of the loaded data created is written to a location that cannot be accessed by the standby database via the path provided with the LOAD command, what will happen?

- ○ A.   The load operation will fail on both the primary and the standby server.
- ○ B.   The load operation will automatically be converted to COPY NO and the standby database will be marked corrupt.
- ✓ C.   The table space in which the table is stored is marked invalid on the standby database and the standby server will stop replaying log records that pertain to this table space.
- ○ D.   The table space in which the table is stored is marked invalid on the primary database and the primary server will stop sending log records that pertain to this table space to the standby server.

Answers

Question 1

The correct answers are **B** and **D**. To enable log file mirroring, you simply assign the fully qualified name of the mirror log location (path) to the *mirrorlogpath* database configuration parameter. Alternately, on UNIX systems, you can assign the value 1 to the DB2_NEWLOGPATH registry variable—in this case, the name of the mirror log location is generated by appending the character "2" to the current value of the *logpath* database configuration parameter. Ideally, the mirror log path used should refer to a physical location (disk) that does not see a large amount of disk I/O and that is separate from the physical location used to store primary log files.

Question 2

The correct answer is **D**. When archival logging is used and archived log files are not moved from the active log directory to another location, the disk where the active log directory resides can quickly become full. By default, when this happens, transactions will receive a disk full error and be rolled back. If the *blk_log_dsk_ful* database configuration parameter is set to YES, applications will hang (instead of rolling back the current transaction) if the DB2 Database Manager receives a disk full error when it attempts to create a new log file in the active log directory. (This gives you the opportunity to manually move or delete files to make more room available.) The DB2 Database Manager will then attempt to create the log file every five minutes until it succeeds – after each attempt, a message is written to the Administration Notification Log.

Question 3

The correct answer is **B**. When a transaction failure takes place, all work done by partially completed transactions that had not yet been externalized to the database is lost. As a result, the database may be left in an inconsistent state (and therefore will be unusable). *Crash recovery* is the process used to return such a database to a consistent and usable state. Crash recovery is performed by using information stored in the transaction log files to complete any committed transactions that were in memory (but had not yet been externalized to storage) when the transaction failure occurred, roll back any incomplete transactions found, and purge any uncommitted transactions from memory.

Question 4

The correct answer is **A**. If a problem occurs with a table space container during the restart process, the DROP PENDING TABLESPACES ([*TS_Name*]) option can be used to place one or more table spaces in "Drop Pending" state. This allows the database to be successfully restarted, after which the offending table space can be dropped and, if necessary, recreated. A list of troubled table space names can found in the administration notification log if a database restart operation fails because of table space container problems.

Question 5

The correct answer is **C**. The Recover utility performs the restore and roll-forward operations needed to recover a database to a specific point in time, based on information found in the recovery history file. The Recovery utility is invoked by executing the RECOVER DATABASE command. The basic syntax for this command is:

```
RECOVER [DATABASE | DB] [DatabaseAlias]
<TO [PointInTime] <USING [UTC | LOCAL] TIME> |
    END OF LOGS>
<USER [UserName] <USING [Password]>>
<USING HISTORY FILE ([HistoryFile])>
<OVERFLOW LOG PATH ([LogDirectory] ,... )>
<RESTART>
```

where:

DatabaseAlias	Identifies the alias assigned to the database associated with the backup image that is to be used to perform a version recovery operation.
PointInTime	Identifies a specific point in time, identified by a timestamp value in the form *yyyy-mm-dd-hh.mm.ss.nnnnnn* (year, month, day, hour, minutes, seconds, microseconds) that the database is to be rolled forward to. (Only transactions that took place before and up to the date and time specified will be reapplied to the database.)
UserName	Identifies the name assigned to a specific user that the recovery operation is to be performed under.
Password	Identifies the password that corresponds to the name of the user that the recovery operation is to be performed under.
HistoryFile	Identifies the name assigned to the recovery history log file that is to be used by the Recovery utility.

LogDirectory   Identifies the directory that contains offline archived log files that are to be used to perform the roll-forward portion of the recovery operation.

Thus, if you wanted to perform a full recovery operation on a database named SAMPLE (which already exists) using information stored in the recovery history file, you could do so by executing a RECOVER DATABASE command that looks something like this:

```
RECOVER DATABASE sample
TO END OF LOGS
```

On the other hand, if you wanted to restore a database named SAMPLE and roll it forward to an extremely old point in time that is no longer contained in the current recovery history file, you could do so by executing a RECOVER DATABASE command that looks something like this (assuming you have a copy of an older recovery history file available):

```
RECOVER DATABASE sample
TO 2005-01-31-04.00.00
USING HISTORY FILE (/home/user/old2005files/db2rhist.asc)
```

It is important to note that if the Recover utility successfully restores a database, but for some reason fails while attempting to roll it forward, the entire recovery operation must be performed again. There is no way to restart a recovery operation from a point of failure.

Question 6

The correct answer is **D**. When invalid table space containers are encountered, they can be redefined at the beginning of the recovery process by performing what is known as a *redirected restore*. (A redirected restore operation can also be used to restore a backup image to a target machine that is different than the source machine, or to store table space data into a different physical location.)

The steps used to perform a redirected restore operation are as follows:

1.   Start the redirected restore operation by executing the RESTORE DATABASE command with the REDIRECT option specified. (When this option is specified, each invalid table space container encountered is flagged, and all table spaces that reference invalid table space containers are placed in the "Restore Pending" state. A list of all table spaces affected can be obtained by executing the LIST TABLESPACES command.) At some point, you should see a message that looks something like this:

```
SQL1277N Restore has detected that one or more table space containers are
inaccessible, or has set their state to 'storage must be defined'.
DB20000I The RESTORE DATABASE command completed successfully.
```

2. Specify new table space containers for each table space placed in "Restore Pending" state by executing a SET TABLESPACE CONTAINERS command for each appropriate table space. (Keep in mind that SMS table spaces can only use PATH containers, while DMS table spaces can only use FILE or DEVICE containers.)

3. Complete the redirected restore operation by executing the RESTORE DATABASE command again with the CONTINUE option specified.

To simplify things, all of these steps can be coded in a UNIX shell script or Windows batch file, which can then be executed from a system prompt. Such a file would look something like this:

```
db2 "RESTORE DATABASE sample FROM C:\backups TO D:\DB_DIR INTO
sample_2 REDIRECT"

db2 "SET TABLESPACE CONTAINERS FOR 0 USING
(PATH 'D:\DB_DIR\SYSTEM')"

db2 "SET TABLESPACE CONTAINERS FOR 1 USING
(PATH 'D:\DB_DIR\TEMP')"

db2 "SET TABLESPACE CONTAINERS FOR 2 USING
(PATH 'D:\DB_DIR\USER')"

db2 "RESTORE DATABASE sample CONTINUE"
```

Question 7

The correct answer is **D**. As the size of a database grows, the time and hardware needed to back up and recover the databases also grows substantially. Thus, creating full database backup images is not always the best approach when dealing with large databases because the storage requirements for multiple copies of such backup images can be enormous. A better alternative is to create a full backup image periodically and one or more *incremental backup* images on a more frequent basis. An incremental backup is a backup image that only contains pages that have been updated since the previous backup image was made.

Two types of incremental backup images can be produced: *incremental* and *delta.* An incremental backup image is a copy of all database data that has changed since the most recent, successful, full backup image was created. An incremental backup image is also known as a *cumulative* backup image, because the last incremental backup image in a series of incremental backup images made over a period of time will contain the contents of all of the previous incremental backup images. The predecessor of an incremental backup image is always the most recent successful full backup image of the same object.

A delta backup image, on the other hand, is a copy of all database data that has changed since the last successful backup (full, incremental, or delta) of the database or table space in question.

For this reason, a delta backup image is also known as a *differential*, or *non-cumulative*, backup image. The predecessor of a delta backup image is the most recent successful backup image that contains a copy of each of the objects found in the delta backup image.

If the INCREMENTAL option is specified with the BACKUP DATABASE command, an incremental backup image will be produced—an incremental backup image is a copy of all data that has changed since the last successful, full backup image was produced. If the INCREMENTAL DELTA option is specified, a delta backup image will be produced—a delta backup image is a copy of all data that has changed since the last successful backup image of any type (full, incremental, or delta) was produced.

Question 8

The correct answer is **A**. The UTIL_IMPACT_PRIORITY option of the BACKUP DATABASE command is used to indicate that the execution of a backup operation is to be throttled such that its affect on concurrent database activity can be controlled. This parameter can be assigned a numerical value within the range of 1 to 100, with 100 representing the highest priority and 1 representing the lowest. (Backup operations that have been assigned a UTIL_IMPACT_PRIORITY value of 25 will impact database workloads by 25% and will take longer to complete; backup operations that have been assigned a UTIL_IMPACT_PRIORITY value of 75 will impact database workloads by 75% and will finish sooner.)

Question 9

The correct answer is **B**. When incremental backup images are taken, database recovery involves restoring the database using the most recent full backup image available and applying the most recent incremental backup image produced. On the other hand, when delta backup images are taken, database recovery involves restoring the database using the most recent full backup image available and applying each delta backup image produced since the full backup image used was made, in the order in which they were created.

Question 10

The correct answer is **B**. Roll-forward recovery takes version recovery one step farther by rebuilding a database or one or more individual table spaces using a backup image, and replaying information stored in transaction log files to return the database/table spaces to the state they were in at an exact point in time. In order to perform a roll-forward recovery operation, you must have archival logging enabled, you must have a full backup image of the database available, and you must have access to all archived log files that have been created since the full backup image was made.

Question 11

The correct answer is **A**. Roll-forward recovery operations can be performed on individual table spaces while a database remains on-line. However, before a database can be restored, it must first be taken offline. Therefore, roll-forward recovery can be accomplished while users are connected to the database—but only at the table space level.

Question 12

The correct answer is **B**. The OVERFLOW LOG PATH option of the ROLLFORWARD DATABASE command is used to identify the directory that contains offline archived log files that are to be used to perform the roll-forward operation. The Roll-forward utility looks in the active log directory first, and then in the directory specified with the OVERFLOW LOG PATH option for log files needed to perform a roll-forward recovery operation.

Question 13

The correct answer is **B**. If you want to restore a table space from a backup image and the table space name has changed since the backup image was created, you should reference the table space by its new name. Table space metadata is stored in an external file and DB2 uses the information stored in this file to correctly identify the table space to restore.

Question 14

The correct answer is **A**. Whenever the DB2 Database Manager detects that an index is no longer valid, it automatically attempts to rebuild it. However, the point in time at which the DB2 Database Manager attempts to rebuild an invalid index is controlled by the INDEXREC parameter of the database or the DB2 Database Manager configuration file. There are three possible settings for this parameter:

SYSTEM. Invalid indexes are to be rebuilt at the time specified in the INDEXREC parameter of the DB2 Database Manager configuration file. (This setting is only valid for database configuration files.)

RESTART. Invalid indexes are to be rebuilt, either explicitly or implicitly, when the database is restarted (i.e., when crash recovery is performed on the database).

ACCESS. Invalid indexes are to be rebuilt the first time they are accessed after they have been marked as being invalid.

So when is the best time to rebuild invalid indexes? If the time needed to perform a crash recovery operation on a database is not a concern, it is better to let the DB2 Database Manager rebuild invalid indexes while it is in the process of returning the database to a consistent state; the time needed to restart a database will be longer due to the index re-creation process, but once the database had been restored, query processing will not be impacted. On the other hand, if indexes are rebuilt as they are accessed, crash recovery will be performed faster, but users may experience a decrease in performance—queries against tables that contain associated invalid indexes will have to wait for the invalid index(es) to be rebuilt before they can be processed. Furthermore, unexpected locks may be acquired and held long after an invalid index has been recreated, especially if the transaction that caused the index recreation to occur is not committed (or rolled back) for some time.

Question 15

The correct answer is **D**. While the *indexrec* parameter of the database or the DB2 Database Manager configuration file can be used to control when indexes are rebuilt as part of a crash recovery operation, it has no affect on how indexes are rebuilt during roll-forward recovery operations. To control that behavior, you must assign the appropriate value to the *logindexbuild* database configuration parameter. There are two possible settings for this parameter:

ON. Index creation, recreation, and reorganization operations are to be recorded in the database's transaction log files so indexes can be reconstructed during roll-forward recovery operations or high availability disaster recovery (HADR) log replay operations.

OFF. Index creation, recreation, and reorganization operations will not be recorded in the database's transaction log files.

Question 16

The correct answer is **A**. Before a split mirror copy of a DB2 database can be used, it must first be initialized; a split mirror database copy is initialized by executing the system command db2inidb. The syntax for this command is:

```
db2inidb [DatabaseAlias]
AS [SNAPSHOT | MIRROR | STANDBY]
<RELOCATE USING [ConfigFile]>
```

where:

DatabaseAlias   Identifies the alias assigned to the database the split mirror copy that is to be initialized references.

ConfigFile   Indicates that the database files contained in the split mirror copy are to be relocated according to information stored in the configuration file specified.

As you can see, a split mirror database copy can be initialized in one of three ways:

SNAPSHOT. The split mirror copy of the database will be initialized as a read-only clone of the primary database.

MIRROR. The split mirror copy of the database will be initialized as a backup image that can be used to restore the primary database.

STANDBY. The split mirror copy of the database will be initialized and placed in roll-forward pending state so that it can be continuously synchronized with the primary database. (New logs from the primary database can be retrieved and applied to the copy of the database at any time.) The standby copy of the database can then be used in place of the primary database if, for some reason, the primary database goes down.

Thus, if you wanted to initialize a split mirror copy of a database named MYDB and make it a read-only clone of the primary database, you could do so by executing a db2inidb command that looks like this:

```
db2inidb mydb AS STANDBY
```

Question 17

The correct answer is **C**. After ensuring the systems to be used as primary and secondary server are identical and that a TCP/IP connection exists between them, you can establish an HADR environment by performing the following tasks, in the order shown:

1. Determine the host name, host IP address, and the service name or port number for both the primary and the secondary database server.
2. Create the standby database by restoring a backup image or initializing a split mirror copy of the database that is to serve as the primary database.
3. Set the HADR configuration parameters on both the primary and the standby databases.
4. Connect to the standby instance and start HADR on the standby database.
5. Connect to the primary instance and start HADR on the primary database.

Question 18

The correct answer is **B**. Both the primary and the standby database must be a single-partition database and they both must have the same database name; however, they do not have to be stored on the same database path.

IBM recommends that you use identical host computers for the HADR primary and standby databases. (If possible, they should be from the same vendor and have the same architecture.) Furthermore, the operating system on the primary and standby database servers should be the same version, including patch level. You can violate this rule for a short time during a rolling upgrade, but use extreme caution when doing so. A TCP/IP interface must also be available between the HADR host machines, and a high-speed, high-capacity network should be used to connect the two.

The DB2 software installed on both the primary and the standby database server must have the same bit size (32 or 64) and the version of DB2 used for the primary and standby databases must be identical; for example, both must be either version 8 or version 9. During rolling upgrades, the modification level (for example, the fix pack level) of the database system for the standby database can be later than that of the primary database for a short while. However, you should not keep this configuration for an extended period of time. The primary and standby databases will not connect to each other if the modification level of the database system for the primary database is later than that of the standby database. Therefore, fix packs must always be applied to the standby database system first.

The amount of storage space allocated for transaction log files should also be the same on both the primary and the standby database server; the use of raw devices for transaction logging is not supported. (Archival logging is only performed by the current primary database.) Table space properties such as table space name, table space type (DMS, SMS, or Automatic Storage), table space page size, table space size, container path, container size, and container type (raw device, file, or directory) must be identical on the primary and standby databases. When you issue a table space statement such as CREATE TABLESPACE, ALTER TABLESPACE, or DROP TABLESPACE on the primary database, it is replayed on the standby database. Therefore, you must ensure that the table space containers involved in such statements exist on both systems before you issue the table space statement on the primary database. (If you create a table space on the primary database and log replay fails on the standby database because the containers are not available, the primary database does not receive an error message stating that the log replay failed.) Automatic storage databases are fully supported, including replication of ALTER DATABASE statements. Similar to table space containers, the storage paths specified must exist on both the primary and the standby server.

Question 19

The correct answer is **A**. Load operations against primary databases in a HADR environment can have an impact on indexes as well as tables and table spaces. If a load operation is performed on the primary database with the COPY YES option specified, affected indexes will be replicated as follows:

- If the indexing mode is set to REBUILD and the table being loaded has been assigned the LOG INDEX BUILD attribute, or if the table being loaded has been assigned the DEFAULT attribute and the *logindexbuild* database configuration parameter on the primary database is set to ON, the primary database will include the rebuilt index object in the copy file so the standby database can replicate the index object. If the index object on the standby database is marked invalid before the load operation is performed, it will become usable again after the load operation as a result of the index rebuild.

- If the indexing mode is set to INCREMENTAL and the table being loaded has been assigned the LOG INDEX BUILD attribute, or if the table being loaded has been assigned the NULL attribute and the *logindexbuild* database configuration parameter on the primary database is set to ON, the index object on the standby database is only updated if it is not marked invalid before the load operation. Otherwise, the index is marked invalid on the standby database.

IBM recommends you set the *logindexbuild* database configuration parameter to ON for HADR databases to ensure that complete information is logged for index creation, recreation, and reorganization. Although this means that index builds might take longer on the primary system and that more log space may be required, the indexes will be rebuilt on the standby system during HADR log replay and will be available when a failover takes place. If index operations on the primary system are not logged and a failover occurs, any invalid indexes that remain after the failover is complete will have to be rebuilt before they can be accessed—while indexes are being recreated, they cannot be accessed by any application.

Question 20

The correct answer is **C**. Since load operations are not recorded in a database's transaction log files, whether or not a load operation can be duplicated is dependent upon whether a copy of the loaded data was saved as part of the load process (which is the case if the COPY YES option of the LOAD command is specified). If a load operation is performed on the primary database with the COPY YES option specified, the command will execute on the primary database and the data will be replicated to the standby database—provided the copy of the loaded data created can be accessed by the standby database via the path or device provided with the LOAD command. If the standby database cannot access the data, the table space in which the table is stored is marked invalid on the standby database and the standby database will stop replaying log records that pertain to this table space. To ensure that the load operation can access the copy on the standby database, it is recommended that you use a shared location for the output file location specified with the COPY YES option. Alternatively, you can deactivate the standby database while the load operation is performed, perform the load operation on the primary database, place a copy of the output file produced in the standby path, and then activate the standby database.

If a load operation is executed on the primary database with the NONRECOVERABLE option specified, data will be loaded into the appropriate table in the primary database and the corresponding table on the standby database will be marked invalid and the standby database will stop replaying log records that pertain to this table. You can reissue the LOAD command with the COPY YES and REPLACE options specified to restore the table on the standby database, or you can drop the table and recover the space.

Because executing a load operation with the COPY NO option specified is not supported by HADR, an attempt to perform such an operation is automatically converted to a load operation that behaves as if the NONRECOVERABLE option was specified. To prevent this behavior, you can set the DB2_LOAD_COPY_NO_OVERRIDE registry variable on the primary database to COPY YES, in which case all load operations performed will behave as if the COPY YES option was specified. When setting this variable, make sure that the device or directory specified on the primary database can be accessed by the standby database using the same path, device, or load library.

CHAPTER 8

Security

Eight and one-half percent (8.5%) of the DB2 9 for Linux, UNIX, and Windows Database Administration exam (Exam 731) is designed to test your knowledge about the mechanisms DB2 uses to protect data and database objects against unauthorized access and modification. The questions that make up this portion of the exam are intended to evaluate the following:

- Your ability to identify the methods that can be used to restrict access to data stored in a DB2 database

- Your ability to identify the authorization levels used by DB2

- Your ability to identify the privileges used by DB2

- Your ability to identify how specific authorizations and/or privileges are given to a user or group

- Your ability to identify how specific authorizations and/or privileges are taken away from a user or group

- Your knowledge of the mechanisms and steps needed to implement label-based access control (LBAC)

This chapter is designed to introduce you to the various authorizations and privileges that are available with DB2 9 and to the tools that are used to give (grant) one or more of these authorizations and/or privileges to various users and groups. This chapter will also show you how to revoke one or more authorizations or privileges a user or group currently holds and how to implement LBAC to control access columns and rows in a table.

Controlling Database Access

Identity theft—a crime in which someone wrongfully obtains another person's personal data (such as a Social Security number, bank account number, and credit card number) and uses it in some way that involves fraud or deception for economic gain—is the fastest-growing crime in our nation today. Criminals are stealing information by overhearing conversations made on cell phones, by reading faxes and emails, by hacking into computers, by waging telephone and email scams, by stealing wallets and purses, by stealing discarded documents from trash bins, by stealing mail, and by taking advantage of careless online shopping and banking habits. But more frightening is the fact that studies show that up to 70 percent of all identity theft cases are inside jobs—perpetrated by a coworker or an employee of a business you patronize. In these cases, all that is needed is access to your personal data, which can often be found in a company database.

Every database management system must be able to protect data against unauthorized access and modification. DB2 uses a combination of external security services and internal access control mechanisms to perform this vital task. In most cases, three different levels of security are employed: The first level controls access to the instance under which a database was created, the second controls access to the database itself, and the third controls access to the data and data objects that reside within the database.

Authentication

The first security portal most users must pass through on their way to gaining access to a DB2 instance or database is a process known as authentication. The purpose of authentication is to verify that users really are who they say they are. Normally, authentication is performed by an external security facility that is not part of DB2. This security facility may be part of the operating system (as is the case with AIX, Solaris, Linux, HP-UX, Windows 2000/NT, and many others), may be a separate add-on product (for example, Distributed Computing Environment [DCE] Security Services), or may not exist at all (which is the case with Windows 95, Windows 98, and Windows Millennium Edition). If a security facility does exist, it must be presented with two specific items before a user can be authenticated: a unique user ID and a corresponding password. The user ID identifies the user to the security facility, and the password, which is information known only by the user and the security facility, is used to verify that the user is indeed who he or she claims to be.

Because passwords are a very important tool for authenticating users, you should always require passwords at the operating system level if you want the operating system to perform the authentication for your database. Keep in mind that on most UNIX operating systems, undefined passwords are treated as NULL, and any user who has not been assigned a password will be treated as having a NULL password. From the operating system's perspective, if no password is provided when a user attempts to log on, this will evaluate to being a valid match.

Where Does Authentication Take Place?

Because DB2 can reside in environments composed of multiple clients, gateways, and servers, each of which may be running on a different operating system, deciding where authentication is to take place can be a daunting task. To simplify things, DB2 uses a parameter in each DB2 Database Manager configuration file (the *authentication* parameter) to determine how and where users are authenticated. Such a file is associated with every instance, and the value assigned to this parameter, often referred to as the *authentication type*, is set initially when an instance is created. (On the server side, the authentication type is specified during the instance creation process; on the client side, the authentication type is specified when a remote database is cataloged.) Only one authentication type exists for each instance, and it controls access to that instance, as well as to all databases that fall under that instance's control.

With DB2 9, the following authentication types are available:

SERVER. Authentication occurs at the server workstation, using the security facility provided by the server's operating system. (The user ID and password provided by the user wishing to attach to an instance or connect to a database are compared to the user ID and password combinations stored at the server to determine whether the user is permitted to access the instance or database.) By default, this is the authentication type used when an instance is first created.

SERVER_ENCRYPT. Authentication occurs at the server workstation, using the security facility that is provided by the server's operating system. However, the password provided by the user wishing to attach to an instance or connect to a database stored on the server may be encrypted at the client workstation before it is sent to the server workstation for validation.

CLIENT. Authentication occurs at the client workstation or database partition where a client application is invoked, using the security facility that is provided by the client's operating system, assuming one is available. If no security facility is available, authentication is handled in a slightly different manner. The user ID and password provided by the user wishing to attach to an instance or connect to a database are compared to the user ID and password combinations stored at the client or node to determine whether the user is permitted to access the instance or the database.

KERBEROS. Authentication occurs at the server workstation, using a security facility that supports the Kerberos security protocol. This protocol performs authentication as a third-party service by using conventional cryptography to create a shared secret key. The key becomes the credentials used to verify the identity of the user whenever local or network services are requested; this eliminates the need to pass a user ID and password across the network as ASCII text. (If both the client and the server support the Kerberos security protocol, the user ID and password provided by the user wishing to attach to an instance or connect to a database are encrypted at the client workstation and sent to the server for validation.) It should be noted that the KERBEROS authentication type is supported only on clients and servers that are using the Windows 2000, Windows XP, or Windows .NET operating system. In addition, both client and server workstations must either belong to the same Windows domain or belong to trusted domains.

KRB_SERVER_ENCRYPT. Authentication occurs at the server workstation, using either the KERBEROS or the SERVER_ENCRYPT authentication method. If the client's authentication type is set to KERBEROS, authentication is performed at the server using the Kerberos security system. On the other hand, if the client's authentication type is set to anything other than KERBEROS, or if the Kerberos authentication service is unavailable, the server acts as if the SERVER_ENCRYPT authentication type was specified, and the rules of this authentication method apply.

DATA_ENCRYPT. Authentication occurs at the server workstation, using the SERVER_ENCRYPT authentication method. In addition, all user data is encrypted before it is passed from client to server and from server to client.

DATA_ENCRYPT_CMP. Authentication occurs at the server workstation, using the SERVER_ENCRYPT authentication method; all user data is encrypted before it is passed from client to server and from server to client. In addition, this authentication type provides compatibility for down-level products that do not support the DATA_ENCRYPT authentication type. Such products connect using the SERVER_ENCRYPT authentication type, and user data is not encrypted.

GSSPLUGIN. Authentication occurs at the server workstation, using a Generic Security Service Application Program Interface (GSS-API) plug-in. If the client's authentication type is not specified, the server returns a list of server-supported plug-ins (found in the *srvcon_gssplugin_list* database manager configuration parameter) to the client. The client then selects the first plug-in found in the client plug-in directory from the list. If the client does not support any plug-in in the list, the client is authenticated using the KERBEROS authentication method.

GSS_SERVER_ENCRYPT. Authentication occurs at the server workstation, using either the GSSPLUGIN or the SERVER_ENCRYPT authentication method. That is, if client authentication occurs through a GSS-API plug-in, the client is authenticated using the first client-supported plug-in found in the list of server-supported plug-ins. If the client does not support any of the plug-ins found in the server-supported plug-in list, the client is authenticated using the KERBEROS authentication method. If the client does not support the Kerberos security protocol, the client is authenticated using the SERVER_ENCRYPT authentication method.

It is important to note that if the authentication type used by the client workstation encrypts user ID and password information before sending it to a server for authentication (i.e., SERVER_ENCRYPT, KRB_SERVER_ENCRYPT, etc.), the server must be configured to use a compatible authentication method. Otherwise, it will not be able to process the encrypted data received, and an error will occur.

It is also important to note that if the authentication type is not specified for a client workstation, the SERVER_ENCRYPT authentication method is used by default. If such a client tries to communicate with a server that does not support the SERVER_ENCRYPT authentication method, the client will attempt to use the authentication type that is being used by the server—provided the server has been configured to use only one authentication type. If the server supports multiple authentication types, an error will be generated.

Security Plug-ins

In DB2 9, authentication is done using security plug-ins. A security plug-in is a dynamically loadable library that provides authentication security services; DB2 9 supports two mechanisms for plug-in authentication:

- User ID/password authentication

  This involves authentication using a user ID and password. The following authentication types are implemented using user ID/password authentication plug-ins:

  - CLIENT

  - SERVER

  - SERVER_ENCRYPT

  - DATA_ENCRYPT

  - DATA_ENCRYPT_CMP

- GSS-API authentication

  GSS-API was formally known as Generic Security Service Application Program Interface, Version 2 (IETF RFC2743) and Generic Security Service API Version 2: C-Bindings (IETF RFC2744). The following authentication types are implemented using GSS-API authentication plug-ins:

  - KERBEROS

  - GSSPLUGIN

- KRB_SERVER_ENCRYPT

- GSS_SERVER_ENCRYPT

KRB_SERVER_ENCRYPT and GSS_SERVER_ENCRYPT support both GSS-API authentication and user ID/password authentication; however, GSS-API authentication is the authentication type preferred.

Each plug-in can be used independently or in conjunction with one or more of the other plug-ins available. For example, you might specify only a server authentication plug-in to use and allow DB2 to use the defaults for client and group authentication. Alternatively, you might specify only a group or client authentication plug-in. The only situation where both a client and server plug-in are required is for GSS-API authentication. (In some cases—for example, if you are using Microsoft Active Directory to validate a user—you may need to create your own custom security plug-in and make it available for DB2 to use.)

The default behavior for DB2 9 is to use a user ID/password plug-in that implements an operating-system-level mechanism for authentication.

Trusted Clients Versus Untrusted Clients

If both the server and the client are configured to use the CLIENT authentication type, authentication occurs at the client workstation (if the database is a nonpartitioned database) or at the database partition from which the client application is invoked (if the database is a partitioned database), using the security facility provided by the client workstation's operating system. But what happens if the client workstation is using an operating system that does not contain a tightly integrated security facility, and no separate add-on security facility has been made available? Does such a configuration compromise security? The answer is no. However, in such environments, the DB2 Database Manager for the instance at the server must be able to determine which clients will be responsible for validating users and which clients will be forced to let the server handle user authentication. To make this distinction, clients that use an operating system that contains a tightly integrated security facility (for example, OS/390, VM, VSE, MVS, AS/400, Windows NT, Windows 2000, and all supported versions of UNIX) are classified as trusted clients, whereas clients that use an operating system that does not provide an integrated security facility (for example, Windows 95, Windows 98, and Windows Millennium Edition) are treated as untrusted clients.

The *trust_allclnts* parameter of a DB2 Database Manager configuration file helps the DB2 Database Manager for an instance on a server anticipate whether its clients are to be treated as trusted or untrusted. If this configuration parameter is set to YES (which is the default), the DB2 Database Manager assumes that any client that accesses the instance is a trusted client and that some form of authentication will take place at the client. However, if this configuration parameter is set to NO, the DB2 Database Manager assumes that one or more untrusted clients will try to access the server; therefore, all users must be authenticated at the server. (If this configuration parameter is set to DRDAONLY, only MVS, OS/390, VM, VSE, and OS/400 clients will be treated as trusted clients.) It is important to note that, regardless of how the *trust_allclnts* parameter is set, whenever an untrusted client attempts to access an instance or a database, user authentication always takes place at the server.

In some situations, it may be desirable to authenticate users at the server, even when untrusted clients will not be used. In such situations, the *trust_clntauth* configuration parameter of a DB2 Database Manager configuration file can be used to control where trusted clients are to be validated. When the default value for this parameter (which is CLIENT) is accepted, authentication for trusted clients will take place at the client workstation. If, however, the value for this parameter is changed to SERVER, authentication for all trusted clients will take place at the server.

Authorities and Privileges

Once a user has been authenticated, and an attachment to an instance or a connection to a database has been established, the DB2 Database Manger evaluates any authorities and privileges that have been assigned to the user to determine what operations the user is allowed to perform. Privileges convey the rights to perform certain actions against specific database resources (such as tables and views). Authorities convey a set of privileges or the right to perform high-level administrative and maintenance/utility operations on an instance or a database. Authorities and privileges can be assigned directly to a user, or they can be obtained indirectly from the authorities and privileges that have been assigned to a group of which the user is a member. Together, authorities and privileges act to control access to the DB2 Database Manager for an instance, to one or more databases running under that instance's control, and to a particular database's objects. Users can work only with those objects for which they have been given the appropriate authorization—that is, the required authority or privilege. Figure 8–1 provides a hierarchical view of the authorities and privileges that are recognized by DB2 9.

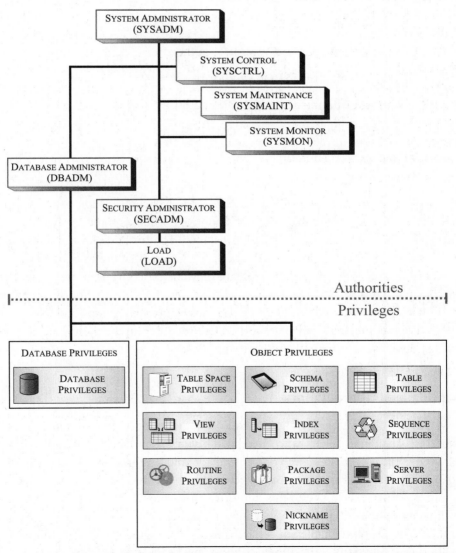

Figure 8–1: Hierarchy of the authorities and privilages available with DB2 9.

Authorities

DB2 9 uses seven different levels of authority to control how users perform administrative and maintenance operations against an instance or a database:

- System Administrator (SYSADM) authority

- System Control (SYSCTRL) authority

- System Maintenance (SYSMAINT) authority

- System Monitor (SYSMON) authority

- Database Administrator (DBADM) authority

- Security Administrator (SECADM) authority

- Load (LOAD) authority

Four of these levels apply to the DB2 Database Manager instance (and to all databases that are under that instance's control), whereas three apply only to specific databases within a particular instance. The instance-level authorities can be assigned only to groups; the names of the groups that are assigned these authorities are stored in the DB2 Database Manager configuration file that is associated with the instance. Conversely, the database-level authorities can be assigned to individual users and, in some cases, groups; groups and users that have been assigned database-level authorities are recorded in the system catalog tables of the database to which the authority applies.

System Administrator authority

System Administrator (SYSADM) authority is the highest level of administrative authority available. Users who have been given this authority are allowed to run any DB2 utility, execute any DB2 command, and perform any SQL/XQuery operation that does not attempt to access data protected by label-based access control (LBAC). Users with this authority also have the ability to control all database objects within an instance, including databases, database partition groups, buffer pools, table spaces, schemas, tables, views, indexes, aliases, servers, data types, functions, procedures, triggers, packages, and event monitors.

Additionally, users who have been given this authority are allowed to perform the following tasks:

- Upgrade (migrate) an existing database from a previous version of DB2 to DB2 Version 9.

- Modify the parameter values of the DB2 Database Manager configuration file associated with an instance—including specifying which groups have System Administrator, System Control, System Maintenance, and System Monitor authority. (The DB2 Database Manager configuration file is used to control the amount of system resources allocated to a single instance.)

- Give (grant) Database Administrator authority and Security Administrator authority to individual users and/or groups.

- Revoke Database Administrator authority and/or Security Administrator authority from individual users and/or groups.

System Administrator authority can be assigned only to a group; this assignment is made by storing the appropriate group name in the *sysadm_group* parameter of the DB2 Database Manager configuration file associated with an instance. (This is done by executing an UPDATE DATABASE MANAGER CONFIGURATION command with the SYSADM_GROUP parameter specified, along with the name of the group that is to receive System Administrator authority.) Individual membership in the group itself is controlled through the security facility provided by the operating system used on the workstation where the instance has been defined. Users who possess System Administrator authority are responsible both for controlling the DB2 Database Manager associated with an instance and for ensuring the safety and integrity of the data contained in databases that fall under the instance's control.

Users who hold System Administrator authority are implicitly given the rights granted by System Control, System Maintenance, System Monitor, and Database Administrator authority. However, they are not implicitly given the rights granted by Security Administrator authority.

System Control authority

System Control (SYSCTRL) authority is the highest level of system or instance control authority available. Users who have been given this authority are allowed to perform maintenance and utility operations both on a DB2 Database Manager instance and on any databases that fall under that instance's control. However, because System Control authority is designed to allow special users to maintain an instance that contains sensitive data that they most likely do not have the right to view or modify, users who are granted this authority do not implicitly receive authority to access the data stored in the databases that are controlled by the instance. On the other hand, because a connection to a database is required in order to perform some of the utility operations available, users who are granted System Control authority for a particular instance also receive the privileges needed to connect to each database under that instance's control.

Users with System Control authority (or higher) are allowed to perform the following tasks:

- Update a database, node, or distributed connection services (DCS) directory (by cataloging/uncataloging databases, nodes, or DCS databases).

- Modify the parameter values in one or more database configuration files. (A database configuration file is used to control the amount of system resources that are allocated to a single database during normal operation.)

- Force users off the system.

- Create or destroy (drop) a database.

- Create, alter, or drop a table space.

- Make a backup image of a database or a table space.

- Restore an existing database using a backup image.

- Restore a table space using a backup image.

- Create a new database from a database backup image.

- Perform a roll-forward recovery operation on a database.

- Start or stop a DB2 Database Manager instance.

- Run a trace on a database operation.

- Take database system monitor snapshots of a DB2 Database Manager instance or any database under the instance's control.

- Query the state of a table space.

- Update recovery history log files.

- Quiesce (restrict access to) a table space.

- Reorganize a table.

- Collect catalog statistics using the RUNSTATS utility.

Like System Administrator authority, System Control authority can be assigned only to a group. This assignment is made by storing the appropriate group name in the *sysctrl_group* parameter of the DB2 Database Manager configuration file that is associated with a particular instance. (This is done by executing an UPDATE DATABASE MANAGER CONFIGURATION command with the SYSCTRL_GROUP parameter specified, along with the name of the group that is to receive System Control authority.) Again, individual membership in the group itself is controlled through the security facility that is used on the workstation where the instance has been defined.

System Maintenance authority

System Maintenance (SYSMAINT) authority is the second highest level of system or instance control authority available. Users who have been given this authority are allowed to perform maintenance and utility operations both on a DB2 Database Manager instance and on and any databases that fall under that instance's control. System Maintenance authority is designed to allow special users to maintain a database that contains sensitive data that they most likely do not have the right to view or modify. Therefore, users who are granted this authority do not implicitly receive authority to access the data stored in the databases on which they are allowed to perform maintenance. However, because a connection to a database must exist before some utility operations can be performed, users who are granted System Maintenance authority for a particular instance automatically receive the privileges needed to connect to each database that falls under that instance's control.

Users with System Maintenance authority (or higher) are allowed to perform the following tasks:

- Modify the parameter values of one or more DB2 database configuration files

- Make a backup image of a database or a table space

- Restore an existing database using a backup image

- Restore a table space using a backup image

- Perform a roll-forward recovery operation on a database

- Start or stop a DB2 Database Manager instance

- Run a trace on a database operation

- Take database system monitor snapshots of a DB2 Database Manager instance or any database under the instance's control

- Query the state of a table space

- Update recovery log history files

- Quiesce (restrict access to) a table space

- Reorganize a table

- Collect catalog statistics using the RUNSTATS utility

Like System Administrator and System Control authority, System Maintenance authority can be assigned only to a group. This assignment is made by storing the appropriate group name in the *sysmaint_group* parameter of the DB2 Database Manager configuration file that is associated with a particular instance. (This is done by executing an UPDATE DATABASE MANAGER CONFIGURATION command with the SYSMAINT_GROUP parameter specified, along with the name of the group that is to receive System Maintenance authority.) Again, individual membership in the group itself is controlled through the security facility that is used on the workstation where the instance has been defined.

System Monitor authority

System Monitor (SYSMON) authority is the third highest level of system or instance control authority available with DB2. Users who have been given this authority are allowed to take system monitor snapshots for a DB2 Database Manager instance and/or for one or more databases that fall under that instance's control. System Monitor authority is designed to allow special users to monitor the performance of a database that contains sensitive data that they most likely do not have the right to view or modify. Therefore, users who are granted this authority do not implicitly rece͏ ͏ to access the data stored in the databases on which they are al͏ ͏hot monitor information. However, because a connection to ͏ the snapshot monitor SQL table functions can be used, ͏nitor authority for a particular instance ͏ded to connect to each database under that

͏ are allowed to perform the

͏itches

͏em as well.

͏(shortly), they
͏ When a user is
͏available for that database as well.

͏databases privileges
͏ for a particular database (shortly), we will look at shortly). When a user is
͏ executing the appropriate
͏ (which is made by executing the appropriate
͏ statement. This assignment is made by executing the appropriate
͏ groups. This assignment is made by executing the appropriate GRANT SQL statement (which we will look at shortly). When a user is
͏ System Maintenance, and System
͏ System Control, System Maintenance, and System
͏ Database Administrator authority can be assigned to both
͏ administrator, Database Administrator authority can be assigned to both
͏ individual users and groups. This assignment
͏ form of the GRANT SQL statement. System Database Administrator authority
͏ given Database Administrator authority receive all database privileges
͏ automatically receive all database privileges

individual membership in the group itself is controlled through the security facility that is used on the workstation where the instance has been defined.

Database Administrator authority

Database Administrator (DBADM) authority is the second highest level of administrative authority available (just below System Administrator authority). Users who have been given this authority are allowed to run most DB2 utilities, issue database-specific DB2 commands, perform most SQL/XQuery operations, and access data stored in any table in a database—provided that data is not protected by LBAC. (To access data protected by LBAC, a user must have the appropriate LBAC credentials.) However, they can perform these functions only on the database for which Database Administrator authority is held.

Additionally, users with Database Administrator authority (or higher) are allowed to perform the following tasks:

- Read database log files

- Create, activate, and drop event monitors

- Query the state of a table space

- Update recovery history log files

- Quiesce (restrict access to) a table space

- Reorganize a table

- Collect catalog statistics using the RUNST

Unlike System Admi

Monitor

Any time a user with SYSADM or SYSCTRL authority creates a new database, that user automatically receives DBADM authority on that database. Furthermore, if a user with SYSADM or SYSCTRL authority creates a database and is later removed from the SYSADM or SYSCTRL group (i.e., the user's SYSADM or SYSCTRL authority is revoked), the user retains DBADM authority for that database until it is explicitly removed (revoked).

Security Administrator authority

Security Administrator (SECADM) authority is a special database level of authority that is designed to allow special users to configure various label-based access control (LBAC) elements to restrict access to one or more tables that contain data to which they most likely do not have access themselves. Users who are granted this authority do not implicitly receive authority to access the data stored in the databases for which they manage data access. In fact, users with Security Administrator authority are allowed to perform only the following tasks:

- Create and drop security policies

- Create and drop security labels

- Grant and revoke security labels to and from individual users (using the GRANT SECURITY LABEL and REVOKE SECURITY LABEL SQL statements)

- Grant and revoke LBAC rule exemptions

- Grant and revoke SETSESSIONUSER privileges (using the GRANT SETSESSIONUSER SQL statement)

- Transfer ownership of any object not owned by the Security Administrator (by executing the TRANSFER OWNERSHIP SQL statement)

No other authority, including System Administrator authority, provides a user with these abilities.

Security Administrator authority can be assigned only to individual users; it cannot be assigned to groups (including the group PUBLIC). This assignment is made by executing the appropriate form of the GRANT SQL statement, and only users with System Administrator authority are allowed to grant this authority.

Load authority

Load (LOAD) authority is a special database level of administrative authority that has a much smaller scope than DBADM authority. Users who have been given this authority, along with INSERT and in some cases DELETE privileges, on a particular table are allowed to bulk-load data into that table, using either the AutoLoader utility (db2atld command) or the LOAD command/API. Load authority is designed to allow special users to perform bulk-load operations against a database with which they most likely cannot do anything else. This authority provides a way for Database Administrators to allow more users to perform special database operations, such as Extraction-Transform-Load (ETL) operations, without having to sacrifice control.

In addition to being able to load data into a database table, users with Load authority (or higher) are allowed to perform the following tasks:

- Query the state of a table space using the LIST TABLESPACES command.

- Quiesce (restrict access to) a table space.

- Perform bulk-load operations using the LOAD utility. (If exception tables are used as part of a load operation, the user must have INSERT privilege on the exception tables used as well as INSERT privilege on the table being loaded.)

- Collect catalog statistics using the RUNSTATS utility.

Like Database Administrator authority, Load authority can be assigned to both individual users and groups. This assignment is made by executing the appropriate form of the GRANT SQL statement.

Privileges

As mentioned earlier, privileges are used to convey the rights to perform certain actions on specific database resources to both individual users and groups. With DB2 9, two distinct types of privileges exist: database privileges and object privileges.

Database privileges

Database privileges apply to a database as a whole, and in many cases, they act as a second security checkpoint that must be cleared before access to data is provided. Figure 8–2 shows the different types of database privileges available.

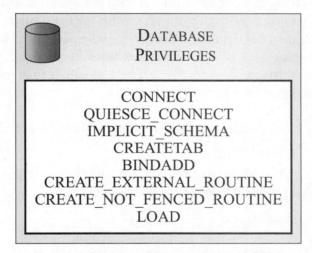

DATABASE
PRIVILEGES

CONNECT
QUIESCE_CONNECT
IMPLICIT_SCHEMA
CREATETAB
BINDADD
CREATE_EXTERNAL_ROUTINE
CREATE_NOT_FENCED_ROUTINE
LOAD

Figure 8–2: Database privileges available with DB2 9.

As you can see in Figure 8–2, eight different database privileges exist. They are:

CONNECT. Allows a user to establish a connection to the database.

QUIESCE_CONNECT. Allows a user to establish a connection to the database while it is in a quiesced state (i.e., while access to it is restricted).

IMPLICIT_SCHEMA. Allows a user to create a new schema in the database implicitly by creating an object and assigning that object a schema name that is different from any of the schema names that already exist in the database.

CREATETAB. Allows a user to create new tables in the database.

BINDADD. Allows a user to create packages in the database (by precompiling embedded SQL application source code files against the database or by binding application bind files to the database).

CREATE_EXTERNAL_ROUTINE. Allows a user to create user-defined functions (UDFs) and/or procedures and store them in the database so that they can be used by other users and applications.

CREATE_NOT_FENCED_ROUTINE. Allows a user to create unfenced UDFs and/or procedures and store them in the database. (Unfenced UDFs and stored procedures are UDFs/procedures that are considered "safe" enough to be run in the DB2 Database Manager operating environment's process or address space. Unless a UDF/procedure is registered as unfenced, the DB2 Database Manager insulates the UDF/procedure's internal resources in such a way that they cannot be run in the DB2 Database Manager's address space.)

LOAD. Allows a user to bulk-load data into one or more existing tables in the database.

At a minimum, a user must have CONNECT privilege on a database before he or she can work with any object contained in that database.

Object privileges

Unlike database privileges, which apply to a database as a whole, object privileges apply only to specific objects within a database. These objects include table spaces, schemas, tables, views, indexes, sequences, routines, packages, servers, and nicknames. Because the nature of each database object available varies, the individual privileges that exist for each object can vary as well. The following sections describe the different sets of object privileges that are available with DB2 9.

Table space privileges. Table space privileges control what users can and cannot do with a particular table space. (Table spaces are used to control where data in a database physically resides.) Figure 8–3 shows the only table space privilege available.

Figure 8–3: Table space privilege available with DB2 9.

As you can see in Figure 8–3, only one table space privilege exists. That privilege is the USE privilege, which, when granted, allows a user to create tables and indexes in the table space. The owner of a table space (usually the individual who created the table space) automatically receives USE privilege for that table space.

The USE privilege cannot be used to provide a user with the ability to create tables in the SYSCATSPACE table space or in any temporary table space that might exist.

Schema privileges. Schema privileges control what users can and cannot do with a particular schema. (A schema is an object that is used to logically classify and group other objects in the database; most objects are named using a naming convention that consists of a schema name, followed by a period, followed by the object name.) Figure 8–4 shows the different types of schema privileges available.

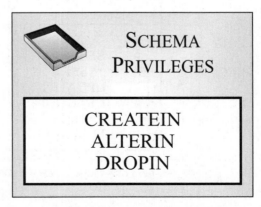

Figure 8–4: Schema privileges available with DB2 9.

As you can see in Figure 8–4, three different schema privileges exist. They are:

CREATEIN. Allows a user to create objects within the schema.

ALTERIN. Allows a user to change the comment associated with any object in the schema or to alter any object that resides within the schema.

DROPIN. Allows a user to remove (drop) any object within the schema.

Objects that can be manipulated within a schema include tables, views, indexes, packages, user-defined data types, user-defined functions, triggers, stored procedures, and aliases. The owner of a schema (usually the individual who created the schema) automatically receives all privileges available for that schema, along with the right to grant any combination of those privileges to other users and groups.

Table privileges. Table privileges control what users can and cannot do with a particular table in a database. (A table is a logical structure used to present data as a collection of unordered rows with a fixed number of columns.) Figure 8–5 shows the different types of table privileges available.

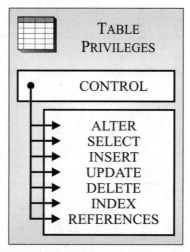

Figure 8–5: Table privileges available with DB2 9.

As you can see in Figure 8–5, eight different table privileges exist. They are:

CONTROL. Provides a user with every table privilege available, allows the user to remove (drop) the table from the database, and gives the user the ability to grant and revoke one or more table privileges (except the CONTROL privilege) to and from other users and groups.

ALTER. Allows a user to execute the ALTER TABLE SQL statement against the table. In other words, allows a user to add columns to the table, add or change comments associated with the table or any of its columns, create or drop a primary key for the table, create or drop a unique constraint for the table, create or drop a check constraint for the table, create or drop a referential constraint for the table, and create or drop triggers for the table (provided the user holds the appropriate privileges for every object referenced by the trigger).

SELECT. Allows a user to execute a SELECT SQL statement against the table. In other words, this privilege allows a user to retrieve data from a table, create a view that references the table, and run the Export utility against the table.

INSERT. Allows a user to execute the INSERT SQL statement against the table. In other words, this privilege allows a user to add data to the table and run the Import utility against the table.

UPDATE. Allows a user to execute the UPDATE SQL statement against the table. In other words, this privilege allows a user to modify data in the table. (This privilege can be granted for the entire table or limited to one or more columns within the table.)

DELETE. Allows a user to execute the DELETE SQL statement against the table. In other words, allows a user to remove rows of data from the table.

INDEX. Allows a user to create an index for the table.

REFERENCES. Allows a user to create and drop foreign key constraints that reference the table in a parent relationship. (This privilege can be granted for the entire table or limited to one or more columns within the table, in which case only those columns can participate as a parent key in a referential constraint.)

The owner of a table (usually the individual who created the table) automatically receives all privileges available for that table (including CONTROL privilege), along with the right to grant any combination of those privileges (except CONTROL privilege) to other users and groups. If the CONTROL privilege is later revoked from the table owner, all other privileges that were automatically granted to the owner for that particular table are not automatically revoked. Instead, they must be explicitly revoked in one or more separate operations.

View privileges. View privileges control what users can and cannot do with a particular view. (A view is a virtual table residing in memory that provides an alternative way of working with data that resides in one or more base tables. For this reason, views can be used to prevent access to select columns in a table.) Figure 8–6 shows the different types of view privileges available.

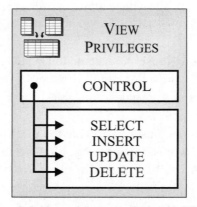

Figure 8–6: View privileges available with DB2 9.

As you can see in Figure 8–6, five different view privileges exist. They are:

CONTROL. Provides a user with every view privilege available, allows the user to remove (drop) the view from the database, and gives the user the ability to grant and revoke one or more view privileges (except the CONTROL privilege) to and from other users and groups.

SELECT. Allows a user to retrieve data from the view, create a second view that references the view, and run the Export utility against the view.

INSERT. Allows a user to execute the INSERT SQL statement against the view. In other words, allows a user to add data to the view.

UPDATE. Allows a user to execute the UPDATE SQL statement against the view. In other words, this privilege allows a user to modify data in the view. (This privilege can be granted for the entire view or limited to one or more columns within the view.)

DELETE. Allows a user to execute the DELETE SQL statement against the view. In other words, this privilege allows a user to remove rows of data from the view.

In order to create a view, a user must hold appropriate privileges (at a minimum, SELECT privilege) on each base table the view references. The owner of a view (usually the individual who created the view) automatically receives all privileges available—with the exception of the CONTROL privilege—for that view, along with the right to grant any combination of those privileges (except CONTROL privilege) to other users and groups. A view owner will receive CONTROL privilege for a view only if he or she also holds CONTROL privilege for every base table the view references.

> If a user who holds SELECT privilege on one or more tables creates a view based on one or more of those tables and his or her SELECT privileges are later revoked, the view will become inoperative, and any privileges that have been granted for that view will be revoked automatically.

Index privileges. Index privileges control what users can and cannot do with a particular index. (An index is an ordered set of pointers that refer to one or more key columns in a base table; indexes are used to improve query performance.) Figure 8–7 shows the only index privilege available.

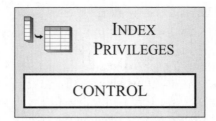

Figure 8–7: Index privilege available with DB2 9.

As you can see in Figure 8–7, only one index privilege exists. That privilege is the CONTROL privilege, which, when granted, allows a user to remove (drop) the index from the database. Unlike the CONTROL privilege for other objects, the CONTROL privilege for an index does not give a user the ability to grant and revoke index privileges to and from other users and groups. That's because the CONTROL privilege is the only index privilege available, and only users who hold System Administrator (SYSADM) or Database Administrator (DBADM) authority are allowed to grant and revoke CONTROL privileges for an object.

The owner of an index (usually the individual who created the index) automatically receives CONTROL privilege for that index.

Sequence privileges. Sequence privileges control what users can and cannot do with a particular sequence. (A sequence is an object that can be used to generate values automatically. Sequences are ideal for generating unique key values, and they can be used to avoid the possible concurrency and performance problems that can occur when unique counters residing outside the database are used for data generation.) Figure 8–8 shows the different types of sequence privileges available.

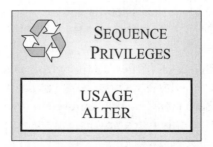

Figure 8–8: Sequence privileges available with DB2 9.

As you can see in Figure 8–8, two different sequence privileges exist. They are:

USAGE. Allows a user to use the PREVIOUS VALUE and NEXT VALUE expressions that are associated with the sequence. (The PREVIOUS VALUE expression returns the most recently generated value for the specified sequence; the NEXT VALUE expression returns the next value for the specified sequence.)

ALTER. Allows a user to perform administrative tasks such as restarting the sequence, changing the increment value for the sequence, and adding or changing the comment associated with the sequence.

The owner of a sequence (usually the individual who created the sequence) automatically receives all privileges available for that sequence, along with the right to grant any combination of those privileges to other users and groups.

Routine privileges. Routine privileges control what users can and cannot do with a particular routine. (A routine can be a user-defined function, a stored procedure, or a method that can be invoked by several different users.) Figure 8–9 shows the only routine privilege available.

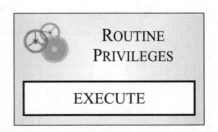

Figure 8–9: Routine privilege available with DB2 9.

As you can see in Figure 8–9, only one routine privilege exists. That privilege is the EXECUTE privilege, which, when granted, allows a user to invoke the routine, create a function that is sourced from the routine (provided the routine is a function), and reference the routine in any Data Definition Language SQL statement (for example, CREATE VIEW and CREATE TRIGGER).

• •

Before a user can invoke a routine (user-defined function, stored procedure, or method), he or she must hold both EXECUTE privilege on the routine and any privileges required by that routine. Thus, in order to execute a stored procedure that queries a table, a user must hold both EXECUTE privilege on the stored procedure and SELECT privilege on the table against which the query is run.

• •

The owner of a routine (usually the individual who created the routine) automatically receives EXECUTE privilege for that routine.

Package privileges. Package privileges control what users can and cannot do with a particular package. (A package is an object that contains the information needed by the DB2 Database Manager to process SQL statements in the most efficient way possible on behalf of an embedded SQL application.) Figure 8–10 shows the different types of package privileges available.

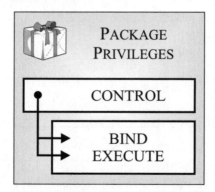

Figure 8–10: Package privileges available with DB2 9.

As you can see in Figure 8–10, three different package privileges exist. They are:

CONTROL. Provides a user with every package privilege available, allows the user to remove (drop) the package from the database, and gives the user the ability to grant and revoke one or more table privileges (except the CONTROL privilege) to and from other users and groups.

BIND. Allows a user to rebind or add new package versions to a package that has already been bound to a database. (In addition to the BIND package privilege, a user must hold the privileges needed to execute the SQL statements that make up the package before the package can be successfully rebound.)

EXECUTE. Allows a user to execute the package. (A user who has EXECUTE privilege for a particular package can execute that package, even if the user does not have the privileges that are needed to execute the SQL statements stored in the package. That is because any privileges needed to execute the SQL statements are implicitly granted to the package user. It is important to note that for privileges to be implicitly granted, the creator of the package must hold privileges as an individual user or as a member of the group PUBLIC—not as a member of another named group.)

The owner of a package (usually the individual who created the package) automatically receives all privileges available for that package (including CONTROL privilege), along with the right to grant any combination of those privileges (except CONTROL privilege) to other users and groups. If the CONTROL privilege is later revoked from the package owner, all other privileges that were automatically granted to the owner for that particular package are not automatically revoked. Instead, they must be explicitly revoked in one or more separate operations.

> Users who have EXECUTE privilege for a package that contains nicknames do not need additional authorities or privileges for the nicknames in the package; however, they must be able to pass any authentication checks performed at the data source(s) in which objects referenced by the nicknames are stored, and they must hold the appropriate authorizations and privileges needed to access all objects referenced.

Server privileges. Server privileges control what users can and cannot do with a particular federated database server. (A DB2 federated system is a distributed computing system that consists of a DB2 server, known as a *federated server*, and one or more data sources to which the federated server sends queries. Each data source consists of an instance of some supported relational database management system—such as Oracle—plus the database or databases that the instance supports.) Figure 8–11 shows the only server privilege available.

Figure 8–11: Server privilege available with DB2 9.

As you can see in Figure 8–11, only one server privilege exists. That privilege is the PASSTHRU privilege, which, when granted, allows a user to issue Data Definition Language (DDL) and Data Manipulation Language (DML) SQL statements (as pass-through operations) directly to a data source via a federated server.

Nickname privileges. Nickname privileges control what users can and cannot do with a particular nickname. (When a client application submits a distributed request to a federated database server, the server forwards the request to the appropriate data source for processing. However, such a request does not identify the data source itself; instead, it references tables and views within the data source by using nicknames that map to specific table and view names in the data source. Nicknames are not alternate names for tables and views in the same way that aliases are; instead, they are pointers by which a federated server references external objects.) Figure 8–12 shows the different types of nickname privileges available.

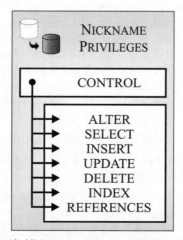

Figure 8–12: Nickname privileges available with DB2 9.

As you can see in Figure 8–12, eight different nickname privileges exist. They are:

CONTROL. Provides a user with every nickname privilege available, allows the user to remove (drop) the nickname from the database, and gives the user the ability to grant and revoke one or more nickname privileges (except the CONTROL privilege) to and from other users and groups.

ALTER. Allows a user to execute the ALTER NICKNAME SQL statement against the table. In other words, this privilege allows a user to change column names in the nickname, add or change the DB2 data type to which a particular nickname column's data type maps, and specify column options for a specific nickname column.

SELECT. Allows a user to execute a SELECT SQL statement against the nickname. In other words, this privilege allows a user to retrieve data from the table or view within a federated data source to which the nickname refers.

INSERT. Allows a user to execute the INSERT SQL statement against the nickname. In other words, this privilege allows a user to add data to the table or view within a federated data source to which the nickname refers.

UPDATE. Allows a user to execute the UPDATE SQL statement against the nickname. In other words, this privilege allows a user to modify data in the table or view within a federated data source to which the nickname refers. (This privilege can be granted for the entire table or limited to one or more columns within the table to which the nickname refers.)

DELETE. Allows a user to execute the DELETE SQL statement against the nickname. In other words, allows a user to remove rows of data from the table or view within a federated data source to which the nickname refers.

INDEX. Allows a user to create an index specification for the nickname.

REFERENCES. Allows a user to create and drop foreign key constraints that reference the nickname in a parent relationship.

The owner of a nickname (usually the individual who created the table) automatically receives all privileges available for that nickname (including CONTROL privilege), along with the right to grant any combination of those privileges (except CONTROL privilege) to other users and groups. If the CONTROL privilege is later revoked from the nickname owner, all other privileges that were automatically granted to the owner for that particular table are not automatically revoked. Instead, they must be explicitly revoked in one or more separate operations.

Granting Authorities and Privileges

There are three different ways that users (and in some cases, groups) can obtain database-level authorities and database/object privileges. They are:

Implicitly. When a user creates a database, that user implicitly receives Database Administrator authority for that database, along with most database privileges available. Likewise, when a user creates a database object, that user implicitly receives all privileges available for that object, along with the ability to grant any combination of those privileges (with the exception of the CONTROL privilege) to other users and groups. Privileges can also be implicitly given whenever a higher-level privilege is explicitly granted to a user (for example, if a user is explicitly given CONTROL privilege for a table space, the user will implicitly receive the USE privilege for that table space as well). It's important to remember that such implicitly assigned privileges are not automatically revoked when the higher-level privilege that caused them to be granted is revoked.

Indirectly. Indirectly assigned privileges are usually associated with packages; when a user executes a package that requires additional privileges that the user does not have (for example, a package that deletes a row of data from a table requires the DELETE privilege on that table), the user is indirectly given those privileges for the express purpose of executing the package. Indirectly granted privileges are temporary and do not exist outside the scope in which they are granted.

Explicitly. Database-level authorities, database privileges, and object privileges can be explicitly given to or taken from an individual user or a group of users by anyone who has the authority to do so. To grant privileges explicitly on most database objects, a user must have System Administrator (SYSADM) or Database Administrator (DBADM) authority, or CONTROL privilege on that object. Alternately, a user can explicitly grant any privilege that user was assigned with the WITH GRANT OPTION specified. To grant CONTROL privilege for any object, a user must have System Administrator (SYSADM) or Database Administrator (DBADM) authority; to grant System Administrator (SYSADM) or Database Administrator (DBADM) authority, a user must have System Administrator (SYSADM) authority.

Granting and Revoking Authorities and Privileges from the Control Center

One way to explicitly grant and revoke database-level authorities, as well as many of the object privileges available, is by using the various authorities and privileges management dialogs that are provided with the Control Center. These dialogs are activated by highlighting the appropriate database or object name shown in the Control Center panes and selecting either Authorities or Privileges from the corresponding database or object menu. Figure 8–13 shows the menu items that must be selected in the Control Center in order to activate the Table Privileges dialog for a particular table. Figure 8–14 shows how the Table Privileges dialog might look immediately after a table is first created. (A single check mark under a privilege means that the individual or group shown has been granted that privilege; a double check mark means the individual or group has also been granted ability to grant that privilege to other users and groups.)

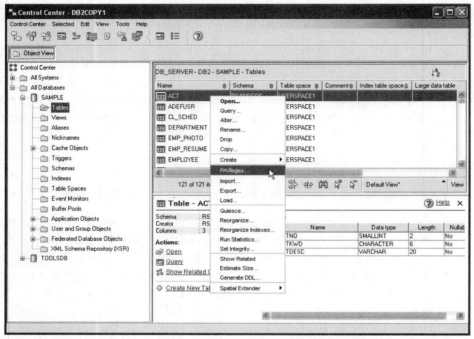

Figure 8–13: Invoking the Table Privileges dialog from the Control Center.

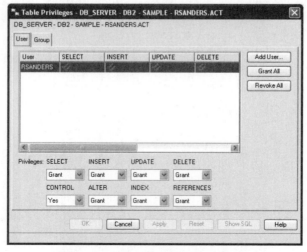

Figure 8–14: The Table privilages dialog.

To assign privileges to an individual user from the Table Privileges dialog (or a similar authorities/privileges dialog), you simply identify a particular user by highlighting the user's entry in the recognized users list—if the desired user is not in the list, the user can be added by selecting the "Add User" push button—and assigning the appropriate privileges (or authorities) using the "Privileges" (or "Authorities") drop-down list(s) or the "Grant All" or "Revoke All" push buttons. To assign privileges to a group of users, you select the "Group" tab to display a list of recognized groups and repeat the process (using the "Add Group" push button instead of the "Add User" push button to add a desired group to the list if the group is not already there).

Granting Authorities and Privileges with the GRANT SQL Statement

Not all privileges can be explicitly given to users or groups with the privileges management dialogs available. In situations where no privileges dialog exists (and in situations where you elect not to use the privileges dialogs available), database-level authorities and database/object privileges can be explicitly given to users and/or groups by executing the appropriate form of the GRANT SQL statement. The syntax for the GRANT SQL statement varies according to the authority or privilege being granted. The following subsections show the syntax used to grant each database-level authority and database/object privilege available.

Database-level authorities and privileges

```
GRANT [Privilege, ...] ON DATABASE
TO [Recipient, ...]
```

where:

Privilege   Identifies one or more database privileges that are to be given to one or more users and/or groups. The following values are valid for this parameter: DBADM, SECADM, CONNECT, CONNECT_QUIESCE, IMPLICIT_SCHEMA, CREATETAB, BINDADD, CREATE_EXTERNAL_ROUTINE, CREATE_NOT_FENCED_ROUTINE, and LOAD.

Recipient	Identifies the name of the user(s) and/or group(s) that are to receive the database privileges specified. The value specified for the *Recipient* parameter can be any combination of the following:
<USER> [*UserName*]	Identifies a specific user to which the privilege(s) specified are to be given.
<GROUP> [*GroupName*]	Identifies a specific group to whom the privilege(s) specified are to be given.
PUBLIC	Indicates that the privilege(s) specified are to be given to the group PUBLIC. (All users are members of the group PUBLIC.)

Checking is not performed to ensure that the names of users and/or groups specified in the *Recipient* parameter are valid. Therefore, it is possible to grant privileges to users and groups that do not yet exist.

Table space privileges

```
GRANT USE OF TABLESPACE [TablespaceName]
TO [Recipient, ...]
<WITH GRANT OPTION>
```

where:

TablespaceName	Identifies by name the table space that the USE privilege is to be associated with.
Recipient	Identifies the name of the user(s) and/or group(s) that are to receive the USE privilege. Again, the value specified for the *Recipient* parameter can be any combination of the following: <USER> [*UserName*], <GROUP> [*GroupName*], and PUBLIC.

If the WITH GRANT OPTION clause is specified, each *Recipient* is given the ability to grant the privilege received to others.

Schema privileges

```
GRANT [Privilege, ...] ON SCHEMA [SchemaName]
TO [Recipient, ...]
<WITH GRANT OPTION>
```

where:

Privilege   Identifies one or more schema privileges that are to be given to one or more users and/or groups. The following values are valid for this parameter: CREATIN, ALTERIN, and DROPIN.

SchemaName   Identifies by name the schema with which all schema privileges specified are to be associated.

Recipient   Identifies the name of the user(s) and/or group(s) that are to receive the schema privileges specified. The value specified for the *Recipient* parameter can be any combination of the following: <USER> [*UserName*], <GROUP> [*GroupName*], and PUBLIC.

Table privileges

```
GRANT [ALL <PRIVILEGES> |
       Privilege <( ColumnName, ... )> , ...]
ON TABLE [TableName]
TO [Recipient, ...]
<WITH GRANT OPTION>
```

where:

Privilege   Identifies one or more table privileges that are to be given to one or more users and/or groups. The following values are valid for this parameter: CONTROL, ALTER, SELECT, INSERT, UPDATE, DELETE, INDEX, and REFERENCES.

ColumnName   Identifies by name one or more specific columns with which
UPDATE or REFERENCES privileges are to be associated. This
option is used only when the *Privilege* parameter contains the
value UPDATE or REFERENCES.

TableName   Identifies by name the table with which all table privileges
specified are to be associated.

Recipient   Identifies the name of the user(s) and/or group(s) that are to
receive the table privileges specified. The value specified for the
Recipient parameter can be any combination of the following:
<USER> [*UserName*], <GROUP> [*GroupName*], and PUBLIC.

It is important to note that only users who hold System Administrator (SYSADM) or
Database Administrator (DBADM) authority are allowed to grant CONTROL privilege
for a table. For this reason, when the ALL PRIVILEGES clause is specified, all table
privileges *except* CONTROL privilege are granted to each *Recipient*; CONTROL
privilege must be granted separately.

View privileges

```
GRANT [ALL <PRIVILEGES> |
        Privilege <( ColumnName, ... )>  , ...]
ON [ViewName]
TO [Recipient, ...]
<WITH GRANT OPTION>
```

where:

Privilege   Identifies one or more view privileges that are to be given to one
or more users and/or groups. The following values are valid for
this parameter: CONTROL, SELECT, INSERT, UPDATE, and DELETE.

ColumnName   Identifies by name one or more specific columns with which
UPDATE privileges are to be associated. This option is used only
when the *Privilege* parameter contains the value UPDATE.

ViewName   Identifies by name the view with which all view privileges
                 specified are to be associated.

Recipient   Identifies the name of the user(s) and/or group(s) that are to
                 receive the view privileges specified. The value specified for the
                 Recipient parameter can be any combination of the following:
                 <USER> [*UserName*], <GROUP> [*GroupName*], and PUBLIC.

Again, only users who hold System Administrator (SYSADM) or Database
Administrator (DBADM) authority are allowed to grant CONTROL privilege for a
table. Therefore, when the ALL PRIVILEGES clause is specified, all view privileges
except CONTROL privilege are granted to each *Recipient*; CONTROL privilege must
be granted separately.

Index privileges

```
GRANT CONTROL ON INDEX [IndexName]
TO [Recipient, ...]
```

where:

IndexName   Identifies by name the index with which the CONTROL privilege
                 is to be associated.

Recipient   Identifies the name of the user(s) and/or group(s) that are to
                 receive the CONTROL privilege. The value specified for the
                 Recipient parameter can be any combination of the following:
                 <USER> [*UserName*], <GROUP> [*GroupName*], and PUBLIC.

Sequence privileges

```
GRANT [Privilege, ...] ON SEQUENCE [SequenceName]
TO [Recipient, ...]
<WITH GRANT OPTION>
```

where:

Privilege	Identifies one or more sequence privileges that are to be given to one or more users and/or groups. The following values are valid for this parameter: USAGE and ALTER.
SequenceName	Identifies by name the sequence with which all sequence privileges specified are to be associated.
Recipient	Identifies the name of the user(s) and/or group(s) that are to receive the sequence privileges specified. Again, the value specified for the *Recipient* parameter can be any combination of the following: <USER> [*UserName*], <GROUP> [*GroupName*], and PUBLIC.

Routine privileges

```
GRANT EXECUTE ON [RoutineName |
                  FUNCTION <SchemaName.> * |
                  METHOD * FOR [TypeName] |
                  METHOD * FOR <SchemaName.> * |
                  PROCEDURE <SchemaName.> *]
TO [Recipient, ...]
<WITH GRANT OPTION>
```

where:

RoutineName	Identifies by name the routine (user-defined function, method, or stored procedure) with which the EXECUTE privilege is to be associated.
TypeName	Identifies by name the type in which the specified method is found.
SchemaName	Identifies by name the schema in which all functions, methods, or procedures—including those that may be created in the future—are to have the EXECUTE privilege granted.
Recipient	Identifies the name of the user(s) and/or group(s) that are to receive the EXECUTE privilege. The value specified for the *Recipient* parameter can be any combination of the following: <USER> [*UserName*], <GROUP> [*GroupName*], and PUBLIC.

Package privileges

```
GRANT [Privilege, ...] ON PACKAGE <SchemaName.>[PackageID] TO [Recipient,
...]
<WITH GRANT OPTION>
```

where:

Privilege   Identifies one or more package privileges that are to be given to one or more users and/or groups. The following values are valid for this parameter: CONTROL, BIND, and EXECUTE.

SchemaName   Identifies by name the schema in which the specified package is found.

PackageName   Identifies by name the package with which all package privileges specified are to be associated.

Recipient   Identifies the name of the user(s) and/or group(s) that are to receive the package privileges specified. The value specified for the *Recipient* parameter can be any combination of the following: <USER> [*UserName*], <GROUP> [*GroupName*], and PUBLIC. (DB2 for Linux, UNIX, and Windows does not allow users to grant package privileges to themselves.)

Server privileges

```
GRANT PASSTHRU ON SERVER [ServerName]
TO [Recipient, ...]
```

where:

ServerName   Identifies by name the server with which the PASSTHRU privilege is to be associated.

Recipient   Identifies the name of the user(s) and/or group(s) that are to receive the PASSTHRU privilege. The value specified for the *Recipient* parameter can be any combination of the following: <USER> [*UserName*], <GROUP> [*GroupName*], and PUBLIC.

Nickname privileges

```
GRANT [ALL <PRIVILEGES> |
        Privilege <( ColumnName, ... )>  , ...]
ON [Nickname]
TO [Recipient, ...]
<WITH GRANT OPTION>
```

where:

Privilege   Identifies one or more nickname privileges that are to be given
                   to one or more users and/or groups. The following values are
                   valid for this parameter: CONTROL, ALTER, SELECT, INSERT,
                   UPDATE, DELETE, INDEX, and REFERENCES.

ColumnName   Identifies by name one or more specific columns with which
                   UPDATE or REFERENCES privileges are to be associated. This
                   option is used only when the *Privilege* parameter contains the
                   value UPDATE or REFERENCES.

Nickname   Identifies by name the nickname with which all privileges
                   specified are to be associated.

Recipient   Identifies the name of the user(s) and/or group(s) that are to
                   receive the nickname privileges specified. The value specified
                   for the *Recipient* parameter can be any combination of the
                   following: <USER> [*UserName*], <GROUP> [*GroupName*], and
                   PUBLIC.

Only users who hold System Administrator (SYSADM) or Database Administrator
(DBADM) authority are allowed to grant CONTROL privilege for a nickname.
Therefore, when the ALL PRIVILEGES clause is specified, all nickname privileges
except CONTROL privilege are granted to each *Recipient*; CONTROL privilege must
be granted separately.

GRANT SQL statement examples

Now that we've seen the basic syntax for the various forms of the GRANT SQL
statement, let's take a look at some examples.

Example 1. A server has both a user and a group named TESTER. Give the group TESTER the ability to bind applications to the database SAMPLE:

```
CONNECT TO sample;
GRANT BINDADD ON DATABASE TO GROUP tester;
```

Example 2. Give all table privileges available for the table PAYROLL.EMPLOYEE (except CONTROL privilege) to the group PUBLIC:

```
GRANT ALL PRIVILEGES ON TABLE payroll.employee TO PUBLIC
```

Example 3. Give user USER1 and user USER2 the privileges needed to perform DML operations on the table DEPARTMENT using the view DEPTVIEW:

```
GRANT SELECT, INSERT, UPDATE, DELETE ON deptview
TO USER user1, USER user2
```

Example 4. Give user JOHN_DOE the privileges needed to query the table INVENTORY, along with the ability to give these privileges to other users whenever appropriate:

```
GRANT SELECT ON TABLE inventory
TO john_doe
WITH GRANT OPTION
```

Example 5. Give user USER1 the ability to run an embedded SQL application that requires a package named GET_INVENTORY:

```
GRANT EXECUTE ON PACKAGE get_inventory TO USER user1
```

Example 6. Give user USER1 the ability to use a stored procedure named PAYROLL.CALC_SALARY in a query:

```
GRANT EXECUTE ON PROCEDURE payroll.calc_salary TO user1
```

Example 7. Give user USER1 and group GROUP1 the ability to define a referential constraint between the tables EMPLOYEE and DEPARTMENT using column EMPID in table EMPLOYEE as the parent key:

```
GRANT REFERENCES(empid) ON TABLE employee TO USER user1,
GROUP group1
```

Example 8. Give the group PUBLIC the ability to modify information stored in the ADDRESS and HOME_PHONE columns of the table EMP_INFO:

```
GRANT UPDATE(address, home_phone) ON TABLE emp_info
TO PUBLIC
```

Revoking Authorities and Privileges with the REVOKE SQL Statement

Just as there is an SQL statement that can be used to grant database-level authorities and database/object privileges, there is an SQL statement that can be used to revoke database-level authorities and database/object privileges. This statement is the REVOKE SQL statement, and as with the GRANT statement, the syntax for the REVOKE statement varies according to the authority or privilege being revoked. The following sections show the syntax used to revoke each database-level authority and database/object privilege available.

Database-level authorities and privileges

```
REVOKE [Privilege, ...] ON DATABASE
FROM [Forfeiter, ...] <BY ALL>
```

where:

Privilege   Identifies one or more database privileges that are to be taken from one or more users and/or groups. The following values are valid for this parameter: DBADM, SECADM, CONNECT, CONNECT_QUIESCE, IMPLICIT_SCHEMA, CREATETAB, BINDADD, CREATE_EXTERNAL_ROUTINE, CREATE_NOT_FENCED_ROUTINE, and LOAD.

Forfeiter   Identifies the name of the user(s) and/or group(s) that are to lose the database privileges specified. The value specified for the *Forfeiter* parameter can be any combination of the following:

<USER> [*UserName*]	Identifies a specific user from whom the privilege(s) specified are to be taken.
<GROUP> [*GroupName*]	Identifies a specific group from which the privilege(s) specified are to be taken.
PUBLIC	Indicates that the privilege(s) specified are to be taken from the group PUBLIC. (All users are members of the group PUBLIC.)

The BY ALL clause is optional and is provided as a courtesy for administrators who are familiar with the syntax of the DB2 for OS/390 REVOKE SQL statement. Whether it is included or not, all privileges specified will be revoked from all users and/or groups specified.

It is important to note that when Database Administrator (DBADM) authority is revoked, privileges held on objects in the database by the *Forfeiter* specified are not automatically revoked. The same is true for all other database authorities that were implicitly and automatically granted when DBADM authority was granted.

Table space privileges

```
REVOKE USE OF TABLESPACE [TablespaceName]
FROM [Forfeiter, ...] <BY ALL>
```

where:

TablespaceName	Identifies by name the table space with which the USE privilege is associated.
Forfeiter	Identifies the name of the user(s) and/or group(s) that are to lose the USE privilege. Again, the value specified for the *Forfeiter* parameter can be any combination of the following: <USER> [*UserName*], <GROUP> [*GroupName*], and PUBLIC.

Schema privileges

```
REVOKE [Privilege, ...] ON SCHEMA [SchemaName]
FROM [Forfeiter, ...] <BY ALL>
```

where:

Privilege	Identifies one or more schema privileges that are to be taken from one or more users and/or groups. The following values are valid for this parameter: CREATIN, ALTERIN, and DROPIN.
SchemaName	Identifies by name the schema with which all schema privileges specified are to be associated.
Forfeiter	Identifies the name of the user(s) and/or group(s) that are to lose the schema privileges specified. The value specified for the *Forfeiter* parameter can be any combination of the following: <USER> [*UserName*], <GROUP> [*GroupName*], and PUBLIC.

Table privileges

```
REVOKE [ALL <PRIVILEGES> |
        Privilege, ...]
ON TABLE [TableName]
FROM [Forfeiter, ...] <BY ALL>
```

where:

Privilege	Identifies one or more table privileges that are to be taken from one or more users and/or groups. The following values are valid for this parameter: CONTROL, ALTER, SELECT, INSERT, UPDATE, DELETE, INDEX, and REFERENCES.
TableName	Identifies by name the table with which all table privileges specified are to be associated.

Forfeiter   Identifies the name of the user(s) and/or group(s) that
                              are to lose the table privileges specified. The value
                              specified for the *Forfeiter* parameter can be any
                              combination of the following: <USER> [*UserName*],
                              <GROUP> [*GroupName*], and PUBLIC.

It is important to note that only users who hold System Administrator (SYSADM) or
Database Administrator (DBADM) authority are allowed to revoke CONTROL
privilege for a table. For this reason, when the ALL PRIVILEGES clause is specified,
all table privileges *except* CONTROL privilege are revoked from each *Forfeiter*;
CONTROL privilege must be revoked separately.

View privileges

```
REVOKE [ALL <PRIVILEGES> |
        Privilege, ...]
ON [ViewName]
FROM [Forfeiter, ...] <BY ALL>
```
where:

Privilege   Identifies one or more view privileges that are to be
                              taken from one or more users and/or groups. The
                              following values are valid for this parameter: CONTROL,
                              SELECT, INSERT, UPDATE, and DELETE.

ViewName   Identifies by name the view with which all view
                              privileges specified are to be associated.

Forfeiter   Identifies the name of the user(s) and/or group(s) that
                              are to lose the view privileges specified. The value
                              specified for the *Forfeiter* parameter can be any
                              combination of the following: <USER> [*UserName*],
                              <GROUP> [*GroupName*], and PUBLIC.

Again, only users who hold System Administrator (SYSADM) or Database
Administrator (DBADM) authority are allowed to revoke CONTROL privilege for a
table. For this reason, when the ALL PRIVILEGES clause is specified, all table

privileges *except* CONTROL privilege are revoked from each *Forfeiter*; CONTROL privilege must be revoked separately.

Index privileges

```
REVOKE CONTROL ON INDEX [IndexName]
FROM [Forfeiter, ...] <BY ALL>
```

where:

IndexName   Identifies by name the index with which the CONTROL privilege is associated.

Forfeiter   Identifies the name of the user(s) and/or group(s) that are to lose the CONTROL privilege. The value specified for the *Forfeiter* parameter can be any combination of the following: <USER> [*UserName*], <GROUP> [*GroupName*], and PUBLIC.

Sequence privileges

```
REVOKE [Privilege, ...] ON SEQUENCE [SequenceName]
FROM [Forfeiter, ...] <BY ALL>
```

where:

Privilege   Identifies one or more sequence privileges that are to be taken from one or more users and/or groups. The following values are valid for this parameter: USAGE and ALTER.

SequenceName   Identifies by name the sequence with which all sequence privileges specified are to be associated with.

Forfeiter   Identifies the name of the user(s) and/or group(s) that are to lose the sequence privileges specified. The value specified for the *Forfeiter* parameter can be any combination of the following: <USER> [*UserName*], <GROUP> [*GroupName*], and PUBLIC.

Routine privileges

```
REVOKE EXECUTE ON [RoutineName |
                      FUNCTION <SchemaName.> * |
                      METHOD * FOR [TypeName] |
                      METHOD * FOR <SchemaName.> * |
                      PROCEDURE <SchemaName.> *]
      FROM [Forfeiter, ...]    <BY ALL>
      RESTRICT
```

where:

RoutineName   Identifies by name the routine (user-defined function, method, or stored procedure) with which the EXECUTE privilege is associated.

TypeName   Identifies by name the type in which the specified method is found.

SchemaName   Identifies by name the schema from which all functions, methods, or procedures—including those that may be created in the future—are to have the EXECUTE privilege revoked.

Forfeiter   Identifies the name of the user(s) and/or group(s) that are to lose the EXECUTE privilege. The value specified for the *Forfeiter* parameter can be any combination of the following: <USER> [*UserName*], <GROUP> [*GroupName*], and PUBLIC.

The RESTRICT clause guarantees EXECUTE privilege will not be revoked if the routine specified is used in a view, trigger, constraint, index, SQL function, SQL method, or transform group or is referenced as the source of a sourced function. Additionally, EXECUTE privilege will not be revoked if the loss of the privilege would prohibit the routine definer from executing the routine (i.e., if the user who created the routine is identified as a *Forfeiter*).

Package privileges

```
REVOKE [Privilege, ...] ON PACKAGE <SchemaName.>[PackageID]
      FROM [Forfeiter, ...] <BY ALL>
```

where:

Privilege	Identifies one or more package privileges that are to be taken from one or more users and/or groups. The following values are valid for this parameter: CONTROL, BIND, and EXECUTE.
SchemaName	Identifies by name the schema in which the specified package is found.
PackageName	Identifies by name the specific package with which all package privileges specified are to be associated.
Forfeiter	Identifies the name of the user(s) and/or group(s) that are to lose the package privileges specified. The value specified for the *Forfeiter* parameter can be any combination of the following: <USER> [*UserName*], <GROUP> [*GroupName*], and PUBLIC.

Server privileges

```
REVOKE PASSTHRU ON SERVER [ServerName]
FROM [Forfeiter, ...] <BY ALL>
```

where:

ServerName	Identifies by name the server with which the PASSTHRU privilege is associated.
Forfeiter	Identifies the name of the user(s) and/or group(s) that are to lose the PASSTHRU privilege. The value specified for the *Forfeiter* parameter can be any combination of the following: <USER> [*UserName*], <GROUP> [*GroupName*], and PUBLIC.

Nickname privileges

```
REVOKE [ALL <PRIVILEGES> |
       Privilege, ...]
ON [Nickname]
FROM [Forfeiter, ...] <BY ALL>
```

where:

Privilege   Identifies one or more nickname privileges that are to be taken from one or more users and/or groups. The following values are valid for this parameter: CONTROL, ALTER, SELECT, INSERT, UPDATE, DELETE, INDEX, and REFERENCES.

Nickname   Identifies by name the nickname with which all privileges specified are to be associated.

Forfeiter   Identifies the name of the user(s) and/or group(s) that are to lose the nickname privileges specified. The value specified for the *Forfeiter* parameter can be any combination of the following: <USER> [*UserName*], <GROUP> [*GroupName*], and PUBLIC.

Only users who hold System Administrator (SYSADM) or Database Administrator (DBADM) authority are allowed to revoke CONTROL privilege for a nickname. For this reason, when the ALL PRIVILEGES clause is specified, all nickname privileges *except* CONTROL privilege are revoked from each *Forfeiter*; CONTROL privilege must be revoked separately.

REVOKE SQL statement examples

Now that we've seen the basic syntax for the various forms of the REVOKE SQL statement, let's take a look at some examples.

Example 1. A server has both a user and a group named Q045. Remove the ability to connect to the database named SAMPLE from the group Q045:

```
CONNECT TO sample;
REVOKE CONNECT ON DATABASE FROM GROUP q045;
```

Example 2. Revoke all table privileges available for the table DEPARTMENT (except CONTROL privilege) from the user USER1 and the group PUBLIC:

```
REVOKE ALL PRIVILEGES ON TABLE department FROM user1, PUBLIC
```

> If all table privileges are revoked from the group PUBLIC, all
> views that reference the table will become inaccessible to the
> group PUBLIC. That's because SELECT privilege must be held
> on a table in order to access a view that references the table.

Example 3. Take away user USER1's ability to use a user-defined function named CALC_BONUS:

```
REVOKE EXECUTE ON FUNCTION calc_bonus FROM user1
```

Example 4. Take away user USER1's ability to modify information stored in the ADDRESS and HOME_PHONE columns of the table EMP_INFO:

```
REVOKE UPDATE(address, home_phone) ON TABLE emp_info FROM user1 BY ALL
```

Example 5. Take away user USER1's ability to read data stored in a table named INVENTORY:

```
REVOKE SELECT ON TABLE inventory FROM user1
```

Example 6. Prevent users in the group PUBLIC from adding or changing data stored in a table named EMPLOYEE:

```
REVOKE INSERT, UPDATE ON TABLE employee FROM PUBLIC
```

Requirements for Granting and Revoking Authorities and Privileges

Not only do authorization levels and privileges control what a user can and cannot do; they also control what authorities and privileges a user is allowed to grant and revoke. A list of the authorities and privileges that a user who has been given a specific authority level or privilege is allowed to grant and revoke can be seen in Table 8.1.

Table 8.1 Requirements for Granting/Revoking Authorities and Privileges		
If a User Holds...	**The User Can Grant...**	**The User Can Revoke...**
System Administrator (SYSADM) authority	System Control (SYSCTRL) authority System Maintenance (SYSMAINT) authority System Monitor (SYSMON) authority Database Administrator (DBADM) authority Security Administrator (SECADM) authority Load (LOAD) authority Any database privilege, including CONTROL privilege Any object privilege, including CONTROL privilege	System Control (SYSCTRL) authority System Maintenance (SYSMAINT) authority System Monitor (SYSMON) authority Database Administrator (DBADM) authority Security Administrator (SECADM) authority Load (LOAD) authority Any database privilege, including CONTROL privilege Any object privilege, including CONTROL privilege
System Control (SYSCTRL) authority	The USE table space privilege	The USE table space privilege
System Maintenance (SYSMAINT) authority	No authorities or privileges	No authorities or privileges
System Monitor (SYSMON) authority	No authorities or privileges	No authorities or privileges
Database Administrator (DBADM) authority	Any database privilege, including CONTROL privilege Any object privilege, including CONTROL privilege	Any database privilege, including CONTROL privilege Any object privilege, including CONTROL privilege
Security Administrator (SECADM) authority	No authorities or privileges	No authorities or privileges
Load (LOAD) authority	No authorities or privileges	No authorities or privileges
CONTROL privilege on an object (but no other authority)	All privileges available (with the exception of the CONTROL privilege) for the object on which the user holds CONTROL privilege	All privileges available (with the exception of the CONTROL privilege) for the object on which the user holds CONTROL privilege
A privilege on an object that was assigned with the WITH GRANT OPTION option specified	The same object privilege that was assigned with the WITH GRANT OPTION option specified.	No authorities or privileges

Authorities and Privileges Needed to Perform Common Tasks

So far, we have identified the authorities and privileges that are available, and we have examined how these authorities and privileges are granted and revoked. But to use authorities and privileges effectively, you must be able to determine which authorities and privileges are appropriate for an individual user and which are not.

Often, a blanket set of authorities and privileges is assigned to an individual, based on his or her job title and job responsibilities. Then, as the individual begins to work with the database, the set of authorities and privileges he or she has is modified as appropriate. Some of the more common job titles used, along with the tasks that usually accompany them and the authorities/privileges needed to perform those tasks, can be seen in Table 8.2.

Table 8.2 Common Job Titles, Tasks, and Authorities/Privileges Needed

Job Title	Tasks	Authorities/Privileges Needed
Department Administrator	Oversees the departmental system; designs and creates databases.	System Control (SYSCTRL) authority or System Administrator (SYSADM) authority (if the department has its own instance)
Security Administrator	Grants authorities and privileges to other users and revokes them, if necessary.	System Administrator (SYSADM) authority or Database Administrator (DBADM) authority (Security Administrator [SECADM] authority if label-based access control is used)
Database Administrator	Designs, develops, operates, safeguards, and maintains one or more databases.	Database Administrator (DBADM) authority over one or more databases and System Maintenance (SYSMAINT) authority, or in some cases System Control (SYSCTRL) authority, over the instance(s) that control the databases
System Operator	Monitors the database and performs routine backup operations. Also performs recovery operations if needed.	System Maintenance (SYSMAINT) authority or System Monitor (SYSMON) authority
Application Developer/ Programmer	Develops and tests database/DB2 Database Manager application programs; may also create test tables and populate them with data.	CONNECT and CREATE_TAB privilege for one or more databases, BINDADD and BIND privilege on one or more packages, one or more schema privileges for one or more schemas, and one or more table privileges for one or more tables; CREATE_EXTERNAL_ROUTINE privilege for one or more databases may also be required
User Analyst	Defines the data requirements for an application program by examining the database structure using the system catalog views.	CONNECT privilege for one or more databases and SELECT privilege on the system catalog views

Table 8.2 Common Job Titles, Tasks, and Authorities/Privileges Needed (continued)		
Job Title	Tasks	Authorities/Privileges Needed
End User	Executes one or more application programs.	CONNECT privilege for one or more databases and EXECUTE privilege on the package associated with each application used; if an application program contains dynamic SQL statements, SELECT, INSERT, UPDATE, and DELETE privileges for one or more tables may be needed as well
Information Center Consultant	Defines the data requirements for a query user; provides the data needed by creating tables and views and by granting access to one or more database objects.	Database Administrator (DBADM) authority for one or more databases
Query User	Issues SQL statements (usually from the Command Line Processor) to retrieve, add, update, or delete data (may also save results of queries in tables)	CONNECT privilege on one or more databases; SELECT, INSERT, UPDATE, and DELETE privilege on each table used; and CREATEIN privilege on the schema in which tables and views are to be created
Adapted from Table 78 on pages 608–609 of the *IBM DB2 Version 9 for Linux, UNIX, and Windows Administration Guide—Implementation* manual.		

Securing Data with Label-Based Access Control (LBAC)

Earlier, we saw that authentication is performed at the operating system level to verify that users are who they say they are, and authorities and privileges control access to a database and the objects and data that reside within it. Views, which allow different users to see different presentations of the same data, can be used in conjunction with privileges to limit access to specific columns. But what if your security requirements dictate that you create and manage several hundred views? Or, more importantly, what if you want to restrict access to individual rows in a table? If you're using DB2 9, the solution for these situations is label-based access control.

So just what is label-based access control (LBAC)? LBAC is a new security feature that uses one or more security labels to control who has read access and who has write access to individual rows and/or columns in a table. The United States and many other governments use LBAC models in which hierarchical classification labels such as CONFIDENTIAL, SECRET, and TOP SECRET are assigned to data based on its sensitivity. Access to data labeled at a certain level (for example, SECRET) is restricted to those users who have been granted that level of access or higher. With

LBAC, you can construct security labels to represent any criteria your company uses to determine who can read or modify particular data values. And LBAC is flexible enough to handle the most simple to the most complex criteria.

One problem with the traditional security methods DB2 uses is that security administrators and DBAs have access to sensitive data stored in the databases they oversee. To solve this problem, LBAC-security administration tasks are isolated from all other tasks—only users with Security Administrator (SECADM) authority are allowed to configure LBAC elements.

Implementing Row-Level LBAC

Before you implement a row-level LBAC solution, you need to have a thorough understanding of the security requirement needs. Suppose you have a database that contains company sales data, and you want to control how senior executives, regional managers, and sales representatives access data stored in a table named SALES. Security requirements might dictate that access to this data should comply with these rules:

- Senior executives are allowed to view, but not update, all records in the table.

- Regional managers are allowed to view and update only records that were entered by sales representatives who report to them.

- Sales representatives are allowed to view and update only records of the sales they made.

Once the security requirements are known, you must then define the appropriate security policies and labels, create an LBAC-protected table (or alter an existing table to add LBAC protection), and grant the proper security labels to the appropriate users.

Defining a security label component

Security label components represent criteria that may be used to decide whether a user should have access to specific data. Three types of security label components can exist:

- A *set* is a collection of elements (character string values) where the order in which each element appears is not important.

- An *array* is an ordered set that can represent a simple hierarchy. In an array, the order in which the elements appear is important—the first element ranks higher than the second, the second ranks higher than the third, and so on.

- A *tree* represents a more complex hierarchy that can have multiple nodes and branches.

To create security label components, you execute one of the following CREATE SECURITY LABEL COMPONENT SQL statements:

```
CREATE SECURITY LABEL COMPONENT [ComponentName]
SET {StringConstant,...}
```

or

```
CREATE SECURITY LABEL COMPONENT [ComponentName]
ARRAY [StringConstant,...]
```

or

```
CREATE SECURITY LABEL COMPONENT [ComponentName]
TREE (StringConstant ROOT < StringConstant UNDER StringConstant >)]
```

where:

ComponentName Identifies the name that is to be assigned to the security label component being created.

StringConstant Identifies one or more string constant values that make up the valid array, set, or tree of values to be used by the security label component being created.

Thus, to create a security label component named SEC_COMP that contains a set of values whose order is insignificant, you would execute a CREATE SECURITY LABEL COMPONENT statement that looks something like this:

```
CREATE SECURITY LABEL COMPONENT sec_comp
SET {'CONFIDENTIAL', 'SECRET', 'TOP_SECRET'}
```

To create a security label component that contains an array of values listed from highest to lowest order, you would execute a CREATE SECURITY LABEL COMPONENT statement that looks something like this:

```
CREATE SECURITY LABEL COMPONENT sec_comp
ARRAY ['MASTER_CRAFTSMAN', 'JOURNEYMAN', 'APPRENTICE']
```

And to create a security label component that contains a tree of values that describe a company's organizational chart, you would execute a CREATE SECURITY LABEL COMPONENT statement that looks something like this:

```
CREATE SECURITY LABEL COMPONENT sec_comp
TREE ('EXEC_STAFF' ROOT,
            'N_MGR' UNDER 'EXEC_STAFF',
            'E_MGR' UNDER 'EXEC_STAFF',
            'S_MGR' UNDER 'EXEC_STAFF',
            'W_MGR' UNDER 'EXEC_STAFF',
            'C_MGR' UNDER 'EXEC_STAFF',
            'SALES_REP1' UNDER 'N_MGR',
            'SALES_REP2' UNDER 'W_MGR')
```

Defining a security policy

Security policies determine exactly how a table is to be protected by LBAC. Specifically, a security policy identifies the following:

- What security label components will be used in the security labels that will be part of the policy

- What rules will be used when security label components are compared (at this time, only one set of rules is supported: DB2LBACRULES)

- Which optional behaviors will be used when accessing data protected by the policy

Every LBAC-protected table must have one (and only one) security policy associated with it. Rows and columns in that table can be protected only with security labels that are part of that security policy; all protected data access must adhere to the rules of that policy. You can have multiple security policies within a single database, but you can't have more than one security policy protecting any given table.

To create a security policy, execute the CREATE SECURITY POLICY SQL statement as follows:

```
CREATE SECURITY POLICY [PolicyName]
COMPONENTS [ComponentName ,...]
WITH DB2LBACRULES
<[OVERRIDE | RESTRICT] NOT AUTHORIZED
    WRITE SECURITY LABEL>
```

where:

PolicyName   Identifies the name that is to be assigned to the security policy being created.

ComponentName Identifies, by name, one or more security label components that are to be part of the security policy being created.

The [OVERRIDE | RESTRICT] NOT AUTHORIZED WRITE SECURITY LABEL option specifies the action to be taken when a user who is not authorized to write the security label explicitly specified with INSERT and UPDATE statements attempts to write data to the protected table. By default, the value of a user's security label, rather than an explicitly specified security label, is used for write access during insert and update operations (OVERRIDE NOT AUTHORIZED WRITE SECURITY LABEL). If the RESTRICT NOT AUTHORIZED WRITE SECURITY LABEL option is used, insert and update operations will fail if the user isn't authorized to write the explicitly specified security label to the protected table.

Therefore, to create a security policy named SEC_POLICY that is based on the SEC_COMP security label component created earlier, you would execute a CREATE SECURITY POLICY statement that look something like this:

```
CREATE SECURITY POLICY sec_policy
COMPONENTS sec_comp
WITH DB2LBACRULES
```

Defining security labels

Security labels describe a set of security criteria and are used to protect data against unauthorized access or modification. Security labels are granted to users who are allowed to access or modify protected data; when users attempt to access or modify protected data, their security label is compared to the security label protecting the data to determine whether the access or modification is allowed. Every security label is part of exactly one security policy, and a security label must exist for each security label component found in the security policy.

Security labels are created by executing the CREATE SECURITY LABEL SQL statement. The syntax for this statement is:

```
CREATE SECURITY LABEL [LabelName]
     [COMPONENT [ComponentName] [StringConstant] ,...]
```

where:

LabelName   Identifies the name that is to be assigned to the security label being created. The name specified must be qualified with a security policy name and must not match an existing security label for the security policy specified.

ComponentName Identifies, by name, a security label component that is part of the security policy specified as the qualifier for the *LabelName* parameter.

StringConstant   Identifies one or more string constant values that are valid elements of the security label component specified in the *ComponentName* parameter.

Thus, to create a set of security labels for the security policy named SEC_POLICY that was created earlier, you would execute a set of CREATE SECURITY LABEL statements that looks something like this:

```
CREATE SECURITY LABEL sec_policy.exec_staff
COMPONENT sec_comp 'EXEC_STAFF'

CREATE SECURITY LABEL sec_policy.n_mgr
COMPONENT sec_comp 'N_MGR'

CREATE SECURITY LABEL sec_policy.e_mgr
COMPONENT sec_comp 'E_MGR'

CREATE SECURITY LABEL sec_policy.s_mgr
COMPONENT sec_comp 'S_MGR'

CREATE SECURITY LABEL sec_policy.w_mgr
COMPONENT sec_comp 'W_MGR'

CREATE SECURITY LABEL sec_policy.c_mgr
COMPONENT sec_comp 'C_MGR'

CREATE SECURITY LABEL sec_policy.sales_rep1
COMPONENT sec_comp 'SALES_REP1'

CREATE SECURITY LABEL sec_policy.sales_rep2
COMPONENT sec_comp 'SALES_REP2'
```

Creating a LBAC-protected table

Once you have defined the security policy and labels needed to enforce your security requirements, you're ready to create a table and configure it for LBAC protection. To configure a new table for row-level LBAC protection, you include a column with the data type DB2SECURITYLABEL in the table's definition and associate a security policy with the table using the SECURITY POLICY clause of the CREATE TABLE SQL statement.

So to create a table named SALES and configure it for row-level LBAC protection using the security policy named SEC_POLICY created earlier, you would execute a CREATE TABLE statement that looks something like this:

```
CREATE TABLE corp.sales (
      sales_rec_id    INTEGER NOT NULL,
      sales_date      DATE WITH DEFAULT,
      sales_rep       INTEGER,
      region          VARCHAR(15),
      manager         INTEGER,
      sales_amt       DECIMAL(12,2),
      margin          DECIMAL(12,2),
      sec_label       DB2SECURITYLABEL)
   SECURITY POLICY sec_policy
```

To configure an existing table named SALES for row-level LBAC protection using a security policy named SEC_POLICY, you would execute an ALTER TABLE statement that looks like this instead:

```
ALTER TABLE corp.sales
    ADD COLUMN sec_label DB2SECURITYLABEL
    ADD SECURITY POLICY sec_policy
```

However, before you can execute such an ALTER TABLE statement, you must be granted a security label for write access that is part of the security policy that will be used to protect the table (which, in this case is SEC_POLICY). Otherwise, you won't be able to create the DB2SECURITYLABEL column.

Granting security labels to users

Once the security policy and labels needed to enforce your security requirements have been defined, and a table has been enabled for LBAC protection, you must grant the proper security labels to the appropriate users and indicate whether they are to have read access, write access, or full access to data that is protected by that label. Security labels are granted to users by executing a special form of the GRANT SQL statement. The syntax for this form of the GRANT statement is:

```
GRANT SECURITY LABEL [LabelName]
TO USER [UserName]
[FOR ALL ACCESS | FOR READ ACCESS | FOR WRITE ACCESS]
```

where:

LabelName   Identifies the name of an existing security label. The name
                specified must be qualified with the security policy name that
                was used when the security label was created.

UserName   Identifies the name of the user to which the security label is to
                be granted.

Thus, to give a user named USER1 the ability to read data protected by the security label SEC_POLICY.EXEC_STAFF, you would execute a GRANT statement that looks like this:

```
GRANT SECURITY LABEL sec_policy.exec_staff
TO USER user1 FOR READ ACCESS
```

Putting row-level LBAC into action

To enforce the security requirements listed earlier, we must first give users the ability to perform DML operations against the SALES table by executing the following GRANT statements, as a user with SYSADM or DBADM authority:

```
GRANT ALL PRIVILEGES ON TABLE corp.sales TO exec_staff;
GRANT ALL PRIVILEGES ON TABLE corp.sales TO n_manager;
GRANT ALL PRIVILEGES ON TABLE corp.sales TO e_manager;
GRANT ALL PRIVILEGES ON TABLE corp.sales TO s_manager;
GRANT ALL PRIVILEGES ON TABLE corp.sales TO w_manager;
GRANT ALL PRIVILEGES ON TABLE corp.sales TO c_manager;
GRANT ALL PRIVILEGES ON TABLE corp.sales TO sales_rep1;
GRANT ALL PRIVILEGES ON TABLE corp.sales TO sales_rep2;
```

Next, we must grant the proper security labels to the appropriate users and indicate whether they are to have read access, write access, or full access to data that is protected by that label. This is done by executing the following GRANT statements, this time as a user with SECADM authority:

```
GRANT SECURITY LABEL sec_policy.exec_staff
TO USER exec_staff FOR READ ACCESS;

GRANT SECURITY LABEL sec_policy.n_mgr
TO USER n_manager FOR ALL ACCESS;

GRANT SECURITY LABEL sec_policy.e_mgr
TO USER e_manager FOR ALL ACCESS;

GRANT SECURITY LABEL sec_policy.s_mgr
TO USER s_manager FOR ALL ACCESS;

GRANT SECURITY LABEL sec_policy.w_mgr
TO USER w_manager FOR ALL ACCESS;

GRANT SECURITY LABEL sec_policy.c_mgr
TO USER c_manager FOR ALL ACCESS;

GRANT SECURITY LABEL sec_policy.sales_rep1
TO USER sales_rep1 FOR ALL ACCESS;

GRANT SECURITY LABEL sec_policy.sales_rep2
TO USER sales_rep2 FOR ALL ACCESS;
```

Now, suppose user SALES_REP1 adds three rows to the SALES table by executing the following SQL statements:

```
INSERT INTO corp.sales VALUES (1, DEFAULT, 1, 'NORTH', 5,
     1000.50, 500.00,
     SECLABEL_BY_NAME('SEC_POLICY', 'SALES_REP1'));

INSERT INTO corp.sales VALUES (2, DEFAULT, 1, 'NORTH', 5,
     2000.00, 400.00,
     SECLABEL_BY_NAME('SEC_POLICY', 'SALES_REP1'));

INSERT INTO corp.sales VALUES (3, DEFAULT, 1, 'NORTH', 5,
     4500.90, 850.00,
     SECLABEL_BY_NAME('SEC_POLICY', 'SALES_REP1'));
```

Because SALES_REP1 has been given read/write access to the table using the
SEC_POLICY.SALES_REP1 security label, the statements execute successfully. Next,
user SALES_REP2 adds two additional rows to the SALES table by executing the
following SQL statements:

```
INSERT INTO corp.sales VALUES (4, DEFAULT, 1, 'WEST', 20,
     1000.50, 500.00,
     SECLABEL_BY_NAME('SEC_POLICY', 'SALES_REP2'));

INSERT INTO corp.sales VALUES (5, DEFAULT, 1, 'WEST', 20,
     3200.00, 600.00,
     SECLABEL_BY_NAME('SEC_POLICY', 'SALES_REP2'));
```

SALES_REP2 has also been given read/write access to the table using the
SEC_POLICY.SALES_REP2 security label, so the rows are successfully inserted.

Now, when user EXEC_STAFF queries the SALES table, all five records entered will
appear (because the security label SEC_POLICY.EXEC_STAFF is the highest level in
the security policy's security label component tree). However, if user EXEC_STAFF
attempts to insert additional records or update an existing record, an error will be
generated because user EXEC_STAFF is allowed only to read the data (only read
access was granted).

When user N_MANAGER queries the table, only records entered by the user
SALES_REP1 will be displayed; the user W_MANAGER will see only records entered
by the user SALES_REP2; and the users E_MANAGER, S_MANAGER, and C_MANAGER
will not see any records at all. (SALES_REP1 reports to N_MANAGER, SALES_REP2
reports to W_MANAGER; no other managers have a sales representative reporting to
them.)

And finally, when SALES_REP1 or SALES_REP2 queries the SALES table, they will see only the records they personally entered. Likewise, they can update only the records they entered.

Implementing Column-Level LBAC

To illustrate how column-level LBAC is employed, let's assume you want to control how Human Resources (HR) staff members, managers, and employees are going to access data stored in a table named EMPLOYEES. For this scenario, the security requirements are as follows:

- Name, gender, department, and phone number information can be viewed by all employees.

- Hire date, salary, and bonus information (in addition to name, gender, department, and phone number information) can be seen only by managers and HR staff members.

- Employee ID and Social Security Number information can be seen only by HR staff members. Additionally, HR staff members are the only users who can create and modify employee records.

Once again, after the security requirements have been identified, the next steps are to define the appropriate security component, policies, and labels; create the table that will house the data; alter the table to add LBAC protection; and grant the proper security labels to the appropriate users.

Defining security label components, security policies, and security labels

Because an array of values, listed from highest to lowest order, would be the best way to implement the security requirements just outlined, you could create the security component needed by executing a CREATE SECURITY LABEL COMPONENT statement (as a user with SECADM authority) that looks something like this:

```
CREATE SECURITY LABEL COMPONENT sec_comp
ARRAY ['CONFIDENTIAL', 'CLASSIFIED', 'UNCLASSIFIED']
```

After the appropriate security label component has been created, you can create a security policy named SEC_POLICY that is based on the SEC_COMP security label component by executing a CREATE SECURITY POLICY statement (as a user with SECADM authority) that looks like this:

```
CREATE SECURITY POLICY sec_policy
COMPONENTS sec_comp
WITH DB2LBACRULES
```

Earlier, we saw that security labels are granted to users who are allowed to access or modify LBAC-protected data; when users attempt to access or modify protected data, their security label is compared to the security label protecting the data to determine whether the access or modification is allowed. But before security labels can be granted, they must first be defined. To create a set of security labels for the security policy named SEC_POLICY that was just created, you would execute the following set of CREATE SECURITY LABEL statements (as a user with SECADM authority):

```
CREATE SECURITY LABEL sec_policy.confidential
COMPONENT sec_comp 'CONFIDENTIAL'

CREATE SECURITY LABEL sec_policy.classified
COMPONENT sec_comp 'CLASSIFIED'

CREATE SECURITY LABEL sec_policy.unclassified
COMPONENT sec_comp 'UNCLASSIFIED'
```

Keep in mind that every security label is part of exactly one security policy, and a security label must exist for each security label component found in that security policy.

Creating a LBAC-protected table and granting privileges and security labels to users

Earlier, we saw that in order to configure a new table for row-level LBAC protection, you must associate a security policy with the table being created with the SECURITY POLICY clause of the CREATE TABLE SQL statement. The same is true if column-level LBAC protection is desired. Therefore, to create a table named EMPLOYEES and associate it with a security policy named SEC_POLICY, you would need to execute a CREATE TABLE statement that looks something like this:

```
CREATE TABLE hr.employees (
    emp_id      INTEGER NOT NULL,
    f_name      VARCHAR(20),
    l_name      VARCHAR(20),
    gender      CHAR(1),
    hire_date DATE WITH DEFAULT,
    dept_id     CHAR(5),
    phone       CHAR(14),
    ssn         CHAR(12),
    salary      DECIMAL(12,2),
    bonus       DECIMAL(12,2))
  SECURITY POLICY sec_policy
```

Then, in order to enforce the security requirements identified earlier, you must give users the ability to perform the appropriate DML operations against the EMPLOYEES table. This is done by executing the following GRANT SQL statements (as a user with SYSADM or DBADM authority):

```
GRANT ALL PRIVILEGES ON TABLE hr.employees TO hr_staff;
GRANT SELECT ON TABLE hr.employees TO manager1;
GRANT SELECT ON TABLE hr.employees TO employee1;
```

Finally, you must grant the proper security label to the appropriate users and indicate whether they are to have read access, write access, or full access to data that is protected by that label. This is done by executing a set of GRANT statements (as a user with SECADM authority) that looks something like this:

```
GRANT SECURITY LABEL sec_policy.confidential
TO USER hr_staff FOR ALL ACCESS;

GRANT SECURITY LABEL sec_policy.classified
TO USER manager1 FOR READ ACCESS;

GRANT SECURITY LABEL sec_policy.unclassified
TO USER employee1 FOR READ ACCESS;
```

Creating LBAC-protected columns

Once you've defined the security policy and labels needed to enforce your security requirements and have granted the appropriate privileges and security labels to users, you are ready to modify the table associated with the security policy and configure its columns for column-level LBAC protection. This is done by executing an ALTER TABLE statement that looks something like this:

```
ALTER TABLE hr.employees
      ALTER COLUMN emp_id SECURED WITH confidential
      ALTER COLUMN f_name SECURED WITH unclassified
      ALTER COLUMN l_name SECURED WITH unclassified
      ALTER COLUMN gender SECURED WITH unclassified
      ALTER COLUMN hire_date SECURED WITH classified
      ALTER COLUMN dept_id SECURED WITH unclassified
      ALTER COLUMN phone SECURED WITH unclassified
      ALTER COLUMN ssn SECURED WITH confidential
      ALTER COLUMN salary SECURED WITH classified
      ALTER COLUMN bonus SECURED WITH classified;
```

Here is where things get a little tricky. If you try to execute the ALTER TABLE statement shown as a user with SYSADM or SECADM authority, the operation will fail, and you will be presented with an error message that looks something like this:

```
SQL20419N For table "EMPLOYEES", authorization ID " " does not have LBAC
credentials that allow using the security label "CONFIDENTIAL" to protect
column "EMP_ID".  SQLSTATE=42522
```

That's because the only user who can secure a column with the "CONFIDENTIAL" security label is a user who has been granted *write access* to data that is protected by that label. In our scenario, this is the user HR_STAFF. So what happens when user HR_STAFF attempts to execute the preceding ALTER TABLE statement? Now a slightly different error message is produced:

```
SQL20419N For table "EMPLOYEES", authorization ID "HR_STAFF" does not
have LBAC credentials that allow using the security label "UNCLASSIFIED"
to protect column "F_NAME".  SQLSTATE=42522
```

Why? Because, by default, the LBAC rules set associated with the security policy assigned to the EMPLOYEES table allows the user HR_STAFF to write data only to columns or rows that are protected by the same security label that he/she has been granted.

DB2LBACRULES rules

An LBAC rule set is a predefined set of rules that is used when comparing security labels. Currently, only one LBAC rule set is supported (DB2LBACRULES), and as we have just seen, this rule set prevents both write-up and write-down behavior. (Write-up and write-down apply only to ARRAY security label components and only to write access.) Write-up is when the security label protecting data to which you are attempting to write is higher than the security label you have been granted; write-down is when the security label protecting data is lower.

Which rules are actually used when two security labels are compared is dependent on the type of component used (SET, ARRAY, or TREE) and the type of access being attempted (read or write). Table 8.3 lists the rules found in the DB2LBACRULES rules set, identifies which component each rule is used for, and describes how the rule determines if access is to be blocked.

Table 8.3 Summary of the DB2LBACRULES Rules			
Rule Name Component	Component	Access	Access is blocked when this condition is met
DB2LBACREADARRAY	ARRAY	Read	The user's security label is lower than the protecting security label.
DB2LBACREADSET	SET	Read	There are one or more protecting security labels that the user does not hold.
DB2LBACREADTREE	TREE	Read	None of the user's security labels are equal to or an ancestor of one of the protecting security labels.
DB2LBACWRITEARRAY	ARRAY	Write	The user's security label is higher than the protecting security label or lower than the protecting security label.
DB2LBACWRITESET	SET	Write	There are one or more protecting security labels that the user does not hold.
DB2LBACWRITETREE	TREE	Write	None of the user's security labels are equal to or an ancestor of one of the protecting security labels.
Adapted from Table 78 on pages 608–609 of the *IBM DB2 Version 9 for Linux, UNIX, and Windows Administration Guide—Implementation* manual.			

Granting exemptions

So how can the remaining columns in the EMPLOYEES table be secured with the appropriate security labels? The Security Administrator must first grant user HR_STAFF an exemption to one or more security policy rules. When a user holds an exemption on a particular security policy rule, that rule is not enforced when the user attempts to access data that is protected by that security policy.

Security policy exemptions are granted by executing the GRANT EXEMPTION ON RULE SQL statement (as a user with SECADM authority). The syntax for this statement is:

```
GRANT EXEMPTION ON RULE [Rule] ,...
FOR [PolicyName]
TO USER [UserName]
```

where:

Rule   Identifies one or more DB2LBACRULES security policy rules for which exemptions are to be given. The following values are valid for this parameter: DB2LBACREADARRAY, DB2LBACREADSET, DB2LBACREADTREE, DB2LBACWRITEARRAY WRITEDOWN, DB2LBACWRITEARRAY WRITEUP, DB2LBACWRITESET, DB2LBACWRITETREE, and ALL. (If an exemption is held for every security policy rule, the user will have complete access to all data protected by that security policy.)

PolicyName   Identifies the security policy for which the exemption is to be granted.

UserName   Identifies the name of the user to which the exemptions specified are to be granted.

Thus, to grant an exemption to the DB2LBACWRITEARRAY rule in the security policy named SEC_POLICY created earlier to a user named HR_STAFF, you would execute a GRANT EXEMPTION statement that looks something like this:

```
GRANT EXEMPTION ON RULE DB2LBACWRITEARRAY
WRITEDOWN FOR sec_policy
TO USER hr_staff
```

Once this exemption is granted along with the appropriate security label, user HR_STAFF will then be able to execute the ALTER TABLE statement shown earlier without generating an error. (Alternately, the following CREATE TABLE statement could be used to create the EMPLOYEES table and protect each column with the appropriate security label, provided user HR_STAFF has the privileges needed to create the table.)

```
CREATE TABLE hr.employees (
      emp_id      INTEGER NOT NULL SECURED WITH confidential,
      f_name      VARCHAR(20) SECURED WITH unclassified,
      l_name      VARCHAR(20) SECURED WITH unclassified,
      gender      CHAR(1) SECURED WITH unclassified,
      hire_date   DATE WITH DEFAULT SECURED WITH classified,
      dept_id     CHAR(5) SECURED WITH unclassified,
      phone       CHAR(14) SECURED WITH unclassified,
      ssn         CHAR(12) SECURED WITH confidential,
      salary      DECIMAL(12,2) SECURED WITH classified,
      bonus       DECIMAL(12,2) SECURED WITH classified)
   SECURITY POLICY sec_policy
```

Putting column-level LBAC into action

Now that we have established a column-level LBAC environment, let's see what happens when different users try to access data stored in protected columns of the EMPLOYEES table. Suppose the user HR_STAFF adds three rows to the EMPLOYEES table by executing the following SQL statements.

```
INSERT INTO hr.employees VALUES(1, 'John', 'Doe', 'M',
    DEFAULT, 'A01', '919-555-1212', '111-22-3333',
    42000.50, 8500.00);

INSERT INTO hr.employees VALUES(2, 'Jane', 'Doe', 'F',
    DEFAULT, 'B02', '919-555-3434', '222-33-4444',
    38000.75, 5000.00);

INSERT INTO hr.employees VALUES(3, 'Paul', 'Smith', 'M',
    DEFAULT, 'C03', '919-555-5656', '333-44-5555',
    39250.00, 3500.00);
```

User HR_STAFF1 has been given read/write access to all columns in the table (with the SEC_POLICY.CLASSIFIED security label and the DB2LBACWRITEARRAY WRITEDOWN exemption), so the statements execute successfully. If user HR_STAFF attempts to query the table, he or she will be able to see every column and every row because he or she has been granted the highest security level in the array.

Now, when user MANAGER1 attempts to read every column in the table, an error will be generated stating that he or she does not have "READ" access to the column "SSN." However, MANAGER1 will be able to execute the following query because he or she has been granted read access to each column specified:

```
SELECT f_name, l_name, hire_date, salary, bonus
FROM hr.employees
```

Now, if user EMPLOYEE1 attempts to execute the same query, an error will be generated stating that he or she does not have "READ" access to the column "BONUS." But an attempt by EMPLOYEE1 to execute the following query will be successful:

```
SELECT f_name, l_name, gender, dept_id, phone
FROM hr.employees
```

Additionally, if user MANAGER1 or user EMPLOYEE1 attempt to insert additional records or update existing information, they will get an error stating they do not have permission to perform the operation against the table.

Combining Row-Level and Column-Level LBAC

There may be times when you would like to limit an individual user's access to a specific combination of rows and columns. When this is the case, you must include a column with the data type DB2SECURITYLABEL in the table's definition, add the SECURED WITH [*SecurityLabel*] option to each column in the table's definition, and associate a security policy with the table using the SECURITY POLICY clause of the CREATE TABLE SQL statement or the ADD SECURITY POLICY clause of the ALTER TABLE statement. Typically, you will also create two security label components—one for rows and one for columns—and use both components to construct the security policy and labels needed.

For example, assume that you created two security label components by executing the following commands:

```
CREATE SECURITY LABEL COMPONENT scom_level
ARRAY ['CONFIDENTIAL', 'CLASSIFIED', 'UNCLASSIFIED'];

CREATE SECURITY LABEL COMPONENT scom_country
TREE ('NA' ROOT, 'CANADA' UNDER 'NA', 'USA' UNDER 'NA');
```

You would then create a security policy by executing a CREATE SECURITY POLICY command that looks something like this:

```
CREATE SECURITY POLICY sec_policy
COMPONENTS scom_level, scom_country
WITH DB2LBACRULES
```

Then you could create corresponding security labels by executing commands that look something like this:

```
CREATE SECURITY LABEL sec_policy.confidential
COMPONENT scom_level 'CONFIDENTIAL';

CREATE SECURITY LABEL sec_policy.uc_canada
COMPONENT scom_level 'UNCLASSIFIED'
COMPONENT scom_country 'CANADA';

CREATE SECURITY LABEL sec_policy.uc_us
COMPONENT scom_level 'UNCLASSIFIED'
COMPONENT scom_country 'USA';
```

Finally, after associating the appropriate security labels with individual columns, you would grant the proper security label to each user and conduct a few tests to ensure data access is controlled as expected.

Practice Questions

Question 1

> Which of the following is NOT a security mechanism that is used to control access
> DB2 data?
>
> ○ A. Authorization
> ○ B. Privileges
> ○ C. Validation
> ○ D. Authentication

Question 2

> Which of the following identifies which users have SYSMAINT authority?
>
> ○ A. The DB2 registry
> ○ B. The DB2 Database Manager configuration
> ○ C. The database configuration
> ○ D. The system catalog

Question 3

> Which of the following database privileges are NOT automatically granted to the
> group PUBLIC when a database is created?
>
> ○ A. CONNECT
> ○ B. BINDADD
> ○ C. IMPLICIT_SCHEMA
> ○ D. CREATE_EXTERNAL_ROUTINE

Question 4

User USER1 needs to remove a view named ORDERS_V, which is based on a table named ORDERS, from the SALES database. Assuming user USER1 does not hold any privileges, which of the following privileges must be granted before user USER1 will be allowed to drop the view?

○ A. DROP privilege on the ORDERS_V view

○ B. CONTROL privilege on the ORDERS table

○ C. DROP privilege on the ORDERS_V view

○ D. CONTROL privilege on the ORDERS_V view

Question 5

Which of the following identifies how authentication is performed for an instance?

○ A. The operating system used by the instance

○ B. The communications configuration used by the instance

○ C. The DB2 registry

○ D. The DB2 Database Manager configuration

Question 6

After the following SQL statement is executed:

    GRANT ALL PRIVILEGES ON TABLE employee TO USER user1

Assuming user USER1 has no other authorities or privileges, which of the following actions is USER1 allowed to perform?

○ A. Drop an index on the EMPLOYEE table.

○ B. Grant all privileges on the EMPLOYEE table to other users.

○ C. Alter the table definition.

○ D. Drop the EMPLOYEE table.

Question 7

A user named USER1 is granted DBADM authority. Assuming no other authorities/privileges have been granted and all privileges have been revoked from the group PUBLIC, if the following SQL statement is executed:

    REVOKE DBADM ON DATABASE FROM user1

What authorities/privileges will user USER1 have?

○ A.   None

○ B.   CONNECT

○ C.   SYSCTRL

○ D.   EXECUTE

Question 8

User USER1 wants to call an SQL stored procedure that dynamically retrieves data from a table. Which two privileges must user USER1 have in order to invoke the stored procedure?

❑ A.   EXECUTE privilege on the stored procedure.

❑ B.   CALL privilege on the stored procedure.

❑ C.   SELECT privilege on the table the stored procedure retrieves data from.

❑ D.   EXECUTE privilege on the package for the stored procedure.

❑ E.   SELECT privilege on the stored procedure.

Question 9

Which of the following privileges allow a user to remove a foreign key that has been defined for a table?

○ A.   ALTER privilege on the table.

○ B.   DELETE privilege on the table.

○ C.   DROP privilege on the table.

○ D.   UPDATE privilege on the table.

Question 10

Which of the following privileges allows a user to generate a package for an embedded SQL application and store it in a database?

- ○ A. BIND
- ○ B. BINDADD
- ○ C. CREATE_EXTERNAL_ROUTINE
- ○ D. CREATE_NOT_FENCED_ROUTINE

Question 11

Which of the following statements is NOT true about DB2 security?

- ○ A. A custom security plug-in must be created if Microsoft Active Directory will be used to validate users.
- ○ B. Only users with Security Administrator authority are allowed to grant and revoke SETSESSIONUSER privileges.
- ○ C. Users and groups must exist before they can be granted privileges.
- ○ D. If a user holding SELECT privilege on a table creates a view based on that table and their SELECT privilege is later revoked, the view will become inoperative.

Question 12

User USER1 has the privileges needed to invoke a stored procedure named GEN_RESUME. User USER2 needs to be able to call the procedure—user USER1 and all members of the group PUBLIC should no longer be allowed to call the procedure. Which of the following statement(s) can be used to accomplish this?

- ○ A. GRANT EXECUTE ON ROUTINE gen_resume TO user2 EXCLUDE user1, PUBLIC
- ○ B. GRANT EXECUTE ON PROCEDURE gen_resume TO user2;
  REVOKE EXECUTE ON PROCEDURE gen_resume FROM user1, PUBLIC;
- ○ C. GRANT CALL ON ROUTINE gen_resume TO user2 EXCLUDE user1, PUBLIC
- ○ D. GRANT CALL ON PROCEDURE gen_resume TO user2;
  REVOKE CALL ON PROCEDURE gen_resume FROM user1, PUBLIC;

Question 13

Which of the following is NOT used to limit access to individual rows in a table that is protected by Label-Based Access Control (LBAC)?

- ○ A. One or more security profiles
- ○ B. A security policy
- ○ C. One or more security labels
- ○ D. A DB2SECURITYLABEL column

Question 14

Which of the following statements is NOT true about Label-Based Access Control (LBAC)?

- ○ A. LBAC can be used to restrict access to individual rows and columns.
- ○ B. Users that have been granted different LBAC security labels will get different results when they execute the same query.
- ○ C. Only users with SYSADM or SECADM authority are allowed to create security policies and security labels.
- ○ D. Security label components represent criteria that may be used to decide whether a user should have access to specific data.

Question 15

Which of the following SQL statements allows a user named USER1 to write to LBAC-protected columns that have been secured with a LBAC label that indicates a lower level of security than that held by USER1?

- ○ A. GRANT EXCEPTION ON RULE DB2LBACWRITEARRAY WRITEDOWN FOR sec_policy TO USER user1
- ○ B. GRANT EXEMPTION ON RULE DB2LBACWRITEARRAY WRITEDOWN FOR sec_policy TO USER user1
- ○ C. GRANT EXCEPTION ON RULE DB2LBACWRITEARRAY WRITEUP FOR sec_policy TO USER user1
- ○ D. GRANT EXCEPTION ON RULE DB2LBACWRITEARRAY WRITEUP FOR sec_policy TO USER user1

Answers

Question 1

The correct answer is **C**. The first security portal most users must pass through on their way to gaining access to a DB2 instance or database is a process known as authentication. The purpose of authentication is to verify that users really are who they say they are. Once a user has been authenticated and an attachment to an instance or a connection to a database has been established, the DB2 Database Manager evaluates any authorities and privileges that have been assigned to the user to determine what operations the user is allowed to perform. *Privileges* convey the rights to perform certain actions against specific database resources (such as tables and views). *Authorities* convey a set of privileges or the right to perform high-level administrative and maintenance/utility operations on an instance or a database.

Question 2

The correct answer is **B**. Like System Administrator (SYSADM), System Control (SYSCTRL), and System Monitor (SYSMON) authority, System Maintenance (SYSMAINT) authority can only be assigned to a group. This assignment is made by storing the appropriate group name in the *sysmaint_group* parameter of the DB2 Database Manager configuration file that is associated with a particular instance.

Question 3

The correct answer is **D**. To connect to and work with a particular database, a user must have the authorities and privileges needed to use that database. Therefore, whenever a new database is created, unless otherwise specified, the following authorities and privileges are automatically granted:

- Database Administrator (DBADM) authority, along with CONNECT, CREATETAB, BINDADD, CREATE_NOT_FENCED, IMPLICIT_SCHEMA, and LOAD privileges, are granted to the user who created the database.

- USE privilege on the table space USERSPACE1 is granted to the group PUBLIC.

- CONNECT, CREATETAB, BINDADD, and IMPLICIT_SCHEMA privileges are granted to the group PUBLIC.

- SELECT privilege on each system catalog table is granted to the group PUBLIC.

- EXECUTE privilege on all procedures found in the SYSIBM schema is granted to the group PUBLIC.

- EXECUTE WITH GRANT privilege on all functions found in the SYSFUN schema is granted to the group PUBLIC.

- BIND and EXECUTE privileges for each successfully bound utility are granted to the group PUBLIC.

(For more information, refer to Chapter 3 – "Data Placement")

Question 4

The correct answer is **D**. The CONTROL view privilege provides a user with every view privilege available, allows the user to remove (drop) the view from the database, and gives the user the ability to grant and revoke one or more view privileges (except the CONTROL privilege) to/from other users and groups.

Question 5

The correct answer is **D**. Because DB2 can reside in environments comprised of multiple clients, gateways, and servers, each of which may be running on a different operating system, deciding where authentication is to take place is determined by the value assigned to the *authentication* parameter in each DB2 Database Manager configuration file. The value assigned to this parameter, often referred to as the authentication type, is set initially when an instance is created. (On the server side, the authentication type is specified during the instance creation process; on the client side, the authentication type is specified when a remote database is cataloged.) Only one authentication type exists for each instance, and it controls access to that instance, as well as to all databases that fall under that instance's control.

Question 6

The correct answer is **C**. The GRANT ALL PRIVILEGES statement gives USER1 the following privileges for the EMPLOYEE table: ALTER, SELECT, INSERT, UPDATE, DELETE, INDEX, and REFERENCES. To drop an index, USER1 would need CONTROL privilege on the index—not the table the index is based on; USER1 cannot grant privileges to other users because the WITH GRANT OPTION clause was not specified with the GRANT ALL PRIVILEGES statement used to give USER1 table privileges; and in order to drop the EMPLOYEE table, USER1 would have to have CONTROL privilege on the table—CONTROL privilege is not granted with the GRANT ALL PRIVILEGES statement.

Question 7

The correct answer is **B**. When a user is given Database Administrator (DBADM) authority for a particular database, they automatically receive all database privileges available for that database as well (CONNECT, CONNECT_QUIESCE, IMPLICIT_SCHEMA, CREATETAB, BINDADD, CREATE_EXTERNAL_ROUTINE, CREATE_NOT_FENCED_ROUTINE, and LOAD). When Database Administrator authority is revoked, all other database authorities that were implicitly and automatically granted when DBADM authority was granted are not automatically revoked. The same is true for privileges held on objects in the database.

Question 8

The correct answers are **A** and **C**. Before a user can invoke a routine (user-defined function, stored procedure, or method) they must hold both EXECUTE privilege on the routine and any privileges required by that routine. Thus, in order to execute a stored procedure that queries a table, a user must hold both EXECUTE privilege on the stored procedure and SELECT privilege on the table the query is ran against.

Package privileges control what users can and cannot do with a particular package. (A package is an object that contains the information needed by the DB2 Database Manager to process SQL statements in the most efficient way possible on behalf of an embedded SQL application.)

Question 9

The correct answer is **A**. The ALTER table privilege allows a user to execute the ALTER TABLE SQL statement against a table. In other words, this privilege allows a user to add columns to the table, add or change comments associated with the table or any of its columns, create or drop a primary key for the table, create or drop a unique constraint for the table, create or drop a check constraint for the table, create or drop a referential constraint for the table, and create triggers for the table (provided the user holds the appropriate privileges for every object referenced by the trigger).

The UPDATE privilege allows a user to execute the UPDATE SQL statement against the table. In other words, this privilege allows a user to modify data in the table. The DELETE privilege allows a user to execute the DELETE SQL statement against the table. In other words, it allows a user to remove rows of data from the table.

Question 10

The correct answer is **B**. The BINDADD database privilege allows a user to create packages in the database (by precompiling embedded SQL application source code files against the database or by binding application bind files to the database).

The BIND package privilege allows a user to rebind or add new package versions to a package that has already been bound to a database. (In addition to the BIND package privilege, a user must hold the privileges needed to execute the SQL statements that make up the package before the package can be successfully rebound.) The CREATE_EXTERNAL_ROUTINE database privilege allows a user to create user-defined functions (UDFs) and/or procedures and store them in the database so that they can be used by other users and applications. The CREATE_NOT_FENCED_ROUTINE database privilege allows a user to create unfenced UDFs and/or procedures and store them in the database. (Unfenced UDFs and stored procedures are UDFs/procedures that are considered "safe" enough to be run in the DB2 Database Manager operating environment's process or address space. Unless a UDF/procedure is registered as unfenced, the DB2 Database Manager insulates the UDF/procedure's internal resources in such a way that they cannot be run in the DB2 Database Manager's address space.)

Question 11

The correct answer is **C**. The GRANT statement does not check to ensure that the names of users and/or groups that are to be granted authorities and privileges are valid. Therefore, it is possible to grant authorities and privileges to users and groups that do not exist.

Question 12

The correct answer is **B**. The syntax used to grant the only stored procedure privilege available is:

```
GRANT EXECUTE ON [RoutineName] |
                 [PROCEDURE <SchemaName.> *]
TO [Recipient, ...]
<WITH GRANT OPTION>
```

The syntax used to revoke the only stored procedure privilege available is:

```
REVOKE EXECUTE ON [RoutineName |
                  [PROCEDURE <SchemaName.> *]
FROM [Forfeiter, ...] <BY ALL>
RESTRICT
```

where:

RoutineName	Identifies by name the routine (user-defined function, method, or stored procedure) that the EXECUTE privilege is to be associated with.
TypeName	Identifies by name the type in which the specified method is found.
SchemaName	Identifies by name the schema in which all functions, methods, or procedures—including those that may be created in the future—are to have the EXECUTE privilege granted on.
Recipient	Identifies the name of the user(s) and/or group(s) that are to receive the EXECUTE privilege. The value specified for the *Recipient* parameter can be any combination of the following: <USER> [*UserName*], <GROUP> [*GroupName*], and PUBLIC.
Forfeiter	Identifies the name of the user(s) and/or group(s) that are to lose the package privileges specified. The value specified for the *Forfeiter* parameter can be any combination of the following: <USER> [*UserName*], <GROUP> [*GroupName*], and PUBLIC.

Thus, the proper way to grant and revoke stored procedure privileges is by executing the GRANT EXECUTE ... and REVOKE EXECUTE ... statements.

Question 13

The correct answer is **A**. To restrict access to rows in a table using Label-Based Access Control (LBAC), you must define a security label component, define a security policy, create one or more security labels, create an LBAC-protected table or alter an existing table to add LBAC protection (this is done by adding the security policy to the table and defining a column that has the DB2SECURITYLABEL data type), and grant the proper security labels to the appropriate users. There are no LBAC security profiles.

Question 14

The correct answer is **C**. Security Administrator (SECADM) authority is a special database level of authority that is designed to allow special users to configure various label-based access control (LBAC) elements to restrict access to one or more tables that contain data to which they most likely do not have access themselves. Users with Security Administrator authority are only allowed to perform the following tasks:

- Create and drop security policies.

- Create and drop security labels.

- Grant and revoke security labels to/from individual users (using the GRANT SECURITY LABEL and REVOKE SECURITY LABEL SQL statements).

- Grant and revoke LBAC rule exemptions.

- Grant and revoke SETSESSIONUSER privileges (using the GRANT SETSESSIONUSER SQL statement).

- Transfer ownership of any object not owned by the Security Administrator (by executing the TRANSFER OWNERSHIP SQL statement).

No other authority provides a user with these abilities, including System Administrator authority.

Question 15

The correct answer is **B**. When a user holds an exemption on an LBAC security policy rule, that rule is not enforced when the user attempts to read and/or write data that is protected by that security policy.

Security policy exemptions are granted by executing the GRANT EXEMPTION ON RULE SQL statement (as a user with SECADM authority). The syntax for this statement is:

```
CREATE EXEMPTION ON RULE [Rule] ,...
FOR [PolicyName]
TO USER [UserName]
```

where:

Rule   Identifies one or more DB2LBACRULES security policy rules that exemptions are to be given for. The following values are valid for this parameter: DB2LBACREADARRAY, DB2LBACREADSET, DB2LBACREADTREE, DB2LBACWRITEARRAY WRITEDOWN, DB2LBACWRITEARRAY WRITEUP, DB2LBACWRITESET, DB2LBACWRITETREE, and ALL. (If an exemption is held for every security policy rule, the user will have complete access to all data protected by that security policy.)

PolicyName   Identifies the security policy for which the exemption is to be granted.

UserName   Identifies the name of the user to which the exemptions specified are to be granted.

Thus, to grant an exemption to the DB2LBACWRITEARRAY rule in a security policy named SEC_POLICY to a user named USER1, you would execute a GRANT EXEMPTION statement that looks something like this:

```
GRANT EXEMPTION ON RULE DB2LBACWRITEARRAY
WRITEDOWN FOR sec_policy
TO USER user1
```

DB2 9 for Linux, UNIX, and Windows Database Administration Exam (Exam 731) Objectives

The DB2 9 for Linux, UNIX, and Windows Database Administration exam (Exam 731) consists of 69 questions, and candidates have 90 minutes to complete the exam. A score of 59% or higher is required to pass this exam.

The primary objectives that the DB2 9 Database Administrator for Linux, UNIX, and Windows exam (Exam 731) is designed to cover are as follows:

DB2 Server Management (20.5%)

- Ability to configure/manage DB2 instances (e.g., scope)
- Ability to obtain/modify database manager configuration information
- Ability to obtain/modify database configuration information
- Knowledge of the DB2 FORCE APPLICATION command.
- Ability to configure client/server connectivity
- Ability to schedule jobs
- Ability to use Automatic Maintenance (i.e., RUNSTAT, Backup, REORG)
- Ability to configure client/server connectivity using DB2 Discovery

- Skill in interpreting the Notify log

- Ability to obtain and modify DB2 registry variables

- Ability to use Self-Tuning Memory Manager and the AUTOCONFIGURE command

- Ability to use Throttling utilities

Data Placement (17.5%)

- Ability to create a database

- Skill in discussing the use of schemas

- Skill in discussing the various table space states

- Ability to create and manipulate the various DB2 objects available

- Ability to create and discuss the characteristics of an SMS table space

- Ability to create and discuss the characteristics of an automatic storage table space

- Knowledge of partitioning capabilities (e.g., table partitioning, hash partitioning, MDC, hybrid)

- Knowledge of XML structure (indexing for performance)

- Knowledge of data row compression

Database Access (11.5%)

- Knowledge of the creation and management of indexes

- Ability to create constraints on tables (e.g., referential integrity, informational, unique)

- Ability to create views on tables

- Skill in examining the contents of the System Catalog tables

- Ability to use the GUI Tools for administration
- Knowledge of how to enforce data uniqueness

Analyzing DB2 Activity (13%)

- Ability to capture and analyze Explain/Visual Explain information
- Ability to capture snapshots using Get Snapshots or SQL functions
- Ability to create and activate event monitors
- Ability to configure Health Monitor using the Health Center
- Ability to identify the functions of Problem Determination Tools (e.g, db2pd, db2mtrk)

DB2 Utilities (14.5%)

- Ability to use Export utility to extract data from a table
- Ability to use Import utility to insert data into a table
- Ability to use the Load utility to insert data into a table
- Knowledge to identify when to use Import versus Load
- Ability to use the REORG, REORGCHK, REBIND, and RUNSTATS utilities
- Ability to use db2move, db2look, and db2batch
- Knowledge of the functionality of the DB2 Design Advisor (db2advis utility)
- Ability to use the DB2 Control Center

High Availability (14.5%)

- Ability to perform database-level and table space-level BACKUP and RESTORE operations

- Knowledge to identify and explain issues on index re-creation
- Knowledge of database logging
- Knowledge of crash recovery
- Knowledge of version recovery
- Knowledge of roll-forward recovery
- Knowledge of and ability to perform HADR
- Knowledge of and ability to perform log mirroring
- Knowledge of configurable online parameters

Security (8.5%)

- Knowledge of DB2 authentication
- Knowledge of DB2 authorities and privileges available
- Ability to set user and group privileges
- Knowledge of the DB2 security infrastructure (e.g., LBAC and security plug-ins)

B

Sample Test

Welcome to the section that really makes this book unique. In my opinion, one of the best ways to prepare for the DB2 9 for Linux, UNIX, and Windows Database Administration exam (Exam 731) is by answering sample questions that are presented in the same format that you will see when you take the certification exam. In this section you will find 150 sample questions, along with comprehensive answers for every question. (It's not enough to know which answer is correct; it's also important to know why the answer is correct and why the other choices are wrong!)

If you worked through the Practice Questions presented at the end of each chapter, many of these questions will be familiar; if you skipped that part, all of those questions can be found here, along with several new ones. All of the questions presented here were developed by analyzing the final set of questions that were chosen for the DB2 9 for Linux, UNIX, and Windows Database Administration exam (Exam 731). (I was a member of the team that developed the DB2 9 for Linux, UNIX, and Windows Database Administration certification exam so I had access to every question!) I hope you find this material helpful.

—Roger E. Sanders

DB2 Server Management

Question 1

A DB2 server contains two instances named TEST and PROD. The instance named TEST is the default instance. Which of the following commands must be executed before an attempt is made to start the instance named PROD?

○ A. db2set DB2_INSTANCE=prod

○ B. UPDATE DBM CFG USING DB2INSTANCE prod

○ C. set DB2INSTANCE=prod

○ D. UPDATE DBM CFG USING DB2_INSTANCE prod

Question 2

Which of the following DB2 Database Manager configuration parameters is used to control the maximum number of applications that can be executing concurrently in an instance?

○ A. NUM_INITAGENTS

○ B. MAXCAGENTS

○ C. MAX_COORDAGENTS

○ D. MAXAGENTS

Question 3

A database administrator executes the following commands:

```
CONNECT TO sample;
UPDATE DB CFG FOR sample USING SORTHEAP 25;
UPDATE DB CFG FOR sample USING UTIL_HEAP_SZ 32;
COMMIT;
```

Assuming sufficient memory is available, when will the changes take place?

○ A. The next time the instance is stopped and restarted.

○ B. The next time the SAMPLE database is stopped and restarted.

○ C. Immediately after the commands are executed.

○ D. The changes will not take place because the database was not placed in quiesce mode first.

Question 4

A database administrator wants a database on a server to be seen by DB2 Discovery. Which of the following is true?

○ A. The database must be activated before it can be seen by DB2 Discovery.

○ B. The database must be cataloged on the server before it can be seen by DB2 Discovery.

○ C. The DAS on the server must be running and the DISCOVER configuration parameter for the DAS must be set to KNOWN or SEARCH.

○ D. The DISCOVER configuration parameter for the database must be set to KNOWN or SEARCH.

Question 5

Which of the following configuration parameters can be used to control how the Task Center behaves when the Scheduler is stopped and restarted?

○ A. JOURNAL_TASKS

○ B. SCHED_RESTART

○ C. EXEC_EXP_TASK

○ D. SCHED_ENABLE

Question 6

Where are changes made by the Self-Tuning Memory Manager recorded?

○ A. In memory tuning log files.

○ B. In the DB2 Diagnostics Log File

○ C. In the Administration Notification Log

○ D. In the Journal

Question 7

Which of the following authorities should a user have in order to quiesce an instance named DB2INST1?

○ A. SYSADM

○ B. SECADM

○ C. SYSMAINT

○ D. SYSMON

Question 8

Which of the following commands will assign the value TCPIP to the variable DB2COMM for all instances on a DB2 server?

- ○ A.   db2set DB2COMM=TCPIP
- ○ B.   db2set –g DB2COMM=TCPIP
- ○ C.   db2set –all DB2COMM=TCPIP
- ○ D.   set DB2COMM=TCPIP

Question 9

A database administrator successfully executed the following commands:

```
UPDATE DBM CFG USING SHEAPTHRES 37500
UPDATE DB CFG FOR sample USING SORTHEAP 2500
```

Assuming each sort operation performed against the SAMPLE database consumes 10 MB of memory, what is the maximum number of sort operations that can be run concurrently?

- ○ A.   5
- ○ B.   10
- ○ C.   15
- ○ D.   20

Question 10

After running the AUTOCONFIGURE command, a database administrator noticed that the SORTHEAP database configuration parameter for a database named SAMPLE had not been set to AUTOMATIC, even though the SELF_TUNING_MEM configuration parameter had been set to ON.

In order to get the desired results, which of the following commands must be executed before the AUTOCONFIGURE command is run again?

- ○ A.   UPDATE DBM CFG USING SHEAPTHRES 0
- ○ B.   UPDATE DB CFG FOR sample USING SHEAPTHRES_SHR AUTOMATIC
- ○ C.   UPDATE DBM CFG USING SHEAPTHRES AUTOMATIC
- ○ D.   UPDATE DB CFG FOR sample USING SHEAPTHRES_SHR 0

Question 11

Which of the following must exist before the Task Center can be used to schedule a daily database backup operation for a database named SAMPLE?

○ A. A special database named TOOLSDB

○ B. A special set of tables known as the tools catalog

○ C. A table space named SYSTOOLSPACE in the SAMPLE database

○ D. A schema named TOOLSCAT in the SAMPLE database

Question 12

A database administrator wants to ensure that backup operations performed against a database named SAMPLE will not impact a production workload by more than 20 percent. Which of the following commands can be used to achieve this objective?

○ A. UPDATE DBM CFG USING UTIL_IMPACT_LIM 80

○ B. UPDATE DBM CFG USING UTIL_IMPACT_PRIORITY 80

○ C. UPDATE DBM CFG USING UTIL_IMPACT_LIM 20

○ D. UPDATE DBM CFG USING UTIL_IMPACT_PRIORITY 20

Question 13

Which of the following components of an administration notification log/DB2 diagnostic log entry header record can be used in conjunction with the LIST APPLICATIONS command to obtain the name of the application that caused the entry to be generated?

○ A. PID

○ B. TID

○ C. APPID

○ D. APPHDL

Question 14

Which of the following commands will start a default instance named DB2INST1?

○ A. START db2inst1

○ B. START DB MANAGER

○ C. db2start -i db2inst1

○ D. START DBMGR

Question 15

If the following command is executed:

    db2set DB2COMM=

What will happen?

○ A.   The value assigned to the DB2COMM registry variable will be displayed.

○ B.   A list of communications protocols that are recognized by the server will be assigned to the DB2COMM registry variable.

○ C.   The value assigned to the global DB2COMM variable will be copied to the DB2COMM registry variable for the default instance.

○ D.   The DB2COMM registry level variable for the default instance will be deleted.

Question 16

Which of the following commands can be used to obtain information about how memory has been allocated for a database named SAMPLE?

○ A.   GET DB CFG FOR sample SHOW DETAIL

○ B.   GET MEMORY USAGE FOR sample

○ C.   GET DBM CFG

○ D.   GET CFG DETAILS FOR sample

Question 17

Which of the following commands disables roll-forward recovery for a database named SAMPLE and causes the database to create a duplicate copy of the transaction log files in a separate location?

○ A. UPDATE DB CFG FOR sample USING LOGARCHMETH1 LOGRETAIN;
      UPDATE DB CFG FOR sample USING NEWLOGPATH D:\dup_logs;

○ B. UPDATE DB CFG FOR sample USING LOGARCHMETH1 OFF;
      UPDATE DB CFG FOR sample USING MIRRORLOGPATH D:\dup_logs;

○ C. UPDATE DB CFG FOR sample USING LOGARCHMETH1 LOGRETAIN;
      UPDATE DB CFG FOR sample USING LOGSECOND D:\dup_logs;

○ D. UPDATE DB CFG FOR sample USING LOGARCHMETH1 OFF;
      UPDATE DB CFG FOR sample USING LOGARCHMETH2 DISK:
      D:\dup_logs;

Question 18

Which of the following database configuration parameters is used to force an application to wait indefinitely to obtain a lock on a table?

○ A. LOCKLIST

○ B. LOCKTIMEOUT

○ C. DLCHKTIME

○ D. MAXLOCKS

Question 19

A database administrator successfully changes the value of the SORTHEAP database configuration parameter while a running application is accessing the database. When will the application see the effects?

○ A. When a new SQL statement is executed.

○ B. When a new transaction is started.

○ C. When a new database connection is established.

○ D. When the application terminates and is restarted.

Question 20

Which of the following commands will recommend and make configuration changes for an instance named DB2INST1?

○ A. AUTOCONFIGURE USING db2inst1 APPLY

○ B. AUTOCONFIGURE USING mem_percent 60 APPLY db2inst1

○ C. AUTOCONFIGURE USING mem_percent 60 APPLY DBM ONLY

○ D. AUTOCONFIGURE USING mem_percent 60 APPLY DB AND DBM

Question 21

Given the following information about a DB2 server:

Instance name: db2inst1
Port number: 60000
Service name: db2c_db2inst1
Host name: db2host
Host TCP/IP address: 10.205.15.100
Protocol: TCP/IP
Database name: PROD_DB

Assuming the following entry has been made to the services file:

```
db2c_db2inst1                    60000/tcp
```

Which two of the following commands must be executed to correctly configure communications for the server?

❏ A.   UPDATE DBM CFG USING SVCENAME db2c_db2inst1

❏ B.   UPDATE DBM CFG USING SVCEPORT 60000

❏ C.   db2set DB2COMM=TCPIP

❏ D.   UPDATE DBM CFG USING NNAME db2host

❏ E.   db2set DB2COMM=TCP/IP

Question 22

A database server has one instance named DB2INST1 and two databases named SALES and PAYROLL. Which of the following commands will allow the DB2INST1 instance and the SALES database, but prevent the PAYROLL database from being seen by DB2 Discovery?

○   A. UPDATE DBM CFG USING DISCOVER_INST SEARCH;
       UPDATE DB CFG FOR sales DISCOVER_DB SEARCH;
       UPDATE DB CFG FOR payroll USING DISCOVER_DB DISABLE;

○   B. UPDATE DBM CFG USING DISCOVER_INST ENABLE;
       UPDATE DB CFG FOR sales DISCOVER_DB ENABLE;
       UPDATE DB CFG FOR payroll USING DISCOVER_DB DISABLE;

○   C. UPDATE DBM CFG USING DISCOVERY SEARCH;
       UPDATE DB CFG FOR sales DISCOVER_DB ENABLE;
       UPDATE DB CFG FOR payroll USING DISCOVER_DB DISABLE;

○   D. UPDATE DBM CFG USING DISCOVERY ENABLE;
       UPDATE DB CFG FOR sales DISCOVER_DB ENABLE;
       UPDATE DB CFG FOR payroll USING DISCOVER_DB DISABLE;

Question 23

Which of the following statements about the DB2 Diagnostics Log File is NOT true?

○ A. Once created, the DB2 Diagnostics Log File grows continuously.

○ B. If the DB2 Diagnostics Log File is deleted, a new one will be created.

○ C. The db2diag utility can be used to filter and format the information stored in the DB2 Diagnostics Log File.

○ D. If the DB2DIAG_RESTART DB2 Database Manager configuration parameter is set to YES, the DB2 Diagnostics Log File will be deleted and recreated whenever an instance is restarted.

Question 24

A LIST APPLICATIONS command returned the following output:

Auth Id	Application Name	Appl. Handle	Application Id	DB Name	# of Agents
RSANDERS	db2taskd	148	*LOCAL.DB2.070601164915	SAMPLE	1
RSANDERS	db2stmm	147	*LOCAL.DB2.070601164914	SAMPLE	1
RSANDERS	db2bp.exe	146	*LOCAL.DB2.070601164913	SAMPLE	1

Which two of the following commands will terminate all of the applications that are currently running?

❏ A. FORCE APPLICATION (146, 147, 148)

❏ B. FORCE APPLICATION (LOCAL.DB2.070601164915, LOCAL.DB2.070601164914, LOCAL.DB2.070601164913)

❏ C. FORCE APPLICATION (db2taskd, db2stmm, db2bp.exe)

❏ D. FORCE APPLICATION ALL

❏ E. FORCE ALL APPLICATIONS

Question 25

A database administrator wants to temporarily disable the Task Center. Which of the following can be used to achieve this objective?

○ A. Assign the value OFF to the SCHED_ENABLE registry variable

○ B. Assign the value OFF to the SCHED_ENABLE parameter in the DB2 Database Manager configuration

○ C. Assign the value OFF to the SCHED_ENABLE parameter in the database configuration for the TOOLSDB database

○ D. Assign the value OFF to the SCHED_ENABLE parameter in the DAS (ADMIN) configuration

Question 26

Which of the following activities can NOT be performed with Automatic Maintenance?

○ A.   Database-level backups

○ B.   Snapshot monitoring

○ C.   Statistics collection and statistics profiling

○ D.   Table and index reorganization

Question 27

A database administrator needs to create a new DB2 9 database and wants offline table and index reorganization operations to be performed automatically whenever the database's data becomes fragmented. Which of the following is the minimum set of steps required to meet this objective?

○ A.   Create the new database using the CREATE DATABASE command
        Define an appropriate maintenance window

○ B.   Create the new database using the CREATE DATABASE command
        Assign the value ON to the AUTO_MAINT database configuration parameter
        Define an appropriate maintenance window

○ C.   Create the new database using the CREATE DATABASE command
        Assign the value ON to the AUTO_REORG database configuration parameter
        Define an appropriate maintenance window

○ D.   Create the new database using the CREATE DATABASE command
        Assign the value ON to the AUTO_MAINT database configuration parameter
        Assign the value ON to the AUTO_REORG database configuration parameter
        Define an appropriate maintenance window

Question 28

A LIST UTILITIES SHOW DETAIL command returned the following output:

```
    ID                              = 1
    Type                            = BACKUP
    Database Name                   = SAMPLE
    Partition Number                = 0
    Description                     = offline db
    Start Time                      = 06/02/2007 10:35:31.442019
    State                           = Executing
    Invocation Type                 = User
    Throttling:
        Priority                    = 20
    Progress Monitoring:
        Estimated Percentage Complete = 46
            Total Work              = 49310404 bytes
            Completed Work          = 22696620 bytes
            Start Time              = 06/02/2007 10:35:31.466054
```

Which of the following commands will allow the backup operation to continue running unthrottled?

- ○ A. SET UTIL_IMPACT_PRIORITY 1 TO 0
- ○ B. SET UTIL_IMPACT_LIM 1 TO 0
- ○ C. SET UTIL_IMPACT_PRIORITY 1 TO 100
- ○ D. SET UTIL_IMPACT_LIM 1 TO 100

Question 29

Which of the following memory consumers can NOT be tuned automatically by the Self-Tuning Memory Manager as the database workload changes?

- ○ A. Buffer pools
- ○ B. Locking memory
- ○ C. Utility memory
- ○ D. Database shared memory

Question 30

A notification log entry indicates that an error was generated by a function named sqlpsize. What does the fourth letter in the function name indicate?

- ○ A. The error occurred during a buffer pool management/manipulation operation
- ○ B. The error occurred during a data management operation
- ○ C. The error occurred during a data protection operation
- ○ D. The error occurred during a sort operation

Data Placement

Question 31

Which of the following features is NOT automatically enabled when a new DB2 9 database is created?

- ○ A. Automatic maintenance
- ○ B. Self tuning memory manager
- ○ C. Data row compression
- ○ D. Utility throttling

Question 32

Which of the following is NOT a valid table space state?

○ A.   Load pending

○ B.   Online and not accessible

○ C.   Load in progress

○ D.   Offline and not accessible

Question 33

Which of the following is NOT true about Global Temporary Tables?

○ A.   Indexes can be created on Global Temporary Tables

○ B.   Global Temporary Tables reside in user temporary table spaces

○ C.   Statistics can be collected on Global Temporary Tables

○ D.   Global Temporary Tables are visible to all users connected to a database

Question 34

Which of the following statements will create a table named PARTS that is partitioned such that rows with part numbers that fall in the range of 0 to 33 are stored in one partition that resides in one table space, rows with part numbers in the range of 34 to 66 are stored in another partition that resides in another table space, and rows with part numbers in the range of 67 to 99 are stored in a third partition that resides in a third table space?

○ A.   CREATE TABLE parts (partno INT, desc VARCHAR(25))
        IN tbsp0, tbsp1, tbsp2
        PARTITION BY (partno NULLS FIRST)
           (STARTING 0 ENDING 33,
           STARTING 34 ENDING 66,
           STARTING 67 ENDING 99)

○ B.   CREATE TABLE parts (partno INT, desc VARCHAR(25))
        PARTITION BY (partno NULLS FIRST)
           (PART part0 STARTING 0 ENDING 33,
           PART part1 STARTING 34 ENDING 66,
           PART part2 STARTING 67 ENDING 99)

○ C.   CREATE TABLE parts (partno INT, desc VARCHAR(25))
       PARTITION BY (partno NULLS FIRST
           (STARTING 0 ENDING 33,
           STARTING 34 ENDING 66,
           STARTING 67 ENDING 99)
           IN tbsp0, tbsp1, tbsp2)

○ D.   CREATE TABLE parts (partno INT, desc VARCHAR(25))
       PARTITION BY (partno NULLS FIRST)
           (STARTING 0 ENDING 33 IN tbsp0,
           STARTING 34 ENDING 66 IN tbsp1,
           STARTING 67 ENDING 99 IN tbsp2)

Question 35

Which two of the following utilities can be used to create a compression dictionary?

❑ A.   reorg

❑ B.   db2pd

❑ C.   inspect

❑ D.   runstats

❑ E.   db2buildcd

Question 36

An instance named DB2INST1 exists on a server and the DFTDBPATH Database
Manager configuration parameter for that instance contains the value "/home".
If no databases exist on the server and the following command is
executed:

    CREATE DATABASE my_db

Where will the metadata files for the database reside?

○ A.   In the /home/NODE0000/SQL00001 subdirectory

○ B.   In the /home/DB2INST1/NODE0000/SQL00001 subdirectory

○ C.   In the /home/ NODE0000/MY_DB subdirectory

○ D.   In the /home/DB2INST1/NODE0000/MY_DB subdirectory

Question 37

If the following CREATE TABLESPACE statement is executed:

```
CREATE REGULAR TABLESPACE sales_ts
PAGESIZE 4096
MANAGED BY DATABASE USING
    (FILE 'D:\tbsp1.tsf' 10 G, FILE 'D:\tbsp2.tsf' 6 G, FILE
'D:\tbsp3.tsf' 4 G)
EXTENTSIZE 32
PREFETCHSIZE 96
```

What is the maximum amount of data that can be stored in the SALES_TS table space?

○ A.   10 GB

○ B.   12 GB

○ C.   16 GB

○ D.   20 GB

Question 38

Which two of the following commands can be used to obtain detailed information, including status, about all table spaces that have been created for a database named SALES?

❑ A.   SELECT * FROM syscat.tablespaces

❑ B.   LIST TABLESPACES SHOW DETAIL

❑ C.   LIST TABLESPACE CONTAINERS SHOW DETAIL

❑ D.   GET SNAPSHOT FOR TABLESPACES ON sales

❑ E.   GET SNAPSHOT FOR TABLESPACE CONTAINERS ON sales

Question 39

Which of the following statements about schema objects is NOT true?

○ A.   After connecting to a new database, all users who have successfully authenticated with the server have the ability to create a new schema.

○ B.   Like table spaces, schemas are used to physically group and store objects in a database.

○ C.   If a schema is explicitly created with the CREATE SCHEMA statement, the schema owner is granted CREATEIN, DROPIN, and ALTERIN privileges on the schema, as well as the ability to grant these privileges to other users.

○ D.   Ownership of a schema that is explicitly created can be assigned during the creation process.

Question 40

In order to use data row compression with a table, which of the following must exist?

○ A. A compression index

○ B. A compression dictionary

○ C. A user-defined compression algorithm

○ D. A table that only contains character data type columns

Question 41

Which of the following options can be used with the REORG command to construct a new compression dictionary before compressing data stored in a table?

○ A. KEEPDICTIONARY

○ B. RESETDICTIONARY

○ C. GENERATEDICTIONARY

○ D. NEWDICTIONARY

Question 42

If the following CREATE DATABASE command is executed:

```
CREATE DATABASE sales ON C: USING CODESET UTF-8 TERRITORY US
RESTRICTIVE
```

Which of the following privileges will be automatically granted to the group PUBLIC?

○ A. No privileges are granted

○ B. CONNECT, CREATETAB, BINDADD, and IMPLICIT_SCHEMA privileges on the database

○ C. SELECT privilege on each system catalog table

○ D. EXECUTE privilege on all procedures found in the SYSIBM schema

Question 43

If the following CREATE TABLESPACE statement is executed:

```
CREATE REGULAR TABLESPACE sales_ts
PAGESIZE 8 K
MANAGED BY SYSTEM USING
    ('/mnt/data1', '/mnt/data2', '/mnt/data3')
EXTENTSIZE 32
PREFETCHSIZE 128
```

How much space does DB2 allocate for the SALES_TS table space when all existing pages in the table space become full?

○ A. 8 KB

○ B. 32 KB

○ C. 128 KB

○ D. 256 KB

Question 44

Given the following CREATE TABLESPACE statement:

```
CREATE REGULAR TABLESPACE payroll_ts
MANAGED BY AUTOMATIC STORAGE
EXTENTSIZE 32
PREFETCHSIZE 128
```

Which of the following statements is NOT true?

○ A. When created, the PAYROLL_TS table space will be a DMS table space with file containers.

○ B. The database the PAYROLL_TS table space is to be created for must be enabled for automatic storage.

○ C. When created, the PAYROLL_TS table space will be an SMS table space with directory containers.

○ D. The MANAGED BY AUTOMATIC STORAGE clause is unnecessary and could have been left out of the CREATE TABLESPACE command.

Question 45

If the following CREATE DATABASE command is executed:

```
CREATE DATABASE sales ON /mnt/data1, /mnt/data2
COLLATE USING IDENTITY
CATALOG TABLESPACE MANAGED BY SYSTEM USING ('mnt/syscat');
```

Which of the following statements is NOT true about the resulting database?

○ A.   Automatic storage is enabled for the database

○ B.   An SMS table space will be used to hold the system catalog

○ C.   User data will be stored on /mnt/data1 and /mnt/data2

○ D.   Metadata for the database will be stored on /mnt/data2

Question 46

Which of the following is NOT a true statement about SMS table spaces?

○ A.   Regular data and long data cannot be split across multiple table spaces.

○ B.   Storage space is allocated by the operating system as it is needed.

○ C.   Containers can be added to or deleted from existing table spaces using the ALTER TABLESPACE command.

○ D.   Only directory containers can be used for storage; file and device containers cannot be used.

Question 47

If the following CREATE INDEX statements are executed:

```
CREATE INDEX cust_zip_idx ON customer(custinfo)
GENERATE KEY
USING XMLPATTERN '/customerinfo/addr/zip-pcode'
AS SQL DOUBLE;
CREATE INDEX cust_city_idx ON customer(custinfo)
GENERATE KEY
USING XMLPATTERN '/customerinfo/addr/city'
AS SQL VARCHAR(40);
```

And the following XML documents are inserted into the CUSTOMER table:

```
<?xml version="1.0" encoding="UTF-8" ?>
<customerinfo xmlns="http://crecord.dat" id="1000">
   <name>John Doe</name>
   <addr country="United States">
     <street>25 East Creek Drive</street>
     <city>Raleigh</city>
     <state-prov>North Carolina</state-prov>
     <zip-pcode>27603</zip-pcode>
   </addr>
```

```
      <phone type="work">919-555-1212</phone>
      <email>john.doe@yahoo.com</email>
    </customerinfo>

  <?xml version="1.0" encoding="UTF-8" ?>
  <customerinfo xmlns="http://crecord.dat" id="1010">
    <name>Jane Smith</name>
    <addr country="United States">
      <street>2120 Stewart Street</street>
      <city></city>
      <state-prov>South Carolina</state-prov>
      <zip-pcode>29501</zip-pcode>
    </addr>
    <phone type="work">843-555-3434</phone>
    <email>jane.smith@aol.com</email>
  </customerinfo>
```

How many index keys will be generated?

○ A.   1

○ B.   2

○ C.   3

○ D.   4

Question 48

Which of the following statements is NOT valid when discussing data row compression?

○ A.   Data row compression can lead to disk I/O savings and improved buffer pool hit ratios.

○ B.   Compressing data at the row level is advantageous because it allows repeating patterns that span multiple columns within a row to be replaced with shorter symbols.

○ C.   Data row compression for a table can be enabled by executing the ALTER TABLE statement with the COMPRESS YES option specified.

○ D.   Only data in a table enabled for data row compression is compressed; data in corresponding indexes and transaction logs is not compressed.

Question 49

If the following CREATE DATABASE command is executed:

    CREATE DATABASE payroll ON C:

Which of the following commands will add new storage containers to the
PAYROLL database?

○ A. ALTER TABLESPACE ADD STORAGE D:\data1, D:\data2
○ B. ALTER DATABASE ADD STORAGE D:\data1, D:\data2
○ C. ALTER TABLESPACE ADD CONTAINERS D:\data1, D:\data2
○ D. ALTER DATABASE ADD CONTAINERS D:\data1, D:\data2

Question 50

Which of the following options can be specified with the CREATE TABLESPACE
statement to create a DMS table space that can automatically expand beyond its
original storage definition?

○ A. AUTORESIZE YES
○ B. RESIZE YES
○ C. EXTEND YES
○ D. EXPAND YES

Question 51

A user named USER1 logs on to an AIX server and connects to a database
named SALES that belongs to an instance named DB2INST1 by executing the
following command:

    CONNECT TO sales USER db2admin USING ibmdb2;

After connecting to the database, user USER1 creates a table by executing the following
statement:

    CREATE TABLE test_tab (col1 INTEGER, col2 CHAR(12));

Assuming the CREATE TABLE statement executed successfully, what schema was the
table TEST_TAB created in?

○ A. ROOT
○ B. DB2INST1
○ C. USER1
○ D. DB2ADMIN

Question 52

Which of the following is NOT a true statement about range-clustered tables?

- ○ A.   Range-clustered tables require less buffer cache because they rely on a special index for organizing data.
- ○ B.   Storage for a range-clustered table must be pre-allocated and available when the table is created.
- ○ C.   Range-clustered tables can result in significant performance advantages during query processing because fewer input/output (I/O) operations are needed.
- ○ D.   Range-clustered tables are created by specifying the ORGANIZE BY KEY SEQUENCE clause with a CREATE TABLE statement.

Question 53

If the following statements are executed in the order shown:

```
CREATE TABLE sales
     (invoice_no      INTEGER,
      sales_date      DATE,
      sales_amt       NUMERIC(5,2))
     IN tbsp0, tbsp1, tbsp2, tbsp3
     PARTITION BY RANGE (sales_date NULLS FIRST)
          (STARTING '1/1/2006' ENDING '12/31/2006'
           EVERY 3 MONTHS);
  CREATE INDEX sales_idx ON sales (invoice_no);
```

Which of the following table spaces will contain the data for the SALES_IDX index?

- ○ A.   TBSP0
- ○ B.   TBSP1
- ○ C.   TBSP2
- ○ D.   TBSP3

Question 54

Which of the following statements about XML indexes is true?

- ○ A.   XML indexes can contain relational data columns.
- ○ B.   An index over XML data can be used to improve the efficiency of XQuery expressions performed against XML columns.
- ○ C.   Unique XML indexes can be created by combining multiple XML columns.
- ○ D.   The entire contents of an XML document stored in an XML column are indexed.

Database Access

Question 55

Given the following CREATE TABLE statement:

```
CREATE TABLE department
  (deptid          INTEGER,
   deptname      CHAR(25),
   budget            NUMERIC(12,2))
```

Which of the following statements prevents two departments from being assigned the same DEPTID, but allows null values?

○ A.   ALTER TABLE department ADD CONSTRAINT dpt_cst PRIMARY KEY (deptid)

○ B.   CREATE INDEX dpt_idx ON department(deptid)

○ C.   ALTER TABLE department ADD CONSTRAINT dpt_cst UNIQUE (deptid)

○ D.   CREATE UNIQUE INDEX dpt_idx ON department(deptid)

Question 56

Which of the following CREATE VIEW statements will ensure that every attempt to insert or update a record in table T1 via the view V1 must pass some criteria before the row can be inserted/updated?

○ A.   CREATE VIEW v1 AS SELECT c1, c2 FROM t1 WHERE c1 < 100

○ B.   CREATE VIEW v1 AS SELECT c1, c2 FROM t1 WHERE c1 < 100 ENFORCED

○ C.   CREATE VIEW v1 AS SELECT c1, c2 FROM t1 WHERE c1 < 100 WITH VALIDATION

○ D.   CREATE VIEW v1 AS SELECT c1, c2 FROM t1 WHERE c1 < 100 WITH LOCAL CHECK OPTION

Question 57

Given the following table:

SALES

REGION	SALES_REP_ID	AMOUNT
East	1200	24000
East	1420	32000
West	1200	29000
South	2120	34000

If the following SQL statements are executed:

```
CREATE UNIQUE INDEX indx1 ON sales(sales_rep_id);
INSERT INTO sales VALUES ('North', 1420, 27500);
SELECT * FROM sales;
```

How many rows will be returned by the last query?

○ A. 3

○ B. 4

○ C. 5

○ D. 6

Question 58

Which of the following is NOT a valid Control Center view?

○ A. Basic

○ B. Intermediate

○ C. Advanced

○ D. Custom

Question 59

Which of the following tools is NOT accessible through the Control Center?

○ A. The Health Center

○ B. The Command Editor

○ C. The Command Line Processor

○ D. The License Center

Question 60

Given the following CREATE TABLE statement:

```
CREATE TABLE employee
   (empid           INTEGER NOT NULL,
    name            VARVHAR(25),
    gender          CHAR(1) NOT NULL,
    CONSTRAINT gender_ok CHECK(gender IN ('M', 'F')) NOT ENFORCED
            ENABLE QUERY OPTIMIZATION)
```

What effect, if any, will the following command have when it is executed?

```
ALTER TABLE employee ALTER CHECK gender_ok DISABLE QUERY
OPTIMIZATION
```

- ○ A. The GENDER_OK constraint will become an enforced check constraint and will be used to check the validity of insert and update operations.
- ○ B. The GENDER_OK constraint will become an enforced check constraint and any data that resides in the EMPLOYEE table will be checked immediately for constraint violations.
- ○ C. The ability for the DB2 Optimizer to use the GENDER_OK constraint for query optimization will be disabled.
- ○ D. All data access plans that used the GENDER_OK constraint for query optimization will be marked inoperative.

Question 61

Given the following CREATE TABLE statement:

```
CREATE TABLE tab1
   (c1           SMALLINT,
    c2           SMALLINT,
    c3           SMALLINT,
    c4           CHAR(4))
```

If the column C1 must be unique and the following queries are frequently issued against table TAB1:

```
SELECT c1, c2 FROM tab1 ORDER BY c1;
SELECT c1, c2, c3 FROM tab1 ORDER BY c1;
```

Which of the following statements will improve performance by providing index-only access?

- ○ A. CREATE INDEX indx1 ON tab1 (c1)
- ○ B. CREATE UNIQUE INDEX indx1 ON tab1 (c1) INCLUDE (c2)
- ○ C. CREATE INDEX indx1 ON tab1 (c1, c2, c3)
- ○ D. CREATE UNIQUE INDEX indx1 ON tab1 (c1) INCLUDE (c2, c3)

Question 62

> If the following query is executed:
>
> ```
> SELECT TABNAME, CARD
> FROM SYSCAT,TABLES
> WHERE TABNAME = 'EMPLOYEES'
> ```
>
> Which of the following can be determined based on the results?
>
> ○ A. Whether or not the EMPLOYEES table needs to be reorganized to reduce data fragmentation.
>
> ○ B. Whether or not the amount of storage available for the table space where the EMPLOYEES table resides needs to be increased.
>
> ○ C. Whether or not statistics for the EMPLOYEES table have been collected.
>
> ○ D. Whether or not storage space can be saved by enabling the EMPLOYEES table for data row compression.

Question 63

> Which of the following best describes the function of the Activity Monitor?
>
> ○ A. Captures specific information about typical workloads (queries or sets of SQL operations) performed against a database and recommends changes based upon the information provided.
>
> ○ B. Constantly monitors the health of a DB2 Database Manager instance using several health indicators to evaluate specific aspects of instance and database performance.
>
> ○ C. Monitors application performance, application concurrency, resource consumption, and SQL statement usage on a database or a database partition.
>
> ○ D. Configures clients so they can access databases stored on remote DB2 servers.

Question 64

> Which of the following can NOT be used to set DB2 environment/registry variables?
>
> ○ A. Configuration Assistant
>
> ○ B. Design Advisor
>
> ○ C. Command Editor
>
> ○ D. Command Line Processor

Question 65

What are informational constraints used for?

- ○ A. To influence DB2 Optimizer data access plan selection without slowing down DML operations
- ○ B. To provide information to an application about any constraints that have been defined
- ○ C. To define non-checked primary keys
- ○ D. To influence DB2 Optimizer data access plans for foreign key-primary key relationships

Question 66

Which of the following statements is NOT true concerning inoperative views?

- ○ A. A view can become inoperative when a privilege the view definition is dependent upon is revoked.
- ○ B. Privileges granted on a view are revoked when the view is marked inoperative.
- ○ C. An inoperative must be recovered before it can be dropped.
- ○ D. An inoperative view can be recreated by re-executing the statement initially used to create it (found in the TEXT column of the SYSCAT.VIEW catalog view).

Question 67

If the following query is executed:

```
SELECT TABNAME, OVERFLOW
FROM SYSCAT,TABLES
WHERE TABNAME = 'SALES'
```

Which of the following can be determined based on the results?

- ○ A. Whether or not the SALES table needs to be reorganized to reduce data fragmentation.
- ○ B. Whether or not the amount of memory available for sort operations needs to be increased.
- ○ C. Whether or not statistics for the SALES table need to be updated.
- ○ D. Whether or not the size of the lock list should be increased to reduce the amount of lock escalations seen.

Question 68

Given the following CREATE TABLE statement:

```
CREATE TABLE products
    (prodid          INTEGER NOT NULL PRIMARY KEY,
     category        CHAR(3) CHECK(category
                     IN ('323', '441', '615', '832', '934')),
     description     VARCHAR(200),
     quantity        INTEGER CHECK (quantity > 0),
     sellprice       NUMERIC(7,2) WITH DEFAULT,
     buyprice        NUMERIC(7,2) WITH DEFAULT,
    CONSTRAINT zeroloss CHECK (sellprice > buyprice))
```

Assuming the table is empty, which of the following INSERT statements will succeed?

- ○ A. INSERT INTO products (prodid, category, description, buyprice) VALUES (1, '832', 'medium white shirt', 6.99)
- ○ B. INSERT INTO products (prodid, category, quantity, sellprice, buyprice) VALUES (2, '323', 5, 28.99, 26.99)
- ○ C. INSERT INTO products (prodid, category, description, quantity) VALUES (1, '934', 'black shoe', 10)
- ○ D. INSERT INTO products (prodid, category, description, quantity, sellprice, buyprice) VALUES (2, '615', 'dark blue socks', 3, 20.00, 25.65)

Question 69

Given the following CREATE TABLE statement:

```
CREATE TABLE employee
    (empid           INTEGER NOT NULL,
     lname           VARVHAR(20),
     gender          CHAR(1) NOT NULL,
    CONSTRAINT gender_ok CHECK(gender IN ('M', 'F')) NOT ENFORCED
            ENABLE QUERY OPTIMIZATION)
```

And the following INSERT statement:

```
INSERT INTO employee VALUES (1, 'Smith', 'M'), (2, 'Doe', 'F'),
    (3, 'Jones', 'U')
```

Which of the following queries will return an empty result set?

- ○ A. SELECT COUNT(gender) FROM employee
- ○ B. SELECT * FROM employee WHERE gender = 'M'
- ○ C. SELECT * FROM employee WHERE gender = 'F'
- ○ D. SELECT * FROM employee WHERE gender = 'U'

Question 70

Which of the following objects can NOT be created from the Control Center?

○ A. Buffer pool

○ B. Event monitor

○ C. Trigger

○ D. User-defined function

Question 71

Which of the following operations can NOT be performed using the Tools Settings notebook?

○ A. Define replication environments.

○ B. Change the font used to display text and menu options.

○ C. Set the default scheduling scheme.

○ D. Configure Health Status Beacons.

Question 72

Which two of the following are valid indexes that are supported by DB2?

❑ A. Spatial grid indexes

❑ B. Static bitmap indexes

❑ C. Dynamic bitmap indexes

❑ D. Page-based indexes

❑ E. Multidimensional range-clustered indexes

Question 73

Given the following CREATE TABLE statement:

```
CREATE TABLE tab1
   (c1        SMALLINT,
    c2        CHAR(4))
```

Table TAB1 is accessed frequently by two applications; one application returns the data in column C1 in ascending order, the other application returns the data in column C1 in descending order. To improve performance, a database administrator executes the following commands:

```
CREATE INDEX indx1 ON tab1(c1 ASC);
CREATE INDEX indx2 ON tab1(c1 DESC);
```

Which of the following will occur?

○ A.   Index INDX1 will be created and the first application will use it when retrieving data; the index INDX2 will be created and the second application will use it when retrieving data.

○ B.   Index INDX1 will be created. When an attempt is made to create index INDX2, DB2 will alter index INDX1 to allow reverse scans and index INDX1 be used by both applications when retrieving data.

○ C.   Index INDX1 will be created. When an attempt is made to create index INDX2, DB2 will alter index INDX2 to allow reverse scans and drop index INDX1; index INDX2 will be used by both applications when retrieving data.

○ D.   Index INDX1 will be created and allow reverse scans by default. When an atempt is made to create index INDX2, DB2 will issue a duplicate index warning message. Index INDX1 be used by both applications when retrieving data.

Question 74

Which of the following best describes the function of the db2ls command?

○ A.   It retrieves information about the DB2 products that have been installed on a particular server.

○ B.   It locks a DB2 system and limits access to users who hold System Administrator authority.

○ C.   It generates a list of all remote servers that have been cataloged on a client workstation.

○ D.   It returns the location of the system catalog for a particular database.

Analyzing DB2 Activity

Question 75

A user issues the following commands:

```
UPDATE DBM CFG USING DFT_MON_SORT ON;
UPDATE MONITOR SWITCHES USING UOW ON;
UPDATE DBM CFG USING DFT_MON_TIMESTAMP ON;
UPDATE MONITOR SWITCHES USING BUFFERPOOL ON;
```

Assuming no other monitor switches have been set, if the DB2 instance is stopped and restarted, which of the following database monitor switches will be set?

- ○ A. SORT, UOW
- ○ B. UOW, BUFFERPOOL
- ○ C. SORT, TIMESTAMP
- ○ D. TIMESTAMP, BUFFERPOOL

Question 76

Which two of the following can be used to capture Explain snapshot data for SQL statements issued from the Command Line Processor (CLP) in the same session?

- ❑ A. EXPLAIN PLAN FOR SNAPSHOT FOR [*SQLStatement*]
- ❑ B. SET CURRENT EXPLAIN MODE EXPLAIN
- ❑ C. SET CURRENT EXPLAIN SNAPSHOT EXPLAIN
- ❑ D. EXPLAIN ALL
- ❑ E. EXPLSNAP ALL

Question 77

A database administrator executed the following command while several applications were interacting with a database named SAMPLE:

```
GET SNAPSHOT FOR LOCKS ON sample
```

And received the following output:

```
Database name                      = SAMPLE
Database path                      = C:\DB2\NODE0000\SQL00002\
Input database alias               = SAMPLE
Locks held                         = 0
Applications currently connected   = 1
Agents currently waiting on locks  = 0
Snapshot timestamp                 = 05/14/2007 14:57:04.559027
```

```
Application handle              = 110
Application ID                  = *LOCAL.DB2.070514185703
Sequence number                 = 00001
Application name                = db2taskd
CONNECT Authorization ID        = DBUSER
Application status              = Connect Completed
Status change time              = Not Collected
Application code page           = 1252
Locks held                      = 0
Total wait time (ms)            = Not Collected
```

Why was the value "Not Collected" returned for the total lock wait time?

○ A. The RESET MONITOR command was executed just before the snapshot was taken.

○ B. The LOCK snapshot monitor switch was off when the snapshot was taken.

○ C. No locks were held at the time the snapshot was taken.

○ D. The UOW snapshot monitor switch was off when the snapshot was taken.

Question 78

Which of the following is NOT a true statement about event monitors?

○ A. An unlimited number of event monitors may be defined.

○ B. An event monitor must be activated before it will start collecting data.

○ C. Up to, but no more than 16 event monitors can be active at the same time.

○ D. An active event monitor must be stopped before it can be dropped.

Question 79

If a query used in an OLTP environment joins two tables on their primary key, which of the following operators will most likely represent this join in an access plan graph produced by Visual Explain?

○ A. HSJOIN

○ B. MSJOIN

○ C. NLJOIN

○ D. SJOIN

Question 80

Which of the following can be used to display the precompile options that were used to create a bind file?

- ○ A.   db2advis
- ○ B.   db2bfd
- ○ C.   db2mtrk
- ○ D.   db2rbind

Question 81

Which of the following statements is NOT true about the DB2 Problem Determination tool (db2pd)?

- ○ A.   db2pd is used to obtain quick and immediate information from the DB2 database system memory sets.
- ○ B.   db2pd does not require a connection to an active database in order to obtain information about it.
- ○ C.   db2pd can be used to obtain information about an instance that has stopped prematurely.
- ○ D.   Because db2pd works directly with memory, it is possible to retrieve information that will change as it is being collected.

Question 82

What is the RESET MONITOR command used for?

- ○ A.   To reset all snapshot monitor counters to zero.
- ○ B.   To reset individual snapshot monitor counters to zero.
- ○ C.   To turn all snapshot monitor switches off.
- ○ D.   To turn all snapshot monitor switches except the TIMESTAMP switch off.

Question 83

An application that contains two embedded dynamic SQL statements has been bound to a database. Which of the following can be used to capture Explain information for both statements in the application that can be examined with Visual Explain?

- ○ A.   EXPLSNAP ALL and SET CURRENT EXPLAIN MODE EXPLAIN
- ○ B.   EXPLAIN ALL and SET CURRENT EXPLAIN SNAPSHOT ALL
- ○ C.   EXPLSNAP NO and SET CURRENT EXPLAIN SNAPSHOT YES
- ○ D.   EXPLAIN NO and SET CURRENT EXPLAIN MODE YES

Question 84

A database named SAMPLE contains a DMS table space that spans five files.
Three of the files are 4 GB in size and two of the files are 3 GB in size. A database
administrator wants an alert to be generated whenever the 3 GB files are 80% full
and the 4GB files are 85% full. What is the best way to accomplish this using the
Health Center?

○ A.   Change the Global level settings for all table space containers; change the
In-stance level settings for the 3 GB table space containers.

○ B.   Change the Instance level settings for all table space containers; change
the Global level settings for the 3 GB table space containers.

○ C.   Change the Global level settings for all table space containers; change the
Object level settings for the 4 GB table space containers.

○ D.   Change the Instance level settings for all table space containers; change
the Object level settings for the 4 GB table space containers.

Question 85

Which of the following commands instructs the DB2 Optimizer to use the maximum
amount of optimization techniques available when generating data access plans for
dynamic SQL statements that will interact with a database named SAMPLE?

○ A.   db2set –g DB2_QUERYOPT=9

○ B.   UPDATE DBM CFG USING QUERYOPT 9

○ C.   UPDATE DB CFG FOR sample USING QUERYOPT 9

○ D.   SET CURRENT QUERY OPTIMIZATION = 9

Question 86

Which of the following can be used to determine how many pages have been written
to the transaction log files associated with a particular database?

○ A.   db2pd

○ B.   db2advis

○ C.   db2look

○ D.   db2mtrk

Question 87

Which of the following queries can be used to obtain information about how buffer pools defined for a database named SAMPLE are being utilized?

○ A.   SELECT * FROM SNAPSHOT_INFO ('sample', BUFFERPOOL)

○ B.   SELECT * FROM SNAPSHOT_BP ('sample', −1)

○ C.   SELECT * FROM TABLE (SNAPSHOT_INFO ('sample', BUFFERPOOL))
         AS snap_info

○ D.   SELECT * FROM TABLE (SNAP_GET_BP ('sample', −1)) AS snap_info

Question 88

Which of the following is NOT a true statement about DEADLOCKS event monitors?

○ A.   By default, a DEADLOCKS event monitor is automatically created when a
         DB2 9 database is created.

○ B.   Once created, the default DEADLOCKS event monitor cannot be deleted.

○ C.   The default DEADLOCKS event monitor is activated when a connection to
         the database is first established.

○ D.   Event monitor data is collected at the time a deadlock cycle is detected.

Question 89

Which of the following is NOT a valid level that health indicator settings can be defined for?

○ A.   Server

○ B.   Global

○ C.   Instance

○ D.   Object

Question 90

Which of the following options can be specified with the CREATE EVENT MONITOR statement to indicate that each agent that generates an event that is being monitored will not wait for an event buffer to be externalized to disk before continuing if it determines that both event buffers are full?

○ A.   BLOCKED

○ B.   NONBLOCKED

○ C.   BUFFERED

○ D.   NONBUFFERED

Question 91

Which two of the following are key tasks that can be performed using the Health Center?

- ❑ A.   View alerts for an instance or a database.
- ❑ B.   Clear all previous alert entries recorded in the Journal.
- ❑ C.   View the history of threshold settings for a database.
- ❑ D.   Quiesce the Health Monitor.
- ❑ E.   View the history of alerts for an instance or a database.

Question 92

Which two of the following utilities can be used to present Explain information in a meaningful format?

- ❑ A.   db2bfd
- ❑ B.   db2expln
- ❑ C.   db2look
- ❑ D.   db2exfmt
- ❑ E.   db2advis

Question 93

If a query used in a decision support environment joins two tables, which of the following operators will most likely be used to represent this join in an access plan graph produced by Visual Explain?

- ○ A.   HSJOIN
- ○ B.   MSJOIN
- ○ C.   NLJOIN
- ○ D.   SJOIN

Question 94

Which of the following best describes the functionality of db2mtrk?

- ○ A.   It reports how memory is being managed by the Self Tuning Memory Manager.
- ○ B.   It estimates the memory requirements for a database, based on values assigned to the memory-related Database Manager configuration parameters.
- ○ C.   It produces report of memory status for instances, databases and agents.
- ○ D.   It recommends memory-related Database Manager configuration parameter values that will improve memory utilization.

DB2 Utilities

Question 95

Which of the following IMPORT command options will cause the Import utility
to acquire a table-level lock after every commit?

○ A. ALLOW NO ACCESS

○ B. ALLOW READ ACCESS

○ C. ALLOW WRITE ACCESS

○ D. ALLOW FULL ACCESS

Question 96

A database administrator wants to delete all records found in a table named DEPARTMENT.
If the DEPARTMENT table resides in a database that is stored on an AIX server, which of
the following commands can be used to accomplish this objective?

○ A. LOAD FROM null OF DEL INSERT INTO department

○ B. LOAD FROM null OF DEL REPLACE INTO department

○ C. LOAD FROM /dev/null OF DEL INSERT INTO department

○ D. LOAD FROM /dev/null OF DEL REPLACE INTO department

Question 97

The table EMPLOYEES was created by executing the following command:

```
CREATE TABLE employees (empid   INTEGER NOT NULL PRIMARY KEY,
                        name    VARCHAR(25))
```

Assuming the file EMPDATA.DEL contains the following data:

```
100, "Kim Moutsos"
100, "Dwaine Snow"
200, "Rebecca Bond"
300, "Phil Gunning"
400, "Paul Zikopoulos"
```

If the following commands are executed:

```
CREATE TABLE emp_exp LIKE EMPLOYEES;
LOAD FROM empdata.del OF DEL
     INSERT INTO EMPLOYEE
     FOR EXECPTION emp_exp;
```

Which of the following statements is true?

○ A.   The table EMPLOYEES will contain four rows; the table EMP_EXP will be empty.

○ B.   The table EMPLOYEES will contain five rows; the table EMP_EXP will contain five rows.

○ C.   The table EMPLOYEES will contain four rows; the table EMP_EXP will contain one row.

○ D.   The table EMPLOYEES will contain five rows; the table EMP_EXP will contain one row.

Question 98

In an attempt to improve query performance, a database administrator created an index for a table named EMPLOYEE, which contains 500,000 records. Performance of ad-hoc queries ran against the EMPLOYEE table has improved, but performance of a batch application that runs at night has not improved. Which of the following operations should correct this problem?

○ A.   REORGCHK

○ B.   REORG

○ C.   FLUSH PACKAGE CACHE

○ D.   REBIND

Question 99

The Design Advisor can be used to analyze SQL from which two of the following?

❑ A.   The EXPLAIN_STATEMENT table

❑ B.   A file containing a workload

❑ C.   The SYSIBM.SYSPLANS system catalog table

❑ D.   The EXPLAIN_STREAM table

❑ E.   The ADVISE_WORKLOAD table

Question 100

Which of the following is NOT a true statement about the Import utility?

○ A.   Worksheet Format (WSF) formatted files are supported.

○ B.   All row transactions are recorded in the database's transaction log files.

○ C.   System catalog tables can be targets.

○ D.   Data can be imported into a host database through DB2 Connect.

Question 101

Which of the following is NOT a method by which the Export utility can be invoked?

- ○ A.   Control Center
- ○ B.   Command Line Processor
- ○ C.   ADMIN_CMD stored procedure
- ○ D.   Replication Center

Question 102

Which of the following IMPORT command options can be used to prevent an import operation from filling up a database's transaction log files and failing?

- ○ A.   ALLOW NO ACCESS
- ○ B.   NOTIMEOUT
- ○ C.   COMMITCOUNT AUTOMATIC
- ○ D.   ALLOW WRITE ACCESS

Question 103

Which of the following set of steps could be used to build a test database that has the same structure and statistics of a production database, but contains less data?

- ○ A.   1) Extract the data from the production database using the db2move utility (EXPORT mode).

    2) Create a test database and populate it using the db2move utility (IMPORT mode).

- ○ B.   1) Generate the SQL needed to create the objects in the production database using the db2look utility.

    2) Create a test database and run the script produced by db2look to create the database objects.

    3) Extract the data from the production database using the db2move utility (EXPORT mode).

    4) Populate the test database using the db2move utility (IMPORT mode).

    5) Run the RUNSTATS utility on each table in the test database.

- ○ C.   1) Run the RUNSTATS utility on each table in the production database.

    2) Generate the SQL needed to create the objects in the production database and reproduce the statistics profile using the db2look utility.

    3) Create a test database and run the script produced by db2look to create the database objects and duplicate the statistics.

    4) Insert, Import, or Load test data into the database.

○ D.   1) Generate the SQL needed to create the objects in the production
         database using the db2look utility.

   2) Create a test database and run the script produced by db2look to
      create the database objects.

   3) Load test data into the database using the LOAD command with the
      STATISTICS USE PROFILE option specified so that statistics will be
      collected.

Question 104

Which of the following commands invokes the Design Advisor and instructs it to make
recommendations for a database named SAMPLE, based on information collected by the
snapshot monitor?

○ A.   db2advis −d SAMPLE -k

○ B.   db2advis −d SAMPLE -qp

○ C.   db2advis −d SAMPLE -g

○ D.   db2advis −d SAMPLE -h

Question 105

Which of the following operations can NOT be performed on a table that contains
a primary key that is referenced by a foreign key in another table?

○ A.   IMPORT ... INSERT

○ B.   IMPORT ... REPLACE

○ C.   IMPORT ... INSERT_UPDATE

○ D.   IMPORT ... CREATE

Question 106

Which two of the following utilities can be used to update the catalog statistics for a table?

❏ A.   EXPORT

❏ B.   IMPORT

❏ C.   LOAD

❏ D.   REORGCHK

❏ E.   REORG

Question 107

Which of the following LOAD command modifiers can be used when working with identity column data?

○ A. IDENTITYRESET

○ B. IDENTITYOVERRIDE

○ C. IDENTITYSUPRESS

○ D. IDENTITYRETAIN

Question 108

Given the following command:

```
LOAD FROM salesdata.del OF DEL INSERT INTO sales
MODIFIED BY DELPRIORITYCHAR
ALLOW READ ACCESS
STATISTICS USE PROFILE
```

Which of the following is NOT true?

○ A. During the load operation, statistics will be collected and the statistics profile for the SALES table and its associated indexes will be updated; if a statistics profile does not exist one will be created.

○ B. Only data in the SALES table that existed prior to the invocation of the LOAD command can be read by other applications while the load operation is in progress.

○ C. The priority for evaluating delimiters is character delimiter, record delimiter, column delimiter rather than record delimiter, character delimiter, column delimiter.

○ D. If the load operation aborts, the original data stored in the SALES table will be accessible for read access.

Question 109

Which of the following illustrates the proper order in which the DB2 data management utilities available should be used?

○ A. RUNSTATS, REORG table, REORG indexes, REORGCHK, REBIND

○ B. RUNSTATS, REORGCHK, REORG table, REORG indexes, RUNSTATS, REBIND

○ C. REORGCHK, REORG indexes, REORG table, RUNSTATS, REBIND

○ D. RUNSTATS, REBIND, REORGCHK, REORG table, REORG indexes, RUNSTATS

Question 110

Which of the following commands can be used to display the status of a load operation?

○ A. LOAD STATUS

○ B. LOAD MESSAGES

○ C. LOAD QUERY

○ D. LOAD STATISTICS

Question 111

In which of the following scenarios should the Load utility be used instead of the Import utility?

○ A. Data needs to be added to a table and any associated triggers need to be fired.

○ B. A large amount of data needs to be added to a table quickly without incurring a significant amount of transaction logging.

○ C. Data stored in a Worksheet (WSF) formatted file needs to be added to a table.

○ D. A large amount of data needs to be added to a table and constraint checking needs to be enforced during population.

Question 112

Which of the following tasks is the db2batch utility best suited for?

○ A. Benchmarking SQL and XQuery operations.

○ B. Copying 50 tables created under a single schema from one database to another.

○ C. Reorganizing table data and clustering its rows.

○ D. Updating access plan information stored in packages.

High Availability

Question 113

What type of recovery operation is used to reapply transactions that were committed but not externalized to storage, roll back transactions that were externalized to storage but not committed, and purge transactions from memory that were neither committed nor externalized to storage?

- ○ A. Quick recovery
- ○ B. Crash recovery
- ○ C. Version recovery
- ○ D. Roll-forward recovery

Question 114

If a database named SAMPLE was backed up on Sunday, which of the following commands will produce a backup image on Wednesday that contains a copy of just the data that has changed since the backup image on Sunday was created?

- ○ A. BACKUP DATABASE sample INCREMENTAL TO C:\backups
- ○ B. BACKUP DATABASE sample DELTA TO C:\backups
- ○ C. BACKUP DATABASE sample DELTA INCREMENTAL TO C:\backups
- ○ D. BACKUP DATABASE sample INCREMENTAL DELTA TO C:\backups

Question 115

Which of the following is NOT needed to recover a database to a specific point in time?

- ○ A. Access to a full database backup image
- ○ B. Access to a backup copy of the recovery history file
- ○ C. Access to archive log files produced since a backup image was made
- ○ D. Access to all delta backup images produced since the last full backup image was made

Question 116

A database named COMPANY was backed up on June 1 and on June 15 the following SQL statement was executed:

```
RENAME TABLESPACE emp_info TO hr_info
```

On July 1, a failed operation made recovery of the HR_INFO table space necessary.

Which of the following commands must be used to roll forward the table space?

- ○ A.   ROLLFORWARD DATABASE company TO END OF LOGS AND STOP TABLESPACE (emp_info)
- ○ B.   ROLLFORWARD DATABASE company TO END OF LOGS AND STOP TABLESPACE (hr_info)
- ○ C.   ROLLFORWARD DATABASE company TO END OF LOGS AND STOP TABLESPACE (emp_info TO hr_info)
- ○ D.   ROLLFORWARD DATABASE company TO END OF LOGS AND STOP TABLESPACE (RENAME emp_info TO hr_info)

Question 117

In a split mirror environment, which of the following commands is used to initialize a mirrored copy of a database named MYDB as a read-only clone of the primary database?

- ○ A.   db2inidb mydb AS SNAPSHOT
- ○ B.   db2inidb mydb AS MIRROR
- ○ C.   db2inidb mydb AS DUPLICATE
- ○ D.   db2inidb mydb AS STANDBY

Question 118

Which of the following is NOT a requirement for an HADR environment?

- ○ A.   The operating system on the primary server and the standby server must be the same (including fix pack level).
- ○ B.   The database path on the primary server and the standby server must be the same.
- ○ C.   The DB2 software version and bit size (32 or 64) used on the primary server and the standby server must be the same.
- ○ D.   Table spaces and table space containers on the primary server and the standby server must be identical.

Question 119

Which two of the following commands can be used to enable dual logging for a database named SAMPLE?

- ❏ A. db2set DB2_NEWLOGPATH=D:\logs_copy
- ❏ B. db2set DB2_NEWLOGPATH=1
- ❏ C. UPDATE DB CFG FOR sample USING failarchpath D:\ logs_copy
- ❏ D. UPDATE DB CFG FOR sample USING mirrorlogpath D:\ logs_copy
- ❏ E. UPDATE DB CFG FOR sample USING logarchmeth2 MIRRORPATH: D:\ logs_copy

Question 120

Which of the following commands will restore a database using information found in the recovery history log file?

- ○ A. RESTART DATABASE
- ○ B. RESTORE DATABASE
- ○ C. RECOVER DATABASE
- ○ D. REBUILD DATABASE

Question 121

Which of the following commands can be used to backup a database named PAYROLL, in such a way that workloads against the database are not impacted by more than 25%?

- ○ A. BACKUP DATABASE payroll ONLINE TO D:\backups UTIL_IMPACT_PRIORITY 25
- ○ B. BACKUP DATABASE payroll ONLINE TO D:\backups UTIL_IMPACT_LIM 25
- ○ C. BACKUP DATABASE payroll ONLINE TO D:\backups UTIL_IMPACT_PRIORITY 75
- ○ D. BACKUP DATABASE payroll ONLINE TO D:\backups UTIL_IMPACT_PRIORITY 75

Question 122

The following command was executed in an attempt to return a database named SAMPLE to the state it was in at 9:30 AM on July 1, 2007:

```
ROLLFORWARD DB sample TO 2007-07-01-09.30.00.000000 AND STOP
```

During execution, the following error was returned:

SQL4970N Roll-forward recovery on database SAMPLE cannot reach the specified stop point (end-of-log or point-in-time) because of missing or corrupted log file(s) on database partition(s) "0". Roll-forward recovery processing has halted on log file S0000007.LOG.

Which of the following options can be added to the ROLLFORWARD command to resolve the problem?

○ A. END OF LOGS

○ B. OVERFLOW LOG PATH

○ C. ALTERNATE LOG PATH

○ D. MIRROR LOG PATH

Question 123

Which of the following commands will ensure that index creation, recreation, and reorganization operations against a database named SAMPLE will be logged so that indexes can be reconstructed during roll-forward recovery operations or high availability disaster recovery (HADR) log replay procedures?

○ A. UPDATE DB CFG FOR sample USING INDEXREC ON

○ B. UPDATE DB CFG FOR sample USING LOGINDEXMAINT ON

○ C. UPDATE DB CFG FOR sample USING INDEXOPS ON

○ D. UPDATE DB CFG FOR sample USING LOGINDEXBUILD ON

Question 124

If the following SQL statement is executed:

```
UPDATE DB CFG FOR sample USING BLK_LOG_DSK_FUL YES
```

What will happen?

○ A. The SAMPLE database will be configured to use infinite logging.

○ B. The SAMPLE database will not automatically allocate additional storage space when the active log directory becomes full.

○ C. Log files for the SAMPLE database will be backed up automatically whenever a full backup image of the SAMPLE database is made.

○ D. Transactions running against the SAMPLE database will not be rolled back if they receive a disk full error.

Question 125

A power failure occurred while several applications were interacting with a database named SAMPLE. When power was restored, the database could not be restarted because a user temporary table space named USER_TMPTS is damaged. What must be done to successfully recover the database?

○ A.   Restart the database by executing the command RESTART DATABASE sample DROP PENDING TABLESPACES; drop and recreate the USER_TMPTS table space

○ B.   Restart the database by executing the command RESTART DATABASE sample DROP PENDING TABLESPACES; recreate the USER_TMPTS table space

○ C.   Restart the database by executing the command RESTART DATABASE sample DROP TABLESPACE (USER_TMPTS); recreate the USER_TMPTS table space

○ D.   Restart the database by executing the command RESTART DATABASE sample RECREATE TABLESPACES (USER_TMPTS)

Question 126

A database administrator has HADR enabled and wants to do a load operation on the primary server. If the LOAD command is executed with the COPY YES option specified and the copy of the loaded data created is written to a location that cannot be accessed by the standby database via the path provided with the LOAD command, what will happen?

○ A.   The load operation will fail on both the primary and the standby server.

○ B.   The load operation will automatically be converted to COPY NO and the standby database will be marked corrupt.

○ C.   The table space in which the table is stored is marked invalid on the standby database and the standby server will stop replaying log records that pertain to this table space.

○ D.   The table space in which the table is stored is marked invalid on the primary database and the primary server will stop sending log records that pertain to this table space to the standby server.

Question 127

While cleaning up files stored on an older AIX server, a database administrator found a shell script that contained the following commands:

```
db2 "RESTORE DATABASE sample FROM C:\backups TO
D:\DB_DIR INTO sample_2 REDIRECT"

db2 "SET TABLESPACE CONTAINERS FOR 0 USING
(PATH 'D:\DB_DIR\SYSTEM')"

db2 "SET TABLESPACE CONTAINERS FOR 1 USING
(PATH 'D:\DB_DIR\TEMP')"

db2 "SET TABLESPACE CONTAINERS FOR 2 USING
(PATH 'D:\DB_DIR\USER')"

db2 "RESTORE DATABASE sample CONTINUE"
```

What was this file designed to perform?

○ A.   A MULTIPLE TABLE SPACE RECOVERY OPERATION

○ B.   A REVERTED RESTORE OPERATION

○ C.   A PARTIAL TABLE SPACE RECONSTRUCTION OPERATION

○ D.   A REDIRECTED RESTORE OPERATION

Question 128

Which of the following statements about incremental backups is NOT true?

○ A.   The predecessor of an incremental backup image is always the most recent successful full backup image of the same object (database or table space).

○ B.   Database recovery involves restoring the database using the most recent full backup image available and applying each incremental backup image produced since the last full backup, in the order in which they were created.

○ C.   Before an incremental backup image can be created, a full backup image must already exist.

○ D.   Along with updated data and index pages, each incremental backup image also contains all of the initial database metadata that is normally found in a full database backup image.

Question 129

Which of the following statements about roll-forward recovery is NOT true?

○ A. Roll-forward recovery cannot be accomplished while users are connected to the database.

○ B. Recovery must be to a point in time that is greater than the minimum recovery time obtained with the LIST TABLESPACES command.

○ C. Recovery to a specific point in time can only be done on a database that is using archival logging.

○ D. By default, all recovery times specified are interpreted as Coordinated Universal Time (UTC)—otherwise known as Greenwich Mean Time (GMT) values.

Question 130

Which of the following commands can cause queries against a database named SAMPLE that utilize indexes to run slower than usual the first time they are executed after a crash recovery operation has been performed?

○ A. UPDATE DBM CFG USING INDEXREC ACCESS;
        UPDATE DB CFG FOR sample USING INDEXREC ACCESS;

○ B. UPDATE DBM CFG USING INDEXREC SYSTEM;
        UPDATE DB CFG FOR sample USING INDEXREC FIRSTEXEC;

○ C. UPDATE DBM CFG USING INDEXREC RESTART;
        UPDATE DB CFG FOR sample USING INDEXREC RESTART;

○ D. UPDATE DBM CFG USING INDEXREC FIRSTEXEC;
        UPDATE DB CFG FOR sample USING INDEXREC SYSTEM;

Question 131

Given two servers named SVR1 and SVR2 with a database named SALES on SRV1, in what order should the following steps be performed to set up an HADR environment using SRV2 as a standby server?

    a) Backup the SALES database on SVR1.
    b) Determine the host name, host IP address, and the service name or port number for SVR1 and SVR2.
    c) Start HADR on SVR2.
    d) Set the HADR configuration parameters on SVR1 and SVR2.
    e) Restore the SALES database on SVR2.
    f) Start HADR on SVR1.

○ A. b, a, e, d, f, c

○ B. b, d, f, c, a, e

○ C. b, a, e, d, c, f

○ D. f, c, b, d, a, e

Question 132

The LOG INDEX BUILD attribute for a table named EMPLOYEES was set to ON just before the table was populated with a load operation. If the database the EMPLOYEES table resides in has been configured for HADR, what will happen when the database fails over to the standby server?

- ○ A. Indexes defined for the EMPLOYEES table may be rebuilt.
- ○ B. Insert operations on the standby server (after the failover to the standby server) will take longer.
- ○ C. Indexes defined for the EMPLOYEES table will not be rebuilt.
- ○ D. An attempt to create a unique index on the EMPLOYEES table (after the failover to the standby server) will fail.

Security

Question 133

Which of the following identifies which users have SYSMAINT authority?

- ○ A. The DB2 registry
- ○ B. The DB2 Database Manager configuration
- ○ C. The database configuration
- ○ D. The system catalog

Question 134

Assuming USER1 has no authorities or privileges, which of the following will allow USER1 to create a view named VIEW1 that references two tables named TAB1 and TAB2?

- ○ A. CREATEIN privilege on the database
- ○ B. REFERENCES privilege on TAB1 and TAB2
- ○ C. CREATE_TAB privilege on the database
- ○ D. SELECT privilege on TAB1 and TAB2

Question 135

After the following SQL statement is executed:

    GRANT ALL PRIVILEGES ON TABLE employee TO USER user1

Assuming user USER1 has no other authorities or privileges, which of the following actions is USER1 allowed to perform?

- ○ A.   Drop an index on the EMPLOYEE table
- ○ B.   Grant all privileges on the EMPLOYEE table to other users
- ○ C.   Alter the table definition
- ○ D.   Drop the EMPLOYEE table

Question 136

Which of the following privileges allow a user to remove a foreign key that has been defined for a table?

- ○ A.   ALTER privilege on the table
- ○ B.   DELETE privilege on the table
- ○ C.   DROP privilege on the table
- ○ D.   UPDATE privilege on the table

Question 137

Which of the following is NOT used to limit access to individual rows in a table that is protected by Label-Based Access Control (LBAC)?

- ○ A.   One or more security profiles
- ○ B.   A security policy
- ○ C.   One or more security labels
- ○ D.   A DB2SECURITYLABEL column

Question 138

User USER1 wants to utilize an alias to remove rows from a table. Assuming USER1 has no authorities or privileges, which of the following privileges are needed?

- ○ A.   DELETE privilege on the table
- ○ B.   DELETE privilege on the alias
- ○ C.   DELETE privilege on the alias; REFERENCES privilege on the table
- ○ D.   REFERENCES privilege on the alias; DELETE privilege on the table

Question 139

Which of the following is NOT a security mechanism that is used to control access to DB2 data?

○ A. Authorization

○ B. Privileges

○ C. Validation

○ D. Authentication

Question 140

Which of the following identifies how authentication is performed for an instance?

○ A. The operating system used by the instance

○ B. The communications configuration used by the instance

○ C. The DB2 registry

○ D. The DB2 Database Manager configuration

Question 141

User USER1 wants to call an SQL stored procedure that dynamically retrieves data from a table. Which two privileges must user USER1 have in order to invoke the stored procedure?

❑ A. EXECUTE privilege on the stored procedure

❑ B. CALL privilege on the stored procedure

❑ C. SELECT privilege on the table the stored procedure retrieves data from

❑ D. EXECUTE privilege on the package for the stored procedure

❑ E. SELECT privilege on the stored procedure

Question 142

What does the following statement do?

```
GRANT ALTER ON SEQUENCE gen_empid TO user1 WITH GRANT OPTION
```

○ A. Gives USER1 the ability to change the comment associated with a sequence named GEN_EMPID, along with the ability to give this CONTROL authority for the sequence to other users and groups.

○ B. Gives USER1 the ability to change the values returned by the PREVIOUS_VALUE and NEXT_VALUE expressions associated with a sequence named GEN_EMPID, along with the ability to give CONTROL authority for the sequence to other users and groups.

○ C. Gives USER1 the ability to change the comment associated with a sequence named GEN_EMPID, along with the ability to give this authority to other users and groups.

○ D. Gives USER1 the ability to change the values returned by the PREVIOUS_VALUE and NEXT_VALUE expressions associated with a sequence named GEN_EMPID, along with the ability to give this authority to other users and groups.

Question 143

Which of the following statements is NOT true about DB2 security?

○ A. A custom security plug-in must be created if Microsoft Active Directory will be used to validate users.

○ B. Only users with Security Administrator authority are allowed to grant and revoke SETSESSIONUSER privileges.

○ C. Users and groups must exist before they can be granted privileges.

○ D. If a user holding SELECT privilege on a table creates a view based on that table and their SELECT privilege is later revoked, the view will become inoperative.

Question 144

Which of the following SQL statements allows a user named USER1 to write to LBAC-protected columns that have been secured with a LBAC label that indicates a lower level of security than that held by USER1?

○ A. GRANT EXCEPTION ON RULE DB2LBACWRITEARRAY WRITEDOWN FOR sec_policy TO USER user1

○ B. GRANT EXEMPTION ON RULE DB2LBACWRITEARRAY WRITEDOWN FOR sec_policy TO USER user1

○ C. GRANT EXCEPTION ON RULE DB2LBACWRITEARRAY WRITEUP FOR sec_policy TO USER user1

○ D. GRANT EXEMPTION ON RULE DB2LBACWRITEARRAY WRITEUP FOR sec_policy TO USER user1

Question 145

Which of the following database privileges are NOT automatically granted to the group PUBLIC when a database is created?

○ A.   CONNECT

○ B.   BINDADD

○ C.   IMPLICIT_SCHEMA

○ D.   CREATE_EXTERNAL_ROUTINE

Question 146

A user named USER1 is granted DBADM authority. Assuming no other authorities/privileges have been granted and all privileges have been revoked from the group PUBLIC, if the following SQL statement is executed:

```
REVOKE DBADM ON DATABASE FROM user1
```

What authorities/privileges will user USER1 have?

○ A.   None

○ B.   CONNECT

○ C.   SYSCTRL

○ D.   CREATETAB

Question 147

User USER1 needs to remove a view named ORDERS_V, which is based on a table named ORDERS, from the SALES database. Assuming user USER1 does not hold any privileges, which of the following privileges must be granted before user USER1 will be allowed to drop the view?

○ A.   DROP privilege on the ORDERS_V view

○ B.   CONTROL privilege on the ORDERS table

○ C.   DROP privilege on the ORDERS_V view

○ D.   CONTROL privilege on the ORDERS_V view

Question 148

Which of the following privileges allows a user to generate a package for an embedded SQL application and store it in a database?

○ A. BIND

○ B. BINDADD

○ C. CREATE_EXTERNAL_ROUTINE

○ D. CREATE_NOT_FENCED_ROUTINE

Question 149

User USER1 has the privileges needed to invoke a stored procedure named GEN_RESUME. User USER2 needs to be able to call the procedure—user USER1 and all members of the group PUBLIC should no longer be allowed to call the procedure. Which of the following statement(s) can be used to accomplish this?

○ A. GRANT EXECUTE ON ROUTINE gen_resume TO user2 EXCLUDE
user1, PUBLIC

○ B. GRANT EXECUTE ON PROCEDURE gen_resume TO user2;
REVOKE EXECUTE ON PROCEDURE gen_resume FROM user1, PUBLIC;

○ C. GRANT CALL ON ROUTINE gen_resume TO user2 EXCLUDE user1,
PUBLIC

○ D. GRANT CALL ON PROCEDURE gen_resume TO user2;
REVOKE CALL ON PROCEDURE gen_resume FROM user1, PUBLIC;

Question 150

Which of the following statements is NOT true about Label-Based Access Control (LBAC)?

○ A. LBAC can be used to restrict access to individual rows and columns.

○ B. Users that have been granted different LBAC security labels will get
different results when they execute the same query.

○ C. Only users with SYSADM or SECADM authority are allowed to create
security policies and security labels.

○ D. Security label components represent criteria that may be used to decide
whether a user should have access to specific data.

Answers

DB2 Server Management

Question 1

The correct answer is **C**. The default instance for a system is defined by the DB2INSTANCE environment variable and in many cases this is the instance that all instance-level operations are performed against. If you need to perform an operation against a different instance, you must first change the value assigned to the DB2INSTANCE variable (by executing the command set DB2INSTANCE=[*InstanceName*] (export DB2INSTANCE=[*InstanceName*] on Linux and UNIX) where *InstanceName* is the name assigned to the instance that you want to make the default instance or you must *attach* to that instance. Applications and users can attach to any instance by executing the ATTACH command.

Question 2

The correct answer is **B**. The MAXCAGENTS DB2 Database Manager configuration parameter is used to specify the maximum number of DB2 Database Manager agents that can be concurrently executing a DB2 Database Manager transaction. (An agent facilitates the operations between the application and the database.) NUM_INITAGENTS specifies the initial number of idle agents that are to be created in the agent pool when the DB2 Database Manager is started; MAX_COORDAGENTS specifies the maximum number of coordinating agents that can exist on a node at one time; and MAXAGENTS specifies the maximum number of DB2 Database Manager agents that can exist simultaneously, regardless of which database is being used.

Question 3

The correct answer is **C**. The value assigned to a particular database configuration file parameter can be changed by executing the UPDATE DATABASE CONFIGURATION command. The syntax for this command is:

```
UPDATE [DATABASE | DB]
[CONFIGURATION | CONFIG | CFG]
```

```
FOR [DatabaseAlias]
USING [[Parameter] [Value] |
       [Parameter] [Value] AUTOMATIC |
       [Parameter] AUTOMATIC |
       [Parameter] MANUAL ,...]
<IMMEDIATE | DEFERRED>
```

where:

DatabaseAlias   Identifies the alias assigned to the database that configuration information is to be modified for.

Parameter   Identifies one or more database configuration parameters (by keyword) whose values are to be modified. (In many cases, the keyword for a parameter is the same as the parameter name itself.)

Value   Identifies the new value(s) that are to be assigned to the database configuration parameter(s) specified.

If the DEFERRED clause is specified with the UPDATE DATABASE CONFIGURATION command, changes made to the database configuration file will not take until all connections to the corresponding database with have been terminated and a new connection is established. If the IMMEDIATE clause is specified instead, or if neither clause is specified, all changes made to the database configuration file will take effect immediately—provided the necessary resources are available.

Question 4

The correct answer is **C**. In addition to enabling remote administration of DB2 servers, the DAS instance assists the Control Center and the Configuration Assistant in providing a means for discovering information about the configuration of other DAS instances, DB2 instances, and databases using DB2 Discovery. (The Configuration Assistant and the Control Center use such information to simplify and automate the configuration of client connections to DB2 servers; neither tool will be able to "discover" a server if the DAS instance for that server is not running.) If the *discover* DAS configuration parameter is set to SEARCH, the server will respond to both search and known discovery requests; if this parameter is set to KNOWN, the server will only respond to known discovery requests; and if this parameter is set to DISABLE, the server will not respond to discovery requests.

A database can be "hidden" from a discovery request by setting its *discover_db* configuration parameter to DISABLE. (By default, this configuration parameter is set to ENABLE.)

Question 5

The correct answer is **C**. The EXEC_ESP_TASK DAS configuration parameter is used to identify whether or not expired tasks are to be executed when the Scheduler is turned on. (The Scheduler only detects expired tasks when it is started.) For example, if you have a job scheduled to run every Saturday, and the Scheduler is turned off on Friday and then restarted on Monday, the job scheduled for Saturday is now an expired task. If EXEC_EXP_TASK DAS configuration parameter is set to YES, the Saturday job will run immediately when the Scheduler is restarted. JOURNAL_TASKS and SCHED_RESTART are not valid DAS configuration parameters; the SCHED_ENABLE DAS configuration parameter is used to identify whether or not the Scheduler is running.

Question 6

The correct answer is **A**. Changes made by the Self Tuning Memory Manager are recorded in memory tuning log files, which reside in the *stmmlog* subdirectory of the instance. (The first file created will be assigned the name *stmm.0.log*, the second will be assigned the name *stmm.1.log*, and so on.) Each memory tuning log file contains summaries of the resource demands for each memory consumer at the time a tuning operation was performed. Tuning intervals can be determined by examining the timestamps for the entries made in the memory tuning log files.

Question 7

The correct answer is **A**. Only users with System Administrator (SYSADM) authority or System Control (SYSCTRL) authority are allowed to quiesce an instance. Once an instance has been placed in a quiesced state, only users with System Administrator (SYSADM), System Control (SYSCTRL), or System Maintenance (SYSMAINT) authority, users who are members of the group specified (if a group name was specified when the instance was placed in quiesced mode), and users with the user name specified (if a user name was specified when the instance was placed in quiesced mode) are allowed to connect to the instance.

Question 8

The correct answer is **B**. The db2set system command is used to determine which registry variables have been set and what they have been set to, or to assign values to one or more registry variables. The –g option indicates that a global profile variable is to be displayed, set, or removed so Answer B is correct. The –all option indicates that all occurrences of the registry variable (environment, node, instance, and global) are to be displayed, so answer C is not valid and answer A will only set the DB2COMM variable for the default instance.

Question 9

The correct answer is **C**. The SHEAPTHRESH DB2 Database Manager configuration parameter is used to specify the instance-wide soft limit on the total amount of memory (in pages) that is to be made available for sorting operations; the SORTHEAP database configuration is used to specify the maximum number of private memory pages to be used for private sorts, or the maximum number of shared memory pages to be used for shared sorts. Each sort operation consumes 10 MB or 2,500 pages (10,000 K / 4K page size = 2,500 4K pages). The total amount of memory available for sorts is 37,500 pages and each sort operation can consume up to 2,500 pages of memory, so 37,500 / 2,500 = 15.

Question 10

The correct answer is **A**. The AUTOCONFIGURE command (and the Design Advisor) will always recommend that a database be configured to take advantage of the Self Tuning Memory Manager. However, if you run the AUTOCONFIGURE command against a database in an instance where the SHEAPTHRES configuration parameter has been assigned a value other than zero, the sort memory heap database configuration parameter (SORTHEAP) will not be configured for automatic tuning. Therefore, you must execute the command UPDATE DATABASE MANAGER CONFIGURATION USING SHEAPTHRES 0 before you execute the AUTOCONFIGURE command if you want to enable sort memory tuning.

Question 11

The correct answer is **B**. In order to use the Task Center, you must first create a set of tables known as the tools catalog. If you did not create a tools catalog when you installed DB2, you can create one by executing the CREATE TOOLS CATALOG command. The tools catalog can reside in its own database, or in a database that contains other data.

Question 12

The correct answer is **C**. To control utility throttling, you must establish an impact policy. The impact policy refers to the instance-wide limit that all throttled utilities can cumulatively have on the production workload; once such a policy is established, it's the system's responsibility to ensure that the policy is obeyed. The impact policy for all throttling-enabled utilities running within an instance is controlled through the *util_impact_lim* DB2 Database Manager configuration parameter. (This parameter is dynamic, so it can be changed without stopping and restarting the instance; it can even be set while throttling-enabled utilities are running.) To define the impact policy for *all* throttled utilities, you simply assign a value between 1 and 100 to the *util_impact_lim* configuration parameter.

Thus, to set the instance-wide limit that all throttled utilities can cumulatively have on a production workloads to 20 percent (or in other words, to ensure performance degradation from all throttled utilities will not impact the system workload by more than 20 percent), you would assign the *util_impact_lim* configuration parameter the value 20 by executing an UPDATE DATABASE MANAGER CONFIGURATION command that looks like this:

```
UPDATE DATABASE MANAGER CONFIGURATION USING UTIL_IMPACT_LIM 20
```

In this example, it is assumed that the backup operation is the only utility running.

Question 13

The correct answer is **C**. Every entry in the administration notification log file and the DB2 diagnostic log file begins with a specific set of values that are intended to help identify the particular event the entry corresponds to. Because this block of information is recorded for all entries and because it is always recorded in a specific format, it is referred to as the *entry header*. Figure B–1 illustrates how a typical administration notification log entry header looks.

All entry headers consist of the following components (refer to the numbered bullets in Figure B–1):

```
❶ 2007-04-27-13.59.03.745000-240  ❷ I1907855H435   ❸ LEVEL: Info
❹ PID     : 3072                   ❺ TID : 3512      ❻ PROC : db2syscs.exe
❼ INSTANCE: DB2                     ❽ NODE : 000       ❾ DB   : SAMPLE
❿ APPHDL  : 0-514                   ⓫ APPID: *LOCAL.DB2.070427175900
⓬ AUTHID  : RSANDERS
⓭ FUNCTION: DB2 UDB, buffer pool services, sqlbAlterBufferPoolAct, probe:90
⓮ MESSAGE : Altering bufferpool "IBMDEFAULTBP" From: "250" To: "350" <automatic>
```

Figure B–1 Individual components of an administration notification log/DB2 diagnostic log entry header.

0.   A timestamp that identifies when the entry was made.

1.   The db2diag.log file's record ID. This ID specifies the file offset at which the current message is being logged (for example, "907855") and the message length (for example, "435") for the platform where the DB2 diagnostic log was created.

2.   The diagnostic level associated with the error message. Valid values are: Info, Warning, Error, Severe, and Event.

3. The unique identifier that has been assigned (by the operating system) to the process that generated the entry. This value is more applicable in a UNIX environment where DB2 operates using multiple processes. In a Windows environment, DB2 operates with multiple threads rather than multiple processes; therefore, the process ID provided is usually that of the main DB2 executable. (If the application is operating in a Distributed Unit Of Work (DUOW) environment, the Process ID shown will be the DUOW correlation token.)

4. The unique identifier that has been assigned (by the operating system) to the thread that generated the entry.

5. The name of the process that generated the entry.

6. The name of the instance that generated the entry.

7. The number that corresponds to the node that generated the entry. If a non-partitioned database is being used, the node number will always be 000.

8. The name of the database for which the entry was generated.

9. The application handle that has been assigned to the application for which the process that generated the event is working. This value consists of the coordinator partition number followed by the coordinator index number, separated by a dash.

10. The unique identifier that has been assigned to the application for which the process that generated the event is working. To find out more about a particular application ID:

   - Use the LIST APPLICATIONS command on a DB2 server or the LIST DCS APPLICATIONS command on a DB2 Connect gateway to obtain a list of application IDs. Search this list for the application ID; once found, you can obtain information about the client experiencing the error, such as its node name and its TCP/IP address.

   - Use the GET SNAPSHOT FOR APPLICATION command to view a list of application IDs.

   - Execute the command db2pd –applications -db [DatabaseName].

11. The authorization ID of the user who was working with the instance/database when the entry was generated

12. The product name ("DB2 UDB"), component name ("buffer pool services"), and function name ("sqlbAlterBufferPoolAct") that generated the message (as well as the probe point (90) within the function). If the entry was generated by a user application that executed the db2AdminMsgWrite() API, this component of the entry header will read "User Application." (Applications can write messages to the administration notification log file and the DB2 diagnostic log file by invoking the db2AdminMsgWrite() API.)

13. A message that describes the event that was logged.

Question 14

The correct answer is **B**. If they are not already running, the DB2 Database Manager background processes that are associated with a particular instance can be started by executing the START DATABASE MANAGER command. The basic syntax for this command is:

```
START [DATABASE MANAGER | DB MANAGER | DBM]
```

or

```
db2start </D>
```

Thus, if you wanted to start the DB2 Database Manager background processes for the default instance, (regardless of its name) you could do so by executing a command that looks like this:

```
START DB MANAGER
```

Question 15

The correct answer is **D**. You can remove the value assigned to any registry variable by providing just the variable name and the equal sign as input to the db2set command. Thus, if you wanted to disable the DB2COMM instance level registry variable for an instance named TEST, you could do so by executing a db2set command that looks like this:

```
db2set -i TEST DB2COMM=
```

Question 16

The correct answer is **A**. The contents of the database configuration file for a particular database can be displayed by executing the GET DATABASE CONFIGURATION command. The syntax for this command is:

```
GET [DATABASE | DB] [CONFIGURATION | CONFIG | CFG]
FOR [DatabaseAlias]
<SHOW DETAIL>
```

where:

DatabaseAlias   Identifies the alias assigned to the database that configuration information is to be displayed for.

Thus, if you wanted to view the contents of the database configuration file for a database named SAMPLE, you could do so by executing a GET DATABASE CONFIGURATION command that looks like this:

```
GET DB CFG FOR sample SHOW DETAIL
```

Question 17

The correct answer is **B**. The LOGARCHMETH1 database configuration parameter is used to specify the media type of the primary destination for archived log files and whether or not archival logging is to be used. If this parameter is set to OFF, circular logging is used and roll-forward recovery is not possible; if this parameter is set to LOGRETAIN, archival logging is used and roll-forward recovery is possible. The MIRRORLOGPATH database configuration parameter specifies the location where a second copy of active log files is to be stored.

NEWLOGPATH specifies an alternate path to use for storing recovery log files; LOGSECOND specifies the number of secondary log files that can be used for database recovery; and LOGARCHMETH2 specifies the media type of the secondary destination for archived logs.

Question 18

The correct answer is **B**. The LOCKTIMEOUT database configuration parameter is used to specify the number of seconds that an application will wait to obtain a lock—if this parameter is assigned the value -1, applications will wait indefinitely to obtain a needed lock. The LOCKLIST database configuration parameter is used to specify the maximum amount of memory (in pages) that is to be allocated and used to hold the lock list; the DLCHKTIME configuration parameter is used to specify the frequency at which the DB2 Database Manager checks for deadlocks among all applications connected to the database; and the MAXLOCKS configuration parameter is used to specify a percentage of the lock list held by an application that must be filled before the DB2 Database Manager performs lock escalation.

Question 19

The correct answer is **A**. If the IMMEDIATE clause is specified with the UPDATE DATABASE CONFIGURATION command, or if neither clause is specified, all changes made to the database configuration file will take effect immediately—provided the necessary resources are available. Applications running against a database at the time configuration changes are made will see the change the next time an SQL statement is executed.

Question 20

The correct answer is **D**. The AUTOCONFIGURE command is designed to capture specific information about your database environment and recommend and/or make changes to configuration parameters based upon the information provided. The basic syntax for this command is:

```
AUTOCONFIGURE
USING [ [Keyword] [Value] ,...]
APPLY [DB ONLY | DB AND DBM | NONE]
```

where:

Keyword   One or more special keywords that are recognized by the AUTOCONFIGURE command. Valid values include: mem_percent, workload_type, num_stmts, tpm, admin_priority, is_populated, num_local_apps, num_remote_apps, isolation, and bp_resizable.

Value   Identifies the value that associated with the keyword provided.

If the APPLY DB ONLY clause is specified with the AUTOCONFIGURE command, database configuration and buffer pool changes recommended by the Design Advisor will be applied to the appropriate database configuration file; if the APPLY DB AND DBM clause is specified, database configuration and buffer pool changes recommended will be applied to the database configuration file and instance configuration changes recommended will be applied to the appropriate DB2 Database Manager configuration file. If the APPLY NONE clause is specified instead, change recommendations will be displayed, but not applied.

Question 21

The correct answers are **A** and **C**. If you choose to manually configure communications, the steps you must follow can vary according to the communications protocol being used. For example, if you wanted to configure a server to use TCP/IP, you would have to perform the following steps:

1. Assign the value TCPIP to the DB2COMM registry variable.

   The value assigned to the DB2COMM registry variable is used to determine which communications managers will be activated when the DB2 Database Manager for a particular instance is started. The DB2COMM registry variable is assigned the value TCPIP by executing a db2set command that looks something like this:

   ```
   db2set DB2COMM=tcpip
   ```

2. Assign the name of the TCP/IP port that the database server will use to receive communications from remote clients to the *svcename* parameter of the DB2 Database Manager configuration file.

   The *svcename* parameter should be set to the service name associated with the main connection port so that when the database server is started, it can determine which port to listen on for incoming connection requests. This parameter is set by executing an UPDATE DATABASE MANAGER CONFIGURATION command that looks something like this:

   ```
   UPDATE DBM CFG USING SVCENAME db2c_db2inst1
   ```

3. Update the services file on the database server.

   The TCP/IP services file identifies the ports that server applications will listen on for client requests. If you specified a service name in the *svcename* parameter of the DB2 Database Manager configuration file, the appropriate service name-to-port number/protocol mapping must be added to the services file on the server. (If you specified a port number in the *svcename* parameter, the services file does not need to be updated.)

   An entry in the services file for a DB2 database server might look something like this:

   ```
   db2c_db2inst1        50001/tcp
   ```

Question 22

The correct answer is **B**. The *discover_inst* DB2 Database Manager configuration parameter is used to specify whether or not information about a particular instance found on a server will be included in the server's response to a discovery request. If this parameter is set to ENABLE, the server will include information about the instance in its response to both search and known discovery requests. If this parameter is set to DISABLE, the server will not include information about the instance (nor will it include information about any databases that come under the instance's control) in its response to discovery requests.

The *discover_db* database configuration parameter is used to specify whether or not information about a particular database found on a server will be included in the server's response to a discovery request. If this parameter is set to ENABLE, the server will include information about the database in its response to both search and known discovery requests. On the other hand, if this parameter is set to DISABLE, the server will not include information about the database in its response to discovery requests.

Question 23

The correct answer is **D**. Once created, the DB2 Diagnostics Log File (db2diag.log) grows continuously. As a result, the most recent entries are always found near the end of the file. If storage space for this file becomes an issue, the existing file can be deleted — a new db2diag.log file will be created automatically the next time one is needed. To aid in problem determination, DB2 9 provides a utility that can be used to filter and format the information available in the db2diag.log file. This utility is known as the db2diag utility and it is activated by executing the db2diag command.

There is no DB2DIAG_RESTART DB2 Database Manager configuration parameter.

Question 24

The correct answers are **A** and **D**. You can terminate one or more running applications prematurely by executing the FORCE APPLICATION command (assuming you have SYSADMN or SYSCTRL authority). The basic syntax for this command is:

```
FORCE APPLICATION ALL
```

or

```
FORCE APPLICATION ( [ApplicationHandle] ,... )
```

where:

ApplicationHandle   Identifies the handle associated with one or more applications whose instance attachments and/or database connections are to be terminated.

Thus, if you wanted to force all users and applications connected to databases stored on a server named DB_SERVER to terminate their database connections, you could do so by executing a FORCE APPLICATION command that looks something like this:

```
FORCE APPLICATION ALL
```

On the other hand, if you wanted to force a specific application whose handle is 148 to terminate its processing, you could do so by executing a FORCE APPLICATION command that looks like this:

```
FORCE APPLICATION (148)
```

Question 25

The correct answer is **D**. To a certain extent, the behavior of the task center is controlled through parameters found in the DAS instance configuration file. The SCHED_ENABLE DAS configuration parameter is used to identify whether or not the Scheduler is running. The Scheduler allows tools such as the Task Center to schedule and execute tasks at the administration server. Therefore, setting the SCHED_ENABLE parameter to OFF temporarily disables the Task Center.

Question 26

The correct answer is **B**. Automatic maintenance can be used to perform the following maintenance operations:

- **Create a backup image of the database.** Automatic database backup provides users with a solution to help ensure their database is being backed up both properly and regularly, without having to worry about when to back up, or having any knowledge of the syntax for the BACKUP command.

- **Data defragmentation (table or index reorganization).** This maintenance activity can increase the efficiency with which the DB2 Database Manager accesses tables. Automatic reorganization manages offline table and index reorganization without users having to worry about when and how to reorganize their data.

- **Data access optimization (running RUNSTATS).** The DB2 Database Manager updates the system catalog statistics on the data in a table, the data in a table's indexes, or the data in both a table and its indexes. The DB2 Optimizer uses these statistics to determine which path to use to access data in response to a query. Automatic statistics collection attempts to improve the performance of the database by maintaining up-to-date table statistics. The goal is to allow the DB2 Optimizer to always choose an access plan based on accurate statistics.

- **Statistics profiling.** Automatic statistics profiling advises when and how to collect table statistics by detecting outdated, missing, and incorrectly specified statistics and by generating statistical profiles based on query feedback.

Question 27

The correct answer is **A**. When a DB2 9 database is created, automatic maintenance is enabled by default. Enablement of the automatic maintenance features available for a database that is not using automatic maintenance is controlled via the automatic maintenance-specific database configuration parameters that are available (AUTO_MAINT, AUTO_DB_BACKUP, AUTO_TBL_MAINT, AUTO_RUNSTATS, AUTO_STATS_PROF, AUTO_PROF_UPD, and AUTO_REORG). These parameters represent a hierarchical set of switches that can be set to ON or OFF.

Question 28

The correct answer is **A**. If you want to change the impact priority (level of throttling) of a utility that is already running, you can do so by executing the SET UTIL_IMPACT_PRIORITY command. With this command, you can:

- throttle a running utility that was started in unthrottled mode

- unthrottle a running throttled utility (disable throttling)

- reprioritize a running throttled utility (this is useful if multiple simultaneous throttled utilities are running and one is more important than the others)

The syntax for the SET UTIL_IMPACT_PRIORITY command is:

```
SET UTIL_IMPACT_PRIORITY [UtilityID]
TO [Priority]
```

where:

UtilityID   Identifies the running utility, by ID, whose priority is to be changed. (The ID assigned to a running utility can be obtained by executing the LIST UTILITIES command.)

Priority   Specifies an instance-level limit on the impact associated with running the utility specified. A value of 100 represents the highest priority; a value of 1 represents the lowest. Setting *Priority* to 0 will force a throttled utility to continue running unthrottled; setting *Priority* to a non-zero value will force an unthrottled utility to continue running in throttled mode.

Thus, if you wanted force a throttled backup operation that has been assigned a utility ID of 1 to continue running unthrottled, you could do so by executing a SET UTIL_IMPACT_PRIORITY command that looks like this:

```
SET UTIL_IMPACT_PRIORITY 1 TO 0
```

Question 29

The correct answer is **C**. When a database has been enabled for self tuning, the memory tuner responds to significant changes in database workload characteristics, adjusting the values of memory configuration parameters and buffer pool sizes to optimize performance. The following memory consumers can be enabled for self tuning:

- Buffer pools (controlled by the ALTER BUFFERPOOL and CREATE BUFFERPOOL statements)

- Package cache (controlled by the *pckcachesz* configuration parameter)

- Locking memory (controlled by the *locklist* and *maxlocks* configuration parameters)

- Sort memory (controlled by the *sheapthers_shr* and the *sortheap* configuration parameter)

- Database shared memory (controlled by the *database_memory* configuration parameter)

Question 30

The correct answer is **C**. To find out more about the type of activity being performed by the function that produced an entry in the administration notification log, look at the fourth letter of its name. The following shows some of the letters used in the fourth position of DB2 function names, along with the type of activity each function performs:

b: Buffer pool management and manipulation.

c: Communications between clients and servers.

d: Data management.

e: Database engine processes.

o: Operating system calls (such as opening and closing files).

p: Data protection (such as locking and logging).

r: Relational database services.

s: Sorting operations.

x: Indexing operations.

Data Placement

Question 31

The correct answer is **C**. Whenever a new DB2 9 database is created, the following features are enabled by default:

- Automatic maintenance (database backups, table and index reorganization, data access optimization, and statistics profiling).

- Self tuning memory manager (package cache, locking memory, sort memory, database shared memory, and buffer pool memory)

- Utility throttling

- The Health Monitor

Question 32

The correct answer is **B**. The table space states available are shown in Table 1.

Table 1: Table Space States and Their Corresponding Hexadecimal Values	
Table Space State	**Hexadecimal Value**
Normal	0x0
Quiesced:SHARE	0x1
Quiesced:UPDATE	0x2
Quiesced:EXCLUSIVE	0x4
Load pending	0x8
Delete pending	0x10
Backup pending	0x20
Roll forward recovery in progress	0x40
Roll forward recovery pending	0x80
Restore pending	0x100
Recovery pending (no longer used)	0x100
Disable pending	0x200
Reorg in progress	0x400
Backup in progress	0x800
Storage must be defined	0x1000
Restore in progress	0x2000

Table 1: Table Space States and Their Corresponding Hexadecimal Values (continued)	
Table Space State	**Hexadecimal Value**
Restore in progress	0x2000
Offline and not accessible	0x4000
Drop pending	0x8000
Storage may be defined	0x2000000
StorDef is in 'Final 'state	0x4000000
StorDef was changed prior to roll forward recovery	0x8000000
DMS rebalancer is active	0x10000000
Table space deletion in progress	0x20000000
Table space creation in progress	0x40000000
Load in progress*	
A single table space can be in more than one state at a given point in time. If this is the case, multiple table space state hexadecimal values will be ANDed together to keep track of the multiple states. The Get Table Space State command (db2tbst) can be used to obtain the table space state associated with any given hexadecimal value. *The Load utility will place a table space in the "Load in progress" state if the COPY NO option is specified when data is being loaded into a recoverable database. The table space remains in this state for the duration of the load operation and is returned to normal state when the load operation completes. This state does not have a hexadecimal value.	

Question 33

The correct answer is **D**. A declared temporary table is a special table that is used to hold temporary data on behalf of a single application. Like base tables, indexes can be created on and statistics can be collected for declared temporary tables. Unlike base tables, whose descriptions and constraints are stored in the system catalog tables of the database to which they belong, declared temporary tables are not persistent and can only be used by the application that creates them—and only for the life of the application. When the application that creates a declared temporary table terminates, the rows of the table are deleted, and the description of the table is dropped. (However, data stored in a temporary table can exist across transaction boundaries.) Another significant difference focuses on where the data for each type of table is stored. Before an application can create and use a declared temporary table, at least one user temporary table space must be created for the database the application will be working with and the privileges needed to use that table space must be granted to the appropriate users. (User temporary table spaces are not created by default when a database is created.) Base tables, on the other hand are created in regular table spaces; if no table space is specified when a base table is created, its data is stored in the table space USERSPACE1, which is created by default when a database is created.

Question 34

The correct answer is **D**. Data from a given table is partitioned into multiple storage objects based on the specifications provided in the PARTITION BY clause of the CREATE TABLE statement. The syntax for this optional clause is:

```
PARTITION BY <RANGE>
    ([ColumnName] <NULLS LAST | NULLS FIRST> ,...)
    (STARTING <FROM>
            <(> [Start | MINVALUE | MAXVALUE] < ,...)>
            <INCLUSIVE | EXCLUSIVE>
      ENDING <AT>
            <(> [End | MINVALUE | MAXVALUE] < ,...)>
            <INCLUSIVE | EXCLUSIVE>
            EVERY <(>[Constant] <DurationLabel><)>
    )
```

or

```
PARTITION BY <RANGE>
    ([ColumnName] <NULLS LAST | NULLS FIRST> ,...)
    (<PARTITION [PartitionName]>
      STARTING <FROM>
            <(> [Start | MINVALUE | MAXVALUE] < ,...)>
            <INCLUSIVE | EXCLUSIVE>
      ENDING <AT>
            <(> [End | MINVALUE | MAXVALUE] < ,...)>
            <INCLUSIVE | EXCLUSIVE>
            <IN [TableSpaceName]>
    )
```

where:

ColumnName	Identifies one or more columns, by name, whose values are to be used to determine which data partition a particular row is to be stored in. (The group of columns specified make up the partitioning key for the table.)
PartitionName	Identifies the unique name that is to be assigned to the data partition to be created.
Start	Specifies the low end of the range for each data partition.
End	Specifies the high end of the range for each data partition.
Constant	Specifies the width of each data partition range when the automatically generated form of the syntax is used. Data partitions will be created starting at the STARTING FROM value and will contain this number of values in the range. This form of the syntax is only supported if the

partitioning key is comprised of a single column that has been assigned a numeric, date, time, or timestamp data type.

DurationLabel   Identifies the duration that is associated with the *Constant* value specified if the partitioning key column has been assigned a date, time, or timestamp data type. The following values are valid for this parameter: YEAR, YEARS, MONTH, MONTHS, DAY, DAYS, HOUR, HOURS, MINUTE, MINUTES, SECOND, SECONDS, MICROSECOND, and MICROSECONDS.

TableSpaceName   Identifies the table space that each data partition is to be stored in.

Thus, if you wanted to create a table named DEPARTMENTS that is partitioned such that rows with numerical values that fall in the range of 0 to 9 are stored in one partition that resides in one table space, rows with numerical values that fall in the range of 10 to 19 are stored in another partition that resides in another table space, and so on, you could do so by executing a CREATE TABLE SQL statement that looks something like this:

```
CREATE TABLE departments
     (dept_no    INT,
      desc       CHAR(3))
     PARTITION BY (dept_no NULLS FIRST)
          (STARTING  0 ENDING  9 IN tbsp0,
           STARTING 10 ENDING 19 IN tbsp1,
           STARTING 20 ENDING 29 IN tbsp2,
           STARTING 30 ENDING 39 IN tbsp3)
```

Question 35

The correct answers are **A** and **C**. Although a table can be enabled for data row compression at any time by setting its COMPRESS attribute to YES, data stored in the table will not be compressed until a compression dictionary has been built. A compression dictionary is built (and data in a table is compressed) by performing an offline table reorganization operation; such an operation is initiated by executing the REORG command with either the KEEPDICTIONARY or the RESETDICTIONARY option specified.

Because an offline reorganization operation is needed to construct a compression dictionary and perform data compression, the initial overhead required to compress data can be quite high. Therefore, it can be beneficial to know which tables will benefit the most from data row compression and which tables will not. In DB2 9, the Inspect utility can help you make that determination. The Inspect utility is invoked by executing the INSPECT command and if this command is executed with the ROWCOMPESTIMATE option specified, the Inspect utility will examine each row in the table specified, build a compression dictionary from the data found, and then use this dictionary to estimate how much space will be saved if the data in the table is compressed.

Question 36

The correct answer is **B**. Information about every DB2 9 database created is stored in a special hierarchical directory tree. Where this directory tree is actually created is determined by information provided with the CREATE DATABASE command—if no location information is provided, this directory tree is created in the location specified by the DFTDBPATH DB2 Database Manager configuration parameter associated with the instance the database is being created under. The root directory of this hierarchical tree is assigned the name of the instance the database is associated with. This directory will contain a subdirectory that has been assigned a name corresponding to the partition's node. If the database is a partitioned database, this directory will be named NODExxxx, where xxxx is the unique node number that has been assigned to the partition; if the database is a non-partitioned database, this directory will be named NODE0000. The node-name directory, in turn, will contain one subdirectory for each database that has been created, along with one subdirectory that contains the containers that are used to hold the database's data.

The name assigned to the subdirectory that holds the containers that are used to house the database's data is the same as that specified for the database; the name assigned to the subdirectory that contains the base files for the database corresponds to the database token that is assigned to the database during the creation process (the subdirectory for the first database created will be named SQL00001, the subdirectory for the second database will be named SQL00002, and so on).

Question 37

The correct answer is **B**. When multiple containers are used with SMS or DMS table spaces, the maximum amount of data that each container can hold is determined by the smallest container used. For example, if a table space uses one container that is 10M in size and a second container that is 12M in size, 2M of the second container will not be useable; the maximum amount of storage available to the table space will be 20M.

In this example, the smallest container used is 4 GB in size so the table space and 3 containers are used so the maximum size is: 3 x 4 GB = 12 GB.

Question 38

The correct answers are **B** and **D**. Information about all table spaces that have been created for a particular database can be obtained by executing the LIST TABLESPACES command. The syntax for this command is:

```
LIST TABLESPACES
<SHOW DETAIL>
```

If this command is executed without the SHOW DETAIL option specified, the following information will be displayed for every table space that has been created for a database:

- The internal ID that was assigned to the table space when it was created.

- The name that has been assigned to the table space.

- Table space type (SMS table space or DMS table space).

- The type of data the table space is designed to hold (i.e., regular data, large data, or temporary data).

- The current state of the table space.

On the other hand, if the LIST TABLESPACES command is executed with the SHOW DETAIL option specified, the following additional information about each table space is provided:

- **Total number of pages.** The total number of pages the table space is designed to hold. For DMS table spaces, this is the sum of all pages available from all containers associated with the table space. For SMS table spaces, this is the total amount of file space currently being used.

- **Number of useable pages.** The number of pages in the table space that user data can be stored in. For DMS table spaces, this number is calculated by subtracting the number of pages required for overhead from the total number of pages available. For SMS table spaces, this number is equal to the total number of pages the table space is designed to hold.

- **Number of used pages.** The number of pages in the table space that already contain data. (For SMS table spaces, this value is equal to the total number of pages the table space is designed to hold.)

- **Number of free pages.** The number of pages in the table space that are currently empty. (This information is only applicable for DMS table spaces.)

- **High water mark.** The number of pages that mark the current "high water mark" or "end" of the table space's address space (i.e., the page number of the first free page following the last allocated extent of the table space). (This information is only applicable to DMS table spaces.)

- **Page size.** The size, in bytes, that one page of data in the table space will occupy.

- **Extent size.** The number of pages that are contained in one extent of the table space.

- **Prefetch size.** The number of pages of data that will be read from the table space in advance of those pages currently being referenced by a query, in anticipation that they will be needed to resolve the query (prefetched).

- **Number of containers.** The number of containers used by the table space.

- **Minimum recovery time.** The earliest point in time that may be specified if a point-in-time roll-forward recovery operation is to be performed on the table space.

- **State change table space ID.** The ID of the table space that caused the table space being queried to be placed in the "Load Pending" or "Delete Pending" state. (This information is only displayed if the table space being queried has been placed in the "Load Pending" or "Delete Pending" state.)

- **State change object ID.** The ID of the object that caused the table space being queried to be placed in the "Load Pending" or "Delete Pending" state. (This information is only displayed if the table space being queried has been placed in the "Load Pending" or "Delete Pending" state.)

- **Number of quiescers.** The number of users and/or applications that have placed the table space in a "Quiesced" (restricted access) state. (This information is only displayed if the table space being queried has been placed in the "Quiesced:SHARE", "Quiesced:UPDATE" or "Quiesced:EXCLUSIVE" state.)

- **Table space ID and object ID for each quiescer.** The ID of the table spaces and objects that caused the table space being queried to be placed in a "Quiesced" state. (This information is only displayed if the number of users and/or applications that have placed the table space in a "Quiesced" state is greater than zero.)

You can also obtain detailed information about all table spaces that have been created for a particular database by capturing and displaying snapshot monitor data. The command that is used to capture table space-specific snapshot monitor information is:

```
GET SNAPSHOT FOR TABLESPACES ON [DatabaseAlias]
```

Question 39

The correct answer is **B**. While table spaces are used to physically store objects in a database, schemas are used to logically classify and group other objects in the database, regardless of where they are physically stored.

Question 40

The correct answer is **B**. In order to use data row compression with a table, two prerequisites must be satisfied:

1. Compression must be enabled at the table level.

2. A compression dictionary for the table must be built

Question 41

The correct answer is **B**. A compression dictionary is built (and data in a table is compressed) by performing an offline table reorganization operation; such an operation is initiated by executing the REORG command with either the KEEPDICTIONARY or the RESETDICTIONARY option specified. If the REORG command is executed with either option specified and a compression dictionary does not exist, a new dictionary will be built; if the REORG command is executed with either option specified and a dictionary already exists, data in the table will be reorganized/compressed and the existing dictionary will either be recreated (RESETDICTIONARY) or left as it is (KEEPDICTIONARY).

Question 42

The correct answer is **A**. Whenever a new database is created, by default, the following authorities and privileges are granted automatically:

- Database Administrator (DBADM) authority, along with CONNECT, CREATETAB, BINDADD, CREATE_NOT_FENCED, IMPLICIT_SCHEMA, and LOAD privileges, are granted to the user who created the database.

- USE privilege on the table space USERSPACE1 is granted to the group PUBLIC.

- CONNECT, CREATETAB, BINDADD, and IMPLICIT_SCHEMA privileges are granted to the group PUBLIC.

- SELECT privilege on each system catalog table is granted to the group PUBLIC.

- EXECUTE privilege on all procedures found in the SYSIBM schema is granted to the group PUBLIC.

- EXECUTE WITH GRANT privilege on all functions found in the SYSFUN schema is granted to the group PUBLIC.

- BIND and EXECUTE privileges for each successfully bound utility are granted to the group PUBLIC.

However, if the RESTRICTIVE clause is specified with the CREATE DATABASE command, privileges are only granted to the database creator—no privileges are granted to the group PUBLIC.

Question 43

The correct answer is **D**. In DB2 9, the initial allocation of space for an object in a DMS table space is two extents; the initial allocation of space for an object in an SMS table space is one extent. In this example, one extent is comprised of thirty-two 8 K pages or 256 KB (8 KB x 32 = 256 KB).

Question 44

The correct answer is **C**. If a database is enabled for automatic storage, the MANAGED BY AUTOMATIC STORAGE clause can be specified with the CREATE TABLESPACE command to create an automatic storage table space (or this clause can be left out completely; in which case automatic storage is implied). No container definitions are provided in this case because the DB2 Database Manager assigns the containers automatically.

Although automatic storage table spaces appear to be a different table space type, it is really just an extension of the existing SMS and DMS types. If the table space being created is a REGULAR or LARGE table space, it is created as a DMS with file containers. If the table space being created is a USER or SYSTEM TEMPORARY table space, it is created as an SMS with directory containers.

Question 45

The correct answer is **D**. The syntax for the CREATE DATABASE command used is this example can be broken down into something that looks like this:

```
CREATE [DATABASE | DB] [DatabaseName]
<AUTOMATIC STORAGE [YES | NO]>
<ON [StoragePath ,...] <DBPATH [DBPath]>>
<COLLATE USING [CollateType]>
<CATALOG TABLESPACE [TS_Definition]>
```

where:

DatabaseName	Identifies the unique name that is to be assigned to the database to be created.
StoragePath	If AUTOMATIC STORAGE YES is specified (the default), identifies one or more storage paths that are to be used to hold table space containers used by automatic storage. Otherwise, identifies the location (drive and/or directory) where the directory hierarchy and files associated with the database to be created are to be physically stored.
DBPath	If AUTOMATIC STORAGE YES is specified (the default), identifies the location (drive and/or directory) where the directory hierarchy and metadata files associated with the database to be created are to be physically stored. (If this parameter is not specified and automatic storage is used, the metadata files will be stored in the first storage path specified in the *StoragePath* parameter.)
CollateType	Specifies the collating sequence (i.e., the sequence in which characters are ordered for the purpose of sorting, merging, and making comparisons) that is to be used by the database to be created. The following values are valid for this parameter: COMPATABILITY, IDENTITY, IDENTITY_16BIT, UCA400_NO, UCA400_LSK, UCA400_LTH, NLSCHAR, and SYSTEM.
TS_Definition	Specifies the definition that is to be used to create the table space that will be used to hold the system catalog tables (SYSCATSPACE).

So in this case, automatic storage is enabled by default, and the storage paths /mnt/data1 and /mnt/data2 will be used to hold table space containers used by automatic storage. And since no database path was specified, the metadata files associated with the database will be stored in the first storage path specified (/mnt/data1).

Question 46

The correct answer is **C**. Additional containers cannot be added to an SMS table space (using the ALTER TABLESPACE SQL statement) once the table space has been created. (Additional containers can be added to a DMS table space after it has been created; when new containers are added, existing data can automatically be rebalanced across the new set of containers to retain optimal I/O efficiency.)

Question 47

The correct answer is **C**. When the documents specified are inserted into the CUSTINFO column of the CUSTOMER table, the values 27603 and 29501 will be added to the CUST_ZIP_IDX index and the value "Raleigh" will be added to the CUST_CITY_IDX index.

Question 48

The correct answer is **D**. Index data is not affected by data row compression; only data stored on a page in a base table can be compressed. However, because records in a compressed table are moved between storage and memory in compressed form (the compression dictionary is moved into memory as well so decompression can take place), records for compressed tables that are written to transaction log files will be compressed as well.

Question 49

The correct answer is **B**. If a database is enabled for automatic storage (which is the default behavior in DB2 9), container and space management characteristics of its table spaces are determined by the DB2 Database Manager. And, although the ALTER TABLESPACE command can be used to add new containers to existing DMS table spaces, it cannot be used to add new containers to automatic storage stable spaces. To perform this type of operation, you must use the ALTER DATABASE statement instead. The basic syntax for this statement is:

```
ALTER DATABASE [DatabaseName]
ADD STORAGE ON '[Container]' ,... )
```

where:

DatabaseName   Identifies the database, by name that is to have new containers added to its pool of containers that are used for automatic storage.

Container   Identifies one or more new storage locations (containers) that are to be added to the collection of storage locations that are used for automatic storage table spaces.

Thus, if you wanted to add the storage locations D:\data1 and D:\data2 to a database named SAMPLE that is configured for automatic storage and resides on a Windows system, you could do so by executing an ALTER DATABASE SQL statement that looks like this:

```
ALTER DATABASE sample ADD STORAGE ON 'D:\data1', 'D:\data2'
```

Question 50

The correct answer is **A**. DMS table spaces are made up of file containers or raw device containers, and their sizes are set when the containers are assigned to the table space. A table space is considered full when all of the space within the containers has been used. However, with DMS table spaces, you can add or extend containers using the ALTER TABLESPACE statement to provide more storage space to a given table space.

DMS table spaces also have a feature called "auto-resize." As space is consumed in a DMS table space that can be automatically resized, the DB2 Database Manager can automatically extend one or more file containers associated with the table space. (SMS table spaces have similar capabilities for growing automatically but the term "auto-resize" is used exclusively for DMS.) The auto-resize feature of a DMS table space is enabled by specifying the AUTORESIZE YES option with the CREATE TABLESPACE statement that is used to create the table space. For example, the following CREATE TABLESPACE statement could be used to create an auto-resize DMS table space:

```
CREATE TABLESPACE tbsp1 MANAGED BY DATABASE
     USING (FILE '/db2files/data1.dat' 10 M) AUTORESIZE YES
```

You can also enable the auto-resize feature after a DMS table space has been created by executing the ALTER TABLESPACE statement with the AUTORESIZE YES option specified. For example:

```
ALTER TABLESPACE tbsp1 AUTORESIZE YES
```

Question 51

The correct answer is **D**. If no schema/qualifier name is specified when an object is created, that object is assigned to the default schema, which is usually the user ID of the individual who is currently connected to the database and is creating the object. In this example, the default schema is DB2ADMIN because that is the user ID that was used to establish the database connection and create the TEST_TAB table object.

Question 52

The correct answer is **A**. Range-clustered tables require less cache buffer allocation because there are no secondary objects to maintain; indexes are not required nor are they supported.

Question 53

The correct answer is **A**. When an index is created for a range partitioned table, the data for that index will be stored in the table space that is used to hold the first partition's data, unless otherwise specified. Since, in the example, the following CREATE INDEX SQL statement was used to create an index for the SALES table:

```
CREATE INDEX sales_idx ON sales (invoice_no);)
```

Data for the index named SALES_IDX will be stored in the table space named TBSP0. If you wanted the index data to be stored in the table space that is used to hold the last partition's data (the table space named TBSP3), the following CREATE INDEX SQL statement would have to be executed instead:

```
CREATE INDEX sales_idx ON sales (invoice_no) IN tbsp3
```

Question 54

The correct answer is **B**. Just as an index over relational data can be used to improve query performance, an index over XML data can be used to improve the efficiency of queries on XML documents that are stored in an XML column. In contrast to traditional relational indexes, where index keys are composed of one or more columns you specify, an index over XML data uses a particular XML pattern expression to index paths and values found in XML documents stored in a single column—the data type of that column must be XML. All or part of the contents of an XML column can be indexed.

Database Access

Question 55

The correct answer is **D**. By default, records that are added to a base table can have the same values assigned to any of the columns available any number of times. DB2. The unique constraint can be used to ensure that the value(s) assigned to one or more columns when a record is added to a base table are always unique; once a unique constraint has been defined for one or more columns, any operation that attempts to place duplicate values in those columns will fail. Unique constraints are usually defined during the table creation process, but can be added later with the ALTER TABLE SQL statement.

When a unique constraint is defined the DB2 Database Manager looks to see if an index for the columns the unique constraint refers to already exists. If so, that index is marked as being unique and system-required. If not, an appropriate index is created and marked as being unique and system-required. This index is then used to enforce uniqueness whenever new records are added to the column(s) the unique constraint was defined for.

Although a unique, system-required index is used to enforce a unique constraint, there is a distinction between defining a unique constraint and creating a unique index. Even though both enforce uniqueness, a unique index allows NULL values and generally cannot be used in a referential constraint. A unique constraint on the other hand, does not allow NULL values and can be referenced in a foreign key specification.

Question 56

The correct answer is **D**. If the WITH LOCAL CHECK OPTION clause of the CREATE VIEW SQL statement is specified (or if the Local Check option is selected on the Create View dialog), insert and update operations performed against the view that is created are validated to ensure that all rows being inserted into or updated in the base table the view refers to conform to the view's definition (otherwise, the insert/update operation will fail). So what exactly does this mean? Suppose a view was created using the following CREATE VIEW statement:

```
CREATE VIEW priority_orders
AS SELECT * FROM orders WHERE response_time < 4
WITH LOCAL CHECK OPTION
```

Now, suppose a user tries to insert a record into this view that has a RESPONSE_TIME value of 6. The insert operation will fail because the record violates the view's definition. Had the view not been created with the WITH LOCAL CHECK OPTION clause, the insert operation would have been successful, even though the new record would not be visible to the view that was used to add it.

Question 57

The correct answer is **C**. If the UNIQUE clause is specified when the CREATE INDEX statement is executed, rows in the table associated with the index to be created must not have two or more occurrences of the same values in the set of columns that make up the index key. If the base table the index is to be created for contains data, this uniqueness is checked when the DB2 Database Manager attempts to create the index specified—if records with duplicate values for the index key are found, the index will not be created; if no duplicates are found, the index is created and uniqueness is enforced each time an insert or update operation is performed against the table.

In this example, records with duplicate SALES_REP_ID numbers were found when the CREATE INDEX statement was executed so the statement failed and the next insert operation was successful, bringing the total number of rows in the SALES table to 5.

Question 58

The correct answer is **B**. The Control Center interface presents itself using one of three different views:

> **Basic.** The basic view displays essential objects such as databases, tables, views, and stored procedures and limits the actions you can perform to those objects. This is the view you should use if you only want to perform core DB2 database operations.

> **Advanced.** The advanced view displays all objects available in the Control Center and allows you to perform all actions available. This is the view you should use if you are working in an enterprise environment and/or if you want to connect to DB2 for i5/OS or DB2 for z/OS.

> **Custom.** The custom view gives you the ability to tailor the object tree and actions allowed to meet your specific needs.

Question 59

The correct answer is **C**. The Command Line Processor (CLP) is a text-oriented application that allows users to issue DB2 commands, system commands, and SQL statements, as well as view the results of the statements/commands executed. Unlike most other Graphical User Interface tools available, the Command Line Processor cannot be invoked from the Control Center.

Question 60

The correct answer is **C**. To tell the DB2 Optimizer to ignore an informational constraint when selecting the best data access plan to use to resolve a query, you simply disable query optimization for the constraint. This can be done at the time the constraint is created, or it can be done later by executing an ALTER TABLE statement, identifying the constraint to be altered, and specifying the DISABLE QUERY OPTIMIZATION option.

Question 61

The correct answer is **D**. If the UNIQUE clause is specified when the CREATE INDEX statement is executed, rows in the table associated with the index to be created must not have two or more occurrences of the same values in the set of columns that make up the index key. The INCLUDE clause is used to identify one or more secondary columns whose values are to be stored with the values of the primary columns specified, but are not to be used to enforce data uniqueness.

Thus, if you wanted to create an index for a base table named TAB1 to improve the performance of a query that retrieves information from columns named C1, C2, and C3 while ensuring that all values entered into the C1 column are unique, you could do so by executing a CREATE INDEX statement that looks something like this:

```
CREATE UNIQUE INDEX indx1
ON tab1 (c1)
INCLUDE (c2, c3)
```

Question 62

The correct answer is **C**. The CARD column of the SYSCAT.TABLES system catalog table contains the number of rows found in each table the last time statistics were collected for the table. If this column contains the value -1 instead of the number of rows stored in the table, statistics have not been collected. Thus, if you wanted to know whether or not statistics have been collected for the EMPLOYEES table, you could find this out by executing a query against the system catalog that looks something like this:

```
SELECT TABNAME, CARD AS num_rows
FROM SYSCAT.TABLES
WHERE TABNAME = 'EMPLOYEES'
```

Question 63

The correct answer is **C**. The Activity Monitor is an interactive GUI application that allows users to monitor application performance, application concurrency, resource consumption, and SQL statement usage on a database or a database partition. With the Activity Monitor, you can:

- View transactions running on a selected application.

- View SQL statements running on a selected application.

- View the text of SQL statements running on a selected application.

- View locks and lock-waiting situations that currently affect a selected application.

- View information about a selected application for which you are viewing lock information.

- View information about the locks held and the locks waited on by a selected application in your database.

- View information to help you interpret report data.

- View recommendations provided by Activity Monitor.

In addition to collecting monitor data, the Activity Monitor can present the data collected using a set of predefined reports, which are based on a specific subset of monitor data. (For example, one report might contain a graphical representation that identifies a locking problem that's causing poor concurrency on a database.) Additionally, the Activity Monitor can make recommendations for most reports that will assist in diagnosing the cause of database performance problems, and in tuning queries for optimal utilization of database resources.

The Design Advisor captures specific information about typical workloads (queries or sets of SQL operations) performed against a database and recommends changes based upon the information provided; The Health Monitor constantly monitors the health of a DB2 Database Manager instance using several health indicators to evaluate specific aspects of instance and database performance; and the Configuration Assistant is an interactive GUI application that allows users to configure clients so they can access databases stored on remote DB2 servers.

Question 64

The correct answer is **B**. The Design Advisor is a special tool that is designed to capture specific information about typical workloads (queries or sets of SQL operations) performed against your database and recommend changes based upon the information provided. When given a set of SQL statements in a workload, the Design Advisor will make recommendations for:

- New indexes

- New materialized query tables (MQTs)

- Conversions of base tables to multidimensional clustering (MDC) tables

- Redistribution of table data

- Deletion of indexes and MQTs that are not being used by the specified workload

Because the Configuration Assistant maintains a list of databases to which users/applications can connect, it can act as a lightweight alternative to the Control Center in situations where the complete set of GUI tools available has not been installed. Therefore, it can be used to set DB2 environment/registry variables. The db2set command can also be used to set DB2 environment/registry variables and this command can be executed from the Command Editor or the Command Line Processor.

Question 65

The correct answer is **A**. Unlike other constraints, informational constraints are not enforced during insert and update processing. However, the DB2 SQL optimizer will evaluate information provided by an informational constraint when considering the best access plan to use to resolve a query. As a result, an informational constraint may result in better query performance even though the constraint itself will not be used to validate data entry/modification. (Informational constraints are defined by appending the keywords NOT ENFORCED ENABLE QUERY OPTIMIZATION to a normal constraint definition.)

Question 66

The correct answer is **C**. If you do not wish to recover an inoperative view, you can explicitly drop it with the DROP VIEW statement. Alternately, you can create a new view and assign it the same name as that of the inoperative view, but give it a different definition.

Question 67

The correct answer is **A**. Whenever an object is created, altered, or dropped, DB2 inserts, updates, or deletes records in the catalog that describe the object and how that object relates to other objects. Thus, if you want to obtain information about a particular database, often, you can do so by connecting to that database and querying the system catalog. For example, suppose you wanted to find out whether a table named EMPLOYEES needed to be reorganized to eliminate fragmentation. You could do so by executing a query against a system catalog table named SYSCAT.TABLES that looks something like this:

```
SELECT TABNAME, OVERFLOW FROM
FROM SYSCAT.TABLES
WHERE TABNAME = 'EMPLOYEES'
```

If the results of this query indicate that a high number of overflow records exist for the EMPLOYEES table, the data is fragmented and the table probably needs to be reorganized.

Question 68

The correct answer is **B**. The first INSERT statement will fail because the resulting SELLPRICE will be 0 (since no value was provided) and a SELLPRICE of 0 is less than a BUYPRICE of 6.99 which violates the ZEROLOSS check constraint. The third INSERT statement will fail because the CATEGORY '423' is not in the set of values that are allowed for the CATEGORY column. Also, the resulting SELLPRICE and BUYPRICE will be 0 (since no value was provided) and a SELLPRICE of 0 is not greater than a BUYPRICE of 0 which violates the ZEROLOSS check constraint. And finally, the last INSERT statement will fail because a SELLPRICE of 20.00 is less than a BUYPRICE of 25.65 which violates the ZEROLOSS check constraint.

Question 69

The correct answer is **D**. Because the DB2 Optimizer evaluates informational constraints when selecting the best data access plan to use to resolve a query, records that have been inserted into a table that violate one or more informational constraints may not be returned by some queries. Thus, if the query "SELECT * FROM employee WHERE gender = 'U'" were to be executed against the EMPLOYEE table shown, no records would be returned because the access plan chosen would assume that no records with a GENDER value of anything other than 'M' or 'F' exists in the table.

Question 70

The correct answer is **D**. While most objects can be created from the Control Center, if you have paid attention to the Control Center screen shots presented in this Chapter, you may have noticed that user-defined functions (UDFs) cannot. User-defined functions must be created by executing the CREATE FUNCTION SQL statement from the Command Line Processor or the Command Editor, or by using the DB2 Developer Workbench.

Question 71

The correct answer is **A**. Tools Settings notebook is an interactive GUI application that is used to customize settings and set properties for the various DB2 administration tools available. To present and collect this information in an organized manner, the Tools Settings notebook uses several different pages/tabs—some pages/tabs will only be displayed after the tools for which they apply have been installed. The pages available with the Tools Settings notebook are:

General page. This page is used to specify whether the local DB2 instance should be started automatically when the DB2 tools are started, whether to use a statement termination character, and whether to use filtering when the maximum number of rows returned for a display sample contents request is exceeded.

Documentation page. This page is used to specify whether hover help and infopop help features in the DB2 administration tools should display automatically, and also to specify the location from which the contextual help is accessed at the instance level.

Fonts page. This page is used to change the font in which text and menus appear in the DB2 administration tools.

OS/390 and z/OS page. This page is used to set column headings and define the online and batch utility execution options for OS/390 and z/OS objects.

Health Center Status Beacon page. This page is used to specify the type of notification you will receive when an alert is generated in the Health Monitor. You can be notified through a pop-up message or with the graphical beacon that displays on the lower-right portion of the status line for each DB2 center, or using both methods of notification.

Scheduler Settings page. This page is used to set the default scheduling scheme. Select Server Scheduling if you want task scheduling to be handled by the scheduler that is local to the database server; select Centralized Scheduling if you want the storage and scheduling of tasks to be handled by a centralized system, in which case you need to select the centralized system from the Centralized Scheduler list. (To enable another scheduler, select a system and click Create New to open a window in which you can create a database for the DB2 Tools Catalog on a cataloged system. If the system you want is not cataloged, you must catalog it first.)

Command Editor page. This page is used to specify how you will generate, edit, execute, and manipulate SQL and XQuery statements, IMS commands, and DB2 commands. This page is also used to specify how you want to work with the resulting output.

IMS page. This page is used to set your preferences when working with IMS. From this page, you can set preferences for using wizards, for syntax support, and for returning results.

The Replication Center is used to define replication environments.

Question 72

The correct answers are **A** and **C**. With DB2 9, several types of indexes are available:

Relational indexes. Indexes that are optimized for a single dimension.

Spatial Grid indexes. Indexes that are optimized for two dimensional data. (Each spatial grid index is created on the X and Y dimensions of a geometry; used by the DB2 Spatial Extender.)

Dynamic Bitmap indexes. Indexes that are produced by ANDing the results of multiple index scans using Dynamic Bitmap techniques. (ANDed predicates can be applied to multiple indexes to keep underlying table accesses to a minimum.)

Block Based indexes. Indexes that contain pointers to rows in a single dimension of a Multidimensional Clustering (MDC) table.

XML indexes. User-defined indexes over XML data that use a particular XML pattern (which is a limited XPath expression) to index paths and values in XML documents stored within a single column.

Question 73

The correct answer is **D**. If you create two indexes on the same table, one specifying ASC and the other DESC, and if you do not specify the DISALLOW REVERSE SCANS option in the CREATE INDEX statement used, both indexes will default to ALLOW REVERSE SCANS. As a result, the latter index will not be created and DB2 will issue a duplicate index warning message. (The ALLOW REVERSE SCANS option allows the same index to be used in two different queries that require the data to be in ascending and descending order.)

Question 74

The correct answer is **A**. The system catalog can only be used to obtain information about a specific database. If you want to obtain information at the system level, you must resort to executing administrative system commands or querying the administrative views available. For example, to obtain information about the DB2 products that have been installed on a particular server, you would have to execute the system command db2ls –q -a (if you are on a Linux or UNIX server).

When executed, the db2ls command lists the DB2 products and features installed on your system, including the DB2 Version 9 HTML documentation. You can use the db2ls command to find out where DB2 products are installed on a system, what DB2 product levels are installed, and what specific DB2 products and features were installed using a particular installation path.

Analyzing DB2 Activity

Question 75

The correct answer is **C**. Snapshot monitor switch settings can be changed at the instance level by modifying the appropriate DB2 Database Manager configuration parameters with the UPDATE DATABASE MANAGER CONFIGURATION command. Snapshot monitor switch settings made at the instance level remain persistent across instance restarts.

Snapshot monitor switch settings can be changed at the application level by executing the UPDATE MONITOR SWITCHES command. Switch settings made at the application level are not persistent across instance restarts.

Question 76

The correct answers are **A** and **C**. One way to collect Explain snapshot data for an SQL statement that is entered using the Command Line Processor is by executing the EXPLAIN SQL statement with the FOR SNAPSHOT option specified (followed by the SQL statement that Explain snapshot data is to be collected for). Another is by setting the value of the CURRENT EXPLAIN SNAPSHOT special register to YES or EXPLAIN, and then executing the desired SQL statements. (If the CURRENT EXPLAIN SNAPSHOT special register is set to EXPLAIN, Explain snapshot data will be collected and the specified statement will not be executed; if the CURRENT EXPLAIN SNAPSHOT special register is set to YES, Explain snapshot data will be collected and the statement will be executed as well.)

Question 77

The correct answer is **B**. The snapshot monitor switches, together with the options available with the GET SNAPSHOT command, determine the type and volume of data that will be returned when a snapshot is taken. If a particular snapshot monitor switch has not been turned on and a snapshot of the monitoring data that is associated with that switch is taken, the monitoring data captured may not contain any values at all. (If you look closely at the snapshot monitoring data collected and notice that some values were "Not Collected," chances are the corresponding snapshot monitor switch was turned off when the snapshot was taken. In this example, when the snapshot of LOCK information was taken, the LOCK snapshot monitor switch was turned off.

Question 78

The correct answer is **C**. While there is no limit to the number of event monitors that can be defined for a single database, no more than 32 event monitors can be active at one time.

Question 79

The correct answer is **C**. The NLJOIN operator in a Visual Explain access plan graph represents a nested-loop join that accesses an inner table once for each row of the outer table. Nested-loop joins are preferred for join operations performed in an OLTP environment.

Question 80

The correct answer is **B**. The DB2 Bind File Description Tool can be used to examine and to verify the SQL statements within a bind file, as well as to display the precompile options used to create the bind file. The DB2 Bind File Description Tool is invoked by executing the db2bfd command.

Question 81

The correct answer is **C**. The DB2 Problem Determination tool (db2pd) is used to obtain quick and immediate information from the DB2 database system memory sets, without acquiring any latches. Two benefits to collecting information without latching include faster data retrieval and no competition for engine resources. However, because the DB2 Problem Determination tool works directly with memory, it is possible to retrieve information that is changing as it is being collected; hence the data retrieved might not be completely accurate. (A signal handler is used to prevent the DB2 Problem Determination tool from aborting abnormally when changing memory pointers are encountered. However, this can result in messages such as "Changing data structure forced command termination" to appear in the output produced.) Nonetheless, this tool can be extremely helpful for problem determination.

There is no minimum connection requirement for executing the db2pd command; if a database-level option is specified, that database must be active before the requested information can be returned. The db2pd command cannot be used to obtain information about a stopped instance.

Question 82

The correct answer is **A**. There may be times when it is desirable to reset all counters to zero without turning snapshot monitor switches off and back on and without terminating and reestablishing database connections. The easiest way to quickly reset all snapshot monitor counters to zero is by executing the RESET MONITOR command. The basic syntax for this command is:

```
RESET MONITOR ALL
```
or
```
RESET MONITOR FOR <DCS> [DATABASE | DB] [DatabaseAlias]
```

where:

DatabaseAlias   Identifies the alias assigned to the database that snapshot monitor counters are to be reset for.

Thus, if you wanted to reset the snapshot monitor counters for all databases under an instance's control to zero, you could do so by attaching to that instance and executing a RESET MONITOR command that looks like this:

```
RESET MONITOR ALL
```

On the other hand, if you wanted to reset just the snapshot monitor counters associated with a database named SAMPLE to zero, you could do so by executing a RESET MONITOR command that looks like this:

```
RESET MONITOR FOR DATABASE sample
```

Question 83

The correct answer is **C**. Only Explain snapshot data can be viewed by Visual Explain and since both EXPLAIN and EXPLSNAP are bind options, their setting has no affect on the application because it has already been bound to the database. (If the application had not been bound, setting the EXPLSNAP bind option to YES or ALL would have caused Explain snapshot data to be collected for the statements when the application was bound.) Therefore, the CURRENT EXPLAIN SNAPSHOT special register must be used to capture Explain snapshot data for the application and the correct way to set this register is by executing the SQL statement SET CURRENT EXPLAIN SNAPSHOT YES.

Question 84

The correct answer is **C**. Health indicator settings can be set at the instance level, global level, or object level. Instance level settings apply to the instance. Global settings apply to objects such as databases, table spaces, and table space containers in the instance that do not have customized settings defined. Object settings are customized settings that apply to individual objects such as databases, table spaces, and table space containers. Therefore, to generate an alert whenever the 3 GB files are 80% full and the 4GB files are 85% full, you would change the Global level settings for all table space containers (80% full) and then change the Object level settings for the 4 GB table space containers (85% full).

Question 85

The correct answer is **D**. The CURRENT QUERY OPTIMIZATION special register is used to control the class of optimization techniques used when binding dynamic SQL statements; the value of the can be changed by executing the SET CURRENT QUERY OPTIMIZATION SQL statement. The basic syntax for this statement is:

```
SET CURRENT QUERY OPTIMIZATION <=> [OptimizationLevel]
```

where:

OptimizationLevel   Specifies the optimization level (class) to use when preparing dynamic SQL statements. This parameter must be set to one of the following values.

- 0

  Specifies that a minimal amount of optimization techniques are to be used when the optimizer generates an access plan. This optimization class level is most suitable for simple dynamic SQL statements that access well-indexed tables.

- 1

  Specifies that the amount of optimization techniques to be used when the optimizer generates an access plan should be roughly equal to that provided by DB2 Version 1.

- 2

  Specifies that the amount of optimization techniques to be used when the optimizer generates an access plan should be higher than that provided by DB2 Version 1, but significantly less than those used by level 3 and higher.

- 3

  Specifies that a moderate amount of optimization techniques are to be used when the optimizer generates an access plan.

- 5

  Specifies that a significant amount of optimization techniques are to be used when the optimizer generates an access plan. For complex queries, heuristic rules are used to limit the amount of time spent selecting an access plan. Whenever possible, queries will use summary tables instead of underlying base tables. This is the default optimization class used by DB2.

- 7

  Specifies that a significant amount of optimization techniques are to be used when the optimizer generates an access plan. This level is similar to level 5; however, no heuristic rules are used to limit the amount of time spent selecting access plans for complex queries.

- 9

  Specifies that the maximum amount of optimization techniques are to be used when the optimizer generates an access plan. This optimization class can greatly expand the number of possible access paths that are evaluated before an access plan is chosen. For this reason, this class is typically used to process SQL statements that contain very complex and very long running queries that are executed against very large tables.

Therefore, if you wanted to tell the DB2 optimizer to use the maximum amount of optimization techniques available when generating access plans for dynamic SQL statements, you could do so by executing a SET CURRENT QUERY OPTIMIZATION statement that looks like this:

```
SET CURRENT QUERY OPTIMIZATION = 9
```

Question 86

The correct answer is **A**. The DB2 Problem Determination tool is used to obtain quick and immediate information from the DB2 database system memory sets, without acquiring any latches. The DB2 Problem Determination tool is invoked by executing the db2pd command. The basic syntax for this command is:

```
db2pd
<- version | -v >
<-inst>
<[-database | -db] [DatabaseName] ,...>
<-alldatabases | -alldbs>
<-full>
<-everything>
<-hadr [-db [DatabaseName] | -alldbs]>
<-utilities>
```

```
<-applications [-db [DatabaseName] | -alldbs]>
<-agents>
<-transactions [-db [DatabaseName] | -alldbs]>
<-bufferpools [-db [DatabaseName] | -alldbs]>
<-logs [-db [DatabaseName] | -alldbs]>
<-tablespaces [-db [DatabaseName] | -alldbs]>
<-dynamic [-db [DatabaseName] | -alldbs]>
<-static [-db [DatabaseName] | -alldbs]>
<-fcm>
<-memsets>
<-mempools>
<-memblocks>
<-dbmcfg>
<-dbcfg [-db [DatabaseName] | -alldbs]>
<-catalogcache [-db [DatabaseName] | -alldbs]>
<-tcbstats [-db [DatabaseName] | -alldbs]>
<-reorg [-db [DatabaseName] | -alldbs]>
<-recovery [-db [DatabaseName] | -alldbs]>
<-reopt [-db [DatabaseName] | -alldbs]>
<-osinfo>
<-storagepaths [-db [DatabaseName] | -alldbs]>
<-pages [-db [DatabaseName] | -alldbs]>
<-stack [all | [ProcessID]]>
<-repeat [Interval] <[Count]>>
<-command [CmdFileName]>
<-file [OutFileName]>
<-interactive>
<-h | -help>
```

where:

DatabaseName	Identifies, by name, the database the DB2 Problem Determination tool is to interact with.
ProcessID	Identifies the process, by ID, that a stack trace file is to be produced for.
Interval	Identifies the number of seconds to wait between subsequent calls to the DB2 Problem Determination tool.
Count	Identifies the number of times to repeat calls to the DB2 Problem Determination tool.
CmdFileName	Identifies the name assigned to an ASCII format file that contains DB2 Problem Determination tool command options that are to be used.
OutFile	Identifies the name of the file that information returned by the DB2 Problem Determination tool is to be written to.

So, if you wanted to find out how many pages have been written to the transaction log files associated with a database named SAMPLE, you could do so by executing a db2pd command that looks something like this:

```
db2pd -logs -db sample
```

Question 87

The correct answer is **D**. With earlier versions of DB2, the only way to capture snapshot monitor data was by executing the GET SNAPSHOT command or by calling its corresponding API from an application program. With DB2 UDB version 8.1, the ability to capture snapshot monitor data by constructing a query that referenced one of 20 snapshot monitor table functions available was introduced. If you wanted to take a snapshot that contains data collected on buffer pools associated with the current connected database using the DB2 V8.1 SNAPSHOT_BP() snapshot monitor table function, you could do so by executing the following query:

```
SELECT * FROM TABLE (SNAPSHOT_BP
        (CAST (NULL AS CHAR), -1) AS snap_info
```

Although these functions are still available and can be used in DB2 9, they have been depreciated. Now, snapshot monitor data can be obtained by querying special administrative views or by using a new set of SQL table functions. Each DB2 9 snapshot monitor table function returns the same information as the corresponding administrative view, but the function allows you to retrieve information for a specific database instead of the current connected database. (If no database is specified when a snapshot monitor table function is used, you must be connected to the appropriate database.) The syntax used to construct a query that references a DB2 9 snapshot monitor table function is the same as that used to reference a DB2 8.1 function—only the function names have changed. Therefore, if you wanted to obtain snapshot monitor buffer pool information for a database named SAMPLE using the SNAP_GET_BP() table function you could do so by constructing a query that looks something like this:

```
SELECT * FROM TABLE(SNAP_GET_BP('sample', -1)) AS snap_info
```

Question 88

The correct answer is **B**. If you are familiar with the concept of deadlocks, you may recall that a special process known as the deadlock detector runs quietly in the background and "wakes up" at predefined intervals to scan the locking system in search of a deadlock cycle. If a deadlock cycle exists, the deadlock detector randomly selects one of the transactions involved in the cycle to roll back and terminate. (The transaction that is rolled back and terminated receives an SQL error code, all locks it had acquired are released, and the remaining transaction(s) are then allowed to proceed.) Information about such a series of events can be captured, the moment the deadlock cycle is detected.

By default, whenever a DB2 9 database is created, a deadlock event monitor is defined for that database and this event monitor is activated when a connection to the database is first established, or whenever the database is activated.

Question 89

The correct answer is **A**. Health indicator settings can be set at the instance level, global level, or object level. Instance level settings apply to the instance. Global settings apply to objects such as databases, table spaces, and table space containers in the instance that do not have customized settings defined. Object settings are customized settings that apply to individual objects such as databases, table spaces, and table space containers.

Question 90

The correct answer is **B**. Data collected by event monitors is streamed to buffers before it is externalized to disk (i.e. written to a table or file). If the BLOCKED option is specified with the CREATE EVENT MONITOR command, agents that generate an event that is being monitored will wait for an event buffer to be written to disk before continuing if it determines that both event buffers are full. As a result, although BLOCKED event monitors guarantee that no event monitor data will be lost, their behavior can increase application response time since any suspended agents (along with any dependent agents) will only be allowed to run when the event monitor buffers are clear. If the NONBLOCKED option is specified instead, agents that generate an event that is being monitored will not wait for an event buffer to be written to disk before continuing if it determines that both event buffers are full. Thus, NONBLOCKED event monitors perform faster than BLOCKED event monitors, but are subject to data loss on highly active systems. (If neither option is specified, the event monitor created will be a BLOCKED event monitor.)

Question 91

The correct answers are **A** and **E**. The Health Center is a GUI tool that is designed to interact with the Health Monitor. Using the Health Center, you can select the instance and database objects that you want to monitor, customize the threshold settings of any health indicator, specify where notifications are to be sent, and specify what actions are to be taken if an alert is raised. The Health Center also allows you to start and stop the Health Monitor, view the current status of the database environment, access details about current alerts, obtain a list of recommended actions for resolving any alerts that have been raised, and view a history of alerts that have been generated for an instance or a database.

Question 92

The correct answers are **B** and **D**. When Explain information is collected, the resulting data is stored in one or more Explain tables. You could construct a query to retrieve this data, but a better way to view the Explain information collected is by using one of the Explain Facility tools that have been designed specifically for presenting explain information in a meaningful format. This set of tools is comprised of:

- The db2expln tool

- The db2exfmt tool

- Visual Explain

Question 93

The correct answer is **A**. The HSJOIN operator in a Visual Explain access plan graph represents a hash join, where two or more tables are hashed on the join columns. Hash joins are preferred for join operations performed in a decision support environment.

Question 94

The correct answer is **C**. The DB2 memory tracker utility is used to produce a complete report of memory status for instances, databases and agents. This utility provides the following information about memory pool allocation:

- Current size

- Maximum size (hard limit)

- Largest size (high water mark)

- Type (identifier indicating function for which memory will be used)

- Agent who allocated pool (only if the pool is private)

(This information is also available from the Snapshot monitor.)

The DB2 memory tracker is invoked by executing the db2mtrk command.

DB2 Utilities

Question 95

The correct answer is **C**. If the IMPORT command is executed with the ALLOW WRITE ACCESS option specified, the Import utility will request a table lock after every commit operation is performed. This can cause an import operation to run slowly in environments that have high concurrency. That is not the case if the ALLOW NO ACCESS option is specified. (There is no ALLOW READ ACCESS or ALLOW FULL ACCESS option.)

Question 96

The correct answer is **D**. The Load utility can be used to delete all records in a table without generating corresponding log records by specifying the null device as the input file and invoking the LOAD with the REPLACE option specified. On UNIX the null device is */dev/null*, on Windows it is *nul*. Thus, the following commands could be used to delete all records found in a table named DEPARTMENT:

```
LOAD FROM /dev/null OF DEL REPLACE INTO department (UNIX)

LOAD FROM nul OF DEL REPLACE INTO department (Windows)
```

Question 97

The correct answer is **C**. During the delete phase of a load operation, any rows that violated primary and/or unique key constraints defined on the target table are removed and copied to an exception table (if appropriate) and a message about each offending row is written to the appropriate message file so it can be modified and manually moved to the target table at some point in the future. Since the data in this example contains two records that have an employee ID value of 100, and because the EMPID column in the EMPLOYEES table is a primary key, the first record will be loaded into the EMPLOYEES table and the second will be moved to the EMP_EXP table.

Question 98

The correct answer is **D**. Because the DB2 Optimizer generates an access plan each time a dynamic SQL statement is prepared for execution, applications using dynamic SQL may see performance improvements immediately after new statistical information has been produced. Unfortunately, that is not the case for applications that use static SQL. That's because the DB2 Optimizer only generates access plans for static SQL statements when the package that contains those statement is bound to the database. Therefore, in order for existing packages to take advantage of new statistical information produced by the RUNSTATS utility, they must be rebound to the database so the DB2 Optimizer will evaluate the new information and formulate new access plans (which may or may not perform better that the original access plan used). The easiest way to rebind an existing package—provided the application source code used to produce the package has not changed—is by executing the REBIND command.

Question 99

The correct answers are **B** and **E**. The Design Advisor recommends one or more indexes that would improve query/workload performance using current database statistics, the DB2 Optimizer, snapshot monitor information, and/or a specific query or set of SQL statements (known as a workload) you provide. The indexes/MQTs/MDCs recommended, the statistics derived for them, and the data definition language (DDL) statements required to create them can be written to a user-created table named ADVISE_INDEX, if so desired.

(If the db2advis command is executed with the –p option specified, the plans that were generated while running the Design Advisor will be saved in the ADVISE_WORKLOAD table and the workload query plans that use the final recommendation to be written to the Explain tables. However, input for the Design Advisor does not come from the Explain tables.)

Question 100

The correct answer is **C**. System catalog tables cannot be modified directly by any operation, including an IMPORT operation.

Question 101

The correct answer is **D**. Most of the utilities that are provided with DB2 can be invoked from the Control Center or by executing the appropriate command from the DB2 Command Line Processor or an operating system prompt. And because most DB2 commands have a corresponding application programming interface (API), they can be invoked from an Embedded SQL, or CLI application as well. However, the source code needed to use some of these APIs can be quite complex and all of the APIs available are designed to be used primarily in C and C++ applications. Another approach is to use the ADMIN_CMD() stored procedure, which is a special stored procedure that allows applications to run select administrative commands by using the CALL SQL statement. The ADMIN_CMD() stored procedure also allows you to invoke utilities from Java applications—something that cannot be done easily with the APIs.

Question 102

The correct answer is **C**. The COMMITCOUNT option of the IMPORT command is used to specify the number of rows of data (records) that are to be copied to the table/updatable view specified before a commit operation is to be performed. The COMMITCOUNT AUTOMATIC option should be used for Import operations that fail because transaction logs become full. This guarantees that transaction logs do not become full of uncommitted data.

Question 103

The correct answer is **C**. The db2move utility queries the system catalog tables of the specified database and compiles a list of all user tables found. It then exports the contents and table structure of each table in the database to individual PC Integrated Exchange Format (IXF) formatted files. The set of files produced can then be imported or loaded to another DB2 database on the same system, or they can be transferred to another workstation and be imported or loaded to a DB2 database residing there. Thus db2move can be used to copy the entire contents of a database from one location to another.

One limitation of the db2move utility is that it can only be used to duplicate table and index objects. If the database to be duplicated contains other objects such as aliases, views, triggers, user-defined data types (UDTs), user-defined functions (UDFs), etc., you must to duplicate those objects in the target database as well if you want to have an identical copy of the source database. That is where the db2look utility comes in. When invoked, db2look can reverse engineer an existing database and produce a set of Data Definition Language (DDL) SQL statements, which can then be used to recreate all of the data objects found in the database that was analyzed. The db2look utility can also collect environment registry variable settings, configuration parameter settings, and statistical (RUNSTATS) information on the source system, which can be used to duplicate those settings on the target system.

In this scenario we only want to copy a portion of the data and we want the statistics from the production database to be copied to the test database. Therefore, db2move cannot be used to move the date; instead, db2look must be used to duplicate the objects and statistics found in the production database and then the appropriate amount of data must be added to the tables.

Question 104

The correct answer is **C**. The Design Advisor is a special tool that is designed to identify indexes, Materialized Query Tables (MQTs), and Multidimensional Clustering Tables (MDCs) that could help improve query performance in your database environment. The

Design Advisor is invoked by executing the db2advis command; the –g option of the db2advis command specifies that the SQL statements that make up the workload to be analyzed are to be retrieved from a dynamic SQL snapshot.

The –k option specifies to what degree the workload will be compressed. (Compression is done to allow the advisor to reduce the complexity of the advisor's execution while achieving similar results to those the advisor could provide when the full workload is considered.) The –qp option specifies that the workload is coming from the DB2 Query Patroller, and the –h option displays help information.

Question 105

The correct answer is **B**. When the REPLACE option of the Import utility is used, any existing data is deleted from the target table (which must already exist); then, the new data is inserted. This option cannot be used if the target table contains a primary key that is referenced by a foreign key in another table.

When the INSERT option is used, data is inserted into the target table (which must already exist). Imported data is appended to any data that already exists. When the INSERT_UPDATE option is used, data is either inserted into the target table (which must already exist), or used to update existing rows (if the row being imported has a primary key value that matches that of an existing record). Existing records will only be updated if the target table specified has a primary key defined. When the CREATE option is used, the target table is created along with all of its associated indexes, then data is imported into the new table.

Question 106

The correct answers are **C** and **D**. The Load utility, (when invoked by executing a LOAD ... STATISTICS USE PROFILE command) and the REORGCHK utility (when invoked by executing a REORGCHK UPDATE STATISTICS ... command) will update the catalog statistics that are used by the DB2 Optimizer to generate data access plans.

Question 107

The correct answer is **B**. The LOAD command modifiers that can be used when loading identity column data are IDENTITYIGNORE, IDENTITYMISSING, and IDENTITYOVERRIDE.

The IDENTITYIGNORE modifier indicates that although data for all identity columns is present in the file being loaded, this data should be ignored and the Load utility should replace all identity column data found with its own generated values.

The IDENTITYMISSING modifier indicates that data for identity columns is missing from the file being loaded and that the Load utility should generate an appropriate value for each missing value encountered.

The IDENTITYOVERRIDE modifier indicates that the Load utility is to accept explicit, non-NULL data values for all identity columns in the table. This modifier is useful when migrating data from another database system, or when loading a table from data that was recovered using the DROPPED TABLE RECOVERY option of the ROLLFORWARD DATABASE command. (This modifier should be used only when an identity column that was defined as GENERATED ALWAYS is present in the table that is to be loaded.)

Question 108

The correct answer is **A**. Statistics cannot be collected if the LOAD command is executed with any option other than the REPLACE option specified. Additionally, a statistics profile for the SALES table must already exist (statistics profiles are created by executing the RUNSTATS command); the Load utility will not create one. If a profile does not exist and the Load utility is instructed to collect statistics, a warning is returned statistics are not collected.

Question 109

The correct answer is **B**. The RUNSTATS utility should be run immediately after any of the following occur:

- A large number of insert, update, or delete operations are performed against a specific table.

- An import operation is performed

- A load operation is performed

- One or more columns are added to an existing table

- A new index is created

- A table or index is reorganized

It is also a good idea to run the RUNSTATS utility before running the REORGCHK utility; if query response is slow because of fragmentation and statistics are not up to date, the REORGCHK utility may report that a table/index reorganization operation is unnecessary when it really is. Upon careful evaluation of the output produced by the REORGCHK utility, you may discover that one or more tables and/or indexes need to be reorganized. If that's the case, you can reorganize the tables, followed by the indexes, using DB2's REORG utility. After reorganizing data, statistics should be collected again and any packages that are associated with the table should be rebound (using the REBIND utility) so the DB2 Optimizer can generate new data access plans using the new statistics information collected.

Question 110

The correct answer is **C**. The LOAD QUERY command is used to monitor the progress/status of a load operation. (There are no LOAD STATUS, LOAD MESSAGES, or LOAD STATISTICS commands.)

Question 111

The correct answer is **B**. The Load utility is significantly faster than the Import utility when processing large amounts of data, because the load utility writes formatted pages directly into the database's storage containers. Additionally, when the Load utility is used, a minimal amount of logging is performed—individual row transactions are not recorded in the database's transaction log files.

Worksheet Format (WSF) formatted files are not supported by the Load utility, triggers are not fired during load processing, and only uniqueness checking is performed during processing. All other constraint checking (check constraints, referential integrity constraints, etc.) must be performed after the load operation has completed using the SET INTEGRITY SQL statement.

Question 112

The correct answer is **A**. The db2batch utility is a simple benchmark tool that reads SQL statements and/or XQuery expressions from either an ASCII format file or standard input, dynamically prepares, describes, and executes the statements/expressions found, and returns a result set that includes among other things, the timing of the execution. (db2move is best suited for copying 50 tables from one database to another; REORG is best suited for reorganizing table data and clustering its rows, and REBIND is best suited for updating access plan information stored in packages.)

High Availability

Question 113

The correct answer is **B**. When a transaction failure takes place, all work done by partially completed transactions that had not yet been externalized to the database is lost. As a result, the database may be left in an inconsistent state (and therefore will be unusable). *Crash recovery* is the process used to return such a database to a consistent and usable state. Crash recovery is performed by using information stored in the transaction log files to complete any committed transactions that were in memory (but had not yet been externalized to storage) when the transaction failure occurred, roll back any incomplete transactions found, and purge any uncommitted transactions from memory.

Question 114

The correct answer is **D**. As the size of a database grows, the time and hardware needed to back up and recover the databases also grows substantially. Thus, creating full database backup images is not always the best approach when dealing with large databases because the storage requirements for multiple copies of such backup images can be enormous. A better alternative is to create a full backup image periodically and one or more *incremental backup* images on a more frequent basis. An incremental backup is a backup image that only contains pages that have been updated since the previous backup image was made.

Two types of incremental backup images can be produced: *incremental* and *delta*. An incremental backup image is a copy of all database data that has changed since the most recent, successful, full backup image was created. An incremental backup image is also known as a *cumulative* backup image, because the last incremental backup image in a series of incremental backup images made over a period of time will contain the contents of all of the previous incremental backup images. The predecessor of an incremental backup image is always the most recent successful full backup image of the same object.

A delta backup image, on the other hand, is a copy of all database data that has changed since the last successful backup (full, incremental, or delta) of the database or table space in question. For this reason, a delta backup image is also known as a *differential*, or *non-cumulative*, backup image. The predecessor of a delta backup image is the most recent successful backup image that contains a copy of each of the objects found in the delta backup image.

If the INCREMENTAL option is specified with the BACKUP DATABASE command, an incremental backup image will be produced—an incremental backup image is a copy of all data that has changed since the last successful, full backup image was produced. If the INCREMENTAL DELTA option is specified, a delta backup image will be produced—a delta backup image is a copy of all data that has changed since the last successful backup image of any type (full, incremental, or delta) was produced.

Question 115

The correct answer is **B**. Roll-forward recovery takes version recovery one step farther by rebuilding a database or one or more individual table spaces using a backup image, and replaying information stored in transaction log files to return the database/table spaces to the state they were in at an exact point in time. In order to perform a roll-forward recovery operation, you must have archival logging enabled, you must have a full backup image of the database available, and you must have access to all archived log files that have been created since the full backup image was made.

Question 116

The correct answer is **B**. If you want to restore a table space from a backup image and the table space name has changed since the backup image was created, you should reference the table space by its new name. Table space metadata is stored in an external file and DB2 uses the information stored in this file to correctly identify the table space to restore.

Question 117

The correct answer is **A**. Before a split mirror copy of a DB2 database can be used, it must first be initialized; a split mirror database copy is initialized by executing the system command db2inidb. The syntax for this command is:

```
db2inidb [DatabaseAlias]
AS [SNAPSHOT | MIRROR | STANDBY]
<RELOCATE USING [ConfigFile]>
```

where:

DatabaseAlias   Identifies the alias assigned to the database the split mirror copy that is to be initialized references.

ConfigFile   Indicates that the database files contained in the split mirror copy are to be relocated according to information stored in the configuration file specified.

As you can see, a split mirror database copy can be initialized in one of three ways:

SNAPSHOT. The split mirror copy of the database will be initialized as a read-only clone of the primary database.

MIRROR. The split mirror copy of the database will be initialized as a backup image that can be used to restore the primary database.

STANDBY. The split mirror copy of the database will be initialized and placed in roll-forward pending state so that it can be continuously synchronized with the primary database. (New logs from the primary database can be retrieved and applied to the copy of the database at any time.) The standby copy of the database can then be used in place of the primary database if, for some reason, the primary database goes down.

Thus, if you wanted to initialize a split mirror copy of a database named MYDB and make it a read-only clone of the primary database, you could do so by executing a db2inidb command that looks like this:

```
db2inidb mydb AS STANDBY
```

Question 118

The correct answer is **B**. Both the primary and the standby database must be a single-partition database and they both must have the same database name; however, they do not have to be stored on the same database path.

IBM recommends that you use identical host computers for the HADR primary and standby databases. (If possible, they should be from the same vendor and have the same architecture.) Furthermore, the operating system on the primary and standby database servers should be the same version, including patch level. You can violate this rule for a short time during a rolling upgrade, but use extreme caution when doing so. A TCP/IP interface must also be available between the HADR host machines, and a high-speed, high-capacity network should be used to connect the two.

The DB2 software installed on both the primary and the standby database server must have the same bit size (32 or 64) and the version of DB2 used for the primary and standby databases must be identical; for example, both must be either version 8 or version 9. During rolling upgrades, the modification level (for example, the fix pack level) of the database system for the standby database can be later than that of the primary database for a short while. However, you should not keep this configuration for an extended period of time. The primary and standby databases will not connect to each other if the modification level of the database system for the primary database is later than that of the standby database. Therefore, fix packs must always be applied to the standby database system first.

The amount of storage space allocated for transaction log files should also be the same on both the primary and the standby database server; the use of raw devices for transaction logging is not supported. (Archival logging is only performed by the current primary database.) Table space properties such as table space name, table space type (DMS, SMS, or Automatic Storage), table space page size, table space size, container path, container size, and container type (raw device, file, or directory) must be identical on the primary and standby databases. When you issue a table space statement such as CREATE TABLESPACE, ALTER TABLESPACE, or DROP TABLESPACE on the primary database, it is replayed on the standby database. Therefore, you must ensure that the table space containers involved such statements exist on both systems before you issue the table space statement on the primary database. (If you create a table space on the primary database and log replay fails on the standby database because the containers are not available, the primary database does not receive an error message stating that the log replay failed.) Automatic storage databases are fully supported, including replication of ALTER DATABASE statements. Similar to table space containers, the storage paths specified must exist on both the primary and the standby server.

Question 119

The correct answers are **B** and **D**. To enable log file mirroring, you simply assign the fully qualified name of the mirror log location (path) to the *mirrorlogpath* database configuration parameter. Alternately, on UNIX systems, you can assign the value 1 to the DB2_NEWLOGPATH registry variable—in this case, the name of the mirror log location is generated by appending the character "2" to the current value of the *logpath* database configuration parameter. Ideally, the mirror log path used should refer to a physical location (disk) that does not see a large amount of disk I/O and that is separate from the physical location used to store primary log files.

Question 120

The correct answer is **C**. The Recover utility performs the restore and roll-forward operations needed to recover a database to a specific point in time, based on information found in the recovery history file. The Recover utility is invoked by executing the RECOVER DATABASE command. The basic syntax for this command is:

```
RECOVER [DATABASE | DB] [DatabaseAlias]
<TO [PointInTime] <USING [UTC | LOCAL] TIME> |
    END OF LOGS>
<USER [UserName] <USING [Password]>>
<USING HISTORY FILE ([HistoryFile])>
<OVERFLOW LOG PATH ([LogDirectory] ,... )>
<RESTART>
```

where:

DatabaseAlias   Identifies the alias assigned to the database associated with the backup image that is to be used to perform a version recovery operation.

PointInTime	Identifies a specific point in time, identified by a timestamp value in the form *yyyy-mm-dd-hh.mm.ss.nnnnnn* (year, month, day, hour, minutes, seconds, microseconds) that the database is to be rolled forward to. (Only transactions that took place before and up to the date and time specified will be reapplied to the database.)
UserName	Identifies the name assigned to a specific user that the recovery operation is to be performed under.
Password	Identifies the password that corresponds to the name of the user that the recovery operation is to be performed under.
HistoryFile	Identifies the name assigned to the recovery history log file that is to be used by the Recovery utility.
LogDirectory	Identifies the directory that contains offline archived log files that are to be used to perform the roll-forward portion of the recovery operation.

Thus, if you wanted to perform a full recovery operation on a database named SAMPLE (which already exists) using information stored in the recovery history file, you could do so by executing a RECOVER DATABASE command that looks something like this:

```
RECOVER DATABASE sample
TO END OF LOGS
```

On the other hand, if you wanted to restore a database named SAMPLE and roll it forward to an extremely old point in time that is no longer contained in the current recovery history file, you could do so by executing a RECOVER DATABASE command that looks something like this (assuming you have a copy of an older recovery history file available):

```
RECOVER DATABASE sample
TO 2005-01-31-04.00.00
USING HISTORY FILE (/home/user/old2005files/db2rhist.asc)
```

It is important to note that if the Recover utility successfully restores a database, but for some reason fails while attempting to roll it forward, the entire recovery operation must be performed again. There is no way to restart a recovery operation from a point of failure.

Question 121

The correct answer is **A**. The UTIL_IMPACT_PRIORITY option of the BACKUP DATABASE command is used to indicate that the execution of a backup operation is to be throttled such that its affect on concurrent database activity can be controlled. This parameter can be assigned a numerical value within the range of 1 to 100, with 100 representing the highest priority and 1 representing the lowest. (Backup operations that have been assigned a

UTIL_IMPACT_PRIORITY value of 25 will impact database workloads by 25% and will take longer to complete; backup operations that have been assigned a UTIL_IMPACT_PRIORITY value of 75 will impact database workloads by 75% and will finish sooner.)

Question 122

The correct answer is **B**. The OVERFLOW LOG PATH option of the ROLLFORWARD DATABASE command is used to identify the directory that contains offline archived log files that are to be used to perform the roll-forward operation. The Roll-forward utility looks in the active log directory first, and then in the directory specified with the OVERFLOW LOG PATH option for log files need to perform a roll-forward recovery operation.

Question 123

The correct answer is **D**. While the *indexrec* parameter of the database or the DB2 Database Manager configuration file can be used to control when indexes are rebuilt as part of a crash recovery operation, it has no effect on how indexes are rebuilt during roll-forward recovery operations. To control that behavior, you must assign the appropriate value to the *logindexbuild* database configuration parameter. There are two possible settings for this parameter:

> **ON.** Index creation, recreation, and reorganization operations are to be recorded in the database's transaction log files so indexes can be reconstructed during roll-forward recovery operations or high availability disaster recovery (HADR) log replay operations.

> **OFF.** Index creation, recreation, and reorganization operations will not be recorded in the database's transaction log files.

Question 124

The correct answer is **D**. When archival logging is used and archived log files are not moved from the active log directory to another location, the disk where the active log directory resides can quickly become full. By default, when this happens, transactions will receive a disk full error and be rolled back. If the *blk_log_dsk_ful* database configuration parameter is set to YES, applications will hang (instead of rolling back the current transaction) if the DB2 Database Manager receives a disk full error when it attempts to create a new log file in the active log directory. (This gives you the opportunity to manually move or delete files to make more room available.) The DB2 Database Manager will then attempt to create the log file every five minutes until it succeeds—after each attempt, a message is written to the Administration Notification Log.

Question 125

The correct answer is **A**. If a problem occurs with a table space container during the restart process, the DROP PENDING TABLESPACES ([*TS_Name*]) option can be used to place one or more table spaces in "Drop Pending" state. This allows the database to be successfully restarted, after which the offending table space can be dropped and, if necessary, recreated. A list of troubled table space names can found in the administration notification log if a database restart operation fails because of table space container problems.

Question 126

The correct answer is **C**. Since load operations are not recorded in a database's transaction log files, whether or not a load operation can be duplicated is dependent upon whether a copy of the loaded data was saved as part of the load process (which is the case if the COPY YES option of the LOAD command is specified). If a load operation is performed on the primary database with the COPY YES option specified, the command will execute on the primary database and the data will be replicated to the standby database—provided the copy of the loaded data created can be accessed by the standby database via the path or device provided with the LOAD command. If the standby database cannot access the data, the table space in which the table is stored is marked invalid on the standby database and the standby database will stop replaying log records that pertain to this table space. To ensure that the load operation can access the copy on the standby database, it is recommended that you use a shared location for the output file location specified with the COPY YES option. Alternatively, you can deactivate the standby database while the load operation is performed, perform the load operation on the primary database, place a copy of the output file produced in the standby path, and then activate the standby database.

If a load operation is executed on the primary database with the NONRECOVERABLE option specified, data will be loaded into the appropriate table in the primary database, the corresponding table on the standby database will be marked invalid, and the standby database will stop replaying log records that pertain to this table. You can reissue the LOAD command with the COPY YES and REPLACE options specified to restore the table on the standby database, or you can drop the table and recover the space.

Because executing a load operation with the COPY NO option specified is not supported by HADR, an attempt to perform such an operation is automatically converted to a load operation that behaves as if the NONRECOVERABLE option was specified. To prevent this behavior, you can set the DB2_LOAD_COPY_NO_OVERRIDE registry variable on the primary database to COPY YES, in which case all load operations performed will behave as if the COPY YES option was specified. When setting this variable, make sure that the device or directory specified on the primary database can be accessed by the standby database using the same path, device, or load library.

Question 127

The correct answer is **D**. When invalid table space containers are encountered, they can be redefined at the beginning of the recovery process by performing what is known as a *redirected restore*. (A redirected restore operation can also be used to restore a backup image to a target machine that is different than the source machine, or to store table space data into a different physical location.)

The steps used to perform a redirected restore operation are as follows:

1. Start the redirected restore operation by executing the RESTORE DATABASE command with the REDIRECT option specified. (When this option is specified, each invalid table space container encountered is flagged, and all table spaces that reference invalid table space containers are placed in the "Restore Pending" state. A list of all table spaces affected can be obtained by executing the LIST TABLESPACES command.) At some point, you should see a message that looks something like this:

    SQL1277N Restore has detected that one or more table space containers are inaccessible, or has set their state to 'storage must be defined'.
    DB20000I The RESTORE DATABASE command completed successfully.

2. Specify new table space containers for each table space placed in "Restore Pending" state by executing a SET TABLESPACE CONTAINERS command for each appropriate table space. (Keep in mind that SMS table spaces can only use PATH containers, while DMS table spaces can only use FILE or DEVICE containers.)

3. Complete the redirected restore operation by executing the RESTORE DATABASE command again with the CONTINUE option specified.

To simplify things, all of these steps can be coded in a UNIX shell script or Windows batch file, which can then be executed from a system prompt. Such a file would look something like this:

```
db2 "RESTORE DATABASE sample FROM C:\backups TO D:\DB_DIR INTO
sample_2 REDIRECT"
db2 "SET TABLESPACE CONTAINERS FOR 0 USING
```

```
        (PATH 'D:\DB_DIR\SYSTEM')"
    db2 "SET TABLESPACE CONTAINERS FOR 1 USING
        (PATH 'D:\DB_DIR\TEMP')"
    db2 "SET TABLESPACE CONTAINERS FOR 2 USING
        (PATH 'D:\DB_DIR\USER')"
    db2 "RESTORE DATABASE sample CONTINUE"
```

Question 128

The correct answer is **B**. When incremental backup images are taken, database recovery involves restoring the database using the most recent full backup image available and applying the most recent incremental backup image produced. On the other hand, when delta backup images are taken, database recovery involves restoring the database using the most recent full backup image available and applying each delta backup image produced since the full backup image used was made, in the order in which they were created.

Question 129

The correct answer is **A**. Roll-forward recovery operations can be performed on individual table spaces while a database remains on-line. However, before a database can be restored, it must first be taken offline. Therefore, roll-forward recovery can be accomplished while users are connected to the database – but only at the table space level.

Question 130

The correct answer is **A**. Whenever the DB2 Database Manager detects that an index is no longer valid, it automatically attempts to rebuild it. However, the point in time at which the DB2 Database Manager attempts to rebuild an invalid index is controlled by the *indexrec* parameter of the database or the DB2 Database Manager configuration file. There are three possible settings for this parameter:

> **SYSTEM.** Invalid indexes are to be rebuilt at the time specified in the *indexrec* parameter of the DB2 Database Manager configuration file. (This setting is only valid for database configuration files.)

> **RESTART.** Invalid indexes are to be rebuilt, either explicitly or implicitly, when the database is restarted (i.e., when crash recovery is performed on the database).

ACCESS. Invalid indexes are to be rebuilt the first time they are accessed after they have been marked as being invalid.

So when is the best time to rebuild invalid indexes? If the time needed to perform a crash recovery operation on a database is not a concern, it is better to let the DB2 Database Manager rebuild invalid indexes while it is in the process of returning the database to a consistent state; the time needed to restart a database will be longer due to the index re-creation process, but once the database had been restored, query processing will not be impacted. On the other hand, if indexes are rebuilt as they are accessed, crash recovery will be performed faster, but users may experience a decrease in performance – queries against tables that contain associated invalid indexes will have to wait for the invalid index(es) to be rebuilt before they can be processed. Furthermore, unexpected locks may be acquired and held long after an invalid index has been recreated, especially if the transaction that caused the index recreation to occur is not committed (or rolled back) for some time.

Question 131

The correct answer is **C**. After ensuring the systems to be used as primary and secondary server are identical and that a TCP/IP connection exists between them, you can establish an HADR environment by performing the following tasks, in the order shown:

1. Determine the host name, host IP address, and the service name or port number for both the primary and the secondary database server.

2. Create the standby database by restoring a backup image or initializing a split mirror copy of the database that is to serve as the primary database.

3. Set the HADR configuration parameters on both the primary and the standby databases.

4. Connect to the standby instance and start HADR on the standby database.

5. Connect to the primary instance and start HADR on the primary database.

Question 132

The correct answer is **A**. Load operations against primary databases in a HADR environment can have an impact on indexes as well as tables and table spaces. If a load operation is performed on the primary database with the COPY YES option specified, affected indexes will be replicated as follows:

- If the indexing mode is set to REBUILD and the table being loaded has been assigned the LOG INDEX BUILD attribute, or if the table being loaded has been assigned the DEFAULT attribute and the *logindexbuild* database configuration parameter on the primary database is set to ON, the primary database will include the rebuilt index object in the copy file so the standby database can replicate the index object. If the index object on the standby database is marked invalid before the load operation is performed, it will become usable again after the load operation as a result of the index rebuild.

- If the indexing mode is set to INCREMENTAL and the table being loaded has been assigned the LOG INDEX BUILD attribute, or if the table being loaded has been assigned the NULL attribute and the *logindexbuild* database configuration parameter on the primary database is set to ON, the index object on the standby database is only updated if it is not marked invalid before the load operation. Otherwise, the index is marked invalid on the standby database.

IBM recommends you set the *logindexbuild* database configuration parameter to ON for HADR databases to ensure that complete information is logged for index creation, recreation, and reorganization. Although this means that index builds might take longer on the primary system and that more log space may be required, the indexes will be rebuilt on the standby system during HADR log replay and will be available when a failover takes place. If index operations on the primary system are not logged and a failover occurs, any invalid indexes that remain after the failover is complete will have to be rebuilt before they can be accessed – while indexes are being recreated, they cannot be accessed by any application.

Security

Question 133

The correct answer is **B**. Like System Administrator (SYSADM), System Control (SYSCTRL), and System Monitor (SYSMON) authority, System Maintenance (SYSMAINT) authority can only be assigned to a group. This assignment is made by storing the appropriate group name in the *sysmaint_group* parameter of the DB2 Database Manager configuration file that is associated with a particular instance.

Question 134

The correct answer is **D**. In order to create a view, a user must hold appropriate privileges (at a minimum, SELECT privilege) on each base table the view references. CREATEIN is a schema privilege – not a database privilege; REFERENCES privilege allows a user to create and drop foreign key constraints that reference the table in a parent relationship; and CREATETAB privilege allows a user to create new tables in the database (there is no CREATE_TAB privilege).

Question 135

The correct answer is **C**. The GRANT ALL PRIVILEGES statement gives USER1 the following privileges for the EMPLOYEE table: ALTER, SELECT, INSERT, UPDATE, DELETE, INDEX, and REFERENCES. To drop an index, USER1 would need CONTROL privilege on the index—not the table the index is based on; USER1 cannot grant privileges to other users because the WITH GRANT OPTION clause was not specified with the GRANT ALL PRIVILEGES statement used to give USER1 table privileges; and in order to drop the EMPLOYEE table, USER1 would have to have CONTROL privilege on the table—CONTROL privilege is not granted with the GRANT ALL PRIVILEGES statement.

Question 136

The correct answer is **A**. The ALTER table privilege allows a user to execute the ALTER TABLE SQL statement against a table. In other words, this privilege allows a user to add columns to the table, add or change comments associated with the table or any of its columns, create or drop a primary key for the table, create or drop a unique constraint for the table, create or drop a check constraint for the table, and create triggers for the table (provided the user holds the appropriate privileges for every object referenced by the trigger).

The UPDATE privilege allows a user to execute the UPDATE SQL statement against the table. In other words, this privilege allows a user to modify data in the table. The DELETE privilege allows a user to execute the DELETE SQL statement against the table. In other words, allows a user to remove rows of data from the table.

Question 137

The correct answer is **A**. To restrict access to rows in a table using Label-Based Access Control (LBAC), you must define a security label component, define a security policy, create one or more security labels, create an LBAC-protected table or alter an existing table to add LBAC protection (this is done by adding the security policy to the table and defining a column that has the DB2SECURITYLABEL data type), and grant the proper security labels to the appropriate users. There are no LBAC security profiles.

Question 138

The correct answer is **A**. The DELETE table privilege allows a user to remove rows of data from a table. Aliases are publicly referenced names, so no special authority or privilege is required to use them. However, tables or views referred to by an alias have still have the authorization requirements that are associated with these types of objects.

Question 139

The correct answer is **C**. The first security portal most users must pass through on their way to gaining access to a DB2 instance or database is a process known as authentication. The purpose of authentication is to verify that users really are who they say they are. Once a user has been authenticated and an attachment to an instance or a connection to a database has been established, the DB2 Database Manager evaluates any authorities and privileges that have been assigned to the user to determine what operations the user is allowed to perform. *Privileges* convey the rights to perform certain actions against specific database resources (such as tables and views). *Authorities* convey a set of privileges or the right to perform high-level administrative and maintenance/utility operations on an instance or a database.

Question 140

The correct answer is **D**. Because DB2 can reside in environments comprised of multiple clients, gateways, and servers, each of which may be running on a different operating system, deciding where authentication is to take place is determined by the value assigned to the *authentication* parameter in each DB2 Database Manager configuration file. The value assigned to this parameter, often referred to as the authentication type, is set initially when an instance is created. (On the server side, the authentication type is specified during the instance creation process; on the client side, the authentication type is specified when a remote database is cataloged.) Only one authentication type exists for each instance, and it controls access to that instance, as well as to all databases that fall under that instance's control.

Question 141

The correct answers are **A** and **C**. Before a user can invoke a routine (user-defined function, stored procedure, or method) they must hold both EXECUTE privilege on the routine and any privileges required by that routine. Thus, in order to execute a stored procedure that queries a table, a user must hold both EXECUTE privilege on the stored procedure and SELECT privilege on the table the query is ran against.

Package privileges control what users can and cannot do with a particular package. (A package is an object that contains the information needed by the DB2 Database Manager to process SQL statements in the most efficient way possible on behalf of an embedded SQL application.)

Question 142

The correct answer is **C**. The ALTER sequence privilege allows a user to perform administrative tasks like restarting the sequence, changing the increment value for the sequence, and *add or change the comment associated with the sequence*. And when the GRANT statement is executed with the WITH GRANT OPTION clause specified, the user/group receiving privileges is given the ability to grant the privileges received to others. There is no CONTROL privilege for a sequence and the USAGE privilege is the sequence privilege that allows a user to use the PREVIOUS VALUE and NEXT VALUE expressions that are associated with the sequence. (The PREVIOUS VALUE expression returns the most recently generated value for the specified sequence; the NEXT VALUE expression returns the next value for the specified sequence.)

Question 143

The correct answer is **C**. The GRANT statement does not check to ensure that the names of users and/or groups that are to be granted authorities and privileges are valid. Therefore, it is possible to grant authorities and privileges to users and groups that do not exist.

Question 144

The correct answer is **B**. When a user holds an exemption on an LBAC security policy rule, that rule is not enforced when the user attempts to read and/or write data that is protected by that security policy.

Security policy exemptions are granted by executing the GRANT EXEMPTION ON RULE SQL statement (as a user with SECADM authority). The syntax for this statement is:

```
CREATE EXEMPTION ON RULE [Rule] ,...
FOR [PolicyName]
TO USER [UserName]
```

where:

Rule	Identifies one or more DB2LBACRULES security policy rules that exemptions are to be given for. The following values are valid for this parameter: DB2LBACREADARRAY, DB2LBACREADSET, DB2LBACREADTREE, DB2LBACWRITEARRAY WRITEDOWN, DB2LBACWRITEARRAY WRITEUP, DB2LBACWRITESET, DB2LBACWRITETREE, and ALL. (If an exemption is held for every security policy rule, the user will have complete access to all data protected by that security policy.)
PolicyName	Identifies the security policy for which the exemption is to be granted.
UserName	Identifies the name of the user to which the exemptions specified are to be granted.

Thus, to grant an exemption to the DB2LBACWRITEARRAY rule in a security policy named SEC_POLICY to a user named USER1, you would execute a GRANT EXEMPTION statement that looks something like this:

```
GRANT EXEMPTION ON RULE DB2LBACWRITEARRAY
WRITEDOWN FOR sec_policy
TO USER user1
```

Question 145

The correct answer is **D**. To connect to and work with a particular database, a user must have the authorities and privileges needed to use that database. Therefore, whenever a new database is created, unless otherwise specified, the following authorities and privileges are automatically granted:

- Database Administrator (DBADM) authority, along with CONNECT, CREATETAB, BINDADD, CREATE_NOT_FENCED, IMPLICIT_SCHEMA, and LOAD privileges, are granted to the user who created the database.

- USE privilege on the table space USERSPACE1 is granted to the group PUBLIC.

- CONNECT, CREATETAB, BINDADD, and IMPLICIT_SCHEMA privileges are granted to the group PUBLIC.

- SELECT privilege on each system catalog table is granted to the group PUBLIC.

- EXECUTE privilege on all procedures found in the SYSIBM schema is granted to the group PUBLIC.

- EXECUTE WITH GRANT privilege on all functions found in the SYSFUN schema is granted to the group PUBLIC.

- BIND and EXECUTE privileges for each successfully bound utility are granted to the group PUBLIC.

Question 146

The correct answer is **B**. When a user is given Database Administrator (DBADM) authority for a particular database, he automatically receives all database privileges available for that database as well (CONNECT, CONNECT_QUIESCE, IMPLICIT_SCHEMA, CREATETAB, BINDADD, CREATE_EXTERNAL_ROUTINE, CREATE_NOT_FENCED_ROUTINE, and LOAD). When Database Administrator authority is revoked, all other database authorities that were implicitly and automatically granted when DBADM authority was granted are not automatically revoked. The same is true for privileges held on objects in the database.

Question 147

The correct answer is **D**. The CONTROL view privilege provides a user with every view privilege available, allows the user to remove (drop) the view from the database, and gives the user the ability to grant and revoke one or more view privileges (except the CONTROL privilege) to/from other users and groups.

Question 148

The correct answer is **B**. The BINDADD database privilege allows a user to create packages in the database (by precompiling embedded SQL application source code files against the database or by binding application bind files to the database).

The BIND package privilege allows a user to rebind or add new package versions to a package that has already been bound to a database. (In addition to the BIND package privilege, a user must hold the privileges needed to execute the SQL statements that make up the package before the package can be successfully rebound.) The CREATE_EXTERNAL_ROUTINE database privilege allows a user to create user-defined functions (UDFs) and/or procedures and store them in the database so that they can be used by other users and applications. The CREATE_NOT_FENCED_ROUTINE database privilege allows a user to create unfenced UDFs and/or procedures and store them in the database. (Unfenced UDFs and stored procedures are UDFs/procedures that are considered "safe" enough to be run in the DB2 Database Manager operating environment's process or address space. Unless a UDF/procedure is registered as unfenced, the DB2 Database Manager insulates the

UDF/procedure's internal resources in such a way that they cannot be run in the DB2 Database Manager's address space.)

Question 149

The correct answer is **B**. The syntax used to grant the only stored procedure privilege available is:

```
GRANT EXECUTE ON [RoutineName] |
                 [PROCEDURE <SchemaName.> *]
TO [Recipient, ...]
<WITH GRANT OPTION>
```

The syntax used to revoke the only stored procedure privilege available is:

```
REVOKE EXECUTE ON [RoutineName |
                  [PROCEDURE <SchemaName.> *]
FROM [Forfeiter, ...] <BY ALL>
RESTRICT
```

where:

RoutineName	Identifies by name the routine (user-defined function, method, or stored procedure) that the EXECUTE privilege is to be associated with.
TypeName	Identifies by name the type in which the specified method is found.
SchemaName	Identifies by name the schema in which all functions, methods, or procedures—including those that may be created in the future—are to have the EXECUTE privilege granted on.
Recipient	Identifies the name of the user(s) and/or group(s) that are to receive the EXECUTE privilege. The value specified for the *Recipient* parameter can be any combination of the following: <USER> [*UserName*], <GROUP> [*GroupName*], and PUBLIC.
Forfeiter	Identifies the name of the user(s) and/or group(s) that are to lose the package privileges specified. The value specified for the *Forfeiter* parameter can be any combination of the following: <USER> [*UserName*], <GROUP> [*GroupName*], and PUBLIC.

Thus, the proper way to grant and revoke stored procedure privileges is by executing the GRANT EXECUTE ... and REVOKE EXECUTE ... statements.

Question 150

The correct answer is **C**. Security Administrator (SECADM) authority is a special database level of authority that is designed to allow special users to configure various label-based access control (LBAC) elements to restrict access to one or more tables that contain data to which they most likely do not have access themselves. Users with Security Administrator authority are only allowed to perform the following tasks:

- Create and drop security policies.

- Create and drop security labels.

- Grant and revoke security labels to/from individual users (using the GRANT SECURITY LABEL and REVOKE SECURITY LABEL SQL statements).

- Grant and revoke LBAC rule exemptions.

- Grant and revoke SETSESSIONUSER privileges (using the GRANT SETSESSIONUSER SQL statement).

- Transfer ownership of any object not owned by the Security Administrator (by executing the TRANSFER OWNERSHIP SQL statement).

No other authority provides a user with these abilities, including System Administrator authority.

Index

More DB2 Books from MC Press

DB2 9 Fundamentals Certification Study Guide
ISBN: 978-158347-072-5
Author: Roger E. Sanders
http://www.mc-store.com/5088

DB2 9 Linux, UNIX, and Windows Database Adminstrator Upgrade Certification Study Guide
ISBN: 978-158347-078-7
Author: Roger E. Sanders
http://www.mc-store.com/5091

DB2 9 for z/OS Database Adminstrator Certification Study Guide
ISBN: 978-158347-074-9
Authors: Susan Lawson and Dan Luksetich
http://www.mc-store.com/5089
Available: November 2007

DB2 9 for Linux, UNIX, and Windows Advanced Database Administrator Certification Study Guide
ISBN: 978-158347-080-0
Authors: Roger Sanders and Dwaine Snow
http://www.mc-store.com/5093
Available: May 2008

DB2 9 for Developers
ISBN: 978-158347-071-8
Author: Philip K. Gunning
http://www.mc-store.com/5086
Available: January 2007